To Walt Young — A persistent critic of Denver Schools.

Phil Goodstein
8/25/00
Denver

Photo by John Schoenwalter

*President Bill Clinton and Pope John Paul II met in Denver in 1993 when the Mile High City portrayed itself as the center of the world during World Youth Day. Such an event was a point of pride of the modern community.*

The cover photo, © 2000 by John Schoenwalter, is of *On the War Trail* by Alexander Phimister Proctor in the Civic Center. The alarmed, angry Indian is stopped, atop a hill, ready to attack. Today, the statue looks smack at the center of corporate Denver, the force controlling the city's modern destiny.

The back cover photo of the author is by Neal Paul. It is taken in Fairmount Cemetery, showing where the bodies are buried.

# DIA and Other Scams

## Volume Two

## Denver in Our Time:

## A People's History of the Modern Mile High City

By Phil Goodstein

Denver
New Social Publications
2000

*To Maxine Lankford:*
*A sturdy part of the Denver opposition and an ardent aide.*

*Denver in Our Time*
Volume One: *Big Money in the Big City*
Volume Two: *DIA and Other Scams*



New Social Publications
Box 18026; Denver, Colorado 80218
(303)333-1095

Printed in Denver, Colorado

First Edition: September 2000

Library of Congress Control Number 00-131682
ISBN 0-9622169-8-4

# Contents

# A Note on Usage

In recent years the city has continually renamed streets. At times, the primary result has been to confuse locals and erase the city's heritage. To combat this, historic street names, such as 32nd Avenue for Martin Luther King Boulevard and 23rd Street for Park Avenue West have generally been retained in noting locations. Avenues east of Broadway are automatically assumed to be east; only those west of Broadway are so specifically designated as "West." Similarly, streets not specially listed as "South," are north of Ellsworth Avenue.

Corporations, utilities, and banks have also frequently changed their names and identities. The title best reflecting the era has been used. Mountain Bell, for example, provided phone service prior to 1985. By the time this book was ready for publication, its successor, US West, had just been swallowed by Qwest. Rumors were hot and heavy about the latter joining with some European communications outfit. Public Service Corporation of Colorado, which had become part of New Century Energies in 1997, was then in the process of merging with a Minnesota-based utility to form Xcel Energy.

Middle schools are referred to by their old title as junior high schools. Recalling Thomas Hornsby Ferril, who stridently sought to retain local customs, the big lake in City Park is simply "City Park Lake," not Ferril Lake.

Those attempting to trace some of these changes should note listings in the index. An effort has been made there to cross-reference changed names and developments with volume one by the designation "V-1."

# Abbreviations

| | |
|---|---|
| ACLU: | American Civil Liberties Union |
| AHEC: | Auraria Higher Education Center |
| AT&T: | American Telephone & Telegraph |
| CANS: | Citizens Association for Neighborhood Schools |
| CARL: | Colorado Alliance of Research Libraries |
| CCD: | Community College of Denver |
| CCR: | Commission on Community Relations |
| CDM: | collaborative decision-making teams |
| CHS: | Colorado Historical Society |
| CHUN: | Capitol Hill United Neighborhoods |
| *CJ*: | *Cervi's Journal* |
| CNB: | Colorado National Bank |
| CORE: | Congress of Racial Equality |
| CRLS: | Colorado Rural Legal Services |
| CSO: | Colorado Symphony Orchestra |
| CSU: | Colorado State University |
| CU: | University of Colorado |
| CWC: | Colorado Woman's College |
| DAC: | Denver Athletic Club |
| *DBJ*: | *Denver Business Journal* |
| DCPA: | Denver Center for the Performing Arts |
| DCTA: | Denver Classroom Teachers Association |
| DDI: | Downtown Denver Incorporated |
| DHA: | Denver Housing Authority |
| DIA: | Denver International Airport |
| DLPC: | Denver Landmark Preservation Commission |
| *DP*: | *Denver Post* |
| DPL: | Denver Public Library |

| | |
|---|---|
| DPS: | Denver Public Schools |
| DPO: | Denver Planning Office |
| DRCOG: | Denver Regional Council of Governments, pronounced "doctor cog." |
| DU: | University of Denver |
| DUDE: | downtown urban design element |
| DURA: | Denver Urban Renewal Authority |
| DUWC: | Denver Union Water Company |
| DWD: | Denver Water Department |
| EIS: | environmental-impact statement |
| EOP: | Equal Opportunity Program |
| EPA: | Environmental Protection Agency |
| FBI: | Federal Bureau of Investigation |
| FSLIC: | Federal Savings and Loan Insurance Corporation |
| G-7: | Group of Seven |
| GPHC: | Greater Park Hill Community Incorporated |
| GW: | George Washington High School |
| HNTB: | Howard Needles Tammen & Bergendoff |
| INC: | Inter–Neighborhood Cooperation |
| LARASA: | Latin American Research and Service Agency |
| LWV: | League of Women Voters |
| MALDEF: | Mexican American Legal Defense and Educational Fund |
| MDC: | Mizel Development Corporation |
| MOED: | Mayor's Office of Economic Development |
| NEPHCA: | Northeast Park Hill Civic Association |
| PHAC: | Park Hill Action Committee |
| PHIA: | Park Hill Improvement Association |
| R-1: | Jefferson County Reorganized School District One |
| *RMN*: | *Rocky Mountain News* |
| ROTC: | Reserve Officers Training Corps |
| RTD: | Regional Transportation District |
| *SCJ*: | *Straight Creek Journal* |
| SWP: | Socialist Workers Party |
| TABOR: | Taxpayers Bill of Rights |
| TCI: | Tele-Communications Incorporated |
| UCD: | University of Colorado at Denver |
| UMAS: | United Mexican American Students |
| V-1: | volume one of *Denver in Our Time* |
| *WW*: | *Westword* |
| YMCA: | Young Men's Christian Association |
| YWCA: | Young Women's Christian Association |

# Introduction

The pope came to town. So did the president. A few years later, the prime ministers of Britain, France, Japan, and other world powers descended on the Mile High City for the Summit of the Eight. Former Mayor Federico Peña held cabinet posts under President Bill Clinton. His successor, Wellington Webb, headed the United States Conference of Mayors. Governor Roy Romer served as chairman of the National Democratic Committee during the late 1990s. By that time, Denver was home to a gigantic, super-expensive new airport.

Such were Denver's points of pride at the end of the 20th century. After wildly growing during the oil boom of the 1970s, an economic downturn paralyzed the metropolis in the 1980s. Within a few years, it was once more full steam ahead. Military contractors and computer and telecommunications businesses increasingly drove the local economy. Countless new real estate subdivisions popped up as developers grew ever more influential.

The last decades of the 20th century saw a significant transformation in the nature of the city government. Denver became a national model, a city where racial and ethnic considerations were primary in who was elected mayor. Federico Peña, the city's leader between 1983 and 1991, built the foundations of a new urban machine. His successor, Wellington Webb, elected in 1991, strengthened it.

As was the case in the 1950s, 1960s, and 1970s, during the last two decades of the century, Denver haters, individuals hostile to the city, controlled the area's commanding business organizations, notably the Denver Partnership and Chamber of Commerce. They readily demeaned existing facilities, such as Stapleton Airport and Currigan Hall, as feeble remnants of a cow town. However, unlike the postwar generation, they had a slight appreciation of some of the area's natural charms. During the 1980s and 1990s, the city had a renewed commitment to civic beauty. Preservation activists managed to save a number of landmark buildings.

Often this was at a cost. A kind of colonial, missionary arrogance permeated the Mile High City, especially where newcomers sought to settle in older, poorer neighborhoods. In some ways, their very presence and success were thanks to the massive civil rights upheavals sweeping the city during the 1960s and 1970s. During those decades, emerging from hidden parts of the Queen City, the black and Chicano communities loudly demanded recognition and respect. All this sets the contours for this concluding part of *Denver in Our Time*.

In volume one, *Big Money in the Big City*, I sought to explore exactly how Denver has grown since World War II. The key focus was on who runs the city. I examined the nature of great fortunes, the role of the media, the reason for the town's intense sports fixation, the nature of cultural facilities and higher education, the push for urban renewal, the impact of the oil boom, and the emergence of lower downtown and the central Platte floodplain. In closing, I noted how voices of opposition have occasionally been heard.

Here, I seek to examine exactly how the city is run and the way the numerous contradictions in the community paved the way for Denver International Airport (DIA). I begin by noting the area's racial upheavals (chapter one). These heavily impacted Denver Public Schools and the suburbs. Eventually, problems in the latter culminated in the Columbine High School Massacre in April 1999 (all covered in chapter two). Meanwhile, out of the Chicano civil rights movement (chapter three), Peña launched his successful campaign for mayor in 1983 (chapter four). How his administration managed to transform that year's populist insurgency into corporate consolidation (chapters five and seven) is a key theme of this volume.

A new convention center (chapter six) and airport (chapter thirteen) were Peña's foremost goals/accomplishments. I look at how he reached them and at what cost. This further leads to examinations of the impact on downtown (chapter nine) and the nature of such institutions as the Denver Public Library (chapter ten) and the doings of the Denver Board of Water Commissioners (chapter eleven). Along the way, I trace the city's political evolution, notably the rise of Wellington Webb (chapter twelve). All the while, the savings and loan scandal of the 1980s (chapter eight) cast a heavy shadow over the Mile High City.

A history of modern Denver is anything but a provincial enterprise. The city has been an exemplar for the country. Not only has it illustrated the workings of a public/private partnership, but it also shows how ethnic and racial tensions have been used to cloak class divisions in the forging of the modern metropolis.

A review of volume one attacked me for not pretending to have any objectivity. In some ways, this is true. I do not accept the status quo as eternal. There are intense class and social chasms in the community. Different interests have different perspectives and values. As an opponent of war and imperialism, I reject policies designed to enhance militarism and violence. This leads to my views on such events as the Summit of the Eight (chapter ten) and the Joe P. Martinez statue in the Capitol Park (chapter three).

My personal biases aside, it is necessary to ask who benefits from various programs, building efforts, and growth campaigns. By realizing where Denver has been and the impact of previous schemes, residents can begin to grasp their past. Only when they know it, can they see where they can go. Through probing the community's values, citizens get a sense of place. They so gain power in rebuilding their world and shaping their future. Insofar as I help everyday individuals get a step closer to this task, I am fulfilling my responsibility as a historian.

While this book is the concluding part of a two-part work, I realize it must also stand alone. Some of the references made in volume one are not explained. In particular, I use "17th Street" to refer to the area's commanding banks, brokerages, real estate firms, and business interests. The power of the Denver Metro Chamber of Commerce, also developed in volume one, is taken as a given.

No sooner had I begun work on this study than I realized a chronological approach would not work; rather, I have focused on specific themes. This is sometimes problematic, assuming the reader has a certain knowledge of modern Denver, especially what is spelled out in *Big Money in the Big City*. The totality of *Denver in Our Time* is from World War II until the beginnings of the 21st century. In *DIA and Other Scams* the focus is primary on the era beginning with the election of Federico Peña as mayor in 1983. Denver International Airport, which opened in 1995 after Peña had committed himself to it in 1984–85, haunted most of the political and economic decisions during this time. Readers wishing to know more about DIA might want to turn immediately to chapter thirteen.

Parts of this book are all too broad. This reflects the immense gaps in the existing literature. Specific volumes are needed on many of the chapters, including the rise of black Denver, the nature of Denver Public Schools, the many faces of the Hispano community, and the nature of water in the region. *DIA and Other Scams* is only an introduction to these topics, ones, I hope, others will address.

Here and there, parts of the text are repetitious as I look at the same development as it affected different sectors. For example, the close nexus between the savings and loan scandals and DIA makes it necessary to mention some of the same players and events in both chapters eight and thirteen.

The volume also suffers from the pitfalls of contemporary history. Seeking to bring events up to the year 2000, I have sometimes accepted breaking news as accomplished fact. This is problematic. For example, just before volume one went to press, Donald Sturm announced he was buying the Denver Nuggets and Colorado Avalanche. That deal soon collapsed.

I have tried to liven up the text with numerous graphics. Unfortunately, no comprehensive archive exists of photos of the modern era. In places, picture selection more relates to the best images I could find than the intrinsic importance of the shots. In places, photos of key buildings, such as the hyperbolic paraboloid of the May D&F are not included since I placed illustrations of such structures in volume one.

John Schoenwalter immensely aided in picture selection. Not only did he shoot the cover graphic and give me advice on photography, but he scoured his files for historic images while educating me on the basics of the craft. Ann Bingham also looked through her files, sharing some of her shots of the Mile High City. Bill Good helped me in camera procurement. Neal Paul shot the photo on the back.

The intense efforts of past scholars have paved the way for my work. I discuss the writings on the city's past in the bibliography. Instead of cluttering the text with footnotes, I have appended essays on sources to each chapter.

Many individuals assisted me in this effort to whom I owe immense gratitude. I try to acknowledge them in specific chapter notes. Most of all, I want to say thanks to the Denver Public Library (DPL). While I make some extremely critical remarks about it, the institution stands out as the area's foremost educational resource. Librarians there have continually aided me, helping me find the seemingly most arcane documents. (Unless otherwise noted, collections listed at DPL are in the Western History Department.)

Thanks also go to the staff of the Stephen Hart Library of the Colorado Historical Society. Frank Tapp of the Auraria Archives readily welcomed me there, allowing me to use its impressive and rather unknown collections on modern Denver. I also wish to acknowledge the help of Steve Fisher and Thyria Wilson at the University of Denver Archives.

I gathered much of the raw data for this volume in the mid-1980s when working as a reporter. During that time I dealt with numerous public relations officials. Most were quite helpful. Unfortunately, I do not recall all who then assisted me.

George Archuleta did yeoman's work as an editor, reading various drafts, calling my attention to sources, and criticizing some of my views and approaches. Mike Davenport also reviewed the text, sharing his inside experiences in fighting the planning office and Peña administration over the convention center and DIA. Joining me in numerous Naysayer meetings, he is sometimes the specific "cynic" I have in mind when I refer to questioners of the status quo.

Maxine Lankford and Dinah Land volunteered their skills as proofreaders, also making suggestions about the volume. Marilyn Megenity stimulated me, reviewing parts of the text. Perry Deshler saved me immense expenses by letting me use his copy machine. Mike Dobrash and Richard Jones shared their knowledge as professional printers, giving me suggestions on improving the appearance of the book. As ever, Walt Young encouraged me, sharing his critical views of neighborhood groups and city hall. His partner, Angel Garcia, always had a good word for my efforts. Kathi Anderson of Councilman Ed Thomas' office, whose name I embarrassedly got wrong in the acknowledgments to volume one, helped give me direction through the labyrinth of city agencies. Those commenting on my past books and coming on my tours have been a constant source of encouragement, keeping me going on Denver history. Most of all, thanks go to those countless, anonymous individuals who have turned out for demonstrations, decried the smugness of the status quo, and worked to improve the city as part of our common community.

**Phil Goodstein**
**Labor Day, 2000**

# 1

# Black Denver

Blacks, Indians, and Hispanos were present in Denver from the beginning. All were part of the Pikes Peak gold rush in 1858–59. Just like Caucasians, African-Americans sought fortune in Colorado during the 19th century. Relations between different races were never smooth. Not only did white pioneers dismiss American Indians as subhuman, but they likewise looked down on all who did not fit into their narrow, northern European, Protestant background. Virtually from its establishment, institutional and de facto racism existed in Denver. At different times, various groups felt the sting of prejudicial actions by the leaders of the business, political, and social communities.

After American Indians were driven out of the area in the 1860s and 1870s, powerful sections of the ruling elite, led by the *Rocky Mountain News*, targeted Asians. A vicious anti-Chinese riot tore through Denver on October 31, 1880. Though there were only 300 or so people of that nationality in a city of 35,629, demagogues blamed the city's problems on them. At other times Jews felt the wrath of intolerant Denver. High society organizations, notably the Denver Athletic Club and Denver Country Club, were outright in their anti-Semitic practices, refusing to allow Jewish members.

With the help of the Republican Party, the American Protective Association, a virulently anti-Catholic group, seized control of the Colorado government in 1894–96 in the name of defeating Populism. The hate group treated Catholics as an abomination. It sought to deny them any government jobs, blaming them for the economic collapse of 1893.

During World War I, at the behest of former Denver journalist and police commissioner George Creel, a close aide of President Woodrow Wilson, Washington declared anybody and anything German an enemy of crusading American patriotism. Locals jumped on this bandwagon, venting their wrath on the city's large German-American population. The *Denver Post* was in the lead of spewing forth such hatred. The city's political and business leaders tolerated it when not openly encouraging it.

Anti-black, anti-Catholic, anti-Hispanic, anti-foreigner, and anti-Jewish prejudice was the rage in 1923–25 when the Ku Klux Klan swept Denver. At first, 17th Street did little to oppose the white supremist group. On the contrary, it generally endorsed the Klan. That organization elected one of its own, Benjamin Stapleton, mayor in 1923. After a couple of years, the Klan showed itself a venal, inefficient, utterly corrupt, coercive gang. By the spring of 1925, seeing strong community opposition to the Klan and troubled by the outfit's efforts to usurp his power as mayor, Stapleton turned against the group. The association interfered with his primary duty to run a smoothly functioning city hall. The business elite endorsed his decision, also rejecting the discredited clique. Nonetheless, racial and ethnic tensions remained part and parcel of the Mile High City.

Right when the Klan was riding high, leading bankers and bond dealers worked with members of the African-American community through the Urban League and black divisions of the YMCA and YWCA to establish the Denver Interracial Committee in 1924. The body observed the discrimination against and economic problems affecting African-Americans. Not only did it call for ending racist practices through greater employment opportunities for blacks, but the commission was open in its recommendations of Negro uplift to get poor blacks to behave more like middle-class whites.

Even before the rise of the Klan, this had been something of official policy. In 1919, for example, the Community Chest helped sponsor a Colored Employment Bureau to assure jobs for African-Americans. A few companies loudly announced they would not discriminate against job applicants on account of their race. Periodically, Denver had widely publicized brotherhood dinners whereby the Chamber of Commerce painted the city as a tolerant community.

The Interracial Committee functioned through the 1930s. It continually complained about discriminatory practices. Though vague in details, it cited the case of a promising young black woman who obtained a teacher's certificate from Colorado State College in Greeley. She was systematically denied a post because of the color of her skin. Seeing her life's aspirations going for nothing, she killed herself to protest the racism of the state's school systems. Showing an international anti-racist consciousness, the commission called for the United States to boycott the 1936 Berlin Olympics to condemn Nazism.

Even more than the rest of the city, black Denver suffered economically through the Great Depression. During the 1930s, there was little investment in public facilities while residences decayed. Housing conditions grew worse with World War II. As the population burgeoned and lodging stagnated, racists were quick to blame minorities as the cause of shortages. Even so, discrimination against and hatred of blacks was sometimes muted compared to the vehement anti-Hispanic sentiment then pervading the Mile High City.

Photo by John Schoenwalter

*Ghosts still linger from when the Ku Klux Klan controlled Denver in 1923–25. During the mid-1990s, members of the Klan had a number of violent rallies in front of the Capitol.*

## Postwar Conditions

Racist rhetoric and practices contrasted with the ideals for which America claimed to fight against Germany and Japan. Even before the war, blacks increasingly marched against and protested the indignities they experienced daily on account of their skin color. As the Cold War loomed and civil right activists became ever more outspoken, blatant discrimination would no longer do.

Mayor Quigg Newton realized this. After his election in 1947, he sought to redress the longtime covert racism of the Stapleton administration. Shortly after taking office, the new mayor appointed a committee to try to defuse a potential racial powder keg. Newton institutionalized this group as the Mayor's Committee on Human Relations. It was a powerful body evolving into the Commission on Human Relations in 1951 before the city turned it into the Commission on Community Relations in 1959. For years, Minoru Yasui directed it. He was a story in his own right.

Born of Japanese parents in Hood River, Oregon, on October 19, 1916, Yasui graduated from the University of Oregon School of Law in 1939. By the time of Pearl Harbor, he served as a lieutenant in the Army Reserves, having gone through the Reserve Officer Training Corps program while in college. He protested Washington's vindictive efforts aimed at Japanese-American citizens during the war. He deliberately violated racist curfew laws. For his troubles he was deprived of his citizenship. Eventually the ruling was overturned. Yasui arrived in Denver in September 1944. Citing his arrest record, the Colorado Bar Association denied him a license. In January 1946, the Colorado Supreme Court belatedly permitted him to practice in the Centennial State.

A charter member of the Mayor's Committee on Human Relations, Yasui served on the board of the Commission on Community Relations (CCR) from 1959 until 1967. He was its executive director from 1967 until 1983. During his tenure, he occasionally clashed with mayors Tom Currigan and Bill McNichols. Mostly, he upheld their policies against those protesting what they believed were racist and brutal city policies. He died on November 12, 1986. Already in 1976, the city named a monthly award to the individual doing the most to assist in brotherhood and volunteer work after Yasui.

Over the years, the Commission on Community Relations was something of a patronage machine for city hall. It hired numerous community activists as consultants. The body often operated as an advocacy office showing dissidents they

Photo by John Schoenwalter

*Martin Luther King Day has become a leading event in black Denver. Mayor Wellington Webb stands on the podium next to the statue of King in City Park in 1993.*

could work within the system. The city transformed CCR into the Agency for Human Rights and Community Relations in May 1984. The latter had a wide-ranging presence, including commissions on aging, women, domestic violence, and people with disabilities. It had the power to review police violence and affirmative action. The Newton-established body's policies shaped it. The Mayor's Committee on Human Relations examined city practices in the late 1940s, discovering racism in many municipal institutions.

In November 1947, the bureau issued *A Report on Minorities*. It estimated that there were 15,000 blacks, 30,000 Hispanics, 2,500 Japanese-Americans, and 16,500 Jews in a Denver of 387,412 residents. (There was no listing for American Indians.) Unfortunately, the agency observed, city hall led the way for discriminatory racial policies at its central public bathhouse at 20th and Curtis streets.

Despite a public accommodations law making it illegal to deprive anyone of access to swimming pools on account of color, the city set aside different days for Negroes, Spanish, Japanese, and "whites." The last bathed first. The water was changed immediately before and after other groups were permitted in the public swimming pool. (In 1941, Mayor Stapleton had refused to heed the demands of neighborhood improvers near Curtis Park to segregate that park's pool at 32nd and Curtis streets. For years, however, the city ignored court rulings mandating no discrimination at public facilities such as the central bathhouse.)

Most outright segregation and discrimination disappeared under the impact of the Newton commission. Even so, the body was blunt in its veiled racism. Its studies of black and brown Denver readily condemned the non-middle-class values and lifestyles of many poor African-Americans and Hispanos. A key goal, echoed by various middle-class Negroes and Spanish-Americans, was for members of these groups to emulate the lifestyle of ruling white Denver.

This remained a culture of discrimination. Leading restaurants and hotels bluntly targeted African-Americans. Typical was the Brown Palace. Owned by the Boettcher family, it long only tolerated blacks on the premises as servants. For some years, it did not even allow African-Americans to ride on the elevators. This exploded in April 1929 when the inn refused to let a black messenger for Governor Billy Adams get on the elevator after the governor called him and requested he bring an urgent dispatch to Adams who was living at the Brown Palace. Other leading hotels, including the Cosmopolitan and Albany, did not treat blacks any better.

The Denver Athletic Club and the Denver Country Club continued to practice overt racism and religious discrimination. Both Elitch's and Lakeside sometimes refused to admit blacks and Hispanics because of the color of their skin. Leading theaters restricted where African-Americans could sit during performances. During the peak of its opulence in the late 19th century, for example, the Tabor Grand Opera House was vehement in restricting when blacks could attend, segregating them in the balcony.

Until World War II, the Orpheum Theater, at 1537 Welton Street, only permitted blacks to sit in the top row of the highest balcony, a place derogatorily called "Nigger Heaven." Under the pressure of civil rights protesters, management changed this policy when whites loudly made a point of sharing the balcony with African-Americans. "Race bars" was the term given to drinking establishments specifically catering to Negroes. Various black-owned taxi firms came and went in response to the lack of cab service for African-Americans.

Despite the presence of Jim Crow policies into the 1960s, racial discrimination was always ostensibly illegal in Colorado. The Centennial State joined the union in 1876 at the close of Reconstruction, a time when the country made strong paper commitments to civil rights. In the enabling act of 1875, when Congress authorized statehood for Colorado, the federal government required the territory adopt the principles of the Civil Rights Act of 1875. The state constitution included strong language prohibiting any "distinction in civil or political rights on account of race or color." In 1885, the state adopted a public accommodations act banning discrimination in inns, restaurants, bars, hotels, and comparable institutions.

These measures were rarely enforced. No district attorney ever filed a criminal complaint against an individual or institution accused of violating the anti-discrimination law. At most, aggrieved parties had the right to sue for civil damages under it. They rarely achieved much relief. On the contrary, the police occasionally arrested civil rights protesters who demanded restaurants, theaters, and hotels obey the letter of the constitution.

Blacks also suffered at the hand of trade unions. While a few labor organizations, notably the Western Federation of Miners, admitted blacks as full, equal members, others preferred a divided and defeated working-class to integrated unions. Some labor groups, such as the Printing Pressman and Denver Painters Union, banned Negro members. Others only permitted blacks in Jim Crow locals, e.g., Waiters and Waitresses local #17 and the Denver Musicians Protective Asso-

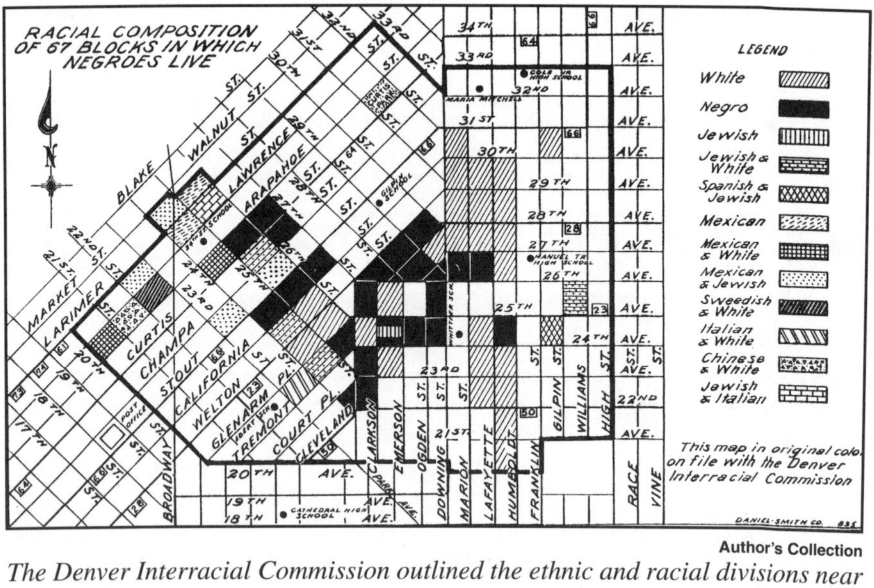


Author's Collection

*The Denver Interracial Commission outlined the ethnic and racial divisions near Five Points, the heart of black Denver, in the mid-1920s.*

ciation. Not surprisingly, many blacks had no use for such unions. Employers, in turn, readily played the race card, fanning divisions between black and white workers in labor disputes.

During the first half of the 20th century, African-Americans came and went from city jobs. On the whole, they were only hired for the most menial of positions. Given black suffrage in Colorado (no attempts were ever made to infringe upon it), politicians sometimes recognized leading Negroes, naming them to various commissions.

A few blacks and Spanish-Americans served on the fire and police departments during the pre-World War II era. In 1930, ten African-Americans were counted as Denver's finest. This was up from two patrolmen and one detective in the 1920s. By 1940, there were no blacks on the police department. Mayor Stapleton explained none were qualified for the job. Under political pressure, he found a couple of black veterans whom he added to the force shortly after World War II.

The Denver Fire Department was conspicuously segregated. Station #3 at 2500 Washington Street, organized in 1893, was the black company. For more than 50 years, all African-Americans desiring to become firefighters either had to work there or stay off the force. The department was only integrated in the 1950s. Even then, strict quotas remained limiting the number of blacks and Mexican-Americans allowed to become police officers or firefighters.

While Emily Griffith Opportunity School sometimes filled its classes on a racial quota basis, there was little ostensible discrimination in the public schools. Class, not race, was the crucial dividing line in most neighborhood and educational facilities. Since most blacks were poor, it was not surprising their children attended classes with the sons and daughters of poor and working-class whites. In 1934, the only school in town with more than a 50-percent black enrollment was Whittier, at 25th Avenue and Downing Street, located where Five Points and old East Denver come together. Generally, the more black students in a school, the less its funding. The school question eventually exploded, showing much of the racist rot of the city.

## The Rise of Black Denver

During the 1950s, 1960s, and 1970s, tensions over school segregation ripped the city apart. Neighborhoods drastically changed as increasing numbers of African-Americans settled in the Mile High City. While most of the blacks were newcomers, they arrived in a city with a rich African-American heritage.

A less than savory reminder of the black participation in the Pikes Peak gold rush was the appellation "Nigger Hill" for a mining area in Summit County. It recalled an escaped slave, Barney Ford, had staked claim to a mine there in the early 1860s. The courts ruled against Ford when he sought to assert his right to the land. His skin color was the major reason for their decision.

Back in Denver, Ford and other African-Americans fought the conservative John Evans–William Newton Byers–Jerome Chaffee faction of the Colorado Republican Party in the mid-1860s. The Denver crowd wanted Colorado to join the union without complete universal manhood suffrage; i.e., right at the time when blacks were winning the franchise in the wake of the Civil War, leading to the adoption of the 15th Amendment, some of Colorado's most honored pioneers sought to exclude African-Americans from casting ballots. With the assistance of Republicans in Golden and Central City, who feared and hated the Denver Republicans, Ford was successful in helping block statehood at this time.

Many African-Americans passed through the city in the 19th century. Among them were cowboys and former calvary soldiers. There were about three dozen blacks in boomtown Denver in 1860. By 1870, 257 African-Americans lived in a Denver of 4,759 inhabitants.

The number of blacks remained quite small into the 20th century. Less than 5 percent of the total population was African-American. Given the anti-discriminatory specifications of the Colorado constitution, Jim Crow did not officially exist. Nonetheless, there were certain places where blacks knew they could not or should not go—racism existed despite the law. Generally, African-Americans lived a world apart from ruling white Denver.

Among the centers of black Denver were its churches. Early settlers established Shorter African Methodist Episcopal (AME) and Zion Baptist in the 1860s. Founders dedicated the former as St. John's AME in July 1868. When the congregation occupied a new building in 1878, members renamed it in honor of Bishop James A. Shorter (1800–80), a powerful figure in the African Methodist Episcopal Church. Five locals joined with preacher William Norrid to start Zion Baptist as African Baptist Church on November 15, 1865. It evolved into Colored Baptist Church before emerging as Zion Baptist. The two congregations helped launch the inaugural school for black children in 1868 when the first Denver Public Schools initially refused to admit African-American children.

Over the decades, Shorter and Zion churches were defining institutions of black Denver. Everybody of account, especially of the business and professional classes, belonged to them. Their ministers were not just spiritual leaders, but powers in their own right. Both churches eventually developed extensive outreach efforts, complete with senior citizen homes and social-welfare programs. Other black churches often originated as splinters from these pioneer congregations.

The various locations of Shorter Church reflected the pockets of black Denver. After initially gathering in a shack near the Platte River, it occupied a simple building at 19th and Market streets in 1868. The congregation moved to 18th and Stout streets ten years later. In 1886, it bought lots for $10,000 at 17th Street and Glenarm Place, opposite where the Denver Athletic Club (DAC) was planning its new home. After the congregation broke ground for its sanctuary, massive pressure from DAC and affluent white homeowners in the area forced the church to sell the land for $14,000. Shortly thereafter, Shorter erected a substantial home near the intersection of Park Avenue, 20th Avenue, 23rd Street, and Washington Street. On April 9, 1925, a mysterious fire, allegedly set by the Ku Klux Klan, destroyed the church. On Easter, April 14, 1926, Shorter held its first services in an elaborate new sanctuary on the site.

By the 1970s, members viewed the existing church as old and as unfashionable as everything else in historic Denver. Reflecting the drift of African-Americans to

Photo by Phil Goodstein

*Zion Baptist Church, at the northwest corner of 24th Avenue and Ogden Street, is the city's pioneer African-American congregation.*

the northeast, many of Shorter's affluent parishioners lived north of City Park and in Park Hill. Simultaneously, the Denver Urban Renewal Authority eyed the 23rd and Washington land for a massive urban renewal project. With the congregation wanting a larger facility, in September 1978, thanks to the help of a trustee, Omar Blair, who was also a member of the school board, Denver Public Schools sold land at 31st Avenue and Jackson Street to the church. Shorter dedicated the last part of its impressive, seven-acre, $7 million complex there in June 1990. Its address was 3100 Richard Allen Court—Jackson Street from 29th Avenue to Martin Luther King Boulevard was renamed in 1980 to honor the founder of the African Methodist Episcopal Church.

## Five Points

The white establishment was always cognizant of black politicians. John T. Gunnell, a Republican, was the first African-American to serve in the state House of Representatives in 1881–82. In the wake of the Populist sweep in 1892, the Republicans recruited blacks to successfully run for office in 1894, including one who served in the General Assembly. Through much of the mid-20th century, Ben Hooper, a firm supporter of Ben Stapleton, represented black Republicans. Oglesive L. "Sonny" Lawson was the leader of Democratic African-Americans.

In July 1972, the city memorialized the latter with Sonny Lawson Park on the block bordered by 23rd, 24th, Welton, and California streets. It had been a small spot of open space since the 19th century, officially becoming a city park on October 2, 1911. The greenery, including a lighted softball field, memorialized a pharmacist, known as Doc Lawson, who was born in Denver on September 12, 1893. After receiving his degree from the Northwestern University School of Pharmacy in 1913, working for the Western Chemical Corporation, and serving in the assessor's office for five years, Lawson opened Radio Pharmacy at 2601 Welton Street in 1923–24 with H. A. Maxwell. The political establishment frequently tabbed Lawson as the black representative on various boards. In 1948, for example, he was the first African-American to serve on the Denver Library Commission. In 1955, he joined the board overseeing the city's Career Service Authority. He was something of the political godfather to Denver's first black city councilman, Elvin Caldwell, and Colorado's inaugural black state senator, George L. Brown. Lawson died at age 75 on July 14, 1969.

The activist's store was in the heart of Five Points, the intersection of Welton, Washington, and 27th streets and 26th Avenue where the diagonal downtown roads intersect with the east-west, north-south grid of the rest of the city. Five Points emerged as the center of black Denver in the early 1900s. In part, this was the result of an early urban renewal effort targeting African-Americans.

Development first occurred in the area near 26th Avenue and Washington Street in the early 1880s. At that time, Denver was rapidly growing to the northeast. Luxurious Victorian houses dotted the area to past Fuller Park, established at 29th Avenue and Williams Street in 1879. Generally, this part of Denver was a white upper-middle-class, suburban residential enclave.

Streetcar service arrived with the settlers. The transit company, seeking a convenient moniker to note the destination of its vehicles, christened the area "Five Points" in 1881. Residents immediately protested. Five Points, they noted, was the name of a notorious slum in New York City. Their neighborhood was not at all like it; on the contrary, it was a stately area. Despite their protests, the Five Points designation stuck.

The area around Five Points and the adjacent Curtis Park never emerged as a permanent upper-class abode. Middle-class development surged with the laying of a streetcar track along 28th Avenue in 1891. Much of the building halted in 1893 when the economy collapsed. The section never recovered. By the early 20th century, the Five Points, Fuller Park, and Curtis Park neighborhoods faded as Capitol Hill and sections near the Denver Country Club grew as the city's distinguished residential abodes. Nonetheless, many middle-class and proud, sturdy, independent white working-class families remained in these parts of old East Denver for generations.

Blacks lived in diverse sections of the Mile High City in the late 19th and early 20th centuries. Cherry Creek was the home to African-American truck farmers, gardeners, and maids and servants for the Country Club. There was also a significant black population in West Denver near West 14th Avenue and Fox Street. A few black families settled on the fringes of the Barnum neighborhood around West Third Avenue and Lowell Boulevard. Most African-Americans dwelt on the fringes of downtown near 20th and 23rd streets along Lawrence and Arapahoe streets.

Homeowners often targeted blacks who sought to move into previously all-white abodes. Typical was the hatred expressed by residents on the 400 block of Kalamath Street in September 1912 when they heard a Negro family might buy a lot to build a home there. They successfully banded together, insisting on a racially pure area.

The city's extension of Broadway in the 1910s led to the emergence of Five Points as the heart of African-American Denver. Broadway initially ended at 20th Avenue and Welton Street. To the southeast was Capitol Hill; northeast was the highly diverse old East Denver. Not only was the original East High School nearby on the block surrounded by 19th, California, 20th, and Stout streets, but so were various factories, printing plants, lumber yards, and residences. The last ranged from 1870s mansions to rowhouses to veritable hovels. Numerous blacks lived in the area. By the early 20th century, real estate interests already viewed much of the section as an ancient vestige of Denver's past in need of replacement.

In the name of business improvement and a better connection between downtown and Brighton Boulevard and the stockyards, city hall pushed an extension of Broadway through old East Denver to 25th Street where it connected with a new Broadway Viaduct. Authorized in 1909, the effort was finally completed in 1921. In the process, the city displaced many African-Americans from their homes. Most moved a few blocks northeast to Five Points.

**Photo by Phil Goodstein**

*A storefront stands before a stone house on the 2500 block of Welton Street along the Welton Center stretch of Five Points.*

Photo by John Schoenwalter

*Famous jazz vibraphonist Milt Jackson was among many leading African-American musicians who performed in the Mile High City. Though generally welcoming black entertainers, for years the city engaged in blatant discriminatory housing policies.*

World War I and the changing nature of urban retail patterns also impacted the neighborhood. Already in the early 20th century, hotels and business blocks emerged along Welton Center, the stretch of Welton Street between 24th and 28th streets. As Welton Center blossomed, houses along Welton Street started to give way to commercial buildings and storefronts. By the time the Ku Klux Klan dominated Denver in the 1920s, these businesses primarily served black customers. Five Points was increasingly the place for African-Americans to go. If nothing else, customers knew they would not suffer from racial discrimination in these shops, unlike the fate they might suffer if they dared venture into the enclaves of elite white Denver. Though Five Points was never 100-percent black, for decades it was *the* African-American neighborhood. Many of the businesses and a good deal of the property were owned by local black investors.

Five Points flourished in the 1920s, 1930s, 1940s, and 1950s as a center of regional black culture. Leading Negro entertainers stayed in homes and hotels there, finding them far more comfortable than the snooty, downtown hotels. Usually, there was no ostensible rule against blacks staying at such places as the Albany or Shirley-Savoy. African-Americas knew better than to challenge the racist customs.

Black musicians touring the country found Denver a convenient stop as they headed to and from Kansas City. Jazz clubs and cabarets popped up along Welton Center. Five Points also attracted the so-called black-and-tan crowd—whites who found Negroes far more liberated, honest, and free than the stuffy Babbitts of white Denver. Cab drivers frequently drove fares to Five Points when riders asked to be taken to places where they could meet women and gamble.

Now and then, Denver tolerated black musicians outside Five Points. Sometimes, such performers were the only African-Americans allowed into white institutions when they came to entertain audiences. After World War II, the Denver Symphony Orchestra employed Jack Bradley, the only black professional classical musician who was a member of a leading symphony in the country. A few white families opened their homes to black musicians, allowing them to stay in elite residential sections which were virtually lily white.

## Segregation and Bombings

Blacks were victims of racial violence. Regardless of the Colorado Constitution, restrictive covenants existed to keep African-Americans out of such areas as Park Hill, Hilltop, and Crestmoor. There were other areas where white residents insisted blacks simply did not belong. Neighborhood improvement associations, leaders of which often had close ties with the Ku Klux Klan, were in the vanguard of fighting residential integration. The presence of black neighbors, they loudly feared, would undermine property values. The Board of Realtors seconded them. It virtually prohibited members from selling African-Americans houses in certain parts of town. Such pressures increased after World War I when many blacks moved to Denver from the South.

Typical of the operations of neighborhood groups was the action of the Clayton Improvement Association in the area to the north and west of City Park. In 1920, after a black fireman, Claude De Priest, previously of 2516 Lafayette Street, bought a house at 2649 Gaylord Street, the neighborhood association threatened him: "If you continue to reside at your present address, you do so at your own peril." De Priest thereupon sold the house. About the same time, a white mob threatened Mrs. Emma Davis, an African-American who had moved to 2450 Gaylord Street.

Those failing to heed such threats were targeted for bombings and burnings. Such was the fate of mail carrier Walter R. Chapman. In July 1921, he moved to 2112 Gilpin Street. A few African-Americans had already made inroads in this mostly white, middle-class area. Among them was Richard Porter, a black member of the police department who sold Chapman the Gilpin Street house. Neighbors were glad to see Porter leave, but did not want Chapman to move in. They warned him to stay away; otherwise, something might happen. The something was a bomb thrown in his front yard on July 7 while Chapman was on the porch of the house with his wife.

Escaping injury, Chapman soon moved out. Another African-American, Charles E. A. Starr, an employee of the city's Department of Parks and Improvements, purchased the house. He likewise received racial threats. On the eve of Starr's plans to sell the structure to a white family, a second bomb blew out every window in the house on November 15, 1921. Starr, along with his wife and ten-year-old daughter escaped unharmed from the blast. In spite of his professed resolve to remain to defy the bombers, within a year, Starr abandoned the area.

CAPITOL HILL URGES NEGRO SEGREGATION

Improvement Association Names Committee to Wait on Legislature

The Capitol Hill Improvement association appointed a committee at a meeting last night to act with committees of other improvement associations to wait on the state legislature in reference to securing legislative steps for Negro segregation. The association also went on record in favoring the plot of ground at East Nineteenth avenue and Franklin street for the erection of the Denver Gas and Electric Light company's new gas storage tank. The meeting was held in the Nash Mortuary, 2205 East Colfax avenue, and was attended by more than one hundred residents of the Capitol hill district.

**Author's Collection**

*The February 13, 1923,* Rocky Mountain News *reported how neighborhood improvement groups were leading advocates of segregation.*

Other bombings followed. Essex E. Carrington found his home a target. An executive with the American Woodmen, a black fraternal-insurance society headquartered at 21st Avenue and Downing Street, he moved to 2253 Vine Street in late 1926. Locals immediately mailed Carrington a notice, informing him he had better leave the neighborhood. Shortly thereafter, around 2:00 AM on December 10, a deafening explosion tore a huge hole through his front porch. On January 2, while Carrington's wife, Lula, was standing on the porch, six shots were fired at her. She escaped unwounded even as bullets were found in both the porch and house. Later that night, gunfire blew out a light on the rear sleeping porch.

The Carringtons vowed to stay. More trouble followed. Around 6:00 PM on January 15, 1927, Carrington noticed somebody throw a bundle on the porch. He immediately ran out, flinging the package toward the street where it exploded, breaking windows in the adjacent house at 2255 Vine Street. Shortly thereafter, the Carringtons moved to 2836 Humboldt Street. Other bombings and cross burnings occurred.

High and Race streets emerged as something of a Mason-Dixon Line, dividing black and white Denver. Some black activists, noting the nearby Grasshopper Hill (approximately the site of the old Presbyterian Hospital near 20th and Williams streets), called it "Struggle Hill." Not until after World War II was the color line peacefully breached in this part of the city. ("Struggle Hill" also applied to Park Hill in the 1960s.)

Racial hatreds and antagonisms were open. Among the most virulent groups was another neighborhood syndicate, the Capitol Hill Improvement Association, the supposed voice and conscience of Capitol Hill. At a gathering on February 12, 1923, it called for Jim Crow laws in Colorado. Some of its members were outraged when black pupils at East High School (around 20 in a student body of more than 2,000) were allowed to attend the senior prom. Working with other intolerant homeowner clubs, the Capitol Hill Improvement Association hoped to amend the Colorado constitution on the model of states in the deep South to specify segregation as a way of life. Nothing came of this venture.

Despite the violence aimed at blacks wishing to move east of High Street during the 1920s, some African-Americans slowly breached the color line. A directory of the membership of the black branch of the YWCA during the mid-1930s, for example, shows blacks living at 1868 Gaylord, 3556 Gaylord, 3042 Vine, 2635 Fillmore, and 2525 Birch Street. Some of the addresses listed are problematic—they may indicate live-in addresses of black maids rather than homes. As late as the 1950–51 *East Denver Directory*, the overwhelming bulk of addresses for African-Americans was west of Race Street. In other words, for years racism and possible physical assaults successfully kept blacks from moving into the areas close to City Park.

## The Depression and World War II

As with the rest of the country, black Denver suffered hard times during the Great Depression. When farmers in eastern Colorado killed thousands of jackrabbits, the *Denver Post* took the lead in dumping them on Five Points. They were, the newspaper explained, the favorite food of the neighborhood's residents. In the late 1930s, the Denver Housing Authority (DHA) claimed it was helping poor blacks when it sought to isolate them in a segregated Arapahoe Courts project at 28th and Arapahoe streets. (DHA simultaneously placed low-income Mexican-Americans in the Las Casitas project near West 11th Avenue and Eliot Street.) The Platte Valley project at 3050 Champa Street followed as another DHA effort for African-Americans after World War II.

The war drastically changed the local black community. Job opportunities brought many people of color to the Mile High City. More African-Americans came via the United States Army. As with numerous whites, many blacks stayed in the city in the wake of the conflict. African-American veterans from the South and Midwest appreciated Denver. Despite its racial shortcomings, they found it far better, cleaner, and more tolerant than other places they had known. They hoped to begin anew in the Queen City.

The number of professional African-Americans surged after the Air Force Finance Center (later the Finance and Accounting Center) relocated to the Mile High City in 1951, when it emerged as an independent entity from the Army Finance Center in St. Louis. The military complex occupied 37.5 acres on the east side of the 3900 block of York Street. For years, this had been open space, adjacent to the railroad tracks, land sometimes used as a circus grounds. In 1942, the property was built up as the Denver Medical Depot. Now it was something of a nerve center for the recently integrated Air Force. Many aspiring middle-class blacks, who found the military a means of upward mobility, came to Denver with it.

The location of the Accounting Center impacted residential patterns. As with the rest of Denver, housing was at a premium in Five Points by the end of World War II. Seeking to live close to their jobs at the federal complex, blacks readily destroyed the old unofficial color line at High and Race streets. Before long, middle-class African-Americans had moved east of York Street. By the 1960s, the area north of City Park was predominantly black.

Harrington School, at 38th Avenue and Adams Street, was illustrative of this shift. Opened in 1926 as Adams Street School, it was virtually 100-percent white when it was renamed for teacher Mary Lyons Harrington in 1950. By 1952, 31 percent of its students were black. By 1960, it had a 100-percent minority enrollment.

Numbers confirm the rapidly changing population pattern. From 7,836 blacks in a Denver of 322,412 residents in 1940, the population of African-Americans in the city more than doubled to 15,901 in 1950 in a Denver of 415,786. By 1960, the number had doubled again to 30,251 in a community of 493,887. Growth continued to 47,011 in 1970, 59,252 in 1980, and 60,046 in 1990 when the black population was about 13 percent of Denver's 467,610 residents. In addition to blacks within the City and County of Denver, the census listed another 28,876 African-Americans in the surrounding Adams, Arapahoe, Boulder, Douglas, and Jefferson counties. Most of those areas remained overwhelmingly white. The projected 2000 census had Denver at 15 percent black compared to a 4 percent African-American population in Adams County, 6 percent in Arapahoe County, and 1 percent each in Boulder, Jefferson, and Douglas counties.

Professional African-Americans took immense pride in their dwellings, touting their residences as much as any middle-class white homeowner. They were socially active and politically involved. The East Denver Improvement Association emerged as a black residential association for the area east of Downing Street. African-Americans increasingly served in the General Assembly. Elvin Caldwell was the first black to win election to city council in 1955.

Caldwell was, so to speak, old Denver. His mother was from a middle-class family in Selma, Alabama. He was born on April 11, 1919, and grew up in the Mile High City. After graduating from East High School in 1937, Caldwell went on to attend both the University of Denver and University of Colorado. In 1950, he gained election as a Democrat to the state House of Representatives. (Denver

DPL

*Elvin Caldwell was Denver's first black city councilman.*

representatives were then elected at large, meaning Caldwell carried the city to gain the post.) Believing he could be more effective in city than state politics, he left the legislature for council.

Not only was the black politician repeatedly reelected, but he also closely allied himself with different mayors on crucial issues. Caldwell served a number of terms as council president. In that capacity, he was an official of the George W. Clayton Boys College. Located at the northwest corner of 32nd Avenue (a road renamed Martin Luther King Boulevard in January 1980) and Colorado Boulevard, it recalls George W. Clayton. A key real estate investor in the 19th century, Clayton owned land throughout the city, including tracts in University Hills, Stapleton Airport, North City Park, Park Hill, and Capitol Hill. Based on his 1892 will, on his death in 1899, Clayton's $3 million estate went to Denver to create a city-sponsored home "for the education and maintenance of poor, white, male, orphan children." The will specifically defined an orphan as a boy who had lost his father.

To gain admission to Clayton College, a boy had to be between six and ten, sound in mind and body, and have "reputable parentage," i.e., no juvenile delinquents or waifs were accepted. The mother or guardian of the child had to agree to give Clayton College a total indenture over the boy. The charge lived on campus where he was educated until he was from 14 to 19. The hope: an orphan graduated from the college would emerge as a productive member of society.

No sooner was Clayton College opened in 1912 than it was engulfed in scandal. City fathers drained many of the school's assets—Clayton's rich real estate holdings—through questionable land deals benefiting friends of leading politicians. Every few years, Clayton College popped up in the news for some alleged transgression or mismanagement. Black Denver long protested its racism. Caldwell finally forced the city to eliminate the race provision from the Clayton charter in 1965. Eventually, Clayton College came to host numerous social-welfare programs primarily geared for African-Americans.

The city councilman vehemently denounced hippies in the late 1960s. He was a firm supporter of Mayor Bill McNichols through the 1970s. Anybody needing to get something done in his council district had to go through Caldwell or one of his associates. The politician had investments in the Rossonian Hotel at the Five Points intersection proper where he ran the Rossonian Lounge, a bar accused of sometimes violating the liquor code.

In April 1980, during his seventh term, Caldwell left council to join the McNichols cabinet as manager of safety, the city official overseeing the fire and police departments. Caldwell resigned the post in the spring of 1983 as McNichols sought reelection as mayor. Allegations surfaced about payoffs to the manager of safety in connection with dubious bingo operations on the police department. Many in the black community were glad to see Caldwell finally retire.

## The Black Panther Party

Among those clashing with Caldwell were members of the Black Panthers. The local chapter described him as "bright, light, and nearly white." In 1969, it called for a "people's tribunal" to condemn Caldwell for failing to serve "the needs and desires of the people." The city councilman responded by firmly endorsing police actions against the Panthers. Branding the group a subversive, revolutionary conspiracy, he wrote the police: "So far as I am personally concerned, I won't be satisfied until every Black Panther is run out of Denver."

In a sense, the Panthers were an aberration in black Denver. Virtually from the beginning, community leadership was always firmly in the hands of church-going,

DPL

*Lauren Watson led the Denver Black Panther Party.*

middle-class individuals. Patriotic veterans after World War II fully endorsed such leadership. Their primary goal was equal opportunity within the larger society. They had no trouble with the condescending improvement programs urged by the Commission on Community Relations. Such individuals were at one with it in wanting to uplift their lower-class brothers. The Panthers questioned this approach. The organization reflected another side of the African-American community: poverty-stricken, angry young men and women.

Huey Newton and Bobby Seale organized the Black Panther Party for Self Defense in Oakland in 1966. While inspired by the civil rights movement and Martin Luther King, its members, mostly youths who had grown up in ghettoes, realized the tactics of nonviolent civil disobedience, with the goal of the total end of Jim Crow discrimination had little applicability in attacking the racism and poverty at the heart of their everyday existences in northern urban centers. Nor did the Panthers think the cultural nationalism of "Black is Beautiful" sufficient to redress the massive social chasms in the United States. They were also disdainful of affirmative-action programs and black capitalism. At the best, they argued, such efforts would only create a few more Uncle Toms, doing nothing for the overwhelming victims of racism and wage slavery.

Opposed to such reforms, the Panthers called for a total social-economic transformation of society. They celebrated petty ghetto criminals as unwitting rebels and potential revolutionaries. The party looked to Mao Tse-tung, Ernesto "Che" Gueverra, Fidel Castro, and other Third World revolutionaries for inspiration. Though the Panthers lacked any realistic program for change or social transformation, their daring and vision provided a political spark and hope to young African-Americans who would otherwise most likely spend their lives in a hideous cycle of poverty, crime, and prison.

The Panther message touched a raw nerve in the Mile High City. Even as the civil rights movement triumphed and many blacks were able to rise to positions of importance in private businesses and public agencies, social divisions remained. Far from benefiting from the affluence of the black middle-class, Five Points suffered badly during the 1960s.

As much as whites who, after World War II, dismissed old buildings and neighborhoods as dilapidated and hopeless, places to flee as soon as possible, many middle-class blacks thought the same about the areas near Five Points. As economic affluence and fair housing legislation provided the way, they wanted out of there. A kind of black flight from Five Points ensued as the African-American middle class moved ever further to the east. Its numbers did not like living next to poor blacks any more than the white middle class did.

Black landlords, who owned most of the area's business buildings and apartments, were little different than white landlords. Though these investors, such as Thomas Bean, LeRoy Smith, McKinley Harris, and Charles Cousins, lived in or near the area and had their businesses there, their aspirations were the same as those of any other developer: the hope the real estate would emerge as part of the central business district, filled with skyscrapers. In the meanwhile, black critics charged they did little to improve existing properties, including some of the worst rental units in the city. Others saw them as civil rights pioneers.

The collapse of Five Points businesses was an unwitting result of the breaking of Jim Crow restrictions and discrimination at department stores, supermarkets, and chain restaurants. To show they were fully equal with whites, many blacks proudly patronized these corporate stores, turning their backs on the small businesses of old black Denver. Many of the latter failed. Empty storefronts increasingly predominated in Five Points.

The historic black area also felt the sting of banks. For many years, the city's leading financial institutions shamelessly discriminated against borrowers seeking to buy or improve properties in Five Points and other relatively poor, inner-city neighborhoods. Nor did city hall care. The bulk of its public works budget was primarily geared for annexations while it more or less ignored basic maintenance in the black section. Sleazy bars and after-hour drinking joints increasingly displaced yesterday's swinging jazz spots. Slumlords, black and white, predominated in the neighborhood. Rat-filled firetraps were often the only housing available to poor residents there.

The number of black juvenile delinquents soared. Some young African-Americans got into trouble simply because of their race—the police picked them up as the "usual suspects." Others were preyed upon by fellow blacks. They sometimes had to affiliate with a club or so-called gang or carry a weapon for their own protection. Cole Junior High School, at 3240 Humboldt Street, had a reputation as an extremely tough school. Dropout and suspension rates were sky-high there and at Manual High School at 28th Avenue and Williams Street. The latter primarily stood out for its excellent basketball program. Compared to the sports emphasis, academics were a second-thought.

As the country struggled with the civil rights movement, living conditions worsened in Five Points. Class divisions widened within the African-American community. Denverites were attuned to national upheavals. All this helped the Black Panthers plant seeds in town in late 1967. The local branch was led by 27-year-old, California-born Lauren R. Watson, who had grown up in the Mile High City. He joined the party during his participation in a national anti-war demonstration in San Francisco that fall. (While the Panthers opposed the Vietnam War, most of the patriotic, middle-class black veterans supported it. Establishment black Denver continued to view the military as a road of achievement and opportunity. Many of these Negroes were deeply troubled by Martin Luther King's condemnation of American involvement in Vietnam.)

Like the national movement, the Denver Panthers aimed to "serve the people." The organization expected members to attend political educational classes, submit to party discipline, and work with the rest of the black community in building the revolutionary movement. The Panthers sponsored a free breakfast program, tried to drive drugs and drug-dealers from their community, and undertook other social-welfare efforts. As was the case throughout the country, the police targeted the Panthers as criminals and troublemakers.

Typical was the Denver Police Department's wedding "present" for Watson. He was married on December 7, 1968, at the local Panther headquarters at 3401 Franklin Street. In addition to decking up the hall for the ceremony, the Panthers filled their office with Christmas decorations and gifts for a party they planned for poor black children. Shortly after the nuptials ended and the Panthers locked up the building, 43 police officers raided it. They systematically looted the premises, knocking over a Christmas tree, smashing ornaments, and scattering the presents. Someone bashed open the Coke machine. The police left the office littered with broken chairs and tables.

By this time, Watson and members of the Panthers had been accused of assorted crimes, including provoking an arson attack on a white-owned dry cleaning establishment at 2018 28th Avenue on September 12, 1968. Following that incident, the police raided the Panther headquarters, then at 2835 Welton Street. They discovered five cases of pop bottles, along with some guns, political statements, and a radio to monitor police calls. The police insisted the bottles were evidence the Panthers were making Molotov cocktails.

The raid led to an explosion in the heart of black Denver. Violence flared during the nights of September 12–13 and 13–14. Massive police reinforcements poured into Five Points. Many Panthers were beaten or maced, including Watson who was arrested. Elvin Caldwell praised the police actions.

When the cases came to court, few of the prosecution's assertions held up and the defendants were freed. This set a pattern. Time and again, hysteria campaigns were launched against the Panthers, but little of substance was proven against the group. Personally, Watson got a good deal of publicity when he was featured as the defendant in one of the first live televised trials in the country. The jury acquit-

**Photo by Phil Goodstein**

*A sculpture of a black fireman, by artist Emanuel Martinez, stands before fire house ten at 32nd Avenue and Steele Street.*

ted him. The Oakland headquarters of the Panthers dismissed the Denver radical as the local head of the group in a national shake-up of the party in August 1969.

By the early 1970s, the local branch was hurting. As with the organization elsewhere, it heavily suffered from continuing legal and police attacks. Nor did its members have a clear vision of precisely what could and should be done. Its infantile rhetoric celebrating violence and petty criminals only increased state repression. Increasingly, the party's main focus was keeping its members out of prison. Two national Panther leaders, Rory B. Hithe and Landon R. Williams, spent nearly two years in the Denver County Jail from June 1969 until April 1971 as the party fought their extradition to New Haven, Connecticut, where they were accused of plotting the murder of a Panther turncoat.

Eventually, most of the charges in New Haven collapsed. This did the party little good. By then many Panthers were dead or serving time for other supposed crimes. As the upheavals of the 1960s settled down in the 1970s, the group collapsed. Middle-class African-Americans increasingly accepted affirmative action as a prime means of allowing some blacks to climb on the shoulders of their brothers and sisters. The Panther alternative to increasing the quota of Uncle Toms was forgotten. The problems of crime, drugs, juvenile delinquency, and the lack of educational accomplishment remained. The African-American community remained highly polarized. Some poverty-stricken individuals and families were in worse shape than ever.

## Black Politicians

By the beginning of the 21st century, daily newspapers and television stations widely publicized the successes of blacks in making their way in white society. Grassroot efforts by African-American activists led to a community appreciation of the area's black culture and history. Ruling Denver feted businessman Barney Ford. It also appreciated Clara Brown. Born a slave in Virginia in 1800, she was freed in 1857, coming to Colorado during the Pikes Peak gold rush. Working as a laundress in mining camps—during which she managed to wash gold dust from the dirty clothes—she eventually brought much of her family to the Centennial State. The message: by hard work, blacks could succeed in the system.

Nobody emphasized this more than the Young Turks. A group of black politicians, mostly in their 20s and 30s, proudly took this title as they gained control of the Democratic Party in East Denver in the early 1970s. Some were blunt in stating race should be a paramount consideration in who was returned to office. Many were attorneys. In 1971, these lawyers formed the Sam Cary Bar Association, a club named in honor of the state's first black lawyer (1886–1961). As long as they were in opposition, the Young Turks, including Wellington Webb, Norm Early, and Dan Muse, readily voiced the glowing ideals of the civil rights movement. Once in power, they generally sanctioned the status quo.

George Leslie Brown blazed the way. Born in Lawrence, Kansas, on July 1, 1926, he was an outstanding high school student. In 1943 he joined the Air Corps. After World War II service, Brown earned a degree in journalism from the University of Kansas, coming to Denver to work as a reporter for the *Denver Post* in 1950. On the job, he exposed some of the city's racist practices.

In 1955, Brown was a key supporter of Elvin Caldwell's bid for city council. After Caldwell left the legislature in the wake of his triumph, the Democratic Party, at the behest of Sonny Lawson, named Brown to fill Caldwell's seat in the state House of Representatives. The next year, the journalist won a narrow, disputed, city-wide election to become the first African-American state senator west of the Mississippi. Brown used the post to speak out as the representative of black Denver.

Photo by Phil Goodstein

*A stained-glass window in the Capitol, installed for the state's Centennial in 1976, honors Clara Brown as personifying 19th-century black Colorado.*

Other African-Americans came and went from the state House of Representatives during the 1940s, 1950s, 1960s, and 1970s. The Democrats recognized Brown in 1974 when they selected him to run for lieutenant governor under Richard Lamm. (Brown had already eyed the post in 1966 and unsuccessfully sought the Democratic nomination in 1970.) The senator's presence on the ticket helped Lamm sweep to victory. Mainstream Denver noted Brown's success in achieving the high office as evidence of how blacks could realize the American dream.

No sooner was he the number-two man in the state government than Brown appeared pompous. Such was the impression many had when he told the press about his World War II fate in Alabama at the conference of the nation's lieutenant governors in Point Clear, Alabama, in late August 1975. After he crashed near Talladega, Alabama, as an flight cadet from Tuskegee during the war, Brown asserted, a local farmer captured him and branded a "K" on his chest, a sign of the Ku Klux Klan's oppression. The branding story, it quickly came out, was a fabrication. The "K" was a sign of Brown's membership in a prominent black fraternity, Kappa Alpha Psi, at the University of Kansas.

Brown clashed with Governor Lamm. The latter claimed his lieutenant was a lax, irresponsible administrator who overspent his budget. (The politician had had financial problems for years. Creditors frequently hounded him for unpaid bills.) Eventually, Lamm withheld part of his number-two man's salary to punish Brown for questionable travel expenses. Some of the lieutenant governor's supporters screamed this was racism on Lamm's part. After seeking renomination in 1978, Brown withdrew from the race in the summer when it was obvious the party would not give him a place on the ticket. Upon the expiration of his term, Brown joined military contractor Grumman, moving to Long Island. Out of office, he sued the governor, settling with him in 1980 for the payment of the withheld salary.

Once blacks won specific seats on city council and in the General Assembly, some African-American politicians insisted they were permanent black seats. To assure this, they occasionally consciously acted to make sure there would not be any open seats which they and their associates might lose. When ready to leave office, incumbents might resign in midterm to arrange the proper succession. Informal gatherings at Pierre's Supper Club at 22nd Avenue and Downing Street often sanctioned such choices.

Not everybody fit in the black political clique. Hiawatha Davis was an outsider. Born in 1944, he graduated from Manual High School. Far from embracing the military tradition of the black veterans, he resisted the Vietnam War, spending 18 months in prison for draft evasion in 1967–68. By the early 1970s, he was a black nationalist who repeatedly clashed with Elvin Caldwell. In 1971, as "Hi" Davis, he ran unsuccessfully for council against the incumbent. He then worked for Denver Opportunity, a foremost Great Society agency.

Within a few years, Davis' politics changed as he emerged as Caldwell's protege. When Caldwell left council in 1980, Davis ran as his heir apparent, supported by the East Denver Ministerial Alliance. A Young Turk, attorney and state Representative King Trimble, upset Davis in the special election on June 24, 1980, 1,346–1,114. Davis unsuccessfully protested the results, charging his opponent had engaged in unethical campaign practices. When Trimble did not seek reelection in 1983, Davis finally won the post.

In office, Davis emerged as part of the city hall crowd. He forever suffered from financial problems. Opponents accused him of engaging in conflict-of-interest deals as he served on the board of the Denver Housing Authority while on council. In September 1999, shortly after gaining election to his fifth term, Davis resigned when Mayor Wellington Webb appointed him to direct the Agency for Human Rights and Community Relations. He died of cancer on May 24, 2000.

As black Democrats prospered, Republicans also sought to appeal to African-American voters. The GOP touted the success of Vikki Buckley. A former welfare mother, she rose in the Colorado Secretary of State's office in the 1980s and 1990s. In 1994, she won the post in a close election amidst charges her Democratic opponent, Sherrie Wolff, had engaged in past unethical actions. Then-Democratic United States Senator Ben Campbell openly blasted Wolff, the former director of his state office, shortly before the election. His move assisted Buckley's triumph.

From the time Buckley took over the Secretary of State's office, critics claimed she was above her head in the job. Staff turnover was immense. Key matters were neglected for months at a time. Election petitions for issues favored by Buckley were approved in a perfunctory manner while she might rule off the ballot those she opposed. The courts often reversed her decisions. Despite this, running against a smug Democratic reformer tied to Colorado Common Cause, Ric Bainter, Buckley won a tight race for reelection in 1998.

Simultaneously, the Republicans gained the governorship. They did so with the assistance of Joe Rogers, an African-American who cynically stressed racial issues as he ran as the GOP candidate for lieutenant governor. Both his and Buckley's message was forthright: thcy could succeed in the system as Republicans. The Democratic turnout in the 1998 election was not as great as usual in key black precincts. Many African-Americans apparently did not vote or voted Republican, primarily attracted by the color of thc Republican candidates' skin. Possibly, this was just enough to assure the triumph of Bill Owens and Vikki Buckley—at least Rogers claimed as much.

No sooner was Buckley reinaugurated as Secretary of State than she was again engulfed by controversy. Rather than depending on an assistant Secretary of State, she hired a Michigan black wheeler-dealer, Sam Riddle, as her advisor. Right as she faced new troubles, Buckley died from a heart attack in July 1999. Rogers made her demise a matter of black and white when he lamented Colorado did not come to a complete standstill to honor her. The commonwealth had never so honored any white secretary of state. Buckley's funeral was highly theatrical, complete with a horse-drawn hearse and men dressed up as black Civil War soldiers to emphasize her support of African-American militarism.

Among the black groups supporting Joe Rogers was the Greater Metro Denver Ministerial Alliance. It reflected the key role clerics frequently played in community and political ventures. Not all African-Americans supported the preachers' activities. Already in the early 20th century as a visible black clergy emerged, some civil rights advocates complained there were too many preachers and small isolated churches. Still, the church remained a center of power. In 1930–31, 15

**Photo by Phil Goodstein**

*New Hope Baptist Church, at 3701 Colorado Boulevard, is among the congregations whose pastor is affiliated with the East Denver Ministerial Alliance.*

African-American clergy formed the East Denver Ministerial Alliance, a group providing leadership to black businesses and politicians. (At that time, "East Denver" was frequently used by blacks as a virtual code word when they did not wish to speak of African-American Denver.)

Many disliked the preachers' group. During the 1979 mayoral election, for example, challenger Felicia Muftic complained the organization, then having about 70 members, had demanded money from her in return for its support. Unsuccessful auditor candidate John Lay similarly reported the association had wanted money from his campaign. Jim Monaghan, who had managed Richard Lamm's 1978 gubernatorial campaign, noted the Ministerial Alliance had asked for $10,000 to $15,000 to launch a get-out-the-vote campaign for his candidate. Newspapers quoted an anonymous insider who blasted the clerical group for operating in a "slick, aloof, cryptic style."

Black critics of the Ministerial Alliance spoke out in the spring of 1990 during a special election to fill a vacancy to District 11 on city council for the Park Hill/Montbello area. Against ten black candidates, the Ministerial Alliance believed the one white challenger had too good of a chance to represent the area. The preachers' association stressed the campaign was a matter of race—District 11 was an African-American seat. It so tabbed a couple of favorites from the black field, excluding other candidates from its forum. Some whom the group scorned claimed the organization was nothing more than a racial political machine. They lamented its lack of a broad social view or mission; on the contrary, these individuals asserted, the clerics were on a power trip to strengthen their personal influence within the larger community.

By the time a black candidate won the 1990 District 11 race, the organization had evolved into the Greater East Denver Ministerial Alliance. Within a few years, it changed its name to the Greater Metro Denver Ministerial Alliance, an organization representing more than 50 predominantly African-American congregations. This was only a minority of the 140-plus black churches in the area.

## The Black American West Museum

The more blacks such as Buckley and Rogers managed to make it in the system, race divisions cut ever deeper in the community. Controversies raged over affirmative-action. With a limited number of posts, government contracts, and awards, some struggling whites believed they were suffering discrimination so a few favored blacks could get ahead. While such racial controversies brewed, the white establishment openly collaborated with African-American veterans and the likes of Buckley and Rogers to herald the experiences of black soldiers in the post-Civil War West. They so created a travesty of an original promising idea. No institution better illustrated the initial impulse of celebrating African-Americans in the region and giving them their full due than the Black American West Museum.

Located in the Justina Ford House at 3091 California Street, the museum claims to "tell it like it was." The institution is the brainchild of Paul W. Stewart. Born in Iowa in 1925, he later moved to Evanston, Illinois, before he came to Colorado in

Photo by Phil Goodstein

*The Justina Ford House after it was moved to 3091 California Street where it is the home of the Black American West Museum.*

1962. After failing as a prospector, he settled in as a Denver barber. A cousin, Earl W. Mann, who served in the state legislature as a Republican between 1943 and 1948 and 1951 and 1954, oriented Stewart to the Mile High City.

(Mann, a World War I lieutenant, was badly gassed in the conflict, coming to Denver to recover his health after his discharge. During the rest of his life, he proudly signed his articles in the *Colorado Statesman* "Lieutenant Earl Mann." After holding posts as a federal deputy marshal and a bailiff for the United States District Court, he worked as a clerk for the Denver Water Department for 25 years. Mann died at age 82 in May 1969.)

A childhood memory gnawed at Stewart. He recalled playing cowboys and Indians in an integrated neighborhood as a boy. The barber always had to be an Indian since everybody knew that there were no such thing as black cowboys. Hollywood confirmed the image, making cowboys into the heroic knights of the West. Eventually, Stewart met a black cowboy and proved his playmates wrong.

There was a rich lore of black cowboys. Anything but a romantic job, driving, herding, and branding cattle was an extremely arduous, poorly paying profession. Seen in this light, it was not surprising many blacks landed up in the field. As many as one-third of all cowboys might have been African-Americans. There were also black calvary soldiers who were in the vanguard of killing Indians and driving Native Americans from their historic homes in the 1860s and 1870s. (The Cheyenne called such troopers "Black White Men." The enlistees were also known as Buffalo Soldiers. The latter has become the preferred term for these men whom white society has increasingly celebrated as the vanguard of African-Americans in the West.)

Stewart slowly discovered the dimensions of black cowboys. Beginning in 1957, he began to collect all the lore and artifacts he could on the subject. By the 1960s, the barber was something of a walking encyclopedia on black cowboys. His shop at 2511 34th Avenue was crammed with memorabilia about western African-Americans.

Fired by the upheavals of the civil rights movement and renewed interest in black pride, in August 1971 Stewart featured his items when he opened what he

Photo by Phil Goodstein

*A bust recalls Justina Ford, the "Baby Doctor," at the RTD light rail station at 30th Avenue and Downing Street.*

called the Black Institute Museum at 221–223 24th Street. Before long the Denver Housing Authority forced him out, condemning and destroying the building. In August 1974, Stewart relocated to 2925 Colfax Avenue as the Black American West Foundation. The gallery later moved to the campus of Clayton College. The city encouraged Stewart to transfer the museum to Five Points at 26th and Welton streets in November 1984.

By this time, Stewart was a national figure. His book on black cowboys was well received and placed in school libraries everywhere. He expanded the museum to include oral histories, legacies of black agricultural settlements, and how blacks were always part of the West. After years of struggling, with the assistance of a sizable federal community block development grant, the museum found a permanent home in the relocated Justina Ford House in 1988.

Justina Ford was the "Baby Doctor." At least two generations of Denverites called her that. Born Justina Carter in Knoxville, Illinois, on January 22, 1871, she wanted to become a physician from the time she was a girl. After receiving her medical degree from Harring Medical College in Chicago, she directed a black hospital in Normal, Alabama, before coming to Denver in 1902. Over great odds, she was certified as the first African-American woman doctor in Colorado, receiving physician license 3800 on October 7, 1902. There were seven other black physicians in Denver at the time.

Settling in a two-story, brick Victorian house at 2334 Arapahoe Street, Ford was on call for the community. During the next 50 years, she delivered approximately 7,000 babies. She never learned to drive and took a cab everywhere, constantly going when she was called. Patients who could not afford to pay for her services compensated her by working at her house or giving her produce. So she could deal with immigrant patients, Ford learned about ten languages, conversing with people from all backgrounds and nationalities who were hurting in poor sections of the Mile High City.

The doctor never had it easy. There was a color line at many hospitals. Often, she was the only medical resource for people living on the fringes of downtown. Ford not only delivered babies, but specialized in first aid. A small, plump woman, she was involved in numerous community ventures. The physician was widely mourned on her death at age 81 on October 14, 1952.

During the 1960s and 1970s, the residential remnants of the area near the Justina Ford House increasingly disappeared. Businesses, parking lots, and shelters were located nearby. Those who had grown up in the neighborhood and had been helped by Dr. Ford remembered her and her home. It was a shrine recalling a saint. The Denver Public Library honored her in 1975 when it named its new East Denver branch at 28th Avenue and High Street the Ford-Warren Library. (The previous East Denver branch, at 34th Avenue and High Street, dated from 1913. It denoted the first bishop of the Methodist Church in Colorado, Henry White Warren.)

The oil blight threatened the last vestiges of the residential neighborhood near 24th and Arapahoe streets in 1982. A real estate investment partnership acquired the Justina Ford House, seeing it as a site for further downtown expansion. By the summer of 1983, the outsiders decided business growth required the demolition of the Baby Doctor's residence for a parking lot. The proposed corporate vandalism outraged Moses Valdez.

In contrast to the majority of preservationists who fashioned themselves high-society aspirants, often engaging in the make-believe of trying to recreate a snobbish Victorian world, Valdez was a veteran demolition worker. Once a supporter of the radical Chicano Crusade for Justice, he appreciated the city's heritage and worked to save working-class institutions, theaters, churches, and apartments. Most of all, he did not want to see the home of the Baby Doctor destroyed, leading him to launch a campaign to save the Justina Ford House.

Historic Denver Incorporated agreed the home had a lot of architectural charm. The developer was insistent it go. A compromise was reached: a parking lot displaced the house, but the structure remained standing. Workers moved the 33-foot-high, 40-foot-long, 20-foot-wide house to the west corner of 31st and California streets in February 1984. At this time, the Black American West Museum had an option on the property and helped raise money to move and restore the house. It took four years to renovate the building into the museum, complete with a small room set aside as Dr. Ford's medical office.

In addition to displays on cowboys and the African-American experience in Colorado, the museum included material on blacks in the military. The Colorado Historical Society echoed this, with special displays on Buffalo Soldiers and black cowboys. The emphasis on the African-American soldiers after the Civil War, ironically, came at a time when the injustice of the government's mistreatment of the Indians was increasingly noted. Little was said in the celebration of the Buffalo Soldiers about their relationship with Native Americans.

## Daddy Bruce

By the time the Black American West Museum was functioning in the Justina Ford House, the city had designated the street on which Stewart had had his barber shop, 34th Avenue, "Bruce Randolph Avenue." It honored a colorful figure in modern black Denver, "Daddy Bruce" Randolph. Born in Arkansas on February 15, 1900, he had had a checkered career in his home state and Texas. Plagued by failures and business reverses, he relocated in Denver in 1962 to work in his son's barbershop.

A veteran restaurateur, Randolph developed an outstanding barbecue recipe. Before long, he was cooking out of his son's backyard barbecue pit. In 1963, he acquired space at the northwest corner of 34th Avenue and Gilpin Street where he opened a small restaurant. As he thrived, he recalled his hard times and noted the problems suffered by others. In 1967, he offered a free meal for those in need on Thanksgiving. During the next 20 years, his holiday feast became a cherished rite of fall. Not only did thousands have their Thanksgiving dinner compliments of Daddy Bruce, but hundreds of others volunteered to help him.

Besides the Thanksgiving affair, Daddy Bruce also distributed free clothing to the neighborhood. He received it from those not trusting religious-based charities who knew Daddy Bruce would distribute the largess without charge. Though Randolph's business fortunes were never ideal, he was beloved by the community.

Photo by Phil Goodstein

*The city renamed 34th Avenue between Downing and Dahlia streets "Bruce Randolph Avenue" in November 1985 to honor "Daddy Bruce" Randolph whose restaurant is shown at the northwest corner of Gilpin Street and the road.*

To note Denver's need to honor some of its black citizens, the city christened 34th Avenue between Downing and Dahlia streets in his honor for Thanksgiving 1985. Randolph's barbecue pit closed in 1993 and he died in 1994. (Bruce Randolph was Denver's second Daddy Bruce. The first was Francis T. Bruce, an African-American who served on the police force in the 1890s.)

A far more important figure in the civil rights movement was Clarence Holmes. A Denver native, born on May 21, 1892, his father moved to the Mile High City in 1890 after working as a waiter in the House of Representatives' dining room in Washington. After graduating from Manual High School, Holmes attended Howard University in Washington. Upon earning a dental degree there in 1920, he returned to Denver to practice his trade. After a five-year stop in Pueblo between 1926–1931, Holmes emerged as a premier Five Points dentist, serving black and white patients alike. He was also a neighborhood landlord, his mother having left him major real estate holdings. Holmes operated properties at 2307 and 2334 Downing Street, next to his home at 2330 Downing Street, as guest houses for travelers.

While still in college, Holmes helped establish the local branch of the National Association for the Advancement of Colored People (NAACP) in 1915. The organization quickly made waves. When the movie extolling the first Ku Klux Klan, *The Birth of a Nation*, was about to arrive for showing at the Tabor Grand in December 1915, the NAACP called for banning the film, one depicting blacks as veritable barbarians. City hall, run by a reform commission, ruled it illegal to screen any movie designed to incite racial hatreds. Though the courts overturned the order and the film was shown in near-riot conditions, the law remained on the books. The city again enforced it during a revival showing of *The Birth of a Nation* in 1939 at the Jewel Theater at South Broadway and Jewell Avenue. Rather than contesting the constitutionality of the measure, the arrested theater manager agreed to a plea bargain with the city. (Despite the NAACP's protest of this film, which helped spawn the second Ku Klux Klan, in June 1925—right at the peak of the Klan's power in Denver—the national NAACP held its convention in the Mile High City. The Klan did nothing to protest the group or interfere with visitors spending top dollar during their stay.)

During the late 1930s and early 1940s, Holmes was sometimes arrested when he tried to test and implement existing Colorado laws guaranteeing all citizens equal access to public accommodations. During this period, Holmes participated in some sit-ins at theaters and restaurants to show the need for full racial equality. Concerned whites often supported these efforts. Here and there, embarrassed owners junked Jim Crow practices.

Protests against open discrimination soared shortly after Pearl Harbor when locals established an active chapter of the Congress of Racial Equality (CORE). When its members were arrested protesting the segregation at the Broadway Theater in the Cosmopolitan Hotel at 18th Avenue Broadway, an impressive defense by the American Civil Liberties Union kept the police from further interfering with CORE's peaceful picket lines. The civil rights organization dissipated in Denver about the end of World War II.

Holmes realized the rich led the way in discriminatory practices. Though he had no trouble gaining admission to the Denver Dental Society, he was refused membership in the Pueblo Dental Society because of his race. One time, a leading

**Photo by Phil Goodstein**

*The Sportland YMCA, at 31st Avenue and Madison Street, appears fenced off to the community, in the same manner the organization once deliberately excluded blacks from its facilities.*

country club refused the Denver Dental Society admission for a banquet because it had black members. This led the dentist to dismiss the country club element in an old leftist line as "a bunch of crumbs held together by their own dough."

The activist was a charter member of the Denver Cosmopolitan Club. Advocates of racial unity established it in 1931. Meeting at Grace Community Church at the southwest corner of West 13th Avenue and Bannock Street, members claimed to work for the betterment of all. An interracial, interfaith social organization, the Cosmopolitan Club's slogan was "Humanity above race, nationality, or creed." For years, it was something of the city's conscience in emphasizing brotherhood over narrow racial and religious distinctions. Well into the 1960s, its annual banquet was a keynote of middle-class advocates of civil rights.

The dentist emphasized patriotism and military service. He was long a member of the local draft board and a leader of black Republicans. In the latter position, Holmes unsuccessfully sought election to city council in 1955 against Elvin Caldwell. The activist also served on the Mayor's Committee on Human Relations, the Colorado Committee on Racial Equality, and the Denver Interracial Committee. He died at age 85 in March 1978. Neighbors have suggested naming a small park at 30th Avenue and High Street in his memory.

## The YMCA and YWCA

Holmes pushed the black branch of the YMCA, the Glenarm Y at 28th Street and Glenarm Place. Organized in 1912, it was both a product of black activists and a result of racism. Many around the central YMCA supported it. If blacks had their own branch, some supporters of the central Y were sure, they would not come to the main building at 16th Avenue and Lincoln Street.

The Glenarm Y occupied an impressive three-story structure, complete with a swimming pool and gym. At a time when most movie houses were segregated, it offered special Friday night films. For years, it was essentially the recreational center of black Denver. Churches held an annual Glenarm YMCA Day to raise funds for the organization.

World War II badly strained the Glenarm Y. During the conflict the association was a center for black soldiers and armament workers. It continued to suffer after the war. As formerly exclusive all-white facilities were opened to blacks, some former supporters turned their back on the Five Points center. The Denver YMCA eventually closed the Glenarm Y, incorporating it into the East Denver YMCA at 31st Avenue and Madison Street. The city, drawing on federal funds, later built the Glenarm Recreation Center at 28th and Glenarm where the YMCA had once stood. The new structure supplanted a previous city facility at 2563 Glenarm Place.

The new home of the East Denver YMCA at 3540 31st Avenue was a story in its own right—Sportland Beach. Local investors, led by theater impresario Arthur M. Oberfelder, bought the land at 31st and Madison from Clayton College in 1934 when they announced plans for an exclusive, Olympic-class swimming pool, bathing beach, playground, and clubhouse complex. Many flocked to the facility, especially youths living in Park Hill. For some years, Sportland Beach was an elite, suburban swimming hole of white Denver.

Sportland Beach was badly hurt by World War II and various polio scares resulting in the shutting of all public swimming pools. It closed in 1948. The owners sold it to the YMCA. The latter renovated it as the Sportland Branch. Despite the increasing African-American influx into this area, the Sportland YMCA refused to admit blacks. Only in 1954, stinging from exposés about its racism and pressure from community protests and the Community Chest which helped fund the YMCA, did Sportland open its pool to African-Americans. (Lakeside was the only other public facility in town retaining a whites-only policy at its swimming pool. Management explained it forbade blacks for safety's safe: it feared a "rough element" would riot if African-Americans were allowed to use the pool.)

The Phyllis Wheatley Branch of the YWCA complemented the Glenarm Y. Noting the void of opportunities for young black women, middle-aged, middle-class African-American women, led by Isabel Chapman, worked to establish a Colored Club within the greater Denver YWCA in 1915. Meeting at Shorter Church, they formed a group the YWCA chartered in October 1916. The nascent organization rented a storefront at 318 25th Street. Rapidly growing after World War I, the Colored Club emerged as the black branch in 1920. The section named itself in honor of a colonial Boston freed slave, who spelled her name Phillis (1753–1784). Having published her first poem at age 13, she gained the support of British noble patrons. Phillis Wheatley emerged as the inaugural African-American poet.

The Colored Club hired its first full-time secretary in the spring of 1920. With the help of a grant from philanthropist Mary Reed, the Phyllis Wheatley YWCA was able to purchase a 12-room, three-story, red-brick house at 2460 Welton Street that March. The Barth family had originally occupied the residence, a mansion later the home of the Denver Bible Institute. The YWCA moved in on June 3, 1920. The branch included dorm rooms, meeting space, and recreational facilities. It offered classes on the Bible, sewing, and music. Most of all, the Phyllis Wheatley Y featured an employment bureau. Surging from 172 members in 1921 to 731 in 1930, it emerged as a center of middle-class female black Denver.

Beginning in 1926, the Wheatley branch operated Camp Nizhoni in the mountains at Lincoln Hills near Pinecliff. Lincoln Hills was a project of a developer who hoped to turn his mountain land into a national summer resort, one specifically catering to affluent blacks. To pull them in, he offered the Camp Nizhoni land free to the Wheatley YWCA if it agreed to have its facility there. (The black branch had sponsored assorted summer camps in various mountain locations since 1921.) Lincoln Hills faded away as a summer resort during the upheavals of World War II.

For years, the Denver YWCA sponsored a committee on Interracial Relations and often strenuously objected to discriminatory practices. Typical of the racism it encountered was the way local hotels responded to a planning meeting the group held in 1942 for the National YWCA Committee for a New Society: the inns refused to accommodate national black officers coming to Denver.

By 1945, the Wheatley YWCA was not sure of what to do about the so-called Segregated Senior Prom. During World War II, black high school seniors made it a point of having their own prom/celebration despite no rules prohibiting them

CHS

*The Phyllis Wheatley branch of the YMCA occupied this mansion at the south corner of 24th and Welton streets.*

from attending their high school proms. The YWCA urged them to attend the latter. At the most, it admitted a special friends and relatives party was appropriate for graduating students.

While advocating integration and actively fighting discriminatory practices, the Denver YWCA recognized the dilemma of having a black branch. Beginning in 1938, it continually pondered whether it should maintain the separate Negro division. It transformed the Wheatley Y into a general part of the organization in 1950 when it designated the former Colored Club the Welton Branch. The new moniker was to note its multiracial constituency. The YWCA put the Welton Street house on the market in the early 1960s as it pondered the best means of serving the burgeoning middle-class population—whites as well as blacks—east of York Street. The YWCA abandoned the Wheatley building in 1964. The 24th and Welton landmark was eventually torn down.

During the heyday of the pre-World War II segregated city, the Negro Woman's Club Home Association served black Denver by running a dormitory for women and a day nursery at 24th Avenue and Clarkson Street. Other black women's clubs, including a section of the Federated Women's Clubs, Carnation Art Club, and Sojourner Truth Club, formed key sections of the social life of the African-American community. The Denver Colored Civic Association devoted its efforts to employment opportunities and the advancement of black businesses. African-Americans often created parallel institutions to those of white society. Among them was the Syrian Temple at the southeast corner of 28th Avenue and Downing Street, the headquarters of black Shriners.

In addition to a flourishing chapter of the NAACP, activists formed a branch of the Urban League in 1946. It stemmed from the Colored Citizens Association, a group attorney Thomas Campbell helped establish in 1919. Newspapers geared at African-Americans came and went. The *Colorado Statesman* was in the lead. Beginning publication in 1895, editor Joseph D. D. Rivers echoed Booker T. Washington about Negro uplift and self-sufficiency. The weekly focused on church, society, and sports news in addition to covering local and national civil rights issues. Other black newspapers appeared, often taking shots at the *Statesman* as too conservative a publication. The latter published until 1961. Showing no memory of the weekly, in February 1977, the *Colorado Democrat* changed its name to the *Colorado Statesman*, subsequently becoming the inside gossip newspaper for region's politicos.

## The Civil Rights Commission

As the civil rights revolution started to shake the nation in the mid-1950s, Denverites were embarrassed by reports showing racism in the area. As a modern city with an urge to grow, political and business leaders sought to project the face of a happy, cooperative community to both residents and the world. Simultaneously, the labor movement was making great strides in Colorado. It helped elect ever

Photo by John Schoenwalter

*A delegation marches in support of better schools during a Martin Luther King Day parade in 1993. Mass activism by countless blacks and whites forced the city to redress its discriminatory heritage.*

more liberal Democrats to the General Assembly in the 1956 election. Seeing how the civil rights provisions of the Colorado constitution had long had little meaning, the legislature sought to make the spirit of the 1870s finally applicable to the Centennial State. This led the General Assembly to create a state Anti-Discrimination Commission in 1957.

The legislature charged the new body with overseeing the enforcement of existing laws prohibiting discrimination. Two years later, following a Democratic sweep in 1958, the General Assembly expanded the Anti-Discrimination Commission's scope, giving it power to enforce fair housing. This was part of a 1959 fair housing act, a model for the country. Under the pressure of the civil rights movement, the solons strengthened the Colorado law in 1965. Local civil rights advocates viewed it as exemplary legislation, the strongest housing act in the nation.

The Anti-Discrimination Commission evolved into the Colorado Civil Rights Commission in the mid-1960s. James Reynolds led it from 1963 until 1980. Prototypical of black Denver, he had come to the Mile High City in 1950 as an airman at Lowry Air Force Base. Staying in Denver, Reynolds suffered random discrimination, including finding himself banned from a Lowry social affair at the Brown Palace because he was black. Soon a civil rights activist, he helped reestablish a Denver chapter of CORE in 1961. During the early 1960s, he led picket lines against major companies engaging in discriminatory hiring practices against African-Americans. Among the firms he and CORE targeted were the Denver Dry and Zone Cab.

Over the years, the Colorado Civil Rights Commission received a good deal of flak. In the 1970s, some Chicanos decried it as favoring blacks at the price of Mexican-Americans. Generally, though, commanding politicians supported Reynolds as a steady-handed director who lent a state presence to anti-discrimination efforts. Warren Alexander, another black activist, worked with Reynolds on the body.

When Reynolds retired in 1980, newspaper reports made it appear black Park Hill state Senator Regis Groff, a man closely tied with the black political elite and the governor's office, had the personal say in who would succeed Reynolds. Among those mentioned for the job were deputy district attorney Norm Early and state Representative Federico Peña. Neither was interested in the post.

Another effort to institutionalize the civil rights movement was the Metro Denver Fair Housing Center. It stemmed from a 1965 push by church and civic groups to make fair housing a reality. The Religious Council on Human Relations for Metro Denver backed it in association with a Commission to Oppose Discrimination. Initially a volunteer effort, the Housing Center called on Realtors and the business community to try to make residential integration work in both the city and suburbs. City, state, and federal funds poured into its coffers. The Housing Center moved into an impressive modern building at 1525 Josephine Street in August 1968.

By this time the organization had close links with the Office of Economic Opportunity of the Great Society. The Ford Foundation gave it a considerable grant.

Such sponsorship led critics to charge the Housing Center was not working for fair housing for the people of Denver; on the contrary, the Capitol Hill Tenants Union—a group fighting for decent housing for renters in the 1970s—accused the organization of shilling for the Denver Urban Renewal Authority. Simultaneously, the organization was beset by internal squabbles, leading to mass losses of funding and support. It reorganized itself as the Metro Housing Center Incorporated in September 1971. Within a year, it collapsed. The Urban League came to occupy its quarters at 1525 Josephine, taking over some of the Housing Center's development programs. In 1999, with financial support from Public Service and US West and governmental grants, the Urban League moved to new quarters in a former Public Service plant at 5900 39th Avenue on the fringes of Park Hill.

## Black Culture

Black culture in Denver was extremely uneven. An African-American bookstore, the Hue-Man Experience, emerged. A Negro history week grew into a black history month during February. During it, newspapers and schools sought to enlighten students about African-American history. Little was said in the process about such groups as the Panthers.

White faces frequently predominated when national touring shows featuring black themes played in town. African-American activists decried this, working to create their own cultural institutions. Sometimes white Denver eagerly embraced them. Such was the case with the Cleo Parker Robinson Dance Ensemble. The troupe originated in Model City efforts in 1970. Over the years, its namesake formed excellent ties with the white cultural establishment. In 1990, the city leased the company the old Shorter Church at 23rd and Washington streets for a dollar a year. The stolid Denver Center for the Performing Arts incorporated the Cleo Parking Robinson Dance Ensemble into its empire in January 1998. Robinson served on the ultra-establishment New World Airport Commission, the body loudly celebrating the coming of Denver International Airport in the early 1990s.

Much more uneven was Eulipions, an African-American theatrical group dating from 1982. Occupying a number of sites, it performed dramas of African-American playwrights and emphasized an annual black nativity. Eventually, leading politicians, including friends and supporters of Mayor Wellington Webb, were on its board. With corporate and foundation grants, Eulipions bought the former home of the Rocky Mountain Consistory Number Two at 18th Avenue and Sherman Street from the Masons in 1995 in an extremely convoluted deal.

El Jebel Shrine constructed Eulipions' new home in 1906–07. The hall included both a performance auditorium and a rooftop garden. After a fire badly damaged the building in 1924, the Shriners sold the temple to the Rocky Mountain Consistory. As the latter organization faded, Eulipions moved in.

No sooner was Eulipions in the new home than it suffered severe financial problems. Bills were not paid and loans were called. Members of the board squabbled with one another. In 1999, two different factions openly competed for the soul of the organization. One board, dominated by the faction close to Webb,

Photo by Phil Goodstein

*Shorter African Methodist Episcopal Church called this building, at 23rd and Washington streets, its home from 1926 until the late 1970s. The structure subsequently became the studio of the Cleo Parker Robinson Dance Ensemble.*

resolved to sell the building. The other vehemently protested the action. By this time, Eulipions had virtually no community outreach or performances seeking to educate the rest of Denver about the African-American legacy.

By the 1990s, the black community had dispersed throughout Denver. Some middle-class blacks wanted to get away from other African-Americans. A number of black professionals settled in southeast Denver near Thomas Jefferson High School. Others moved to the suburbs. Though sections of Denver remained almost exclusively white, the vestiges of Jim Crow had virtually disappeared. Social and economic problems remained.

Illustrative was the heavy black presence in old Aurora. The area between Yosemite and Peoria streets between Colfax Avenue and Stapleton Airport was never much. While it was the site of the Aurora city hall, it was mostly filled with post-World War II frame structures, trailer courts, and simple apartment buildings. Many servicemen and young veterans had lived there in the 1950s and 1960s. As they moved out and the houses rapidly aged, blacks moved in.

Businesses on Colfax reflected the transformation. A stretch from approximately Dayton to Galena streets had once been Aurora's downtown, complete with department and drug stores, sporting goods shops, groceries, nightclubs, and banks. By the late 1970s, this section was filled with pawn shops, dumpy bars, and a wide array of ethnic restaurants. Korean-owned establishments predominated. The road's enterprises reflected the low-income levels of many nearby residents.

Among those fleeing this section of old Aurora was the city government. Wanting to be at one with the new sections of the suburb and the real estate interests it served, city hall relocated to near the Buckingham Mall in September 1970. To compensate old Aurora for the loss of the seat of government, the city added ornate landscaping to Colfax. Though physically this stretch of the road in old downtown Aurora looked appealing, boosters continually lamented crime and the presence of hookers, pimps, and junkies in the idyllic suburb.

Aurora responded with hysterical, police-state measures to prohibit loitering and publishing photos of men accused of dealing with prostitutes. The city changed zoning near the former Fitzsimons Hospital in the late 1990s, prohibiting trailer courts and businesses catering to low-income individuals. It openly hoped the prohibitions against the poor would nourish an Aurora Cherry Creek North, especially after the University of Colorado Health Sciences Center announced its intention to relocate to the abandoned Army medical center in 1996. The latter hoped to include virtual Disneyland-like services for patients.

Another suburban spread of black Denver was Montbello. Private investors worked closely with the city to develop the area northeast of Stapleton Airport as an ideal community in the mid-1960s. Developers named streets after Air Force bases, noting the community aimed to attract military veterans. While sponsors originally envisaged Montbello as a white suburb, within a few years blacks flocked into it. With open spaces and large yards, African-Americas saw homes there a respite from the old, crowded ghetto. In no time, the class tensions, social conditions, and economic and family problems of blacks and whites struck heavily at Montbello residents.

The way out appeared in better education. This was a recurring theme of the civil rights movement. No place more illustrated it than the black experience in Park Hill. Tensions in that neighborhood set the stage for convulsions over busing in Denver Public Schools, a crucial event in shaping the modern city.

## A Note on Sources:

Background on racist organizations and hatreds in the area, including the anti-Chinese riot, the American Protective Association, the anti-German hysteria of World War I, and the Ku Klux Klan are in Goldberg, *Hooded Empire*; Perkin, *First Hundred Years*; Lyle Dorsett, "The Ordeal of Colorado's Germans during World War I," *Colorado Magazine*, 51:4 (Fall 1974), 277–93; and my *Seamy Side of Denver*. An interesting favorable retrospection on the American Protective Association is Frank Thomas Johnson, *Autobiography of a Centenarian*.

The papers of the Commission on Community Relations are at DPL. The Auraria Archives house the Minoru Yasui papers, which include a good deal of material about CCR, the Mayor's Committee on Human Relations, civil rights issues, and the Colorado Anti-Discrimination Commission. Bill Hosokawa has a sketch of Yasui in *Nisei* (New York: Morrow, 1992), 312–14. Also see Kerry S. Hada and Andrew S. Hamano, "Minoru Yasui," *Colorado Lawyer*, 27:7 (July 1998), 9–12.

Richard Delgado and Jean Stefancic, "Home-Grown Racism: Colorado's Historic Embrace—and Denial—of Equal Opportunity in Higher Education," *University of Colorado Law Review*, 70:3 (Summer 1999), 703–812, is a sloppy piece of special pleading that reeks with moral self-righteousness. The article, reprinted as a monograph, focuses on notorious instances of racism in Colorado over the years. The goal is plain: using past injustices to provide for special affirmative action programs. Dates cited often do not confirm the point of the text. The tract heavily relies on hearsay and vague, anonymous sources whereby the authors appear unsure of their evidence. Its best part is where Delgado and Stefancic note how self-proclaimed brotherhood advocates after World War II systematically degraded the black and Chicano communities for not properly embracing the white middle-class ethic.

DPL has sought to gather together special holdings on black Denver, preparing to house them at an African American Research Library. There is an existing collection on African-Americans in Colorado at DPL assembled by Juanita Gray. The Ford-Warren branch of DPL has an extensive photo display, complete with biographical portraits, of many of the leaders of the black community. There are also materials on African-Americans in the Centennial State at CHS. The Black American West Museum likewise has archives on the subject.

A good, brief overview of the first hundred years of black Denver is a two-part article by James Atkins, "The Negro in Denver," *Denver: Monthly Magazine of the Good Life in Colorado*, June 1965, pp. 17–20, and July 1965, pp. 39–40. Atkins' papers are at CHS. They include information on the civil rights movement during the 1950s and 1960s. He was also the author of *Human Relations in Colorado* (Denver: Office of Instructional Services, 1961).

James Rose Harvey, "Negroes in Colorado," (Master's Thesis, University of Denver, 1941), is an early look at black Denver. A fascinating portrait of the area, commissioned by the Denver Interracial Committee and conducted by the National Urban League, is Ira De A. Reid, *The Negro Population of Denver, Colorado* (New York: National Urban League, 1929). Chapter 26 in Leonard and Noel, *Mining Camp*, has some useful materials on the subject. Singular, *Talked to Death*, discusses the Halpern family and how it hosted black artists at its home at 370 Albion. Ida Uchill shared her knowledge of this aspect of Denver culture.

Jim Raughton reviewed this chapter, providing me with information about blacks in the Whittier neighborhood. He also arranged for me to read the paper by graduate student Dutch Hodges at UCD, "Whittier: A Historical Resource to Denver." The latter gave me copies of two research papers by Moya Hansen of CHS on black Denver, "Try Being a Black Woman!" and "Pebbles on the Shore."

From the late 19th century until its demise in 1961, the *Colorado Statesman* reported on black Denver. The *African Advocate* was an early black nationalist/return to Africa publication in 1890. Other local African-American newspapers and magazines include *New American Weekly*, *Denver Independent*, *Denver Star*, *Denver Blade*, *African American Voice*, and *Denver Weekly News*. The last was something of the stalwart of the middle-class African-American community in the 1980s and 1990s into the 2000s. *Denver Call* was a local edition of a national

Kansas City-based black newspaper in the 1950s. Front-page articles frequently focused on the doings of African-American politicians. Other features dealt with the city's jazz scene. *Rage* was a local black militant magazine that briefly appeared in the early 1970s. *Black Lifestyles* and *Odyssey West* were other local black magazines.

*Urban Spectrum* is a contemporary monthly magazine-like paper. It has included a wide mix of columnists and views. Articles have ranged from mainstream celebrations of the black middle class and a column by Mayor Wellington Webb to severe criticisms of African-Americans who uphold and support the establishment.

Shorter Community AME Church gives its history in *This Far by Faith* (Denver: Shorter Community AME, 1990). Zion Baptist tells its story its *Precentennial Booklet: Zion Baptist Church, 1865–1959* ([Denver]: Zion Baptist, [1959]); and *The 115th Anniversary of Zion Baptist Church* (Denver: Zion Baptist, 1980). There are also materials on Zion Baptist and the Colorado black church in the archives of the Western States Missionary Baptist Convention at DPL. The Cleo Parker Robinson Dance Ensemble has put together a short brochure, *Shorter AME Church Building*. Newspapers have reported controversies concerning the East Denver Ministerial Alliance.

A gap-filled look at the black political establishment, which tells much and understands little, is T. R. Witcher, "The Young and the Restless," *WW*, April 1, 1999, pp. 25–33. Loren R. Ginsburg, "Sam Cary," *Colorado Lawyer*, 23:7 (July 1994), 1487–88, is a paean to Colorado's first black attorney. Doug McNair, *Colorado Black Leadership Profiles* (Denver: Western Images, 1989), is a public relations effort with brief, shallow portraits of leading politicians and entrepreneurs of modern black Denver.

In the summer of 1969, the *Denver Post Empire* ran an 11-part series by Cary Stiff on blacks in Colorado. A retrospective on the civil rights upheavals in Denver was a six-part series, "The Tarnished Dream/Black Denver, 1968–1988," *RMN*, May 22–27, 1988. An early look at civil rights controversies in the region is Eugene H. Berwanger, "William J. Hardin: Colorado Spokesman for Racial Justice, 1863–1873," *Colorado Magazine*, 52:1 (Winter 1975), 52–62. Also see Lynda Faye Dickson, "The Early Club Movement among Black Women in Denver," (Ph.D. dissertation, University of Colorado, 1982).

Forbes Parkhill, *Mister Barney Ford* (Denver: Sage, 1963); and Marian Talmadge and Iris Gilmore, *Barney Ford: Black Baron* (New York, Dodd, Mead & Company, 1973), look at Barney Ford. Eleanor Gehres, "Barney Ford, Governor Alexander Cummings, Negro Suffrage, and the Colorado Statehood Bill of 1866," (paper at the University of Denver, 1971, on file at DPL), is an excellent overview of the topics mentioned.

Billie Arlene Grant, Ernestine Smith, and Gladys Smith, *Growing Up Black in Denver* (n.p.: n.p., 1988), is a set of portraits of Denver African-American natives. Many interviewed in the book recall specific instances of racism in modern Denver. Shelley Rhym, *Through My Eyes: The Denver Negro Community, March 1934–January 1968* ([Denver]: [Core City Ministries], 1968), is a rambling memoir and political commentary on black Denver, initially printed in the March 3, 1968, *DP*. *Westward Soul* (Denver: Black American West Foundation, 1976), is a photo book of black Colorado pioneers.

Alexander L. Crosby, *In These Ten Cities* (New York: National Public Affairs Committee, 1951), contains a portrait of Denver, berating housing discrimination under the Ben Stapleton administration while hailing Denver as a model city after the election of Quigg Newton. William Loren Katz *The Black West* (New York: Touchstone, 1987), has little specifically on Denver. Eugene H. Berwanger treats Reconstruction-era black Denver in Monroe Lee Billington and Roger D. Hardaway, eds., *African Americans on the Western Frontier* (Niwot: University Press of Colorado, 1998). Dave Hays informed me of his research on discriminatory practices and protests against them in Boulder in the late 1930s/early 1940s.

John Harris, long the member of the Denver Planning Office responsible for Five Points and black Denver, shared his rich memories of the African-American experience in the Mile High City from the 1940s to the 1980s. Billie Bramhall, another planner active in Five Points efforts, gave me her perspective. Bill Good reminisced on Five Points after World War II, including the black-and-tan crowd. Lee Hawkins chatted about black Realtors. Sid Wilson reviewed the text, sharing his experiences as a black tour guide. Lauren Watson chatted about the Panthers. Walter Gerash allowed me to examine his file on the Panthers. Cathy Donohue recalled her encounters with Elvin Caldwell while on city council. Tom Bastien remembered various black legislators and the origins of the fair housing bill. Steve LeMaster informed me about his days at Clayton College. CHS has a collection on George Clayton and the facility.

*The East Denver Directory of Business and Citizenry* sporadically appeared from the 1920s into the 1950s. The volumes are veritable yearbooks of leading African-American businesses, clubs, and figures. There is also a listing of residents on a block-by-block basis. The directory includes photos of some of the key places and individuals of black Denver. Linda Lebsack called my attention to this source.

Evelyn C. White, "Paul Stewart's Romance in the West," *Smithsonian*, August 1989, pp. 58–65, is a revealing portrait of Stewart's work and the Black American West Museum. Staffers there have discussed it when I have visited there, including Daphne Rice. Paul W. Stewart and Wallace Yvonne Ponce, *Black Cowboys* (Broomfield: Phillip Publishing Company, 1986), is Stewart's look at African-American cowboys. Also see Philip Dunham and Everett L. Jones, *The Negro Cowboys* (Lincoln: University of Nebraska Press, 1965); and Keith Schrum, "Of Myth and Men: The Trail of the Black Cowboy," *Colorado Heritage*, Autumn 1998, pp. 2–17.

Mark Harris, "Forty Years of Justina Ford," *Negro Digest*, March 1950, pp. 42–45, is an introductory biographical sketch of the Baby Doctor. Moses Valdez recalled his efforts to save the Justina Ford House. Roseanne Taht shared her memories of Justina Ford. DPL has a clipping file on Ford. Billie Arlene Grant, *Daddy Bruce Randolph: The Pied Piper of Denver* (Aurora: Accent Advantage, 1986), is extremely superficial. The first Daddy Bruce is noted in *Westward Soul*.

DPL has the Clarence Holmes papers, complete with a detailed discussion of the Cosmopolitan Club. Gwen Crenshaw discussed DPL's African American Research Library. She reviewed a draft of this chapter.

J. David Penwell, "Civil Rights in Colorado," *Denver Law Journal*, 46:2 (Spring 1969), 181–210, looks at the history of civil rights legislation in the state. *Colorado Anti-Discrimination Commission* v. *J. L. Case*, 380 P.2d 34, is the Colorado Supreme Court ruling upholding the constitutionality of the 1959 fair housing act and powers of the Civil Rights Commission. DPL has a clipping file on James Reynolds. Jerry McCracken recalled his participation as a white in CORE in the early 1960s. *Rebels Remembered* is a video documentary on CORE in the area.

There is a treasure trove on black Denver, addresses, and civil rights discussions in the YWCA papers at CHS. Boxes 1, 8, 11, 19, and 24 especially contain materials on the Colored Club. The Denver Area Welfare Council issued a special review, "A Study of the Place of the Welton Street Branch in the Denver YWCA," at the behest of the YWCA in 1954. It urged a greater integration of the branch into the larger East Denver community. Nina Mjagakij, *Light in the Darkness* (Lexington: University Press of Kentucky, 1994), focuses on the YMCA's black policies.

DPL has a detailed clipping file on Cleo Parker Robinson. T. R. Witcher, "All the World's an Empty Stage," *WW*, January 6, 2000, pp. 12–18, looks at the uneasy fate of Eulipions. *Urban Spectrum* also commented on the Eulipions controversy. I discuss the El Jebel Shrine Temple in my *Ghosts of Denver*.

Little has been published on the specifically black dimension of Aurora. Overviews of the city include Carl and Leona McFadden, *Early Aurora*; Steven F. Mehls, Carol J. Drake, and James E. Fell Jr., *Aurora: Gateway to the Rockies*; and Dave Hicks, *Aurora from the Beginning*. Pam Ladowig shared her views as a longtime resident of old Aurora. The January 23, 2000, *RMN*, p. 34A, noted the CU Health Sciences Center plans for Disneyland-like services at Fitzsimons.

DPO documents discuss the evolution of Montbello. Neighborhood activists have loudly spoken out concerning the area's problems. Bettina Basamow shared stories of her long residence there, branding it an island separated from the rest of the city. I briefly discuss the specific history of Montbello in the chapter on DIA below.

# 2

# The Agony of Denver Public Schools

Virtually from the time of the Pikes Peak gold rush, Denver was fixated on its schools. To prove to one and all—primarily to themselves—that the Mile High City was not a cow town, locals sought to create a distinguished educational system. The 1870s and 1880s saw the emergence of landmark schools serving the sons and daughters of the ruling elite. The latter were mostly college graduates in an era when less than 5 percent of the population attended school for more than 12 years. Children of workers usually dropped out of school and joined the labor force at an early age. As late as 1950, high schools had only a 50-percent graduation rate.

Denver touted its academies. Civic leaders and publicists viewed universal public education as evidence of the city's public spirit and democratic beliefs. On December 1, 1902, Denver School District One emerged as the body operating all of the City and County of Denver's public schools. An elected seven-person board ran the system. Members served staggered six-year terms.

Schools acutely mirrored the city's diversity. Besides fine academies, there were ramshackle buildings. Some schools had excellent graduation rates, others were little more than prisons. The names of four of the high schools—East, North, South, and West—denoted the geographic divisions of the city. In addition to them, Manual High School, a spinoff from East High School in 1894, offered vocational education to young men and women.

Many of the schools were stately edifices. Architects avidly competed for commissions to design the educational temples. The city stressed the beauty of its academies in the 1920s when it undertook a major wave of school building. The result was new homes for East, West, and South highs, all next to commanding parks. Real estate interests heralded the attractive structures, citing them as symbols of the city's faith in education and its proud commitment to the future.

The Chamber of Commerce seconded this point. During the 1920s, it loudly argued Denver had to grow from a city of 250,000 in 1920 to 500,000 by 1930. By providing classroom capacity for a city of 500,000, it hoped Denver would reach the magical number. Ideally, students would graduate from the schools ready to embrace the Chamber's vision for Denver.

Members of old, affluent families prominently served on the school board. Some of the elite saw the schools as their personal enclave. While ruling Denver established such private academies as Graland and Kent in the 1920s, more often than not, the children of the wealthy attended the public schools. A kind of natural integration occurred in the high schools where the poor mixed with the rich. The latter predominated in elaborate social hierarchies.

The Ku Klux Klan was then a foremost champion of public schools. It wanted to make attendance at them mandatory. The group's prime target was a strong, separate Catholic school system. The Denver Public Schools (DPS) leadership expected both Catholics and Jews to adapt to the prevailing Protestant traditions in the schools, complete with heavy religious indoctrination during Christmas ceremonies.

In 1924, during the heyday of the Klan, Superintendent Jesse Newlon introduced separate but equal practices in DPS. Noting racial tensions at Morey Junior High School and Manual High School, he ordered segregated social functions for students based on race. This was a means of keeping a black girl out of a swimming class at Morey and refusing to allow a couple of young African-American women to participate in social functions at Manual. After the Denver District Court refused to intervene, in January 1927 the Colorado Supreme Court ordered DPS to cease and desist from this activity since it was a violation of both the letter and spirit of the state constitution.

Newlon's action was in tune with a racist tradition in the schools. In 1866, territorial Governor Alexander Cummings, an outsider who clashed with the local establishment, decried actions by Denver leaders to prevent black children from attending the area's inaugural public schools. Before long, DPS was ostensibly integrated—the system dropped its early race bar.

Discrimination continued. In the late 19th century, for example, crusading *Rocky Mountain News* journalist Minnie Reynolds revealed DPS went out of its way to deny a black girl the academic honors she had earned because of her race. The system more or less simply tolerated minority students who were ignored if at all possible. For some years, the district primarily only hired Christians as teachers, having a strict quota on the number of Jews allowed on the faculty. DPS reserved the right to review the living quarters of single women teachers.

The school system was a bulwark of staunch conservatism. Flags flew in classrooms and days began with the Pledge of Allegiance. There was little questioning of the status quo. The stated goal was to train students to channel their energy and

Author's Collection

*North High School, near Decatur Street along Speer Boulevard, shortly after its completion in 1911.*

direct their attention to the tasks at hand. With bells dominating movement, pupils were expected to obey. There was no place for randomness, independence, and self-directed learning.

The board of education advertised DPS's military orientation. It allowed individuals not certified to teach to shove junior Reserve Officer Training Corps (ROTC) programs at high school students. Denver Public Schools were not for anybody who wished to rock the boat. They were part and parcel of the establishment.

The school system expanded with the city after World War II. A frenzied building campaign saw countless educational structures arise in the rapidly emerging sections of new Denver. Frequently these were faceless edifices, mass produced for mass education. To discourage children from daydreaming and looking out the windows, there were few windows in the buildings. As it emphasized constructing new schools, DPS increasingly neglected old structures in poor neighborhoods.

Enrollment soared in the 1950s and 1960s as those born after World War II came of school age. From about 56,000 students in 1950 in a city of 415,786, there were 90,518 students in a Denver of 493,887 in 1960. DPS reached a peak enrollment of 96,848 in 1968 when the town's population was a little more than 500,000 residents.

## Kenneth K. Oberholtzer

During much of the post-World War II epoch, Superintendent Kenneth K. Oberholtzer ran DPS, according to former school board member A. Edgar Benton, "with an iron hand in a velvet glove." Oberholtzer took the job at age 43 in 1947, having previously served as the head of the Long Beach, California, schools. An extremely competent, hard-working man who made his job his life, the superintendent sold himself to the media. They greatly extolled him, readily asserting Denver had a foremost educator leading a distinguished school district.

Under Oberholtzer, DPS was an extremely hierarchical system. He had three assistants to whom he assigned crucial parts of the administration. As with the chief, the aides were of German heritage. They ran DPS so efficiently that some joked DPS was modeled on the Prussian Army. Teachers and administrators were expected unquestioningly to follow the superintendent's orders.

A catechism of tests was the keynote of Oberholtzer's leadership. Both in the spring and fall, DPS set aside days for blocks of examinations when students took national, computer-scored tests. Getting students to learn how to take the exams, it sometimes appeared, was a foremost teaching goal. DPS not only used the test results to measure achievement, but it also heavily relied upon them for placement.

Under Oberholtzer, a pupil had to pass a high school competency exam to earn a diploma. Beginning in the tenth grade, the schools geared themselves to making sure students were up for this task. (From the establishment of junior high schools in 1917–18 until the opening of middle schools in 1981, Denver high schools were only for tenth through twelfth grades.)

The competency test was DPS's response to complaints about how graduates left high school unprepared for the world. Already in the 1950s, the country was torn by massive anxieties about why "Johnny can't read." Others berated the educational system for allowing the Russians to be first in space. Both conservatives

DPL

Time *featured Denver Superintendent Kenneth Oberholtzer on the cover of its February 20, 1950, issue.*

and liberals constantly moaned something had to be done to improve the schools. Efforts to reform them were unending.

The superintendent was a staunch advocate of "general education," of preparing students for life. In addition to providing rigorous academic classes for future college students, he saw DPS offer courses to assure its graduates emerged as properly prepared members of the labor force. Tracking systems divided students into regular, accelerated, and modified sections. Frequently these pairings, made in elementary school based on test results and parental pressure, followed pupils through their high school days. The result was more or less to perpetuate the status quo: children of college graduates were prepared to go to leading universities while the sons and daughters of blue-collar workers were set for a life comparable to that of their parents.

While the school board stoutly backed Oberholtzer, criticism of him was widespread. A February 20, 1950, cover story in *Time* reported the superintendent's doings and the controversies surrounding his approach. It generally portrayed him on the cutting edge of modern school administration. Among his innovations was Boettcher School of the Air.

In 1956, the city's four television stations—channels Two, Four, Seven, and Nine—not wanting another commercial rival, helped DPS procure an educational outlet for the Rocky Mountain area, KRMA, Channel Six. DPS used it as a teaching tool. Initially, in association with Boettcher School near the northeast corner of 18th Avenue and Downing Street, an institution designed for handicapped and medically incapacitated children, it beamed classes to shut-ins.

Before long, KRMA had heavy instructional programming. During parts of the school day, teachers, whose elementary classrooms had televisions, tuned the sets to Channel Six. Students would watch the television instructor in preference to a live teacher. During the evening, Channel Six broadcast lectures. Viewers could enroll in television classes. They were expected to submit homework and attend schools where they took tests, earning credit for watching the broadcasts. This never worked ideally. By the 1970s, DPS increasingly dismissed KRMA as a financial drain. Citing endless budget shortages, DPS severed its affiliation with Channel Six in 1986. The latter emerged as a typical public broadcasting station with no specific educational mission. (By that time, like other ostensible public educational institutions, such as the Zoo and Botanic Gardens, KRMA was dominated by a private membership organization whose members often treated it as their personal possession.)

Howard L. Johnson, who served as superintendent from 1970 until 1973, launched KRMA when he was principal of Emily Griffith Opportunity School. Johnson's rise in the system was typical. He first came to notice as a highly successful baseball and football coach at South High School in the 1930s. Named an assistant superintendent in 1960, Johnson closely worked with Oberholtzer. Increasingly, coaches rather than master instructors emerged as principals and administrators.

On the surface, the schools flourished into the 1960s. DPS frequently bused pupils to relieve overcrowding at some schools. Extended sessions and temporary classrooms were also common. Student bodies were quite large, with more than a thousand students in a few elementary schools. Some children got lost in this gigantic wash; others were able to survive precisely thanks to the anonymity it provided. Generally, DPS was a model district, precisely the kind of place critics such as Paul Goodman condemned for imposing "compulsory mis-education" on the youth of America.

A measure of the changing nature of DPS was the opening of Thomas Jefferson, George Washington, and Abraham Lincoln high schools in 1960. John F. Kennedy High School joined them six years later. All were designed for new Denver. Not only did they relieve the extreme overcrowding in the old, neighborhood-based high schools, but they sought to provide for future city growth.

The locations of Thomas Jefferson and John F. Kennedy high schools reflected this. DPS built both at the borders of the City and County of Denver. The city was sure its schools were so superior to those in the suburbs it expected residents of unincorporated areas to petition to join Denver with these marvelous institutions next door.

Denver Public Schools offered a ticket of opportunity into the business community. High school principals sometimes served as recruiting agents, pinpointing promising youths and arranging scholarships or job opportunities for them. Well into the 1960s, members of corporate Denver remained foremost figures on the board of education. They sought the unpaid post as their community service. With Oberholtzer firmly in command as superintendent, ruling Denver saw its school system as a municipal gem.

## Racial Tensions

After the initial racism of the 1860s and 1870s, the schools were never officially segregated. In the same manner that there were a few integrated neighborhoods, there were some integrated grammar schools. Twenty-fourth Street School, at 24th and Walnut streets before relocating to 24th and Arapahoe streets in 1919 (renamed Crofton Elementary School in January 1959), was known as "the school of all nations" and the "57 varieties school." Native-born whites joined with blacks, children from Mexico, Japanese-American students, and youths from many parts of Europe in attending it. All were poor. That was the key defining mark: the neighborhood schools generally reflected the class composition of the surrounding areas. Usually the worse the socioeconomic character of the area, the worse the academic performance and the higher the dropout rate.

Nobody claimed the world was fair and equal. The schools reflected the stratified city. Pioneer educator Emily Griffith achieved great renown in the 1910s for her efforts to reach out to poorer students, giving them an opportunity to learn whatever they wished as adults.

Sometimes, open prejudice existed. Illustrative was the library at Fairmont Elementary School at 520 West Third Avenue. It stood out thanks to a 1925 gift of $2,500 worth of books from retiring school board member Ella Strong Denison. The award, she specified, was to go to a school "in a community of predominating

American families," i.e., those of northern European origins, one with "a fairly stable population, and not over-privileged children."

In other places, parents were expected to help improve the schools. Naturally, more affluent families could and did assist their children's academies to a far greater extent than did people who could barely read and make ends meet. Even at that, the schools were far more integrated than any other city institution. The 1948 *East Denver Directory*, a self-portrait of Negro Denver, noted how African-Americans lived in all parts of the city whereby at least one or two black children were present in virtually all schools.

Middle-class blacks embraced DPS, valuing it as a source of advancement. The many well-educated African-American veterans who settled in Mile High City after World War II wanted the best for their children. They had no trouble with the conservative, militaristic orientation of the schools; on the contrary, their sons were often enrolled in ROTC programs. The reality of the schools, they lamented, frequently proved far short of their democratic, integrated rhetoric.

More than anything else, the African-American middle class wanted respect, dignity, and equal opportunity. Aspiring blacks saw the schools as the ideal means of achieving these goals. As black Denver rapidly grew in the 1950s, many of the newcomers were pained to discover the Queen City was not the tolerant, open, non-discriminatory community they thought. No place was this more apparent than in the schools.

Civil rights advocates complained DPS ignored its facilities in historic East Denver, i.e., black Denver. Elementary schools such as Wyatt, Whittier, Mitchell, and Ebert, all institutions with heavy black enrollments, they insisted, were neglected compared to new suburban academies. African-American activists noted

Photo by Phil Goodstein

*Crofton School, at 2409 Arapahoe Street, was once known as the "school of all nations," noting its extremely mixed student body.*

how the district invariably assigned black and inexperienced teachers to posts at minority schools. They claimed the administration foisted old textbooks, already used in newer white schools, on their children. That was the reason, they concluded, the black East Denver schools usually had the worst academic performances within the district.

Black Denver shared the commonplace assumption that old was bad. The bulk of DPS funds went into building new suburban schools. Only in them—sleek, modern buildings—many believed, could good education take place. Not class divisions, but institutional racism was why the school system left their children behind. Many African-Americans longingly sought to move to better, newer neighborhoods where their offspring could attend classes next to white youths, assuring them the advantages of modern middle-class white schools. The ideal location was Park Hill.

## Park Hill

Greater Park Hill refers to the neighborhood east of Colorado Boulevard, between Colfax and approximately I-70, stretching to roughly Quebec Street. Though community boosters have sought to present it as a united mass, Park Hill is much more and much less than this. There are numerous subsections of the area. The foremost division is between old and new Park Hill.

Old Park Hill, the southwestern section of the neighborhood, along Montview Boulevard, dates from the 1880s. Its heart is between 17th and 23rd avenues from Colorado Boulevard to Monaco Street Parkway. Investors, with heavy city assistance, slowly laid out and developed the equivalent of 20th Avenue, Montview Boulevard, between 1892 and 1911, as an idyllic drive. The Downing family owned much of the land adjacent to it.

Caroline Eudora Downing platted Downington, the area between Forest and Monaco streets from Colfax Avenue to Montview Boulevard, on December 24, 1886. By the early 20th century, an investment consortium, a prominent member of which was Warwick Downing (no direct relationship to Caroline Downing), owned much of Downington. Warwick Downing then served as manager of parks and improvements under Mayor Robert Speer. He saw Park Hill get the lion's share of parkways. In particular, the parkways on Montview, 17th Avenue, Monaco Street, and Forest Street were part of Downington. The subdivision included restrictive covenants. Property deeds required residents to build high-class houses, mandating that only whites were allowed in the area. Realtors refused to sell homes in the neighborhood to blacks.

Park Hill projected itself as an elite enclave. Numerous physicians, attorneys, and business executives lived in the romantic suburb filled with tree-lined streets, broad sidewalks, and wide parking strips separating the streets from the sidewalks. This section east of City Park was the neighborhood for those wishing to escape the bustle of Capitol Hill and who had little truck with the Denver Country Club.

Residents saw themselves as a God-fearing, devout people. A heavy church presence helped define Park Hill. Montview Boulevard Presbyterian Church at the southeast corner of Montview Boulevard and Dahlia Street, dating from 1902,

Photo by Phil Goodstein

*The resegregation of Park Hill Elementary School, at 5050 19th Avenue, in 1960 triggered Denver's busing wars.*

and Park Hill Methodist Church at Montview Boulevard and Forest Street, originating at 23rd Avenue and Dexter Street in 1910, were in the lead. Both became among the largest, most prosperous congregations in the city. St. Thomas Episcopal at 22nd Avenue and Dexter Street, and Blessed Sacrament Catholic Church at Montview Boulevard and Eudora Street, joined them as central Park Hill religious institutions. Other congregations, notably City Park Baptist at 17th Avenue and Forest Street, Messiah Lutheran at 18th Avenue and Colorado Boulevard, Park Hill Congregational at 26th Avenue and Leyden Street, and Park Hill Christian at 26th Avenue and Hudson Street, followed after World War II. A strong Masonic link was found in the Park Hill Masonic Temple across the street from Montview Boulevard Presbyterian Church at 4819 Montview Boulevard.

The neighborhood was conservative and straitlaced. Something of a dandelion police existed, assuring lawns were uniformly well maintained. Residents opposed anything smacking of commercialism. The Park Hill Improvement Association, formed in 1908, worked to preserve and enhance the area.

"What Georgetown is to Washington, what Beverly Hills is to Los Angeles, Park Hill is to Denver" stated a neighborhood promotional flyer. Another was in the same vein: "Living is how you feel about where you live. In Park Hill, you can be pardoned for feeling quietly pleased with yourself, just a bit smug." The result was to make Park Hill the kind of place idealized by such television shows as "Ozzie and Harriet" and "Father Knows Best."

The neighborhood's schools reinforced the Park Hill élan. Foremost was Park Hill Elementary at 19th Avenue and Elm Street. Opened as an eight-room school in 1901, it replaced a two-room Park School at the northwest corner of 18th Avenue and Forest Street dating from 1893. Park School was officially renamed Park

Hill School on May 6, 1904. DPS expanded the quickly overcrowded building in 1912 and again in 1928. Complete with a gym and auditorium, Park Hill School was among the city's largest elementary schools. The extremely attractive stuccoed structure, with elaborate terra cotta trim, featured busts of Shakespeare and Beethoven staring at passersby along Elm and Fairfax streets. In no time, Park Hill Elementary was a community gathering place. Troop 28 of the Boy Scouts met there, claiming to have the highest per capita rate of Eagle Scouts in the country during the postwar era. (Boys not likely to make Eagle Scout were often discouraged from enrolling in the troop.)

Stedman Elementary, at 29th Avenue and Dexter Street, opened in 1924. The district slated the property for Park Hill Heights School in the 1910s. The name reflected the designation of the northern part of old Park Hill, the section between roughly 26th and 35th avenues from Colorado Boulevard to Dahlia Street. To the north was the farm of Clayton Boys College.

Photo by Phil Goodstein

*Stedman School at 2940 Dexter Street was once the pride of Park Hill Heights.*

The agricultural land became a golf course, the Park Hill Country Club, in 1930. A privately run facility open to the public, for years the sporting spot practiced blatant discrimination against blacks and Asians. Despite a 1962 ruling by the state Anti-Discrimination Commission finding it guilty of violating the Colorado constitution and the state's open-accommodations act, the Park Hill Country Club persisted in denying blacks access to the links. (Max Zall, who was later city attorney under mayors Tom Currigan and Bill McNichols, represented the racist social organization which claimed it had to keep African-Americas from the course since golf was "a gentleman's game.")

Not until 1966, under the pressure of the civil rights movement, did the country club allow blacks to play there. The facility evolved into the Park Hill Golf Course. By the 1970s, accusations were made about sweetheart deals to its concessionaire from the city. Bill McNichols, incidentally, was long a prime patron of its clubhouse, dining there regularly until shortly before his death in 1997.

The golf club reflected the transformation of Park Hill Heights. The board of education ordered portable classrooms placed on the Dexter Street site in 1917 when it designated the academy Stedman Elementary. The school commemorated Dr. Arnold Stedman (1839–1913). At the time of his death, the city mourned the school's namesake as the dean of the Denver medical community who had been a local physician since 1870. Besides leading the local medical society, Dr. Stedman had sat on the school board.

Stedman School proper opened in 1924. Quickly filled to capacity, DPS completed an expansion of it in 1929. While never quite on the same level as Park Hill Elementary, the Park Hill Heights school was a distinguished neighborhood center. A strong rivalry existed between it and Park Hill Elementary. Residents of Park Hill Heights claimed they were over and above those of Park Hill proper.

Students from Park Hill and Stedman elementary schools went on to Smiley Junior High School at 25th Avenue and Holly Street. The board of education placed it on the drawing board shortly after Denver adopted the principle of junior highs in 1917–18. The administration originally called the land the Holly Street Site and later Park Hill Junior High. The academy honored a longtime principal of East High School who had subsequently served as superintendent, William H. Smiley (1854–1934).

When it opened its doors in 1928, Smiley was at the edge of the city. Open fields leading to the land about to become Stapleton Airport were to the north and east of it. The Smiley site reflected how real estate interests believed the boom of the 1920s would never end whereby the school would quickly be in the center of burgeoning Park Hill.

Like Park Hill Elementary, Smiley Junior High stressed academic achievement. It was also something of a high-society school with an arcane student pecking order. Sports, primarily touch football, were roughhouse there. For years, "Smiley rules" were a code for touch football of tough young athletes. Park Hill residents and teams tended to dominate prep competitions.

The neighborhood underwent drastic changes after World War II. The open spaces to the north and east of Smiley rapidly filled with homes. The sections

Photo by Phil Goodstein

*Hallett Elementary School at 2950 Jasmine Street was a modern school for new Park Hill. It rapidly went from an overwhelmingly white to a virtually all-black enrollment in the mid-1960s, reflecting the transformation of the neighborhood.*

growing up in the 1950s, notably the area east of Dahlia Street and north of 29th Avenue, were quite unlike the prewar enclaves. Ranch-style houses predominated. Instead of tree-lined streets with broad sidewalks, there were often no sidewalks and few trees. Other than for its name, there was nothing Park Hill about these sterile areas stretching toward Stapleton Airport. They were parts of faceless ticky-tacky suburbia.

New Park Hill was the rage. Recently married veterans moved there, occupying what Realtors call starter homes. They were simple structures for young couples that quickly became obsolete as children arrived. For the time being, the North Park Hill abodes had the charm of new houses.

Many airport workers lived in new Park Hill. Residents took pride in the area. They organized the Northeast Park Hill Civic Association (NEPHCA) in 1955 to improve the neighborhood. Among the people dwelling there was Tom Currigan at 2915 Ivy Street. By the time he served as mayor from 1963 until 1968, he had left new Park Hill for a house at 444 South Oneida Way.

Currigan's successor, Bill McNichols (1969–83), had lived at 3395 Grape Street and 2115 Quince Street during the epoch when new Park Hill was emerging. He also abandoned the enclave. While mayor, he was at 754 Krameria Street. Much more typical was the home of Mayor Richard Batterton (1959–63) who lived in the heart of old Park Hill at 2009 Hudson Street. Federico Peña (1983–91) moved to 1740 Leyden Street in Downington during his second term as mayor.

The exodus of such notables as Currigan and McNichols from new Park Hill was indicative. Within a few years, the small simple homes for young couples were not large enough for their growing families. Now and then, residents gave up on the area. Some of the domiciles had been shabbily built and were falling apart by the time they were ten or 15 years old. Others were in excellent shape. Many residents, more affluent than in their new Park Hill days, relocated to substantial houses in old Park Hill.

Simultaneously, jet aircraft began operating out of Stapleton Airport in 1959. Caring little about the amenities of residential Denver, federal aviation officials, backed by city hall, allowed the planes to fly smack over Park Hill. Twenty-sixth Avenue not only emerged as a dividing line between South and North Park Hill, but was a virtual extension of a major east-west runway. Noise from the airport chased many residents from the postwar sections of the neighborhood. Those in old Park Hill likewise complained about the noise. It helped bond them together in fighting city hall to preserve the Park Hill ideal.

## The Black Influx

Right about this time—the late 1950s/early 1960s—blacks started to move into Park Hill. The neighborhood still had a magical allure. A home in Park Hill was a symbol of success. The Park Hill in which most African-Americans settled was not the old, distinguished Park Hill, but the postwar suburban area, right under the flight paths of the airport. The coming of blacks heavily impacted the neighborhood, shaping its modern fabric, schools, and the city as a whole.

A few blacks had lived in Park Hill for years. The Frank Brickler family, for example, located at 2946 Dahlia Street in the early 20th century. On the fringes of the neighborhood, its home was across the street from the Columbia Water Company, a firm providing bottled water from an artesian well. There were also dog pounds and private airports on the outskirts of Park Hill. While blacks came and went from these facilities on the northern and eastern edges of the neighborhood, the postwar impact on Park Hill was quite different.

Already in 1956, Park Hill residents feared blacks were beginning to swarm into their exclusive enclave. The baby boom strained the neighborhood's educational facilities. African-American children were increasingly present in Park Hill schools. With more students than classroom capacity west of Colorado Boulevard, DPS bused black pupils to Park Hill Elementary. Often these boys and girls arrived well before the start of the school day and had to stay considerably after school to meet the bus schedule.

Parents obviously wanted better conditions for their children. Since their offspring went to Park Hill schools, they figured they ought to move to the neighborhood proper. As much as any white couple before 1960, blacks saw buying a home in Park Hill as the realization of the American dream. African-American veterans from Lowry Air Force Base also acquired homes in the neighborhood.

Some in old Park Hill feared the coming of blacks. Rumors abounded concerning a black invasion, about how the neighborhood verged on becoming "Dark Hill." Many argued for toleration. Fervently agreeing that Park Hill was the city's finest neighborhood, existing residents noted they should be willing to share their space with others. These individuals were ready to welcome blacks to Park Hill as long as they were part and parcel of upper-middle-class America. If they were well-educated, churchgoing, and would maintain their properties in pristine condition, Park Hill could be their home.

This was the message coming out of numerous fellowship meetings centered at Montview Boulevard Presbyterian Church. From 1922 until 1946, Dr. William L. Barrett led it. He built the church into a congregation of nearly 2,400 members. Calling itself the "church of a thousand welcomes," Montview Presbyterian developed an impressive physical plant. Something was always going on there, including concerts, lectures, political meetings, and social-welfare efforts.

In 1947, the church called Arthur L. Miller to its ministry. The cleric quickly emerged as a leading Denver preacher. In 1959–60, he was the moderator of the General Assembly of the United Presbyterian Church. His daughter, Bea Ann, married a young politician-attorney, Roy Romer, on June 10, 1952. The couple settled a block from the church at 2045 Eudora Street.

Miller oversaw a massive church expansion in 1958. He remained the congregation's leader until he retired in November 1967. During this epoch, he was an advocate of racial understanding. When some Park Hill residents panicked as the first wave of blacks started to attend neighborhood schools in 1956–58, the church urged whites to work with blacks to shape Park Hill's future. Many residents agreed. They liked where they were in old Park Hill. They were not about to abandon their distinguished homes, churches, and schools at the drop of a hat; on the contrary, they would do their all to keep it the proud neighborhood it had always been.

Members of Montview Boulevard Presbyterian Church took the lead in establishing the Park Hill Action Committee (PHAC) in 1960. The goal was plain: racial understanding and the prevention of any black/white frenzy. The white activists behind the effort reached out to seven other churches—Park Hill Methodist, City Park Baptist, St. Thomas Episcopal, Blessed Sacrament, Messiah Lutheran, Park Hill Congregational, and Park Hill Christian—to fund the group. (Some accounts insist only seven churches were involved, stating Blessed Sacrament was not part of the initial effort.) PHAC's primary purpose was to assure peaceful, friendly relations between old Park Hill whites and blacks starting to come to new Park Hill.

The neighborhood achieved great acclaim for its efforts. Motorcades by presidents Lyndon Johnson and Richard Nixon passed through it. (Johnson, seeing all the blacks standing in front of the fine structures along Monaco Street Parkway near 32nd Avenue in 1964, purportedly turned to his host, stating it was wonderful how the homeowners had allowed their servants to view his procession—the blacks were the homeowners.) CBS Television featured Park Hill as a model integrated community. The *Wall Street Journal* and *New Yorker* wrote it up. When Martin Luther King visited Denver in April 1962, he spoke at Park Hill Methodist. He preached at Montview Boulevard Presbyterian Church during a January 1964 Mile High appearance.

Below the surface, there were severe tensions in integrated Park Hill. Despite the integration rhetoric, Park Hill was internally segregated. Most of the black population lived north of 26th Avenue. By the early 1960s, ever more African-Americans were moving into that area. Among those fearing this influx were

Photo by Phil Goodstein

*Montview Boulevard Presbyterian Church, at Montview Boulevard and Dahlia Street, helped give birth to the Park Hill Action Committee in 1960.*

recently settled members of the black middle class. Park Hill, they concluded once they had established themselves there, had enough African-Americans. With the addition of any more, the neighborhood would become resegregated. In 1965, to keep more blacks out, these African-American pioneers of integrated Park Hill issued what was known as the Blue Flyer, a statement printed on blue paper urging blacks to move to other parts of the city rather than to their neighborhood.

The warning had little effect. Blacks continued to pour into Park Hill. Many were no longer members of the middle class. African-Americans from all backgrounds were calling the neighborhood home. Within a few years, new Park Hill went from an overwhelmingly white to a predominantly black area. Some Realtors—blacks as well as whites—frantically encouraged whites to flee because African-Americans were moving in.

The commercial face of Park Hill also changed. Two shopping centers, Dahlia Square at 34th Avenue and Dahlia Street, and the Park Hill Shopping Center at 34th Avenue and Holly Street, were anchors of the postwar section. They included supermarkets, bowling alleys, lounges, drive-in restaurants, and dime stores. By the late 1960s, many of the businesses had closed and the shopping centers started to have run-down appearances.

Typical of the despair and lack of promise of new Park Hill was the fate of Dahlia Square. After King Soopers closed its grocery there in the early 1970s, the entire commercial area rapidly declined. McDonald's also exited the center. Other chain stores abandoned new Park Hill. The former gem of the postwar neighborhood mostly became a vacant battle zone. Promises were unending about the imminence of a complete renewal of the area. In 1999, Mayor Wellington Webb vowed massive city assistance to renovate the center as part of his administration's commitment to helping Denver's poorest neighborhoods. (City hall claimed the existing location was inappropriate. It wished to move the square to nearby Martin Luther King Boulevard as part of an urban renewal project.)

The fate of the shopping center was illustrative of the city's poor and minority neighborhoods. By the 1970s, black enclaves were generally devoid of national pharmacies or supermarkets. Nor were modern movie complexes added to these residential sections. Those living in African-American areas had to drive for miles to get to middle-class shopping and entertainment areas. (Many blacks had once patronized historic, moderately priced downtown shops. The city responded by pushing for their replacement with fancy, high-class boutiques.)

As the Dahlia and Park Hill shopping centers declined, groups of black adolescents frequently hung out around them. Various gangs marked them as their turfs. Though Denver never experienced a race riot as such during the height of the crisis of the 1960s, there were occasional rumbles at the Park Hill Shopping Center between African-American teenagers and the police.

The Northeast Park Hill Civic Association tried to respond. As new Park Hill changed from a white to a black neighborhood, NEPHCA mirrored the transformation. Middle-class black activists were in the forefront of the organization. Often they were highly motivated individuals who firmly supported the establishment. They included assistant city and federal attorneys. More than one was a volunteer instructor in ROTC programs at East and Manual high schools. These community leaders had no use for radicals, troublemakers, or young punks. On the contrary, their goal was to see new Park Hill achieve its original promise as part of the greater Park Hill community.

One effort was Skyland Park, bordered by 33rd and 35th avenues and Holly and Ivy streets, directly east of the Park Hill Shopping Center. The city dedicated the park in August 1957 as the playground for new Park Hill. A swimming pool, added in the mid-1960s, was immediately integrated. A recreation center followed in November 1969. Among those pushing the last was a leader of NEPHCA who was a former employee of the city's recreation program, Bill Roberts.

Elected as Park Hill's first African-American councilman in 1971, Roberts personified the neighborhood's black political activists. Reared in Toccoa, Georgia, a small manufacturing town on the South Carolina border, he patriotically enrolled in the Army. He arrived in Denver in 1958 when he was stationed at Fitzsimons. Upon his discharge in 1961, Roberts stayed in the area, going to work for the city's Department of Parks and Recreation. As the civil rights upheavals shook the area, he signed on with the Commission on Community Relations in 1968. Two years later, in November 1970, Roberts became the project director for the Metropolitan Denver Minority Construction Plan, a federal Department of Labor effort to recruit more blacks into the construction trades.

Roberts fought for equal rights for blacks. Simultaneously, he was an aspiring member of the ruling elite. For example, when Colorado was convulsed by the debate over whether to host the 1976 Winter Olympics in 1971–72, Roberts served on the Denver Organizing Committee, the sponsor of the games. By then, Roberts had gone from working to recruit minorities to the building trades to running his own construction company. He proudly noted how, in the 1980s, his firm received the largest government construction contract ever awarded to a minority firm in the state as part of a Colorado Springs water pumping project. His proudest accomplishment on council was establishing a city commission to assist the elderly.

Before winning the council seat, Roberts had helped engineer a merger between NEPHCA and PHAC in 1970 when the two associations formed Greater Park Hill Community Incorporated (GPHC). Members of both groups were conscious of race during their four years of negotiations preceding the combination. Leaders were selected by the color of their skins. The threats to Park Hill went beyond race, demanding cooperation between the two organizations. Park Hill, GPHC asserted, was one of 25 truly integrated neighborhoods in the country.

The improvement group was a religiously based constituency group stemming from PHAC's church origins. Though GPHC's bylaws did not define "participating church," each such body was allowed to appoint two governors to the board of directors. In addition to the church delegates, the GPHC board included representatives from geographic subsections in addition to commissioners at large.

With a strong backing from the mainline churches, GPHC was more than simply a homeowners' group. It featured a health-testing program focusing on sickle-cell anemia. For some years, it ran a thrift shop. An annual house tour generated a good deal of revenue. Members socialized during wine-tasting parties. The group held an annual Park Hill Day of fun and games at Smiley Junior High School.

Photo by Phil Goodstein

*The nearly abandoned Dahlia Square at 34th Avenue and Dahlia Street reflects the troubled development of North Park Hill.*

So people would know what it was about and happenings in the neighborhood, GPHC published a monthly newspaper, *Greater Park Hill News*.

Though far less visible than GPHC, the Park Hill Improvement Association (PHIA) continued to function. It had little to do with the social affairs of GPHC, but PHIA was at one with it on many issues. Both vehemently opposed the granting of any liquor licenses in the area. They pushed for exclusive R-0 zoning for most of old, and a good deal of new, Park Hill. This was a regulation permitting only members of families and close relatives to occupy single-family houses. While a number of religious monasteries were in the neighborhood, Park Hill did not tolerate any hippie pads or experimental living ventures. GPHC, for instance, successfully declared war on a commune at 4131 26th Avenue in 1973. A history of the organization called the closure of the house a Park Hill triumph.

Strong racial divisions continued in Park Hill. Few blacks showed up at programs featuring the history of the neighborhood. The physical design of new Park Hill was such it never came close to looking like the older sections. In places, 29th Avenue was a literal dividing point between two different worlds: affluent, mostly white middle-class Park Hill to the south, and lower-income, predominantly black Park Hill to the north. Overwhelmingly black gangs grew in the latter. Shootings and drug-dealing marred the Park Hill idyll. Residents were angry and hurt by this violence, especially as it moved into old Park Hill when a black youth was murdered in a gang-related shooting near 19th Avenue and Cherry Street on Halloween 1993.

## Barrett School

By this time, the schools of Park Hill had completely changed. From leaders of academic achievement, they were extremely troubled. Ironically, an urgent goal of the black middle-class—having their children share an outstanding Park Hill education—backfired.

As new Park Hill emerged after World War II, schools came with it. Hallett School at 28th Avenue and Jasmine Street opened in 1951. Philips Elementary at Montview Boulevard and Monaco Street Parkway followed the next year. Both were quickly overcrowded, leading to the construction of Smith School at 36th Avenue and Jasmine Street in 1955. Virtually all neighborhood schools were expanded in the 1950s and 1960s. An architecturally intrusive addition to Park Hill Elementary in 1968 increased the school's capacity to 1,200 students.

Park Hill Elementary was also at the center of severe court and political fights over integration. As enrollment swelled to 859 students in a school designed for 660 pupils in the late 1950s, the board of education proposed a new school for the overwhelmingly black North City Park neighborhood. Not only were pupils bused from west of Colorado Boulevard to Park Hill Elementary, but DPS had owned land between 29th and 32nd avenues from Colorado Boulevard to Jackson Street since 1949. Periodically, it had pondered placing a junior high school there. Black activists, who feared a segregated academy at the corner, killed the junior high proposal in 1962—they saw it a nefarious means to preserve Smiley as a white school. Nor were middle-class African-Americans happy about plans for an elementary school at 29th Avenue and Jackson Street. They noted it was primarily designed to keep black children out of Park Hill schools. The school board could just as well build the new school east of Colorado Boulevard as west of it since DPS also owned land east of Colorado Boulevard. A school there, advocates insisted, would emerge as a fine integrated facility.

Despite the realization any school west of Colorado Boulevard would be overwhelmingly black, DPS opened Harry M. Barrett Elementary School in 1960 at the northeast corner of 29th and Jackson. The school honored a former principal of East High School. The board of education carefully drew the academy's borders with Colorado Boulevard, two blocks away, as the eastern terminus. The line was selected to assure black children from the area, who had previously attended Stedman or had been bused to Park Hill Elementary, would go to Barrett. DPS channeled white students to Park Hill Elementary and Stedman. In this light, it was not surprising that 89.6 percent of Barrett's 533 students were black when it held its first classes in a structure designed for 450 pupils. Within a few years, the school was 100 percent minority, consisting of 93 percent black children and 7 percent Hispanics. Compared to 8.5 percent black teachers in the school system as a whole, 52.6 percent of Barrett's faculty were African-Americans. (Skilled, veteran teachers were a rarity at it and most of the poor, minority schools—they transferred from them as soon as they had enough seniority.)

Barrett's impact on Park Hill Elementary was immediate. From 859 students in the 1959–60 school year, about 200 of whom were black, Park Hill was down to 706 students in the 1960–61 school year with a virtually all-white enrollment. While a handful of blacks attended Park Hill Elementary during the early 1960s, the school was virtually resegregated upon the completion of Barrett. Many black parents and integration activists believed this a deliberate Jim Crow policy by the school board and old white Park Hill.

Photo by Phil Goodstein

*The school board deliberately gerrymandered the borders of Barrett School at 2900 Jackson Street in 1960 to ensure it would have an overwhelmingly black enrollment.*

Middle-class African-Americans were outraged to see their children taken from the ideal, integrated Park Hill Elementary and placed in a black school. They feared the education was not as good. As much as the white middle class, they did not want their children mixing with lower-class elements whom they feared pulled down the quality of the learning experience as a whole.

Segregated schools, however, seemed the fate of Park Hill blacks. Stedman School reflected the rapidly changing racial composition of Park Hill Heights. While DPS undertook efforts to keep it a white school—Stedman had only a 4 percent black enrollment in 1960 after the opening of Barrett—the board of education eventually concluded it was hopeless to hold the race line at Stedman in face of the mass black influx into North Park Hill. In 1964, the school board gerrymandered the Park Hill Heights school's attendance borders so white students, who would have previously attended Stedman, were sent elsewhere. By 1968, Stedman had a 94.6 percent African-American enrollment.

Nor were some of the district's other actions successful in preserving the white schools of new Park Hill. At first, many of Stedman's white students landed up at Hallett School, 99 percent white in 1960. Hallett was 90 percent black by 1968. The few remaining white children in northeast Park Hill were then sent to Philips School.

Racial tensions also marred Smiley Junior High School. By the mid-1960s, it had a very integrated enrollment. Blacks and whites mixed in gym classes and shop and home economics courses. The mind-boggling social studies program was geared to achieve integrated classes. Science and mathematics classes were often highly segregated. Few blacks were in accelerated classes while modified sections were overwhelmingly black. Sometimes, white students gathered at the 25th Avenue entrance to the school while black students called the 26th Avenue entrance their own. There was limited social mingling between blacks and whites.

## The Changing School Board

The school board sanctioned both the internal and external segregation of the schools. For years, it held its meetings at 2:00 PM. By the time it was formally in session, its members had usually already reached a consensus on key matters during a previous, private superintendent's conference. The commission neither expected nor desired much citizen input. While the body ostensibly oversaw Superintendent Oberholtzer, he mostly ran it.

The board of education could not ignore the growing racial tensions in the city amidst the national civil rights upheavals. Neighborhood activists and black leaders demanded a greater accountability from DPS. As riots tore northern cities, politicians and reformers decried the fate of "urban disadvantaged children." Under the pressures of black militants, the country increasingly condemned racial segregation as a brutal, shameful practice. Reformers saw schools as a key means of redressing racism and injustice. What was more, the highly influential 1966 Coleman Report claimed integration produced "astounding" results in improving educational performance of both black and white children.

DPS had to change. Ironically, a conservative Republican, Palmer L. Burch, was the catalyst for the transformation of the school board. Born in Ordway in 1907, he graduated from high school in Frederick, Colorado, in 1923, receiving a degree from Central Business College, a Denver trade school, the next year. He soon plunged into real estate, becoming a key executive with Horace W. Bennett & Company. After serving as president of the Denver Association of Building Owners and Managers and the Board of Realtors, Burch won election to the Colorado House of Representatives in 1946 and again in 1950, 1952, 1954, and 1956. The commercial real estate investor was the unsuccessful Republican candidate for governor in 1958. Out of office in 1959, after pondering a race for mayor, he won election to the school board.

Author's Collection

*Palmer Burch shook up the school board in the 1960s.*

Burch immediately transformed the body. He not only questioned the budget, but noted the board needed to reach out to the public. To assure day workers could participate in the body's deliberations, he convinced the majority to move school board meetings to the evening. While he had served in the legislature, the insurgent member had arranged, beginning in 1959, for DPS to hold school board elections in conjunction with Denver municipal elections. Previously, the board had completely controlled the nonpartisan elections, calling them to assure its self-perpetuation.

Citizens eagerly embraced the new system. Opposed to the 104,810 votes cast in the 1959 election—Burch received 60,092 of them—only 14,998 ballots had been counted in the 1957 school board election. More and more contenders sought to win seats on the board of education. Often there were upwards of a dozen candidates. The two or three top vote-getters were elected even if they only had small pluralities and far less than a majority of the total votes. Usually, the victors were well-financed individuals with excellent ties to 17th Street and the political establishment.

About the time Burch was agitating the board, Rachel Bassette Noel emerged as the leader of blacks demanding fair play from DPS. Born in 1919, she grew up in Hampton, Virginia, earning her bachelor's degree at Hampton Institute. She followed it with a master's degree in sociology from Fisk University. After marrying a medical student, Edmond F. Noel, she came to Denver with him in November 1949. Having recently gained his degree, Dr. Noel believed the Mile High City was an ideal place to establish a practice.

The Noels were part and parcel of the postwar black middle class. They located in a house directly north of the City Park Golf Course. Rachel Noel naturally insisted her children get the best education possible. She was in the forefront of opposing efforts to build a segregated school near 32nd Avenue and Colorado Boulevard while she was a leader of the PTA. Noel worked as a consultant for the city's Commission on Community Relations. Her children proudly attended East High School.

When a vacancy occurred on the school board in 1963, black Denver pushed Noel for the post. The *Denver Post* loudly championed her. (Art Branscombe, a *Post* editorial and education writer, was an activist in Park Hill integration battles, a leader of PHAC, and a fierce advocate of desegregation.) For nearly six months, the board was at a three-to-three deadlock over whether Noel should join it. Some of the conservative incumbents opposed her, fearing she was too friendly to labor. (About this time, the Denver Federation of Teachers launched a vigorous drive for meaningful union representation of the district's instructors.) To the outrage of the *Post* and advocates of having a black on the school board, the incumbents bypassed Noel.

The scorned candidate used her rejection as a launching pad to run for the job in the May 1965 elections. With a well-organized campaign, Noel led a field of 22 candidates, sweeping Park Hill and most of old East Denver as she became the first African-American woman elected to any public post in Colorado. Simultaneously, other individuals dedicated to integration won seats on the school board, forming a majority of the seven-member body.

Seventeenth Street attorney Ed Benton won the race to fill a vacancy on the board in 1961. He immediately started rocking the boat, noting the system's discriminatory practices. Added to community upheavals and the national civil rights movement, DPS responded in 1962 when the board of education conceded not all its schools were equal. To redress this problem, it established a Special Study Committee on Equality of Educational Opportunity. Numerous civic activists, many with close ties to old Denver and members of the school board, served on the body, one for which more than 500 individuals volunteered.

Powerbroker attorney and television station owner William W. Grant III initially headed the commission. Shortly after it started its work, he resigned to unsuccessfully run for mayor in 1963. Another attorney, James Voorhees, took charge of what became known as the Voorhees Committee. (Voorhees used his leadership of it to win a post on the school board in 1965.)

The body showed itself urgently concerned about providing avenues whereby poor students could become part of mainstream society. In its report, released in February 1964, the commission observed members of minority groups tended to drop out more frequently than non-minority students. This, it feared, would result in future crime, welfare, and unemployment. A high school diploma was necessary for lifelong success. The duty of the schools was to help all students achieve the piece of sheepskin.

The Voorhees Committee urged DPS to consider racial, ethnic, and social-economic factors when establishing school borders and opening new academies. The city had to have a heterogeneous school community. DPS must take the lead in pushing for racial tolerance and understanding. The board of education adopted Policy 5100 on May 6, 1964, endorsing the findings of the Voorhees Committee.

The same year the school board gerrymandered a few school borders to preserve the racial status quo. That was the stated policy of Oberholtzer. While he lived in an exclusive white neighborhood near the Wellshire Golf Course at 3244 South Gregg Court, he was a member of Montview Boulevard Presbyterian Church. Despite the congregation's activism on racial questions, he pretended they did not exist for DPS. (Many members of Montview Presbyterian moved out of Park Hill. Some of them also lived near the Wellshire Golf Course and joined Wellshire Presbyterian Church at 2999 South Colorado Boulevard, a congregation established in 1951.) Oberholtzer explained his policy was one of strict neutrality on racial matters. Far from redressing discrimination and past racism, his goal was to keep conditions as they were.

Photo by Phil Goodstein

*A stained glass window at Shorter Church honors Rachel Noel.*

Even while Oberholtzer was ignoring racial problems, the school board stated it wanted a more integrated system. Denver was mostly a segregated city. Other than Park Hill and some old working-class neighborhoods near the smelters, stockyards, and Cherry Creek, most areas were either black or white. (Hispanics were largely a world in themselves, having little to do with either the black or white perspectives on integration.) The affluent neighborhoods were overwhelmingly white as were their schools.

Despite the superintendent's waffling on racial matters, the school board pushed the question. Following the pro-desegregation results of the 1965 election, the body governing DPS established an advisory committee on integration. Drawing members from the Congress of Racial Equality, the National Association for the Advancement of Colored People, the Hispanic GI Forum, the Jewish Anti-Defamation League, PHAC, and others concerned about the quality and racial makeup of the schools, the committee argued integration was not simply a matter of abstract justice; it was a vital component of successful education. Students in integrated schools, proponents insisted, learned better—both academically and socially—than did pupils in segregated institutions. Busing was a means of desegregating the system.

## Busing Controversies

Busing was widely used throughout Denver in the 1960s. Not only were suburban children bused for miles to get to their schools, so were children in newer parts of the Queen City where neighborhood schools were not yet open or past capacity. Increasingly, civil rights exponents viewed busing as a method to overcome racial problems. By going to school together, blacks and whites would get to know one another and live together. It was also a steppingstone by which black youths could experience the superior quality of white middle-class academies. Ideally, they would graduate and proceed to college as all-American kids.

Initially, busing for integration was a volunteer effort. The first steps toward it failed. Smiley Junior High School was a case in point. As the baby boomers came of junior high age, Smiley was so overcrowded it had to go on split sessions in the fall of 1966. The school board allowed black students attending Smiley the chance to get on the bus and go to other junior highs in the name of bringing racial balance to them. Only 14 students signed up for the program.

Members of PHAC openly advocated split-sessions as a means of keeping Smiley integrated. The alternative, they feared, was a new, segregated academy at 32nd Avenue and Colorado Boulevard. Despite the building of Hallett, Smith, and Philips schools and major additions to Smiley and Park Hill Elementary, they claimed their part of town was not receiving its fair share of school dollars. While new academies continued to open in postwar sections of the city, the administration supposedly ignored their neighborhood. They wanted nothing more than what the rest of Denver was receiving: good new schools with adequate capacity for the students. In such a manner, Park Hill schools would emerge as premier examples of the wonders of integrated education.

By 1966, as racial concerns increasingly haunted DPS, the school board formed another committee, led by attorney Bill Berge, to look into the question. It concluded no new schools should be built in the northeast corridor because of the rapidly changing racial composition of the area. Segregated schools, it admitted,

Photo by Phil Goodstein

*Park Hill integration controversies heavily impacted Smiley Junior High School at 2540 Holly Street.*

were inferior by their very nature. Instead of doing anything to foster them, DPS should push a cultural arts center in northeast Denver, an educational complex drawing students to specialized classes from throughout the region.

This policy, never implemented, quickly evolved into advocacy of educational parks. Proponents saw neighborhood schools in the middle of residential sections as obsolete. They wanted to displace them with learning centers, massive complexes pulling in students from diverse areas. Supporters pictured the educational parks as combined campuses, including elementary, junior high, and high schools. They would serve city-wide constituencies, redressing overcrowding, obsolete equipment, and racial imbalance. Most students would ride the bus to them.

Educational parks were a central issue in the 1967 school board race. Far from capturing the fancy of the city, they became a bone of contention. Those proud of the existing neighborhood schools feared the educational parks were nothing but coercive schemes of the high priests of the knowledge business who had no feeling for the city or traditional learning climates. Bill Berge, who opposed the program, joined with Stephen Knight of an affluent, influential, old Denver family on a ticket advocating neighborhood schools in the May election. The two swept to victory over supporters of educational parks. A five-to-two pro-integration majority remained on the school board.

As controversy raged over DPS racial policies, just before Christmas 1966, Oberholtzer announced he would retire as superintendent on July 31, 1967. After having unquestioned control of the system since the late 1940s, he found himself increasingly challenged. Seeing a transformation of the system was imminent, the educator realized it was time to move on. He died in California at age 89 on December 17, 1993.

The school board could not find a successor to Oberholtzer in the district. Scouring the country, it brought in Robert D. Gilberts, the superintendent of the Madison, Wisconsin, school system to succeed him. A consultant's report then described DPS as having "a very minor minority problem." This was not only an extreme understatement, but it was quickly obvious the old order had only worked because of Oberholtzer's extreme efficiency.

Gilberts headed the system for three stormy years until 1970. Over the next 20 years, superintendents came and went as the system veered from one extreme to another. The post was highly politically charged. The superintendent was no longer an educational leader, but simply an administrative fixer. Busing and integration controversies continually haunted DPS.

During 1967–69, numerous perspectives were presented on busing. Some believed it a necessary evil, a measure only to redress overcrowding. Others insisted on voluntary busing: black parents could have their children ride the bus to seemingly better white schools while DPS forced nobody, black or white, to get on a bus to fulfill the abstract integration ideal. A loud section of the community, especially in Park Hill, argued for mandatory busing. The old system was so discriminatory that drastic actions were needed to assure better education for all.

National racial developments intensified Denver integration controversies. Shortly after the death of Martin Luther King, the school board adopted resolution

1490 by a five-to-two margin on May 16, 1968. Referred to as the Noel Resolution after Rachel Noel, who introduced and pushed it, the measure drew on Policy 5100, the 1964 proposal to take racial, ethnic, and social-economic factors into account when establishing school borders and building new academies. The May 1968 decision specifically called for Superintendent Gilberts to devise a comprehensive integration program by September 30, 1968. The motion further specified the board of education would consider the plan for adoption no later than December 31, 1968. Desegregation, the measure stressed, was a paramount educational goal. Insofar as busing was needed to achieve it, the majority of the school board was ready to employ this means. Speak Out on School Integration was a community-based group heartily supporting the effort. Citizens for One Community joined it, trying to build a multiracial coalition for desegregation. Many students supported the effort in Students for One Community.

Numerous residents opposed the busing policy. On November 14, 1967, the electorate overwhelmingly rejected a $32.5 million DPS bond issue, 20,381–43,983, to expand school facilities. The proposal, or so opponents claimed, was not for bricks and mortar, but called for an entire redesign of the school system, including educational parks, whereby race and busing were foremost considerations. Others voted against the bond issue to mark their lack of confidence in the school board. Prior to the election, members of the Junior Chamber of Commerce (the Jaycees) passed out tens of thousands of flyers questioning the bond issue's integration overtones.

Board of education meetings became highly controversial and heavily attended. To accommodate all comers, the school board transferred its sessions to high school auditoriums. After moving them about the city, it selected the auditorium at South High School as its permanent home, explaining the school was centrally located. On occasion, concerned citizens filled virtually all of the hall's 1,600 seats. Channel Six broadcast them. A loud bell on the podium rang after three minutes during public hearings—the limit to which the school board would listen to an individual member of the public.

(Blacks claimed the choice of South High School was deliberately racist. The school celebrated Confederate lore, including having murals showing Confederate battle flags. Its students were deemed "Rebels," though the administration did not tolerate any student rebels at the school. The school covered up the Confederate murals during board of education meetings.)

The morass in DPS was highlighted in 1968 when the latest reports of student achievement numbed the school board and the city. Under Oberholtzer, Denver test scores were usually well above the national norm. Suddenly, they were only average. Schools with heavy black enrollments had the worst results. Advocates of integration pointed to this. Only by having these students attend good white schools was it possible to improve their educational achievements. Such policies would further prevent the school board from unfairly distributing materials and supplies primarily to white schools. Parents of students in white schools, in contrast, feared such poorly performing students would bring down the educational quality of their children's academies.

Photo by Phil Goodstein

*The school board held numerous sessions at South High School during which it debated busing for integration.*

Educational issues increasingly polarized the city. Some parents decided to move out of Denver altogether to escape DPS turmoil. Commentators increasingly viewed the Cherry Creek School District in the southeastern suburbs as the region's premier school system. They pointed to Cherry Creek High, rather than East High, as the defining public school of greater Denver.

## The Gilberts Plan

In response to the Noel Resolution, Superintendent Gilberts, with the assistance of staff members Joseph Brzeinski and Charles Armstrong, submitted "Planning Quality Education—A Proposal for Integrating the Denver Public Schools" in the fall of 1968. Deemed the Gilberts Plan, it called for the gradual integration of the city's schools over the course of four years. The system would primarily accomplish the effort by busing blacks into previously all-white schools. White students, who wanted to attend black schools, were welcomed to do so.

To bring whites into heavily black schools, DPS sought to transform Manual High School into a college preparatory academy. The institution had been under fire since 1950 when the school board resolved to build a new home for the school, then at 27th Avenue and Franklin Street. No sooner was the replacement structure operating at 28th Avenue and Williams Street in 1953 than some blacks claimed Manual was deliberately segregated, providing inferior education and programs for African-Americans compared to those offered to whites at other Denver high schools. They noted how the board of education had set York Street as Manual's eastern boundary. In the 1970s, a few civil rights activists called for renaming the school Martin Luther King High School, not liking the historic manual training connotation of the academy's name.

The integration program sought to provide such attractive programs at Manual that white students would willingly get on the bus and ride across town to attend the previously overwhelmingly black school. DPS also modified attendance borders so some black students, who otherwise might go to Manual, went to George Washington High School, an institution excelling in academic achievement. Reviving the educational park idea of the 1967 elections, the Gilberts Plan further proposed clustering school facilities.

The Denver Chamber of Commerce lined up behind the Gilberts Plan. Few others were happy with it. The Denver Federation of Teachers, then unsuccessfully struggling for union recognition against the Denver Classroom Teachers Association, blasted it as a meaningless gesture, a program that did not really integrate anything. Nor did exponents of neighborhood schools think much of the superintendent's proposal. They continued to insist the school board was on a foolish path. All the Gilberts Plan would accomplish was the destruction of existing, well-functioning white schools for an arcane, unproven ideal.

Civil rights exponents also opposed the Gilberts Plan. They argued it was far too gradual. It was not a real solution to segregation, but rank tokenism. At the most, the proposal would artificially mix black and white children for a few hours a week while changing nothing of substance. Activists in Park Hill were especially harsh. Jules Mondschein, a sociology professor at the University of Denver and a white leader of PHAC, asserted: "If we don't get racially balanced schools, Denver's through as a city."

Armageddon rhetoric escalated. The school question literally seemed a matter of black and white. Nor did compromise proposals work. The effort at voluntary busing and open enrollment produced little results. If anything, some bright students from Thomas Jefferson High School opted to take the bus to East High, finding that campus far more dynamic than their school. Meanwhile, racial violence erupted in some of the schools. Adolescents were aping their elders, making race a defining consideration in all interactions.

Despite the numerous complaints, the majority of the school board stuck with the Gilberts Plan. To affirm busing was in Denver's future, DPS ordered 39 additional school buses in January 1969. Critics of the integration efforts denounced this purchase. The school district, they gloomily lamented, was committing suicide. The money spent on the buses could easily go into improving academic performance.

Supporters of the busing program readily took on opponents. Often they dismissed foes as racists. They pointed out numerous children were already bused to schools around the metropolitan area. What the anti-busing constituency lamented, they asserted, was not busing per se, but having blacks bused into their neighborhoods. In this atmosphere, there was little give and take.

The board of education ratified its commitment to integration via busing in April 1969. After months of controversy and public hearings on the Gilberts Plan, the body adopted three proposals. The first, resolution 1520, sought to protect

East High and Smiley Junior High as integrated academies. The second, resolution 1524, called for specific improvement at Cole Junior High School, a troubled, overwhelmingly black school at 3240 Humboldt Street. The last, resolution 1531, passed by a five-to-two vote on April 24, 1969, mandated busing for elementary students for the 1969–70 school year.

Park Hill Elementary, not surprisingly, was the school most benefiting from the integration proposal. By this time, it had an enrollment of about 71 percent white, 24 percent black, and 5 percent Hispanic children. Under the busing scenario, Park Hill Elementary would be stabilized at 79 percent white, 13 percent black, and 8 percent Hispanic. In other words, despite the massive changing racial composition of Park Hill as a whole, the landmark school of the neighborhood would remain the standard-bearer of old white Park Hill.

The concern for Smiley and East was also indicative. Smiley was the Park Hill school. Even more, for years East High had been *the* Denver school. Generations of Denverites, including members of the elite, proudly called it their alma mater. It pulled students from both the North City Park and Country Club areas. Many living in the latter section, including board of education president James Voorhees whose daughter attended the high school, wanted to see East remain a vibrant integrated academy. Without busing, those living in the high-class areas of Capitol Hill feared, East was on its way to becoming an all-minority institution. Seen in this light, many in the Country Club neighborhood endorsed busing. Among the leaders of Speak Out on School Integration and supporters of busing were the wives of Denver businessmen and bankers who lived in high-class sections of greater Capitol Hill.

Author's Collection

*A campaign flyer for Monte Pascoe and Edgar Benton in the controversial May 1969 school board election.*

Auraria Archives

*James Perrill and Frank Southworth successfully led the anti-busing campaign in May 1969.*

All viewed the approaching May 1969 school board election as a decisive referendum on busing. Two of the five supporters of busing on the seven-member body were up for reelection, Ed Benton and Allegra Saunders. The two had not gotten along. The latter had joined the board in 1963. A resident of the Berkeley neighborhood, her husband George E. Saunders, was Colorado Secretary of State from 1935 until 1941. She developed a political career of her own in the 1950s when she served eight years as Denver's representative on the state Board of Education. Denver's leading woman politician by this time, Saunders gained election to the state Senate in 1958 where she served until 1962, chairing the education committee.

As busing controversies heated up, Benton found Saunders wavering and unreliable. He replaced her with water attorney Monte Pascoe as his running mate. The two were longtime walking companions. Pascoe had managed Benton's 1963 bid for the school board. Unhappy about being dumped by the pro-busing forces, Saunders ran for reelection to the school board as an independent.

Benton and Pascoe projected themselves as the morally righteous. Their campaign slogan said as much: "Doing the right thing isn't always easy, but it is always worth doing." Their supporters insisted the city's soul was at stake. Only outright racists and the ignorant opposed the integration program. If nothing else, busing advocates were firmly convinced they were doing the right thing.

Jim Perrill was the key political opponent of busing. A 44-year-old civic activist whose daughter attended East High, Perrill was a former state senator, municipal judge, and administrative assistant of Mayor Richard Batterton. Frank Southworth, the city's manager of revenue under Batterton, joined Perrill on the anti-busing ticket. The two had collaborated on various ventures since they had worked together under Denver's last Republican mayor. A commercial Realtor, Southworth was receptive to Perrill's suggestions about the need to stop busing and preserve the quality of neighborhood schools. In the process, he and Perrill hoped to revitalize the ever smaller and more irrelevant Denver Republican Party.

The issue was clear: the ticket of Benton-Pascoe and integration, against that of Perrill-Southworth which called for maintenance of the existing system of neighborhood schools. The contest achieved mass national attention. Right in the middle of it, in March 1969, riots wracked West High School where Chicano activists were decrying the racism of the schools. There was little connection between the Hispanic protesters and the middle-class blacks advocating integration. The former did not believe mixing a few of their children in overwhelmingly white, middle-class schools would accomplish much. If anything, it would only dilute their proud culture and language.

Nor did all African-Americans endorse busing. They too wanted neighborhood schools. Many of them had no more confidence in DPS than did Chicano militants. This was the time when the Black Panthers were trying to operate their own schools for black children. That group did not trust the establishment in any form, least of all its racist school system.

While the Democratic Party officially lined up behind the ticket of Benton and Pascoe, it was rent with disagreements. Just before the election, more than a quarter of the city's Democratic captains loudly voiced their opposition to the pro-busing campaign. While some members of the GOP established a Republicans for Benton-Pascoe, the party establishment eagerly supported Perrill and Southworth.

Nearly 110,000 voters, out of a total registration of 215,000, turned out on election day, May 20, 1969. Anti-busing forces overwhelming triumphed. Southworth led the pack with 75,596, closely followed by Perrill's 73,932. Benton was far behind in third place with 31,098. Pascoe got 28,948. Six other candidates got the rest, including Saunders who received 4,666. While Benton and Pascoe carried black neighborhoods and Park Hill, the rest of Denver, including Hispanic enclaves, went for the anti-busing candidates. Cable television magnate Bill Daniels saw the triumph of the Perrill-Southworth ticket as a salvation for Denver as he hosted a party for the victors. He subsequently donated considerable sums to those advocating a public bankrolling of private schools.

## The Keyes Case

Champions of neighborhood schools celebrated the victory of the Perrill-Southworth ticket. Advocates of desegregation were angry and outraged. Instead of seeing that the victors had strong merits to their case, civil rights activists insisted the results showed Denver was a hopelessly racist city. As the anti-busing vote mounted on election night, integration champions talked about suing the school district if the majority reversed the Noel Resolution and Gilberts Plan. Nonetheless, the four-to-three anti-busing board of education immediately moved to shelve the school busing plan. On June 9, 1969, it rescinded the controversial resolutions 1520, 1524, and 1531.

As threatened, those pushing integration immediately filed suit against Denver Public Schools for operating and maintaining a deliberately segregated system. Black activist Fred N. Thomas of 2875 Bellaire Street was in the lead. Born in Harlem on September 7, 1919, he arrived in Denver in 1951 as an equal-opportunity officer at the Air Force Finance Center. He subsequently worked in civil rights compliance for the Department of Health Education and Welfare and the regional division of the federal civil rights commission. After retiring from the federal government in 1975, he signed on with Johns Manville as vice president of corporate compliance.

Thomas served on the boards of many civic associations and headed PHAC in 1967–68. Specifically concerning himself with the schools, he protested the unequal treatment of black schools in North Park Hill. In the wake of the defeat of Benton and Pascoe, Thomas suggested Park Hill secede from DPS and set up its own independent, integrated school district. Lawyers convinced him and his cohorts that they had a solid federal case against the board of education.

Thomas agreed to take the burden as the lead plaintiff in the lawsuit. Just before lawyers filed it on June 19, 1969, Governor John Love named Thomas to the Colorado Commission on Higher Education. Fearing his new job would interfere with the legal action, Thomas recruited another middle-class Park Hill African-American, Wilfred Keyes, as the lead plaintiff.

A chiropractor whose wife was a special education teacher in DPS, Keyes was born in Kansas City, Missouri, on April 14, 1925. After graduating from a segregated Kansas City high school and serving in the Army during World War II, he arrived in Denver in 1951. Initially, he worked at the notorious Spears Chiropractic Hospital at Tenth Avenue and Ivanhoe Street. Its head, Leo Spears, claimed the ability to cure cancer, tuberculosis, and other deadly diseases with chiropractic. Spears readily sued those who doubted his veracity though he always walked away the loser in the courtroom. Keyes remained a Spears employee for a decade, later becoming an insurance salesman. The plaintiff was among the upwardly mobile African-Americans settling in new Park Hill.

Taking an active interest in his daughter's education, Keyes was disturbed by the somewhat beat-up equipment and books in his child's school. The teachers explained they received the books secondhand from academies in southeast Denver. The plaintiff consequently joined the campaign to do something about the de facto racism at the heart of DPS. All he wanted, he later stated, was open enrollment so his nine-year-old daughter could attend a better school than the one she was assigned in new Park Hill.

Four other blacks, one Hispanic, and two white parents joined Keyes—Maxine N. Becker, Christine A. Colley, Irma J. Jennings, Josephine Perez, Edward J. Starks Jr., Robert R. Wade, and Eugene R. Weiner—in the lawsuit. Thomas recruited them, wanting all races and ethnic groups represented in the case. The plaintiffs argued DPS had systematically engaged in de facto segregatory practices. Such actions were just as bad and as illegal as outright de jure segregation. Only court oversight, including the use of busing for desegregation, could remedy the injustice.

Two extremely contrasting attorneys handled the Keyes case, Craig Barnes and Gordon Greiner. While Barnes, who lived in the University Park neighborhood, was active in the New Politics, anti-war wing of the Democratic Party, Greiner was a straitlaced resident of Lookout Mountain and a staunch conservative. If anything, he called himself a "John Birch Society Republican." Barnes had worked for the 17th Street law firm of Holland & Hart in the mid-1960s. Realizing he and other lawyers pushing the suit lacked the necessary trial experience for the complex case, he convinced Greiner, a partner with Holland & Hart who was a veteran litigator, to climb aboard. Before long, the 17th Street attorney moved to Park Hill, grew a beard, and came to identify with the liberal wing of the Democratic Party.

**Photo of picture at Park Hill Library**

*Fred Thomas took the lead in suing DPS in 1970.*

Greiner, Barnes, Thomas, and others met over Memorial Day weekend 1969 when they planned the suit. The NAACP Legal Defense Fund agreed to help pay for it. Thomas served as treasurer of the Denver Equal Educational Opportunity Fund, the organization specifically financing the legal challenge.

Despite integration advocates' public discussions about the suit, their legal action caught the school board unprepared. DPS's ineptness came out during discovery. The plaintiffs noted the school system did not really know exactly what it did, the nature of its past studies and decisions, or the full extent of the materials in the documents it provided the court.

Federal District Court Judge William E. Doyle presided over the suit. A Denver native and onetime Democratic Party activist, he was the brother-in-law of former United States Senator John Carroll. In March 1968, in an unsolved case, someone threw a bomb at Doyle's house. The police attributed the attack, which did little damage, to radicals who were unhappy about the jurist harshly presiding in the successful governmental prosecution of draft-card burner Mendel Cooper in February 1968. Otherwise, Doyle was generally viewed as a liberal on the bench. A loyal Catholic, he had sent his children to parochial schools and had no direct involvement with DPS.

Integration exponents moved for a preliminary injunction to force the school district to implement the busing program. Doyle held a hearing on it on July 17, 1969. Rachel Noel was the desegregation forces' lead witness. She detailed the background of the case and the past racial injustices in the system. Other past and present school board members testified. So did former Superintendent Oberholtzer. All admitted DPS had consciously acted to maintain a de facto segregation of Park Hill schools.

The relationship between Park Hill Elementary and Barrett was crucial to the plaintiffs' case. Those challenging the anti-busing majority's actions noted the cynical gerrymandering of the two schools' borders. This, they argued, was crystal-clear proof DPS had engaged in segregation patterns comparable to the Jim

Crow policies the Supreme Court had ruled unconstitutional in its landmark *Brown* v. *Board of Education* decision.

The plaintiffs further claimed DPS had maintained a deliberate pattern of segregation by ignoring, neglecting, and refusing to improve old, minority schools. They cited the tracking system as another means by which DPS discriminated against blacks. Finally, those calling for busing asserted DPS had failed black students even under the separate but equal standard: the separate schools provided to African-Americans were nowhere equal to white schools. The very principle of neighborhood schools meant segregated, unequal schools.

DPS denied all charges. The Barrett border was logically at Colorado Boulevard—the district did not want young children crossing the exceedingly busy, dangerous street, one on which two students at Gove Junior High were killed during a gym class in March 1965. Old did not mean bad. Some of the most attractive schools in Denver were the historic buildings. Besides, Park Hill had numerous new schools, including the ones with overwhelming black enrollments. Tracking simply encouraged academic excellence for gifted and talented students. Nor did Denver have a dual system. No pupil was denied admission to any school because of race. The suit was nothing but sour grapes by the losers in the May election.

DU Archives

*Judge William E. Doyle ruled in favor of advocates of busing in 1969.*

Though the DPS case sounded quite impressive on the surface, its witnesses contradicted one another. The Voorhees Committee of 1962–64 had noted the school board realized how changing residential patterns and civil rights concerns forced the district to reach out and take special measures to assure equal educational opportunity for all students. At the best, DPS had engaged in a pattern of benign neglect, pretending not to see mounting racial problems. At the worst, it had deliberately shifted school attendance borders in Park Hill to keep some schools white while others were given over to blacks. Numerous other instances of de facto segregation existed in the city where the board had deliberately sought to isolate blacks, Hispanos, and the poor in inferior schools.

The evidence surprised and offended Doyle. After listening to the testimony, he ruled in favor of the plaintiffs on July 31, 1969. DPS had been on the right path with the Gilberts Plan. Resolutions 1520, 1524, and 1531, the jurist declared, were "bona fide attempts of the board to recognize the constitutional rights of the persons affected by the prior segregation." Opposed to those measures, the rescission was "a clear and palpable act which obviously resulted in perpetuation of segregation and deprivation of the rights of these plaintiffs." Concluding de facto segregation existed, Doyle agreed the separate schools were unequal schools. Therefore, the board of education was to implement the elementary school busing plan as of September 1969.

The school board argued the judge's decision was nebulous. He had not claimed DPS was an illegal dual system where students were divided by race. At the very least, the district wanted a formal trial on the matter before committing itself to an unpopular, massive busing program. The board of education so appealed to the Tenth Circuit Court. The higher court overturned Doyle's order on August 5, 1969, ordering him to reconsider the matter. Nine days later, Doyle issued a slightly revised opinion, once more instructing DPS to begin busing for the 1969–70 school year based on the Gilberts Plan.

The Tenth Circuit Court again vacated Doyle's order on August 27: a three-judge panel ruled it was unclear, hasty, and questionable if busing would redress the problem. The plaintiffs thereupon asked for emergency action from the United States Supreme Court. Two days later, Justice William Brennan, overseeing the Tenth Circuit, reinstated Doyle's ruling. The appellate court's stay had been "improvidently granted." In a civil rights case, it was necessary to leave the benefit of doubt with the District Court finding a constitutional issue in favor of the plaintiffs. While it was true this would impact the coming school year scheduled to begin on September 2, Brennan noted, there had been too much foot-dragging in the past to give validity to this argument. He ordered DPS immediately to start busing for integration as proposed by the Gilberts Plan.

Brennan's opinion set the stage for numerous legal battles over school busing during the next 25 years. Time after time the matter came to court. The school-busing trial was held before Doyle beginning on February 2, 1970. During the 14-day proceeding, the plaintiffs produced the preponderance of evidence showing the past de facto segregation of the schools. Or so the judge ruled.

Handing down his decision on March 21, 1970, Doyle agreed DPS had engaged in a systematic program of discrimination against blacks by which it limited their educational opportunities. Not only did DPS keep blacks out of white schools, but the separate minority schools were not equal to those attended by white children. Observing the direct link between high minority enrollments and lack of academic performance, the judge concluded there were at least 15 "inferior" core city schools—all had substantial black or Hispanic enrollments. The jurist ordered DPS to take special actions to improve these schools while it implemented the complete Gilberts Plan of busing students to achieve racial balance.

Here and there, Doyle was critical of the plaintiffs, ruling for DPS. For example, he rejected the integration advocates' charge the construction of the new Manual High School in 1953 was a deliberate act of racism. On the contrary, members of the community, including African-American parents, had long urged the erection of a new Manual building.

Similarly, in light of the claim black students learned better with black teachers as role models, Doyle did not believe, as the plaintiffs asserted, DPS had done anything wrong in primarily assigning black teachers to African-American schools. Nonetheless, he noted DPS's failure to act only increased the problems of school

DPL

*Standing in front of the old DPS headquarters at 14th Street and Tremont Place, Chicanos protest the arrest of New Mexico land activist Baltazar Martinez, who was accused of bombing a DPS garage in February 1970 at the peak of the busing controversies. The district attorney soon dropped the charges.*

segregation. The board had engaged in "eye-closing and head-burying" practices. The district had violated the constitutional rights of the plaintiffs. Remedies were glaringly needed to redress past and present injustices.

The judge called for more discussion and testimony before deciding on the precise means of redressing the discrimination. Ideally, Doyle hoped a voluntary transfer policy, combined with open enrollment and vigorous improvements at minority schools, would overcome the unequal educational opportunities at the latter. Reviewing the whole matter on May 21, 1970, the jurist concluded a drastic remedy was required to overcome the district's racist rot. Seeing no better program, Doyle ruled mandatory busing was necessary to achieve a unitary, desegregated, equal system. Implementation would occur in stages from the fall of 1970 through the fall of 1972.

Once more the school board majority appealed. Nor were the plaintiffs completely happy with Doyle's decision. They did not think it went far enough—the judge had hedged on many of their claims. Seeing the electorate was hopelessly opposed to busing, integration forces believed direct federal court supervision of DPS was vital in assuring a thorough cleansing of all discriminatory practices from the system.

The Tenth Circuit Court of Appeals waffled on the question when it reviewed the Keyes case on June 11, 1971. While it noted Doyle had made the proper finding of facts about the de facto character of racial segregation, it was not sure the remedy of forced busing was either constitutional or proper. Unlike other places where courts had ordered forced integration, Denver did not have a dual system, i.e., one set of schools exclusively for whites and another for blacks. While court oversight of DPS was needed, the appellate panel remanded the case to Doyle to reconsider whether busing was the appropriate remedy. Meanwhile, busing continued.

The whole matter came before the United States Supreme Court on October 12, 1972. In a landmark decision, announced on June 21, 1973, *Keyes* v. *School District Number One,* Justice Brennan, writing for the majority, ruled de facto segregation was just as harmful and illegal as de jure segregation. If anything, Brennan argued Doyle had not gone far enough. The evidence showed DPS had engaged in a cynical and deliberate effort to keep the schools segregated on account of race. While it was true the evidence only pointed to specific segregation in the Park Hill area, the finding of segregation there was indicative of a dual system as a whole.

Denver Public Schools, the court ordered, must eliminate this segregation through a comprehensive integration program. Since the school board had shown it could not and would not implement this policy, the United States District Court must oversee the school system. The Supreme Court further ordered DPS to aggressively recruit minority faculty and staff members. Their numbers should mirror the composition of the student body.

Members of the court were divided by the Keyes case. Justice William O. Douglas wrote a concurring opinion. He was even more blunt in describing the segregation of DPS than Brennan. There was no difference, Douglas insisted, between de jure and de facto segregation. Actions at DPS should be a national model illustrating the urgent necessity of integrating all school systems.

Justice Lewis Powell, while agreeing with Brennan that the Mile High City had a deliberately segregated system, dissented in part. Observing *Keyes* v. *School District Number One* was the first school desegregation case before the Supreme Court not involving an openly segregated school system in the South, he urged caution. If crude court-ordered busing were foisted on DPS, integration would not necessarily result. On the contrary, forced busing could well increase segregation through shifting population patterns, encouraging white flight to the suburbs, and parents removing white students from the public schools to private academies. Busing was only a tool; it could not magically eliminate vestiges of segregation.

Future Chief Justice William Rehnquist dissented. There was quite a difference, he insisted, between de jure and de facto segregation. It was a "long leap" of constitutional law to argue the Denver case was comparable to the deliberate segregation in the South. While there might have been individual cases of gerrymandering in the Park Hill area, they did not justify system-wide consequences.

Though these other opinions were duly published, Brennan's ruling was the law. All educational matters were secondary to achieving racial balance. It took the United States District Court and DPS years to determine precisely what the Keyes case meant and how to redress the system's discriminatory past.

## Busing and Bombings

By the time the Supreme Court had the final word, the busing controversy had torn the city apart. A bomb ripped a DPS garage near West Seventh Avenue and Eliot Street on February 3, 1970, damaging or destroying 38 buses. Lacking a better suspect, the police focused on a radical Chicano nationalist from New Mexico, Baltazar Martinez. They had no evidence against him and the crime was never solved.

Other explosions followed. Jim Perrill's house at 1324 Birch Street was firebombed at around 3:00 AM on February 22. The anti-busing leader and his family escaped injury from the act of terrorism doing about $2,000 in damage. Shortly thereafter, around 8:30 PM on February 24, a bomb was thrown into the house of the lead plaintiff in the lawsuit, Wilfred Keyes, at 2651 Ivanhoe Street. He also escaped injury. School board member Bill Berge reported receiving a bomb threat. All board members were given police protection. Nobody ever claimed credit for the bombings and there were no arrests.

Otherwise, there was little blatant citizen violence over desegregation compared to the storms sweeping Boston about the same time. Rather, the high schools felt the brunt of the upheavals as busing became a reality in the fall of 1970. No academy was more heavily impacted than George Washington High School at 655 South Monaco Street Parkway.

The school was the city's leader in academic achievement. It drew on a diverse population ranging from the once-restricted upper-class Crestmoor neighborhood and the aspiring Hilltop to rather plebeian areas south of Alameda Avenue and Leetsdale Drive. About 5 percent of the enrollment was black, mostly the sons and daughters of servicemen stationed at Lowry. Jewish students composed approximately a third of the student body.

Students invariably called the school "GW." (Some occasionally referred to it as "George.") Since it opened in 1960, the southeast Denver high school had an

Photo by Phil Goodstein

*George Washington High School, 655 South Monaco Street Parkway, was the crown jewel of DPS in academic achievement in the 1960s. Racial violence tore the school apart in the fall of 1970 with the coming of forced busing.*

enrollment of more than 3,000 in a large, sprawling complex. In 1968, pupils there scored 76 percent on the median of uniform tests. Opposed to this, Manual students were at 30 percent; those at East were at 54 percent.

The last number was deceiving. The top 5 percent of East students were fully equal to the best at GW. East, with a nearly 40 percent black enrollment, was highly internally segregated. While the white students in the advanced classes did quite well, many of the blacks performed poorly. Opponents of busing feared court-ordered desegregation would pull down the quality of places such as GW.

While some GW students treasured academic achievement, others encouraged a snob atmosphere. Social aspirants went out of their way to join deliberately exclusive fraternities and sororities. There was a great deal of internal social and class segregation within the school. Some blacks, including those living in northeastern Park Hill, who had the option of attending GW or Manual opted for the latter. The cloaked tensions of the 1960s came to a head with busing.

Just before the start of the 1970–71 school year, the court ordered 257 black students transferred to GW. Most had previously attended East High or had been slated to attend that school. They generally shared East students' disdain for GW and were unhappy with the move. Nor did DPS provide them with decent transportation. Instead of riding on school buses to GW, they had to get on city buses. The operator of the latter, Denver Tramway, complained about the rowdiness of the pupils. (A side result of busing was changing school hours whereby students were ordered to report to classes at ever earlier times to meet bus schedules.)

No more than the rest of the city were the students eager advocates of integration. When allowed to sit where they pleased in classrooms, blacks and whites separated themselves. They frequently judged one another primarily by skin color. Forced busing exacerbated existing problems.

Already in 1968, GW had arranged for special police patrols in response to some racial assaults. Generally, though, the 126 blacks in the student body in 1969–70 more or less got along with their peers. Within a month of the opening of school in September 1970, racial tensions overwhelmed the academy.

In what physics teacher Buel C. Robinson described as a place providing an "impersonal, dehumanizing brand of education" and an "assembly-line operation" where computers made key decisions concerning students' fates, racial tensions grew from the first day of classes. Blacks taunted whites and whites taunted blacks. Many teachers were caught in the middle. They were proud of the school's academic achievement. GW had been a veritable prep academy, gearing its graduates for leading colleges. Top students earned college credit for work done during their senior year. Accelerated classes demanded the most from their pupils.

GW was not ready for the new students. Some of the bused-in blacks were from small, segregated southern towns. Others came from broken families. Many were unused to the school's strict discipline and pride in scholarly achievement. In the past, teachers had simply pushed them along to the next level. The high school did nothing to prepare the new pupils for its traditions. Many were quickly far behind in classroom work, bewildered by the new environment. Faculty members noted many African-American pupils were not doing acceptable work. Black students, in turn, protested how the teachers discriminated against them, treating them as hopelessly dumb. This spawned a crisis.

A handful of teachers were outright racists. Onc was noted for deliberately holding key examinations on Jewish holy days. As the school board did its all to block busing, few instructors or administrators reached out to bused students, helping them gain their bearings at GW.

The high school's problems reflected an unrealized part of the original busing plan. Not only were students transported across town in the name of desegregation, but supporters stressed a more positive goal—integration. Via busing, proponents were sure, members of different races would get to know one another. By going to school together, blacks and whites would come to respect each other's traditions, histories, and customs. In this manner, combined with a vigorous improvement of old minority schools, a new generation would come of age freed of their parents' biases.

Far from fostering a flourishing climate of diversity, busing rubbed both white and black students the wrong way. Racial violence ripped GW in the fall of 1970. In an overcrowded school with 3,020 students in a facility designed for 2,520 pupils, busing, combined with racial and social divisions, created a powder keg. Fights broke out between blacks and whites. The administration, finding itself unable to control the students, frequently called the police to the campus. Before long, officers regularly patrolled the school. Many students hated and feared them.

Controversy soared over whether the police should be armed. Civil rights activists, led by state Senator George Brown, insisted on unarmed police. Otherwise, he dreaded, some of the black students might pack guns, leading to a tragedy at the school. The police waffled on the matter. Meanwhile, conditions worsened at GW.

Trouble started in the lunchroom on Thursday, September 24, when a black girl and a white girl started calling each other names. Suddenly they were fighting. In no time, others joined the brawl, lining up on the basis of race. Not only did students throw trays around the lunchroom, but the tension spread through the entire school like wildfire. The administration closed the school at around 1:20 PM. Sixteen were treated for injuries. The police arrested two young black men, one of whom was not a student.

Tensions continued the next day. Once more, a virtual race riot swept GW. The disturbance was particularly intense in the north lobby and the student parking lot. Principal Jack Beardshear ordered the school closed at 11:45 that morning. During the next month, the police escalated their patrols, using dogs to reinforce their control of the campus.

On October 20, right when racial strains were at razor's edge, around 1:00 PM, an out-of-uniform patrolman came across some black students playing a dice game in a stairwell. After breaking up the game, he arbitrarily ordered a participant to submit to a search for drugs. Suddenly, he claimed, the students jumped him. Losing control of the situation, the officer fired two shots, one into the air and the other into the ground. More violence flared.

The school became unhinged. Students threw chairs through windows and vandalized the property. A few rioted in the north courtyard. Amidst the confu-

CHS

*Intense protest met the court order of forcible busing for desegregation.*

sion, the fire alarm sounded, leading to the evacuation of the school. The disturbance continued for about two hours with 250 youths and police officers fighting at its peak. The police arrested eight. Nine were injured.

GW closed for six school days. It reopened on October 29 with split sessions. The academy separated sophomores from juniors and seniors. The administration placed students in new classes with new teachers. Black security personnel patrolled the halls. Except for the front entrance, all doors, including those of classrooms, were locked. Signs informed visitors they must immediately report to the main office. So there would be no more problems in the cafeteria, the school shut the lunchroom.

Some of the faculty and student body lived in fear. Stories circulated about white girls who did not eat breakfast and drank no water before school since they were afraid to use the lavatories. Others claimed their fellow students were armed. Liberal advocates of busing, in turn, came to the school. They insisted they had to supervise the teachers lest the instructors discriminate against black pupils.

The high school never recovered. Its overall standards plunged. Seeing the controversies busing and academic rigor caused, administrators ordered easing class requirements. In a move to relate to African-American students, the school introduced black studies programs. About the same time, it eliminated Dickens and Shakespeare from tenth-grade English classes. The unspoken, cynical consensus: by not demanding as much from the pupils, there would be fewer problems. The bused black students, consequently, did not get any better education at GW than they received before busing. The schooling of white students, though, worsened.

Nor did the court help conditions. As failures continued and racial tensions increased, Judge Doyle ordered all DPS faculty undergo five hours of annual training about the need for desegregation. The courses stressed how teachers must have a special understanding of the new students. Far from free-flowing exchanges probing the roots of academic failure and the means of redressing it, the sessions were extremely hierarchical with black activists readily and angrily accusing the captive faculty members of racism.

Quite a few veteran teachers saw this as nothing more than brainwashing, an indoctrination measure undermining the system's supposed emphasis on learning. That subject, they lamented, was a minor school goal opposed to pretending to provide equal educational opportunity for all. The impact, on the contrary, was worse schools for the students and the city.

Neighborhood residents, noting the decline, quit supporting DPS. Some moved to suburbia. Others helped establish private and religious schools. (Ironically, at the same time Protestant and Jewish academies increased in the wake of busing, the Denver Catholic Archdiocese closed most of its high schools and eliminated elementary school programs at many of its poor, minority parishes.) Relations between the community and its schools became ever more taut.

Photo by Phil Goodstein

*Ebert School, at 410 23rd Street, was among the many architecturally distinguished school buildings the city put up in the 1920s when it was one of the city's distinctive integrated schools. By the late 1960s, civil rights activists and the courts dismissed it, with its heavy black enrollment, as an "inferior" academy.*

Nor did internal integration of the school produce the promised results of high academic achievement for all pupils. The quality of advanced placement classes declined. These were once exclusive classes, DPS's pride and joy in showing the benefits of the heavy testing routine. The system only allowed high-achieving seniors in them. These students were given college-level work and credit if they passed rigorous examinations at the end of the year. Given the strict requirements, most of the students successfully completed the standardized tests.

Some black education activists loudly charged the advanced placement courses were racist since they were overwhelmingly composed of white students. To redress this, the schools offered open enrollment in them. Simultaneously, the percentage of pupils earning passing scores on the standardized tests drastically plunged. The classes were no longer essentially college level, but only glorified high school courses.

The number of pupils going to GW plummeted. By 1974, the school had lost nearly a third of its student body, down to 2,200 pupils. It was simply a glaring example of what happened through DPS as a whole. From a peak of 96,848 students on the eve of busing in 1968, the number of pupils dropped to 85,438 by 1974 when busing was in full force. By 1987, busing, coupled with the passing of the baby-boom generation, brought enrollment down to 57,503.

As court supervision of the schools eased in the 1990s and a so-called baby-boom echo generation came of school age, enrollment increased to about 63,000 students by 1995. By 1998–99, it was at 68,893. In contrast to a Denver that was 61 percent white, 23 percent Hispanic, 13 percent black, 2 percent Asian, and 1 percent American Indian, enrollment in Denver Public Schools was only 24.4 percent white. In contrast, 49.8 percent of the students were Hispanic, 21 percent were black, 3.4 percent were Asian, and little more than 1 percent was American Indian. By the 1999–2000 school year, a majority of DPS students were Latinos. In other words, busing was not the promised solution. It had simply brought out the problems stemming from the racism of the old school system.

## Continuing Controversy

DPS was in paralysis through the 1970s. Busing, apparently, was all that mattered. There was massive shouting about the issue, but little discussion or give and take. Some continued to view it as a civil rights achievement; others were convinced it was evil incarnate. With the court overseeing the system, the school board frequently undertook token measures to comply with the legal mandates at the expense of learning or seeing that desegregation worked. Bureaucratic manipulators increasingly flourished. Disciplinarians overshadowed educators as the key figures in the schools. Many increasingly looked back to the highly regimented Oberholtzer era as a golden age.

Anti-busing candidates swept the 1971 board of education elections, giving anti-busing forces complete control of the body. The Citizens Association for Neighborhood Schools (CANS) loudly projected itself as the embodiment of common sense and righteousness in opposing the court-ordered busing. University of Denver chancellor Maurice Mitchell, who had not bothered to vote in the May

1969 school board election, led the Community Educational Council, an effort to encourage the peaceful, voluntary implementation of court-ordered busing.

In 1973, liberals, blacks, and advocates of integration made some headway in school board elections. A black civil rights activist, Omar D. Blair, who was an equal opportunity officer at Lowry, and Kay Schomp, the wife of a Capitol Hill car dealer who had previously led the local League of Women Voters, won posts on the board. Despite their triumphs, the body was still highly polarized. Nevertheless, the election showed the city had accepted there was no going back from court-ordered busing. CANS started to fade.

After the 1975 election, during which neither Perrill nor Southworth sought reelection, a four-to-three majority emerged on the board accepting busing. Virginia Rockwell, the wife of banker Bruce Rockwell, then won election as a pro-integration activist. In 1969, she had managed the Benton-Pascoe campaign.

Simultaneously, the DPS administration was in turmoil. Just before the 1973 school board election, the seven-member anti-busing group brought in an outsider as superintendent, Louis J. Kishkunas. Previously the head of the Pittsburgh school system, he was a specialist in technical and vocational education. The new superintendent had encountered a good deal of turbulence in the Steel City.

Kishkunas was a darling of the board. Jim Perrill was a close friend, coming to represent Kishkunas as an attorney. Before he left office in May 1975, Perrill saw Kishkunas receive a major extension of his contract. New, pro-desegregation members of the board were not happy with Kishkunas. They claimed he tried to set policy rather than simply operate a smoothly functioning system. He dragged his heels in collaborating with the court in making busing work. The superintendent avoided hard decisions and relied on the old-boy network to sanction the status quo. Teachers lamented the endless bureaucratic stupidity and insensitivity of the hierarchy.

Newspapers failed to report on this; their exclusive focus remained on the busing controversies. In the void, there was less educational integrity than ever in the system. Kishkunas even managed to alienate his supporters on the school board. Finally, after much hesitation and delay, the board dismissed Kishkunas in the middle of his term on December 9, 1976. The tenures of subsequent superintendents were equally stormy. Busing and court supervision were in the forefront of all DPS decisions.

## The Finger Plan

In the wake of the Supreme Court ruling, on December 17, 1973, Judge Doyle modified his initial findings in the Keyes case. De facto segregation in Park Hill, he noted, created the presumption of segregation in the system as a whole. He called for both the plaintiffs and DPS to file integration plans. (Though President Richard Nixon elevated Doyle to the Tenth Circuit Court of Appeals in 1971, the jurist continued to sit as a District Court judge in personally overseeing the litigation. Only in 1976 did District Court Judge Richard P. Matsch take over the case.)

Doyle held a lengthy hearing on precisely how to desegregate the schools in February-March 1974. The judge did not like the plan filed by DPS. Despite the court order, the DPS proposal only called for token busing. Once more, the school board floated the idea of educational parks, now referred to as "educational enrichment centers." With the backing of CANS, DPS continued its obstinacy, not cooperating with the court.

Nor was Doyle happy with the plaintiffs' proposal. It focused primarily on Park Hill, echoing the Gilberts Plan. DPS problems, the jurist observed, were system-wide. The Supreme Court had said as much. Only through the complete integration of all Denver Public Schools was it possible to redress past injustices.

On April 17, 1974, the judge announced his decision. He depended on the findings of his own expert on school integration, Dr. John A. Finger. The latter drew up a three-pronged desegregation proposal. First, it modified the attendance borders of 24 elementary schools. Second, Finger rezoned the borders of an additional 23 schools. This primarily affected the areas from which pupils were bused to their academies. Finally, he paired 37 minority and white schools.

In the last case, the court ordered students bused across town for half a day to a matched school to assure desegregation. Those from one academy, predominantly white, would go to the other, overwhelmingly minority, for second, fourth, and sixth grades. Students in the first, third, and fifth grades would be bused to the other facility. The hope was a certain sense of neighborhood schools would remain despite busing. The Finger Plan further imposed comparable busing plans on junior highs and high schools. At Finger's suggestion, Doyle mandated a quota percentage of enrollments based on race at all schools.

Even while ordering this busing plan, Doyle was receptive to a proposal filed by Dr. Jose A. Cardenas of Texas for the Congress of Hispanic Educators. Seeing how drastically the litigation was impacting DPS, the recently formed group entered the case as the voice of the Mexican-American community during the initial

Photo by Phil Goodstein

*Cole Junior High School, at 33rd Avenue and Humboldt Street, was an extremely troubled, overwhelmingly black school in the 1960s. Advocates of busing believed their program would solve the school's problems.*

Photo by Phil Goodstein

*The school board closed Wyatt School, at the northeast corner of 36th Avenue and Humboldt Street, in 1982 as an ugly, ancient, dilapidated, underperforming minority school. In the late 1990s, the Edison School chain, an investor effort to reap profits in the name of providing education for poor and minority students, got hold of the building, reopening it as an elementary school.*

flurry of lawsuits. Latino Denver had no direct involvement in the busing controversy amidst the 1969 election. As busing transformed DPS, Hispanic leaders wanted a say in making decisions. Before long, the Congress of Hispanic Educators was a key player in the case.

Not just blacks, but also Mexican-American students, the civil rights group noted, got a raw deal from DPS. The system had scorned their children, imposing English-only policies on those in need of bilingual education. Rather than having Hispanic children bused in the abstract name of integration, the Congress called for the school system to provide Latino youths with special lessons on their people's history, customs, and heritage. In particular, it asked the courts to allow five overwhelmingly Mexican-American schools to offer pupils special bilingual/bicultural programs. Doyle agreed to exempt these schools from busing and desegregation.

The judge's decision failed to satisfy either the plaintiffs or DPS. Both appealed. The Tenth Circuit Court agreed Doyle had imposed an awkward program on DPS. Instead of half-day busing, on August 11, 1975, it ordered full-time busing. It divided elementary schools into primary (grades one through three) and intermediate (grades four through six) divisions. DPS, it decreed, must bus all students from one level to a paired school; the system was to transport all the pupils from the other division to the sister school. The appellate court further threw out Doyle's exemption of Hispanic schools from busing. They could no more be separate and equal from the rest of the system than any other schools.

The United States Supreme Court declined to hear an appeal from the Tenth Circuit Court's ruling. After the case was returned to the District Court, the school board accepted a consent degree in 1976. Seeing no alternative to court supervision of the schools, it reluctantly agreed to obey the court and implement the busing program featuring paired schools. By this time, the court had reduced the quota of white students at each school because their numbers constantly decreased as their parents sent them to private and suburban academies.

Paired schools did not work ideally. Typical was the linkage between Steele Elementary at South Marion Street and Alameda Avenue with Crofton Elementary at 24th and Arapahoe streets. The latter was next to a housing project. It received little extra financial support from parents and had few middle-class students. Steele, in contrast, was in the burgeoning Washington Park neighborhood. Parents eagerly pushed it as their area's school. Few of their children attended Crofton—many of the youths went to private schools during the time the court wished them transported across town. While there was a joint Crofton-Steele PTA, most of the activities were at Steele School. An annual house tour, for example, only focused on the Washington Park neighborhood.

Court-ordered desegregation did bring some relief to the school system. There was no longer any overt discrimination or gerrymandering of school boundaries. Minority areas received money for new buildings. In the name of educational improvement, DPS managed to destroy such architecturally impressive edifices as Ashland School at West 29th Avenue and Bryant Street, Cheltenham School at West Colfax and Irving Street, and Wyman School at 16th Avenue and Williams Street. In each case, ugly, faceless modern structures replaced them. Poor, black, and Hispanic parents frequently applauded these moves. They were at one with suburban educators: learning could only take place in a sterile, properly engineered, modern environment.

DPS further closed historic lower-income academies such as Boulevard School at West 24th Avenue and Federal Boulevard, Alameda School at West Byers Place and South Bannock Street, and Emerson School at 14th Avenue and Ogden Street. Regardless of the building specifics, academic achievement continued to stagnate in the system as a whole. Minority students performed as poorly as ever.

These results reflected the class divisions of the city. The schools were overwhelmingly geared to a middle-class accomplishment ethic. They were designed to reward those who were well-behaved as they worked to become part of the existing society. Many of the minority students came from poverty-stricken and dysfunctional families. Sometimes English was not their mother tongue. Their parents often had severe difficulties making ends meet. Not coming from a culture valuing the hierarchical education system and failing to receive home nurturing comparable to middle-class white students, they suffered in the school system. Simply changing attendance boundaries or the age of the buildings did nothing to redress this.

## The Poundstone Amendment

Busing controversies heavily impacted Colorado politics. In 1974, amidst the Watergate election and the Democratic sweep of the state government, anti-busing forces successfully passed an initiated amendment to the Colorado constitution prohibiting busing for racial purposes. The same election saw the passage of the Poundstone Amendment. This constitutional measure, drafted by suburban lobbyist Freda Poundstone, who was close to Coors interests, drastically limited Denver's ability to annex land from surrounding Jefferson, Adams, and Arapahoe counties. A companion measure created a six-member Denver/suburban commission to authorize annexations—it was equally composed of Denver and suburban representatives, assuring the defeat of all annexation proposals. The primary purpose of the amendments was to quarantine suburban students from the morass of Denver Public Schools.

The Poundstone Amendment struck at the heart of postwar Denver. During the previous 30 years, the city had primarily grown through annexing land. Until the busing controversy, Denver used its schools as lures to get suburbanites to join the city. With busing, however, many parents living outside of Denver wanted to keep their children out of DPS. Families fled to the suburbs precisely to escape the busing upheavals. They then incorporated such communities as Lakewood and Wheat Ridge to keep out DPS and busing. Far from encouraging integration and racial understanding, the turmoil in DPS accelerated white flight and the polarization of the metropolis. Between 1970 and 1980, suburban growth soared while Denver's total population declined from 514,678 in a metropolis of 1,239,545 to 492,365 in a community of 1,620,902. By 1990, Denver was down to 467,610 in a sprawling area of 1,980,140.

Busing directly influenced Denver residential patterns. While many young white couples lived in the city, they frequently moved to the suburbs when their children came of school age. They were blunt: they did not want their offspring buffeted by the crude, court-controlled school system. Consequently, a gap opened in the age levels in middle-class white neighborhoods. There were fewer children than ever on city streets.

Both suburban developers and Realtors steered new arrivals away from Denver, noting the extreme problems of the Queen City's schools. Many suburban districts meanwhile sought to recreate the rigid world of DPS under Oberholtzer—a system where the superior was always right and the schools closed their eyes to social and racial problems. Before long, suburban schools also had their share of discipline problems, lack of academic achievement, and accusations of internal segregation where children of rich parents got far better buildings and programs than the sons and daughters of the poor.

As enrollment shrank and the community lost confidence in the school system, the size of the DPS administration swelled. The district took over a highrise as its offices at Ninth Avenue and Grant Street in 1974–75. There ever more bureaucrats supervised fewer students. In addition to functionaries at headquarters, the number of experts in the knowledge business, including assistant principals and social workers, soared in the schools. Paraprofessionals and reading specialists were

Author's Collection

*The old Manual High School, at 27th Avenue and Franklin Street, was built in the 1890s, a time Denver primarily segregated its high schools by economic class. The district designed it for students desiring manual training as opposed to the college aspirants of East High School. Fire destroyed the structure in 1953.*

added to the system. The more support personnel present, the greater were the laments about the lack of educational achievement, high dropout rates, poor test scores, and an abysmal level of cultural illiteracy.

Under court and political pressures, administrators expected equal disciplining of blacks and whites. Translated, this meant for every black student an instructor sent to the office, he or she was expected to send a white one. Principals increasingly sanctioned teachers for breaking such rules. The hierarchy further created even more bureaucratic regulations in the name of assuring racial equality. Not surprisingly, teacher morale became progressively worse.

In some cases, assistant principals—the officials in charge of school discipline—were blunt. They did not care what, if anything, was taught. Rather, a teacher's foremost responsibility was to maintain calm and prevent vandalism. The system rewarded teachers who were best at accomplishing these goals.

The schools as learning centers gave way to a heavy emphasis on welfare programs. Those lamenting societal problems—including crime, battered children, the unemployability of certain people, and social breakdown—insisted the schools redress them. On occasion, teachers were required to act as spies, reporting suspicious circumstances to the police. At other times, educators were nothing more than glorified baby-sitters, keeping students off the streets. Security measures were continually tightened at the schools. Some principals operated their campuses as if they were prison complexes. The presence of armed police officers in the school reinforced the reality that many students were nothing more than involuntary inmates with no interest in or enthusiasm for the daily routines to which they were subjected. Rarely did the schools show any respect for their students as young citizens who were emerging as the next generation.

Despite all the turmoil in the system, many students managed to learn. Both on paper and in practice, programs existed for high academic achievers. Manual High School stood out. With principal Jim Ward taking the lead, skilled, earnest, and veteran teachers worked to make integration work at the northeast Denver high school. Scholarly achievement soared, especially among white adolescents from the area around George Washington High School who now attended Manual. The school's international studies programs reaped great acclaim. It portrayed itself as the first black school in the country integrated by busing white students into it.

Thanks to desegregation and the innovative programs, some black students gained great confidence in working with whites. Even so, Manual continued to have a high dropout rate. There was all too little interaction between the brought-in learners and neighborhood youths. Some locals, only living a few blocks from the school, were bused as far away as Kennedy High School in far southwest Denver. Simultaneously, the school's traditional innovative efforts to provide students with excellent manual training disappeared.

DPS saw it had to do something at places like Manual. The board of education increasingly realized it no longer ran an educational monopoly. Middle-class parents, it knew, had a choice and would remove their children from the system if the district did not provide a satisfactory educational program. To retain such students, it sought to win over those who still believed in the public schools.

The school board opened a Career Education Center at West 26th Avenue and Eliot Street in 1976 to provide specialized vocational skills for high school students. Irv Moskowitz, who served as superintendent from 1994 until 1999, was its first principal. DPS christened it the Fred N. Thomas Career Education Center in November 1980. It honored the man who had taken the lead in suing the system over discrimination in 1969. The move came nine months after Thomas' death in February 1980 at age 60. Ten years later, in July 1990, the city named a 23-acre park at 23rd Avenue and Quebec Street in memory of Thomas. DPS also established a series of community schools, offering noncredit classes to adults.

The district further introduced magnet programs in selected elementary schools, including Montessori and old-fashioned fundamentalist approaches. These academies usually required parents to work closely with the schools. With involved, concerned parents, students at the magnet schools did much better than those attending academies where social-welfare and baby-sitting were the foremost concerns. More than ever, class and culture, not race or ethnicity, were the defining elements in determining the success of students and schools.

## The Prostration of Schools

DPS policies encouraged this. Instead of probing the social and economic problems of integrating poor people into middle-class society, DPS pushed slick public relations efforts to convince parents and businesses that the school system was actually working. A side result was the open prostration of the schools to the corporate community. Far more than helping young people learn, the school board advertised it primarily existed to cater to the economic masters of society.

Photo by Phil Goodstein

*In the name of providing greater business participation in the schools, DPS turned some of its buses into moving billboards for corporate Denver.*

As busing controversies plagued the city during the 1970s, Washington, through the Department of Health, Education, and Welfare, sought to assist Denver by fostering greater "community participation" in the schools. Funds to make this a reality materialized in 1978. Translated, it meant turning the school system over to 17th Street.

From the onset of the busing crisis, many community leaders were silent in providing guidance and direction for the city and the schools. Mayor Bill McNichols was invisible as the controversy fractured the city. Demagogic politicians projected themselves as champions of neighborhood schools and children. The construction/development/real estate lobby—the most powerful voice of local business—greatly profited from the suburban growth fueled, in part, by the breakdown of DPS. Increasingly, the city and its school system were in a void.

Proponents of the district, including busing backers and the Denver Chamber of Commerce, were insistent a good school system was in the direct economic interest of business. Far from simply money-making machines exploiting the community, corporations had to become partners in the schools. Those urging greater business involvement often interpreted this to mean having the schools educate students about business and indoctrinating pupils with corporate values.

Employers were often frustrated by the schools. All too often, high school graduates, whether from Denver or the suburbs, were functionally illiterate—they did not known how to balance a checkbook or make change. Nor did the educational system prepare students for the world of business. Graduates lacked responsibility, timeliness, and team commitment. The schools failed properly to train graduates as wage workers—or such was corporate America's indictment of the schools. It relentlessly denied the educational system turned out graduates in the image of the existing economic order.

With the funds provided by the federal grant, business activists agreed to adopt schools. In the late 1970s, DPS developed a national model for the "Adopt-a-

School" program. It asked corporations to sponsor a specific school. Principals welcomed leading executives into their schools, having them tell the students about what business expected from youths as future employees. Companies adopting the schools sometimes helped "disadvantaged" students attending them get jobs in their firms. The administration pressured teachers to embrace the program. (Some instructors complained the corporate speakers were anything but inspiring, literate role models.)

There was no debate on this matter. Nor were there classes on the history, contributions, and nature of trade unionism. On the contrary, Coors Brewery, an avid sponsor of the Adopt-a-School program, used the effort to denounce unions. The assumption: the business ethic was the community's ethic, one instilled into students with direct corporate support. While taxes on businesses were kept low, corporations agreed to give a little extra money—which was tax deductible—to the schools.

Corporate and philanthropic interests moved to institutionalize this "community" involvement. Their goal was to make business values a permanent part of the schools. Toward this end, they established a private foundation to assure the continuation of the Adopt-a-School program after the initial federal grant ran out. Eventually, a powerful Public Education & Business Coalition advocated the total corporate domination of education. Members of its board were drawn from such stalwarts as Gates Rubber, Columbia Hospitals, Norwest Banks, US West, United Airlines, Johns Manville, and AT&T. Sponsors of and activists in the foundation further included executives from such law firms and accounting practices as Holland & Hart, Sherman & Howard, Brownstein Hyatt Farber & Strickland, Holme, Roberts & Owen, and Deloitte & Touche. To assure proper media support, the publisher of the *Denver Post* was also on the Public Education & Business

Photo by Phil Goodstein

*During the 1970s, in the name of providing equal educational opportunity in old, central city schools, DPS replaced historic structures with bland, sterile, modern edifices such as the new Wyman School at 17th Avenue and Williams Street.*

Coalition's board. Though many of the companies and firms changed their names and their specific executives left the corporate-school conclave, the effort kept going. Clearly, 17th Street got the educational system it wanted and deserved.

As if this private effort were not enough, a government mandate gave the business community a direct say in running the schools through collaborative decision-making (CDM) bodies. Ironically, this stemmed from a labor dispute. In November 1969, right in the middle of the turmoil over busing, a strike by the Denver Classroom Teachers Association (DCTA), the Denver branch of the National Educational Association, shut down parts of the school system for two weeks. Tensions between management and labor continued to haunt the system during the turmoil of the 1970s and 1980s. With a strike looming in early 1991 among the generally conservative, order-obeying teachers, Governor Roy Romer intervened. Not only did he decree the instructors had no right to withhold their labor power to protest bad management and poor working conditions, but in settling the dispute he changed the essence of the school administration.

With amazingly little opposition and no legal challenge, the governor announced all Denver Public Schools were henceforth under collaborative decision-making teams. A national fad, these were adult student councils including the principal, representatives of the faculty, and parents. Most of all, an unelected representative of the business community was part of each committee. In this manner, the governor gave the corporate sector a direct say in the daily management of the schools.

Sponsors, including commercial interests and out-of-state foundations, projected Romer's proposal as democracy in action, a means for reducing the existing tensions between management, labor, and parents. It was nothing of the sort. Labor problems remained. The governor did nothing to prevent a brief strike in 1994 or ease the poor relations between teachers, employees, and the DPS administration.

Those drawn to CDMs (sometimes called community decision-making bodies) were usually individuals who were already active in wanting to manage the schools or who gloried in bureaucratic manipulations. The councils simply allowed them to assert their influence further. Principals frequently packed the bodies, hand-picking the "volunteers" from the faculty for them. The business representation guaranteed a subservience to the status quo and corporate values, not learning or encouraging students to question the world, were at the heart of the schools. That Romer could so easily impose CDMs showed how divorced the schools had become from the community they were supposed to serve.

CDMs did not live up to their promise. A DPS review of the bodies in 1999 showed many of the adult student councils were nothing like what advocates envisaged. The analysis noted that more than a third of the district's schools lacked full CDMs. Nor were they appropriately racially balanced. As opposed to a 50 percent Hispanic enrollment, only 20 percent of the CDM members were of Spanish heritage. Fifteen percent of the CDM participants were African-American opposed to a 22 percent black enrollment. Whites, on the other hand, consisted of 65 percent of the CDM positions contrasted to their 24 percent of the student body.

In the fall of 1999, DPS hired Aaron Gray, a Methodist minister who resigned from the school board in 1996 to take a post with a church in Parker, as the district's community relations director. His assignment was to strengthen the dysfunctional, non-representative bodies. (The school board initially wanted a Latino for the post, noting the need for racial/ethnic representation. It concluded the African-American Gray was too good to pass up for the job.)

With this background, the next step was not surprising. Schools became poster boards of big business. School systems signed contracts to advertise soft drinks and telecommunication services. Not only were the names of corporate America's commodities splashed about the schools, but lunchrooms sometimes became nothing more than fast-food outlets. A Denver school board member even pondered selling advertising on report cards. Those backing these moves explained the schools direly needed the advertising revenue. They implied the community was too cheap to pay for decent schools. Only through a dependence on commercial funds and business oversight, administrators told the public, could the schools survive.

Actually, the sellout of the schools was a response to a lack of voter trust in them. As business domination soared while academic achievement stagnated, voters increasingly lost faith in the school system. Both in Denver and the suburbs, the electorate was hesitant to endorse massive spending proposals advocated by PTAs and school administrators.

The schools never seemed to have enough money. Regardless of how much voters appropriated for education, the learning experts always wanted more. The latter, however were not able to show any correlation between the amount spent on the schools and the excellence of their product. Nor were the economics of school financing addressed. Tax increases for the schools invariably bore down on homeowners. Real estate speculators, who heavily profited from growth and made immense demands on school systems through the creation of new, isolated residential communities, were largely immune from paying for the costs they imposed on the educational establishment. The Colorado Supreme Court ruled illegal extra fees on builders to pay for the schools their developments required.

## The Disconnected School Board

The corporate control of the schools advanced at the same time the board of education became ever more divorced from the electorate. For years, many had lamented the precise composition of this seven-member body. Ostensibly nonpartisan, all elections were at large. Race was a primary factor in who won the school board contests. Black Denver realized this. It deliberately recruited its candidate in each election and organized for him or her. Many white liberals, including much of the old integration crowd, firmly supported this policy. After the 1973 election, there was usually at least one black on the school board.

Hispanics did not do as well. Latino Denver was neither united by the call for desegregation nor did it have any central, strong, controlling political force comparable to the East Denver Ministerial Alliance. Bert Gallegos, elected to the school board in 1971, personified conservative Spanish-Americans who vehemently rejected busing. Chicano militants, in turn, insisted they needed their own schools.

In 1973, Bernie Valdez, appointed to the board in the wake of Gallegos' resignation in 1972, won election in his own right as both an anti-busing and the Mexican-American candidate. Naomi Bradford, who stemmed from a poor California Spanish-Indian family, won a post on the board in 1975. A vehement opponent of forced busing, she had served as a leader of CANS. Though Bradford was also on the board of Hispanics of Colorado, a conservative organization mostly composed of state employees, other members of the Latino community did not accept her as their representative on the school board. Rather, they openly opposed her, especially when Bradford loudly opposed bilingual education programs. She won reelection to the board in 1981 and 1987.

In contrast to Bradford, former state Senator Paul Sandoval had excellent ties with the Democratic Party and Latino education activists. He gained a board seat in 1983. Claiming burnout, he quit the board in 1988, a year before the end of his term. Both the establishment Hispanic leadership and ruling Denver agreed another Mexican-American should succeed him. The school board named former state Representative Rich Castro to fill the empty slot.

Author's Collection

*Rich Castro served as the semiofficial Latino member of the school board in 1988–89.*

Castro lost when he sought to retain the post the next year. Work-within-the-system Latinos again met with failure during the early 1990s when they insisted a Hispanic should be elected to the board primarily because of ethnicity rather than community involvement or commitment to education. There was frequently minimal turnout for Latino candidates in Chicano districts.

The solution, with no community vote, was a cynical shift in the date and nature of school board elections. They had previously been in May of odd-numbered years. Holding the school board elections as part of municipal elections forced candidates and voters specifically to focus on the schools. That was junked in 1992. Instead of redressing the inequities of at-large elections through providing for some form of proportional representation, with virtually no debate, the Republican-dominated General Assembly decided, as of 1993, that the school board would consist of representatives of five districts and two at-large members. The openly stated goal was to assure at least one black and one Hispanic were on the board. The same legislation specified, beginning in 1997, the shifting of school board elections from May to November of odd-numbered years. Terms were reduced from six years to four years. Rather than giving the people of Denver through the school board the power to determine the exact boundaries of the districts, the legislature retained this power.

The schools were ever more isolated from non-parents thanks to the district balkanization. Collaborative decision-making team activists emerged as leading

Photo by Phil Goodstein

*Looking up 19th Street at the Federal Building, left, Federal Courthouse, center, and the 1999 Broadway glasstower. The courthouse was the true home of Denver Public Schools decisions between 1969 and 1995 when the United States District Court oversaw the district.*

candidates and board members. Critics of the school system found the new board members no better than the old ones. A few even charged DPS was emerging as a veritable political machine whereby successful candidates arranged for backers to get jobs as reading assistants and support personnel.

Members of the Hispanic community loudly bickered over whether their member really represented them. When two work-within-the-system Latinos gained election in 1999—James Mejia, a close political associate of Wellington Webb who won an at-large seat, and Lucia Guzman, a Protestant minister who was the former executive director of the Colorado Council of Churches—advocates of ethnic politics made it sound as if salvation had finally arrived.

Resignations from the school board were common—transient Denverites showed voters no respect since they moved from the city or cavalierly quit the job despite their commitment of public service in seeking the post. In case of a vacancy, the board appointed a replacement. Sometimes, the new member was the choice of the person leaving the board, especially when racial politics were involved. In other cases, the individual named to the board might have been an unsuccessful candidate in a previous school board contest. In other words, despite the electorate's verdict, the person rejected by the voters still joined the board. The result was to further remove direct community involvement in the schools.

## The End of Busing

Much of this transformation occurred about the same time the United States District Court finally ceded control of DPS back to the board of education. After years of appeals, hearings, controversies, and manipulations, in August 1994 Judge Richard Matsch listened to a DPS plea for the court to drop its supervision of the district. After long pondering the matter, the judge issued his ruling on September 12, 1995. The board of education, Matsch concluded, had finally listened to the court. It had started off in a state of denial. Through the first half of the 1970s, it had categorically refused to cooperate with the court, leading to harsh judicial orders to ensure desegregation. Finally, beginning in 1976, DPS began to cooperate. Numerous programs introduced in the 1980s and 1990s—including closing Stevens School, a popular, naturally integrated academy at 12th Avenue and Columbine Street—showed the district had eradicated past vestiges of segregation. DPS had so finally proven itself a unitary school system. In this light, Matsch released Denver Public Schools from direct court supervision. Mandatory busing was no longer necessary.

Despite the end of court-ordered busing, Matsch warned the board: if DPS reverted to its old segregated, racist practices, the court would again intervene in the system. In reviewing the whole matter, the jurist noted how public and court opinions had changed about the value of integration. What the courts had prohibited was segregation. The constitution did not require integration. Nor could the court mandate equal educational performance. The continuing inequities within the school system between black and white students, including differing test scores, disciplinary infractions, and participation in certain programs and activities, were not caused by systematic, discriminatory practices as had been the case in the 1960s. While these unequal results obviously needed redress, it was no longer the role of the court to directly supervise the operations of DPS.

Some African-Americans decried the judge's decision. Though not trusting the white establishment, they continued to look to the federal courts for relief from a school system producing an inferior education for their children. There was little popular resonance to their appeals.

Simultaneously, Latinos targeted DPS. Their offspring were the dominant constituency in the student body. Included were the sons and daughters of immigrants who did not speak English. This group, including children of poor, migrant families who moved frequently, had a 50-percent dropout rate. In the same manner that middle-class black parents embraced busing as a cure to the educational woes, some Mexican-American activists argued bilingual education would drastically reduce the dropout rates of their children.

A dispute at Valverde School, at West Alameda Avenue and South Tejon Street in 1991, when Hispanic students were forced to sit on the floor of the cafeteria during lunch as a collective punishment, led to the creation of Padres Unidos, a group of Hispanic parents demanding DPS show special sensitivity to the problems of Latino students. It pinpointed numerous cases of the system's discrimination and callousness to their children. Members, including Anglo supporters, called for a bilingual North Denver Montessori school.

Under such pressure, the courts ordered bilingual programs. The efforts had minimal positive results. Critics charged DPS administered awkward, unfeeling schemes primarily designed to keep Hispanic students isolated from their English-speaking peers. When bilingual champions appealed to the Office of Civil Rights of the federal Department of Education, it responded in 1997 by ordering further supervision and even more clumsy, hierarchical bilingual attempts. Seemingly, the more "reforms" made to incorporate English-challenged students, the worse the system became. By 2000, more than 20 percent of all DPS pupils did not speak English as their first language.

Inferior education was not unique to the sons and daughters of African-Americans and Latinos. All schools graduated culturally unaware students by the 1980s, 1990s, and into the 2000s. Nor was this unique to Denver. An unending educational crisis was lamented everywhere. Time and again, politicians called for increased funding for the schools, strengthening requirements, and imposing an even more severe regimen of standardized tests. An openly stated goal was to transform the schools into technical training institutions, filled with all sorts of computer wizardry. Many advocates of such reforms showed no conception of why the system continually failed to deliver as promised.

In 1999, the board of education declared it essentially ran a factory system. This came out in a new contract with the teachers union. DPS committed itself to merit pay for master teachers. It promised to reward them for outstanding performance. Other than by worshipping test scores, advocates of this program were extremely vague on precisely how they hoped to measure learning and the teachers' true accomplishments.

All the while, the meaning of the exams was exceedingly nebulous. Some years, administrators gloated when they were able to report positive test results. They readily cited them, proving their outstanding improvements as permanent solutions to the crises of the schools. A year later, however, test scores might show major relapses at the same academies. The larger issue of whether the examinations measured literacy or a love of learning was far beyond the comprehension of those touting merit pay and wonder-working educational reforms.

Much of the controversy about the nature of the schools and educational processes was dismal. Ignoring more than a century of debate, political ideologues touted panaceas. Time and again, narrow-minded savants assured the public, if only the schools embraced standards-based education, or phonetics, or fundamentals, or career enhancement, or some other buzzword, the educational problems would magically disappear.

Seeing increased problems with youths, solons drastically strengthened state laws overseeing adolescents. The government subjected people under age 21 to numerous restrictions while the government sought to crack down on alleged sexual abuse of juveniles. The result was often a witch-hunting atmosphere where social

Photo by Phil Goodstein

*Members of Padres Unidos, a modern Latino activist group focusing on education, participate in a demonstration decrying police brutality in 2000.*

workers emerged as leading school figures. Such societal problems as dysfunctional families, single-parents, divorce, drugs, alcohol, and spousal abuse were either attributed to the schools or, conversely, the educational system was seen as the primary means of redressing them.

Revolts against the educational establishment were common. In 1993, Colorado adopted the principle of charter schools. These were independently run, but publicly supported academies for students whose parents did not believe their children were getting an adequate education in the public schools. Gamesmanship, controversies, and parental divisions quickly rocked these quasi-public/private schools. Religious academies expanded and efforts at home schooling popped up. Conservative politicians called for vouchers as an alternative to the public schools.

Suburbanites were in the vanguard of pushing these proposals. Not only had busing failed within Denver, but so had the universal public school idea. Far from academies of democracy, the schools had become political footballs. Nor was there any connection between the reform efforts and actual learning. The nurturing of independent-minded, autonomous, questioning, committed adolescents was often the very last goal of those heralding their commitment to education.

If anything, the suburban schools were worse than those in Denver in attacking free thought of students and seeking to regiment youths. Instead of encouraging students to challenge and discover the world, some of the bogus educators insisted on denying the teaching of evolution. In 1999, the administration in suburban Douglas County even required elementary teachers get parents' written permission before reading aloud to their classes fantasy Harry Potter books. Such idyllic suburban academies, not surprisingly, also churned out alienated, functionally illiterate graduates. Demagogues responded by loudly demanding prayer in the schools. Nor were the suburban academies any safer than those in the city. If anything, they were deadly. Such was the case at Columbine High School.

## The Columbine Massacre

Eric Harris and Dylan Klebold pulled away the curtains cloaking the reality of suburban schools on April 20, 1999. The two, students at the overwhelmingly white, upper-middle-class Columbine High School, with an enrollment of 1,680, at 6201 South Pierce Street in unincorporated, southwestern Jefferson County, physically invaded the academy. With numerous bombs and guns in hand, they opened up on their fellow students. They killed 12 pupils and one teacher and wounded 23 other students before committing suicide.

Former Boy Scouts, the killers were outcasts. Columbine was an all-American school where a celebration of sports, physical appearance, and high-society popularity were the dominant themes. Athletes and cheerleaders mocked and bullied those who did not fit the mold. In doing so, they often emulated their parents. The latter were sure they were the elect, living in a world deliberately isolated from the crime, decay, and violence of the wicked city.

Harris was the son of a former Air Force pilot. He was greatly disappointed when his application to join the Marines was rejected. The military did not want him since he had previously taken a prescribed drug for a mental condition. The want-to-be soldier joined with Klebold in celebrating the decadence of a so-called Gothic culture, one idealizing Nazis as rebels against the smugness embodied by the dominant Columbine student body. They selected Adolph Hitler's birthday as the date for their attack.

Klebold and Harris were both from two-parent households. Their families showered them with material possessions. Klebold's parents, for example, gave the boy a BMW—comparable to the snob cars driven by others in the Columbine student body and neighborhood.

Columbine High School was illustrative of the morass of the educational system. As was often the case in DPS, its head was not a scholar, but an athlete. Principal Frank DeAngelis was a former baseball coach. The school's foremost accomplishment in the wake of the massacre was winning the state football championship in the fall of 1999. By then, story after story had come out about the hidden tensions leading to the Harris-Klebold explosion.

Far from a community of committed young people, the student body was a swarming world of hatred. The principal, those suffering at the hands of the jocks charged, turned a blind eye to transgressions by favored students and athletes while dissidents found themselves subjected to continued punishment for trivial infractions. Though the mascot nickname for Columbine was the "Rebels," the school had no place for students who actually revolted against the social tyranny and brain-dead education marking the place.

Mass lachrymose swept the area after the shootings. Columbine so numbed ruling Denver because it struck home. No one could explain away the killers'

CHS

*An outpouring of grief met the Columbine Massacre, including memorabilia left at Clement Park near the school at West Bowles Avenue and South Pierce Street.*

actions as those of crazed, drug-addicted black and Chicano gang-bangers. The area around the high school was precisely the kind of subdivision the Chamber of Commerce had pushed since the end of World War II. Some of the parents worked as executives and engineers at the nearby Lockheed Martin missile plant, among the area's commanding industrial firms/war contractors. The massacre showed suburbia was no refuge from societal dilemmas.

Cynics noted a Columbine Massacre would probably never happen in an inner-city school. If Harris and Klebold—both of whom had past legal problems—had been poor ghetto kids, they would have felt the sting of the courts, rather than the consolation of counseling. Rather than dismissing counseling as a failure because it did not work in the Columbine case, the champions of giving social workers ever more power in the schools readily embraced it as a way to prevent Columbine from repeating itself.

Counselors and psychologists threw themselves at the community. Newspaper stories stressed the urgent necessity of survivors availing themselves of the experts' grief therapy. Some opportunists readily sought to profit from the whole fiasco, especially since immense contributions poured in to help those hurt by Columbine. Mental health experts appeared to swallow many of the donations to the Columbine community.

Even more than usual in the educational debates, world saviors were quick to offer their solutions. Invariably, they sought to repress the students instead of redressing the terrible morass the killings had revealed. Members of the Jefferson County School Board talked about labeling all students as commodities. Just as the case with much of insecure, dictatorial corporate America, it pondered forcing all pupils to parade about campuses with identification tags. Lest they carry any illicit materials, it also talked about only permitting them to have see-through backpacks. None of these measures would have prevented the shootings.

School administrators cracked down even more drastically than they had in the past on any student dissent. Some sought to turn campuses into veritable prisons. Throughout the debate, a few voices continually sought to remind the reformers the schools were supposedly temples of knowledge, not institutions of incarceration.

Advocates of gun control seized on the murders to push their agenda. Prior to the shootings, the General Assembly was on the verge of adopting sweeping legislation permitting individuals to carry concealed weapons. After Columbine, advocates of this position cowered in fear. Gun-control advocates led by opportunistic Democrats, in turn, readily and cynically employed youths to launch a veritable children's crusade for their pet program.

Nobody was fiercer in insisting on less public access to guns than Mayor Webb. As the level of police violence escalated under him, he pushed laws drastically limiting when and where law-abiding citizens could carry firearms. His agenda included legislation allowing the government to seize a car should the police find a weapon in it. In the wake of Columbine, he came across like a pompous redneck sheriff during the height of the civil rights movement when the National Rifle Association was to convene its previously scheduled convention in Denver. Webb, guarded by armed police officers and cloaking himself in morality, told the group it was not wanted in town. Despite this, the pro-gun group held its conclave.

Photo by Phil Goodstein

*The Columbine Massacre occurred right at the time the United States government was engaged in vicious terror bombings in Kosovo and Iraq. A guerrilla billboard at 23rd and Welton streets noted the connection.*

Even as the killings spurred endless moaning about a culture of violence, virtually nothing was said about how military recruiters were allowed free and ready access to the high schools or how ROTC programs, complete with guns, were a credible part of the curriculum. Compounding the military orientation was that the killings were simultaneous with the vicious American terror bombings against Serbia. No connection was made between Harris' actions and his father's past service as a retired bomber pilot. On the contrary, those mourning the victims of Columbine celebrated military violence. They arranged to have the Air Force send four F-16s screaming over the mass commemoration meeting for the murdered students and teacher.

No governmental or community leader decried such a celebration of violence. Instead, those with power to shape public debate and media presentations—notably newspaper editors and managers of television stations—focused on trifles. Typical was the response to a planned NBC mini-series, "Atomic Train." An action thriller, the television show was about the fate of a train carrying nuclear waste from Idaho to Denver. After the crew loses control of the train, the bomb-packed cars blow up in the Mile High City.

In the wake of Columbine, NBC modified the plot whereby the train only carried "hazardous waste." Even so, broadcasting executives decided a show with social commentary about the dangers of transporting deadly materials was "insensitive" to the community after the high school killings. Consequently, the local NBC affiliate, Channel Nine, did not air the series. Even while pondering this point and the horrors of easy access to guns, the media were filled with endless hoopla for a coming *Star Wars* film, thinking nothing of promoting a movie with the message that evil and extreme violence are the eternal fate of the universe.

Far from redressing such a celebration of violence, many seeking to profit from Columbine insisted fundamentalist Christianity alone could solve educational and social problems. In the same manner advocates of gun restriction had little use for the Second Amendment, those of this position were ready to gut the First Amendment. By placing the Ten Commandments in each classroom, they were sure, troubled students in the future would read them and cease and desist from following in the footsteps of Harris and Klebold. In July 2000, the Colorado Board of Education urged school districts to place the words "In God We Trust" in all classrooms.

Religious debate haunted the aftermath of Columbine. Controversy flared over installing memorial crosses in Clement Park near the high school. Some objected to the presence of 15 crosses—two for the murderers as well as 13 for the victims. All the while, organizers eagerly transformed the public mourning gathering for the victims into a worship service of their narrow brand of religion. Stories came out about how administrators had ignored past anti-Semitic incidents in the system. Some of the worthy Christians who had fled to this part of suburbia were fully in tune with their religion's historic hatred of other races and creeds. Their children at Columbine reflected their views.

Not forgiveness, but an intense vengeance and desire to perpetrate the conditions leading to Columbine were the calls of some touched by the tragedy. All too typical was how a few of the family members of survivors, joined by other self-proclaimed worthy Christians, proudly vandalized and destroyed trees planted by West Bowles Community Church in September 1999. The church planted 15 trees to atone for all the families hurt by the killings, including the Harrises and Klebolds. Against this, after picketing the church, a gang of the Columbine crowd, who painted themselves as professional victims, pounded nails in 13 of the trees; they chopped down the other two.

There was no place in their universe for new perspectives. Nor did they want to allow community institutions to provide condolence. Shortly thereafter, for example, a worthy, self-proclaimed "Christian" attorney, Anthony Sturniolo, loudly advised Columbine families pondering legal action in the wake of the massacre to steer clear of any "Jewish" lawyers. The open hatred, racism, and anti-Semitism of the Columbine community so remained as powerful as ever in the wake of the shootings.

## Jefferson County Schools

Such an intolerance was a theme pervading all aspects of the Columbine Massacre. Jefferson County Reorganized School District One (R-1) emerged in 1950 to unify the 39 small districts in the county west of Denver. It surged with suburban growth in the 1960s, 1970s, and 1980s. As DPS enrollment declined under the pressure of busing, the Jefferson County system became the largest school district in the state, eventually having around 90,000 students. It put up schools everywhere to meet endless residential expansion.

Financial crises continually haunted R-1. No sooner had the district opened a new school than it found it needed yet another one. Unlike Denver, its appeals to the voters for more funds were usually defeated. This mirrored the divided, polarized nature of the county it served.

While parents wanted the best schools for their children, the suburban dwellers often had little orientation to local politics. Instead of seeking to redress the rot sweeping DPS and the increasing urban problems of modern Denver, they turned their backs on the city and their home communities. Often settling in unincorporated regions created by corporate developers, they sought to shelter themselves and their children from social, economic, and moral issues.

Reflecting some of their insecure constituents, suburban representatives sometimes demanded coercive governmental legislation. In the name of protecting children, some politicians were ready to impose a veritable theocracy as the solution to what they perceived as the world's errant course. The Republican Party, largely dominated by real estate interests and fundamentalist Christians, overwhelmingly swept Jefferson County elections. R-1 illustrated the conservative if not reactionary side of the region.

Typical was the fate of Al Wilder, a 26-year-veteran Jefferson County instructor who had also served as an assistant principal. During the 1994–95 school year, he was teaching a class on logic and debate at Columbine High. To give students a view of life outside the system's artificial and standard banalities, Wilder showed the class *1900*, a controversial film by Italian director Bernardo Bertolucci. The movie focuses about life, growing up, fascism, resistance, friendship, and love. It includes a graphic scene about bought sex.

The students were receptive to the film. None were surprised or objected to the frontal nudity. One parent did. On the basis of her complaint, Columbine principal Ron Mitchell, who had previously clashed with Wilder, fired the teacher. The principal announced Wilder had failed to get proper approval for the movie. Even worse, he was insubordinate and neglectful of his duties. Among those firmly supporting the principal in the dismissal of Wilder were activists in the Mormon church. They noted 130 to 140 of their children attended Columbine in 1994–95. Neither the school nor R-1 paid any heed to a student petition to retain Wilder.

A week-long hearing followed in February 1996 before an outside arbitrator, Nancy Cohen. Wilder's attorneys brought out past conflicts between the principal and the instructor. They pointed out a teacher must have the power to decide on specific materials as he seeks to get students to think. Against this, the Jefferson County school board, fully endorsing the principal, harped on Wilder's failures as a teacher. R-1 noted it was "inconceivable" the instructor did not know it was necessary to have administrative approval to show the film.

Though the hearing officer decided Wilder had been neglectful in dealing with most of the allegations against him, she ruled they were no reason to fire him. He had used his professional judgment in showing the film as an appropriate topic for a class on logic and debate. Despite her verdict, the R-1 school board unanimously fired Wilder in March 1996. Such a move was necessary, members noted,

Photo by Phil Goodstein

*Though Columbine High School students are "the Rebels," Jefferson County School District R-1 has done everything to prevent students or teachers from rebelling against a rigid, anti-intellectual administration.*

to protect the children: logic and debate were apparently forbidden topics. On no account were students allowed access to anything beyond their parents' narrow-minded, insecure worlds.

None of the wise commentators pondering the meaning of the Columbine Massacre said anything about this anti-intellectual background of the school. Nor was any link made between the behavior of the students and the region's politicians. In the generation leading up to the massacre, close connections existed between county commissioners and developers. The former invariably gave the latter a free hand. By the early 1990s, the extravagance of the commissioners was obvious when their dysfunctional, gigantic new headquarters—a $71.5 million structure mocked as the "Taj Mahal"—came in vastly above budget. In 1992, voters turned out many Jefferson County Republican incumbents, blaming them for the building. Before long, conditions were back to normal.

All the while, school administrators, both locally and nationally, often showed a complete absence of common sense, vehemently denying due process for students accused of breaking arbitrary rules. Seeking to show how tough and mean they were, officials touted their "zero tolerance" of weapons in schools. Numerous cases of despotism resulted, including expelling an honor student who accidentally brought a paring knife to school in her lunch bag and kicking out a girl who had a Swiss Army knife in her car as part of a first-aid kit. The officials so came across for their petty vindictiveness and unthinking legalism. They showed themselves as anything but educators.

Side by side of this, a police-state mentality treated children as master criminals if not fiends. This came out in Jefferson County shortly after Columbine when, at 10:30 PM on August 30, 1999, the sheriff's department raided the Wuthrich family house in Evergreen. The deputies arrested 11-year-old Raoul Wuthrich, hauling him away in handcuffs. Their action stemmed from a neighbor's accusation in June that she had seen him commit incest with his five-year-old sister when the boy appeared to touch his sibling inappropriately. Instead of having a prompt hearing, the Jefferson County district attorney's office kept the boy in detention for seven weeks before placing him in a foster home. The sloppiness of the county's actions in the matter came out that November when District Court Judge James Zimmerman threw out the case, noting the district attorney's office violated the boy's right to a speedy trial.

Youths were not stupid. They saw what was occurring, how the politicians achieved their goals, and the scornful way in which they were treated. Ruling Jefferson County's actions, in other words, could very well have been a role model for the Columbine students.

School administrators did not tolerate any free student debate, discussion, or questioning on such matters. To show Denver was at one with the suburbs in primarily desiring a brain-dead, rigid system discouraging independent thought, about the time of the Columbine Massacre, the DPS administration prohibited students from using video productions to make any "statement or inference that undermines or attacks Denver Public School policies, practices, personnel, students, or community members." In a word, students had no right to make a docu-

Author's Collection

*The killings at Columbine High School in April 1999 were Colorado's second Columbine Massacre. The first occurred on Monday, November 20, 1927, when members of the state police opened fire on peaceful miners picketing the Columbine Mine near Lafayette, killing six workers and wounding five more. Shown is a 1989 poster memorializing the event.*

mentary pointing to problems with dress codes or the crude police-state measures increasingly embraced by a society hysterically scared of its own children. This only highlighted the extreme lack of respect educators had for students. The pompous administrators were exceedingly irritated when the youths, in turn, showed them little respect. Massive negative publicity forced the board of education to overturn the bureaucratic edict.

(DPS did not practice "zero tolerance" when its number-two man, a former military official, Greg Cook, physically assaulted the district's public relations officer, Mark Stevens, in the fall of 1999. Superintendent Chip Zullinger did not automatically suspend or expel Cook. Rather, he noted there were conflicting accounts and justifications for the confrontation—something the advocates of zero tolerance never allowed to students. Zullinger was not steady in other administrative decisions, having taken the job in August 1999. Nine months later, in May 2000, the school board fired him, awarding him generous severance pay.)

In a final bit of irony, Jefferson County Schools drastically cut busing programs in the aftermath of Columbine. R-1 did not earn kudos by this move to keep young children off school buses—a favorite theme of anti-integration voices during the late 1960s/early 1970s; on the contrary, parents loudly griped about it. They noted how bad and dangerous walking conditions were in their idyllic neighborhoods. In a word, the entire experience of the Jefferson County system was something of a direct legacy and result of those who had all so callously turned their backs on the agony of Denver Public Schools.

## The Fate of Park Hill Schools

Some members of the black and Chicano communities were disgusted by the response to the Columbine killings. They noted comparable violence and breakdown had dominated their children's schools and lives for generations. When activists had tried to redress them in the 1960s through integration proposals, the result was the explosion of the busing controversy and the decline of DPS. Now the same factors had spread to the whitest parts of suburbia.

Even as locals narcissistically reflected on the Columbine shootings, other educational problems remained. Blacks as well as whites agreed it was necessary to change and improve the schools. Some of the former embraced Afrocentric education. In addition to intentionally imposing business values, the schools also pushed white European traditions and Christianity as the unquestioned basics of western civilization. Nationalistic blacks insisted African-Americans had a different reality. Because their children could not relate to the Eurocentric teachings of the schools, they failed.

Other groups had faced the discriminatory biases of the school system for years. Jews, for example, sent their children to Hebrew schools to gain an appreciation of their people's language, religion, and culture. Greek and Japanese families established similar national academies for their youths. In the 1960s, black militants had sought to create their own schools. Chicano activists echoed them in the belief the public schools would invariably indoctrinate their children and whitewash the traditions and histories of their people.

As the demand for special programs and quasi-private, but publicly funded, schools soared, it impacted black Denver. A few saw a means of redressing the miserable educational performances of their children by having DPS provide black youths Afrocentric educations. Appropriately, Park Hill was the focal point.

As the original ideals of busing faded, Park Hill schools remained in crisis. Some in the neighborhood, particularly whites, sent their children to private schools or pushed charter schools. (After the closing of Lowry Air Force Base in 1994, private schools occupied space there, often drawing enrollment from Park Hill.)

While Park Hill Elementary continued to hold its own as an integrated school with acceptable academic accomplishment, all other neighborhood schools were hurting. Performances on standardized tests were below average. Enhanced educational programs did not always help. An idea pondered by integration activists during the 1960s was implemented in 1996: the creation of a mini-Park Hill school district.

Known as the Park Hill Magnet Schools, each of the elementary programs in the neighborhood had a specific slant. Park Hill Elementary, for example, featured a school of international studies; Barrett School emphasized zoology in cooperation with the Denver Zoo; Hallett was a science and technology academy; and Philips was a preparatory school. Missing was an Afrocentric orientation. That was the goal of some black activists.

Since the schools remained badly troubled, newspapers gave massive attention to the call for an Afrocentric Park Hill district. The development was indicative: Despite all the turmoil of the busing wars, school supporters and social engineers firmly retained the belief that, by somehow tinkering with the schools, it was possible to redress racial, ethnic, economic, and class divisions. All the while, the agony of the schools reflected the anguish of the city. In this atmosphere, the Chicano movement surged.

## A Note on Sources:

The chapter obviously has a strong bias about the nature of mainstream education. I have generally followed the writings of Paul Goodman, John Holt, and James Herdon on this subject, notably Goodman's *Compulsory Mis-Education* (New York: Vintage, 1964). A solid critique of education in the late 1960s/early 1970s is in Mitchell Goodman, ed., *The Movement toward a New America* (New York: Knopf, 1970). Also see Holt, *How Children Fail* (New York: Pitman, 1964); idem, *How Children Learn* (New York: Pitman, 1967); Herdon, *The Way It Spozed to Be* (New York: Simon & Schuster, 1968); idem, *Notes from a Schoolteacher* (New York: Simon & Schuster, 1985); and Nat Hentoff, *Our Children are Dying* (New York: Viking, 1966).

My perspective is also slanted as a graduate of DPS. I was at Park Hill Elementary School in 1959–61 when it was resegregated upon the opening of Barrett. I similarly attended Smiley Junior High and East High when the busing and racial controversies were at razor's edge. Generally, I found DPS a turgid, dull, mind-deadening experience. Naturally, I have drawn on my memories in interpreting the schools. In all cases, I have sought to double check recollections with official documents. (Besides growing up in Park Hill, I lived on and off in the neighborhood from 1972 until 1982. During this time, I met members of GPHC, occasionally attended its meetings, and observed how the organization operated.)

There is an immense paper trail about the evolution of DPS. The district has issued numerous newsletters, reports, analyses, and studies. Many are on file at the Government Documents division of DPL, including minutes of school board meetings. DPS has issued annual statistical reports and directories, listing the various schools. Overviews of the specific buildings are in *Histories of the Denver Public Schools*, a volume put together by the administration shortly after World War II. Also see Kenton Forrest, Gene McKeever, and Raymond McAllister, *History of the Public Schools of Denver*. I further checked DPS's files on its schools.

Patricia Ann Shikes, "Three Denver School Superintendents," (Ph.D. dissertation, University of Denver, 1987), contains a lengthy chapter on Oberholtzer. *Time* featured him in its February 20, 1950, issue. There is a smidgen on him in the Palmer Burch papers at CHS. That collection also contains a good deal on school board politics in the late 1950s and early 1960s and information about hiring Ronald D. Gilberts.

During the 1980s and early 1990s, members of the DPS public relations staff were always most helpful in answering my questions about the district and allowing me access to its records. I specifically wish to acknowledge the assistance of Will Howard and Evelyn Converse.

Among the specific DPL publications I drew upon are the *Superintendent's Newsletter*, *Superintendent's Bulletin*, *School Review*, *Instruction News*, and *DPS Review*. For years, DPL had an annual self-examination, publishing a survey, *Denver Looks at its Schools*. "DPS Today" was a chaotic, badly designed advertising supplement to the January 16, 2000, *RMN*, where DPS sought to tout its programs.

There have also been various private reviews of DPS, mostly customer guides for parents and newcomers, e.g., Cynthia Benegar and Heidi Yoder McClain, *Learning in the Mile High City* (Denver: Metro Source Publications, 1986); and Margaret Hicks, *The Guide to Metro Denver Public Schools* (Denver: Magnolia Street Press, 1997). *Washington Park Profile* and *Life on Capitol Hill* are neighborhood newspapers that have had extensive columns reporting on, usually most favorably, about area schools.

Ed Benton discussed his experiences on the school board and the 1969 election. He noted the anti-busing board of education did its all to make sure desegregation would not work. Jerry McCracken granted me an interview about his experiences as a teacher at Smiley, George Washington, and Manual during the 1950s, 1960s, and 1970s. He also observed the labor battles in the district during these years and the role of the Denver Federation of Teachers.

Many other former and present employees of the district shared their memories and views about the system's operations. So did countless alumni. Often their recollections came in informal conversations. Unfortunately, I do not recall all the names. Among those specifically helping me were William Wilbur, Allan Winter, Ann Morgan, Paul Ton, Jim London, and Delia Armstrong. Jackie Friedman told me about her experiences teaching in DPS in the 1940s, including the quota on hiring Jewish instructors.

Newspapers extensively reviewed the George Washington High School upheavals. Among the best surveys was by GW physics teacher, Buel C. Robinson, "Confrontation at George Washington High: Why?" *DP Empire*, January 3, 1971. *Look* examined the crisis in a fluffy article focusing on the school's principal, Jack Beardshear, March 9, 1971, pp. 20–29. There are also materials on the GW explosion in the Commission on Community Relations (CCR) papers at DPL and Minoru Yasui papers in the Auraria Archives.

Ida Uchill read a draft of this chapter, telling me about her experiences as a teacher at George Washington High School in the late 1960s/early 1970s. She further regaled me with tales of her other adventures in teaching for DPS. Doug Gerash recalled what it was like to be a politically active dissident white student at GW during the fall of 1970. Michael Allen, who attended Smiley and GW a few years earlier, also discussed his experiences in the schools. Marilyn Megenity reminisced on her experiences at Hallett, Smiley, and GW. Chuck Michaels remembered being a GW junior at the time of the riot. He reviewed the 1971 GW yearbook for me.

Assorted doctoral studies have been done on the busing controversies. The best are: Mary Jean Taylor, "Leadership Responses to Desegregation in the Denver Public Schools, A Historical Study, 1959–77," (Ph.D. dissertation, University of Denver, 1990); and Frederick D. Watson, "Removing the Barricades from the Northern Schoolhouse Door: School Desegregation in Denver," (Ph.D. dissertation, University of Colorado, 1993). Arguing the city deliberately sought to contain black settlement after 1950, Watson claims by 1956 it was clear Denver had a de facto segregated system.

Harriet Elaine Glosson Adair, "Trends in School Desegregation: An Historical Case Study of Desegregation in Dayton, Ohio; Denver, Colorado; Los Angeles, California; and Seattle, Washington; 1954–1985," (Ed.D. dissertation, Brigham Young University, 1986), is vague on names and specifics. It adds little to the subject. Kenneth Ronald Emerson, "Denver Public Schools and Decentralization: An Implementation Game," (Ph.D. dissertation, University of Colorado at Denver, 1996), looks at the evolution of the district.

A history of Park Hill is badly needed. Bits and pieces on it show up in history books, especially Leonard and Noel, *Mining Camp*. Students at Park Hill Elementary put together an impressive eight-page tabloid newspaper account of the area, *Our Park Hill Story* (Denver: Park Hill Elementary School, 1976). The Park Hill branch of DPL once had a good clipping file on the neighborhood—it lost it during a remodeling of the library in the 1990s. The 1975 League of Women Voters' tour booklet of the neighborhood has some basic materials on Park Hill. The city engineer's office has original plat maps.

Bea and Art Branscombe are the "official" historians of GPHC. They have been working on a book on Park Hill, concentrating on the civil rights struggles, for years. Numerous sections of their work have been published in *Greater Park Hill News,* the organ of GPHC. They sponsored a forum on the subject at Montview Boulevard Presbyterian Church on April 16, 1988. The Branscombes also arranged for a Park Hill hall of fame in the basement of the Park Hill Library. The display includes photos and biographies of past leaders of PHAC, NEPHCA, and GPHC. (Bea Branscombe died in July 2000.)

*Greater Park Hill News*, along with publications of PHAC and NEPHCA, included immense details of the neighborhood. Also see *East Denver Journal*. In the 1950s, it served as the publication of both PHIA and NEPHCA. *The Park Hill Express* reported on the neighborhood before World War I. Other Park Hill newspapers over the years include *Park Hill Bulletin* in the 1920s; *Park Hill Topics* in the 1930s and 1940s; and *Park Hill Scroll* in the early 1960s. The *Black Panther* of March 28, 1970, contains a scathing review of the Negroes of Park Hill, "Disneyland—Denver Style."

Bob Verner talked about growing up in Park Hill in the 1930s. The late Bud Hawkins gave me his observations as a longtime resident. Jerry Kopel recalled his involvement in the neighborhood and the school busing fight. Tom Bastien shared his extensive knowledge of Denver politics, including developments in Park Hill in the 1950s, 1960s, and 1970s.

Early materials on Park Hill are in the Pliny F. Sharp Scrapbook at DPL. A survey of the neighborhood during the 1960s is George E. Bardwell, *Park Hill Areas of Denver, 1950–1966* (Denver: CCR, 1966); and idem, *Characteristics of*

*Negro Residences in Park Hill* (Denver: CCR, 1966). Bardwell, a professor of statistics and mathematics at the University of Denver, proposed an integration plan for DPS and the neighborhood. Materials on him are in the Doris Banks papers at Auraria. The CCR and Yasui papers also contain an immense amount about school busing controversies. A look at the political career of Bill Roberts is noted in passing in T. R. Witcher, "The Young and the Restless," *WW*, April 1, 1999, pp. 25–33.

Some of the churches have issued their own histories including Park Hill Methodist, *Celebrating the Opening of the New Church Edifice* (Denver: Park Hill Methodist, 1924); Hartzell Spence, *One Foot in Heaven* (Denver: Park Hill Methodist, 1940); and *Twenty-Fifth Anniversary of Park Hill Methodist* (Denver: Park Hill Methodist, 1949). The Montview Boulevard Presbyterian story is: *Montview Church, 1902–1932* (Denver: Eames Brothers, 1932); *Montview's Golden Year* (Denver: Montview Boulevard Presbyterian Church, 1952); *Montview Boulevard Presbyterian: The First 75 Years* (Denver: Montview Boulevard Presbyterian Church, 1977); and a sketch in Arthur B. Cooper, *The Story of Our Presbytery of Denver*. George P. Goodier and Clarence Culver Moore, *The Story of St. Thomas Church* (Denver: Peerless Printing, [1966]), treats that parish. Also see Breck, *The Episcopal Church in Colorado*. Blessed Sacrament's issued *Church of the Most Blessed Sacrament* (Denver: Blessed Sacrament, 1975); and a 12-page supplement to the *Denver Catholic Register* upon the dedication of Machebeuf High School, September 24, 1959. Sketches of Blessed Sacrament and Curé d'Ars parish in new Park Hill are in Noel, *Colorado Catholicism*. *Freemasons, Denver: Park Hill Lodge No. 148* (Denver: Smith-Brooks, 1959), is the story of the organization in the neighborhood.

The Voorhees Report is *Report and Recommendations to the Denver Public Schools by the Special Study Committee on Equality of Educational Opportunity in the Denver Public Schools* (Denver: DPS, 1964). Also see *Final Report and Recommendations to the Board of Education by the Advisory Council on Equality of Educational Opportunity* (Denver: DPS, 1967), an update on the Voorhees Report sometimes known as the Berge Report. The Gilberts Plan is outlined in *The Superintendent Reports*. This was an eight-page DPS publication beginning in November 1968. The first issue was a summary of the integration proposal, "Planning Quality Education: A Proposal for Integrating the Denver Public Schools." *Schools for Denver's Children* (Denver: DPS, 1971), is a DPS look at its facilities amidst the busing controversies.

James S. Coleman, et al., *Equality of Educational Opportunity* (Washington: GPO, 1966), is the Coleman Report. The summary report of the United States Civil Rights Commission, *Racial Isolation in the Public Schools* (Washington: GPO, 1967), argued integrated education, by its very nature, is superior to segregated schools. The *Kerner Report* (New York: Dutton, 1968), focusing on racial tensions in the United States, also affirmed the need for school integration.

The Tom Currigan papers at DPL include numerous materials on DPS, including the failed 1967 bond issue, educational parks, and busing. "Preliminary Report of the Committee on Equality of Educational Opportunity in DPS," issued on

June 1, 1963, is also in them. The Currigan collection further contains various documents advocating an integration program, such as the declaration of the Clearing House for Concerned Citizens for the Noel Resolution, statistics compiled by Gordon Bardwell of Speak Out on School Integration, and reports of the City-Wide Committee of Cooperative Endeavor on the riot at George Washington High School in 1970.

The Doris Banks papers at the Auraria Archives, especially box 13, have an immense collection on the 1969 school election. There are also materials in them from Speak Out on School Integration and DPS documents. A statement by Corky Gonzales denouncing school integration is among the papers as is the position statement of the Congress of Hispanic Educators drafted by its local head, Gene Gallegos. The Commission on Community Relations heavily pushed the integration program. Materials on the subject are in its papers at DPL, the Banks papers, and the Yasui papers.

The League of Women Voters put together *Court-Ordered Desegregation of the Denver Public Schools* (Denver: LWV, 1974), a basic guide to the issue. Also see the special report by James Meadows in *CJ*, May 8, 1974. Calvin Trillin had a pro-busing slant in his look at the 1969 school board election, "Denver, Doing the Right Thing Isn't Always Easy," *New Yorker*, May 31, 1969, pp. 85–89. Compare the *Wall Street Journal*, June 15, 1972, on the topic. Bill Hornby, *The Law Out West: Holland & Hart*, provides a sketch of Gordon Greiner and the law firm's involvement in the busing case.

I give a background sketch of William Doyle in volume one, discussing his treatment of draft-card burner Mendel Cooper. Walter Gerash and Steve Savageau shared their memories of the judge. His papers are at the Auraria Archives. They have a smattering of material on the busing controversy.

An extensive court record traces the racial practices in DPS. The 1927 Colorado Supreme Court ruling on separate but equal in DPS is *Jones* v. *Newlon*, 253 P 386. Eighteen separate opinions were published on the Keyes case. Judge Doyle's granting of the preliminary injunction is *Keyes* v. *School District Number One*, 303 FSupp 279 and 289. Justice William Brennan's order affirming it is 396 US 1215. Doyle's ruling on the desegregation suit is 313 FSupp 61; his specific order mandating busing is 313 FSupp 90. The Tenth Circuit decision overturning Doyle is 445 F.2d 990. The landmark Supreme Court case is 413 US 189. Doyle's integration order of 1974 is 380 FSupp 673. The Tenth Circuit ruling modifying it is 521 F.2d 465. Judge Matsch issued a number of rulings on the case, including 474 FSupp 1265, 609 FSupp 1491, 653 FSupp 1536, and 670 FSupp 1513. His order releasing DPS from court supervision is *Keyes* v. *Congress of Hispanic Educators*, 902 FSupp 1275. Briefs in the Keyes case are in Philip B. Kurland and Gerhard Casper, eds., *Landmark Briefs and Arguments of the Supreme Court of the United States: Constitutional Law* (Washington: University Publications of America, 1977), 77:3–600.

There are immense clipping files on busing and DPS at DPL. An attack on the newspaper coverage of DPS in the mid-1970s, asserting neither the *Post* nor *News* knew what was going on in DPS, was Ron Wolf's polemic in *SCJ*, December 16,

1976, pp. 4–5. The middle-class Hispano perspective on educational opportunity in the mid- to late 1970s is found in the newsletter of the Chicano Education Project, *Un Nuevo Día*. The Chicano Education Project sued the state in the 1970s, arguing unequal financing of various districts made for unequal educational opportunity for minority students. Though it won at the district court level, the Colorado Supreme Court overturned the ruling. See *Lujan* v. *Colorado State Board of Education*, 649 P.2d 1005 (1982).

Sarah Nordgren and Andrea Gabriel, "School Days for Big Business," *The Nation*, September 19, 1981, is a portrait of the Adopt-a-School program. The Minoru Yasui papers contain promotional materials for the effort. "Public Schools. Public Interest," was a special report in the April 26, 1998, *DP*, heralding the work of the Public Education & Business Coalition, noting its domination of the schools. An article extolling DPS's commercial deals is in *DP*, July 2, 2000, p. 1B.

An eager advocacy of CDMs is in Citizens for Quality Schools, *The Power of Collaborative Decision Making: A Handbook for Change in the Denver Public Schools* (Denver: Center for Quality Schools, 1997). Operating out of Republic Plaza, it issued a newsletter urgently advocating greater power for CDMs, *Quality Matters*. The review of CDMs and Aaron Gray's role is noted in *RMN*, November 8, 1999. Kevin Tannenbaum recalled going to Smiley. He shared his views as a member of the Morey CDM, specifically labeling it an adult student council.

George Archuleta gave me his detailed views on bilingual education and the numerous efforts at improving schools for Chicano students. He also provided me with materials from Padres Unidos. Maxine Lankford discussed her knowledge of some of the activists in the group. Esther Scher shared her perspectives as a teacher in Tucson, including her participation in its pioneering bilingual program.

The Columbine Massacre was endlessly reported in the media. An overview is Steven G. Grinstead, "Flower Blue," *Colorado Heritage*, Winter 2000, pp. 6–12. A rambling review of the shootings, noting many of the media errors about the event and the jock administration of Columbine is Alan Prendergast, "Doom Rules," *WW*, August 5, 1999, pp. 23–35. Columbine parent Steve Schweitzberger gave me his views on the affair.

Sketches of the origins and evolution of Jefferson County schools are in Dorothy Lombard, "Some Thought Ahead," in *From Scratch: A History of Jefferson County, Colorado*, 13–21; and Barbara A. Martin, "The Creation of R-1," in Pat Wilcox, ed., *76 Centennial Stories of Lakewood*, 158–59. The August 20, 1999, *DP*, p. 2B, notes parent protests of the cut of the Jefferson County school busing program. Walter Gerash talked about the Al Wilder case. Loretta Werth recalled her involvement with the modern Jefferson County Republican Party and her daughter's experiences in the R-1 district. Jerry Milbrath shared his experiences as a teacher in R-1.

DPS records and reportage in *Greater Park Hill News* cover the evolution of Park Hill schools. A report on them, filled with statistics and bureaucratic gibberish is OMNI Research & Training, *Park Hill Magnet Project Evaluation* (Denver: OMNI, 1997).

# 3

# Chicano Power

At the same time middle-class blacks focused on Park Hill and demanded the desegregation of the schools, upheavals swept the city's largest ethnic group, individuals of Mexican descent. By the end of the 20th century, they made up one-quarter of Denver's population. Debates were hot and heavy over English as an official language and bilingual education. The controversies cloaked a history of intrigue, class and social divisions, and cynical efforts to recruit community leaders to stand on the shoulders of their fellows.

Individuals of Spanish heritage were the first permanent settlers of European origin in Colorado—they included both people from Mexico proper and those who had lived in areas the United States wrenched from Mexico in 1848 at the conclusion of the Mexican-American War. While most of these Spanish-Americans settled in the southern part of the state in the 19th century, some were in the Denver area from the time of the Pikes Peak gold rush. The so-called Mexican Diggings of 1857 helped trigger the stampede leading to the creation of the Territory of Colorado in 1861. Generally, Hispanos remained hidden in Denver shadows until the 1910s. At that time, a cynical ploy by Great Western Sugar brought tens of thousands of them to northern Colorado.

Needing cheap laborers to toil for minimum wages in highly seasonal employment, the sugar concern—run by the Boettcher family as part of the national sugar trust—deliberately over-recruited laborers from the American Southwest and Mexico for the beet fields of eastern Colorado early in the 20th century. Great Western made no secret of its primary goal: keeping down labor costs. The giant corporation did nothing to provide health care, schooling, or otherwise assist the social welfare of its field workers. With the full support of county and state authorities, it ruthlessly crushed sporadic farmworker protests.

More than anything, the company's labor policies were premised on the bad conditions elsewhere. It was sure there was an endless supply of Mexican and Mexican-American stoop laborers. Great Western's off-season policy was essentially for the workers to go away during the months they were not needed. As Great Western's dependence on migrant labor became ever more pronounced, increasing numbers of Hispanos remained in the area. They were often without steady employment or resources in the winter.

These agricultural workers drifted to the small towns of northern Colorado. By the 1910s, segregated slums—barrios—had appeared. Discrimination was common. Towns and ruling interests banned Mexicans and Spanish-Americans from clubs and swimming pools. In some places, Hispanics could only attend movies during a special "Mexican night" once a week. Claims have been made signs declared "No Dogs and No Mexicans." No solid documentation exists of this, but it was quite possible: open scorn, hatred, and discrimination against Latinos were part and parcel of the communities dominated by Great Western Sugar.

Some of the farmworkers came to the Mile High City. Frequently marginally employed, they lived in the worst housing and often were victimized by the police. A large number settled in shanties along the Platte River, in Auraria, west of Santa Fe Drive, under the Colfax Viaduct, and near Curtis Park. Many were industrial workers, coming to form the backbone of local unions.

The 1920 census listed 1,390 Hispanics in a city of 256,491 residents. The number quadrupled to 6,837 by 1930—this was still fewer than the 8,792 Latin Americans in Weld County. By 1940, 12,323 individuals of Mexican heritage called Denver home. The Spanish-American population soared even more during World War II. Many arrived in the city during the conflict, drawn by the demand for workers. By 1945, 14,651 Hispanos were reported in the Queen City. This increased to 19,009 in 1950. Their numbers could have been greater—many distrusted the government and did not allow themselves to be counted.

Anti-Hispanic bias was widespread. Politicians readily exploited it. Democrat Edwin C. "Big Ed" Johnson was in the lead. Eying a seat in the United States Senate in 1936 when he served as governor, Johnson laid the blame for unemployment and high welfare costs on "Mexicans." To do something about these problems, he called out the National Guard on April 18, 1936, ordering it to seal the Colorado-New Mexico border to Hispanics. Though the governor quickly ended the so-called bum blockade—partly at the behest of Great Western—Johnson's ploy was successful in helping him win the Senate election.

The politician showed himself an heir to the Ku Klux Klan. It had rapidly grown in Denver in the early 1920s, loudly preaching a hatred of Catholics, Jews, and foreigners. None were more despised than the Spanish-surnamed. Though the Klan rapidly faded, its disdain for Chicanos remained.

While demagogues such as Johnson readily attacked poor Mexican-Americans, mainstream Denver generally ignored the day-to-day living conditions of Hispanos. People of Spanish heritage seemingly occupied a world of their own. While, now and then, a talented member of this community got ahead, most remained economically exploited workers with little chance of achieving the American dream.

Photo by John Gordon, DPL

*Locals celebrated Mexican Independence Day, September 16, as "Chicano Liberation Day" in the late 1960s/early 1970s.*

There was no consensus about the right term to use to describe people of Spanish-Indian descent. Individuals of Mexican heritage have at various times referred to themselves as Mexicans, Mexican-Americans, Spanish-Americans, Ibero-Americans, the Spanish-speaking, the Spanish, Latin Americans, the Spanish-surnamed, Chicanos, Hispanos, Hispanics, and Latinos. They have frequently labeled all other Caucasians "gabachos," "gringos" or "Anglos," including individuals of Irish, Italian, Greek, Slavic, Jewish, Portuguese, and other non-English European origins. "Anglo" was picked up by blacks in the school busing controversy. They readily divided the city among Hispanics, African-Americans, and Anglos. The courts and media echoed them. Many non-English Europeans, including the Irish who had battled the English for centuries, found "Anglo" an exceedingly racist, deprecatory term.

The old-line, well-established Hispano families of southern Colorado called themselves Spanish-Americans or Spanish-Colonials, emphasizing their Old World descent. As often as not, they were open in their hatred of "Mexicans"—people from Mexico. They despised the term Chicano. The word had appeared in the 1920s as an appellation for Mexican-Americans, especially those in the lower classes. It did not last in popular parlance. Conservative members of the community claimed it was a derogatory abbreviation of "Mexicano" or meant chicanery. They were vehement: they were Americans, not Mexicans.

Individuals of Mexican descent proudly called themselves Chicanos amidst the civil rights upheavals of the 1960s. They did not identify with the so-called Anglo culture. Opposed to it, these mostly young men and women related to Mexico and the brave traditions of its Indians and the Native Americans of the Southwest. By labeling themselves Chicanos, these ideologues and activists projected themselves as a New World people formed by the intermingling of Indians and Mexicans. They further celebrated Aztlan, the mythic homeland of fierce Aztec warriors, as the true designation of the southwestern United States. In addition to Texas, this was the land taken from Mexico in the Mexican-American War. Chicanos declared it their true country. All this added up to a volatile mix, one which had been building since World War II.

## Hispanic Leaders

Many Hispanos proudly served in the military during the conflict. The Army appealed to their valor. Mexican-American veterans loudly noted they had won a greater percentage of medals and citations than the percentage of their enrollment in the service. After the war, they were angry to find their patriotism unappreciated.

Returning to the Mile High City, Mexican-American soldiers confronted continuing discrimination. To do something about it, they organized civil rights groups. The American GI Forum was in the lead. The organization sought to assure that Spanish-surnamed veterans were accepted as full, equal members of the community. (The GI Forum moved its national headquarters from Austin, Texas, to Denver in March 1999.) The League of United Latin American Citizens (LULAC), a national Spanish-American civil rights organization dating from 1929, also had a powerful presence in the community.

Numerous other Hispanic political and social associations came and went, including Political Action Spanish Organizations, the Federation of Latin American Groups, and the United Latin Americans Organization. Often they were nothing more than temporary alliances or political front groups for the Democratic Party. Various Hispanic newspapers appeared. Though these publications might have Spanish names and include sections in Spanish, most of the text was in English—the first language of Denver Chicanos. Members of the Mexican-American community eagerly sought to rally their fellows, providing better job and educational opportunities.

White Denver often saluted such efforts. It praised Lino M. Lopez as an example. Born in Texas in 1910, he was the son of migrant workers who lost his mother when he was 12. Shortly thereafter, his family moved to Chicago where, after working his way through high school, he enrolled in Loyola University. Holding a full-time job, it took him seven years to earn his degree. Shortly thereafter, Lopez went to work for the Illinois Welfare Department and the Bishop's Committee for the Spanish-Speaking of the Catholic Church. After a stint in San Antonio, Texas, as a court juvenile officer, Lopez moved to Pueblo in 1948 to direct the Catholic Youth Center. Five years later, he relocated in the Mile High City.

During the next decade, Lopez emerged as a civil rights pioneer, urging greater educational opportunities for the Spanish-surnamed. He helped form numerous community groups and inspired local Hispanic politicians. He worked as a consultant for both the Commission on Community Relations and Denver Public Schools. Lopez left the Mile High City for a job in California in 1963. The educator retired to Denver in 1974, dying in late 1978.

DPL

*Paco Sanchez was the voice of Spanish Denver in the 1950s and 1960s.*

During the 1950s and 1960s, Paco Sanchez was literally the voice of Spanish-speaking Denver. Born in Guadalajara, Mexico, on December 9, 1915, he stemmed from an affluent family. After traveling widely and attending medical school, he worked as an actor, radio announcer, and showman. He arrived in Denver shortly after World War II as the promoter of a Latin dance troupe. Discovering the city lacked a Spanish-language radio station, he focused on broadcasting in his native language. After working on KTLN and KMYR, in June 1954 Sanchez purchased his own station, KFSC, 1220 AM, converting it into an all-Spanish outlet.

Sanchez was a proud adopted citizen of the United States. To stress Mexican-American patriotism and self-help, he launched the Good Citizens Organization in 1954, a group he quickly renamed the Good Americans Organization. All members were required to participate in its credit union. The association pushed better housing for Hispanics, both in Denver and in rural farming communities. Eventually, collaborating with the Denver Urban Renewal Authority (DURA), Denver Housing Authority (DHA), and federal agencies, the Good Americans Organization ran some low-income housing projects. By the 1960s, it was the largest individual Mexican-American organization in the state. (An old fraternal insurance association started in Antonito in 1900, Sociedad Protectora Mutual de los Trabajadores Unidos [Mutual Protection Society of the United Workers], was rapidly fading in Denver at this time—it retained many members in southern Colorado into the 21st century.)

The radio station owner never walked a picket line or engaged in angry confrontations with racist Denver. Nor did he address social issues on KFSC. On the contrary, Sanchez was a voice of accommodation. He was elected to one term in the state House of Representatives as a Democrat in 1968, losing in his effort to regain the nomination in 1970. Both Hispanics and ruling Denver widely mourned him on his unexpected death after surgery on July 12, 1973. The city subsequently named the park along West 12th Avenue near Hooker Street in his memory.

Insofar as there was a political leader of Hispanic Denver in the postwar years, James M. Fresques filled the role. He was born in Clayton, New Mexico, in 1908, an old-line Hispano who was proud of having achieved the American dream. Growing up in Denver, he put himself through high school and pharmacy college. Before long, he ran his own store, Rocky Mountain Pharmacy at 2300 Champa Street. Fresques was Denver's first Mexican-American councilman, winning the post to represent the Curtis Park/Five Points neighborhood in 1939.

A staunch Republican and fierce anticommunist, Fresques sometimes blasted city hall's discriminatory policies. This was the case in September 1945 when the police arrested him for interference. Acting as a member of the public, the city councilman had simply protested a patrolman's unwarranted arrogance in arresting a 20-year-old Hispanic sailor. When the charges against him were dropped that October, Fresques noted Mexican-Americans were "tired of being kicked around by the police department." He lambasted the Ben Stapleton administration's primitive techniques, ones more suited to the 19th century than post–World War II America.

Fresques served as city council president in 1946–47 and again in 1950–51. After moving to the Hilltop neighborhood in the early 1950s while he still represented Curtis Park on council, Fresques unsuccessfully ran for auditor in 1955. He subsequently was manager of welfare under Mayor Will F. Nicholson and was an administrative assistant to Mayor Richard Batterton. From 1961 until 1965, he was the director of the Denver Housing Authority. Under Governor John Love, Fresques helped push improved housing for migrant workers. He died in 1987.

Other Spanish-surnamed politicians came and went, including judges and members of the General Assembly. Though such individuals succeeded in the larger society, police brutality remained common against Chicanos. They were the usual suspects. Crime plagued their community. By the 1960s, 40 per cent of the defendants charged with crimes in the Mile High City were of Hispanic backgrounds. Until legal challenges in 1959 forced jury commissioners to include the Spanish-surnamed in jury pools, counties often deliberately excluded Mexican-Americans from this part of the legal system.

The city frequently destroyed Latino neighborhoods and businesses. DHA and DURA projects targeted Hispanic areas. Though these agencies claimed they were helping the poor, they often simply displaced them in their eager efforts to rebuild the Mile High City in the image of 17th Street. Chicanos, who found themselves forced to move by such efforts as the Skyline, Auraria, and Avondale urban renewal projects, were sure they and their enclaves were deliberately targeted because of their inhabitants' ethnicity. A side effect: Mexican-Americans spread to ever greater sections of the Mile High City. There was no one barrio as such, but numerous Hispanic subsections throughout the older parts of Denver.

Urban renewal and displacement projects fueled a simmering anger and frustration. Violence sometimes flared in Mexican-American Denver. Latino juvenile delinquents justified their vandalism as assertions of national liberation. Young men flaunted their machismo. Some literally tried to fight their way out of this discriminatory morass. The best known individual who employed this approach was Rodolfo "Corky" Gonzales. He personified the Chicano upheavals of the 1960s and 1970s.

## Corky Gonzales

Gonzales was the youngest of eight children, born in Denver on June 18, 1928. He lost his mother when he was two years old. His father, an immigrant from Chihuahua, Mexico, variously worked as a migrant laborer, miner, railroad hand, and fry cook. Known by one and all as "Corky," Gonzales grew up around the city's barrios. A measure of how frequently his family moved was his attendance at four grade schools, three junior high schools, and two high schools.

Much of the information about Gonzales' early life is nebulous. While he claimed to have worked with his father in the fields, associates reported he knew little about the specifics of the job. Nor did Corky have a good command of Spanish, the tongue of most migrant workers in the 1920s and 1930s. While some accounts even cite Gonzales as having been a lumberjack, there is no evidence to support the assertion. It often appeared Corky and his supporters did their all to romanticize the man's early years.

Private Collection

*Corky Gonzales when he was a top-rated boxer in the early 1950s.*

The militant first gained attention as a boxer. At age 19, in 1947, Gonzales won the Golden Gloves and Amateur Athletic Union bantamweight championships. Shortly thereafter, he turned professional. Between 1949 and his retirement from the ring in 1953, Gonzales was a top-ranked contender for the featherweight crown, winning 66 of his 75 pro fights. He used his earnings from the ring, supplemented by money from his wife's family, to purchase a bar, Corky's Corner, near 38th and Walnut streets. His brother joined him in running the tavern. Eventually, Corky also operated as a bail bondsman and owned an insurance agency.

Father Neal Patrick Moynihan of Annunciation Church, at 36th Avenue and Humboldt Street, near Corky's Corner, suggested Gonzales become politically involved. The former boxer continually informed the priest how patrons of his lounge were always complaining about their problems with the police and city hall. The cleric convinced Corky he could do something about them by working in the system through the Democratic Party. On this basis, Gonzales emerged as a Democratic precinct worker. His wife's family, the Romeros, greatly assisted the effort.

In 1955, Corky unsuccessfully sought a seat on city council against Elvin Caldwell. Before long, the Democratic establishment praised him as a leader and a gentleman. When Gonzales was charged with assaulting a police officer during a barroom brawl at Ciro's Tavern at 741 Colfax on July 25, 1958, a veritable who's who of the Democratic Party leadership testified in his behalf as character witnesses, resulting in his acquittal in January 1959. In 1960, Gonzales led the "Viva

Kennedy" movement in Colorado, rallying Hispanic voters for the Democratic presidential candidate. In that capacity he worked closely with the head of the Kennedy campaign in Colorado, future Supreme Court Justice Byron White.

Gonzales built something of a Spanish-American machine within the old East Denver Democratic Party. He led a rather conservative group known as Los Voluntarios (the Volunteers). Formed in 1964, it sought greater recognition for Hispanics within the system, including getting them city jobs. During this time, he called himself Rudolph Gonzales.

The aspiring politician ran for the legislature in 1962. He actively pushed for Spanish-Americans to vote for Democratic Governor Steve McNichols in a special publication, *¡La Verdad!* (McNichols had appointed Gonzales to the state's parks and recreation board in 1957.) The effort did little good. Not only was McNichols defeated for reelection, but Corky came in last among all the Denver legislative candidates.

Nothing illustrated the activist's mixed feelings more in the first half of the 1960s than his personal newspaper, *Viva*. Describing itself as "the battle cry of truth" and "the political voice of the Hispanic community," it readily attacked

DPL

*Young Chicanos serve as body guards for Corky Gonzales during a rally at the Capitol in the early 1970s. Gonzales is just beneath the "war" sign on the far left.*

police brutality and racism. Simultaneously, *Viva* noted the successes of Chicanos within the system. It proudly reported President Lyndon Johnson's naming Gonzales to a federal civil rights advisory commission in the spring of 1964.

Mayor Tom Currigan tabbed the bar owner/bondsman in 1965 to head the local War on Poverty and direct the Neighborhood Youth Corps. This was Corky's reward for helping Currigan win election in 1963. Gonzales then mobilized Spanish-American voters for the Democratic candidate in an organization known as Amigos for Currigan.

Gonzales denied the job was a political payoff. The former boxer, who liked living high and always had money problems, stated he did not need the post, but was accepting it in the hope he could help poor Chicanos. Boasting of his notoriety, he claimed "I'm an agitator and a troublemaker. That's my reputation and that is what I'm going to be. They didn't buy me when they put me in this job."

Corky's tenure as the director of the Youth Corps was stormy. Allegations quickly surfaced about Gonzales favoring Chicanos in awarding contracts while sloppy bookkeeping meant kids in the Youth Corps were sometimes not paid on time. The black East Denver Ministerial Alliance decried Corky's favoritism to Mexican-Americans, seeing African-Americans slighted in the process. (Gonzales was previously on record in attacking local War on Poverty programs for benefiting blacks at the expense of Hispanics.)

The situation blew up in April 1966. The Office of Economic Opportunity in Washington, the *Rocky Mountain News* reported, was closely watching Corky's actions. The newspaper hinted not all was well in the Neighborhood Youth Corps as a result of Gonzales' mismanagement. Corky, always extremely sensitive to criticisms, claimed the paper's account was a base racist libel. He called for a community boycott of the *News*. He openly denounced the daily on the radio and led a picket line around the *News*' headquarters.

Currigan, who had been barraged by complaints about Gonzales and feared that conservative Republican Senator Peter Dominick of Colorado was about to launch a congressional investigation of the city program, was not pleased. On Sunday, April 24, 1966, the mayor fired Gonzales. While claiming he had full confidence in Corky's administration of the Youth Corps, Currigan stated he did not like the way Gonzales responded to the newspaper's attack. A politician, the mayor noted, had to be able to take criticism. Nor was Currigan happy with the way Corky continually operated on his own, outside of the city administration. Even when he was head of the Youth Corps, Gonzales was in the political limelight. By the time he was fired, the Denver Chicano had become a national figure demanding civil rights for Hispanos, including the end to police brutality, discriminatory court sentences, and school policies imposing English-only on students in need of bilingual education.

Corky quickly dropped his effort to sue the *News* for libel. Nor did much come of his call for a boycott of the paper. Rather, Gonzales made his departure from the appointed city post the first step toward Chicano political activism. He proposed "*El Plan del Barrio*," calling for separate public housing for Chicanos, improved business opportunities in Hispanic neighborhoods, and a return of lands taken from

The Political Voice of The Hispanic Community

VIVA 10¢

THE BATTLE CRY OF TRUTH

VOL. 1 DENVER, COLORADO JULY 15, 1964 NO. 4

# President Johnson Appoints Gonzales

## City Council Rejects Bills To Hear Police Brutality

After hearing speakers for the bills to give the Community Relations Commission broader powers in investigating and hearing complaints of Police Brutality, City Council members took the floor to speak on the reasons why they personally were for or against the bills. Councilman Bob Keating, took twenty minutes to talk around the subject and also inject the fact that his father Bert Keating, District Attorney, had been critized, before he said No, he wouldn't support the bills.

Hoot Gibson, Councilman from Southwest Denver, repeatedly asked questions and made statements through the night long

## Nationwide Commission on Civil Rights

Rudolph Gonzales, Editor of Viva, Democratic District Captain and Member of the Colorado advisory committee to the President's Commission on Civil Rights received a three page telegram from President Johnson asking him to serve on a Nation Wide Committee for Community Relations. Gonzales immediately accepted. His statement to the President was short and affirmative. It read, "It is with deep humility and great pride that I gladly accept to serve my community, my state and my country as a member of your National Citizens Committee for Community Relations.

Western Union Telegram reads as follows:

"Enactment of the civil rights bill challenges all Americans to join in an affirmative voluntary effort to preserve order and to achieve the goal of equal tering voluntary observance of the provisions of the bill.

"I deeply hope you will advise me by return telegram that you will serve on the National Citizens committee for Community Relations.

"It is contemplated that after the organization of the community relations service there will be a meeting of this citizens committee at which time the directions of the over-all national program will be fully spelled out and your own role will be more clearly defined.

"I urge you as a private citizen to use your leadership in the meantime to promote a spirit of acceptance and observance in your own community and business area."

LYNDON B. JOHNSON

LAND GRANT

Auraria Archives

Viva *was the newspaper of Corky Gonzales (pictured) in the mid-1960s when he was still in the good graces of the Democratic Party.*

Mexico in 1848 to Mexican-Americans. He further advocated "Brown Power," and a celebration of Chicano cultural nationalism.

A charismatic figure and a powerful, effective speaker, Gonzales touched a raw nerve. Many Chicanos related to him. Having suffered blatant discrimination, they readily believed his dismissal by Currigan stemmed from a racist animus. Some of the middle-aged, working-class Hispanos who had joined Gonzales in Los Voluntarios readily made it known they would follow wherever Corky led them. They opened up their checkbooks to finance his new ventures.

By this time, the handsome, curly-haired, bushy-eyebrowed Corky had sprouted a mustache and looked vaguely like Emiliano Zapata. Henceforth, he denounced those having any ties with the Democratic Party. On April 25, 1966, Corky established his own organization, the Crusade for Justice.

The organization later sometimes referred to itself as *La Crusada para la Justicia*. The Spanish title was apropos. Like most Denver Chicanos, Crusade members primarily spoke English, though freely sprinkling their conversation with assorted Spanish words, including slang and numerous profanities. A strong division existed between English- and Spanish-speaking members of the community. Many of the latter were from Mexico. Members of long-established families from Colorado often scorned the newcomers. Against these conservative Spanish-Americans, by using Spanish, Crusade activists emphasized their Mexican heritage.

From the outset, Corky and the Crusade had a strong nationalist ideology. They saw all Chicanos as brothers and sisters against a racist Anglo establishment. By buying from and selling to one another and building their own cooperatives and institutions, Crusade members believed they were creating Aztlan. *El Gallo*, the Crusade's newspaper, reported both local and national events impacting the Chicano movement.

In 1969, the Crusade established Escuela Tlatelolco. The group named the school for a section of Mexico City—once an Aztec marketplace and merchant city-state—where the Mexican government murdered hundreds of protesters before and during the 1968 Summer Olympics. Besides teaching Chicano youths the traditions of their people, Escuela Tlatelolco served as an alternative to the public and parochial schools. Students enrolled there frequently turned out at Crusade protests. Goddard College in Vermont granted the academy accreditation. At the peak of its operations, nearly 300 students enrolled in Escuela Tlatelolco classes from preschool to the collegiate level.

The Crusade pushed for Chicanos to observe Mexican holidays. Beginning in 1969, Mexican Independence Day, September 16, became a time for public rallies and marches. The Crusade christened it Chicano Liberation Day. It also celebrated Cinco de Mayo, May 5, commemorating the Battle of Puebla in 1862 when a large Mexican peasant army defeated a small force of arrogantly overconfident French imperialist invaders.

After first gathering in a dilapidated, two-story apartment house at 1265 Cherokee Street, the Crusade purchased the abandoned Calvary Baptist Church building at the southwest corner of 16th Avenue and Downing Street in 1968. Dedicated on September 16, the building rapidly emerged as a Chicano social center. Besides a meeting hall, there was a bar, restaurant, and bookstore. The middle-aged members usually gathered on Wednesday evenings for informal sessions known as Fishermen's Meetings. A popular dance troupe entertained members at the hall.

The church and an adjacent apartment house directly to the south, Downing Terrace, became the center for Chicano militancy. Boxing matches, plays, and community meetings were frequently held at the former sanctuary. As the Crusade addressed discriminatory policies in the schools, numerous Chicano adolescents flocked to the organization. It readily recruited them, using the old church as a social center hosting weekly dances.

Many Chicano teenagers saw Gonzales as a role model and hero. He and a former boxing partner taught many of the boys how to box. These adolescents found Corky's political militancy an inspiring alternative to simply fighting one another. Gonzales used the young men as guards for Crusade events. Those working security for the organization boasted of their toughness and ability to physically beat up others.

A strong mythology quickly grew up about Gonzales. In addition to a boxer and a politician, he was a playwright and a poet. He claimed authorship of *I Am Joaquín*, a poem focusing on the plight of Chicanos in Aztlan. (Apparently the booklet's illustrator, Bill Longley, later known as Yermo Vasquez, greatly contributed to the work.)

The Crusade only had a marginal following in the larger Hispanic community. Illustrative was Corky's campaign for mayor in 1967. Running as the Chicano candidate against Currigan, Gonzales only received 4,179 votes opposed to the incumbent's 72,729 total out of 130,365 ballots cast. Despite the small vote, many in the political establishment hated and feared Corky and the Crusade.

Gonzales was active in the 1967 Chicago Conference for a New Politics. In 1968, Corky joined with a rival for leadership of the national Chicano movement, militant New Mexico land nationalist Reies Lopez Tijerina, in heading a Mexican-American delegation in the Poor People's March on Washington. The Crusade allied itself with other groups from Texas to California advocating Mexican-American militancy. Corky's organization played a major role in endorsing a Texas-based effort to establish a national Chicano political party, *El Partido de la Raza Unida*, usually simply called La Raza Unida Party. Its candidates, invariably Crusade members or allies, were on the Colorado ballot during the early 1970s.

(Efforts were made in 1966 to have a comparable Chicano party, the New Hispano Party. Part of a larger New Hispano Movement, it openly opposed the Vietnam War. Despite past vows of refusing to have anything to do with the Democrats, shortly before the election, Gonzales and the Crusade for Justice preferred to

DPL

*A Crusade picket line in front of the old main post office at 18th and Stout streets in the late 1960s.*

support the Democratic candidate for governor, Bob Knous, over Levi Martinez, the New Hispano contender. The party quickly faded after the election.)

Corky's actions were very much in the spirit of the times. He excelled in the politics of confrontation. Rather than sweeping matters under the rug or agreeing to muted compromises, Gonzales believed in head-on attacks. He and the Crusade were vitriolic in denouncing "professional Mexicans." The organization called Spanish-American leaders who were blessed by and firmly supported the establishment "*Tío Tomas*" and "*Tío Tacos*" (Uncle Toms and Uncle Tacos). As often as not, anyone not with Crusade was so branded. Many old-line, conservative Hispanos despised Corky as a troublemaker who brought discredit on all Mexican-Americans. They further charged youthful members of the Crusade were goons whom Gonzales used to assault his critics.

Both the Communist Party and the Socialist Workers Party sought to win Gonzales and the Crusade to their views. The former prizefighter was no socialist; on the contrary, he was a pro-capitalist nationalist. The Crusade banned members of leftist groups from key gatherings. Gonzales hopefully believed, that by gaining a full Chicano independence, his liberated people could successfully solve the problems plaguing their community. Scholars have cited him as an ideologue of *Chicanismo*, a romantic idealization of the Hispanos of the Southwest.

The former prizefighter bitterly criticized American foreign policy. His opposition to the Vietnam War was typical. As much as anything, he was against it because of the high rate of Chicano casualties in Southeast Asia. He and the Crusade were also in sympathy with Fidel Castro and others battling against United States intervention in Central and South America. The Crusade's bookstore offered posters of Ernesto "Che" Guevara. It celebrated him as the ultimate Latino revolutionary. The organization portrayed Chicanos, Mexicanos, and Latinos as a triad representing the best of their people and culture. The Crusade had fraternal relations with Puerto Rican nationalists and a working liaison with the Denver chapter of the Black Panthers.

Gonzales' views on working within the system were mixed. He vehemently denounced the establishment, calling on members to quit their city jobs to work for the Crusade. Simultaneously, he fully milked numerous private foundation and Great Society programs. Corky encouraged supporters to get jobs as VISTA volunteers whereby they were assigned to the Crusade. Others managed to work for the Crusade via funds provided by a Great Society program, Denver Education and Training Administration. Those getting such jobs were expected to kick back parts of their wages to the organization.

The group also had close connections with the governmentally funded *Servicios de la Raza*, stemming from Service Employment Redevelopment, another Great Society effort. *Servicios de la Raza* emerged as a source of funds, jobs, and power for the Crusade. Gonzales' daughter, Nita, eventually dominated it. Numerous politicians, church groups, and liberal-oriented charities donated to Corky's organization, seeing it as a powerful voice redressing the injustice done to Mexican-Americans. The organization never fully opened up its books to the members while it always claimed financial shortages.

The Crusade was more than Gonzales. As the Chicano movement surged, members of the organization went beyond their leader's often provincial interests, seeing the possibility of creating a new society. Tensions split the organization, resulting in numerous resignations and expulsions. Dissidents accused Corky of financial malfeasance.

## The West High Blowout

The Crusade visibly targeted Denver Public Schools. It decried them for shortchanging Chicano youths. Not only was there an extremely high dropout rate among Hispanics, but such students received little support or respect. The schools were more designed as indoctrination institutions to shape Mexican-Americans in the image of the WASP middle-class than temples of learning. Teachers and administrators were often prejudiced against struggling Latino students. Counselors readily suggested high school boys become cannon fodder, encouraging them to show their bravery by joining the Army and going to Vietnam. The organization insisted that as many young Chicanos were pushed out of the schools as simply dropped out.

Tensions were most intense at West High School. This building at 951 Elati Street was in the center of the city's historic West Side. Scandinavian, German, and East European immigrants once inhabited this working-class enclave. As they moved out, Chicanos and natives of Mexico moved in. By the late 1960s, about 34 percent of West's 1,900 students were Hispanic. They far overshadowed the 57 percent white and 9 percent black enrollment in dropout rates and lack of academic achievement. In 1968, West students scored in the 35th percentile in academic achievement contrasted to other high school pupils.

A spark set off an explosion at West in the spring of 1969. Chicano students who supported the Crusade claimed history teacher Harry B. Shafer had stated: "Mexicans are stupid because their parents were stupid and their parents' parents were stupid." The instructor supposedly deliberately mispronounced the names of Chicano students and traced their deficiency to eating too many beans. Shafer, who had been at West for 13 years, insisted he had never uttered the words attributed to him. What he had been discussing in a social issues class, he explained, was the relationship between family background and school success. His goal was to stimulate debate by raising controversial issues.

The climate was such it did not matter what Shafer's intentions were or what he had actually said. He was a symbol. Supporters of the Crusade insisted Shafer personified the racism of the schools. To do something about it, Gonzales forced school officials to meet with him, students, and members of the school board on February 28 about the teacher's comments. Nothing was accomplished. The administration ruled Shafer had done nothing wrong. Shafer's fellow teachers came to his support, arguing he should not have been tried before such a "kangaroo court." Corky's supporters demanded action. As much as anything, they wanted some symbolic gesture to atone for all of the racism and discrimination they had suffered at the hands of the schools in the past. There had been turbulent Chicano protests, "blowouts," against discriminatory schools in San Antonio and Los Angeles. The Crusade did not want Denver to lag.

Through the first half of March, talk of a protest filled the air. By March 19, 1969, it assumed specific form when a walkout was planned for the next day. With the assistance of the Crusade, militant students showed up at school early on March 20, leafleting their fellows about why they should walk out of classes. Fifteen minutes after the school day had begun, at 9:00 AM, students were asked to get up and leave the building. Those pushing the action invited Gonzales to speak to them outside of West.

Their appeal struck a chord. Many Chicano teenagers were well aware of the discrimination they faced. The Crusade appealed to how these adolescents feared and hated the *chotas* and the *jura*—the police. Many had grown up knowing the refrain, "*Me tratas como si fuera hijo de chota*," you treat me as if I were the son of a cop. Opposed to the stolid, conservative Spanish-American establishment, Gonzales and the Crusade offered these adolescents a dynamic opportunity to assert themselves. The youths did not see themselves simply fighting the police and administration; they were battling for liberty.

The walkout began slowly. Initially only a student or two left a classroom. Before long, three and four students were walking out at a time: it was the thing to do. Eventually upwards of 300 students milled in front of the school. Corky, other members of the Crusade, neighborhood activists, friends, and relatives joined the youths who had left West.

Shouting "walkout!" the crowd marched three blocks to the neighborhood junior high school, Baker, at West Sixth Avenue and Elati Street. Some of the students

**Author's Collection**

*West High School, at 951 Elati Street, was the scene of a clash between the police and protesting Chicano students in March 1969.*

Photo by Dave Buresh, CHS

*Corky Gonzales speaks in front of the old West Side Courthouse in 1980, a building establishment Latinos later converted into the Bernard Valdez Hispanic Heritage Center.*

there crawled out of windows to link up with the demonstration. The protesters marched back to West High. Leaders of the group addressed the crowd from its steps, using bullhorns.

The police sent in a 15-member Special Service Unit. Called the "SS" by the Crusade, members of the squad were in full riot gear. The police let the crowd know nobody had better try anything. Numerous other police officers, with helmets on and wielding riot sticks, quickly appeared as reinforcements. The police helicopter hovered overhead. Police Chief George Seaton was on the scene.

The authorities ordered the protesters to move across Elati Street to the Sunken Gardens, a park directly east of the high school. As the crowd began to drift to it, violence suddenly flared. Corky was in the middle of it. Police officer Dennis Dickman claimed Corky assaulted him as the protesters were crossing the road. The former prizefighter twice punched him in his face-visor. In response, Dickman decked the ex-boxer. Before long, five police officers were standing around Corky who was maced three times. The authorities arrested Gonzales, charging him with assault and battery, disturbance, and assaulting a police officer with a deadly weapon, i.e., his fist.

The result was a melee. Sticks and stones were thrown and punches were tossed. The police freely clubbed protesters and dragged young women by the hair. They used tear gas and mace on the crowd. One officer was hit in the head with a shoe. When he was knocked out, somebody made off with his helmet. Chief Seaton bemoaned the presence of numerous young mothers and children. This, he claimed, was a nefarious Crusade ploy to keep the police from using full force in dispersing the rioters. Additional clashes occurred around the school and the park the next day, March 21.

The police account proved extremely nebulous. This was seen when Gonzales came to trial in September. The first case against him ended in a mistrial. The second prosecution began on December 1, 1969. The district attorney relied almost exclusively on the testimony of the police. The different officers had vastly contrasting accounts. One admitted mace was used, another denied it. Two officers stated it was not until Corky was arrested that the crowd became unruly. Dickman's testimony was conflicting.

During a preliminary hearing, Dickman had insisted Gonzales had slugged him with a left-right combination. At the trial, however, he asserted Gonzales had thrown two rights. Dickman further insisted the police had not donned riot equipment until after they had arrested Corky. Yet, he admitted, he had a riot helmet on when Gonzales hit him in his visor.

The defense called reporters who had been present. Other civilian witnesses were called. Corky made a powerful witness in his own defense. The result was to raise severe doubts in the jurors' minds about exactly what had occurred. Consequently, after deliberating for one and a half hours after a four-day trial, the jury found Corky not guilty on all counts on December 4. Most of the charges against others arrested in the incident were eventually dismissed.

The 1969 riot set a pattern. No sooner did Corky and members of the Crusade protest a certain injustice than there was a massive police response. From the start, relations were taut between the Crusade and police. Almost from the time Gonzales' organization began operations, local and federal law enforcement agencies, including Army Intelligence, spied on it. Denver's finest viewed supporters of the Crusade as the usual suspects. They often stopped individuals coming out of the Crusade headquarters. Their actions implied simple association with the Crusade was a crime.

At the same time ruling Denver vented its wrath on Corky and the Crusade, the organization powerfully resonated among young Chicanos. They were impressed by Gonzales' courage in standing up to the establishment. At the time the call for "Black Power" swept young African-American militants, these adolescents rallied to the Crusade's demand for Chicano Power.

Many barrio kids signed on with the Crusade. The organization provided them with a political direction and idealism. (For every actual member of the Crusade, at least another ten youths claimed an affinity with it. Other Latino teenagers belonged to such national Chicano youth groups as the Brown Berets and Black

Berets. Both had only limited presences in Denver. Their activists overlapped with members of the Crusade.) Rather than affiliation with gangs and fighting one another, these adolescents found inspiration and a future through militant *Chicanismo*. In the process, the Crusade changed from mostly a middle-aged, working-class organization to a youth-oriented movement reflecting the values, hopes, and problems of insurgent Mexican-Americans.

## The St. Patrick's Day Massacre

Tensions simmered into the 1970s. They boiled over on Friday night-Saturday morning March 16–17, 1973. As was par for the course, the mostly youthful supporters of the Crusade hung around the building and the adjacent Downing Terrace that evening, many of them consuming alcohol. A birthday party was just winding down at the latter building around 12:35 AM when police officers Carole C. Hogue and Stephen Snyder pulled up and parked their squad car across the street from the apartment building.

Members of the Crusade were uncomfortable with the very presence of the police. The appearance of a squad car was not unusual. Peace officers were always prowling around the Crusade. Snyder and Hogue had passed by the building at least two times previously during the evening of March 16.

A teenage supporter of the Crusade, later only identified as Mascareñas, who had been attending the party, wanted to know what the snooping officers wanted. He approached Snyder to inquire the reason for the police presence. "We're tired of driving," was the patrolman's flippant reply. The youth supposedly responded

CHS

*The ruins of Downing Terrace in the wake of the confrontation at the Crusade for Justice on March 17, 1973.*

by asking: "Well, I want to know why are you sitting there? Are you answering a call for something?"

Others watched the encounter from the apartment building. They observed Snyder tell the reconnoitering youth he had jaywalked when he crossed the street to talk with the police. When the supporter of the Crusade failed to produce any identification, Snyder ordered him into the squad car. Mascareñas peacefully entered the vehicle. Other supporters of the Crusade were upset by what they perceived as the arrest of the jaywalker. To find out what was going on, five of them, led by 20-year-old Luis "Junior" Martinez, approached the squad car.

Martinez was a former member of the Brown Berets who lived at Downing Terrace. He was co-director of the Crusade's dance troupe, Ballet Chicano de Aztlan, and taught a class on dance at Escuela Tlatelolco. Born in San Cristobol, New Mexico, on August 21, 1952, Martinez had had bad encounters with the police in the past. On December 16, 1969, he and a fellow Brown Beret had left the Crusade apartment house around midnight to buy cigarettes at a local store. The police stopped the two young men on the street. The confrontation turned violent and the police beat the two youths. Rather than taking them, as minors, to Juvenile Hall, they were driven to the North Denver precinct station at 2195 Decatur Street. The authorities held them there for three days, not giving them any medical treatment or allowing them to get legal assistance—or so the Crusade claimed. Martinez, in turn, loved taunting the police. His colleagues appreciated Martinez's past triumphs in escaping and mocking the men and women in blue.

When Martinez and others approached the squad car, Snyder told them they had also jaywalked and should leave. Hearing the word "leave," Mascareñas bolted from the squad car. Snyder, seeking to pursue the fleeing jaywalker, threw open the car's door. It hit Martinez. The Chicano militant slammed the door back onto Snyder. The latter got out of the car and approached Martinez. The Chicano began backing away, saying, according to the police report, "Hey, man, leave me alone. I don't want no hassle." The two went through a parking lot and were alone in the alley.

It was 12:45 AM. Hogue, a black woman who had recently sued to gain membership on the police department and was still on rookie, probationary status, immediately grabbed her walkie-talkie and called for help as she got out of the car to assist Snyder in the chase. He turned around, telling her to get back into the car. Hogue again put in a call for emergency help. She simultaneously drove the police car into the parking lot where she had last seen Snyder pursuing Martinez. Observers heard gunshots and the sound of breaking glass.

Within minutes, numerous other squad cars were in front of the Crusade. The response was so immediate it appeared the reinforcements were waiting for the call. Hogue, unable to locate her partner, asked other officers if they had seen Snyder. They spotted him standing on the lawn of an apartment house across the street from Downing Terrace. Blood was pouring down his face. The policeman had been shot through the stomach, in the right leg, and in the face. Before being taken to the hospital, Snyder gave another officer a gun he claimed Martinez had used to shoot him.

The police found Martinez lying in a pool of blood on the lawn at 1550 Downing Street. Snyder had shot him in the right chest and the neck. The latter bullet had ripped an artery, killing Martinez. Powder burns were around the wound, showing Martinez had been shot at less than 18 inches from the gun muzzle.

The patrolman claimed Martinez had ambushed him in the alley, shooting him three times before he was able to pull his weapon and kill Martinez in self-defense. The gun Snyder claimed was Martinez's weapon, a .38 Smith & Wesson revolver, was stolen. The coroner found two .38 cartridges in Martinez's pockets. The autopsy showed the dead youth had been drinking heavily before the shooting.

Hogue noticed the side rearview mirror of the squad car was broken. It had possibly been hit by a bullet while she joined Snyder in the pursuit of Martinez. By this time, she was near where Snyder and Martinez had shot it out, away from the Crusade building. Before long, more than 200 officers, led by Police Chief Art Dill and District Attorney Dale Tooley, surrounded the Crusade property. All Latinos near the Crusade were considered suspects as the police freely used their clubs on people they thought were associated with Corky's organization. (Gonzales was not at the Crusade that night.)

During the next three hours the police systematically invaded all ten units of Downing Terrace. When the midnight visitors kicked in the door of 1547½ Downing Street, the apartment directly south of the old Baptist church, somebody cried there was a sniper inside. The police responded with a massive fusillade at the apartment, using pistols, rifles, and shotguns. The authorities fired upwards of a hundred shots. About this time, approximately 2:00 AM, a blast destroyed the entire second floor of the unit.

The police claimed the explosion was evidence Crusade supporters were making bombs. Some police officers, who had been climbing up the stairs to the second-floor unit, were injured when the detonation occurred. The Crusade insisted the police might well have tossed a grenade into the building.

To find out the cause of the blast, early the next morning Gonzales sought to bring in an independent investigator to examine the ruins of the building. The police denied the outsider access to the crime scene. Instead of studying the bombed-out apartment to determine the origins of the explosion, the authorities, with the assistance of city building inspectors and the fire department, ordered the immediate demolition of the damaged section of the building. To rub salt in the wounds, the contractor called in scabs for the job—his firm usually employed Hispanic workers who were then out on strike.

For almost a year, the Crusade left the exposed section of the building standing to remind one and all of the shootout. In addition to the death of Martinez, four Chicanos were shot, numerous others injured, and 36 arrested. Twelve police officers were hurt in the confrontation, including four of whom were wounded. The Crusade called the encounter the "St. Patrick's Day Massacre."

Not until 10:00 the following morning did the police finish their searches of the premises. The authorities reported they had found more than 100 guns in the apartment house, including an M-16. Eight of the guns were allegedly stolen. At least that was the initial statement.

**Photo by Phil Goodstein**

*A mural at the St. Charles Recreation Center, at 3777 Lafayette Street, recalls Luis "Junior" Martinez who was killed during the police-Chicano confrontation at the Crusade for Justice on March 17, 1973.*

The only evidence of an M-16 was a newspaper photo showing the police carrying such a weapon out of Downing Terrace. When the police specifically had to produce the weapons, they could only account for about 25 guns. Most were not in working condition and were actually stage props used by a Crusade theater group. The organization argued the police might have been the ones firing the M-16. The officers who had been shot, it further asserted, were most likely wounded by their fellow department members.

Police Chief Dill blamed "irresponsible individuals and militants" for the encounter. Despite much bluster, few of the police assertions stood up in court. It only took a jury 30 seconds to acquit one defendant, Ernesto Vigil, who was charged with shooting at Hogue. Mario Manuel Vasquez, who was found lying in the rubble of the exploded apartment at 1547½ Downing Street, was found guilty of three counts of first-degree assault, receiving three indeterminate-to-15 year sentences. He subsequently spent little time in prison.

The shootout got national publicity. The Crusade hailed Martinez as a martyr. Artists painted murals in his memory. Gonzales' organization observed March 17 as a date of remembrance for the murdered militant. Shortly after the confrontation with the police, the Crusade built a substantial masonry security fence around the church building and apartment house. The organization was blunt about the fence's role: it was to keep out the police.

The Crusade became a rallying point for people decrying police brutality. Its Denver Chicano Liberation Defense Committee raised funds to support those who had been arrested in the confrontation. The famed, black communist leader, Angela Davis, packed an auditorium at Loretto Heights College on April 28, 1973, delivering a flat, boring, bombastic speech for the defense. The Crusade received an excellent settlement from the city and insurance companies in the wake of the blast, giving the organization clear title to both the apartment house and the church.

Even while using the confrontation to bolster the cause and recruit new supporters, the St. Patrick's Day shootout adversely impacted the Crusade. Its violent bluster provoked further police hostilities. Many in the Chicano community increasingly turned away from the Crusade as a hopeless, suicidal organization. Activists who had once endorsed Corky's program and ran as candidates under the banner of La Raza Unida Party linked up with the Democrats. Increasingly, the Crusade became something of a closed circle. Outreach into the community waned. A new corps of activists failed to replace those who left the organization as the country regained its equilibrium in the post-Vietnam era.

## Corky's Critics

As Gonzales remained in the headlines, many Latinos despised him more than ever. They dismissed him as a grown-up juvenile delinquent who aided, encouraged, and abetted other juvenile delinquents. Such actions, they asserted, had naturally led to the St. Patrick's Day confrontation, an event in which some Spanish-Americans fully supported the police. Assorted Latino veterans made it a point of flaunting their patriotism, and dedication to the system.

Nor did all Chicano activists like Gonzales. Clashes were intense between different factions of the Mexican-American community in old West Denver. That neighborhood, bordered by approximately West Colfax Avenue, West Alameda Avenue, Broadway, and the Platte River, was predominantly Hispanic by the 1960s.

Photo by Phil Goodstein

*A mural along the wall of the Auraria Community Center at West 12th Avenue and Mariposa Street, a building which was the locus of disputes within the Hispanic community in the early 1970s.*

Housing projects dotted it, schools were inadequate and inferior, and urban renewal schemes were continually formulated to drive residents from it.

To fight back, locals formed the West Side Coalition in 1969, a group reflecting the larger Hispanic community. Chicano militants as well as advocates of working in the system belonged to the council. Though differing on the prescription, both groups agreed city hall continually targeted their community precisely because it was overwhelmingly Mexican-American. A foremost achievement, led by a young community worker, Rich Castro, was a successful drive to prevent the city from turning West 11th and West 12th avenues into one-way arterials in 1970. By this time, Castro allied himself with the Benavidez family.

Waldo Benavidez had been a colleague of Gonzales in Los Voluntarios. Opposing Corky's decision to break irreparably with the Democrats, Benavidez left the Crusade at an early date. For differing with Gonzales, Benavidez claimed he was viciously beaten by Corky's thugs.

By the time Castro was active, Benavidez's wife, Elizabeth "Betty," was chairwoman of the West Side Coalition. Serving as a district captain of the Democratic Party, in 1970 she ousted incumbent Paco Sanchez to become the first Hispanic woman to win election to the state House of Representatives. Waldo Benavidez simultaneously ran the Auraria Community Center at West 12th Avenue at Mariposa Street across the street from Lincoln Park, greenery Chicanos labeled La Alma Park.

The Denver Housing Authority, the city agency operating two nearby housing projects, provided money to open the center in 1966. The goal was to provide a meeting place for those dwelling in the projects. Also receiving War on Poverty and Model City funds, the center always suffered from financial problems and intense factional divisions. Simultaneously, DHA targeted much of the standing housing directly east of Lincoln Park. With the assistance of DURA, it hoped to raze a good deal of the neighborhood to add a couple more projects to West Denver. City policy seemed to want to segregate poor Chicanos from the rest of the city in the enclave.

Historic preservation activists stalemated the urban renewal scheme when they managed to get much of the area placed on the National Register of Historic Places in January 1975. This meant the city faced virtually insurmountable obstacles in getting federal funds to destroy the existing houses. Rich Castro was among those opposing the landmark effort.

Clashes were frequent between supporters of the Benavidezes and those of Escuela de Aztlan at 966 Santa Fe Drive. A private academy for junior high school dropouts, Escuela de Aztlan was generally aligned with the Crusade. The Benavidezes did not like its students, claiming the school's "asshole kids" caused trouble at the community center. The school sometimes sought to bill the community center for the academy's expenses. On Monday, July 2, 1973, three of its supporters sought to physically intimidate Waldo Benavidez when the center refused to pay $300 for a damaged display case at Escuela.

When the police failed to respond to Representative Benavidez's request for protection, she went to Escuela around 4:00 PM on July 2 where she was accused of

Author's Collection

*A Chicano contingent of an anti-war march at Colfax and Clarkson Street in 1971. Numerous members of a college group, the United Mexican American Students, participated in such protests.*

twice brandishing a weapon at the principal of the school, Lois Lujan. The latter was not sure where to turn for help. She feared it was hopeless to go to the police or the West Side Legal Aid Clinic because the Benavidezes had ties to both of them. With the help of volunteer lawyers in North Denver, Lujan swore out a complaint against Betty Benavidez who was arrested on Thursday, July 5. Shortly thereafter, Benavidez disappeared. For a few months, nobody knew where she was. The politician claimed she had to go into hiding on account of threats on her life.

The same evening on which Benavidez was arrested, Rich Castro was shot at West Tenth Avenue and Santa Fe Drive near Escuela de Aztlan. He had gotten out of his car and crossed the street, allegedly shouting at Chicano militants Florencio J. "Fast Freddie" Granado and Willie Montoya: "You fucked-up revolutionaries, you're sticking your nose where it doesn't belong."

Castro, according to Granado's supporters, thereupon started beating Fast Freddie. The latter allegedly shot Castro in self-defense. The wounds were minor whereby Castro was able to drive off and report the shooting at police headquarters. Later that night, supporters of the Benavidezes and Escuela clashed violently near the emergency room of Denver General Hospital. About seven weeks later, on August 27, 1973, the building housing Escuela was severely damaged by arson.

Granado's story was indicative of another side of the Chicano movement, the role of college activists. He had been a leader of the United Mexican American Students (UMAS) at the University of Colorado (CU) in Boulder. The organization stemmed from a Great Society effort, the Equal Opportunity Program (EOP).

A major goal of the War on Poverty was to reach out to the black and Chicano communities. By giving bright, but poor, youths an opportunity to go to college, supporters hoped to integrate them into the system. Estimates claim EOP helped as many as 95 percent of all Chicano students enter college.

To incorporate poor Mexican-Americans into mainstream society, EOP sought working-class Chicanos, offering them a chance at a university education. Among those it recruited were ex-cons, known as *pintos*, meaning "spotted" in Spanish. Idealists believed many of them were not really criminals, but misguided individuals who had not had proper chances to make it. Advocates of EOP argued the *pintos* deserved equal educational opportunity in view of their having been singled out for past punishment by racist school and judicial systems.

About the time the government and CU launched EOP in 1968, eight or nine students took the lead in forming a branch of UMAS to help coordinate the activities of Chicanos on the Boulder campus. (UMAS originated in Los Angeles in 1966. Eventually, most of the chapters became part of the *Movimiento Estudiantil Chicano de Aztlán*, the Chicano Student Movement of Aztlan [MEChA]).

Even as the Boulder UMAS held itself separate from the school and student government, the association received university and federal funding and occupied free office space at the college. Before long, it had hundreds of members. UMAS activists were involved in assorted protests, demanding the end of all vestiges of racism and discrimination. Foremost among them was Granado, a *pinto*.

Fast Freddie Granado was born in San Antonio, Texas, on January 17, 1942. After his father was killed in action during World War II, he grew up in a migrant farmworker's family. During his youth Granado helped harvest crops in Wisconsin, Minnesota, South Dakota, and Michigan as well as in Texas. For most of the year, his family lived in Brownsville, Texas. Granado frequently saw police abuse Chicanos and protect scabs in labor disputes. He got in trouble with the law at a young age, dropped out of school in the ninth grade, and was first incarcerated when he was 16.

Educating himself in prison, Granado eventually earned a GED. He came to Lamar, Colorado, in 1968. In the fall of 1969, at age 27, he entered CU as an EOP student. Joining the campus UMAS, the largest Chicano student organization in Colorado, he emerged as a leader. After serving one year as its third vice president, Granado was elected the group's head for the 1971–72 school year.

UMAS did not just limit itself to student issues. It heartily supported the efforts of migrant farmworkers to build the United Farm Workers. Members were active in the Migrant Action Program, an endeavor to assure better housing and working conditions for agricultural workers. Before long, Granado was an omnipresent principal in all Chicano battles.

His thanks was police harassment. Granado was arrested on numerous occasions. Nor did his personal behavior help. Like many young Chicanos, he was insistent on his machismo. He defined any slight as an ethnic slur demanding satisfaction. Granado's personal and political actions led the university to place him on probation for two years after he participated in a supposedly disruptive protest against legislators on campus.

By the fall of 1971, Granado was no longer in school. He remained active in both the Boulder and Denver Chicano communities, having close ties with the Crusade for Justice and Escuela de Aztlan. When the University of Colorado banned him from the campus, he responded by running as La Raza Unida's candidate for regent in 1972. Right about the time his trial for shooting Rich Castro was scheduled to come to court, Granado was blown up with two others in a car bombing in Boulder on Wednesday, May 29, 1974.

Two days before the blast, three other people linked to the Chicano movement were killed by a comparable explosion in the university city. The police immediately charged the victims had been manufacturing bombs. Supporters of the deceased asserted the Chicanos had been bombed. The cause of neither blast was ever determined. Militants commemorated the dead as martyrs, *los Seis de Boulder* (the Boulder Six).

The explosions came at a time when bombings were common. The police frequently accused radicals of planting bombs. Most of the devices attributed to Chicanos either caused minimal damage or were so badly constructed they did not go off. This hinted provocateurs might have planted them. In face of the revelations of Watergate and Richard Nixon's dirty tricks, some believed an elaborate police conspiracy aimed to discredit the Chicano movement by linking it to bombings. Those of this outlook had good reason for their beliefs as was illustrated by the case of Kiko Martinez.

## The Lawyer and the Letter Bomb

Authorities asserted Martinez was the perpetrator of bomb week. This was the label newspapers gave the stretch of October 25–31, 1973. Bomb after bomb was then discovered around Denver. The supposed bombs were planted in bars and restaurants and arrived in the mail. While the police reported finding ten bombs and receiving calls about 75 others, none of the devices exploded. Flaws in each of the bombs prevented them from performing as planned.

Three letter bombs were politically ominous. The first to receive one was Bob Crider, an anti-busing member of the Board of Education. On Saturday afternoon, October 27, the mailman delivered a large package envelope to Crider's home at 4932 Bryant Street. It had a return address of the Denver Classroom Teachers Association, the local teachers' union. Forty eight-cent stamps were on the package, far more postage than was necessary. Crider opened it, discovering it contained three sticks of dynamite, connected to a blasting cap with a five-second fuse powered by a nine-volt battery. The device did not explode.

The bomb squad dismantled the package. Its members concluded the battery did not have sufficient power to ignite the bomb. The police kept the wrapper from the dynamite and various parts of the bomb, including the mailer envelope, the typed label, the postmark, stamps, wires, and the battery. The police lab dusted them for fingerprints in the hope of discovering who sent the bomb.

A few hours after news of the Crider bomb was announced, at 6:50 PM, the post office called the police to the main station where workers had discovered a nearly identical mailer envelope. It was a comparable bomb, addressed to Carole C.

Photo by Phil Goodstein

*The police claimed radical Chicano attorney Kiko Martinez was Denver's mad bomber in October 1973.*

Hogue, the policewoman who was riding with Stephen Snyder when the confrontation between Snyder and the jaywalker led to the St. Patrick's Day blowout at the Crusade for Justice. The bomb listed the local branch of the American Civil Liberties Union on its return address. This was a few weeks before Ernesto Vigil was set for trial for shooting at Hogue during the St. Patrick's Day incident. The Hogue bomb was also defective.

Amidst this frenzy, on October 30, James Taylor, co-owner of the Two Wheelers Motorcycle Shop, at West 38th Avenue and Navajo Street, received a similar package with five sticks of dynamite. Taylor had protested the rowdiness of Chicano youths in the adjacent La Raza/Columbus Park. A Hispanic police dctective thereupon warned him to beware of unexpected packages. Like the Crider container, the box sent to Two Wheelers had far too much postage on it. After examining the envelope and calling the motorcycle supply company listed on the return address, which denied sending him anything, Taylor suspected the letter was a bomb. The authorities opened it, discovering five sticks of dynamite in a poorly constructed device. Defusing the bomb, the police saved most of the exterior packaging, battery, and the blasting cap.

By this time the city was in a bomb-scare frenzy. Numerous reports of bombs were phoned to the police. Among the alleged bombs were a Bible, a highway flare, and a picnic lunch. Making things worse, the police reported someone had twice intentionally loosened the lugs on its bomb disposal van.

Right before the discovery of the letter bombs, other bombs were found on the night of October 25–26 in bars and restaurants near Glendale. All the devices were discovered in women's purses. They were timed with cheap pocket watches the police traced to a nearby Target store. A salesclerk, Carol Fischer, remembered selling five such watches to a Hispanic man about two weeks earlier. She remembered him getting angry when she inquired why he needed so many watches. An art student, Fischer helped the police draw a sketch of the suspect. The authorities claimed the man in the picture was Francisco Eugenio "Kiko" Martinez. With this clue, the police examined the cardboard and paper from the dismantled letter bombs. A palmprint here and a fingerprint there matched those of Martinez. Robert Shaughnessy, the head of the bomb squad, announced the authorities had "irrefutable evidence" proving Martinez was the city's crazed bomber. (Fischer subsequently denied Martinez was the man who purchased the watches.)

Also known as "Franke" and generally referred to as "Kiko," Martinez was born to a well-established, long-settled Hispano family in Alamosa, Colorado, on November 26, 1946. A good student who was generally nonpolitical, after receiving his bachelor's degree from Adams State College in Alamosa in 1968, Martinez earned his law degree from the University of Minnesota in 1971. He had then come politically of age.

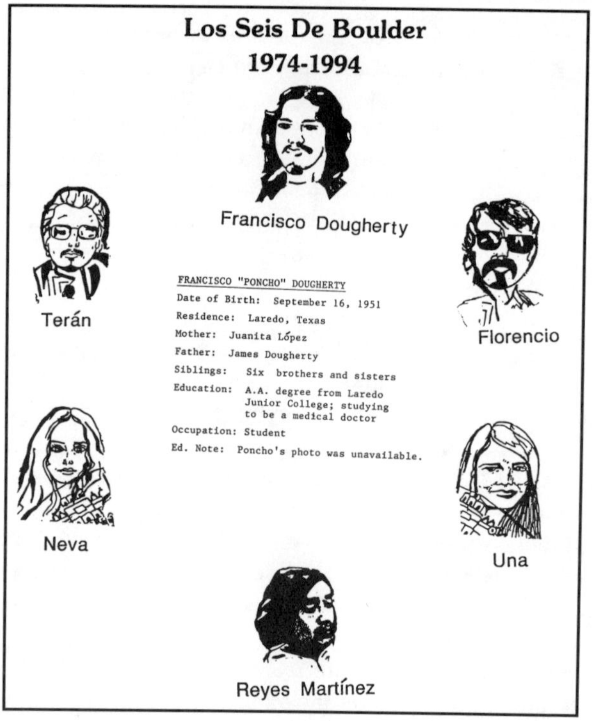


Courtesy George Archuleta

*A memorial to the six Chicanos killed in Boulder in May 1974 includes Reyes Martinez, the brother of Kiko Martinez, at the bottom. "Florencio" on the upper right was Fast Freddie Granado.*

While in law school, Martinez worked as a volunteer in the San Luis Valley for Colorado Rural Legal Services (CRLS), a Great Society program seeking to assure the poor, including Chicanos, did not lack legal representation. After gaining admission to the bar, Martinez returned to the job with CRLS. Headquartered in Boulder, he roamed the Centennial State, primarily helping his ethnic brothers and sisters in the San Luis Valley. Alamosa was always his true home. He wanted to make sure Chicanos had a fighting chance in the world. During this time, he emerged as a nationalist demanding a full recognition of his Mexican and Indian heritage.

Kiko was also in tune with the counterculture. He had long hair, a beard, and went around in bib overalls. He quickly became a visible member of the militant Chicano community. Word was out among activists that if they got in legal trouble, they should contact Martinez. He would do his best to help them. Associates fondly called him "*el abogado de Aztlán*," the attorney of Aztlan.

During 1972–73, Martinez was seemingly everywhere, representing Chicanos in trouble with the law. He frequently clashed with prosecutors and the police. He was arrested in Scottsbluff, Nebraska, in January 1973, for allegedly possessing an explosive device. This was just after a Scottsbluff junior high school was firebombed about the time a coalition of Chicanos and American Indians staged a rally in central Scottsbluff. The prosecution was forced to drop the charges after the defense proved the police had illegally searched Kiko's car.

Martinez had been out of Denver at the start of Bomb Week. Driving home with his wife and infant daughter on the afternoon of October 30, 1973, while listening to the radio, he found out he was targeted as the city's mad bomber. When he approached his residence at 4775 Vine Street, police officers were everywhere. Rather than approaching them, he left his wife and baby at his mother-in-law's house and ran.

The authorities intensified their search, posting a $3,000 reward for information leading to Martinez's arrest. Posters declared him "armed and dangerous." In a front-page special report, the *Denver Post* offered an additional $2,500 reward for the "secret witness" who would turn in Martinez. Despite this, the fugitive vanished from sight.

By 1974, rumors freely floated about Martinez. He was supposedly in Cuba. Another account claimed he was responsible for plotting the assassination of the police chief of Union City, California. Officials in Monte Vista, Colorado, accused him of participating in a barroom brawl. Other reports placed Kiko in El Paso or in a secret training camp for guerrillas in northern New Mexico. For some months, authorities staked out parts of the San Luis Valley looking for Martinez. More than 100 alleged sightings of Kiko were reported. None produced any leads.

In 1974, Kiko's foremost champion died, his younger brother, Reyes. Born on March 5, 1948, Reyes Martinez emulated Kiko. He followed his brother through law school and joined the Colorado bar. By 1973, Reyes was working for Colorado Rural Legal Services. After Kiko disappeared, the police continually harassed Reyes. One day, for example, after he had spoken to a rally in defense of his brother, the authorities spitefully arrested Reyes as being Kiko. When Reyes quickly proved his identity, the police charged him with illegal possession of marijuana, claiming to have found a strange-looking cigarette on him. They dismissed the charges after keeping him in jail overnight. Numerous other Chicano youths from Colorado to California reported police officers had stopped and hassled them on accusations they were Kiko Martinez.

The 26-year-old Reyes Martinez met his end on Monday, May 27, 1974. While in his car near Boulder's Chautauqua Park, an explosion ripped the vehicle apart, killing him, his girlfriend, Una Jaakola, and one other passenger, Neva Romero. This was two days before three other Chicanos, including Freddie Granado, were killed in another car bomb blast in Boulder.

As he remained out of sight, Kiko emerged as something of a folk hero among young Chicano militants. A tape-recording from Martinez and some of his poems and letters circulated among them. Activists viewed him as a refugee who was fighting for oppressed people everywhere. Slowly, however, consciousness of his case faded when Martinez was nowhere to be found.

On September 3, 1980, border guards stopped a man identifying himself as Jose Reynoso Diaz at the Mexico-United States crossing at Nogales, Arizona. Diaz was passing into the United States via a pedestrian bridge. Speaking fluent English, Diaz asserted he was an American citizen from Des Moines, Iowa, a worker at a John Deere plant who was returning home. The border guard searched Diaz's backpack, discovering a Mexican passport, a visa for Diaz to enter the United States, and papers showing Diaz had served in the Mexican Army. Suddenly, Diaz bolted from the border guard. He ran toward the United States rather than Mexico. The guard easily subdued him.

Authorities arrested Diaz, charging him with attempting illegally to enter the United States, a misdemeanor, and claiming false citizenship, a felony. Suddenly, pretending not to understand English and asserting he was an illiterate, Diaz signed an "X" to a form declaring himself a pauper when asked whether he needed a lawyer. The attorney quickly cut a deal for the defendant who pleaded guilty to the charge of attempting illegally to enter the United States in exchange for having the felony charge dropped. The judge sentenced Diaz to ten days in a federal detention center at Florence, Arizona, near the Mexican border. Deportation was to follow the completion of the term.

From the time of his arrest, border guards and immigration authorities were puzzled by Diaz. They found a journal, written in English, in Diaz's pack. It described a boyhood in Alamosa, Colorado. On the possibility somebody in Colorado might have information about Diaz, a photo of the suspect was given to an immigration officer about to attend a law enforcement conference in Denver. A member of the Colorado Bureau of Investigation identified Diaz as Martinez. Diaz's fingerprints were matched with those of Martinez. The police ordered him held in Arizona, pending his extradition to Colorado. This was only hours before prison authorities were to place Martinez on a bus carrying him back to Mexico.

On September 18, banner headlines cried "Colorado's number one fugitive is captured," reporting Martinez's arrest. The accused waived extradition proceedings. Federal District Court Judge Sherman Finesilver ordered him held on a $1 million bond. A bond reduction hearing was held on October 2. By this time, the Chief Judge of the Federal District Court of Colorado, Fred Winner, had assigned himself the case. He reduced the bond to $500,000. Supporters of the defendant established a Free Francisco E. "Kiko" Martinez Defense Committee, headquartered in Alamosa, to raise the bond and costs of the defense. Donors made their checks payable to the Clarence Darrow Fund. Relatives and friends put their property up for the bond. Out on bail, Martinez continued to push the cause of Chicano liberation.

Noting the massive, prejudicial publicity about the case in Denver, Judge Winner moved the trial to Pueblo. Martinez came to court on January 26, 1981. Prosecutors charged him with conspiracy, illegally possessing an explosive device, and mailing it to Policewoman Hogue with the intent to cause death or injury. Two more trials on the other bombing accusations were to immediately follow the first trial. In addition to federal counts, Denver District Attorney Dale Tooley sought to try Martinez on state charges of conspiracy and the bombings. Noted radical defense attorney Leonard Weinglass defended Martinez. Denver civil rights lawyer, Kenneth Padilla, joined Weinglass at the defense table.

The trial began just when American hostages had come home from Iran. Observing Pueblo hosting a parade to honor the return of one of them, Pueblo resident Marine Corporal Bill Gallegos, Judge Winner declared a two-hour recess to allow court personnel, the jury, and trial participants to welcome the military hero. The obvious intent was to contrast the soldier with Martinez, an anti-war protestor who was perceived as the antithesis of the former captive. The defense protested, asking for a mistrial. The judge denied the motion.

The trial was stormy from the beginning. Supporters of Kiko packed the courtroom, a place seating about 80 spectators. Interspersed among them were a dozen or so federal deputy marshals. Members of the FBI and undercover Pueblo police officers were also on duty in the courtroom. Security personnel subjected all entering the courthouse to searches.

After the jury was seated, Weinglass outlined the defense's view of the case. He made what Winner later deemed "one of the most masterful opening statements I had ever heard in my life." Thc judge was secretly angry the prosecution was not doing nearly as good of job as the defense.

During the second day of the trial, a couple of jurors made it known they were unhappy with the behavior of a few pro-Martinez spectators. They objected to members of the audience who wore "Free Kiko" T-shirts. The judge reported the jurors saw one or two spectators making motions of slitting their fingers across the neck. Other members of the audience were allegedly trying to stare down the jury. An artist with sketch pad visibly sat in the front row. Working for a Pueblo Chicano publication, *La Cucaracha*, he drew pictures of trial participants. Supposedly, he was attempting to catch the eye-movements of the jurors. One juror further protested the sunglasses of a law student who was temporarily sitting at the defense table. Winner replaced the two jurors complaining about these events with alternates. The jurist did nothing to impose a dress code on the audience or caution observers about their behavior.

Fearing the jury as a whole was hostile to Kiko, the defense repeatedly called for a mistrial. The judge rejected its motions. When the defense once more asked for a mistrial on the fourth day of the trial, Thursday, January 29, the prosecution specifically stated that it wished the trial to continue. Winner once more denied the request of Martinez's lawyers.

After court adjourned that day, without notifying the defense, the jurist ordered the two Assistant United States Attorneys trying the case, John Barksdale and Dan Christopher, three federal deputy marshals, the judge's secretary, the clerk of the court, two Denver police detectives who were witnesses at the trial, FBI agents, and others to meet with him in secret at the judge's hotel suite. There, exercising what Martinez subsequently called "the naked abuse of raw power," Winner hatched an elaborate plot to get the defense.

The trial, the judge lamented, was getting totally out of hand. He could see no outcome of the case except a mistrial. "You can have a mistrial anytime you want," he told the prosecutors. Winner, a former land-condemnation attorney for the Denver Urban Renewal Authority who had also worked as a First Amendment attorney for *Cervi's Journal*, stated he did not want to declare a mistrial just yet. He first wished to get some evidence on the audience. The jurist hoped to do so by planting a secret camera in the courtroom. It would capture on film the antics of supporters of Kiko who might be misbehaving or intimidating the jury.

Even more, Winner wanted to sound out the defense. He only planned to declare the mistrial after the defense had put on its case. The prosecution would so get a good idea of Martinez's strategy and tactics. As the meeting ended, the judge suggested he and the prosecutors might have some more secret meetings before the conclusion of the trial.

The judge's conduct bewildered the prosecutors. They knew Winner's actions were highly unethical. Unsure of what to do, they called in the United States Attorney for Colorado, Joe Dolan, who was closely following the trial. Upon consulting him, after some hesitation, on the afternoon of January 30, the prosecutors moved to support a previous defense request for a mistrial.

Their motion angered Winner. He called the attorneys into his chambers. "This comes as somewhat of a surprise to me," he declared in response to the government's move. He noted the defense had repeatedly called for a mistrial, but the prosecution had opposed all such suggestions. Defense attorney Weinglass was similarly not sure what to make of this. He wanted to know why the prosecution had suddenly changed its position. Had something happened?

Winner immediately responded. "I am unaware of it," he told the lawyer. The implication was nothing of substance had occurred since the recess of the court on the afternoon of January 29. To make sure the defense had a good chance to ponder the mistrial, Winner declared a recess. He knew if he improperly granted the mistrial, Martinez could not be tried again on the outstanding counts. If, however, Kiko consented to the mistrial, the prosecution could renew the charges.

When court reassembled, the defense endorsed the prosecution's request for a mistrial. Winner specifically asked Martinez if he agreed to it. Kiko said yes. Anytime the defense can force the government into a mistrial, he declared to his supporters, it is a victory for the defense. "This is a partial victory. The final victory will be ours," he concluded.

That evening, Winner hosted a party for the jurors. To advertise his disdain for the defense, he mocked it by wearing a "Free Kiko" T-shirt. Shortly thereafter, he recused himself from the case. The retrial was set for May 18. The jurist vented his wrath against the prosecution and the Department of Justice in a February 3, 1981, letter to Philip Weilens, the director of Federal Court Security of the Department of Justice. Winner protested how Washington had sabotaged his efforts to rig the case against the defense. The trial, he insisted, had brought together

> four terrorist groups which have never before acted jointly. Persons of national notoriety attended the trial, and it is evident that the defense is well financed. If there is an acquittal, efforts to intimidate future juries throughout the United States will accelerate. I believe that this case poses a real threat to our system of justice.

Therefore, a conviction of Martinez, by fair means or foul, was necessary. Through moving for the mistrial at the wrong time, the Assistant United States Attorneys undermined the judge's elaborate plans.

**Photo by Phil Goodstein**

*The United States Courthouse at 18th and Stout streets was heavily guarded, complete with barricades, during the Oklahoma City bombing trials in 1997. The building housed the bombing trial of Kiko Martinez in October-November 1982 after Chief Federal District Court Justice Fred Winner had sought to rig Martinez's first trial in Pueblo in January 1981.*

After excerpts of Winner's letter were printed on the front page of the *Denver Post* on April 4, something had to be done. The Tenth Circuit Court, overseeing the United States District Court of Colorado, appointed a federal judge from Oklahoma, Luther Eubanks, to look into the matter. He ruled the mistrial was improper whereby Kiko could not again be tried on the outstanding charges. Martinez, however, was to stand trial on the two other bombing counts.

The United States Attorney's office was not pleased with the compromise. It was chagrined when it lost its appeal. Meanwhile, the Denver Police Department admitted it had destroyed evidence that might have cleared Martinez of the charge of having sent a bomb to school board member Bob Crider. Given this, and the unethical actions of Judge Winner, the Denver district attorney's office dropped outstanding state charges against Kiko.

Martinez finally came to trial in October 1982, charged with sending the bomb to the Two Wheelers Motorcycle Shop. By this time, the case had achieved so much publicity that Chief Justice Warren Burger had intervened in it, naming a senior judge from Kansas, Frank Theis, to preside at the trial. The Department of Justice sent in two young, eager prosecutors from Chicago, supposed experts on terrorism, to try Kiko in Denver. Assisted by Kenneth Padilla, Walter Gerash, a veteran criminal defense and civil rights attorney, represented Martinez.

The prosecution proved a fingerprint of Kiko's left index finger was on the inside label of the box containing the bomb sent to the motorcycle shop. Nothing, though, specifically connected the print to the explosive device. It could have been an innocent touching, a print Martinez had left years before on the mailer envelope containing the bomb. Given the weak prosecution evidence, combined with defense educating the jury about Kiko's background and the actions of Judge Winner, the jury found Martinez not guilty.

This led the United States Attorney's office to try even harder. It planned to try Martinez for sending the bomb to Crider. A Colorado judge had previously ruled the destruction of evidence in the case meant Kiko could not be tried for the incident. Judge Theis agreed. On September 14, 1984, however, the Eighth Circuit Court of Appeals (sitting for the Tenth Circuit Court which had been besmirched by Judge Winner's actions), ruled the police's photographic evidence of the bomb could be used in a trial of Martinez on the Crider count. Shortly thereafter, Bob Shaughnessy, the former head of the Denver Police Department bomb squad and the only man who understood the mechanism of the bomb and the nature of the destroyed evidence, died. As a result, the United States Attorney was forced to drop the remaining bombing charge against Kiko.

The Department of Justice would not quit. In October 1986, it managed to convince a jury in Tucson that Martinez had committed perjury when he told a federal magistrate his name was Jose Reynoso Diaz after he was detained by the border guard at Nogales. The Colorado Bar Association followed the verdict by moving to disbar the Chicano attorney.

On January 28, 1988, a three-judge panel of the Ninth Circuit Court overturned the conviction. Using an alias, it declared, was not a material misrepresentation of facts, meaning the government had no case. Only when the United States Supreme Court refused to hear the prosecution's appeal was Kiko finally cleared of all charges. He was finally reinstated to the Colorado bar on April 6, 1989. Returning to Alamosa, Martinez resumed his role as a people's lawyer.

## Our Lady of Guadalupe Church

By the time the Martinez case played out, the Chicano movement had fractured. As much as any other group, Spanish-Americans were divided by class, personal background, religious devotion, political commitments, and personal jealousies. The Catholic church at the center of Hispanic Denver, Our Lady of Guadalupe at West 36th Avenue and Kalamath Street, reflected the community's diverse views.

During the 1920s, Hispanos started to move into parts of North Denver. This was the area northwest of the Platte River near downtown, a place literally on the wrong side of the railroad tracks. Irish and Italian immigrants had previously settled there, living mostly in simple duplexes, terraces, and small single-family houses. They worshiped at competing Catholic churches, St. Patrick's, at West 33rd Avenue and Pecos Street, and Mount Carmel, at West 36th Avenue and Navajo Street. Neither congregation wanted "the Spanish" attending it. Consequently, the Theatine Fathers, who had established St. Cajetan's parish in Auraria as a church for Hispanics in 1922, created a North Denver mission in a store at the northwest

Photo by Phil Goodstein

*Numerous Protestant, Spanish-language churches have popped up around Denver, challenging Catholics for the religious loyalty of the Hispanic population. Shown is such a congregation in the former Highland Christian Church at the northwest corner of West 34th Avenue and Bryant Street.*

corner of West 36th Avenue and Kalamath Street in 1936. The priests, members of an order focusing on Latin America, named the congregation for the patron saint of Mexico.

For some years, Our Lady of Guadalupe operated on a shoestring. Priests did little more than administer rites before returning to St. Cajetan's. There was little social idealism or activism in the congregation. It was not a defining center of Mexican-American Denver.

Nor did the Catholic Church have much outreach into the Latino community in other parts of Denver. Father Craig Hart, who was part Hispanic, was assigned to Annunciation Church, at 36th Avenue and Humboldt Street. He noted its extreme indifference to its many Mexican-American parishioners and social justice. During the late 1960s, Hart was the outspoken radical Chicano priest of Denver. He quickly found he could accomplish more by working with the Quaker American Friends Service Committee than the Denver Archdiocese. In the early 1970s, he left the priesthood and married.

As the Hispanic population grew from approximately 13 percent of old North Denver at the end of World War II to 60 percent in 1980, Our Lady of Guadalupe blossomed. It dedicated its Spanish mission-style church at 3565 Kalamath Street on August 12, 1948. As the remnants of Little Italy—the previous designation for the neighborhood—dissipated, this part of North Denver evolved into a barrio. The church was a traditional Catholic center, hosting bingo games, weddings, and baptisms. It had little ties with Chicano activists.

The civil rights movement forced the church to address social issues. Conservative members of the congregation were troubled when their sons and daughters joined the Crusade—the militant organization struck a chord with the youths which was missing in the traditional community. Exacerbating the problem was continual unrest between Mexican-American kids and the police at Columbus Park, a square block between West 38th and West 39th avenues from Navajo Street to Osage Street. Middle-class Italians had promoted it as an open space for their part of town. Contributing to the expansion and development of the land, the Italian community saw it named for Columbus in 1931, whom they venerated as a veritable Italian-American saint. Not believing an "Anglo" in the employ of the king and queen of Spain should be honored by the North Denver park in the heart of the barrio, Chicanos dubbed the ground La Raza Park in 1972—the park of the race.

A swimming pool had been a park amenity since the land was originally used as the North Denver public bathhouse in 1906. By the late 1960s, the city's scorn of neighborhood youths was obvious in the operation of the pool. The Department of Parks and Recreation, led by a longtime North Denver Italian-American, Joe Cianco, poorly maintained the pool. Broken glass lay nearby, and a rusty fence surrounded the water. Rather than keeping the pool open during summer evenings so local kids could literally cool off, the city closed it quite early in the day. When adolescents crawled over the fence, some neighbors complained. They also griped about the noise, alcoholism, and illicit sex in and around the park.

In response, the police frequently used crude, violent tactics with the youths in the open space. From the late 1960s into the early 1980s, there was almost an

Photo by Rob Prince

*Father Jose Lara*

annual police crackdown/riot in the park. Tensions over the swimming pool only disappeared in the mid-1980s when the Federico Peña administration filled in the swimming pool. City hall replaced it with an indoor pool at the nearby Aztlan Recreation Center at 4435 Navajo Street. Activists complained the new pool was neither as large as the old one nor the promised heated, year-round facility.

During the upheavals of the 1970s, Our Lady of Guadalupe was a central part of the Chicano mix. A new pastor, Jose Maria Lara, reoriented the church. A native of Navarra in the Spanish Basque country, he came to America as part of a Theatine mission. The order assigned him to St. Cajetan's. He arrived at Our Lady of Guadalupe in 1969. The priest learned plenty from the community.

Among his teachers were members of the United Farm Workers. The idealism of Cesar Chavez had spread to Colorado. Locals not only endorsed the grape boycott in California, but also sought to organize farmworkers throughout the Centennial State. Under Lara, Our Lady of Guadalupe became a center for the union. The parish also supported other Hispanic workers who sought to organize and improve their wages and working conditions.

The church hosted numerous political meetings. It fostered ethnic pride and heritage by hosting Mexican music and dance classes. Young Chicano artists decorated the buildings with murals in the tradition of Diego Rivera.

Lara frequently dealt with the police. At times, he served as a mediator between Chicano teenagers and the authorities. Some officers were very thankful for the priest's calming presence. At other times, the police denounced him as an irresponsible troublemaker. Nor was Lara popular among all North Denver Spanish-Americans. Some conservative, well-established, middle-class residents and parishioners viewed him as an outsider who cared nothing for the traditions, customs, and tranquility of the neighborhood.

The priest clashed with the Archdiocese. Lara mockingly called Archbishop James Casey a member of the PGA—the priests' golfing association. The native of Spain observed how the church leader was far more at home on the links and at country clubs than he was in protesting injustice or dealing with the poor. Using the Archdiocese and Casey as examples, Lara declared the "institutional church is the enemy of Christ" and "bishops never die, they just get fat and chummy with the rulers of the world."

Believing Our Lady of Guadalupe was possibly the center of a criminal conspiracy, the police planted informers at the church. On Monday, March 22, 1976, one told her handler at the FBI that the sanctuary was actually a bomb factory. The FBI shared this information with the police. The latter contacted the Archdiocese on Tuesday, March 23. The Vicar of Pastoral Personnel, Leo Horrigan, acting for

Archbishop Casey, signed a waiver permitting the police to search the church. He did not inform Lara of this action.

The police assembled a 30-plus-member Special Command Action Team, surrounding Our Lady of Guadalupe at 9:00 that evening. With backups from federal agencies, the authorities were sure they were about to come across a cache of grenades, dynamite, and other explosives. Parishioners, seeing the police swarming about the church, informed Lara, who had just sat down to dinner. He rushed to the sanctuary where he refused to grant entry to the police. They shoved him aside, picked the lock to the front door, and invaded the church. The authorities handcuffed Lara to the sacristy as they swept through Our Lady of Guadalupe, assisted by bomb-sniffing dogs. Far from discovering any explosives, the police found old piñatas and pinto beans from a church food bank. Their informant had fabricated her story—or so the law enforcement officials explained.

In the wake of the fiasco, Archbishop Casey apologized to the church, raising it from mission to parish status on Easter 1976. Lara left Our Lady of Guadalupe in 1979 to study psychology at St. Elizabeth's Hospital in Washington, D.C. He quit the priesthood a year later, returning to the Mile High City. The ex-cleric married in 1982, going to work as a North Denver Realtor. In 1993, Lara concluded America was hopelessly corrupt when he publicly announced he was returning with his family to Spain.

Marshall Gourley led the parish during much of the 1980s and 1990s. Born a Methodist in Iowa, his father was a ranking Air Force officer who taught at the Air Force Academy in the 1960s. The callous militarism of the community at the peak of the Vietnam War upset Gourley. Attracted by the social activism and idealism of liberal Catholics, he converted, learned Spanish, and eventually emerged as the clerical leader of the North Denver Hispanic community

The Archdiocese removed Gourley in 1997 after he was accused of sexually molesting a Harvard-educated former member of the parish. The courts dismissed suits against Gourley and the Archdiocese. Nonetheless, the hierarchy did not reinstate Gourley at Our Lady of Guadalupe. All the while, numerous leftist groups met at the church. President Daniel Ortega of Nicaragua spoke there in the mid-1980s during a visit to the Mile High City. As the Chicano movement faded, the church increasingly reverted to its traditional role.

Even so, Our Lady of Guadalupe retained a social conscience and commitment. Illustrative was its Clinica Tepeyac. A 1992 parish survey showed many of its worshippers were undocumented aliens badly in need of health care. Such individuals, cowed by the Immigration and Naturalization Service and a wave of immigrant bashing, were afraid to go to a city-run system of health clinics. The nearby La Casa de Salute Health Station, at West 36th Avenue and Pecos Street, served North Denver. The city built it in 1973 as part of an innovative program to provide health care to poor individuals, keeping them out of the emergency room of Denver General Hospital. The name was a combination of Italian and Spanish, noting the mixed heritage and nature of the neighborhood. Our Lady of Guadalupe opened its clinic next to its parish house in April 1995 for those who feared the repercussions of seeking treatment at the city facility.

Photo by John Schoenwalter

*Reverend Marshall Gourley, an Anglo, led the Hispanic Our Lady of Guadalupe Church through most of the 1980s and 1990s.*

## Chicano Politicians

Among those unhappy with Lara and the Chicano activists at Our Lady of Guadalupe in the early 1970s was North Denver city councilman Eugene "Geno" DiManna. A former star athlete at Cathedral High School and a onetime minor league baseball player in the Chicago Cubs organization, DiManna had grown up around Denargo Market. After unsuccessfully running for council in 1967, he eyed an open seat in 1971.

In 1968, voters authorized the expansion of city council from nine to 13 members, beginning in 1971. Two of the seats were for members at large. The others were carved into districts representing the different sections of the city. A prime reason for the increase in council membership was to allow more ethnic and racial representation. A successful lawsuit by the advocates of the politics of recognition (electing individuals based on race and ethnicity to show how the system is able to incorporate specific groups) forced the city to readjust council borders. A city official who was also a leader of the Park Hill Action Committee, Bill Bradley, helped draw the borders of the new districts. He and many others favored gerrymandering the districts to assure at least one or two blacks and one or two Hispanics would always serve on council.

In addition to District Eight, which centered in Five Points and had been represented by a black since 1955, District Eleven was created to focus on Park Hill and Montbello. Given the demographics and politics of those areas, a black, Bill Roberts, easily won election from it.

District Three, encompassing Barnum and much of poor, southwest Denver, was viewed as a Mexican-American constituency. Those pushing for ethnic candidates were angry when a Republican businessman, J. Ivan Rosenberg, the publisher of *Southwest Denver Herald-Dispatch*, won the post in 1971, 3,875–3,339, over challenger Manuel "Sam" Sandos. It was supposed to be a Chicano seat. Rosenberg, through his publishing company, later got control of a Hispanic weekly, *La Voz*, well after Sandos displaced him from council in 1975.

Born on June 16, 1927, Sandos was the son of a Greek coal miner and a Hispanic mother. When he was 14, lying about his age, he dropped out of school and joined the Army. Throughout the rest of his life, he was always proud of his service as a paratrooper during World War II.

In the 1960s, Sandos assisted Mayor Currigan on youth affairs, working to establish more youth and health centers in poorer sections of town. He simultaneously was a consultant for the Commission on Community Relations. Bill McNichols endorsed Sandos when the latter ran unsuccessfully for council in 1971. After his defeat, Sandos often fought city hall as a neighborhood activist. On council, he valiantly, but unsuccessfully, fought for a warrant of habitability for renters. He died shortly after leaving council in 1987. By this time, District Three was considered a safe Chicano seat.

Sandos' son, Tim, served as a councilman at large from 1991 until 1995, firmly supporting 17th Street's development agenda. In 1996, he ran for the Democratic nomination for Congress. The candidate expressed dismay when he discovered some feminists considered that, given Pat Schroeder's longtime tenure in Congress, the Denver congressional seat should always remain in the hands of a woman. After losing the primary to Diana DeGette, Sandos worked as a lobbyist for US West.

**Author's Collection**

*The Chicano liberation movement fought to recall North Denver city councilman Geno DiManna between 1972 and 1975.*

Despite Tim Sandos' lament that gender should not be a consideration in who was returned to office, many Chicanos were sure ethnicity was paramount in determining for whom to vote. This came out in the returns in District Nine in 1971. The constituency, encompassing North Denver, was seemingly an improvement on the old district, one splitting the neighborhood along 26th to 34th avenues. The old council district had included land to the north of the roads, snaking around the

Platte River and central business district, from Federal Boulevard to Stapleton Airport.

In the wake of the expansion of council and the redrawing of borders, District Nine took an extremely odd shape, including most of Hispanic North Denver. The new seat stretched from Globeville at 52nd Avenue and Washington Street on the north to South Broadway near Alameda Avenue on the south. It included a large chunk of West Denver. All the neighborhoods in District Nine had considerable Hispanic populations.

Incumbent Ernest Marranzino was from an Italian-Argentine family. He vehemently opposed the gerrymandering. It was, he noted, an effort to enact "legislative segregation." Marranzino, whose father had also served on council, was so disgusted by the result that he did not seek reelection from the new district. His effort to win a post as councilman at large in 1971 was unsuccessful. Chicanos were sure they would put one of their own on council from District Nine that year.

Eight candidates sought the post, including an aspiring Latino politician, Paul Sandoval, who later represented the neighborhood in the state Senate from 1975 until 1982. DiManna won a runoff against Father Peter Garcia, pastor of St. Cajetan's Church, 4,339–4,104, in June. The latter was backed by Hispanics while the former played to old North Denver, demagogically stressing his Italian heritage.

The victor was the last of a dying breed of North Denver Italians. A bar and liquor store owner, DiManna ran Pic's Corner Tavern at West 32nd Avenue and Vallejo Street. The saloon was damaged when someone tossed a hand grenade through a window on May 12, 1972. In the wake of this, the councilman received a police guard at his house at 2345 West 32nd Avenue. He advocated a tough law-and-order approach to the protests of rowdy Chicano youths and encouraged police crackdowns at La Raza Park. Physical confrontations ensued between DiManna and Lara. The latter accused the councilman of beating him.

Time and again, Chicano activists railed DiManna was not representing them or District Nine. Not only was he not a Hispanic, but he had no concern for the poor of the neighborhood. They were angry when he opposed a plan to down zone the West Side near Speer Boulevard and West 14th Avenue. Exponents of the measure noted its primary intent was to prevent an anti-poor, anti-residential, anti-quality of living urban renewal program which would displace many low-income Hispanics. DiManna supported the Denver Urban Renewal Authority against the neighborhood in the controversy.

Beginning in 1972, Chicano militants, including people affiliated with Our Lady of Guadalupe, worked to recall the councilman. DiManna was able to stave off this effort until near the end of his term in February 1975. He felt vindicated when he won the recall election, 2,990–2,420, against challenger Sal Carpio. Using the momentum of the recall, Carpio defeated DiManna for city council by 4,971–4,124 in a June 1975 runoff following an inconclusive primary in May.

Carpio was a leading Latino politician. During the early 1970s, he was active in La Raza Unida, running as its candidate for Congress in 1970 when he got 3.2 percent of the vote. By 1975, he had linked up with Chicanos taking control of the

North Denver Democratic Party. The city councilman was typical of the new generation of North Denver. He understood the Italian dimension of the neighborhood, having attended the Italian-American Mount Carmel High School.

(Members of Italian and Hispanic families sometimes intermarried. By the time Carpio won election, various North Denver residents projected themselves as Italian or Hispanic depending on circumstances. Their integration permeated neighborhood institutions. An Italian pastor, for instance, led St. Patrick's Church by the 1940s. Before long, the congregation included many Mexican-American parishioners. In 1988, the Archdiocese converted St. Patrick's into a mission for an order of Mexican nuns.)

On city council, Carpio was a sharp critic of Mayor McNichols and the city establishment. Time and again, he questioned their priorities and social policies. Growth, he observed, was not benefiting his constituents. The Chicano councilman acutely pointed to the special-interest deals whereby city hall worked hand-in-glove with the corporate community against the citizenry. The North Denver representative led council as its president during 1978–79.

Carpio was unopposed for reelection in 1979 and continued to lead the charge against the mayor. He developed an excellent command of federal urban assistance programs. The councilman became a master of funneling city and federal moneys into District Nine. By the early 1980s, he pondered running for mayor, but did not believe the time was ripe. After he was again returned to council in 1983, Carpio was not able to adjust to the new, pro-business administration of Federico Peña. His service on council became slack as he operated a restaurant, Papa Rox at West 36th Avenue and Tejon Street, in partnership with Paul Sandoval.

Formerly known as Carbone's, Carpio named Papa Rox for a longtime North Denver baker, community leader, and city council member, Roxie Carbone, an Italian immigrant who had been something of a political father to Carpio. The city councilman bought the bar from Roxie Carbone's son, Rich. After Carpio lost the bar and suffered from bouts of alcoholism, the former North Denver city council activist served as director of the Denver Housing Authority during the 1990s and 2000s. Under him, the city agency loudly made social engineering a foremost goal in destroying and designing housing projects.

Debbie Ortega succeeded Carpio on council. A former assistant of the pioneer Chicano politician, she openly played the race card during her 1987 campaign. She readily asserted that her leading opponent, the former wife of Paul Sandoval, Mary Helen Sandoval, was not a true Latina, but had only married into the race. "It's in the blood" was supposedly a slogan Ortega used to win the election. On council, the Latina readily allied herself with those insisting on a dandelion police to spruce up sections of her overwhelmingly poor district.

## The Fate of the Crusade

By the time there were safe Hispanic seats on city council and various Mexican-Americans held leading city posts in the 1980s, the Chicano movement had virtually vanished as a dynamic, independent, radical force. Part of the reason was its very success. It had brought out the institutional racism and discrimination of the system. The establishment responded with affirmative action programs and other efforts designed to reach out and recruit promising members of the community. The election of Peña in 1983 was a sign of this. Though his politics were fully in tune with those of the banking-real estate-growth-development industry, Peña, the son of an affluent Texas cottonbroker, projected himself as a poor Hispanic who was making good. Many Chicanos went out of their way to vote for him. They saw his triumph as their common victory. The mainstream media loudly echoed this stance.

In the wake of Peña's election, Corky and the Crusade became virtually invisible. (Gonzales supported Peña for mayor.) As the Texan took charge at city hall, activities virtually ceased at the Crusade building. Corky abandoned it in the mid-1980s. Escuela Tlatelolco relocated to North Denver. When Gonzales announced he was going to sell the old church to the post office, which planned to level it, only a few dedicated militants and preservationists protested this plan. Arson destroyed the hall on June 16, 1988. By this time, Corky was in poor physical shape, badly injured in a car accident in October 1987.

Corky's daughter, Nita Gonzales, claimed the rite of succession. While she received a great deal of ink from the establishment press and support from newspapers and leading liberal politicians, her campaigns to win election as the Chi-

Photo by Phil Goodstein

*In the 1990s, Escuela Tlatelolco obtained the school building of St. Dominic's Church at 2949 Federal Boulevard, turning it into Centro de Tlatelolco.*

cano candidate to the school board were unsuccessful in 1991 and 1993. Her backers lamented the poor turnout in Hispanic neighborhoods. They insisted Chicanos should have flocked to the polls to elect the only Latina on the ballot. Cynics scoffed, noting Mexican-Americans had not voted for Nita Gonzales precisely because she was Corky's daughter and was widely hated in the community. Only members of the Gonzales family were on the board of the Crusade. Virtually no new outside blood had flown into the organization since the late 1970s.

Former members and supporters of the Crusade charged Corky had run the organization as a family enterprise. Questions were left unanswered about the group's finances. Juan Haro, who had been vice chairman of the Crusade between 1968 and 1976 and La Raza Unida's candidate for mayor in 1971, charged the Gonzales family reeked with "corruption, intimidation, and hypocrisy."

Haro, the owner of a small, neighborhood filling station, incidentally, was the only member of the Crusade ever convicted of a serious, politically charged felony. Authorities arrested him in September 1975, accusing him of plotting to bomb police stations while the convention of the International Association of Chiefs of Police met in Denver. The activist was stopped during the convention while riding in the car of Joseph Cordova Jr. The authorities found hand grenades in Cordova's vehicle.

Cordova had a long criminal record. Out on the streets, the police used him to stage burglaries so they could catch other crooks in action. Not only did the police whitewash Cordova's misdoings, but they gave him more than $10,000 to snoop on the Crusade. It was quite possible Cordova or the police had planted the grenades in order to get Haro. The Crusade leader was acquitted on state charges, but was found guilty of federal charges of illegal possession of explosives. He served 20 months in Leavenworth Federal Penitentiary.

In the late 1990s, Haro emerged as a severe critic of Gonzales and the Crusade. He argued Corky was not what he seemed. Far from a principled, militant opponent of the status quo, Haro insisted that Gonzales, virtually from the beginning, as early as 1946, was actually a police snoop. The former vice chairman of the Crusade contended Gonzales had used the movement's funds for his own high living. Far from pushing for justice in the greater community, the organization was the "Crusade for Just Us." Instead of specifically refuting Haro's accusations, the Gonzales family targeted the publisher of Haro's memoirs, *The Ultimate Betrayal*. Treating the founder of the Crusade as a veritable saint, the Gonzales family got the publisher to ban Haro's book through threats of a libel suit.

After the demise of the 16th and Downing headquarters of the Crusade, Escuela Tlatelolco acquired the former school of St. Dominic's Catholic Church at 2949 Federal Boulevard in the mid-1990s. It openly worked with Denver Public Schools, providing programs for Hispano youths. Receiving immense public funds, Escuela Tlatelolco functioned as an alternative high school, mostly catering to Chicanos who had dropped out of the public schools or did not fit in. The academy claimed a 97-percent graduation rate with most of its students going on to college. Some came out of the Crusade academy parroting a veritable mythology about Corky Gonzales.

During the heyday of the Crusade, youthful supporters frequently simply called Corky "*el jefe*," the chief. Gonzales did nothing to dissuade their use of the term or the adulation of his personage. In a sense, *el jefe* was the appropriate title. In many ways, Gonzales fit into the pattern of dynamic, supposedly revolutionary Latin American insurgents who sought power against venal establishments. No sooner had they succeeded than they were *el caudillo*, the leader. Before long, their new regimes were very much like the old ones while nepotism, corruption, and favoritism were their hallmarks. Parallels are obvious with the rise and fall of the Crusade.

## The Bernard Valdez Hispanic Heritage Center

By the 21st century, numerous programs and organizations existed to celebrate Hispanic heritage. Rather than remaining a revolutionary, nationalistic event, Cinco de Mayo emerged as a commercial festival, sponsored by beer companies and media outlets. The Chicano Humanities and Arts Council emphasized the colorful spirit of the Mexican-American contribution to the arts.

Su Teatro was an innovative effort at community theater. Presenting socially conscious dramas, it emphasized it was "your theater" and could only flourish with the direct involvement of the everyday individuals. Initially performing street theater and to crowds at Columbus Park, it obtained the former Elyria School on the 4700 block of High Street as its home in 1989. Politically charged messages,

Photo by Phil Goodstein

*Santa Fe Theatre, also known as Aztlan Theatre, at the corner of West Tenth Avenue and Santa Fe Drive, is along a strip in West Denver which the city has pushed as a Hispanic cultural-business center.*

including mocking establishment Hispanics and the sterility of the Denver Center for the Performing Arts, remained central to its performances.

The city sponsored many efforts to nourish the Hispanic business community. Generous grants were poured into the sector along Santa Fe Drive between Sixth and Colfax avenues. The Hispanic Chamber of Commerce moved into the nearby Peña Business Plaza at 930 West Seventh Avenue in 1990, a building it obtained with financial assistance from US West and Norwest Banks. The Chamber's leaders had holdings along this strip of Santa Fe, an area including the quarters of a Spanish-language radio station and Museo de las Americas, a museum at 861 Santa Fe Drive focusing on Latin American art and history. Efforts to operate a Spanish-language movie theater in an old neighborhood cinema at West Tenth Avenue and Santa Fe Drive, Santa Fe Theatre—also known as Aztlan Theatre—never worked ideally.

In the 1990s, the northern section of the Santa Fe strip was engulfed in controversy over establishing the Bernard Valdez Hispanic Heritage Center in the West Side Courthouse at the southwest corner of West Colfax Avenue and Speer Boulevard. This structure, dedicated on May 15, 1922, was once the center of the Denver criminal courts. A justice facility had been at the corner since 1874. Nearby, linked to the imposing two-story erection by a tunnel, was the Denver County Jail at West 14th Avenue and Kalamath Street. The courthouse included dormitory rooms to house sequestered jurors.

The criminal courts left the West Side Courthouse for the City and County Building in 1952. The traffic court exited the West Side Courthouse in 1958. For a couple of years, the judicial building was the administrative offices of the Denver Fire Department. The Denver District Attorney's office made the West Side Courthouse its home until November 1984. Hollywood briefly rented the structure for Perry Mason television movies. Otherwise, the courthouse was boarded up with transients and pigeons occupying the 27,000-square foot edifice. (The city demolished the old jail after it opened a new facility at Havana Street and Smith Road in March 1956.)

Numerous proposals were suggested for the former justice center. One was to turn it into a community theater. Another was to transform it into a bus terminal. A third called for making it into condominiums. The last suggestion verged on reality in 1992–93 when investors offered $410,000 for the building. They promised to invest $2.2 million in renovating it as residences.

Just before the deal was set to close, Councilwoman Ramona Martinez intervened. She had succeeded Sam Sandos as the representative from District Three in 1987, and was seeking the Democratic nomination for the United States Senate for 1996. Martinez wanted the city to sell the courthouse to National Image, a Hispanic advocacy group mostly composed of people who worked for the federal government.

Established in Denver in 1973, National Image quickly turned its back on the Mile High City for Washington, D.C. After having its headquarters in the capital for 22 years, it returned to Denver six months before it hoped to make the West Side Courthouse its permanent home. Not only would National Image have its offices in the former courthouse, but it would also provide space for other Hispanic groups. The former justice center would simultaneously house a museum honoring Latinos, host community meetings, and provide display areas for Hispanic art. National Image promised to turn the courthouse into both the physical and cultural heart of Latino Denver. In this manner, the Mile High City would emulate comparable Hispanic cultural centers in San Antonio and Albuquerque.

Not all were happy with the proposal. Such community-based Latino arts groups as Su Teatro, the Chicano Humanities and Arts Council, and Museo de las Americas, noted National Image had no real roots in the Denver activist community; on the contrary, it was a largely conservative, outside outfit. By having the city pour money into National Image's new home, they feared they would receive less funds.

Those questioning the Valdez Center noted how Martinez cynically exploited racial and ethnic issues in pushing the facility. The mid-1990s saw the opening of the Five Points Media Center at 29th and Welton streets in the heart of black Denver. Though it was the home of a community radio station, KUVO, that played Latin music, Martinez implied Hispanics needed a facility of their own to balance the African-American Five Points studio. In particular, the Colorado Hispanic Media Association wished to get space at the Valdez Center. Judy Montero, a legislative aide of Councilwoman Ortega, headed the organization. Ortega collaborated with Martinez in the courthouse project. Controversy raged over the center both within and outside the Hispanic community.

Those questioning the Valdez Center noted some of its Anglo business sponsors. Coors was in the forefront of promising money for the effort. For decades, Chicanos decried the brewery, charging it discriminated against them. Hurting

Photo by Phil Goodstein

*Establishment Latinos got a special deal with the city in the 1990s to turn the abandoned West Side Court House, at West Colfax Avenue and Speer Boulevard, into the Bernard Valdez Hispanic Heritage Center.*

Photo by Phil Goodstein

*A bust of Bernie Valdez is in the Valdez-Perry branch of the Denver Public Library at 47th Avenue and Vine Street.*

under a national boycott for its vicious anti-union policies in the 1970s and 1980s, the beer company changed its line. It heavily courted middle-class Hispanics, advertising in local Latino publications. The brewery even went into southern and southwestern Colorado to recruit Hispanos as scabs. The company required such employees to disavow any association with Corky Gonzales, the Crusade for Justice, or the militant Chicano movement. Coors promised at least $400,000 to help make the cultural center come alive. The money from Coors was enough to guarantee the opposition of many Chicanos to the effort.

Martinez's intervention killed the effort to transform the courthouse into condos. Though National Image had a green light to move ahead, the effort stalled. For some years, neither the money nor interest existed to establish the complex. The city councilwoman's campaign for the Senate similarly went nowhere. By 1997, the building was in worse shape than ever. Other members of council again called for selling the structure at its fair market value. Based on sales of comparable real estate in the vicinity, they estimated it was worth anywhere from $1 million to $2.4 million. The corporate and politically well-connected leaders of

National Image insisted on buying it for the 1993 price, agreeing to pay only $410,001 for it. More delays ensued.

Among those pushing the center was Alvarado Construction. Robert and Linda Alvarado, the proprietors of the firm, were close to the Peña administration and had received numerous city contracts. The Alvarados developed strip shopping areas near West Colfax Avenue and Kalamath Street adjacent to the West Side Courthouse. They also owned numerous Taco Bell and Pizza Hut franchises and had a share of the Colorado Rockies baseball team. Linda Alvarado headed the Hispanic Chamber of Commerce.

In May 1997, Alvarado Construction announced it was forging a partnership with National Image to make the Valdez Center a reality. Coors renewed its commitment to the project. On this basis, on April 10, 1998, after receiving $400,000 from Coors, plus a $200,000 donation from Linda and Robert Alvarado, the purchase was finally consummated. An additional $3 million was needed to renovate the building. US West poured around $500,000 into the project. AT&T added $300,000 more, money Mile Hi Cablevision, its predecessor in running the Denver cable franchise, had once set aside for a special local Hispanic entrepreneurial cable channel. By 2000, sponsors hoped to finish the renovation by the end of the year. The Hispanic Chamber of Commerce, a group formed in 1978, agreed to move to the center, giving it the proceeds from the sale of its Peña Plaza.

The Valdez Center honored a longtime community figure. Born on a farm near Cleveland, New Mexico, in the northern portion of that state in 1912, Bernard "Bernie" Valdez dropped out of school at an early age. He came with his family to Colorado in 1926, working as a migrant farm laborer in the sugar-beet fields. After his father died, the family settled in Limon in 1928 where he began an eight-year effort to put himself through high school. Along the way, he signed on with the Civilian Conservation Corps in 1933, earning his high school diploma in Fort Collins in 1936.

Valdez moved to Denver about this time, helping run a cooperative grocery store. He was also worked to build the Congress of Industrial Organizations. Simultaneously, he attended the forerunner of Colorado State University, receiving his bachelor's degree in sociology in 1939.

After getting out of college, Valdez returned to New Mexico for a few years, working in a cooperative health program. He permanently settled in the Mile High City in 1948. Active in many governmental studies and efforts to redress poverty, discrimination, and unemployment within the Hispanic community, Valdez worked for city, state, and federal agencies. Foremost of his goals was providing for off-season employment of and housing for migrants.

In 1949, Valdez helped launch the Latin American Educational Foundation, an organization providing college scholarships for Mexican-American youths, especially those from Denver. He was a moving force in establishing the Latin American Research and Service Agency (LARASA) in 1964. It was a research/policy analysis organization for the Hispanic community. (Eventually, LARASA and the Latin American Educational Foundation emerged as preferred establishment charities, complete with glittering high-society banquets.) Through the 1950s, 1960s, and 1970s, Valdez was omnipresent in virtually all efforts dealing with the state's Hispanics. Radical critics saw him as a token Latino on numerous government bodies.

The activist worked for DHA for 14 years. Many of its projects, Valdez observed, primarily housed poor Chicanos. People living in them needed more and better recreation programs and opportunities. He readily admitted some DHA efforts were poorly designed and only herded the poor together.

Mayor Tom Currigan named Valdez manager of welfare in 1963. The New Mexico native held the post for 16 years as the job evolved into the manager of social services. During the 1960s, Valdez prominently served on committees probing discrimination in Denver Public Schools. Appointed to the board of education in June 1972, and elected to the post the next year, Valdez opposed busing since he did not believe forced desegregation improved the schools or the lot of Hispanic children. About the time he was running for the job in May 1973, his house was bombed. He was not injured and there was little damage.

**Photo by Phil Goodstein**

*Anti-militarists have mocked the statue of Hispanic war hero Joe P. Martinez in the Capitol Park as "G. I. Jose."*

The community worker frequently clashed with Corky Gonzales and members of the Crusade. On a couple of occasions, members of the Crusade assaulted Valdez, branding him a sellout. He argued the Crusade was not really interested in civil rights, but in the personal advancement of its leader and members.

After his retirement in 1979, Valdez was frequently consulted as an elder statesman of the Hispanic community. Numerous awards were bestowed upon him. A bust memorialized him in the Valdez-Perry branch of the Denver Public Library at 47th Avenue and Vine Street, which opened on March 18, 1996. It honored both him and the family that had given the land for the library. Valdez died in November 1997, praised by ruling Denver as a Hispano who had made good.

## Promoting Militarism

Opposed to the library ideal—celebrating knowledge, books, and self-education—the conservative and establishment Latino community have often encouraged militarism. Strong, patriotic Hispanic veterans organizations exist. They are usually at one with other branches of the American Legion and Veterans of Foreign Wars in fully supporting American interventions around the globe.

Typical of the promotion of Hispanic militarism was how Denver Public Schools renamed Ashland Elementary School, at West 29th Avenue and Bryant Street, Jose Valdez School, in 1974, when a new building opened to the east of the historic North Denver school. Observing the academy had a high percentage of Mexican-heritage students, the school board wanted it named for a Hispano. Far from selecting a social dreamer, activist, author, or educator, it tabbed the first Mexican-American—a New Mexico resident—who had won the Congressional Medal of Honor as the eponym for the institution.

The first Coloradan to receive the Medal of Honor was another Hispanic, 22-year-old Joe P. Martinez of Ault, who was killed in May 1943 while attacking part of the Japanese-held Aleutian Islands. The city commemorated him in the 1960s when it designated a small park near West Ninth Avenue and Quitman Street in the memory of the World War II soldier. This was not enough as ruling Colorado consciously sought to promote Latino patriotism. The state saluted the Ault native with a statue by Emanuel Martinez (a former Crusade activist), unveiled in the State Capitol Park near Colfax and Broadway in July 1988. Ramona Martinez actively pushed it with the support of Coors. (There was no relation between any of the Martinezes.) The sculpture looks like a larger than life GI Joe doll, slinging a carbine. Cynics branded it "GI Jose."

The statue did not fit in with the bulk of Denver memorials. Previous monuments honored idealists and poets such as Robert Burns and Martin Luther King or were abstract portrayals of pioneer women, miners, and trappers. Nor did critics believe it was an appropriate statement of Hispanic heritage.

Leaders of the middle-class Latino community had originally suggested a *charro* for the statue. This proposal outraged those knowledgeable about Mexican history. The *charro*, the heavily dressed-up, ceremonial Mexican cowboy, was the symbol of reaction in late 19th- and early 20th-century Mexico. Men wearing fancy outfits and sombreros serenaded the dictatorship of Porfirio Diaz. The *charros* simultaneously were the champions of the *rurales*, the brutal constabulary which viciously suppressed peasant rebellions. In a word, the *charros* were an embodiment of everything wrong with pre-revolutionary Mexico. Far better than such a statue, those opposing the *charro* insisted, would be a sculpture of a nameless, stooped farmworker as an accurate image of the Hispanic contribution to Colorado. (In 1999, the Colorado Historical Society included a touched-up 1906 photo of three sugar beet workers from Mexico standing in the fields near Holly in preference to a *charro* on a mural portraying the state's past outside the Colorado History Museum at 13th Avenue and Broadway.)

The Anglo establishment saluted the GI Jose monument. Colorado politicians made it clear the piece extolled militarism, not Chicano heroism. This came out a few years after the dedication of the Martinez statue. The politicians overseeing the greenery then vetoed another sculpture by Emanuel Martinez for the Capitol Park because it was "too Hispanic." In this case, the monument sought to portray a brave Mexican-American fireman, joined by black, white, and women firefighters, saving people's lives. Opposed to this, by literally placing GI Jose on a pedestal, ruling Colorado essentially told Hispanics that only by giving their lives to the Army could they gain recognition by serving the system.

Some other Hispanic heroes were also dubious role models. Among them was Casimiro Barela, the *patrón* of much of southeastern Colorado in the late 19th and early 20th centuries. Born in Embudo, New Mexico, on March 4, 1847, he received a Jesuit education. Driving a team of oxen from Mora, New Mexico, he arrived in Las Animas County in 1867. Before long, Barela was part and parcel of the local Democratic Party establishment with ties to the Santa Fe Ring. The latter referred to an unscrupulous set of New Mexico businessmen, land speculators, and interlopers who controlled much of the Southwest.

Based on his political and social connections, Barela quickly emerged as the financial, political, and social leader of the 19th-century Latino community. He served as a broker for the labor of poor Mexican and Spanish-Americans, holding some in veritable peonage and leasing others to mine- and ranch-owners. The prominent Hispano reaped a fortune in cattle ranching, real estate, railroads, and trade. Eventually, he possessed a huge plantation in Brazil. His name shows up in numerous ventures around Trinidad.

Most of all, Barela was a powerful politician. After serving as assessor, justice of the peace, and sheriff for Las Animas County, he won election to the territorial legislature in 1871. In 1875–76, he was a member of the Colorado constitutional convention. Upon statehood, Barela entered the state Senate. His contributions were noted shortly after the turn of the century when a stained-glass panel was installed in the rotunda of the Capitol honoring him as one of Colorado's 16 most worthy pioneers. By this time, having won election after election, Barela was called "the perpetual senator."

The window was dedicated at a time when Barela faced massive opposition. Union activists denounced him as a man who served the corporate establishment, shamefully exploiting his people and all workers. In the early 20th century, Barela openly came down on the side of management during turbulent strikes. To affirm

Photo by Phil Goodstein

*A stained-glass window in the rotunda of the Capitol recalls reactionary Hispano state Senator Casimiro Barela.*

he was at one with the conservative mine-owning elite, he switched his affiliation from the Democrats to the Republicans on June 11, 1904.

Unions and liberal Democrats targeted Barela for defeat in the 1904 election. With charges of massive fraud, corruption, and dirty dealing surrounding him, the Republican Senate majority deemed Barela the victor in the race despite returns showing him trailing Democratic challenger Michael Beshoar 5,143–4,585. In the most controversial election in Colorado—one witnessing the packing of the state Supreme Court and three different governors in one day—the Republicans modified the results of the Senate election to declare Barela the winner by a 4,816–4,609 margin. Among the Perpetual Senator's fervent supporters and financial backers were the Denver & Rio Grande Railroad, the Colorado & Southern Railroad, Rocky Mountain Fuel Company, Colorado Fuel & Iron, and American Smelting and Refining Company. This demonstrated he was essentially the candidate and representative of big business.

Barela continued to ride high in the Senate. Newspapers frequently praised him. He was the Mexican consul for Colorado in the declining years of the venal Porfirio Diaz dictatorship. As such, he helped mineowners bring Mexican scabs into Colorado during labor disputes. The perpetual senator once more won a controversial election in 1908. Hearings in the wake of his triumph showed a long, corrupt trail of money. The New Mexico native had an easier triumph in 1912. Four years later, in 1916, the opposition finally defeated Barela. He died on December 18, 1920, from pneumonia, having recently returned from Mexico City where he had been Governor Oliver Shoup's personal representative to the inauguration of Mexican President Alvaro Obregon. Barela left an estate of $750,000, making him among the wealthiest men in southern Colorado.

The perpetual senator's reactionary role was ignored as he was elevated into a Hispano role-model in the 1980s. Typical was the way Richard Thomas "Rich" Castro commemorated him. After recovering from his gunshot wounds, at age 28, the community activist succeeded Betty Benavidez in the state legislature in 1974. He served until 1984 when he joined the Federico Peña administration as the director of the Agency on Human Rights and Community Relations. (Castro had worked as a consultant for its forerunner, the Commission on Community Relations from 1975 until 1980.) The Latino politician was widely mourned when he suddenly died of a brain hemorrhage at age 44 in April 1991. The city named both an elementary school and social services center in his memory.

While in the General Assembly, Castro argued that a legislative redistricting in 1981 should provide for the widest number of Hispanic districts possible, i.e., Latinos should primarily vote based on ethnicity rather than class. At the time of his death, he was working on a project commemorating Mexican-Americans in the legislature. The politician praised Barela. He recalled frequently going up to the picture of the perpetual senator in the rotunda of the Capitol to draw inspiration when he was faced with hard choices during his years in the legislature. The message: rather than following in the footsteps of the many Mexican-American workers who struck for better wages and working conditions against the companies Barela represented, young Latinos should work within the establishment and follow the pro-business path of Barela.

This image was reinforced by the way daily newspapers and television stations reported about Hispanics—they frequently favored the term Latino by the 1990s/2000s. Far from branding such individuals part of an inferior or criminal element, the media went out of their way to praise them. Many Mexican-Americans held prominent public offices. Others succeeded as businesspeople. Ruling Denver stressed their triumphs.

By 1999, the manager of safety, Fidel "Butch" Montoya, fire chief, Richard Gonzales, and police chief, Tom Sanchez, were all Latinos. Despite the large number of Hispanics serving on public safety bodies, complaints about police brutality against Chicanos remained frequent. For a few years in the mid-1990s, cruising on Federal Boulevard during Cinco de Mayo celebrations almost turned into annual riots between the police and Mexican-American youths. Community monitoring of the cruisers and police helped bring this under control. Meanwhile, some Chicanos were more frightened by Spanish-surnamed policemen than Anglo officers. One Hispanic cop, Kenny Chavez, was notorious for his frequent involvement in shooting incidents. Many in the Latino community, in turn, were embarrassed by the Chicano teenage delinquents as a disgrace to their people. They wanted the police to deal most firmly with them.

## Continuing Divisions

The diverse views on the police reflected the continuing divisions within Mexican-American Denver. The success of some did not hide the immense class divisions remaining between affluent, middle-class citizens and poor, working-class Hispanos. While a good deal of mingling and intermarriage occurred, tensions

Photo by Phil Goodstein

*The mural in front of the Colorado History Museum, at 13th Avenue and Broadway, includes three agricultural workers from Mexico, center, standing in sugar-beet fields near Holly, Colorado, in 1906—the state's tribute to the role of Hispanos in building Colorado.*

existed between Denver natives and immigrants from Mexico. A few old-line Hispanos in the San Luis Valley hated anyone who had come to the region in recent years. They continued to refer to themselves as Spanish-Americans.

Side by side of Hispanos who had been in Colorado for nearly 150 years, an immigrant community was ever more visible in the course of the 1980s, 1990s, and 2000s. There were commercial sections in North Denver along West 32nd Avenue east of Clay Street and Tejon Street north of West 32nd Avenue where Spanish was the first language. Mexican nationals frequently worked as roofers and in other poorly paying, physically demanding jobs. Jests about the immigration service and the Mexicans were frequent both within and without the Chicano community. In addition to migrants from Mexico, Spanish-speaking Denver increasingly included individuals from Central America.

Spanish-language radio stations came and went, including one featuring Denver Bronco games. Television channels broadcasting in Spanish also took to the airwaves. Different Hispanic newspapers popped up, some of which flaunted their Spanish language reportage and Latino ownership.

There were frequent clashes between Hispanics and members of other ethnic groups. Tensions soared in the late 1970s when Vietnamese refugees began to settle in housing projects near Lincoln Park. As a distinctive Vietnamese community emerged along South Federal Boulevard, in an area with a large number of Latinos, members of the two groups feuded.

Strong rivalries existed between blacks and Mexican-Americans. During the late 1960s and early 1970s, there was something of a competition between them to see who could get the biggest share of Great Society programs and public services. The African-American community claimed the East Side—generally defined as old East Denver near Five Points—as a black section despite the presence of a heavy Hispanic population in the adjacent Curtis Park neighborhood. Those who believed the establishment consciously employed a divide-and-conquer strategy cited the way Hispanics and African-Americans fought as evidence supporting their views.

No such nefarious conspiracy existed. The keynote was class. Many in both groups only protested the discrimination against them, not a system built on exploitation. They readily made it known they were for sale and could be bought. A prime purpose of many social programs, affirmative action efforts, and cultural centers was to incorporate these people into the system. Given the success of both Wellington Webb and Federico Peña as ethnic mayors and the general social peace in Denver by the turn of the millennium, it is obvious the ideologues of recognizing middle-class blacks and Latinos succeeded well in making black and Hispanic leaders part of the system. Precisely out of the conflicts of the African-American and Chicano communities in the 1970s came a new political machine shaping modern Denver, an instrument forged by Federico Peña.

## A Note on Sources:

First of all, I wish to thank George Archuleta for his assistance on this chapter. Not only did he read different drafts of it, but he arranged for me to meet with some of the key personalities in the Chicano community, including Bernie Valdez, Kiko Martinez, and Juan Haro. He further called my attention to sources and checked my Spanish. Archuleta noted the problematic character of the *charro* as a symbol for the Mexican-American community and the history of Cinco de Mayo.

A solid history of the Hispanic presence in Colorado is needed. Assorted volumes have appeared, but a serious overview awaits publication. Evelio Echevarria and Jose Otero, eds., *Hispanic Colorado: Four Centuries of History and Heritage* (Fort Collins: Centennial Publications, 1976), is extremely uneven and often superficial. Robert N. McLean and Charles A. Thomson, *Spanish and Mexican in Colorado* (New York: Board of National Missions of the Presbyterian Church, 1924), is condescending. *The Spanish-Speaking Population of Denver* (Denver: Denver Unity Council, 1946), is a sociological survey prepared by the National Opinion Research Center of the University of Denver. *The Spanish-American Population of Denver* (Denver: Denver Area Welfare Council, 1950), surveys the poverty of the community. The best portrait of Spanish-American Denver in the early 1950s is Bill Barrett's novel, *The Shadows of the Images* (Garden City, NY: Doubleday, 1953). Steve Leonard and Vincent C. de Baca have put together an unpublished "Hispanic Bibliography of Colorado," (Denver: Metropolitan State College History Department, n.d.)

Vincent C. de Baca, ed., *La Gente: Hispano History and Life in Colorado* (Denver: CHS, 1998), fails to present a comprehensive overview. Many of the contributions to the volume are more genealogical musings than serious studies on such topics as Hispanic coal miners or the nature of migratory agricultural workers. Far and away the most comprehensive look at the latter is Carey McWilliams, *Ill Fares the Land* (Boston: Little, Brown, 1942). The Farmworker Data Network of the Colorado Migrant Council issued the *Farmworker Journal* in the 1970s. Also see C. E. Hazard, *North of 66* (n.p.: brochure by the Farm Security Administration of the Department of Agriculture, n.d.); and the materials on migrant laborers in the Colorado Council of Churches papers at the Auraria Archives. The University of Colorado School of Nursing also issued papers on "Spanish-Speaking People of the Southwest," in the 1960s for students in its visiting nurse service. Copies are in the Denver War on Poverty collection at the Auraria Archives.

A general overview of the modern Chicano movement is F. Arturo Rosales, *Chicano* (Houston: Arte Publico Press, 1996). Also see Matt S. Meier and Feliciano Ribera, *Mexican Americans/American Mexicans: From Conquistadores to Chicanos* (New York: Hill and Wang, 1993). L. H. Gann and Peter J. Duignan, *The Hispanics in the United States* (Boulder: Westview Press, 1986), is a conservative look at the ethnic movement. An overview of LULAC is Benjamin Marquez, *LULAC: The Evolution of a Mexican American Political Organization* (Austin: University of Texas Press, 1993).

A portrait of Governor Ed Johnson and the "bum blockade" is in Stephen J. Leonard, *Trials and Tribulations*. James M. Fresques' widow, Winona, and his son, John, recalled the man's political career and shared his scrapbook with me. Bernard Valdez made himself available for an interview shortly before his death. A good profile of Valdez is in the April 4, 1976, *DP*, p. 20. Papers by Valdez on Spanish-Americans in Colorado are in the Denver War on Poverty collection at the Auraria Archives. (Valdez was the initial chairman of Denver Opportunity, the body coordinating the local War on Poverty. DPL has the Denver Opportunity papers.) CHS has the nomination form for the West Side Historic District.

The public library also has clipping files on Valdez, Fresques, Lino Lopez, Paco Sanchez and other notable Hispanics. Lopez pushed a fluffy brochure celebrating leading middle-class Latinos of the 1950s by Harold Ellithropre and Charles Mendoza, *Colorado Latin-American Personalities* (Denver: Colorado Anti-Discrimination Commission, 1959). *Montoya* v. *Colorado*, 345 P.2d 1062, is the November 1959 Colorado Supreme Court decision mandating the inclusion of the Spanish-surnamed in jury pools.

Numerous Hispanic newspapers have appeared. Most have been in English. Even those with Spanish titles are usually in English or bilingual. *El Imparcial* appeared in the early 1930s. *Latin American News* came out in 1939. *The Clarion*, also known as *Colorado Clarion* and *Clarin de Colorado*, voiced the views of Spanish Colorado in the late 1940s/early 1950s. Daniel Valdes edited *La Luz* in the early 1970s, a pro-establishment magazine geared to Spanish-American professionals.

*La Voz* is typical of modern Denver, primarily geared to the middle-class Latino community. It has occasionally printed articles of social criticism. Other publications that have come and gone in recent years include *Viva*, *Papel del Bar-*

*rio*, *HOLA Colorado*, *El Hispano*, and *La Semana en Colorado*. The last was distributed in places as a supplement to the *Denver Post*. The *Rocky Mountain News* published *Las Noticias* in the early 1990s. Other Denver and Colorado Hispanic-oriented newspapers in the modern era have included *El Hispano*, *Antena: Spanish News*, *El Heraldo de Colorado*, *El Reportero*, *El Tiempo*, and *El Sol*. A look at the various Chicano publications in the late 1990s was Gayle Worland, "Guerra de los Periódicos," *WW*, July 22, 1999, p. 16.

*Montelibre Monthly*, a newspaper with a noted pro-Cuban, pro-Soviet slant, had a bilingual format when it started publishing in May 1988, heavily focusing on international news of Spanish-speaking countries. It subsequently came primarily to publish in English. *El Camino de Justicia* (in English) was the publication of CRLS beginning in 1970. *¡Ahora!* was the United Farm Workers Organizing Committee's strike bulletin in Center, Colorado, in 1970. *Comercio* was the newsletter of the Hispanic Chamber of Commerce. *Un Nuevo Día* was the magazine of the Chicano Education Project.

Materials on the politics of West Denver in the 1970s are found in *Santa Fe Trail: Westside News* and *West Side Recorder*. The latter was the monthly publication of the West Side Improvement Association, a neighborhood group preceding the West Side Coalition. News on the neighborhood in the 1950s is found in the *West Side Hustler*.

A look at Chicano-police relations in the early 1970s is R. J. Hernandez & Associates, *Chicano Report on Chicano Community-Police Relations* (Denver: R. J. Hernandez & Associates, 1971). Surveys of the Hispanic community in the 1980s are two monographs issued by LARASA, *A Demographic Profile of Denver's Hispanic Population* (Denver: LARASA, 1985); and *Hispanics in Denver County* (Denver: LARASA, 1986). Revealing on the middle-class aspirations of Latinos is the brochure financed by US West, *Hispanic Agenda: 1990 and Beyond* (Denver: LARASA, 1987).

The foremost work on the Crusade for Justice is Juan Haro, *The Ultimate Betrayal* (Pittsburgh: Dorrance Publishing, 1998). Written by a former vice-chairman of the Crusade who was eventually purged from the organization, it is extremely critical. In addition to discussing his own involvement in the organization, Haro included interviews with numerous other ex-members in the volume. All share the plaint that Corky Gonzales ran the Crusade more as a religious cult with him as the glorious, well-paid leader than as a civil rights organization. Haro discussed his views with me in an interview in February 1999. He reviewed a draft of this chapter.

Another former Crusade activist, Ernesto Vigil, looks at the organization and Gonzales from a much different perspective in *The Crusade for Justice: The Chicano Movement in Denver* (Madison: University of Wisconsin Press, 1999). The volume accepts Gonzales as a radical nationalist, readily quoting FBI reports about him and noting his head-on attacks against the political establishment. Often tedious and boring, taking numerous detours into such topics as the operations of the Los Angeles Police Department or the dealings of the FBI at Wounded Knee, the book has glaring gaps about the debates surrounding the Crusade. Celebrating the organization's romantic nationalism, Vigil's tone is frequently that of a juvenile rebel boasting of his comrades' stunts against the police while exalting the successes and violence of the defense squad of the Crusade. (Haro claims Vigil was among Gonzales' enforcers.)

Before the publication of his book, Vigil briefly talked about his involvement in the St. Patrick's Day Massacre. My comments on the Angela Davis speech come from attending it. I reviewed the Haro and Vigil volumes in the September 1999 *Naysayer*. Vigil responded with a vehement personal attack in a letter. In January 2000, he gave me a detailed chronology of the fate of Mario Manuel Vasquez, who was convicted of first-degree assault in the St. Patrick's Day confrontation. Vigil claimed the police turned Vasquez into an informer in the wake of the explosion.

Moses Valdez led the fight to save the Crusade building against Gonzales. He told me many stories about the place in the mid-1980s when he served as its caretaker after the organization abandoned the 16th and Downing complex. Valdez died of a heart attack in 1987 while trying to get the former church declared a landmark. His death came immediately after Valdez had an angry, threatening confrontation with Corky about preserving the structure. This was shortly before Gonzales was badly injured in a car accident. Valdez's widow, Beth, informed me of the circumstances of his death.

Critical portraits of Gonzales and his role in the national Chicano movement and La Raza Unida are in Mario T. Garcia, *Memories of Chicano History: The Life and Narrative of Bert Corona* (Berkeley and Los Angeles: University of California Press, 1994); and Jose Angel Gutierrez, *The Making of a Chicano Militant* (Madison: University of Wisconsin Press, 1998).

The West High incident is mentioned in Haro, *Ultimate Betrayal*; and Vigil, *Crusade for Justice*. It is also briefly noted in Gene Vervalin, *West Denver: The Story of an American High School*.

Walter Gerash allowed me to examine some of his files relating to Chicano rights cases of the 1960s, 1970s, and 1980s, including those of Fast Freddie Granado and Kiko Martinez. Richard Spriggs, who prosecuted Martinez in Denver, also briefly spoke about the case. Numerous legal decisions were published on it, including *United States* v. *Martinez*, 681 F.2d 1248; *United States* v. *Martinez*, 667 F.2d 886; *United States* v. *Martinez*, 744 F.2d 76; *Martinez* v. *Winner*, 548 FSupp 278; *Martinez* v. *Winner*, 778 F.2d 424 and 553; *Martinez* v. *United States*, 785 F.2d 663; and *Martinez* v. *United States*, 837 F.2d 900.

Martinez has given his papers to the University of New Mexico as part of its Grassroots Activism Project. He spoke of his career and the Chicano movement in a special oral history interview at Metropolitan State College on January 26, 2000. The activist reviewed a draft of this chapter. Vince de Baca also gave me his very critical review of the text.

There is a good deal about cases concerning Hispanics in the Samuel Menin papers at the Auraria Archives. The students at Metropolitan State College Chicano Studies Department are building a Chicano oral history file. The MSCD chapter of MEChA has a rich clipping file on the Chicano movement.

"UMAS Speaks" is a mimeographed set of statements of members of the organization in the late 1960s. A copy is in the Auraria Archives. The President's papers at the CU Archives at Norlin Library include an extensive file on the origins and controversies of the EOP and UMAS on campus. *Los Seis de Boulder*, is an English-language booklet commemorating the six people killed in Boulder bomb blasts in 1974.

Noel, *Colorado Catholicism*, examines the Spanish influence on the church. The volume includes uncritical portraits of St. Cajetan's and Our Lady of Guadalupe. I discuss Auraria in volume one, including the fate of St. Cajetan's. *My Seamy Side of Denver* looks at the police raid at Our Lady of Guadalupe. Information on the origins of La Casa de Salute and the health center system is in the Abraham Kauvar papers at the DU Archives.

Materials on the redistricting of city council are in the Doris Banks papers at the Auraria Archives. Kelly, *Old Gray Mayors*, discusses the move. Jerry Kopel recalled the gerrymandering process. Bill Bradley noted his role in the process at a forum on the history of Park Hill in 1988. Materials on the redistricting are also in the Minoru Yasui papers at Auraria. Sal Carpio briefly talked about his role and the North Denver political fights in sporadic conversations with the author in the mid-1980s. Mike Davenport observed the race-baiting in the 1987 District Nine election. Bill Good noted his fights with Debbie Ortega over the dandelion police. Peter Boyles, "Running on Empty," *Denver Magazine*, June 1981, pp. 26–31, is a look at Denver's Hispanic gangs.

DPL has a collection on Su Teatro. Its director, Tony Garcia, frequently speaks about the group's heritage at its various performances. Michelle Dally Johnson, "Trials and Tribulations," *WW*, March 14, 1996, pp. 15–21, is a look at the politics behind the Bernard Valdez Heritage Center. Councilman Ed Thomas allowed me to examine his file on it. Also see, T. R. Witcher, "The Revolution will not be Televised," *WW*, March 30, 2000, pp. 17–23.

Jose Emilio Fernandez, *Cuarena Años de Legislador: O Biografía del Senador Casimiro Barela* (Trinidad: n.p., 1911), is an accolade to the Perpetual Senator. A comparable, uncritical eulogy is found in John H. Monnett and Michael McCarthy, *Colorado Profiles*. Barron B. Beshoar, *Hippocrates in a Red Vest*, in contrast, is quite hard hitting, documenting Barela's dubious electoral triumphs. Bill Haywood in passing notes Barela's role in breaking strikes in his autobiography, *Bill Haywood's Book*.

Rich Castro shared his views with me in various conversations before his death. He beat around the bush when I directly asked him about Barela's reactionary politics. His paper on the colonization of West Denver, with George Rivera Jr. and Aileen F. Lucero, "Internal Colonialism in Colorado: The Westside Coalition and Barrio Control," was posthumously published in a volume dedicated in his memory, *La Gente*, 203–22. There are also materials on him in the Minoru Yasui papers. I have given numerous walking tours of North Denver, noting the heavy Spanish-language presence in the area.

# 4

# From McNichols to Peña

Mayor William Henry McNichols Jr. was riding high in 1979. His only real challenge as he sought reelection came from the candidate of the Socialist Workers Party. The two mainstream opponents had no dynamism or constituency. The mayor easily won the May 15 contest, receiving 58,189 votes (54.4 percent) out of 106,996 ballots cast.

This was quite a change for McNichols, an accidental mayor. Through the 1970s, he was buffeted by forces of opposition. Citizens frequently attacked him for doing nothing or all the wrong things. The 1979 results revealed the mayor was firmly in command of the city.

Born in Denver on April 11, 1910, McNichols became mayor of his home town on January 1, 1969, upon the resignation of incumbent Tom Currigan. A functionary in the Quigg Newton administration who later served as Denver clerk and recorder, Currigan won election as auditor in 1955. In that post, he stood out as a fierce critic of city hall. No sooner did Republican mayors Will F. Nicholson (1955–59) and Richard Batterton (1959–63) launch projects than Currigan publicly scrutinized the financing. Unafraid to fulfill the proper role of the auditor as a loud watchdog of the commonweal, Currigan was the major institutional critic of the mayor. By asking questions about the operations of city hall, he forced the administration to justify every penny it spent.

A Democrat, Currigan used the auditor's post to launch his campaign for mayor in 1963. Incumbent Richard Batterton was badly scarred by the police scandal of 1960–61 when more than 50 of Denver's finest were arrested and accused of stag-

Author's Collection

*Mayor Tom Currigan resigned from office in late 1968, complaining the city did not pay him enough.*

ing burglaries. When rumblings of the misdoings were first heard in 1959–60, Batterton insistently denied them. He later blamed Currigan and the Democrats for the police department's disgrace as he traced the origins of the ignominy to the Newton administration.

Batterton's dismissal of the malfeasance of the police department came on top of his snide hatred of the city. The mayor, a former car dealer, was at one with the postwar generation in readily attacking everything old in Denver as bad and obsolete. His major accomplishment in office was providing the rights-of-way for Interstate 70, a freeway intentionally designed to ruin residential neighborhoods on the northern edge of the city. The incumbent was the best the Republicans had to offer as Batterton sought to remain in office in 1963. The Democrats were sure it was time for them to resume their traditional place in occupying city hall.

Steve McNichols eyed the mayor's post. A Democrat, his father, William McNichols Sr., was city auditor from 1931 until 1955. The younger McNichols served in the state Senate from 1949 until 1954 when he was elected lieutenant governor under Edwin C. Johnson. He held the governor's seat from 1957 until 1963. After he was defeated for reelection in 1962, the politician pondered running for Denver's chief office.

Currigan feared the McNichols challenge. He and the former governor were political clones: corporate Democrats with liberal veneers. If they ran against one another in the ostensibly nonpartisan race, they might undercut one another, allowing Batterton to remain as mayor. This was compounded by the challenge of another pro-business Democrat, Bill Grant. A powerful attorney born in Estes Park in 1910, he owned Channel Four and was a member of a historic Denver family. As a young man, he was worked for Mayor Newton's father, James Q. Newton, in the stock brokerage of Boettcher, Newton & Company from 1933 until 1935. He was later also an aide of Quigg Newton. Both the *News* and *Post* endorsed Grant for mayor.

The auditor and former governor were at one in noting Batterton's strong chance for reelection, especially when the Grant campaign was added to the balance. To regain the mayor's post for the Democrats, the auditor and former governor struck a deal: Steve McNichols would not run for mayor; if Currigan were elected, he would appoint the ex-governor's older brother, Bill McNichols Jr., to a high post in the city government.

Steve McNichols' withdrawal cleared the way for Currigan. After receiving a plurality in the May 1963 election, 56,043 (42 percent), to Batterton's 42,929 (32 percent), and Grant's 33,340 (25 percent), Currigan easily defeated Batterton in a runoff in June, 73,848 (56 percent) to 58,153 (44 percent). Once in city hall, Currigan named Bill McNichols to the number-two post in the administration, manager of public works, which made McNichols de facto deputy mayor.

A 1929 graduate of East High, Currigan's assistant attended both the University of Alabama and the University of Colorado. Over the years, McNichols had drifted from Denver. A decorated World War II combat soldier, he subsequently worked as a car, insurance, and real estate salesman in California and Hawaii. His brother hired him as an administrative assistant. In the post, McNichols showed himself a skilled executive who knew how to get things done.

There was nothing colorful about McNichols. He lacked the polish increasingly associated with politicians. As manager of public works, he primarily succeeded by depending on professional career service employees. McNichols, comfortable with many of the wirepullers of 17th Street, was at one with the world of old, ruling-class Denver.

As mayor, Currigan was an open advocate of business-governmental cooperation. He staked his career on pushing through the Skyline Urban Renewal Project. A firm supporter of Lyndon Johnson and the Great Society, he arranged for Denver to receive assorted federal funds for War on Poverty efforts. Seventeenth Street lined up behind him in 1967 when he was easily reelected.

Currigan's major gripe about serving as mayor was the pay. For years, Denver deliberately kept salaries for elected city officials low. In this manner, everyday residents, willing to sacrifice, would guide the city. Denverites did not pamper council members, the auditor, or mayor. On the contrary, citizens expected public officials to make do on their salaries as much as any other middle-class taxpayers. Voter authorization was necessary to hike the pay of elected officials.

The incumbent said nothing about his low salary during the 1967 campaign. At that time, Republican challenger Don Nicholson exposed the Tom-Tom Club. It was something of a slush fund set up by the mayor's supporters to help Currigan pay the extra costs associated with serving as mayor. Nicholson failed to strike a receptive chord. His campaign was flat. One and all recognized Currigan was essentially ruling Denver's candidate. The voters assumed the mayor would make do with his existing salary.

Money problems haunted Currigan. Three times in the year and a half after his 1967 triumph, the mayor approached the voters for a raise. Each time the answer was the same, NO! After his third defeat in November 1968, Currigan figured if his boss—the electorate—would not give him the raise, he should resign.

The mayor had close relations with Robert Six, the president of Continental Airlines. While the carrier had moved its headquarters from Denver to Los Angeles in June 1963, it still had strong Mile High connections and major operations out of Stapleton Airport. Six frequently visited Currigan at city hall where he derided Currigan for holding a "chickenshit job." Given Currigan's influence in Washington, Six figured the politician would be an ideal addition to Continental. The business executive repeatedly offered Currigan a top post with the airline.

In face of the mayor's limited salary and the repeated voter rejection of pay hikes, Currigan decided he had no loyalty to Denver or responsibility to those who

Author's Collection

*Bill McNichols was mayor from 1969 until 1983.*

had returned him to office. In November-December 1968, he decided to resign as mayor and leave Denver for Los Angeles as Continental's vice president for community affairs.

Before abandoning the city, Currigan wanted to appoint Dale Tooley as his successor. A Denver native, born on November 13, 1933, Tooley was a whirlwind of energy. Seemingly insatiable as a student at the University of Colorado in the mid-1950s, he was not only a playboy, but also a politician on the make, serving as student body president. While still an undergraduate, Tooley entered CU law school. In 1957, he simultaneously received his bachelor and law degrees.

Tooley plunged into Denver Democratic politics. In 1966–68, he chaired the city Democratic Party, the youngest man ever to hold the office. Quite close to Currigan, Tooley served as campaign manager for the mayor's 1967 reelection bid. Simultaneously Tooley emerged an excellent lawyer with the firm of Lesher, Schmidt & Van Cise. An associate there was future Governor Roy Romer, who overwhelmingly lost a bid for the United States Senate in 1966. (In 1962, Tooley had unsuccessfully run for the University of Colorado board of regents.)

Generally, Tooley's politics were at one with Currigan. He was a status quo Democrat, endorsing Lyndon Johnson and the Great Society. Currigan wanted the promising young attorney to succeed him as mayor. To make this happen, Tooley resigned as chairman of the Democratic Party in late 1968.

Before Tooley could become mayor, something had to be done about the deputy mayor, Bill McNichols. Currigan carefully crafted his scheme: remove McNichols as manager of public works/deputy mayor; name Tooley to the post; resign; and have the new mayor—Tooley—reappoint McNichols manager of public works. Only at the last minute did Currigan inform the deputy mayor of these plans. McNichols refused to go along. He demanded Currigan publicly announce his intentions before he would quit. Currigan backed down. The incumbent simply gave up the mayor's post, allowing McNichols to succeed him.

Ominous repercussions swept the city. Foremost, voters agreed to hike the mayor's salary. More than that, the power structure made it sound as if the citizenry was at fault for Currigan's abandonment of city hall. Advocates of highly paid, prince-like politicians convinced the electorate to abdicate its power of determining the mayor's wages in public votes. Instead of letting the people decide how much the mayor and other elected officials should receive, city hall got the voters to turn this power over to a commission. The latter, geared to ensuring top salaries for politicians, determined the pay of officeholders based on the earnings of mayors and council members in other cities.

## McNichols as Mayor

McNichols drifted as mayor. He was the epitome of the old politics at the time when George McGovern and the New Politics movement swept the country. The incumbent eagerly supported 17th Street, embracing the Olympics, growth, development, highways, and sprawl. As with Currigan, under McNichols the poor frequently saw the city destroy their homes and neighborhoods in the name of urban renewal. Nor was the mayor willing to tolerate dissent or alternate lifestyles.

Typical of McNichols' approach was the fate of a youth shelter at St. Andrew's Church at 2013 Glenarm Place. An East Denver Episcopal mission dating from November 30, 1873, St. Andrew's had occupied buildings at 21st and Arapahoe and 26th and Curtis streets, before moving to its permanent home in 1909, a structure designed by acclaimed New York architect Ralph Adams Cram.

For generations, St. Andrew's was a conservative, high Episcopal church, filled with religious statuary. It underwent massive upheavals after 35-year-old Jon Marr Stark became pastor in 1968. He opened the church's doors to vagabond youths. St. Andrew's sponsored a drug/health clinic, low-cost meals, and a coffeehouse. Most of all, it provided a place where wandering hippies, runaways, and homeless teenagers could sleep.

As young people occupied St. Andrew's, upwards of 80 percent of the 200 or so existing parishioners abandoned the church. The changing character of St. Andrew's was confirmed when Reverend Stark organized the Order of the Holy Family under the auspices of the Donati Brothers. Its members dressed in blue and white robes and marched down Broadway and Colfax seeking to spread the gospel. Known as the Mad Monks of Glenarm, they established missions along Colfax and 17th avenues, in Five Points, and on South Broadway. They projected themselves as modern incarnations of the Franciscans and Benedictines.

By the early 1970s, St. Andrew's was feeding upwards of a hundred people an evening and sheltering 50–75 youths a night. Reverend Stark openly admitted many of those coming to the church had substance-abuse problems and were troubled adolescents. Rather than turning them away, the mission of the church was to help those in need. Insofar as possible, St. Andrew's tried to reunite runaways with their families and educate them about how they were destroying their bodies and souls with drugs and alcohol.

The Episcopal diocese helped finance the St. Andrew's youth program. At the peak of the church's operations, ten physicians volunteered their services for its health clinic. Many affiliating with the Holy Family were extremely transient. About 75 percent of those who joined the order moved on in a month or two.

Neighbors were generally tolerant of St. Andrew's. It was surrounded by old houses, shops, and run-down apartments. Nearby 20th Avenue was something of a hippie enclave, complete with bohemian coffeehouses and alternate bars.

Some slumlords did not like the shelter or the hippies. They claimed the people around the church and businesses were "undesirable." Land speculators eyed the area for redevelopment. With the support of the Denver Urban Renewal Authority (DURA), they hoped to obliterate much of the neighborhood for a housing project for the 1976 Winter Olympics. To make way for it, programs such as those at St. Andrew's had to go.

City hall readily responded to property holders' calls for action. On July 25, 1968, the police swept through the area. Their target was the Golden Apple, about two blocks from the church at 2150 Court Place, a hippie hangout attracting numerous teenagers. In response to complaints about loitering near the coffeehouse, the authorities targeted everybody standing in the area. Among those arrested for refusing to move at the police's arbitrary command was Dorothy Davidson, the local head of the American Civil Liberties Union.

The city attorney's office unsuccessfully pushed her prosecution. McNichols eagerly embraced these policies as they had been developed under Currigan. He kept his predecessor's vindictive city attorney, Max Zall, in the post. Under Currigan and McNichols alike, city hall had no place for an establishment like the Golden Apple. The coffeehouse soon went out of business.

The McNichols city hall applied comparable coercive tactics to St. Andrew's. The police were convinced the church was a center of criminal activity. Arrested transients sometimes listed St. Andrew's as their home. Authorities linked people staying there to robberies, burglaries, and even a homicide. To do something about

Photo by Phil Goodstein

*St. Andrew's Episcopal Church at 2013 Glenarm Place was the target of massive police repression under Mayor Bill McNichols in 1971.*

the church, the administration drew up an elaborate plan to raid the shelter and close down the Mad Monks of Glenarm.

Around 4:00 AM on Saturday, July 24, 1971, 50 police officers, including members of the canine corps, gathered at the corner of 22nd and California streets. They prepared to raid St. Andrew's, convinced they would catch drug dealers and other criminals there. With a search warrant in hand, signed at 3:30 that morning by Judge Paul Weddick, they surrounded St. Andrew's, cut holes in screens, and swarmed through the windows into the sanctuary.

The midnight invaders rousted 80 men sleeping at St. Andrew's. Their number-one target, Reverend Stark, was missing—he was at a church conference in Evergreen. Thoroughly searching the St. Andrew's complex, the police discovered a minor amount of drugs, a .22 rifle, and a BB gun. They accused the church of harboring runaways as they booked 24 people for illegal possession of drugs. The authorities kept others in detention as minors.

No sooner did the charges come to court than they collapsed. A basic investigation showed there was no substance to police claims; the raid was totally unjustified. Still, the attack served its purpose. St. Andrew's never recovered from the sweep. While its programs continued, the entire conclave was in decline. Before long, DURA destroyed most of the nearby houses and businesses. The Mad Monks completely abandoned St. Andrew's in 1984.

The raid caused intense community controversy. McNichols was firm in his support of the police: they had done the right thing in attacking the hippie menace.

He similarly endorsed the draconian police measures used to destroy the Woodstock West anti-war protest at the University of Denver in May 1970.

This was typical of McNichols. He relied on a crude, heavy-handed administrative approach. When pedestrians complained it was too dangerous to cross many streets, he responded by ordering the police to target jaywalkers. Given a free hand from city hall, the level of police violence soared in the 1970s. Blacks, Chicanos, youths, and others who did not fit in McNichols' smug, middle-class, pro-business world found themselves living in fear of out-of-control cops. Police violence sometimes led to outbreaks threatening the very cohesion of the city.

The fate of Arthur "Artie" Espinoza was all too typical. A 48-year-old Hispano, he lived in the Curtis Park Housing Project, adjacent to Curtis Park, a three-square-block spread of greenery near 32nd and Curtis streets. Unemployed and suffering from alcoholism, Espinoza frequently staggered about drunk in the park.

July 30, 1977, was an awful day for Espinoza. He shot someone in the morning and got into an altercation with his family. Espinoza left them and was lying on the grass in Curtis Park where he shared a bottle with James Max Hinojos, 32. As the two got ever more intoxicated, around 8:00 PM, the police sought Espinoza.

Plainclothes narcotics detectives John O'Dell and Gary Graham searched the park, looking for Espinoza. While they were on foot, a uniformed officer, Patrolman David Neil, drove his squad car onto the grass of the park. The officers spotted Espinoza, who was face down on the lawn, next to Hinojos.

The detectives approached, pulling their weapons. They saw Espinoza and Hinojos passing a gun between them. When the police identified themselves, Hinojos grabbed the gun and rolled over. The two plainclothes officers emptied their revolvers into him. Patrolman Neil, meanwhile, had driven within ten feet of the men, gotten out of his vehicle, and, using the car door as a shield, had fired one shot at Espinoza. Neil claimed he saw Espinoza reach for something and feared Espinoza was going for a gun. No such weapon was found. When the smoke cleared, Hinojos was dead, killed by six bullets. Espinoza, who had grabbed his crotch and was urinating, was dead, killed by the shot fired by Neil.

An explosion swept the Curtis Park neighborhood. Many poor residents, especially Chicanos, saw this as an act of police brutality and the cold-blooded execution of a couple of drunks. Nor did the initial police response encourage calm. The first police statement to the media reported the officers had stopped a car Hinojos was driving. He suddenly leaped out of the vehicle, pointing a gun at them. The officers had no choice but to shoot him. This gave way to the version that, when the police had approached him in the park, Hinojos had jumped up and pulled a revolver on them. Before long, the authorities settled on the account of Hinojos reaching for the weapon while lying in a drunken stupor in the park. Witnesses did not see any such pistol.

For some days after the shooting, the neighborhood around Curtis Park was extremely tense. Clashes between the police and residents were common. The authorities cleared 200 demonstrators from Curtis Park on the night of the shooting, using mace, tear gas, and dogs against those protesting the deaths of Hinojos and Espinoza.

A police investigation cleared detectives O'Dell and Graham. A grand jury indicted Neil for manslaughter. At his trial, Chicano activists charged the police tampered with the plastic bag holding the bullet killing Espinoza. The jury found Neil not guilty. After years of litigation, including a verdict for more than $900,000 against the police overturned on appeal because one juror did not think the amount sufficient, the Espinoza family won an excellent settlement for the wrongful death of their loved one.

Not only did McNichols see nothing wrong with events such as the Curtis Park shooting, but under the mayor's longtime police chief, Art Dill, the vice and narcotics squad appeared to cozy up to owners of stripper bars. Little was done to rein in out-of-control officers such as James "Buster" Snider and George Adam Homa Jr. A Glendale bar where Dill hung out, Casa Donato at 888 South Colorado Boulevard, was linked to the operations of a couple of rogue former New York detectives, Michael Borrelli and Robert Davis, who were accused of executing a local furniture dealer, Hal Levine, in October 1975. McNichols never called the police department into account.

Other cases of police beatings and the killings of blacks and Chicanos created massive community distrust of the mayor. The city was more divided than ever under McNichols. Minority politicians loudly called for an independent civilian review board of the police. District Attorney Dale Tooley invariably supported McNichols and the police in such controversies.

**Photo by Phil Goodstein**

*The Kingston, at the north corner of 21st Street and Tremont Place, was among the many buildings slated for destruction in the name of urban renewal during the McNichols years. It managed to remain standing after voters defeated the 1976 Winter Olympics.*

Courtesy Walter Gerash

*Dale Tooley was a three-time loser in his efforts to win election as mayor.*

## Denver's Bobby Kennedy

After Tooley found himself left in the cold by Currigan in the unsuccessful effort to make him mayor in 1968, the aspiring politician drifted to the New Politics Democrats. By 1969–70, Tooley projected himself as Denver's Bobby Kennedy, a committed, energetic, young liberal who denounced the Richard Nixon administration and the Vietnam War. He endorsed Craig Barnes' successful challenge to Byron Rogers in the 1970 Democratic congressional primary and lined up behind the candidates advocating school integration in the 1969 election. (Despite this stance, Tooley sent his children to private schools. He took them out of Denver Public Schools in 1968 when it appeared he was about to become mayor. The message: others could be bused, but DPS was not good enough for the mayor's children.)

Tooley announced he was going to run for mayor in 1971 as a dynamic alternative to the stodgy, stagnant, brutal McNichols administration. Given his past post as chairman of the Democratic Party added to the burgeoning New Politics movement, Tooley was the insider for the Democratic nomination. He was the key player in making sure there would be a Democratic nomination.

In 1913, after gaining control of city hall the previous year, reformers amended city charter to eliminate partisan politics from municipal elections. One was not a

Denver Democrat or Denver Republican, they argued, but a Denver lover. Partisan divisions were a hindrance to advancing the city.

Upon returning to office as mayor in 1916, the city's longtime Democratic boss, Robert W. Speer, retained nonpartisan municipal elections. If nothing else, nonpartisanship meant there was no place for organized forces of opposition within the rubric of city politics. The mayor, consequently, did not face any steady institutional criticism.

Despite the nonpartisan cloak, everybody knew who the Republican and Democratic candidates were in mayoral races. Both parties readily mocked the system. In face of this, led by Tooley, reformers asked the voters in September 1968 to permit forthright partisan municipal elections. By allowing the parties to compete in the city, advocates hoped the candidates would be more accountable. The charter amendment, written by Tooley, passed 48,293–27,178. Under it, the Democratic nomination was the prime position for the contender hoping to win the spring 1971 election.

A crucial trigger to the charter change was the severe embarrassment Currigan had suffered in the wake of the 1967 election. In addition to eliminating party affiliations from municipal elections, the 1913 reform sought to keep big money from the polls. A companion charter provision limited all candidates and their supporters to spending a maximum of $1,000 on a campaign. Ruling Denver even more cynically flouted this measure than the bogus nonpartisanship.

The 1963 election was illustrative. A marginal candidate for mayor, attorney Sheldon Greene, noted the major candidates, including Currigan, had grossly violated the charter by spending far more than the $1,000 limit. When he asked for court relief against this breach of the law, a judge ruled the issue was not germane because the election had not yet been held. After the election, the courts declared the subject was moot.

This was the situation in the 1967 campaign. Corky Gonzales emphasized the 1913 law as he ran for mayor as the radical Chicano candidate. He noted Currigan, the Republican-supported challenger Nicholson, and independent city councilman Houston Gibson, all vastly violated the $1,000 spending limit. When Gonzales asked the courts to enforce the law, Judge James C. Flanigan dismissed the suit. He ruled it irrelevant to raise the issue before the election. The jurist instructed Gonzales to wait until after the vote to demand the enforcement of the statute. The hope was Corky and the flagrant violation of the ordinance would simply go away.

After Currigan was overwhelmingly returned to office, Gonzales stuck to his guns. He again filed a complaint asserting Currigan had violated the law. Once more, Judge Flanigan dismissed the case, observing the mayor had not yet taken office for his second term. Only after Currigan was reinaugurated on July 3, 1967, was Gonzales allowed to file suit. As required by law, upon being sworn in for his second term, Currigan signed an affidavit stating he had not violated the spending ordinance. Not only had he not spent more than the $1,000 maximum on the election, but the mayor stated his total campaign costs had not exceeded $75. Apparently all the literature, television and newspaper advertisements, bumperstickers, mailings, billboards, telephone banks, and office space needed for the election had cost less than this sum. The $75, incidentally, was less than half of the $184 Currigan admitted spending on his 1963 bid for mayor.

The press treated Currigan's claim as a cynical joke. It observed the mayor had raised so much money in his campaign that, after the election, his top donors were given a 10-percent refund. Currigan's supporters lambasted the law as archaic and irrelevant. On no account were they willing to admit Gonzales had raised a valid point about the corrupt core of Denver municipal politics.

The Chicano challenger did not let the mayor's deceit pass. He asked newly appointed Republican District Attorney Mike McKevitt to file charges over Currigan's violation of the law. The district attorney brushed him off, explaining he did not have the time or resources to bother with such trifles. Consequently, with help of volunteer attorneys from the National Lawyers Guild, Gonzales filed suit against Currigan. The plaintiff asked the courts to set aside the election since the incumbent had been illegally elected in violation of the spending ordinance.

Currigan's lawyer, Philip Hornbein, sought to deal with the matter on a purely technical basis: the courts had no jurisdiction in the matter. For one thing, the 1913 ordinance was obsolete since the purchasing power of $1,000 was vastly greater at the earlier date than the present. For another, the $1,000 limit was a restriction of free speech. The incumbent, his backers insisted, had been fairly

Author's Collection

*A cartoon in the Crusade for Justice's* El Gallo *mocks Mayor Tom Currigan's amnesia about the finances of his 1967 reelection campaign. Hispanic radio announcer Paco Sanchez is the bootlicker at the lower right.*

reelected as mayor and the whole issue should be dropped as an irrelevant episode from a previous era.

The mayor did not listen to his lawyer. He continued to insist he had not violated the spending ordinance and stuck by his $75 figure. Both issues—the relevance of the 1913 law and whether it had been broken—came to trial in April 1968 before Judge Merle Knous.

Walter Gerash, a flamboyant local people's attorney who was involved in numerous civil rights trials, handled the case for Gonzales. He subpoenaed the Denver political elite for the hearing. The plaintiff called editors Palmer Hoyt of the *Denver Post* and Jack Foster of the *Rocky Mountain News* as witnesses. Both admitted the Currigan campaign had spent more than $1,000 in advertising in their papers. Managers of the city's television stations similarly vouchsafed the Currigan campaign had paid them more than $1,000 for broadcast commercials. Tooley, as chairman of the Denver Democratic Party and manager of the Currigan reelection effort, testified to the campaign's numerous expenses. Roy Romer noted his role in raising money for Democratic candidates in the "nonpartisan" Denver city election. He and Tooley conceded Currigan had spent more than $1,000 on the campaign.

The evidence showed Currigan had spent between $40,000 and $100,000 on the election. Everybody granted this except Currigan. The mayor continually swore he and his supporters had only spent $75 on the campaign. He testified as much at the trial.

Gerash tore into the mayor during his cross-examination. Suddenly, the city's chief executive was nebulous. He could not remember any details. He was unsure of who had paid the campaign's bills. "I can't remember" and "I don't know" were his answers to both general and specific questions. The mayor was suffering amnesia about his finances. So Gonzales' attorney asked Currigan about something the mayor should know, the politics of the campaign.

"Do you think the newspapers accurately reported the campaign?"

"I don't know."

"What do you mean? 'You don't know'?"

"I didn't have time to read the newspapers during the campaign."

Nor did Denver's leader seem aware of the operations of the Tom-Tom Club. Why did the organization have a special party room at the city's airport? Where did it get its money? Did it aid Currigan in his election campaign?

"I don't know."

How about the role of Dale Tooley? As chairman of the Denver Democratic Party, did he help the campaign and give it financial assistance?

"I don't know." This led Tooley to joke outside of the courtroom that "I didn't know that I was that ineffective."

On issue after issue, the mayor's answer was the same: "I don't know." It seemed Currigan had no idea of what was going on in the city or how he had campaigned for mayor the previous year. The only specific fact Currigan swore he remembered about the 1967 campaign was he and his supporters had spent about $75 on it.

The mayor's testimony came after Curigan's attorney had readily conceded it was impossible to run a serious mayoral campaign for less than $50,000. At the end of the testimony, Judge Knous took the matter under advisement. In June 1968, he upheld the contention of the mayor's backers: the $1,000 spending limit was obsolete when he ruled that the campaign spending cap was "unworkable and unreasonable." The judge declared the monetary limit unconstitutional and so dismissed the suit.

A few months later, on November 14, 1968, Judge Knous threw out a second suit by Gonzales against Currigan. This one charged Currigan had violated the nonpartisan character of Denver municipal elections because he was actually the Democratic Party candidate in the 1967 election. Since Denver voters had recently amended the charter to provide for partisan elections in September 1968, Knous observed, the issue was moot. Though the judge conveniently cited the charter amendment to cleanse Currigan's 1967 election, politicos had strong second-thoughts about nonpartisan elections as the 1971 election loomed.

McNichols, who did not have nearly the ties with the Democratic establishment as Tooley, preferred to keep the nonpartisan system. The Republicans echoed him. Partisan elections, they realized, virtually guaranteed the Democrats' permanent hold on city hall. Moreover, unlike Currigan or McNichols, a liberal Democrat—notably Tooley—might win the Democratic nomination and the mayor's post under the charter change. Those fearing such developments challenged the reform in court.

In November 1970, Denver District Judge Saul Pinchick threw out the partisan election measure. The ballot title, he observed, was defective. Nothing in it specifically called for partisan elections. The Colorado Supreme Court agreed, rejecting the amendment in January 1971. Hence, the mayoral race was wide-open. Besides McNichols and Tooley, Republican State Senator Joe Shoemaker announced for the office.

## District Attorney Tooley

Tooley staged an impressive campaign. He was everywhere, shaking hands, personally answering and making phone calls, and addressing all constituencies. Opposed to him, McNichols, a poor orator, ran a quiet, wire-pulling effort. The incumbent appealed to those who wanted a no-nonsense, law-and-order, anti-hippie, anti-minority mayor. Seventeenth Street noted McNichols' firm support of the Olympics. Continental Airlines and other leading corporations favored him as the candidate assuring the continual business domination of Denver.

In a closely fought election in May 1971, Tooley won a slight plurality, 45,308 (34 percent). McNichols was just behind him with 44,035 (33 percent). Shoemaker gathered 39,212 (29 percent). Protest and radical candidates received the rest. Since Tooley failed to gain a majority, a runoff was held between him and McNichols.

The latter's troops mobilized. Noting school busing was extremely unpopular, they readily linked Tooley to pro-busing attorney Craig Barnes. McNichols' backers branded Tooley a radical; according to them, the challenger's backers were the

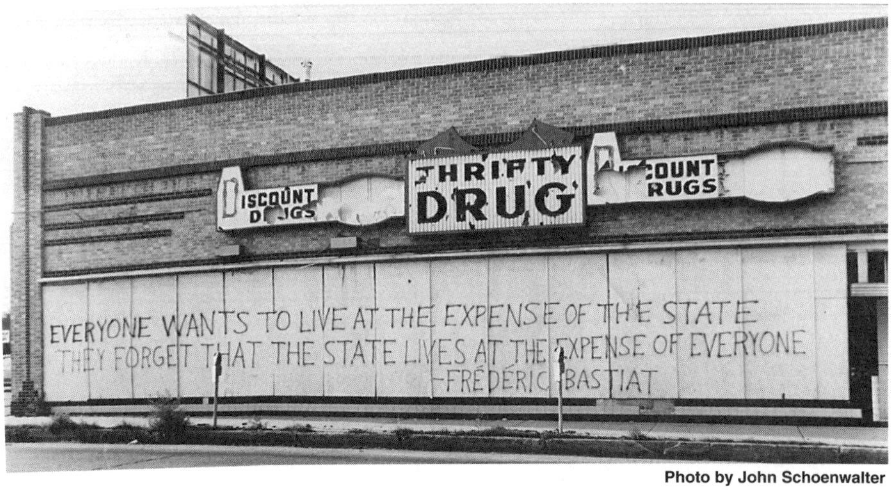


Photo by John Schoenwalter

*Unlike his successors, McNichols sometimes tolerated graffiti such as this comment on an abandoned drugstore at the southeast corner of 20th Avenue and Logan Street.*

"Tooley-Barnes bunch." Tooley's triumph, the mayor's campaign loudly announced, would be a victory of blacks, of school busers, of hippies, and other forces threatening sleek, new modern corporate Denver.

In connection with Republican activist William Chenoweth, advertising executive Sam Lusky, who was extremely personally and politically close to McNichols, developed the phrase the "Tooley-Barnes bunch." When Tooley directly challenged McNichols on the use of smear tactics during their final debate, the mayor brushed the accusation aside. He observed the Republican Party—a group heavily backing him—was responsible for the fear-inducing technique. The Republicans noted their support of McNichols as the mayor "of *our* city."

Tooley did not respond in kind. Nor did he vehemently attack the intolerance, hatred, and hysteria at the heart of the incumbent's campaign. The McNichols brain trust took this as a sign of weakness. In the weekend before the vote, it increased its efforts to besmirch the opposition candidate. The result was McNichols' narrow triumph in the runoff, 62,013 (50.7 percent) to 60,274 (49.3 percent).

Far from apologizing for the way in which he won the election, McNichols took his victory as a vindication of such tactics. He remained blunt as mayor, refusing to recognize those living outside the narrow world of his backers and their business culture. Tooley, on the other hand, underwent a major metamorphosis in the wake of the defeat. By 1972, in his quest for office, he announced his intention of becoming the dynamic district attorney who would set the city straight.

For years, the district attorney's office had been a morass. Bert Keating was the last man elected to the post in 1948. Under him, Denver was an open city for striptease hustlers and other shady business interests. Far from checking misdoing on the part of the police, the district attorney whitewashed it. In failing health, Keating died in early July 1967 (rumors claim he killed himself). Republican

Governor John Love thereupon appointed a young assistant Colorado Attorney General, Mike McKevitt, to replace him. (The district attorney is a county official; hence the governor, not the mayor, is responsible for filling the job in case of a vacancy.)

McKevitt reeked of political ambition. He found an easy target: the hippie menace to society. The district attorney focused on it as he ran for Congress in 1970. When he successfully defeated Craig Barnes to go to Washington, Governor Love named another Republican, Jarvis Seccombe, to lead the district attorney's office. Despite holding the highly visible, powerful post, Seccombe did little to identify himself to the electorate as the city's fighting district attorney. He remained very much an unknown as he sought to keep his job in 1972.

Aggressively targeting Seccombe, Tooley easily won the Democratic nomination. Promising he would push for more and better police, the challenger vowed to actively seek input from minorities to assure they could work within the system. The aspiring politician also addressed what could be done about recidivism and public safety. As was typical of the man, Tooley was once more a whirlwind of energy. He projected his election as a breath of fresh air for the district attorney's office and the city as a whole. The mayor want-to-be overwhelmed Seccombe, 114,456 (54.2 percent) to 81,874 (38.8 percent). Independent candidate Johnny Dee ran a poor third with 14,823 (7 percent).

Tooley kept up his frantic pace as district attorney. Not only did he direct the office's staff, but he also personally tried high-profile cases and actively participated in grand jury investigations. The politician tried to know everybody on his staff of one hundred or so. Members of the district attorney's office developed a special camaraderie.

**Courtesy Walter Gerash**

*Attorney Walter Gerash frequently clashed with District Attorney Dale Tooley during the 1970s, representing clients in politically charged cases.*

The district attorney skillfully pulled federal purse strings, getting numerous grants for his office and law enforcement efforts in the area. Tooley showed up at countless political and community meetings. Whenever a worthy cause needed a boost, the district attorney was there.

Among Tooley's accomplishments as district attorney was cracking down on individuals he believed were playing fast and lose with fiduciary rules and swindling the public. He also focused on rowdy sex businesses. As he undertook a crusade against crooked striptease joints, he discovered the owners and managers of these places were well acquainted with members of the vice squad. Instead of using Denver's finest to gather information about illegal practices in sleazy, dumpy, dive bars, Tooley recruited private attorneys to spy on these establishments.

Generally, though, Tooley worked closely with the police. Not only did he back them up in their violent encounters with Chicanos, but grand jury investigations he conducted into police shootings invariably cleared members of the department. In spite of the district attorney's decision not to prosecute in these cases, individuals brutalized by the police won many sizeable civil suits against the city and department through the 1970s.

The prosecutor sometimes appeared more interested in grabbing the public spotlight than in seeing justice done. Nothing illustrated this more than the case Tooley claimed was his best technical prosecution during his decade as district attorney, the trial of Afshin Shariati.

The defendant was a 20-year-old Iranian student living at 3060 South Federal Boulevard, across the street from Loretto Heights College, on November 11, 1979. This was a week after anti-American protesters in Tehran had seized the United States embassy, taking more than 60 American citizens hostage. Massive outrage swept the United States. Some chauvinists viewed Iranians in this country as the enemy. By beating up Iranians in Denver, jingoes believed they could right the wrong of the hostage crisis.

This was on the mind of 15 young men in four cars—mostly students from John F. Kennedy High School in far southwest Denver—who stormed onto the Loretto Heights campus, baseball bats in hand, shortly after midnight on Sunday, November 11. They could not find any Iranians on the peaceful Catholic women's college that they vandalized. A member of the disappointed gang stated he had heard an Iranian lived across the street in a modern apartment building, a structure without backdoors or internal hallways. The Iranian bashers proceeded there. Three of them discovered the light on in Shariati's third-floor apartment. The Iranian student was studying late into the night while his American-born wife, Toni, was sleeping.

Around 12:30 AM, Shariati suddenly found himself engulfed in an explosion. Blows from baseball bats shattered the front door. Glass came flying through his window followed by beer bottles, possibly Molotov cocktails. Instinctively, Shariati ran into the bedroom. His wife had been awakened by the blast.

As he shouted at her to protect herself from a bomb, Shariati went to the closet where he kept his hunting rifle. He had loaded it earlier in the week, living in fear after hearing numerous reports about violent, deadly attacks on Iranian students in

Courtesy Walter Gerash

*District Attorney Dale Tooley sought to convict Afshin Shariati, pictured, of murder for defending his apartment amidst the turmoil stemming from the occupation of the American Embassy in Tehran in 1979.*

the United States. Grabbing the gun, he immediately made for the door. His wife yelled after him, "You're not leaving without me!" She followed him.

Outside, Shariati did not know what to expect. He was afraid another bomb was imminent and thought attackers were coming toward him from his left. Trembling for his life, he heard a getaway car in the distance. Toni told him: "Shoot the tires so they won't escape."

Guessing where the tires were, Shariati fired at the car. He briefly moved after firing the first shot, afraid he might be the target of a sniper. Within three-four seconds, he fired off a second round. By then the getaway vehicle had sped out of the parking lot. In a frightened, agitated mood, Shariati followed his wife back into the apartment. Six or seven times he went into and out of the apartment, looking down at the parking lot. Finally, he thought he saw something in the parking lot. He went down to it as he told Toni to call the police.

By the time the authorities arrived, Shariati was hovering over the body of 15-year-old Paul Moritzky whom he had killed with his shots. Moritzsky's confederates, Michael Lopez, 16, and Steve R. Roane, 17, who had joined him in attacking Shariati's apartment, were wounded. The police arrested Shariati.

Far from using the killing to show the insanity of the American response to the Iranian invasion and the need for understanding and a peaceful community, Tooley fanned the flames of outrage over the events in Tehran. He sought to make Shariati responsible for all the crimes, charging him with first-degree murder. By prosecuting Shariati, Tooley acted as if he were righting the wrongs in Iran. To get the maximum exposure for his role in dealing with the hostage crisis, Tooley personally prosecuted the case.

While the district attorney got plenty of attention in the trial and proved there was a long enough delay between Shariati's shots to show premeditation, he failed to address the central defense contention: Shariati was acting in defense of himself, his wife, and his home. Nor did it help when a crucial FBI witness failed to produce his complete report in defiance of the judge's orders. When the government agent gave the strong impression he was hiding something, if not lying, Tooley had to intervene with a high official in the Department of Justice in Washington to keep his case from totally unfolding. The jury found Tooley's prosecution unwarranted when it acquitted Shariati in December 1980.

By this time, many saw Tooley as a chameleon. The politician kept changing his colors and positions depending on what he thought was popular. Nonetheless, he was still perceived as the liberal challenger when he again ran for mayor against McNichols in 1975. There was less fire in this race than in 1971. The result was the same: Tooley won a slight plurality over McNichols in the May election, 50,119–49,133—both received about 41 percent of the vote. The Republican candidate, city auditor Charles Byrne, trailed far behind with 19,342 votes. Though the polls predicted a close race and a likely Tooley victory in the runoff, McNichols easily triumphed, 66,106 (57 percent) to 50,275 (43 percent).

Despite the loss, Tooley breezed to reelection as district attorney in 1976 and 1980. By 1979, as Denver boomed under the impact of the oil boom, the prosecutor saw it hopeless to challenge McNichols for the mayor's post. Tooley sat out the race. He never said anything about the insane speculative course Denver was then adopting or advocated an alternative vision for the city. As district attorney, he was anything but a strong critic of McNichols' municipal policies. Still, he was sure 1983 would be his year to finally win city hall.

Others agreed McNichols' end was near in 1983. He was getting old, his administration was tired, unimaginative, and increasingly inefficient. As long as the petroleum bubble lubricated Denver through the 1970s, McNichols soared with it. By the early 1980s, the costs of growth were telling: the library was closed two days a week, charges were imposed on cultural facilities, downtown retail was reeling, relations with the suburbs were worse than ever, the schools were in decay, and the new office buildings were ugly and anti-human. Nor was city hall responsive to the needs and complaints of the citizenry. This was confirmed by McNichols' response to the 1982 Christmas blizzard.

## The Christmas Blizzard

The first three weeks of December 1982 were typical Denver weather. Some days were mild, filled with sunshine and temperatures into the 50s. Other days saw frigid conditions, ice, and snow. Romantics looked forward to snow falling on Christmas for only the eighth time in the 20th century. On December 22, the National Weather Service predicted their wish would probably come true with an accumulation of two to four inches of snow on December 24–25.

By Thursday, December 23, the Weather Service had upgraded the forecast to a storm warning. Weather was apt to blow in "capable of producing heavy snow, strong gusty winds, and possible blizzard conditions." It predicted temperatures in the 10s and 20s by Friday, December 24, while the windchill would go below zero. Even as the gloomy news arrived, people were out in shirt sleeves. Despite heavy passenger loads, traffic flowed smoothly at Stapleton International Airport. The city expected a pleasant holiday.

The prelude to the storm literally blew in late Thursday afternoon, December 23. Winds kicked up. Locals responded by descending on grocery stores. To stock up for the holiday weekend, customers virtually stripped shelves bare in supermarkets. This was only the beginning.

The snow started falling around 11:00 PM on the 23rd. A Pacific storm system, which had already dumped considerable snow on five western states, arrived in the Mile High City for Christmas. The cold front hit a body of warm, moist air from the Gulf of Mexico over the Front Range. The result was a deluge. Within

Photo by John Schoenwalter

*A skier tries to make his way at 23rd Avenue and Dexter Street in the wake of the 1982 Christmas blizzard.*

24 hours, two feet of snow fell. Eventually, 28 inches of wet, heavy snow were on the ground. An additional ten inches accumulated in Wheat Ridge. Drifts in places were up to six-feet deep. Here and there roofs collapsed, especially on modern buildings with flat roofs not designed to handle heavy snow falls.

Residents, who were snug and safe at home, reacted with fascination. Most simply battened down their hatches, staying inside in the expectation the blizzard would prove a typical Denver storm: flurry, bluster, and accumulation followed by sunshine and the quick disappearance of the precipitation. Those who had to go out in the weather found traffic at a near standstill. Before long, Stapleton Airport was closed, hospital personnel were stranded, and the city was paralyzed by the storm.

Denver came to a halt on December 24. Individuals waiting to do last-minute Christmas shopping found the task hopeless. Not only could they not get through on the streets, highways, and buses, but stores were closed. Even the *Rocky Mountain News* and *Denver Post* found the storm too much. Neither publication appeared on Christmas.

The storm spent itself about midnight Christmas eve. Christmas morning was filled with sunshine. Neighbors slowly tried digging out, joking as to what dastardly party had wished for a white Christmas. Cross-country skiers had a field day, sliding about the city. A few ardent ice-skaters managed to clear off bits and pieces of park lakes where they glided about. During the next few days, many followed them, enjoying the winter wonderland.

Driving was extremely hazardous. At the most, the city plowed one lane on such major arterials as 13th Avenue east of Broadway and South Colorado Boulevard. Accidents were everywhere. Many drivers simply abandoned their cars in the middle of the road. Ten-miles-an-hour was a good speed for those who could get through. Chains were indispensable. Streets in residential sections were frequently impassible. Those who made it to 24-hour-a-day convenience and grocery stores often found all perishables had vanished from the shelves.

For some, the blizzard was a magical experience. Having to cancel existing holiday plans because of the storm, they walked brief distances to gather with their fellows. The Mercury Cafe, then at 13th Avenue and Pearl Street, for example, hosted an impromptu Christmas banquet and concert with locals sleeping on the floor, sharing a blizzard camaraderie. Other neighbors likewise spontaneously celebrated the holiday on account of the storm.

Some owners of four-wheel vehicles volunteered their services. They functioned as a free, private taxi service, transporting people to hospitals and making emergency deliveries. Others, vaunting the power of their all-weather tanks, aggressively flew around stranded cars. Instead of helping clear parking lots, these drivers sometimes playfully skidded around on them.

The storm forced airlines to cancel all flights. Inept management and a scorn for travelers were Stapleton's keynotes in the wake of the blizzard. With passengers unable to get into or out of the airport, individuals had no choice but to stay in the terminal. There was no place for them comfortably to lie down. The facility's chairs were intentionally designed to keep those waiting for flights from sleeping at the airport. Before long, travelers, camping on the floor, were out of luck and out of money.

The airport's snack bars and restaurants were not able to feed the nearly 2,000 stranded passengers. Basic janitorial services broke down. Garbage was strewn about the facility. Those out of funds found the traveler aid agencies closed or of little assistance. The nursery at the airport was shut. Officials were unable to open it since people living far from the airport had the key. Traffic backed up on 32nd Avenue west all the way to Colorado Boulevard. The McNichols administration lacked any clue as to how to handle the situation.

City hall was unprepared for the deluge. Existing plans called for mobilizing the Denver Office of Emergency Preparedness to deal with such a snowfall. Instead of immediately reacting in the early hours of December 24 when it was obvious the Christmas blizzard was far more than an ordinary storm, the agency and city hall did nothing. Not until 11:00 AM on Christmas day—nearly 12 hours after the blizzard had spent itself—did the Office of Emergency Preparedness swing into action. It established its command headquarters in the basement of the City and County Building. McNichols arrived on the scene to direct operations.

The mayor confronted a chaotic scene. Despite the intense snowfall, the Department of Public Works had not mobilized all available snow-fighting personnel. McNichols' assistant, Errol Stevens, explained there was too much snow to make the plowing of the roads worthwhile. Consequently, the administration did nothing. Not until 34 hours after the storm had spent itself was the city's snow-removal operation functioning at 100-percent capacity.

During the early hours of December 24, as the snow rapidly accumulated, the city only had 14 plows on the streets. Since only six to eight inches of snow were expected, the Department of Public Works did not order more equipment into operation. (With Christmas falling on a Saturday, the administration treated Friday, December 24, as a holiday. It allowed most city workers to leave their jobs on the afternoon of December 23. Few drivers, consequently, were in the garage when the intensity of the storm became obvious.)

Even if the city had immediately mobilized every resource available, the Department of Public Works still would not have had enough vehicles to handle the blizzard. The agency had 42 snowplows, 15 road graders, and eight front-end loaders available to cope with the snowfall. Opposed to this, St. Louis had 60 snowplows, Kansas City had 120 pieces of snow-removal equipment, and there were 131 trucks prepared to remove snow in Minneapolis.

The Mile High City, McNichols explained, was sufficiently equipped for the blizzard. Not only did Denver snow usually quickly go away, but the snowfall was such an exceptional event that the city would be foolish to invest its capital resources to deal with this rare emergency. The Weather Service seconded this opinion, noting the storm was a "hundred-year blizzard," a snowfall only expected once a century.

DPL

*The December 1913 blizzard kept the streetcars from running. They are shown stalled at Colfax and Downing Street. The Lawrence Phipps House is on the right.*

As snow drifts, icy streets, and airport problems continued to paralyze Denver during the week after Christmas, tensions mounted. The novelty of the storm quickly passed. The nuisance of coping with the ice, cold, and omnipresent snow replaced the excitement of a white Christmas. Critics claimed the mayor had pulled out the city's 1913 snow removal policy as his way of dealing with the disaster.

## Memories of the 1913 Blizzard

December 1913 was the date of the worst blizzard in Denver history. Four and two-tenths inches of snow fell on December 1. About 1.5 inches followed on December 2. December 3 saw 2.4 inches further accumulation. Most of the snow was extremely wet and immediately froze on the ground. Conditions were already severe when the heavens opened up on December 4 at about 6:00 AM. Twenty and nine-tenths inches of snow fell that day. Another 16.5 inches followed on December 5 when the snow ended around 10:00 PM. More snow fell on December 6. The total accumulation was between 45.7 and 47.9 inches. Ten-foot drifts were common throughout the city. Denver was at a standstill.

A new reform administration had taken power in city hall in July 1913. A five-member, nonpartisan commission, it replaced both the mayor and city council. The commission promised economical, efficient government. Other than letting the sun come out and shine, it had no program to deal with the snow. It even boasted of this. In an official municipal magazine, *The City of Denver*, city hall argued the blizzard was such a rarity, a once in a lifetime happening, that the Mile High City should be proud of its lack of action:

> The city's almost total prostration under the effects of a four-foot snowfall was in reality a tribute to the splendid climate of Colorado. The unpreparedness of the people, the city and the public service companies, adds weight and sanction to the tribute. The very helplessness of the people, snowbound for the first time in the experience of a city, was proof to the outer world of the claims Denver always has made for her extraordinary advantages in climatic conditions.

This was why Denver did not have the heavy snow-removal equipment other cities did. All the Queen City needed to do was relax and let the sun melt the snow.

Such explanations did not satisfy the citizenry. Before long, the administration conscripted numerous horses and wagons so workers could haul snow from the central business district. A preferred dumping place was the land between West Colfax and West 14th avenues from Broadway to Bannock Street. This area had recently been cleared of all buildings for the yet-to-be-landscaped Civic Center. In no time, a snow mountain, estimated from 75- to 100-feet-high, filled the future park. A favorite subject among bettors during the spring of 1914 was when the last of the snow would melt. Not until June did traces of the blizzard disappear.

The reform administration never recovered from its inept handling of the snowfall. Similarly, Ben Stapleton was adversely impacted as mayor in November 1946 when Denver was again snowed under. Between Friday, November 2, and Sunday, November 4, 28 inches of snow swamped the region. The storm paralyzed trains, kept the streetcars from running, and stalled truck deliveries. Denver was socked by coal, wood, and gas shortages on account of the storm. Adding to the turmoil: a strike had already shut major grocery stores.

At first, city hall easily handled the snow. Temperatures into the 50s followed the blizzard during midweek. No sooner was the Stapleton administration gloating about how smoothly it had removed the snow, with less than ten inches still on the ground by Thursday, November 7, than another storm hit Denver on Friday. Temperatures plunged as nearly nine more inches of snow fell. The total 42.6 inches of snow accumulating during the month—3.21 inches of precipitation—made that November the wettest in Denver history. Streets were icier and more

Author's Collection

*In response to the Christmas blizzard, some thought the solution was obvious.*

impassible than they had been a week earlier. Fuel shortages escalated. For weeks, the blizzard heavily impacted Denver. As city hall failed to act, some argued the solution was obvious: Mayor Stapleton must go. This set the stage for the triumph of 35-year-old Quigg Newton in the May 1947 election.

Even with this background of blizzards spelling city hall's doom, none of McNichols' opponents immediately made the Christmas blizzard an issue. They realized nobody could have prevented the storm. As much as the advocates of the 1913 snow removal policy, they conceded a heavy stocking up on snowplows for a rare blizzard was not a sound investment. Had they been in office, they knew they could not have done any better than McNichols in making the snow go away.

In no time, however, challengers reversed their stance. The inefficiency of city hall gave the mayor's rivals election fodder. Not only was the administration slow in mobilizing its complete snow-fighting crews and equipment, but few roads were cleared in the days immediately after the blizzard. While travelers were stranded at Stapleton where the city did nothing for them, McNichols ordered workers to make an extra effort to clear a runway so the Denver Broncos could fly to California to play the Raiders. The hated foe clobbered the Denver team, 27–10. Some of the Bronco players were only able to get to Stapleton via helicopter taxi service provided by the city's television stations.

The city failed to plow parking lots at Denver General Hospital or provide for safe access to the facility. Public Works crews, though, did remove snow from lots at the mayor's beloved McNichols Arena where 800 fans attended a Denver Nuggets game on Monday, December 27. (The game was postponed from December 26 and only held after the opponent made a heroic effort to reach Denver for the contest.) Far from concentrating on clearing the snow from the streets, city crews plowed the lots of engineering firm Stearns-Roger in Glendale. Other companies got the city to plow their lots while residents fumed.

Those dissatisfied with the mayor's handling of the storm noted the suburbs did a far better job of plowing residential streets than Denver did. Some citizens, seeing public services as hopeless, hired private contractors to remove the snow. The city, unable to make the Department of Public Works function effectively, also paid private contractors to plow the roads.

By New Year's 1983, all Christmas cheer had vanished. As ice ruts dominated streets through January, testy disdain for McNichols mounted. Walkers had it even worse than drivers. Many sidewalks were not shoveled—city hall did nothing to see this basic amenity was implemented, including along city bridges. Where the city plowed roads, it often blocked sidewalks. The more residents seethed under the snow, the more voters agreed McNichols' day had passed. This set the stage for the impending 1983 mayoral election.

## The 1983 Election

Even before the blizzard, many thought McNichols had been in office too long. Through the 1970s, there had been sporadic attacks on the administration. Allegations of wrongdoing were constant, complete with charges of sweetheart deals to the Broncos at Mile High Stadium, cost overruns on virtually all bond and building projects, giveaways to the Arlberg Club at Winter Park, and conflicts of interest between members of the McNichols administration and contractors, concessionaires, and bond houses. At times, the mayor only seemed to care about his 17th Street buddies and sports facilities—they were the exclusive Denver he saw and served.

An anti-McNichols constituency consistently berated the mayor. Unfocused and largely unorganized, it did not receive any leadership or direction from Tooley. Still, it kept battling city hall. A powerful expression of anti-McNichols feeling came in 1975 when an insurgent group gained election to city council. During the next eight years, these citizen legislators, notably Cathy Donohue, Sal Carpio, and Sam Sandos, frequently questioned the mayor, bypassed him, demanded greater council oversight of city spending, and called for informing neighborhood activists about pending public decisions. In May 1977, those challenging the mayor managed to get the voters to ratify a city charter amendment slightly strengthening the power of council whereby nine votes, rather than ten, could override a veto by the mayor. Shortly after Elvin Caldwell left council to become manager of safety in 1980, a close McNichols supporter on council, Kenneth MacIntosh died. New members gave anti-McNichols forces control of the city legislature.

Generally, council was no more than an irritant to the administration. Whenever council challenged him, McNichols emphasized Denver had a strong mayor form of government—he was to lead and council must follow. Boss Robert Speer instituted the system in 1916 after reformers had failed in city hall. Unlike Speer, who had previously been mayor from 1904 until 1912, the reformers had been incapable of readily doing the bidding of the business community.

Among those calling for the replacement of McNichols were individuals new to Denver. Often acting as arrogant missionaries who sought to take over the city, they had no respect for anything preceding their occupancy. They dismissed the incumbent as a vestige of the past. Besides, McNichols occasionally got in their way. The mayor knew enough about the city, bureaucratic administration, and Denver traditions whereby he sometimes honored local customs when he said no to schemes to completely remodel the city. The newcomers, notably business and real estate investors, wanted to totally reshape Denver in their own image. Showing a condescending scorn for their new community, they continually mocked the Mile High City as a cow town; it rather should be a great city. McNichols, they decreed, was just like Ben Stapleton—a stodgy, immovable character who prevented the Queen City from coming of age.

The mayor had supporters. Many had firmly stood by him from the time he took over from Currigan. They not only applauded his endorsement of the Olympics, but also noted how much of modern Denver was built under McNichols. The incumbent was the mayor who oversaw the construction of the Platte Greenway, McNichols Arena, and the 16th Street Mall. Generally relying on professional engineers, until the Christmas blizzard, McNichols projected himself as a man who got things done. As much as the newcomers, the Denver Planning Office under McNichols spewed out countless documents calling for Denver to recast itself in the image of some place else. Only in such a manner, the planners and administration agreed, could Denver emerge as a great city.

The incumbent's backers did not mention McNichols was also the mayor who was invisible in the school busing fights. "Mayor Bill," as supporters fondly called McNichols, never used his office as a bully pulpit to rein in the hatred and social divisions leading to the decline of Denver Public Schools (DPS). Nor was he an effective leader against the Poundstone Amendment. Outside of the transitory successes of the business community, McNichols neglected his home town while in office. During his mayoralty, parks became increasingly run down, fountains were shut off, and civic beauty was ignored. His critics wanted an executive who was a popular leader, not just a 17th Street administrative fixer.

It was unclear exactly who would challenge McNichols. Many of the newcomers had no more use for Dale Tooley than they did for the incumbent. The district attorney was as much old Denver as the mayor. Similarly, the idealism and liberalism of Tooley's New Politics epoch had disappeared by the time the 1983 mayoral election loomed—he was no longer the shining young idealist. Some residents disliked Tooley because he was district attorney. They saw him responsible for prosecutions aimed at people they knew or causes they supported. Those who had been attracted to Tooley in the 1970s by his liberal idealism now sought a different candidate. Still, Tooley was so sure his time had come that in November 1982, more than a month before the Christmas Blizzard, he announced he was going to resign as district attorney as of January 31, 1983, for the full-time job of running for mayor in the spring of 1983.

Photo by Phil Goodstein

*The city renames Wazee Street at 17th Street in memory of Dale Tooley for a week each year before St. Patrick's Day though Tooley was never particularly active in the city's Irish community. Wellington Webb who, like Tooley, unsuccessfully sought the mayor's post in 1983, looks at the sign.*

Monte Pascoe also entered the mayor's race. Another Denver native, born in 1935, he graduated from Dartmouth. A past chairman of the state Democrats, Pascoe's one previous fling at office was in 1969 when he was on the unsuccessful pro-busing ticket in the controversial school board election. In the interim, he worked as a water attorney while volunteering his time to assorted civic causes.

The candidate was a political associate of Governor Richard Lamm. During the 1970s, the governor appointed Pascoe to numerous state commissions. In 1980, Lamm arranged for the challenger to serve as executive director of the Department of Natural Resources. Pascoe projected himself as the politically astute, intellectual candidate.

Wellington Webb was another contender. Born in Chicago on February 17, 1941, he grew up on the south side of the Windy City. At age 12, suffering from severe asthma, he moved to Denver on a doctor's suggestion to live with his grandmother. The city's climate restored his vigor as Webb grew up as a tall young man who starred in basketball at Manual High School. Otherwise, he was a mediocre student, graduating with a C- average. After attending Northeastern Junior College in Sterling, in 1964 he got a bachelor's in sociology and teacher's certificate from Colorado State College in Greeley. He earned a master's in sociology from the school, by then the University of Northern Colorado, in 1971.

The graduate's initial goal was to teach in DPS, coaching Manual High School's basketball team. Ideally, Webb hoped to take it to three state championships in the course of a 35-year career, retiring to a small house with a white picket fence around it. Back in Denver, Webb could not get a teaching post. After working as a forklift operator for Frito Lay, he got caught up in the upheavals of the civil rights movement. Encouraged by his politically active grandmother, a close supporter of city councilman Elvin Caldwell, he committed himself to the Democratic Party. Through it, Webb established ties with Mayor Currigan and was offered a job with DPS in 1966. The corrupt process disgusted him. Rather than playing the system's game, Webb secured a position at Fort Logan where he taught emotionally troubled children. Eventually, he signed on with the Job Opportunity Center, a Model Cities program.

In the early 1970s, Webb emerged as a coming force in the Democratic Party. He joined with other blacks to push the election of African-Americans to office in a group known as the Young Turks. With their support and encouraged by the National Black Convention held in Gary, Indiana, in 1972 Webb launched a successful campaign for state representative from East Denver. In office, he stood out as a black advocate, intervening in racial tensions over school busing. Webb called for greater civilian control of the police, roundly criticizing the brutality of the department against African-Americans under McNichols. The aspiring politician had no trouble winning reelection in 1974.

Besides successfully running for the legislature in 1976, Webb was the state manager of the Jimmy Carter campaign. The new president appointed Webb regional administrator of the Department of Health, Education, and Welfare in 1977. When Carter sought reelection in 1980, Webb returned to Illinois to run the Carter campaign there. Webb came back to Denver after the election. Governor Lamm

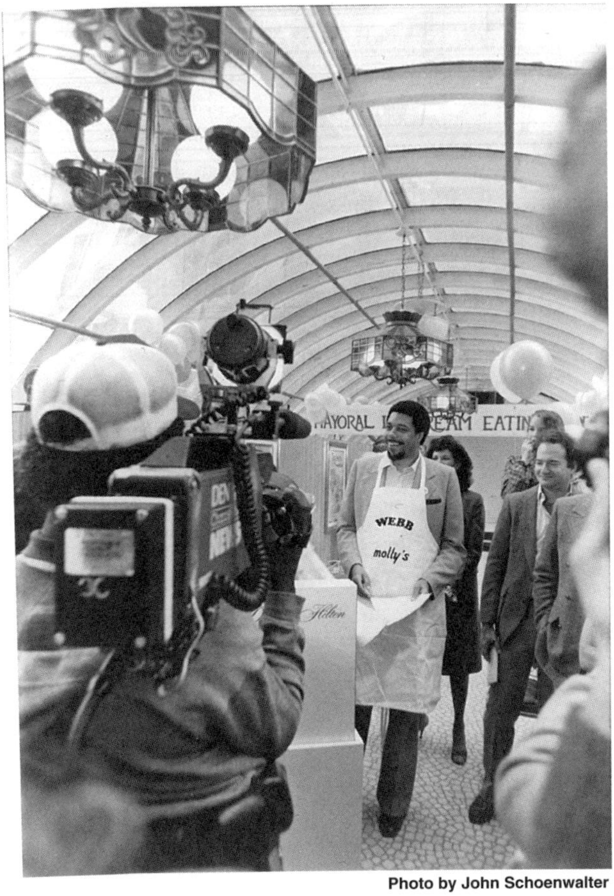


Photo by John Schoenwalter

*Wellington Webb still wore a beard when he challenged for city hall in 1983. He is shown on the bridge between the Hilton and May D&F upon winning a mayoral ice cream-eating contest that spring.*

named him executive director of the Colorado Department of Regulatory Agencies in 1981.

Webb campaigned for mayor in 1983 under the banner of the Committee for Denver's Future. It called for a municipal government "of the best and brightest people available," one critically reviewing municipal programs leading to a reform of much of the existing system. Denver, Webb announced, should emerge as "a modern Athens." He readily supported an expanded convention center and bringing neighborhoods into the public planning process.

While Webb's promises struck a chord among those dissatisfied with city hall, the candidate had a somewhat crude delivery. Still wearing a beard, conservatives feared him as nothing more than a vestige of 1960s black militancy. Though Webb tried to gather multiracial support, he was mostly the African-American candidate. His campaign generally failed to reach the entire city.

## The Rise of Federico Peña

One person just the opposite of Webb in this matter was the Hispanic candidate, Federico Fabian Peña. The third of six children, he was born in Laredo, Texas, on March 15, 1947, and raised in Brownsville. His father, Gustavo, was a prosperous cotton dealer who worked with Mexican businesses on the United States-Mexican border. Peña learned business ethics as a boy—he always embraced the essential corporate principle: business is the heart and soul of a community. After attending the private St. Joseph Academy in Brownsville, the future Denver resident earned his bachelor and law degrees from the University of Texas. On joining the Texas bar, Peña sought a political career. He initially opened a practice in El Paso.

By this time, the attorney's older brother, Alfredo, had settled in Denver as a lawyer. While not an active figure within the Chicano community, Alfredo Peña was involved with it, sometimes volunteering his services to the Mexican American Legal Defense and Educational Fund (MALDEF), a mostly work-within-the-system organization helping Chicanos who faced politically charged crimes. For a while, Alfredo Peña was a partner with Kenneth Padilla, the head of the local branch of MALDEF who defended many Chicano militants during the 1970s.

Pondering a possible political future in California or New York, Federico Peña visited his brother in Denver in 1973. The Texas attorney observed there were great possibilities in the Mile High City. He decided to stay in town, joining Alfredo Peña's law practice. Before long, Federico Peña had good political connections, especially with those close to Governor Lamm.

During the mid-1970s, Peña sometimes showed up as a lawyer for MALDEF. He was also staff attorney for the Chicano Education Project, an establishment push to improve schooling opportunities for Hispanic youth. During the mid-

Auraria Archives

*Federico Peña when he was the staff attorney for the Chicano Education Project in 1977.*

1970s, Peña was active in all of its major litigation while he contributed articles to its magazine, *Un Nuevo Día*. The Chicano Education Project honored him in 1978 when it established an annual Federico F. Peña Community Service Award.

Otherwise, Peña was not politically involved. There was no record of him actively participating in any elections at this time and he is not even listed in some city directories. Claims have confidently been made Peña did not subscribe to either the *Denver Post* or *Rocky Mountain News* and was ignorant of city issues. Still, Peña was the right man at the right time.

North Denver politics were in drastic transition in the mid-1970s. The Italian-American machine, which had long dominated the neighborhood, was in rapid decline. As Hispanos increasingly moved into the area while Chicano protests soared, the Democrats eagerly sought Latino candidates. Peña was among them.

Ruben Valdez encouraged Peña to get involved. Valdez was then the state's leading Hispanic politician. Born in Trinidad on January 27, 1937, he dropped out of Pueblo Centennial High School at age 15. After a stint in the military, Valdez joined the United Steel Workers in San Francisco. Maintaining his union affiliation when he moved to Denver, he learned politics by fighting for the rights of his fellow workers. Before long, Valdez directed the local Service Employment Redevelopment program of the Department of Labor.

The aspiring politician won election to the General Assembly in 1970. Quickly rising in the ranks of the Democrats, Valdez was caucus chairman in 1973–74. When the Democrats won control of the Colorado House in November 1974, he emerged, at age 37, as the body's speaker in 1975–76. After serving as Democratic minority leader in 1977–78, he sought the Democratic nomination for lieutenant governor in 1978.

Four years earlier, the Democrats tabbed a black politician, George Brown, for the post over a woman candidate. In 1978, in contrast, the party decided a woman's time had come when it nominated Nancy Dick of Aspen for lieutenant governor over Valdez. The latter admitted he ran an insipid campaign. After working as a consultant for the Commission on Community Relations while in the legislature, Valdez took a post in the Lamm cabinet. He was subsequently a lobbyist.

As the Hispanic politician sought election as lieutenant governor, Valdez looked for a replacement in the legislature. He joined with state Senator Paul Sandoval in suggesting Peña seek the open seat from North Denver. (Sandoval and Peña had ties through the Chicano Education Project.) Tom Nussbaum and John Parr, both veterans of the Lamm administration, also eagerly encouraged the Texas transplant to run. Peña, who had strong political ambitions, accepted the invitation.

Not all were happy about Peña's bid for the legislature. Also seeking the seat, community activist Anthony Ortiz questioned whether Peña was qualified for the job. He argued Peña was a carpetbagger who had not even sufficiently established his residency in the House district—Peña had only lived there for a year or so. Nor had Peña been involved in neighborhood politics or municipal concerns. Foes asserted the candidate had never voted in any school board, city council, or non-general municipal election. Despite this, with the help of a well-organized, well-financed campaign drawing on the Lamm machine, Peña easily triumphed over

Ortiz, 1,131–371, in the September 12, 1978, primary. He overwhelmed Republican Andy Carney, 3,835–1,050, in the general election.

The turnout in Peña's district was miserable. Opposed to the 4,885 ballots cast in his election—there were 10,822 voters registered in the district—a heavily contested race between Jerry Kopel and Paul Swalm in the area east of Colorado Boulevard along Sixth Avenue saw 13,856 ballots cast out of 22,030 registered voters. The contrasting levels of participation were reflective of how badly the North Denver machine had faded. Bright young Latinos such as Peña were helping revive the Democrats in this part of town.

As the Chicano civil rights movement forced white Denver to recognize Hispanics, Peña emerged as an energetic new face in the political establishment. An excellent speaker and neat dresser, the young legislator appealed to both Chicano militants and conservative, middle-class Latinos who appreciated the Texan's business ties and background. Nobody challenged Peña when he ran for reelection in 1980. By this time, he stood out. Governor Lamm named Peña to various commissions, including a panel studying growth as part of the Front Range Project and a body reviewing the impact of the Rocky Flats nuclear bomb factory.

After one term in the General Assembly, Peña was the foremost beneficiary of a Democratic upheaval. Far from challenging the Republican majority in the House of Representatives, the Democratic leadership often rubber-stamped it. At least this was the gripe of liberal Denver legislators unhappy with House minority leader Bob Leon Kirscht of Pueblo.

**Author's Collection**

*Harold Sudmeyer of the Socialist Workers Party was the only voice challenging the Democratic monopoly on city politics in the 1979 and 1983 mayoral elections.*

As Kirscht led the legislative party during 1979–80, critics complained the Democratic leader went out of his way to compromise on issues while he toned down traditional party principles. He failed to speak out in the House as a proud champion of the minority. Nor did he do well in delegating responsibility. Having both personal and political problems with Kirscht, Denver representatives, led by Wayne Knox, Jerry Kopel, and Miller Hudson, called for his replacement.

None of those openly opposed to Kirscht were eager to run for minority leader. The liberals' inaugural candidate, assistant minority leader Rich Castro, noted he had promised Kirscht he would not challenge the incumbent. Only after Peña had twice passed during a session called to choose a challenger shortly after the 1980 election did the future mayor decide he was the man for the job.

In 1980, there was a 100-percent concordance between Peña and Kirscht on crucial votes. Nonetheless, the Hispanic politician quickly separated himself from the minority leader. Peña drew on his ties with the Lamm administration, observing the governor had not gotten along too well with Kirscht.

Peña supporters played on their candidate's ethnicity in the campaign. They targeted Pueblo representative Leo Lucero. Though he was otherwise loyal to Kirscht and would not support Castro, the insurgents noted Lucero might—and did—vote for Peña as a fellow Latino. (Some within the caucus were concerned about having Mexican-Americans in the two top leadership positions—Castro remained as assistant minority leader. Others paid it no heed or insisted such ethnic politics would strengthen the party's hold as they lined up behind the challenger.)

Building a coalition among the House Democratic Party, Peña got affidavits from supporters promising to back him. Catching Kirscht completely by surprise, the future mayor narrowly triumphed among the 26 House Democrats. (Kirscht, a former Goldwater Republican before his election to the legislature as a Democrat in 1970, immediately bolted back to the Republicans. He later unsuccessfully sought the GOP nomination for governor.)

The conservative Republican leadership in the House feared Peña's triumph. Some thought him a radical Chicano bomb-thrower. They circulated a photo of the attorney, taken in the mid-1970s, when Peña, reflecting the fashions of the day, had relatively long hair and a mustache. The Democratic leader, they were sure was at one with the militants whom he had defended during his MALDEF days.

Peña quickly put their fears at rest. A fast learner, he mastered the issues and tried to build rapport with the Republicans. The future mayor had little success. In 1981, the Republicans systematically declared war on Denver, stripping state funding from the Denver Public Library and other cultural institutions. Peña fought back, defending the Mile High City's interests.

The North Denver Hispano easily charmed journalists. He was a smooth, energetic personality who always had a good word for them. By the end of his first term, the *Post* and *News* both praised him as the best freshman representative. The *Post* subsequently listed Peña as among the state's top ten legislators. Peña was obviously a man with a future.

Reapportionment after the 1980 census strengthened the hold of the suburbs on the legislature. With the exception of 1975–76, Democrats had been in the minor-

Photo by John Schoenwalter

*A supporter consoles Mayor William McNichols, left, on his defeat for reelection in May 1983.*

ity since 1966 and there was little prospect of them winning control of the House. Idealistic Democrats in the legislature rarely accomplished much. Other opportunities than leadership of the minority party were open to a bright young Hispanic politician.

By 1982, many Mexican-Americans were sure the time for a Latino mayor was near. While incumbent city councilman Sal Carpio did not believe it was immediately at hand and Rich Castro also passed on making the run, other politicians and community activists, including Peña mentor Paul Sandoval, argued McNichols was vulnerable in 1983. By building a coalition, a Hispanic could win. Peña agreed with them.

Lamm advisers Nussbaum and Parr took the lead. The more the governor bogged down in bad compromises while unconstrained growth devastated the state, his idealistic supporters were in a quandary. They had started off in the early 1970s by challenging the conservative powers within the Democratic Party around Bill McNichols. With Lamm, they had helped defeat the 1976 Winter Olympics. However, they realized few of their goals as Lamm institutionalized himself in office. He explained some of his lack of accomplishment by noting the extremely weak constitutional position of the governor. Some of his backers pondered rewriting the state constitution to redress this; others hoped to make their man mayor of Denver. They noted that post was stronger and more influential than the governor's.

Initially, insurgent Democrats aspired to put one of their own in city hall during the 1970s. Sam Brown, another anti-Olympics activist, sought the job. He stalled after he was elected state treasurer in 1974. To escape the bad press he received locally, Brown resigned in 1977 to go to Washington to serve as the head of AC-

TION. He announced he hoped to return to Denver as the idealist who would lead the forces of opposition in the 1979 mayor's race. In no time, Brown was the object of massive ridicule in the capital for his inept administration, leading him to leave his political career in near disgrace. Federico Peña, rather, came to the fore as the alternative for city hall.

After leading the Democrats in the House in 1981–82, Peña did not seek re-election in 1982. (The Republican majority gerrymandered him into the same district with Miller Hudson who announced he was leaving the legislature.) Peña likewise exited the General Assembly to run for mayor. As was the case with Tooley, Peña targeted McNichols even before the incumbent was snowed under by the Christmas blizzard.

Critics charged Peña was initially completely ignorant of urban controversies. A newspaper reporter gossiped he had not seen any books in Peña's rather dilapidated house near West 26th Avenue and Grove Street. Those so dismissing Peña underestimated the candidate. Once he resolved to run, Peña devoted himself heart and soul to winning the job. He quickly had a good command of the issues.

Heavily assisted by Lamm lobbyist Eric Sondermann, the challenger readily let Nussbaum and Parr run the campaign. They picked him up in the morning, showing him his schedule. His managers carefully prepared note cards for him, outlining subjects and helping Peña formulate policy. In no time, the ex-legislator came across as eminently qualified for the mayor's office. An outstanding extemporaneous speaker, Peña had an answer, idea, or suggestion for everything. Most of all, he presented a lively approach compared to the stagnant McNichols/Tooley status quo.

From the beginning, Peña waged an aggressive campaign, trying to hit all community forums. Though denying he was an ethnic candidate, he emphasized he was a Latino—a member of a minority struggling to make it within the system. His election, his supporters implied, would show Denver's tolerance and readiness to embrace the future. Besides, unlike Webb, Tooley, McNichols, and Pascoe, Peña was new to Denver. He had fresh approaches and was not fettered by the dead weight of the city's past. In this manner he appealed to other newcomers who were ready to take control of Denver's destiny.

On a more prosaic level, Peña lined up constituencies. Besides Hispanics, he appealed to labor. He promised union members better jobs, wages, working conditions, and municipal assistance. The Denver Area Labor Federation became the first influential group to endorse Peña. The candidate also rallied the women's movement. This was the time of the emerging rainbow coalition—an effort by Jesse Jackson to unite ethnic voters, students, women, and labor within the Democratic Party. Peña was the man to successfully make this happen locally.

Cynics pointed out Peña had another attraction for women voters: he was young, cute, and single. Simultaneously, Peña also lured the homosexual movement. He went out of his way to appeal to it, making special Valentine's Day stops at gay bars. Though not politically well organized, gay and lesbian activists did produce some votes and Peña became their candidate. The Sierra Club and environmentalists likewise endorsed him.

As the campaign heated up, Peña separated himself from Pascoe and Webb as the outside challenger. He stood out as the most effective debater at many candidate forums. As often as not, McNichols and Tooley were absent from them. By failing to show up at these neighborhood meetings, the Tooley-McNichols message was blunt: such outpourings of grassroot democracy did not matter. Scorned attendees realized the two insiders would readily ignore them as mayor in the same manner they lacked the basic courtesy to show up at the debates. Peña believed otherwise, trying to touch voters who had come to hear him speak.

## The Heat of the Campaign

A couple of fringe candidates were also on the ballot. Steve Schweitzberger, born in Denver on March 5, 1950, was proud of volunteering for the Air Force in 1969 at the peak of the Vietnam War. After his military service, he returned to his home town, deriving his income as a landlord in southwest Denver. For years, he had complained about the stilted and unimaginative core of the McNichols administration. The city needed creative ideas. Though not well informed about urban administration, public policy, or city issues, Schweitzberger was full of suggestions on how to redress sprawl and air pollution.

The candidate had sought to run for mayor in 1979, but the election commission ruled him off the ballot since he was not the required 30 years of age. Schweitzberger then failed in his campaign for councilman at large. Terming himself a "freelance activist," Schweitzberger frequently wrote letters to the editor and spoke out at public forums. The want-to-be politician unsuccessfully ran for the Democratic nomination to the legislature in 1980. In 1983, calling on Denverites to "Have a Good Mayor," he provided a different perspective on the city's future. Even as he sought the mayor's post, Schweitzberger made it known that he would happily trade his minuscule support for a job in the next administration.

Taxi driver Harold Sudmeyer, a member of the Socialist Workers Party (SWP), was the only non-Democrat seeking city hall. The Republicans had not mounted a challenger in the 1979 election nor did they do so in 1983. In this manner, the SWP was the only party to challenge the Democratic monopoly of Denver politics.

The SWP embraced a wide variety of radical causes during the 1970s. Sudmeyer was its most visible spokesman. He ran unsuccessfully for lieutenant governor in 1978, for mayor in 1979, and for Congress in 1980. As the socialist candidate in 1983, he called for a municipal workers' government. His campaign pointed out how growth had fueled social breakdown and increased poverty. Most of all, Sudmeyer managed to turn his campaign speeches into harangues about American foreign policy in Nicaragua.

Though Schweitzberger and Sudmeyer threw barbs into some of the candidate forums, the general tone of the election was about who would be the city's best administrator. All five of the establishment Democrats loudly voiced their support of the status quo. They likewise agreed something must be done to deal with air pollution, getting the city wired for cable television, supporting the arts, and better transportation. None questioned Denver's runaway growth. The crucial concern, one and all stated, was which one could best guide the metropolis.

Photo by John Schoenwalter

*Federico Peña gloats on his election triumph in June 1983.*

Peña harped on this. More determined city planning was essential. From a government of, by, and for the people, he insisted city hall should become part of a "public/private partnership." He seemingly could not get through a speech or interview without employing the phrase. Increasingly ignoring labor and minority issues, he sounded like a John Lennon dreamer, calling for voters to "Imagine a Great City." His personal dynamism and successful use of his ethnicity covered the void as to what exactly "great city" meant. Tom Nussbaum cleverly managed the campaign, firing the enthusiasm of numerous youthful volunteers.

The *Rocky Mountain News* endorsed Peña in April. It noted his ability to "lead and communicate a purpose" opposed to McNichols. Peña was also something of the consensus candidate, backed by both capital and labor. Neighborhood activists and academic wise men and women similarly endorsed him. Showing himself at one with the urban programs of the Ronald Reagan administration, Peña claimed credit for pushing enterprise zones in economically depressed areas of Denver while in the legislature. Even as Peña sold himself to the Hispanic community as their ethnic candidate, he emphasized he sought to represent everybody.

The *Denver Post* supported Tooley. McNichols' supporters seized on this. The incumbent's advertisements noted there were two good reasons for voters to re-elect the mayor: the *Post* and *News* opposed him. Otherwise, McNichols did not fit in during the 1983 election. As broadcast images became the keynote of the campaign, he could not compete with Peña or Tooley. He was such a poor speaker he had to hire announcers to voice his views on radio advertisements.

The Peña campaign also had an aggressive get-out-the-vote effort. It encouraged Mexican-Americans who had never previously bothered to register to do so. Peña also employed populist rhetoric among the disenfranchised. "The old powers in Denver are counting on you *not* to vote on May 17th. They will stay in control only if you stay at home. Let's show them," read one of his flyers.

Polls showed a toss-up. Tooley insisted he was actually in the lead. As often as not, he relied more on memories of past campaigns than in actively wooing first-time voters in a rapidly changing city. Instead of promising a fresh face for city hall, he equivocated about how much of a transformation his administration would bring. While Webb and Peña built support, promising to redress numerous complaints about police brutality and misconduct, Tooley was not ready to announce that he would replace longtime police chief Art Dill, a man with whom he had worked closely while district attorney. More than ever, Tooley emerged as McNichols' clone. (Just before the election, Dill resigned as police chief, compromised by an exposé of troubling police bingo operations.)

McNichols attempted to show himself as the activist mayor during a dangerous chemical spill in the rail yards shortly before the election. His message: the city had done fine during the last 14 years with him as mayor. There was no reason to get rid of a well-functioning administration. Voters, though, were reminded of the incumbent as the do-nothing mayor during the Christmas blizzard when it snowed on election day, May 17, 1983.

The storm was telling. Sixty-three percent of the electorate trooped to the polls. Peña won an impressive plurality with 48,320 (36.4 percent). Tooley was second with 41,126 (30.8 percent). Far behind was McNichols with 25,638 (19.1 percent). Webb gathered 9,371 (7 percent); Pascoe 6,835 (5.2 percent); Schweitzberger 1,709 (1.5 percent); and Sudmeyer 204 (.2 percent). Somewhere between 22 and 25 percent of the voters were newcomers who had never previously cast ballots in a Denver municipal election. Clearly, the face of the city's politics had changed.

Since Peña had failed to receive a majority of the total vote cast, a runoff election was held on June 21. Peña surged in the polls. Were it anybody except Tooley challenging him in a head-to-head race, the opposition candidate would have likely won. Republican voters were key to the election. In past runoffs between Democrats, especially the 1971 and 1975 races pitting Tooley against McNichols, they had generally supported the mayor. These voters did not forget their longtime hatred for Tooley. They preferred to support Peña, or not vote at all, rather than see Tooley finally become the city's leader.

Simultaneously, Peña stepped up his registration efforts in the Hispanic community. With the help of a $10,000 grant from the San Antonio-based Southwest Voter Registration Project, he brought nearly 6,000 new voters to the polls. Rumors floated not all were Denver residents or even American citizens. Tooley lamented his opponent's efforts, but could not prove the Peña camp was doing anything wrong. The former district attorney similarly rejected suggestions from some anti-Hispanic backers to play an ethnic card against Peña. The latter, though, readily called on people to vote for him precisely because he was a Latino. The Texas native redoubled his efforts to make his a people's campaign. Even with this cloak, he promised a great city, new leadership, fresh vision, and an eager commitment to the business domination of city hall.

The weekend before the runoff election, Dale Tooley's mother was stricken by a serious heart attack which she survived. Peña joined Tooley in calling off all further campaigning. The election was the end of Tooley's hopes when Peña narrowly defeated him for mayor, 79,542 (51.4 percent) to 75,097 (48.6 percent). The turnout was incredibly high, with 71.5 percent of the voters going to the polls. The Hispanic challenger swept the black, Hispanic, and traditionally liberal precincts of the city. About 18 months after the election, Tooley disclosed he was suffering from inoperable cancer. He died on April 1, 1985, at age 51. By that time, Peña was trying to make Denver a great city.

## A Note on Sources:

George V. Kelly, *Old Gray Mayors*, is the political history of Denver from World War II until the mid-1970s. It details the Currigan years and the Tooley deal. A sanctification of McNichols' policies is the oral history reminiscence of Ben Bezoff at DPL. Robert J. Sterling, in his biography of Robert Six, *Maverick*, describes Six's relations with Currigan. The Tom Currigan papers are at DPL. They include a good deal about the McNichols administration.

Radio reporter Bill Gagnon had numerous exposés of the problems of the city attorney and district attorney offices under Max Zall and Bert Keating in the 1960s, especially on KTLN and KIMN. *Colorado Lawyer* has sanctified Keating and Zall as among the outstanding lawyers in Colorado history: Theodore A. Borillo and Zeke Scher, "Bert M. Keating," 21:7 (July 1992), 1362–64; and Ronald I. Zall and Jon M. Zall, "Max P. Zall," 22:7 (July 1993), 1417–18.

The Doris Banks papers at the Auraria Archives contain an immense store of materials on the Democratic Party in the 1960s and early 1970s, including correspondence with Dale Tooley and support of his 1971 campaign. Tooley told his story in his posthumously published memoirs, *I'd Rather Be in Denver*. A good biographical portrait of him is Dick Spriggs, "Dale Tooley," *Colorado Lawyer*, 26:7 (July 1997), 11–12. Spriggs shared with me his memories of working in the district attorney's office under Tooley. Juan Haro remembered his run for mayor in 1971 and the personalities and issues in that year's race.

The ACLU records at the Auraria Archives includes materials on the arrest of Dorothy Davidson, the Golden Apple, and the raid on St. Andrew's Church. ACLU attorney Bill Reynard recalled his involvement in the Davidson case. There is a portrait of the early history of St. Andrew's in Breck, *The Episcopal Church in Colorado*. Members of St. Andrew's have told me stories about the Mad Monks and invited my tours to come into the building.

Walter Gerash talked about Tooley. He allowed me to look at his files on Corky Gonzales' suit against Currigan and defense of Afshin Shariati. Both trials were widely reported in media. *El Gallo* took special shots at Currigan in the Gonzales case. Afshin Shariati gave me his version of his trial and Tooley's actions. The

Minoru Yasui papers in the Auraria Archives contain materials on the city's response to the Iranian developments.

Scott Robinson reflected on the Espinoza case. *Espinoza v. O'Dell*, 663 P.2d 455, and *O'Dell v. Espinoza*, 456 US 430, are key court rulings on it. *El Gallo* also reported the events. Some of its impact is noted in Vigil, *Crusade for Justice*. Walter Gerash allowed me to look the files of his suits against the police over shootings and brutality in the 1970s. I review some of the police department scandals in my *Seamy Side of Denver*. Ed Thomas and Allen Jones recalled their careers on the department at this time.

*Christmas Blizzard '82* (Indianapolis: News and Features Press, 1983), is a compilation of *Rocky Mountain News* articles on the storm. In addition to it, I have drawn on *Denver Post* reportage and coverage in such weeklies as *Westword*, *City Edition*, and *Up the Creek*. As one who lived through the storm, personal memories are obviously added. Pat Angell recalled working through the blizzard for United Airlines at Stapleton. Marilyn Megenity shared her experiences at the Mercury Cafe.

The Denver Department of Public Works has periodically issued snow control plans, including one in January 1975 and another in October 1984. They are mostly filled with bureaucratic gibberish. There is little in the annual report of the Department of Public Works on the 1982 blizzard.

Jones and Forrest, *Denver: A Pictorial History*, has a good discussion of the 1913 and 1946 blizzards. Gene Fowler, *Salute to Yesterday* (New York: Random House, 1937), is a fictional account of the 1913 blizzard. City hall's boast of not being prepared is in *City of Denver*, 2:7 (January 10, 1914), 3. William E. Heatley, *That Snow Storm* (Denver: Williamson-Haffner, 1914), is a photo book on the snowfall. The April 18, 1920, *Rocky Mountain News* had a story about great blizzards from Denver's past.

Newspaper reports, including the coverage in *Westword* and *City Edition*, and campaign brochures, gave sketches of the candidates in 1983. There are DPL clipping files on the contenders and the race. The *Denver Downtowner* then beat the drum for Peña as the newcomers' candidate. *Un Nuevo Día* included materials on Peña and articles by him. Kieran McConnellogue, "Walking the Walk," *University of Northern Colorado Spectrum*, Fall 1999, pp. 8–11, traces Webb's background. Richard Lamm gives his views on the governor's office in a book he wrote with Duane Smith on the history of the state's governors, *Pioneers & Politicians*. There is a biographical sketch of Ruben Valdez in Colorado Legislative Council, *Presidents and Speakers of the Colorado General Assembly*, 173–74.

Wayne Knox, Miller Hudson, Jerry Kopel, and Jack McCroskey gave me drastically differing accounts of the revolt against Bob Kirscht and the rise of Peña as House minority leader in 1981. They also discussed Denver politics in the 1970s and early 1980s, noting the rise of Peña and the 1983 election. Harold Sudmeyer and Steve Schweitzberger shared their views of that campaign. Bill Himmelmann observed labor's role in backing Peña. Tom Bastien, Paul Swalm, Cathy Donohue, Hiawatha Davis, Cathy Reynolds, Mike Davenport, and Steve Garber also noted this epoch.

# 5

# Imagining a Great City

Federico Peña took office when Denver verged on a precipice. The oil bubble was about to burst. The city had not benefited from the immense growth of the late 1970s/early 1980s when barrel after barrel of black gold coated the community. The ten years before Peña was inaugurated saw the transformation of the central business district. The runaway price of oil fueled ridiculous land prices and brought a corps of carpetbaggers to a wide-open, rootless, directionless community. Even as the metropolitan area expanded, cultural institutions stagnated. Social divisions widened. Speculators and developers increasingly destroyed low-income housing for parking lots. Downtown was more a sacrifice zone to real estate speculation than a people place.

Peña won city hall by appealing to individuals frustrated with the pro-business administration of Bill McNichols. The new mayor, however, never directly addressed the rot at the core of oil-boom city. Far from decrying the direct and blatant negative impact of cancerous growth, Peña gloried in it. Such sprawl, he and his backers were sure, was a permanent part of the local scene. The mayor's policies called for guiding and directing it. Heartily echoing the rhetoric of the Denver Partnership (the commanding downtown business group, previously known as Downtown Denver Incorporated and later renamed the Downtown Denver Partnership), he agreed 17th Street and city hall must be partners in shaping the city.

Nobody seconded this more heartily than the head of the Partnership, Dick Fleming, who quickly emerged as something of the stealth mayor under Peña. Upon winning the runoff, Peña and his backers were unprepared to take over city hall. They had neither a program of action nor a well-conceived understanding of how to forge a new administration.

Photo by Phil Goodstein

*After Peña vowed his commitment to preserving low-income housing in the central city, acres of parking lots came to line the fringes of downtown. Shown is a lot on the 2100 block of California Street that displaced residential units.*

Fleming did. On the morrow of the election, he emerged as a foremost Peña adviser, guiding the politician on how to assume power and act as mayor. As much as serving as head of the Partnership, Fleming was a close Peña associate in working to select people and shape the policies of the new municipal government. This continued for long after Peña was sworn into office.

In this void, it was quickly clear Peña's campaign slogan of "Imagine a Great City" was more than rhetoric. As much as any architect or contractor, his foremost desire was to be a builder, a man remembered by his successes in completely reshaping the metropolis. This meant encouraging development and assuring high land values. He called for freely applying cosmetics to cloak problems and bring out the city's natural beauty. The administration targeted the poor and the misfits for elimination from downtown while the public/private partnership—the unity of Peña with Fleming—ruled the city.

It took a while for Peña's business orientation to sink in. The mayor had campaigned for office as a populist. The candidate pointed to his record in the legislature where he had been a foe of corporate domination. In 1981, for example, he lamented how "developers love to come to Denver because there are no questions asked by the city." He had worked with constituents in his North Denver district, helping them stave off unwanted projects out of scale with the people, places, and rents in the working-class enclave.

As mayor, Peña initially seemed to continue this position. Opposed to the stodgy, anti-neighborhood, anti-activist, anti-quality-of-life character of the McNichols administration, the new regime was a breath of fresh air. New faces, ideas, and forces swept the city. The mayor was everywhere. He reached out to the citizenry. Peña held well-publicized, heavily attended community forums, meetings at which citizens could approach the mayor, ask him about city policies, and inform him of neighborhood problems. A telegenic politician, Peña gloried in the attention he received.

Before long, it was questionable whether Peña knew what he was doing. Despite promises at community forums to redress complaints, conditions often more or less continued as normal. Though individuals dealing with city officials were greeted by smiling faces and vows of action, they frequently received little satisfaction. The mayoral sessions became less regular. Increasingly, they were simply public relations measures.

Many around Peña had a haughty attitude. Newcomers to the city, they sometimes embodied all the arrogance of a colonial force, bringing enlightenment to yokels from allegedly better, more sophisticated communities. As much as the postwar generation, they dismissed old Denver as obsolete and meaningless. Nobody around McNichols, they were sure, had known how to run a city. Part of their mission, they implied, was to recreate the municipal government. In the process, the Peña administration often appeared comparable to inventors who declared their square wheels improvements on the existing technology.

## The Denver Planning Office

Bill Lamont personified the arrogance of city hall. He emerged as Peña's right-hand man, heading the Denver Planning Office (DPO). This was among the many crucial posts for which the mayor lacked a candidate upon taking office. Dick Fleming loudly demanded the city bring in a hot-shot city planning expert of his choosing from the East. Others close to Peña agreed the planning director would be a pivotal leader of the new administration. At times, it appeared those having the mayor's ear would settle for nobody less than the messiah for the job.

Peña tabbed Lamont for the post in November 1983. The appointee had the right pedigree. A native of Chicago, Lamont attended the University of Colorado in the mid-1950s on a football scholarship. After receiving a master's degree in city planning from the University of Illinois, Lamont joined the DPO in 1959. Moving to Boulder in 1961, he later worked as that city's director of community development. By 1983, Lamont had tired of working as a private planning consultant. He talked about going to an undeveloped country in Africa to test his theories about government problem-solving. Instead, he moved back to the Colorado capital to guide Denver's emergence as a great city.

The planning director mouthed all the correct phrases about the need to design cities for people. Lamont quickly came to the fore in the administration as the mayor stumbled in 1983–84 with precisely how to get Denver to work. The DPO chief was the individual in the administration who at least had a grasp of urban design. Under him, the planning office achieved great influence. The mayor looked to it to bring the corporate community together with residents. It was the vehicle to implement Peña's campaign pledges.

DPO stemmed from the Denver Planning Commission. Virtually from the time the Ben Stapleton administration created the latter on February 24, 1926, the bureau had eagerly sought to direct the city's destiny. City hall shaped the commission based on recommendations from Secretary of Commerce Herbert Hoover. The agency embodied the 1920s concept of the public/private partnership.

Never modest in its aspirations, the commission confidently asserted that, by allowing it to determine zoning codes and a harmonious arrangement of buildings, parks, schools, and streets, Denver would flourish. The body openly advocated a kind of state capitalism whereby the city did the bidding of the private sector. While the organization got a good deal of ink and drew pretty pictures, it was mostly a paper operation with little power.

Mayor Quigg Newton (1947–55) realized this. As Denver verged on chaos, unable to cope with the massive growth transforming the city after World War II, Newton replaced the planning commission with the nine-member Denver Planning Board in 1948. It was very similar to its predecessor. Those serving on it without pay were politically well-connected, usually having ties to the corporate community. Still, more than just the name changed.

The planning commission had been an amateur outfit drawing on private consultants. Thanks to Newton, the planning board oversaw the Denver Planning Office, a city agency staffed with professional planners. Bringing the men and women of DPO together with the planning board was the director of planning, a mayoral appointee. This official led DPO in its mission of formulating comprehensive city plans and working to shape Denver's growth.

The federal government bolstered the planning office's authority. As cities increasingly veered out of control in the 1950s and 1960s, racked by internal decay and suburban flight, Washington embraced planning as a cure to their ills. This was at a time when widely circulated books, notably Jane Jacobs' *The Death and Life of Great American Cities*, convincingly illustrated the fundamental flaws of the planning profession. Jacobs and others noted how most city planners lacked the slightest idea of how metropolises actually operated. Nonetheless, Washington mandated that all communities seeking federal urban assistance funds have planning agencies. The better a local planning office was at formulating idealistic programs and running the bureaucratic maze, the more money a city was likely to get from Washington.

As Newton intended, DPO led the charge for urban renewal and superhighways, programs cutting Denver into shreds during the 1960s and 1970s. A never-ending stream of comprehensive city and neighborhood plans flowed from the agency. DPO reviewed all proposed zoning changes and tried to explain city policy to the public. In the name of democratic participation—and to comply with federal regulations—it called on people to attend neighborhood planning sessions.

Despite DPO's impressive self-portrait as the nerve center of the city, most politicians paid it little heed. City council rarely depended on the planning office when considering zoning changes. Some council members were blunt: the professional planners lacked a grasp of the quirks, idiosyncrasies, and traditions of the city; instead of appreciating Denver for what it was, DPO employees often relied on textbook clichés having no connection with how people lived or worked. The agency eagerly embraced urban renewal programs, city efforts displacing many low-income individuals from their longtime homes. The area's actual physical growth and land uses during the 1950s, 1960s, and 1970s were worlds away from what the planners envisaged. Nor did DPO address economic realities and the question of precisely who benefited from various projects. On the contrary, most planners assumed existing power relations and the dominance of business were unquestioned eternals.

DPO

*Bill Lamont was Peña's planning director.*

Mayor Bill McNichols readily used the planning office to push his policies. DPO spewed out continual documents during the 1970s and early 1980s. By following their guidelines, the planners confidently asserted, Denver would quickly evolve into a great city. The planners frequently had little patience with those demanding to know precisely what this meant or why new plans were forever needed when the old ones remained unimplemented or advocated all the wrong things.

Even while DPO presented a confident, optimistic face to the public, it was torn by severe dissension under McNichols. This was exemplified in the parking garage war. In the late 1960s/early 1970s, a powerful environmental and citizens' revolt swept Denver. Activists hoped the city would do something about residents' increasing car dependency. City hall, in contrast, in collaboration with Downtown Denver Incorporated and the Denver Urban Renewal Authority, wanted to erect numerous monstrous parking garages around downtown. The proposal mobilized opponents. They noted the administration's effort would increase congestion, destroy housing, and make the central city ever more car dependent. Some of the DPO staff realized this and also spoke out against the garages.

McNichols, who fully supported the scheme, which collapsed in May 1972, responded by muzzling DPO. Planners were not to speak to the media without official clearance. Far from bringing any critical knowledge about cities to the administration, the mayor simply expected DPO to execute the city's pro-development policies.

Faced with such treatment, morale sagged in DPO. Vacancies were left unfilled. National planners and academic experts condemned this—they were sure the planning office could bring life and vitality to the otherwise brain-dead administration. Some of McNichols' supporters claimed the mayor's treatment of the planning office was the best thing the politician ever did. Under him, nobody took DPO seriously.

This greatly changed under Peña. He considerably beefed up the planning office as the administration used it to shape policy. Lamont was constantly at the mayor's side. When asked questions to which he did not know the answers, the planning director sometimes appeared to fabricate data. He cited population figures, for example, about North Capitol Hill unsupported by any census reports. Scorning the work of Henry Barnes and the Division of Traffic Engineering in the 1940s, 1950s, and 1960s, Lamont erroneously stated downtown traffic lights were not synchronized. In his efforts to reshape the city, the DPO chief loudly talked about totally rewriting the Denver zoning code.

The planning director's pronouncements embodied the Peña team. Manipulators at city hall targeted senior career service personnel who actually ran the city. Most of the latter, led by City Engineer Jack Bruce, were engineers who had signed on in the 1950s and 1960s. The Peña administration dismissed these senior civil servants as hopeless remnants of the past. A systematic cleaning out of such city employees was needed as part of their efforts to reshape Denver. Before long, many veteran municipal workers were at war with the mayor. Eventually, city hall forced most out or into early retirement.

## Yuppie Planners

An extreme, condescending arrogance permeated the Peña administration. Those who did not fit, such as the career civil servants, had to go. The well-educated, affluent, rather youthful backers of Peña projected themselves as the morally elect, the anointed who were to transform their adopted cow town into the Queen City of Mountain and Plain. At the time when the term "yuppie" first appeared in 1984 to describe the backers of the presidential campaign of Colorado United States Senator Gary Hart, the Peña cadre embodied all of its negative connotations. It was the new generation seeking to reshape Denver in its own image.

Far more than a young Hispanic mayor, Peña was the country's first yuppie mayor. Socially and politically, he and his backers were generally at one with Dick Fleming of the Partnership. (Though Lamont and Fleming were ideologically close, both eagerly embracing the public/private partnership, personal tensions rapidly grew between the two powerbrokers.)

As much as Lamont, other members of the planning office exuded a divine eminence making it unnecessary for them to study the specific traditions and actual physical layout of the areas and projects they were designing. Illustrative was the planner overseeing the Cherry Creek neighborhood, Maggie Sperling. Opposed to the executives of the Taubman Corporation, the developer of the new Cherry Creek Mall who fully reviewed its history and land use—including the presence of a tunnel under First Avenue near Clayton Street—Sperling's angry answer to a question about the tunnel was "what tunnel?"

Representatives of the planning office engaged in partisan pleading for certain projects in front of city council while conveniently distorting data to fit their agenda. One evening, for instance, council debated a zoning change near Evans Avenue and South Humboldt Street. The planning office vigorously advocated the measure since it would fill in vacant land with a commercial development. Neighbors opposed the proposal because it would demolish an existing house. After nearly an hour-long public hearing, it became obvious the planning office had failed to observe that a house stood on the allegedly vacant lot.

Such trifles did not bother Lamont and backers of the planning office. Far from addressing the questions about whether city planning had ever accomplished any meaningful, pro-community results, they scorned skeptics of planning schemes as

Photo by Phil Goodstein

*Republic Plaza towers over the blank wall of the Denver Pavilions where developers hoped to build an 86-story highrise. In the mid-1980s, the virtually empty Republic Plaza was the home of Studio 37, the space where the Denver Planning Office and Denver Partnership plotted their plans for downtown.*

hopeless Neanderthals. Instead of debating exactly what the community should be and the problems with the planning process, supporters of the Peña administration and DPO, especially a group known as the Urban Design Forum, encouraged the public to have good thoughts, push brilliant ideas, and so help the mayor imagine a great city. Those behind the highly publicized efforts often had an imperious disdain for any questioning of city policy.

Nothing better illustrated the administration, the doings of DPO, and the character of its backers than the 1986 comprehensive plan for downtown. Actually, it is a misnomer to attribute the document to DPO or call it a plan. It was as much a product of the Denver Partnership as the city agency. The private business group spent upwards of a $1 million in formulating this effort to guide public policies on the central business district.

Meetings discussing the plan were usually held at Studio 37. This was the DPO/Partnership's trendy name for private office space provided gratis to the planners by real estate interests. It was located on the 37th floor of the city's highest office tower, the 56-story Republic Plaza.

A partnership of Philip Anschutz and Canadian oil speculators, Oxford-Ansco, developed the glasstower. By the time Republic Plaza opened in 1984, the office boom had started to go bust. Far from thriving with tenants paying Wall Street rents, the skyscraper was mostly vacant. To attract more growth and customers, the owners turned over the 37th floor to the collaboration of the Partnership and planning office to draft the downtown plan. Even as the plotters of downtown's destiny met in the nearly empty building, a prime premise of their document was the continued high demand for elite office space. As late as 1985, *Denver Today*, a publication of the Partnership, extolled central Denver as among the top ten locations in the country in the rate of office absorption.

The irony of lack of demand and the belief the office boom was a permanent phenomenon did not register on the Partnership or Peña administration. They were self-professed visionaries who did not let facts get in their way. This came across in the way they presented their plan to the public.

After the downtown leaders and city officials had formulated the document to their liking, rather than circulating it as a working draft, subject to correction of errors, amendment, and debate, the Partnership/DPO printed the master plan as a sleek brochure. Not only did interested parties have to buy the proposal, but the message was the text could and would not be changed.

With such parentage, it was not surprising the plan failed to reflect the actual economic forces destroying the oil facade. At a time when downtown office va-

DPO

*The 1986 comprehensive downtown plan included Disneyland sketches, such as this one providing for sailboats on the Platte.*

cancies were soaring, the downtown plan talked about the need for more highrises. It called on the city to limit traffic while increasing parking and automobile access. Fantasy scenarios filled its pages, complete with sailboats on the Platte. The illustrations were more apropos of a comic book or a science fiction story than a serious effort to map the future of a vibrant, diverse urban area.

The plan was incredibly sloppy. To show their sophistication and how they were in tune with the city's traditions, the Partnership and DPO stressed downtown's history. In the process, they revealed their laziness and ignorance. Date after date was erroneous, ranging from the time of the end of the Pikes Peak gold rush to when Robert Speer took office as mayor to the year the Regional Transportation District was established. By stating the 20th Street Viaduct linked downtown with "West Denver" (it went to Highland in the heart of historic North Denver), the planners exposed their lack of knowledge of the city's geography.

The planning office did not care. When the errors were called to his attention, Lamont dismissed correcting them as "too negative." It was obvious DPO had no concern about the accuracy of its pronouncements. On the contrary, it saw itself as a cheerleader for 17th Street. The downtown plan was not a realistic outline mapping the possibilities and potentials of the central business district; it was a propaganda tract for the Partnership and Peña administration.

No sooner had city council officially adopted the plan than members of the business community, planning office, and politicians asserted the city needed a plan for the central business district. A Downtown Redevelopment Committee pushed for a new one. In other words, without saying as much, champions of planning conceded the Denver Partnership/DPO document had no value. (Lamont suddenly quit as planning director in December 1989.)

## The McNichols Administration in Running Shorts

The downtown plan reflected the quality of much of the Peña administration. A groping incompetence permeated it. While rosy vows were made to redress wrongs and fix broken municipal institutions, there was little relationship between promise and performance. As confusion and mumbo-jumbo became city hall's defining characteristics, some started to idealize the days of Mayor Bill as backers of the old order increasingly romanticized McNichols. Those celebrating him—ignoring the massive social breakdowns of his years in office—claimed he at least knew how to get things done.

After Peña showed himself as unable as McNichols to clear the streets following a blizzard that dropped 21.5 inches of snow on November 25–27, Thanksgiving weekend 1983, memories of the previous incumbent's failure faded. Peña became a laughingstock in the wake of the storm when he suggested, rather than plowing the snow, having city trucks pack it down, assuring even icier conditions. Opposed to ice-skating on city parks in the wake of the Christmas Blizzard, he prohibited ice-skating on city property. It was, he explained, too dangerous. His administration also vehemently forbade children from sledding down park hills.

Part of the problem the Peña administration faced was the legacy of the McNichols administration. The former mayor's lack of leadership during the oil

Photo by Phil Goodstein

*The dome of the Greek Assumption Cathedral is in the distance in Glendale, a community of vacant lots, storage facilities, offices, apartments, and stripper bars. During much of the 1970s and 1980s, it was the center of Denver's wild, rowdy, nightlife. Seemingly, it was a model for those calling for Denver to become a "24-hour-city."*

boom and social crises tearing Denver apart during the 1970s left massive chasms. While McNichols had committed himself heart and soul to sports facilities, other institutions, notably schools, parks, and libraries, were falling apart. Despite the real estate growth, the city faced an endless financial squeeze. Nor was downtown inviting; on the contrary, it was usually dead after business hours.

Other than idealistic rhetoric and planning documents, the Peña administration accomplished little at first. Instead of committing himself to basic principles, the mayor avoided making hard decisions. Throughout his first term, he constantly called in outside consultants who told him what he wanted to hear. Most of all, he readily adopted a corporate attitude, marked by his alliance with Fleming and the Partnership. Under Peña, business' demands, hopes, and aspirations were those of the city. He ratified this as he endlessly spouted the glories of the "public/private partnership" whereby the city served the interests of 17th Street.

As the mayor showed himself at one with the moguls' domination of the Mile High City, the joke went out about how McNichols had made decisions. When he faced a dilemma, Mayor Bill turned to a dart board in his office. Part of it said "yes," the other part "no." Peña had a similar dart board, but with a third section reading "Ask Dick Fleming." As much as during the McNichols years, assisting the rich and influential was the administration's first priority. No more than under the former mayor was city hall willing to question the dictates of the region's largest banks and property speculators.

Illustrative of Peña's politics was his failure to support a 1984 citizen initiative calling for a height-limitation ordinance. Proponents, mostly drawn from the neighborhood movement, asserted such a measure was vital. Without it, corporate domination and real estate speculation continually threatened residents with monstrous buildings blocking the sunshine and changing the nature of social geography. Height limitation was also urgent because faceless skyscrapers threatened the view of the mountains and Denver's distinctive personality. Opponents, outspending advocates by more than ten to one, only narrowly defeated the measure.

Peña's silence on the proposal was telling. He and his partners in the business community did not want any fetters on development. Far from nourishing a local character, they repeatedly argued Denver must follow the pattern of other cities. Advocating a clone community, they readily spoke of luring outside capital and bringing in new affluent residents. Only by so selling itself could Denver emerge as a great city. The implication: it was still a hick burg neither having nor deserving any respect.

The mayor was almost hysterical on this point. When a Monday Night Football game on October 15, 1984, showed the city engulfed in a blizzard, Peña exploded. Following in the wake of the 1982 Christmas and 1983 Thanksgiving blizzards, he lamented how the national media unfairly painted Denver as a veritable Siberia. It was almost as if, he implied, a nefarious bad weather bureau existed to keep Denver from achieving its place in the sun. Such a stance, compounded by an utter kowtowing to the corporate elite—just as had been the case in the days of Mayor Bill—led *Denver Post* columnist Tom Gavin to dismiss the new regime as "the McNichols administration in running shorts."

Others, such as a close associate of city councilwoman Cathy Donohue, were equally vicious. She claimed Peña had somehow mixed up the "imagine a great city" slogan of his 1983 campaign with rival Dale Tooley's vow of "no special favors." The result, under the new administration, was to shape Denver as "no special city" where business interests could "imagine a great favor."

All the while, the mayor's rhetoric intensified about making Denver a great city. Planning office shows increased. Among them were non-stop "charettes," a term for conferences lasting up to a week as the planners sought to reinvent neighborhoods and the city. At all of them, the message was the same: Denver had to rebuild itself. Only in such a manner could it emerge as a "24-hour city."

This was a favorite cliché of the mayor and his business backers. The media readily echoed the meaningless phrase. Never adequately defined, a 24-hour city was apparently one filled with endless noise and activity. Once again, rhetoric was used to mask reality. There was something deeply wrong with the Denver created by the massive urban renewal and growth policies of the past generation, but the planners had no idea what it was or how Denver could best serve its existing residents.

Part of the push for a 24-hour city was the realization all the new investment since the 1950s had left downtown a sterile place. During the 1970s and 1980s, most of the swinging nightclubs were outside of the central business district. Many were not even in Denver proper; rather, they were in the town of Glendale. It was an independent, 354-acre enclave, bordered roughly by Alameda Avenue, South Dahlia Street, Leetsdale Drive, South Fairfax Street, Mississippi Avenue, and South Colorado Boulevard. A few landowners there had fiercely resisted Denver's efforts to annex the land after World War II, leading them to incorporate Glendale in 1952.

Wars between Denver and Glendale were constant well into the 1960s. The Mile High City systematically refused to provide any services to the suburb. To generate revenue, Glendale invited bars and nightclubs to make the town their home. In the wake of a 1968 Denver crackdown on rowdy liquor establishments, many watering holes moved to Glendale. During the next 20 years, it was the center of swinging, loud, drug-fueled nightlife. (Among those patronizing such Glendale lounges was Peña. His main birthday party/fund-raising bash in his 1987 campaign for reelection was at a Glendale nightclub.)

Denver, the Peña administration announced, needed Glendale-like watering spots downtown. The implication was that since Denver was not a 24-hour city, it was a dull, stodgy place. The call for a 24-hour city also expressed the regime's scorn for residents. Far from working for a safe, friendly community, one where people were proud of their city and treasured its history, heritage, culture, and idiosyncrasies, Peña sought to transform Denver into a generic town modeled on other metropolises: supposedly 24-hour cities. Why Denver needed rackets at three and four in the morning, combined with the drugs, alcoholism, and unhappiness of Glendale nightlife, was never explained. Seemingly, unless Denver had something happening at all hours of the day and night, it could not be a great city.

Given such an outlook, the planners and advocates of a great city took no account of what would happen if the oil bubble burst. Citing the figures of the late 1970s/early 1980s, they argued growth would never end. Comprehensive planning was necessary to direct it. Without the obtrusive intervention of DPO, Denver would be caught up in events beyond its control. As it was, precisely thanks to its unquestioned faith in growth, development, and sprawl—all supposedly provided for via planning in the name of becoming a great city—Denver found itself in crisis.

## The Devastation of Downtown

As Peña consolidated himself in city hall in 1984–85, the oil boom was no more. The aspirations for high rents, ever taller skyscrapers, and the transformation of Denver into the oil center of the universe had little foundation. Unemployment and office vacancy rates soared. By the mid-1980s, conditions were so bad that a story circulated about how only Quito, Ecuador, had a worse central office market than Denver.

The impending real estate collapse was already visible by the time of Peña's election. After 1982, developers undertook no new oil-inspired office towers. They junked a number already on the drawing board. The speculative real estate market increasingly had no relationship to land and building values. Instead of using the planning department to address this concern so Denver could cope when the inevitable downturn came, Peña's primary goal was to revive the boom. He sought to give business whatever it demanded in the hope of restoring the good days of the McNichols years.

Author's Collection

*The new Public Service Building at the south corner of 15th and Welton streets in 1963. Note the many low-scale neighboring structures, including the Ghost Building to the left of Public Service.*

Though new construction ceased under Peña, the wave of demolition continued. Real estate gamblers, who had bought buildings with smoke-and-mirror financing, lost their holdings. Often, the owners simply abandoned the structures, especially those on the fringes of downtown. Banks and insurance companies foreclosed on these properties. Instead of seeking to renovate the structures and find new tenants such as the low-income renters who had previously occupied many old residential hotels and apartment houses, the financial institutions frequently ordered the demolition of these residences. Especially northeast of 20th Street and south of West Colfax Avenue, a sea of parking lots replaced what had been working-class neighborhoods.

Tax laws encouraged such destruction. Improved land—real estate with structures on it—was taxed more than undeveloped land, including prime parcels of unkempt parking lots. Besides, the parking lots produced revenues. The old buildings did not. In light of this, a greater percentage of downtown buildings were torn down for speculation and parking lots than had been destroyed in the central districts of heavily bombed German and Japanese cities during World War II.

No place was the destruction greater than in a blue-collar section of downtown southwest of 15th Street. In the late 1970s, this area was still lined by simple two-

and three-story structures. Often low-income workers lived in them, residents who patronized adjacent bars and greasy spoons. The businesses also included an outstanding bookstore, Bargain Books, at the west corner of 15th Street and Tremont Place. Nearby were small, customer-oriented, family-owned tailor shops, portrait studios, beauty parlors, laundries, a bowling alley, bicycle shop, florists, typewriter rental establishments, and other places making downtown a neighborhood for people.

A foremost supporter of growth, the area's power utility, Public Service Company of Colorado, took the lead in destroying these structures and businesses. Its longtime home was the Gas & Electric Building at the west corner of 15th and Champa streets, a 1910-vintage edifice the electric company lit up at night to advertise its commodity. Turning its back on the landmark, Public Service moved to a modern tower at the south corner of 15th and Welton streets in 1962. That building was also designed to advertise the utility. Huge panels dominated each side of the top of the building. During the night, they were visible for miles away as they glowed in different colors. Public Service disconnected the lights in the wake of the energy crisis of 1973 as the firm's tower rapidly aged, becoming just another bland downtown office headquarters.

(The Gas & Electric Building became the Insurance Exchange Building after Public Service moved out. Its lights also went dark in the wake of the energy crisis. When insurance companies were in greater disrepute than usual in the mid-1980s, the owner turned the lights back on to brighten the industry's image.)

Directly southeast of the new Public Service quarters, at the west corner of 15th Street and Glenarm Place, was the Ghost Building. Architect William Lang designed this three-story, stone-faced structure in 1890 as the business headquarters of developer Allen M. Ghost. Over the years, apartments were let upstairs while small shops stood at the street level of the Ghost Building.

The structure flourished into the late 1970s. As real estate speculation then raged, Public Service bought the landmark, announcing plans to tear it down. The company was blunt. It did not need the land for utility development or any other immediate purpose. At the most, it explained, it might require the parcel in the future. In the meanwhile, it preferred another parking lot on the land to a functioning residential/commercial building.

Preservationists cried the Ghost Building was the last of its kind, a stone building on 15th Street dating from before the silver crash of 1893. A bad compromise was reached whereby the stones were numbered and removed before Public Service leveled the structure in 1979. The stones sat in a warehouse for more than five years before a developer bought them. He had workers place them on the exterior of a modern three-story office at the west corner of 18th and Stout streets in 1985. The new building resembled the Ghost Building. It was not a successful venture, remaining mostly empty for years.

Public Service abandoned its headquarters in April 1992. By then, the rest of the block was empty. The gas and electric utility held the 15th Street property for speculation until it placed a cooling plant where the Ghost Building had stood in 1997. Some of the firm's technical personnel then occupied the former administrative offices. By 2000, it talked about selling its vacant lots for a convention center hotel.

The *Denver Post* joined Public Service in devastating 15th Street. It moved to Temple Court in 1950. This was the name of a 1901-vintage building architect Frank Edbrooke designed at the south corner of 15th and California streets. Behind it, stretching to 14th Street, was Home Public Market, a middle- and working-class shopping area including a pharmacy, grocery, and ice cream parlor. Though the *Post* pondered destroying both structures for an 18-story tower, it opted to have architect Temple Buell renovate them into its new plant. The newspaper eventually acquired the whole block, having its printing, editorial, and circulation facilities there.

When the Times Mirror Corporation of Los Angeles took over the *Post* in 1981, it eagerly eyed this land. Given the incredibly poor manner in which Times Mirror ran the *Post*, it appeared the Los Angles concern was more interested in real estate speculation than in publishing a vibrant newspaper. Evidence to confirm this view came out when Times Mirror sold the *Post* in 1987. Though it dumped the paper, it hung onto the 15th and California tract. The next year, the *Post* moved out of Temple Court. The entire Times Mirror block was abandoned as a dilapidated, blighted area.

**Photo by Ann Bingham**

*The Ghost Building at 15th Street and Glenarm Place, stripped of its stone work, shortly before its demolition in 1979.*

Photo by Phil Goodstein

*The old* Denver Post *Building, at the south corner of 15th and California streets, shortly before it was destroyed for a parking lot in 1998. By the time it came done, virtually all of the adjacent low-income housing in the area had disappeared.*

By this time, virtually all of the working-class structures along 15th Street had disappeared. The Peña administration encouraged their end. No sooner had the mayor vowed his commitment to preserving low-income housing near the central city than property owners razed most residential facilities in this part of downtown.

Population figures reflected the city's demolition of such residences. After peaking at 515,320 residents in 1970, amidst the oil boom and suburban sprawl, the city shrank to 490,011 citizens in 1980. With Peña policies further eliminating housing, the population declined to 467,610 in 1990. Simultaneously, the number of homeless individuals soared. Far from admitting a close connection between the destruction of housing and the loss of population, the mayor screamed the Census Bureau had not counted all the people in Denver. Even so, by this time a new treasured edifice of ruling Denver had arisen on land workers had once occupied as their homes—the Colorado Convention Center.

## A Note on Sources:

Much of the analysis on Peña's first term comes from firsthand observation as a reporter, including covering city council meetings and DPO affairs in 1983–86. I heard many of Bill Lamont's questionable assertions. He informed me it was "too negative" to correct errors in the downtown plan. Maggie Sperling's answer about the Cherry Creek tunnel was in response to my question. I was also at the city council meeting when it debated the presence of the house on the lot DPO claimed was vacant. The comments about the Urban Design Forum are drawn from attendance at and participation in some of its events in 1984–85. Mike Davenport filled me with numerous stories about the inside workings of the planning community at this time.

A trendy, cliché-filled look at the first two years of the Peña administration is *The Maturing of the Peña Administration: An Analysis of the Decision-Making Process* (Denver: City Club, 1985). An overview, celebrating Peña, is included in "50th Anniversary Commemorative Edition," *DBJ*, September 11, 1998.

I examine the role of Dick Fleming in volume one in the chapter on "Big Money." Volume one also includes a discussion of the oil crash and its impact on downtown. Both daily papers and the business press noted the high vacancy rates. Stories in the *Denver Business Journal* reflected the many panaceas of 17th Street to get the city out of the morass.

I have been greatly influenced in my views of city planning by such critics as Jane Jacobs, *The Death and Life of Great American Cities* (New York: Vintage, 1961); and Lewis Mumford, *The City in History* (New York: Harcourt Brace Jovanovich, 1961). Robert Goodman, *After the Planners* (New York: Simon and Schuster, 1971), is an excellent attack on city planners as the "soft cops" assuring the corporate domination of cities and working-class neighborhoods.

Ronald Wiedenhoeft, *Cities are for People* (New York: Van Nostrand Reinhold, 1981), reports the massive destruction of central American cities compared to the impact of World War II bombings. James H. Kunstler, *The Geography of Nowhere* (New York: Simon & Schuster, 1993), observes the contemporary urban scene. Robert Caro, *The Power Broker* (New York: Vintage, 1975), a biography of Robert Moses, includes an examination of the nature of the planning process, bureaucratic procurements, and the role of federal funds.

Goodman, *After the Planners*, notes the role of Herbert Hoover in pushing planning commissions. Articles on the Denver Planning Commission and its work are in *Municipal Facts*, a city magazine published from 1918 until 1931, especially "City Planning in Denver," January-February 1930, pp. 6–7. The Denver Planning Commission issued the seven-volume *Denver Plan* between 1929 and 1941. It also published *The Denver Planning Primer* in 1934. Many of the organization's reports are on file at both the Government Documents and Western History departments of DPL. The Saco DeBoer papers at DPL and the Irvin McCrary papers at the Auraria Archives contain materials on the commission. Information on city planning in the area, notably on the local American Planning Association and its forerunner, the Denver branch of the American Institute of Planners, are in papers of the latter group at the Auraria Archives.

DPO has been prolific in issuing studies, newsletters, neighborhood analyses, and plans. Over the years, it has also sporadically published annual reports. Under Lamont, it widely reported on its doings in *Denver Planning News*.

Some of the publications of the Partnership are also in the Government Documents section of DPL. The implication is they are quasi-official documents. They include such newsletters as *Downtown* and *Denver Today*. *Downtown Area Plan: A Plan for the Future of Downtown Denver* (Denver: A Joint Venture of the Denver Partnership, Denver Planning Office, and City and County of Denver, 1986), is the heralded 1986 downtown plan.

Phil Milstein discussed his work on the planning board and his rather hostile views of the Denver Partnership under Fleming. His papers are at DPL. Some materials on the planning board are also in Charles Gordon Lee papers at DPL. John Harris of DPO shared his knowledge of its operations. Gordon Appell, who edited the *Denver Planning News* under Lamont, and Dennis Swain of DPO assisted me in covering city planning issues. Billie Bramhall, the number-two person in the planning office under Lamont, gave me an insider's look at the operations of the agency, especially its neighborhood planning division. She claimed the planners made great accomplishments in the Peña administration. Peter Natan added his penetrating observations about cities and the planning office.

Materials on the planning office are also scattered in the Tom Currigan and DURA papers at DPL. Councilmen Ted Hackworth and John Silchia were the most outspoken elected officials criticizing DPO under Peña. Gertie Grant shared her views of trying to work with the planning office as a citizen activist in 1983–86. A satirical look at Peña's snow policies is a story about the Bad Weather Bureau in *City Edition*, January 9, 1985.

Newspaper clippings, issues of *Historic Denver News*, reports of the Denver Landmark Preservation Commission, and files of properties listed on the National Register of Historic Places at CHS chronicle some of the downtown structures, including the fate of the Ghost Building. Also see Noel and Norgren, *City Beautiful*, on the evolution of downtown architecture. Newspapers reported the census controversy.

# 6

# Convention City

Virtually from its establishment in 1858–59, Denver has sought to live off visitors. Leading businesses have devised elaborate schemes to get the most money possible from outsiders. Since the rich have more funds to spend than the poor, city hall and the Chamber of Commerce have engaged in outreach efforts to attract the wealthy to the Mile High City. A foremost means is to pull them into town for conventions.

In 1892, the Knights Templar brought their gathering to town. For the occasion, leading casinos and bordellos collaborated in printing the *Denver Red Book: A Reliable Directory of the Pleasure Resorts of Denver*. Outlining the commercial sex and gambling opportunities in town, it illustrated the true economic potential of business assemblies.

To secure comparable bashes, corporate advocates called for taxpayers to erect a municipal convention hall in the late 19th century. Exponents of the effort made no secret about its purpose: by having a publicly financed facility, nearby hotels and restaurants would flourish. They could raise their prices since the visitors would not have any viable alternative to patronizing them.

The convention center encountered rough sailing. Opponents noted the greed-inspired hall would negatively impact locals who would also have to pay the high prices. More than this, the convention center was nothing but state capitalism. If conventions were so good for business, then the hotel and restaurant industries should pay for their own convention center.

These debates convulsed the city until 1907 when the courts ruled the city had the legal authority to build a convention center. Mayor Robert Speer, a politician closely allied with 17th Street, thereupon oversaw the construction of the Denver Auditorium at the south corner of 14th and Curtis streets. It opened for the 1908 Democratic National Convention.

The Auditorium was much more than an exclusive convention hall. The city used it for countless functions, including concerts, meetings, and basketball games. Modifications of the building were unending. In 1939, the city began work on the Auditorium Annex (also known as the Auditorium Arena) to the southwest of the hall. The expansion was completed in 1953 as a three-part project.

Even as the Auditorium grew, business champions in the 1930s loudly called for a new convention hall. That, they were convinced, was the only way to increase the high-spending visitor business. They seriously pondered filling the abandoned Catholic Mount Calvary Cemetery between Ninth and 11th avenues to the west of York Street with a new auditorium. City hall also contemplated a site by Sloans Lake for the replacement building.

Nothing happened. Convention advocates remained dissatisfied with the Auditorium, a structure they demeaned as the "Old Barn." The Annex did not provide the promised benefits. Nor did conditions improve after a thorough remodeling of the Auditorium in 1954–56. Instead of drawing more business to the center, the refurbishment destroyed the hall's pipe organ, curtain, and acoustics.

Meanwhile, private efforts were underway to bring conventions to town at the Hilton Hotel. It was a key project of a New York speculator/developer, William Zeckendorf. With the assistance of 17th Street kingpin Claude Boettcher and Mayor Benjamin Stapleton, Zeckendorf purchased the park occupying the site of the old, demolished County Courthouse on the block surrounded by 15th and 16th streets and Court and Tremont places in 1945. He promised an elite hotel across the street, on the block bordered by 15th and 16th streets from Court Place to Cleveland Place, would grace his project, one known as Courthouse Square. It took him 15 years to fulfill his pledge.

Nothing happened immediately at Courthouse Square. Legal challenges kept Zeckendorf from destroying the park for a parking lot until 1949. Only in 1956 did work get underway to erect the May D&F. Even so, Zeckendorf was always vowing imminent action on the hotel. In 1953, for example, he confidently predicted a thousand-room, 30-story lodge would complement the new department store. Before long, he painted the hotel as a 15- to 18-story structure. Or, as a 1956 account reported, a 20-story highrise. Ground-breaking was vowed in 1954 and again in 1955 and 1956. Supporters optimistically announced the inn would boost convention business by 80 percent. Not until the Hilton chain agreed to operate the facility in 1958 did Zeckendorf begin work on the 22-story, 750-room hotel. He opened it to grand acclaim in April 1960.

Zeckendorf asserted the Denver Hilton put the Brown Palace to shame. Architect I. M. Pei designed it based on a comparable structure he had put up in Manhattan. Seeing meetings and conventions as very profitable for the hospitality industry, the hotel included numerous meeting rooms and display areas. The wing of the hotel along Cleveland Place included office space. A bridge and a tunnel linked the Hilton with the May D&F.

Author's Collection

*The Auditorium, as seen from 14th and Curtis streets, was initially designed to be lit up at night as part of Denver's efforts to emerge as a city of lights.*

Though not nearly as profitable as Zeckendorf—who eventually went bankrupt—hoped, the Hilton immediately emerged as the city's convention hotel. Many agreed with Zeckendorf: the Hilton eclipsed the Brown Palace. The owner of the Brown Palace, the Boettcher dynasty, thought as much. At the same time the Hilton was going up, it built the 22-story Brown Palace West at the north corner of 17th Street and Tremont Place in 1959. The inn preferred to book visitors there: management was sure the modern structure was much better than the landmark hotel.

No sooner was the annex open than patrons loudly complained to the Brown Palace. Guests did not appreciate rooms in the bland new structure. They wanted to stay at the historic Brown Palace, not a pale imitation of it. Finally, in the 1980s, the company running the Brown Palace, Clarendon Hotels, saw their point. It dropped the name Brown Palace West as the modern building took the name of a corporate hotel chain, Comfort Inn. The Brown Palace ballroom remained in the annex.

## Currigan Hall

By the time Bill McNichols was mayor, private approaches comparable to those of the Hilton and Brown Palace were mostly passé. The belief in state capitalism was stronger than ever. Seventeenth Street insisted gigantic conventions were crucial to business success. A massive public facility was needed for Denver (read the corporate community) to procure them. Only in such a manner could downtown restaurants and hotels get affluent customers. Well before Federico Peña championed this approach as the "public/private partnership," countless efforts had been made to have the city build a super convention center.

Public policy kept changing about the Auditorium. One year, convention advocates dismissed it as an embarrassment from Denver's past. The next, city hall praised the Old Barn as an example of Denver's foresight and public spirit. By the early 1960s, downtown policy makers figured there was a great future for the Auditorium. What the city primarily needed was an adjacent exposition hall, one connecting with the Auditorium and Arena via a bridge. The meeting rooms in the existing facilities would serve conventioneers who toured displays in a hall occupying two square city blocks. On this basis, in June 1964, Mayor Tom Currigan sold a bond issue to the voters who authorized the construction of an $11.5 million, 100,000-square-foot hall to last Denver into the 21st century. It opened at a cost of $13 million in 1969 as Currigan Hall.

The Denver Metro Convention & Visitors Bureau pushed the facility. The agency typified the way private interests set public policy. Dating from 1909, the Bureau stemmed from a section of the Denver Chamber of Commerce and a Denver Convention League, established in 1905. The organization asserted it was the

**DU Archives**

*An aerial overview of downtown in the late 1940s shows Courthouse Square, the park in the center-right of the picture.*

sixth such tourist promotion outfit in the country. It made no secret of its purpose. The pro-business group was an aggressive quasi-public body pulling affluent visitors to Denver so hotels, restaurants, and nightclubs could take guests for every possible penny. This was a time when crooked stock market operators preyed on those staying at fancy hotels. Until well after World War II, authorities tolerated gambling in protected houses in Adams, Arapahoe, and Douglas counties. Those knowing where to look could procure call girls. In addition to these convention amenities, a number of rowdy, criminal stripper bars popped up near the Brown Palace and Hilton Hotel in the 1960s.

The Convention & Visitors Bureau emerged as an independent entity from the Chamber of Commerce in the 1950s. By the 1970s, it achieved great power when it pushed through a public financing mechanism. A 1.75-percent lodging tax was imposed on all hotel rooms. The revenue generated by the tax did not go to the city general fund; on the contrary, it was given to the Convention & Visitors Bureau—a private membership concern. In 1994, the tax provided for $3.6 million of the organization's $4.88 million budget. The agency needed these funds because none of its schemes ever quite delivered their promises.

Such was the case with Currigan Hall. No sooner had it opened than problems appeared. The flat roof leaked badly. The bridge to the Auditorium was not an ideal linkage. The fancy, high-cost hotels geared to conventioneers were upwards of a half mile away. Some of them, including the Albany, Shirley-Savoy, and Cosmopolitan, shut their doors and were demolished within 15 years after the opening of the convention center. Far from stimulating nearby businesses, more parking lots appeared around Currigan Hall. The facility quickly emerged as something of a fortress. It had virtually no connections with nearby stores or working-class residents. Nor was it a magnet for conventions. Other cities built larger, more ornate facilities. The meeting center was often vacant during the middle of the week.

The convention industry's response was simple. It demanded the city expand or supplant Currigan Hall with a bigger facility. A kind of armaments race occurred in the visitor business. City after city, alike in their corporate domination and dedication to state capitalism, sought to have bigger and more elaborate convention centers than their rivals. Trade shows expanded to all possible space. Before long, the most costly affairs demanded more square footage than was available at Currigan Hall, the Auditorium, and the Arena combined.

That was only one reason a bigger convention center was needed. Just as important, the Convention & Visitors Bureau noted, Currigan Hall failed because it could only house one big show at a time. Since it required a day or two to assemble and then another day or two to take down displays, the city could only host one major convention a week. To emerge as a convention city, two or three shows should be going on simultaneously at a gigantic center.

Currigan Hall was also isolated from the Auditorium. The bridge between the two facilities was rarely open. Traffic made crossing Champa Street to get from one to the other a risky proposition. The original idea—the halls at the Auditorium and space at the Arena could be used for assemblies—was rarely implemented.

Author's Collection

*This architect's sketch of Currigan Hall in the mid-1960s emphasized the convention center's bridge link to the Auditorium.*

Nor did many in the convention business realize the meeting rooms at the Auditorium were part and parcel of the convention center complex.

At least members of the Denver Planning Office (DPO) were ignorant of this fact. This came out during a session of area city planners and promoters about a year and a half after Peña took office. Thirty minutes or so after the general session had started in a meeting room of the Auditorium, it was interrupted when the DPO delegation noisily arrived. Its members explained they were late because they had gotten lost: they did not know such rooms existed in the Auditorium. This was at the same time the planning office was explaining a new convention center was vital because Currigan Hall lacked any meeting rooms. Shortly thereafter, in the 1986 master plan for downtown, DPO erroneously asserted Currigan Hall was completed in 1964. The agency's public actions and pronouncements so showed the planners did not have the slightest conception of what the convention center was about.

That did not matter. DPO was chanting official mantra. Seventeenth Street was sure a larger facility would solve the city's convention woes. Responding to business lobbying, McNichols had already called for expanding Currigan Hall in 1977. The Convention & Visitors Bureau—which had sponsored and sold the facility to the public—readily bad-mouthed its own place. Repeating the same lines they had used to get voters to authorize Currigan Hall in 1964, city hall and private concerns agreed: only by having a bigger convention center could downtown businesses flourish.

## The Hall of Peña

As towering highrises displaced residential structures and small downtown businesses during the oil boom, the central business district grew ever more barren. Stores serving the workers and residents of the central city closed when the buildings they occupied were demolished for new towers. The Denver Partnership was blunt about the need for new, exclusive, high-class shops to replace the old middle-income stores.

As the Partnership failed to recruit elite new emporiums and the downtown malaise widened, major property owners and developers increasingly saw a gigantic, ultramodern convention center as the unquestioned solution to the central city's escalating woes. Such a facility, they vowed, would bring new life and spending as it replaced the people and structures eliminated by the oil boom.

Constructing a better convention facility was a central issue in the 1983 mayoral campaign. Challengers criticized McNichols for not moving ahead on it. In office, Peña showed he was eager to make it a reality. The key problem was where to build it.

The new meeting hall was not simply to lubricate the existing tourist-related businesses; it was also to fuel real estate speculation. This became quickly obvious when, in association with the Denver Partnership and people around Marvin Davis, Peña advocated a 300,000-square-foot facility in the middle of the Platte floodplain, to the northwest of Union Station near the right bank of the river. By building the convention center there, exponents hoped to convert the rail yards into a second downtown. Upon the completion of the project, the city planned to sell Currigan Hall. Ideally, land near it would finally become part of the bustling oil district.

Not everybody liked this idea. The strains of the oil bust were becoming increasingly apparent under Peña. As new building ceased after 1983, the convention center looked more and more like a pork-barrel project than a practical measure to assure Denver served its residents or even flourished as a convention city. There were no hotels or restaurants directly adjacent to the floodplain facility, a place critics called the Hall of Peña. Nor was a transportation network in place to connect it with the existing hotels. In addition to the price of putting up the center, a whole new infrastructure was needed to serve it. Far more than a convention center, the project seemed a giveaway to land speculators.

Before Marvin Davis had stepped on the scene, Allan Reiver, a developer notorious for his ruthlessness who had engaged in questionable land deals in lower downtown, had pushed a meeting hall near the river. Dick Fleming of the Denver Partnership, a close Reiver associate, loudly endorsed the effort. In 1981, Reiver convinced a city task force on the expansion of Currigan Hall that a new building behind the train station was preferable to revamping the existing facility. In particular, he hoped to completely develop an 18.5-acre tract for the project as part of a $590 million effort to change the face of downtown. (Before focusing on the rail yards, Reiver had sought to create a second downtown/convention center district around Mile High Stadium.)

Reiver closely collaborated with the American branch of an Argentine conglomerate, SOCMA, in pushing the center. On September 8, 1982, the Denver Union Railway Company—the consortium of railroads owning Union Station and the rail yards—tabbed SOCMA over four rivals for the floodplain development.

The city confirmed this on February 22, 1983, when council approved the SOCMA proposal. It included a complete replacement for Currigan Hall.

No sooner did SOCMA get the green light than numerous problems loomed. Foremost was the financing. At one point, SOCMA president James Capolino talked about making the required deposit for the convention center in Argentine pesos. At the earliest, SOCMA noted, it would only be able to begin work on the hall in 1986. As a September 19, 1983, deadline loomed, differences between the city and developer widened. The entire proposal collapsed on September 13. Before long, SOCMA left the scene while Reiver was swamped by unpaid bills as he turned his attention to trying to create an extremely unsuccessful deluxe shopping/design center, Broadway Plaza, near I-25 and South Broadway.

As Davis' partnership, Miller Klutznick Davis Gray, emerged as the floodplain developer, other landowners feared for their investments. Were the convention center built next to the river, the Hall of Peña might totally shift the direction of downtown's growth. This would leave other speculators holding the bag with land they had purchased to the east of Broadway, southwest of 15th Street, northeast of 20th Street, and south of West Colfax Avenue. Murmurs of dissent became increasingly loud. Skeptics pointed out there were no cost limits on the hall.

Peña was insistent the floodplain center was a done deal. Other landowners did not believe this, mobilizing opposition to it. In the lead was Neil Macey. A veteran suburban politician and lobbyist, he was financed by members of the Dikeou family who owned land along 14th and 15th streets near Currigan Hall. Most of the Dikeou holdings were dilapidated properties the family hoped to sell for top dollar once downtown finally started growing near Currigan Hall. Other speculators in the area agreed. They loudly advertised their properties with gigantic "for sale" banners hung from some of the apartment houses along Stout Street across the road from Currigan Hall. The signs announced the property was ideal for a convention center.

Macey, who suggested a 50,000- to 100,000-square-foot expansion of Currigan Hall, demanded a public vote on the convention center. City hall vehemently opposed such a plebiscite. A convention center, it explained, was an extremely complicated decision. Voters, the populist Peña administration implied, were too stupid to understand the complexities of all of the handouts and giveaways at the heart of the effort. With rhetoric fully worthy of those who had viciously opposed a public vote on Denver's hosting of the 1976 Winter Olympics, the Peña crowd argued only elected officials, appointed policy makers, and others who fully embraced the public/private partnership were sophisticated enough to make this decision affecting Denver's future.

Not all elected officials were of one mind on this. Members of city council dissented from the floodplain hall. Anti-convention center forces announced they might launch a petition drive to put the matter on the ballot. That scared security dealers who knew they would not be able to sell bonds if the center's financing was in limbo.

To head off the initiative anti-convention center forces might win through a petition drive, the Peña administration slated a special election on the convention

Photo by John Schoenwalter

*About the same time Federico Peña pushed a convention center in the Platte flood-plain, speculators demolished the West Court Hotel at 1415 Glenarm Place.*

center for October 15, 1985. Supporters were blunt. The Hall of Peña was Denver's salvation. While there might be some problems with its finances, linkages with downtown, and presence in the floodplain, they would easily be solved in the course of construction. "BUILD IT" they demanded, wearing huge lapel buttons, showing their commitment to the project.

"Shove it!" opponents thought was the appropriate answer to the convention center campaign. They focused on costs—there was no fixed maximum on the price of the hall nor guarantee of the revenue it would produce. By erecting the hall in an isolated spot, far from existing hotels and businesses, a sterile environment would grow up around the convention center, one more deterring visitors than attracting them. "Don't write a blank check" they warned, noting the proposal was a virtual giveaway to Marvin Davis and associates.

Advocates never addressed these points; on the contrary, they waved the flag, pointing to the glamour and profits the center would bring. The hall, they proudly announced, would finally create a 24-hour city, complete with a flourishing nightlife. Affluent conventioneers, they vowed, would readily drop hundreds of dollars a day on rooms, food, and alcohol. The newspapers listed $137.4 million as the expected price.

Supporters of the convention center raised a war chest of $600,000, bombarding the electorate with pleas for the state capitalist project. Approximately half the BUILD IT money came from the coffers of Marvin Davis and his partner, Micky Miller. Foes of the center raised about $100,000. Though they did not get the media exposure the advocates of the center did, they had greater outreach into the community. Pro-convention center forces did nothing to turn out the vote. They believed their pollsters who reported overwhelming support for the measure.

Just before the election, the pollsters hedged their bets. They noted the opposition was rapidly growing. This led them to predict a tight race. Simultaneously, pro-convention center forces started slinging mud. Close Peña campaign adviser Ed Graham had phone solicitors call voters, telling them a ballot against the convention center was the equivalent of an anti-Hispanic vote since a defeat of the project would be a denunciation of the mayor precisely because of his ethnicity. When anti forces loudly complained about the tactic, Peña pretended outrage over such a "repugnant" message.

The phone calls were a sign of desperation. The election was anything but close. Voters overwhelmingly rejected the corporate welfare proposal, 33,661–67,769. Despite the immense advantage of the business and political leadership, which had overwhelmingly endorsed the convention center and had seen the newspapers support it, the public did not buy the Hall of Peña. The outcome was a vote of no confidence in the mayor. Not only did the electorate not trust or believe him, but the taxpayers did not want state capitalism. They were not simply opposed to the location of the facility, but to the very principle they should pay for a pro-business center. (The same day the voters rejected the convention center, city council, at the mayor's behest, "temporarily" hiked the sales tax by .5 cent—it never rescinded the increase.)

Peña retreated after the election. The next day, while he affirmed his commitment to a new meeting hall, he stressed his administration had other goals, notably making a new airport a reality. For nearly a year, the mayor was a virtual non-player in the convention center debate.

Meanwhile, none of the politicians, including those who had fervently opposed the floodplain facility, admitted the vote was against the convention center per se. On the contrary, in the wake of the election they rallied to the project. Council members Cathy Reynolds and Bob Crider, both of whom had opposed the floodplain site and called for an expansion of Currigan Hall, affirmed that the city needed a larger facility. As Peña increasingly stressed DIA, they took the lead in making the convention center a reality.

Advocates of the meeting hall not only proposed a different site than the floodplain, but announced Denver alone should not pay for the facility. Since the center was to benefit the entire metropolitan area, the State of Colorado should help finance the corporate shrine. The mayor and his recent foes united in getting the legislature—controlled by suburban and rural politicians who were open in their disdain for the Mile High City—to go along with them.

Ruling Colorado believed the convention center so urgent that the General Assembly gave the city more than what it asked. Initially, the center's backers only wanted a generous loan from the state. The legislature gave them more. Seeing the hall as a vital public necessity, it appropriated a $36 million grant for the business effort.

Even as the General Assembly earmarked public funds for the convention center, the facility's advocates loudly told residents they would not have to pay for the new hall. Revenue bonds, they announced, would finance the facility. Profits generated by the center would retire the debt. On closer examination, these vows had as little substance as the rest of the convention center promises.

The convention center required the imposition of new taxes to guarantee the bonds. Among them was a 1.75-percent hike in the lodging tax. This included an increased assessment on all who rented rooms in Denver, whether they were staying in a hotel for a convention or were residents who had to rent a room because they were displaced from their homes for the night.

The majority of people renting hotel rooms were not conventioneers. In 1997, for example, out of 8.8 million overnight visitors, 6.4 million were leisure travelers, individuals passing through the area to appreciate its amenities or visit family and friends. Only 2.4 million of those renting a room did so for business purposes. Not all were attending conventions. Nor did all of the latter patronize the city-owned facility. Their meetings were often at hotels and private halls.

These numbers about hotel occupancy took no account of Denverites living from week to week in residential hotels. Often such individuals were only a step

Photo by Ann Bingham

*Ghosts apparently haunt this house at 1128 Bannock Street. The city planned to level it for a convention center in the Golden Triangle after voters rejected the floodplain Hall of Peña.*

above the homeless, staying in cheap motels because they could not afford security deposits on evermore expensive apartments. Not only were they forced to pay the hotel tax to support the convention center, so were locals who stayed at bed and breakfasts. During weekends, locals often made up more than half of the bed and breakfasts' guests.

Other direct assessments on residents followed. Foremost was an increased tax on restaurant meals. Peña also hiked taxes on car rentals. Even more than the case with those renting hotel rooms, Coloradans leased many of the rental vehicles, including low-income non-car owners who needed a vehicle for a few days. Simultaneously, the convention center removed land from the existing property tax rolls. This impacted the general fund as a whole. In other words, the people of Denver very much paid for the convention center. These taxes were so designed to impact the poor more than the rich. While some of the mayor's liberal backers would have loudly protested had McNichols attempted to impose such fees as part of a no-taxes pledge, they were silent when their man pushed the 17th Street measure.

None of this got a full public airing in the wake of the defeat of the floodplain center. On the contrary, the election taught the Peña administration to keep crucial decisions from the public. Usually the more serious an issue was, the less debate the mayor permitted on the matter.

Throughout 1986, 1987, and 1988, the barrage of propaganda for the convention center was unending. No longer was it just a measure to spark downtown visitor businesses, but it was a salvation for the oil-bust city. Even so, it stalled. Once more, land speculation issues were evident as rivals disputed where to build the Hall of Peña.

## The Golden Triangle

Marvin Davis and Philip Anschutz clashed on who was to directly benefit from the convention center. City hall's candidate was Al Cohen, a general contractor/developer who was close to Davis. Cohen had collaborated with the oil man in numerous deals and served on the boards of some of Davis' enterprises. His land for the meeting hall was in the so-called Golden Triangle. This was a real estate speculation zone, referring to property bordered by West Colfax Avenue, Speer Boulevard, and Broadway. For nearly a century, it had been a residential neighborhood. During the last 25 years of the 19th century, parts of it were an elite suburban enclave.

Sometimes known as Evans Addition, after Colorado Governor John Evans, who developed the area from roughly Broadway to the alley of Cherokee-Delaware streets between Colfax and West 11th avenues, the neighborhood never recovered from the economic crash of 1893. Most of the rich inhabitants abandoned the West Denver site for Capitol Hill. In their place, working-class families moved in. In the course of the first third of the 20th century, land on the northern fringe along Colfax emerged as a governmental center, complete with the Civic Center, Denver Public Library, City and County Building, and United States Mint.

# COLORADO CONVENTION CENTER COUNTDOWN

## Colorado Convention Center At The Golden Triangle Poised For Fall 1989 Opening

DENVER—The Colorado Convention Center at the Golden Triangle is poised to become one of the nation's most attractive and competitive facilities, rivaling even the highly successful Georgia World Congress Center in Atlanta.

As the fall construction deadline approaches, designers are putting the finishing touches on a comprehensive plan that includes a stunning exterior design with a crystalline glass-enclosed entryway overlooking the Denver city skyline and the Civic Center Park area.

*Looking north along Broadway, the Colorado Convention Center at the Golden Triangle lies at the doorstep of Downtown Denver within easy walking distance of major hotels, popular tourist attractions and the 16th Street Mall retail and entertainment districts.*

The plan culminates more than three years of site analysis and a year's negotiation and consultation with city officials, prospective users, traffic engineers, urban planners and architectural specialists. The result is a world class convention center that will attract upwards of 250,000 visitors annually, and pump more than $200 million each year into the ailing local and state economies.

The Colorado Convention Center at the Golden Triangle was designed by Thompson Ventulett and Stainback & Associates, the same firm that designed the highly acclaimed Georgia World Congress Center. And Tom Ventulett, managing partner, says the Colorado Center is "nicer and even more attractive than Atlanta's."

Specific plans call for a 300,000 square-foot exhibition hall, a 35,000 square-foot ballroom and 85,000 square feet of meeting space. There will be hotel-quality finish throughout the second floor meeting rooms, including attractive patterned carpet and built-in, state of the art audio-visual equipment. Escalator access to the exhibition floor facilitates delegate registration and the smooth flow of pedestrian traffic throughout the hall.

The plan includes 32 concealed underground truck docks, allowing direct access to the exhibit hall floor, and minimizing impact on the surrounding neighborhood. Phase I plans also call for about 1,215 on-site parking spaces, in addition to thousands of existing spaces, all within a five minute walk of the facility.

Vehicular movement to and from the Center is totally organized. Trucks approach from the west, avoiding conflict with bus movement to the east along Broadway and taxi access on the north.

Roger Smith, president of the Denver Metro Convention & Visitors Bureau, said the center promises to be highly attractive to major exhibitors and meeting planners because it is within easy walking distance of major downtown hotels, popular tourist attractions and the city's retail/entertainment districts.

"Proximity is key, in terms of marketability," Smith said. "The convention business is highly competitive, and the more attractive we are in terms of function, proximity to hotels and entertainment outlets, and overall quality of experience, the better off we'll be financially."

Pending City Council approval and state funding for land acquisition, the Colorado Convention Center at the Golden Triangle will be open for its first convention in the Fall of 1989.

Construction costs of $70.6 million and a 28-month construction time table have been guaranteed by the builder, Al Cohen Construction Company, one of the region's foremost construction firms for 34 years.

**Author's Collection**

*A propaganda brochure for the never-built Golden Triangle convention center.*

For years, speculators eyed properties south of the government zone. The area remained a very mixed neighborhood, filled with apartments, single-family houses, duplexes, offices, and industrial concerns. Car dealerships were common, including the service center of Robert R. Hall Cadillac at the northeast corner of West 11th Avenue and Cherokee Street. In 1929, Rocky Mountain Bank Notes occupied an impressive headquarters a block down at West 11th Avenue and Delaware Street. The Denver Coca-Cola bottling plant was at 1024 Cherokee Street from 1925 until 1948. There were small black and Mexican-American settlements in the neighborhood, a place long the home of many German and Scandinavian immigrants.

In the late 1930s, a Denver Housing Authority study designated properties in the area, especially near West 14th Avenue and Fox Street, as blighted and in need of replacement. Over the years, the city agency pondered putting up some sort of project in the area at the price of destroying the existing houses. The Denver Urban Renewal Authority (DURA) also eyed the Golden Triangle. Nothing happened. Many individuals—particularly lower-income Hispanos—remained in Evans Addition. Hippies and counterculture institutions dotted it by the early 1970s.

In the mid-1960s, structures went up close to West 14th Avenue and Elati-Fox streets as the home for Metropolitan State College. Community College of Denver (CCD) occupied nearby space centered at the northeast corner of West 12th Avenue and Acoma. The Denver Wax Museum opened at 919 Bannock Street in 1964. The Museum for Children joined it at 931 Bannock Street in 1975. The same year, the Denver Catholic Archdiocese, headquartered at 934–38 Bannock Street, relocated to Second Avenue and Josephine Street.

By this time, efforts to completely rebuild sections of Evans Addition near Speer Boulevard for the Olympics had been shot down when the voters rejected the games in November 1972. Then, in the mid-1970s, Metropolitan State College and CCD left the neighborhood for the Auraria Higher Education Center. Most of the residential section had disappeared by this time. Many blocks were primarily huge swaths of parking lots.

The oil boom greatly impacted the neighborhood. As downtown soared in the late 1970s, investors saw Evans Addition as an ideal extension of the central business district. About this time, newspapers and planners started to call the old residential enclave the "Golden Triangle," possibly in emulation of a section of Central Asia where drug dealers reaped immense profits. Another account has it labeled after a comparable area touted as a great real estate success in Pittsburgh.

Among those heavily investing in the neighborhood was Bannock Center Development, a real estate front of Public Service. It announced the impending trans-

Photo by Ann Bingham

*Houses on the 1300 block of Delaware Street in the heart of the Golden Triangle have emerged as the center of the city's bail bond row.*

formation of the southern part of the land as an idyllic, planned, plush community. As speculators drove up property prices, places such as the Wax and Children's museums on the 900 block of Bannock Street were no more.

Assorted development occurred. Some of the single-family homes and townhouses became offices. Property owners also transformed automobile storage and maintenance garages into offices. After the new Denver City Jail and police headquarters opened in 1978 on the block surrounded by West 13th and West 14th avenues and Cherokee and Delaware streets, nearby residential structures, especially along the west side of the 1300 block of Delaware Street, emerged as the quarters of bail bondsmen. Numerous lawyers had offices in the vicinity. Art galleries opened up along parts of Broadway. Politicians frequently established their campaign headquarters in the Golden Triangle. Investors hoped the central business district would finally cross West 13th Avenue as this area became part of greater downtown.

At first, speculators did not want the city in the Golden Triangle. When DURA launched a Civic Center plan, a $43 million effort to level about eight blocks between West 11th and West 13th avenues east of Speer Boulevard in the fall of 1981, property owners protested. They formed the Golden Triangle Association to get DURA off their backs. The landowners shot down the urban renewal effort that December when they convinced city council private money would take the lead in redeveloping the area. As the oil bust deepened, many speculators longed for city assistance via the convention center.

All this added up to the new preferred location for the Hall of Peña: in the heart of the Golden Triangle to the south of the Denver Public Library and Denver Art Museum. The specific site was a superblock bordered by Broadway, West 11th Avenue, Cherokee Street, and West 13th Avenue. Among the existing properties impacted was Evans School at the northwest corner of West 11th Avenue and Acoma Street.

Named for the former governor, Evans School stood on land the politician/speculator donated as a possible site for the Colorado Capitol in the late 1860s. Eventually, Denver Public Schools (DPS) acquired the plot. Architect David W. Dryden designed the $130,000 building in 1904–05. It was originally known as New Broadway School, noting its displacement of the existing Broadway School near the southeast corner of 14th Avenue and Broadway. The academy opened for classes on March 1, 1905, with a capacity for 750 students. For years, it was the near West Denver elementary school.

This started to change in the late 1920s. Industrial uses were already displacing residents from Evans Addition. As local children disappeared from its halls, Evans School brought in pupils from across the city. In 1928, it became the center of programs for deaf elementary students in DPS. Two years later, it added a comparable effort to educate blind children.

By the early 1970s, the board of education dismissed Evans School as a hopelessly antiquated facility. Few families with elementary-aged children lived nearby. It trailed other schools in academic performance. DPS closed Evans School at the end of the 1971–72 school year. Alan and Robert Eber bought it for $650,000 in

1974. The new owners sealed the building. Seeing themselves as preservationists, they oversaw its listing on the National Register of Historic Places in 1980. Nothing was done with the school. Talk was heard the city might destroy it for the convention center. Others called for making it part of the meeting hall, highlighting the historic charm of the neighborhood. With rumors floating about a ghost or two in the old academy, now and then the owners opened up the school for Halloween haunted house tours.

The push for the convention center came right at a time when property values were rapidly plummeting in the Golden Triangle. The speculative exuberance driving prices to ridiculous levels during the oil boom hurt the buyers. Not only were residents displaced from their Evans Addition homes, but new owners lacked money to develop their properties or pay off loans. They saw banks foreclose upon their holdings. To reduce maintenance costs and taxes, financial institutions and speculators razed structures. Among the buildings demolished were surviving landmark houses on the east side of the 1100 block of Acoma Street designed by acclaimed 19th-century architect Robert S. Roeschlaub. Ever more parking lots dotted the area. A new convention center, which would include yet more parking spaces, was the means of redressing the virtual destruction of the neighborhood.

No sooner had the city committed itself to the Golden Triangle hall than other speculative interests wanted the facility on or near their properties. In the forefront of opposing the Golden Triangle site was Philip Anschutz. Like Marvin Davis, he had land in the Platte floodplain. He called on the city to buy it, notably a parcel northwest of the Auraria campus near the equivalent of Fifth and Wynkoop streets, for the convention center. To accomplish this, the oil billionaire launched a powerful counter-initiative to the Golden Triangle hall.

Neither location was ideally suited vis-à-vis existing hotels, restaurants, and tourist facilities. On the contrary, it would be necessary to bus conventioneers to and from them. This was the pattern in other cities where mayors comparable to Peña supported gigantic convention halls in working-class neighborhoods. Architects and politicians designed such facilities as virtual castles with negative impact on surrounding residents.

Plenty of open land was available for a massive convention center in the heart of downtown. Not only was there empty land around Public Service at 15th and Welton streets, and the soon-to-be abandoned *Denver Post* block at 15th and California streets, but the two blocks surrounded by 15th and 16th streets from Tremont Place to Welton Street were empty. Here was ideal land for a convention center: virtually nothing would be razed for it, hotels were nearby, and the 16th Street Mall fronted it. This location was not considered.

The reason the obvious site was scorned was because the vacant blocks were held for speculative purposes and further construction. Their value, owners and downtown property interests hoped, would soar once the convention center was built on marginal lands. But the dispute between the Golden Triangle and Anschutz interests kept anything from happening. Both sides were strong enough to cancel out the other. Neither, though, could make the center a reality. Eventually they accepted a compromise. In 1987, at the behest of the General Assembly with

Photo by Phil Goodstein

*The abandoned Evans School, at West 11th Avenue and Acoma Street, was threatened by the proposed Golden Triangle convention center.*

its grant of convention center money, the contending parties agreed outside experts from the Urban Land Institute would adjudicate the matter.

## The Colorado Convention Center

The arbitrating body, a fervid advocate of urban renewal, convention centers, and other state capitalist policies, had close ties with business investors. The Urban Land Institute was not to question the wisdom of the convention center; rather, it was to confirm and expedite it. The city gave the consultants five choices for the Hall of Peña: the Golden Triangle, the Anschutz location, Stapleton Airport, Currigan Hall, or land adjacent to Currigan Hall.

City hall permitted power brokers, including Anschutz and Cohen, to name an advisory body to help the outside city planners make the choice. During the commission's deliberations, the Golden Triangle and floodplain forces cancelled out each other: both preferred to have the convention center near Currigan Hall opposed to seeing the rival contender triumph. The Urban Land Institute so resolved Denver should erect the convention center adjacent to the existing Currigan Hall–Auditorium complex.

No more than city leaders did the Land Institute's experts care about the people who lived on the property—between approximately Welton and Stout streets from 14th Street to West Colfax Avenue. The outsiders supported city hall's goal of leveling the entire area for what was designated as the Colorado Convention Center. By this time, the area was sometimes called the Silver Triangle (roughly West

Colfax Avenue, 14th Street, and Champa Street), denoting it as the counterpart of the Golden Triangle.

Despite the anti-convention center verdict of the 1985 vote, no election was held on the matter. City hall and corporate Denver accepted the Urban Land Institute verdict as the final word. Both the Golden Triangle and floodplain interests were left holding the bag. Those owning the speculative properties near Currigan Hall, including the Dikeou family, emerged as the victors in the convention center squabble. Developer David French, working with Hensel Phelps Construction and architect Curt Fentress, put together the deal.

Work finally got underway on the Colorado Convention Center in April 1988. The 292,000-square-foot structure was an island, well isolated from the street by parking lots and loading areas. It opened in June 1990, coming in at $132 million, 10 percent more than the initial estimate of $120 million. (The Union Station center was supposed to have cost $60 million to $80 million in 1983.) The city imposed an additional 3-percent tax on lodging, a 2-percent tax on auto rentals, and a .5-percent tax on restaurant meals to pay off the debt.

The Colorado Convention Center was built with precast concrete. Originally, it was to have a brick veneer, matching the existing neighborhood. Not only was that too expensive, but it did not matter—other than Emily Griffith Opportunity School on the 1200 block of Welton Street, virtually the entire neighborhood was demolished for the hall. At the most, the Hall of Peña architecture resembled the loading docks of the abandoned *Denver Post* headquarters along 14th Street between California and Welton streets.

Photo by Phil Goodstein

*Locals have dismissed the main entrance of the Colorado Convention Center as "tinker-toy architecture."*

From the beginning, the edifice failed to capture the imagination of locals. Some mocked it as tinker-toy architecture. Abutments at the entrances stood out, looking like Tinker Toys, to give the bland box some character. To show the hall was actually a statement of public beauty, the city commissioned artists to decorate it with paintings, mosaics, and sculptures. None were as interesting as the graffiti adolescents were allowed to paint on the plywood walls of the barriers and temporary sidewalks around the building as the Hall of Peña went up.

The administration staged a lavish celebration to note the completion of the convention center. Big money visibly sponsored the bash—at $50 a ticket—including Continental Airlines, Boettcher & Company, Hensel Phelps Construction, Miller Klutznick Davis Gray, Prudential, and US West. The public celebration was cosponsored by Coors. The mayor noted minority and women contractors had benefited from the public works venture. They received set-aside contracts to assure their participation in it. This showed how the Peña administration cared about the poor in Denver: a little of the convention center booty had trickled down to favored female-, black-, and Hispanic-owned businesses.

From the start, there were severe problems with the Colorado Convention Center. Rather than spurring entrepreneurs to open new stores, restaurants, and shops to serve the conventioneers, the building generated more parking lots. The only new nightclub near the Hall of Peña was the Diamond Cabaret, a striptease joint—this was the culture it wrought. (The Denver Partnership had not been eager to save the Denver Dry when the department store was shut by a monopolistic merger in 1987. It noted downtown really did not need such retail. It contrast, it endorsed the Diamond Cabaret. This, apparently, is what it supported for downtown opposed to a distinctive historic dry goods store.) An isolated bastion with little connection with the rest of downtown remained the Colorado Convention Center's fate through the end of the 20th century. Meanwhile, with no initial city encouragement or handouts, the bulk of the city's wild nightlife started to move to lower downtown.

Ironically, the Golden Triangle prospered at the same time land by the Colorado Convention Center stagnated. During the late 1990s, Evans Addition started to fill up with high-priced lofts, townhouses, mixed-used towers, and restaurants. Part of its success was due to the collapse of the real estate market. After Public Service had spent more than $50 million buying up 17.5 acres in the southern part of the neighborhood through its Bannock Center Development, it sold the land for about $5.75 million in December 1992. Compared to the actual residential developments in the Golden Triangle, parking lots and the Diamond Cabaret remained the highest and best use of the land in the vicinity of the Hall of Peña into the 21st century.

Even more problematic than land usage was the character of the Colorado Convention Center. The place often resembled a mausoleum. Far from a continually booked facility constantly filled with action, someone wandering through the acclaimed business temple in the middle of the week might find quiet contemplation. Contrary to a 1984 study, predicting more than 90,000 people would attend conventions at the facility during its first year, only about 65,000 were drawn to it.

Hotel occupancy rates continued to stagnate and the hall was vacant more than a third of the time.

Compared to the emptiness of the Colorado Convention Center, the privately run Denver Merchandise Mart at 58th Avenue and Washington Street in Adams County flourished. Dating from 1965, the latter was based on a successful Dallas Trade Mart, designed to host apparel sales representatives from a 14-state region. The Merchandise Mart expanded into an exposition hall in 1973 as it came to host numerous commercial gatherings. By the late 1990s, more people went to shows at the suburban plant than they did to the Hall of Peña.

Those going to affairs at the Merchandise Mart were of no account. At least the Convention Bureau claimed as much. After all, the Merchandise Mart's patrons were mostly Denver residents. Against them, Bureau chief Eugene Dilbeck stated "anything that drives hotel rooms takes priority" over local events.

Dilbeck was a typical Denver executive. His newspaper quotes reeked with disdain for his adopted city. A professional corporate advocate who transferred from city to city at the behest of his business masters, Dilbeck previously held comparable tourist promotion jobs in New Jersey, Texas, and Oklahoma. He came to Denver in the 1990s to make the convention center work after the facility had failed to live up to its initial dreams. The Bureau chief replaced Roger Smith, another outsider who quickly moved on after foisting the Hall of Peña on Denver. Some accounts claim Smith was ousted when the new center did not deliver the promised results. Dilbeck was eager to shape the area's future, including calling for hikes in taxes to assure corporate convention welfare.

Under Dilbeck, the Bureau scorned Currigan Hall. The original Hall of Peña plans dismissed the 1969 structure as a hopeless anachronism, a totally obsolete building with no future. Once the new convention center opened—whether in the Platte floodplain, Golden Triangle, or next to the existing building—backers announced, the city would level or sell Currigan Hall. Despite dismissing it as a white elephant, the administration expected to receive a high price for the building and land. Convention advocates listed potential revenue from the sale of the convention center of Denver's past as a considerable chunk of change with which to pay for the Hall of Peña.

Currigan Hall remained open. Compared to the new facility, it had a certain intimacy and humanity. Its rust-covered sides had architectural charm in contrast to the Colorado Convention Center's sterility. Events drawing locals, such as home and garden, boat, and book expositions, found the 1969 building a far better site than the new hall. Rooms at the Auditorium remained in use in conjunction with Currigan trade shows. The Denver Metro Convention & Visitors Bureau's response was to demand the demolition of Currigan Hall.

Virtually from the time the new center opened, boosters lamented the Hall of Peña was too small. Denver was not the only city fixated by visions of big money from reckless conventioneers. Other towns invested in gargantuan facilities, ones overshadowing the Colorado Convention Center in size and total square footage. In light of this, the stagnation of the panacea project was explained away because it was not big enough. As much as they had when they scorned Currigan Hall to

Photo by Phil Goodstein

*Currigan Hall, on the left, was slated for removal in the early 21st century for the expansion of the dysfunctional Colorado Convention Center, on the right.*

push the modern facility, convention advocates loudly demeaned the Colorado Convention Center. Far from having any pride in it as an alluring civic building, they hatefully dismissed their own creation as "a box with docks."

None was more scornful of the standing building than its architect, Curt Fentress. He urged a mass expansion and reshaping of the convention center in 1999. "We want this building to be a civic building. . . . As designed, it would be an asset to downtown." His 1990 edifice, apparently, failed as both a civic building and asset to downtown.

Nor did Denver International Airport (DIA) help the convention business. The extreme bungling of the project gave the city a deserved black eye. The airport did not have good connections with the central city. In light of the terminal's distance from downtown, people did not want to come to Denver for conventions, knowing they faced high taxi fares. The vehicular dependence of DIA showed how bad a town Denver was for conventions. This was illustrated when two-thirds of the 5,000 people attending a meeting of the National Community Pharmacists Association could not get into downtown during a blizzard in October 1997 because of the poor design of Peña Boulevard. Not the size of the convention center, but the greed, incompetence, and lack of vision of its sponsors, lay at the heart of the Colorado Convention Center as an underused, dysfunctional facility.

The failure of the meeting hall temporarily forced the hotel and visitor industry to admit, in essence, Denver was not the convention city of the world. At the best, the Queen City was only a second-tier convention town lagging well behind New Orleans, Las Vegas, and New York. Though the Denver Metro Convention & Visitors Bureau touted a doubling of the convention center's size as the means of making Denver a first-class convention city, size alone did not determine where conventions were held. San Diego, for example, with a 254,000-square-foot hall—a facility smaller than Denver's—drew 295,000 delegates to its conventions in 1997 compared to 188,450 who came to the Queen City. In 1998, the Mile High hall only attracted 36 major conventions. This was less than one a week, i.e., about the same rate Currigan Hall could handle. Despite this, the Bureau received immense publicity and full support from city hall in its campaign to get more handouts for a larger complex.

In the late 1990s, the Bureau came up with its latest nostrum to cure the stagnation of the Colorado Convention Center: doubling it in size through a massive addition crossing Stout Street where Currigan Hall stood. In the process, it would finally achieve its goal of getting rid of the facility it had sponsored in the 1960s. Only in this manner could the Hall of Peña finally emerge as a successful complex.

At first, the private group wanted the city to float a $200 million bond to pay for this effort, including boosting taxes on residents. Notably, it planned to charge locals more on car rentals and lodging. Before long the price soared to $268 million. The additional funds were needed, explained the Wellington Webb administration in August 1999, because the first estimate did not include such basics as engineering details and technical costs. Further money was additionally asked to reshape the 1990 building.

In justifying the tax hike, the Bureau claimed the existing assessments for the Hall of Peña were generating more revenue than needed to service the unsuccessful project's debt. Rather than seeing these charges on Denverites reduced or have the excess money go into the general fund, the convention industry wanted more subsidies for its business efforts. Even so, the tourist agency's scheme faced obstacles. The car rental business, for example, noted how few of its customers were Colorado Convention Center patrons compared to others, including locals, who leased cars. Likewise, conventioneers remained an extremely minor percentage of those paying extra restaurant taxes for the center.

Supporters readily brushed such facts and objections aside. Public moneys, they made plain, were theirs to use as they liked as part of the public/private partnership. With almost unlimited funding, repeating every convention lie, and facing no organized opposition, the Visitors Bureau, fully backed by the Webb administration, got voters to approve a convention center expansion, 43,492 (55 percent) to 35,305 (45 percent), in November 1999 when Denverites authorized all other building efforts on the ballot by more than 60 percent.

## A Thousand-Room Hotel

Another panacea dominated the convention center debate, the need for a thousand-room hotel. Like "great city" and "24-hour city," "thousand-room hotel" was an incantation. From the 1970s, when it was obvious the recently completed Currigan Hall was not going to magically transform downtown, advocates of state capitalism insisted a thousand-room hotel was vital. Only such a massive facility, they explained, could host the bloated conclaves enriching those who lived off the convention business. Naturally, they expected the city to help finance it.

CHS

*A group poses on the Zeckendorf Plaza ice-skating rink in the early 1960s. The city allowed the Adam's Mark to destroy this amenity as part of the push for a thousand-room hotel. The old Hilton Hotel is in the background.*

Denver's grand inn of the 1960s, the Hilton, swallowed the thousand-room hotel bait. As the push for the Hall of Peña got hot and heavy, complete with promise of a thousand-room hotel, Hilton abandoned Courthouse Square in December 1984. The chain announced it hoped to run the new thousand-room hotel next to the super convention center. Talk was heard the city might destroy the Denver Dry and Neusteter buildings to make way for the lodge.

As problem after problem emerged in making the convention center a working reality, the gigantic hotel was put on hold. The Radisson chain took over the 16th and Court facility. Despite the claim a larger, more modern structure was vital, the Radisson profitably operated the Courthouse Square hostelry as a meeting/convention facility. The owner did not want to see its investment endangered by a larger, city-subsidized convention hotel. Despite this, Reliance Development of New York eagerly pushed for DURA to condemn land along 14th Street where it could put up a 980-room hotel in the late 1980s. It expected the city to guarantee a five-year occupancy of its project.

Other hotels joined Radisson in opposing the measure. Straining under high vacancy rates despite the promises of the Colorado Convention Center, they did not want the rival hotel. They managed to shoot down Reliance's demand for the subsidy. As the convention center failed to deliver its promises in the mid-1990s, the hotel became a reality. After the May D&F abandoned Courthouse Square in 1993 while efforts to bring new retail to 16th Street stagnated, the city declared the area a blighted zone in need of urban renewal. Corporate Denver so looked to DURA to bring forth the thousand-room hotel.

On this basis, HBE Corporation of St. Louis, owned by Fred Kummer, purchased the Radisson in 1994. It immediately demanded a $25 million subsidy from DURA to transform it and the adjacent May D&F building into the 1,200-plus room Adam's Mark Hotel—otherwise, it would walk away from the project. Named for an area near Vail where Kummer had other investments, Adam's Mark was finally the promised prodigious convention hotel. (Civil rights advocates accused the hotel chain of discriminating against African-American workers and guests. Kummer also had a notorious record of union-busting. He used the subsidy and takeover of the hotel to get rid of the union representing its workers.)

With the principle of state capitalism so well established and the quest for the thousand-room hotel so pressing, HBE had few problems getting the city and DURA to give it what it wanted. The only real challenge it faced was the so-called hyperbolic paraboloid at the May D&F. Located at the south corner of 16th Street and Tremont Place, the paraboloid was the distinguishing part of the store which was otherwise nothing more than a big box. Champions of modern architecture saw it as something special—a creative landmark designed by I. M. Pei. Others claimed it looked as if its roof had collapsed. Preservationists focused on trying to make

Photo by Ann Bingham

*The Hilton Hotel later became the Adam's Mark. The Petroleum Building, a 1957 structure, is on the right. The small building in between, the Harris Hotel, a low-cost lodge, was subsequently displaced for a parking lot as the city determinedly pushed for a thousand-room hotel.*

the paraboloid part of Adam's Mark. The St. Louis developer was not interested. With the authorization and money of DURA, Adam's Mark destroyed the wing in the fall of 1996.

(Lovers of modern architecture responded by embracing Currigan Hall. In face of their pressure, after voters authorized a doubling of the Colorado Convention Center's size in 1999, the city talked about somehow moving Currigan Hall or giving the building away to whoever would disassemble and recreate it elsewhere.)

The most important part of Courthouse Square was obliterated in the birthing of Adam's Mark, Zeckendorf Plaza, at the west corner of 16th Street and Court Place. From the opening of the May D&F in 1958 until the mid-1980s, Zeckendorf Plaza was the heart of downtown. In the winter, locals ice-skated there. In the summer, they played miniature golf. The May D&F sponsored numerous other gatherings and events on the open space. None of the new subsidized developments associated with the convention center, a thousand-room hotel, or downtown retail had any place for such a meeting spot.

Adam's Mark erased Zeckendorf Plaza. In its place, the hotel cut through a car-first main entrance. The hotel also blocked part of the sidewalk along Court Place near the old main entrance to the Hilton, creating a very poor, dangerous walking environment. The design openly announced that, despite all the promises of the 16th Street Mall, downtown was more car dependent than ever. It was a sign of desperation of a city yet to grasp what it had done wrong.

No sooner had the long-sought thousand-room hotel formally opened in August 1997 than others demanded special favors for another thousand-room hotel at the site of the abandoned *Denver Post* Building at 15th and California streets. Developer Bruce Berger bought the *Post* site from Times Mirror for about $3.3 million in May 1998. He spent about another $3 million in tearing down the edifice and paving it for a parking lot. In the process, he left more remnants of the old *Post*, including some of its slogans, than anything found at the modern *Denver Post*. By the summer of 1999, Berger valued the property at $22 million in his dealings with the city and DURA.

In 2000, the developer asked for a $55.4 million subsidy to build a twin-towered, 1,100-room hotel there in conjunction with the Marriott chain. The city saw the lodge as part and parcel of the expanded convention center. Negotiations over subsidies and tax abatements for the inn temporarily collapsed in April 2000 when it appeared a parking lot was the best use for the land. By May 2000, the hotel was once more slated to arise. More controversies followed.

## Tourism Taxes

As its determined effort to destroy the paraboloid, Zeckendorf Plaza, and Currigan Hall showed, failure did not faze the tourism and visitor industry. It wanted money any way it could get it. In addition to the Denver lodging tax, it also received funds from the State of Colorado. When these faced a voter review in 1993, those in this field showed what they were about.

At an early date, promoting Colorado was established territorial policy. Public funds were appropriated to market the region. No lie was too extravagant to bring rich suckers to the Mile High City. To serve them, assorted swindlers packed Denver. While the city prohibited con men from preying on locals, it permitted them to target outsiders as easy marks.

The *Denver Post* killed a state-sponsored tourist board in the early 20th century. The newspaper proclaimed itself the official booster of the Centennial State, opposing any publicly funded competition. As the *Post* stagnated after the death of owner/publisher Frederick Bonfils in 1933, so did the open boasting about Colorado's wonders. By the end of World War II, the new generation—described by author John Gunther as "progressive" Coloradans—bemoaned the lack of an "organized booster spirit." Colorado, they wailed, did not actively seek to sell itself. On the contrary, it figured it was so special only sophisticates would come to it, making the state a better place for all. Gunther and the "progressives" decried such a stance, one emphasizing the state should primarily cater to residents rather than affluent outsiders.

The election of Quigg Newton in 1947 marked the triumph of the "progressives." They managed to get the General Assembly to appropriate public funds for private business ventures. The legislature added extra taxes to restaurant meals, hotel rooms, and rental cars to pay for promotional campaigns and a state tourist board. Money from the general fund was spent on marketing Colorado. A state Advertising and Publicity Committee, the Colorado Department of Highways, and the Game and Fish Department all paid for advertisements to attract visitors. Governors Dan Thornton, John Love, and Roy Romer went out of their ways to travel the world to bring business and high-spending visitors to the Centennial State.

Not everybody endorsed this approach. A satirical "Colorado State Song" by U. Utah Phillips in the early 1970s mocked the tourism business. Noting how rich outsiders increasingly destroyed the amenities of the Centennial State, the tune described the jet set as "them lazy, no-good bastards" who love to ski, fly to Colorado, "and buy up all our mountain scenery." The goal of the promotion agencies, the song continued, was to attract to Colorado "many different kinds of bums" who will turn the state into a place just like "all those eastern slums." The preferred message to tourists should be: "visit now and then, bring your money, bring your friends, bring your campers and your Winnebagos too, bring your festivals and dope," but "we all sincerely hope that you don't forget to leave when you get through."

A massive protest against such a sellout of Colorado was a key factor behind the defeat of the 1976 Winter Olympics. However, no sooner was the Richard Lamm administration in place in 1975, coming to power on the wave of the anti-Olympic enthusiasm, than it was business as usual among the visitor industry. The new governor failed to check the mindless promotion of Colorado. Taxpayer moneys continued to flow to those benefiting from tourism. Eventually, the excesses of Denver International Airport and the Colorado Convention Center called this part of the establishment into account.

As the costs of DIA soared ever higher in the early 1990s while the city built the new convention center despite the public referendum rejecting it, many voters rallied to the banner of Douglas Bruce. A typical Colorado interloper, he arrived

Photo by John Schoenwalter

*U. Utah Phillips wrote the "Colorado State Song," in which he argued the visitor industry wanted to attract to Colorado "many different types of bums" who will turn the state into a place "just like all those eastern slums."*

in the state in the early 1980s from southern California. He immediately speculated in slum properties in Denver and Colorado Springs. After a referendum to reduce taxes went down to defeat in 1986, he emerged as the state's foremost anti-tax crusader. Bruce, a former Los Angeles deputy district attorney, saw no reason the government needed a constantly increasing revenue stream, one surpassing both growth and inflation rates.

Taxpayers had been in revolt against an ever-growing, more arrogant government giving away subsidies to the rich since the 1970s. Those hating taxes joined environmentalists and anti-growth forces in rejecting the Olympics. In 1978, after California adopted a sweeping restriction on the Golden State's ability to generate revenue, former Colorado state treasurer Palmer Burch pushed an initiated measure tying Colorado's purse strings. The Chamber of Commerce vehemently opposed it, sending it down to defeat.

The movement for tax limitation would not go away. Bruce, headquartered in Colorado Springs, soon called the idea his own. In 1988, he launched a public initiative severely restricting the amount of taxes the government could collect. The establishment responded by bitterly attacking Bruce. The leading media demeaned his personal life. They sometimes projected him as the devil incarnate, blaming him for everything wrong with the state government.

Bruce was proud of his notoriety. "I'm not just another crackpot anymore," he quipped. "Now I'm the number-one crackpot." He loudly blasted Colorado Secretary of State Natalie Meyer as a "crook." The executive branch was composed of "pimps"; the General Assembly was filled with "prostitutes."

Bruce's tax limitation measure won 42 percent of the vote in 1988 and 49.7 percent in 1990. The anti-tax crusader described the votes for his proposition as "cries for help and cries of outrage by citizens of Colorado." As the lack of success of the convention center became plain while DIA's cost burgeoned, against the full force of powerful businesses benefiting from subsidies, leading politicians, and the media, Bruce convinced voters to pass his initiated Amendment One in 1992 by 54 percent. Known as the Taxpayers Bill of Rights (TABOR), the measure strictly limited the amount of new taxes the government could levy. Under it, voter authorization was necessary for the government to impose any new taxes. The establishment responded by making it more difficult for citizens to place initiated measures on the ballot.

Shortly after voters enacted TABOR, the existing state tourism taxes expired in 1993. A heavy sell-Colorado effort sought their renewal at the polls that November. Once more, tourist and convention promoters told the electorate how vital it was for them to pay $12 million or so in additional taxes so the business community could get the money, profit from it, and continue Colorado's sellout spirit. The question of why, if tourism advertising was so good for business, the visitor industry did not pay for it itself, was not answered. To obscure this inquiry, restaurants screamed the tax was only a token amount—only cheapskates decried paying it. (Shortly thereafter, the same restaurants launched a vehement, successful campaign against a public initiative requiring them to pay their employees a "living wage.")

As much as in the campaign for Denver International Airport or the convention center, there was no serious public debate of essential issues before the November 1993 tourism vote. While Bruce showed himself a man of principle who did not believe in state capitalism and all the extra assessments the visitor business wanted, the supporters of the tax categorically refused to address the larger issue of whether a public subsidy for private concerns was appropriate. On the contrary, spending freely and dominating the media and key politicians, they shrieked the defeat of the tax would force Colorado to revert to its parochial, non-state capitalist past. On election day, 55 percent of the voters said no to them and the continuation of the tourism tax.

Outrage followed. Leading politicians, boosters, and the ski industry howled in protest of the voters' verdict. Instead of seeing a private effort by those who had directly benefited from the tourism taxes to assess themselves for advertising and promotional efforts, the visitor sector sought to get around the amendment. Showing zero respect for the electorate, corporate Colorado demanded additional public handouts. The General Assembly readily granted them. Recreating a state-sponsored tourism board was the order of the day. Moneys were taken from DIA funds to market Colorado. There were no limits to the grasping nature of those seeking to benefit from the tourist and convention trades.

Much of this came after Federico Peña left office as mayor. Even so, he was the man who had helped make sure there were no serious challenges to the corporate domination of the city. This was apparent as he struggled for his political life in his 1987 bid for reelection.

## A Note on Sources:

The National Register nomination of the Auditorium at CHS discusses the origins and history of the building and the many modifications the city has made to it. The Tom Currigan Papers at DPL include immense analyses of downtown problems and proposals in the 1960s. Box 39 is filled with discussions and plans for what became Currigan Hall. The DURA collection at DPL also contains material on the push for the convention center. A celebration of Currigan Hall and downtown in the 1970s is *Downtown Denver: Where It Happens!* (Denver: First National Bank, 1971). Also see Sam Lusky, *The Denver Excitement*.

The Denver Metro Convention & Visitors Bureau has issued numerous studies and brochures. Its newsletter is *Denver Update*. Various Partnership and Bureau publications are on file in the Government Documents section of DPL. Charlenne Orr and Rich Grant talked about the Convention & Visitors Bureau. Jerry Vergatos recalled his family owning businesses in the Silver Triangle and the city relocation procedures. Jim Peiker discussed the bed and breakfast trade, including the large number of locals staying at the inns.

I examine the crooked core of the visitor industry in the late 19th/early 20th centuries in *The Seamy Side of Denver*. The volume notes the *Denver Red Book*, stock market scams, and the nature of protected gambling houses. Also see Philip Van Cise, *Fighting the Underworld*, a book focusing on the dirty tricks of and political protection received by con artist Lou Blounger.

William Zeckendorf notes the origins of the Hilton Hotel and its many problems in his *Autobiography*. There are detailed newspaper clippings about the building at DPL. The saga of the Brown Palace is told by Corinne Hunt, *The Brown Palace Story*. I look at the evolution and fate of the Courthouse Square project, focusing on the May D&F, in volume one.

Reuben Espinosa, Mike Davenport, and Cathy Donohue shared their opposition to the floodplain convention center with me in 1985. Don Bain noted Peña's capitulation on the matter. Dick Fleming and Bill Lamont were loud in asserting it as Denver's destiny. I glance at Allan Reiver's career in my *South Denver Saga*.

A history of Evans Addition is badly needed. I briefly touch on it in my *Ghosts of Denver*. There are materials on its origins in Perkin, *First Hundred Years*. Elaine C. Walsh and Jean W. Smith, *Victoria of Civic Center*, is the story of the most distinguished surviving mansion in the area, the Byers-Evans House. Edgar M.

Wahlberg, *Voices in the Darkness*, recalls the neighborhood church, Grace Methodist. His papers at the Auraria Archives reflect on the composition of the neighborhood in the 1930s when Grace Church was actively involved in numerous social welfare efforts. The Saco DeBoer papers at DPL include materials on declaring the Golden Triangle a slum in the late 1930s.

The National Register listings at CHS include the Rocky Mountain Bank Note Building and Evans School. Also see clippings at DPL, DPS records, and Forrest, *History of the Public Schools,* on the latter structure. The buildings of Robert S. Roeschlaub in the area are discussed in passing in Richard Brettell, *Historic Denver*; and Francine Heber, Kenneth Fuller, and David Wetzel, *Robert S. Roeschlaub: Architect of the Emerging West.*

The DU Archives includes a file on Micky Miller, noting his close links to Al Cohen and Marvin Davis. The Abraham Kauvar papers at DU also have materials on Al Cohen. The Al Cohen proposal was *Colorado Convention Center at the Golden Triangle: Fact Book* (Denver: Cohen Construction, 1987). David French's successful bid was *The Colorado Convention Center: A Proposal* (Denver: French & Company, 1987). The Colorado Convention Center building is featured in Roger A. Chandler, *Fentress Bradburn Architects.*

*Urban Land* is the publication of the Urban Land Institute. The magazine's April 1998 issue is a salute to Denver's accomplishments. The organization's version of urban renewal is Leo Adde, *Nine Cities* (Washington: Urban Land Institute, 1969), which includes at look at Denver. Volume seven of the *Denver Plan* (Denver: Denver Planning Commission, 1941), notes the early urban renewal views of the Land Institute.

I look at the politics and development of the Diamond Cabaret in my *Seamy Side of Denver*. The city and Convention Bureau issued numerous newsletters and press releases on the Colorado Convention Center. Some are in the Government Documents section of DPL. Western History at DPL also includes a thick clipping file on convention center controversies. Stuart Steers, "Give Them a Hand," *WW*, May 18, 2000, p. 15, examines the giveaways on the Bruce Berger hotel project.

Athearn, *The Coloradans*, reflects on the booster/promotion ethic and how it frequently backfired on the state. Perkin, *First Hundred Years*, observes the heavy promotional role of newspapers in early Colorado. The Denver & Rio Grande Railroad issued numerous sleek tourism brochures advertising 19th-century Colorado. Copies are available at DPL and CHS. Also see Robert Athearn, *The Denver & Rio Grande Western Railroad.* Gunther, *Inside the USA*, reports the *Denver Post* veto on a state tourism commission and the attitude of "progressive" citizens on this matter. Utah Phillips chatted about the "Colorado State Song" in a brief informal conversation in 1987. Harry Tuft talked about performing and recording the song with Grubstake on Manasses Records, MR 1001.

A good deal of material on the 1993 tourism tax election is in the Jack McCroskey file at the DU Archives. Greg Lopez had an excellent portrait of Douglas Bruce, *RMN*, January 21, 1993. *Westword* took the lead in demeaning Bruce's personal life, e.g., the article by Alan Pendergast in the October 21, 1999, issue.

# 7

# Desperately Seeking Someone

As the May 1987 municipal election approached, the city was as uneasy as it had been prior to the 1983 showdown. The promise of Federico Peña as a bright new light who would transform the city with a people-friendly government had vanished. Instead of a populist administration, he had imposed arrogant experts on the city. In addition to the convention center, a new airport was a foremost goal. They were crucial, he repeatedly explained, because the oil bust had devastated Denver with massive unemployment, business failures, and foreclosures. These public work projects were magic bullets to revive the boom.

Despite his eager commitment to the corporate community, many business advocates complained Peña had not accomplished anything. He had been all talk, but no action. Neighborhood activists lamented the administration had promised more than it had delivered. Longtime residents were unhappy about Peña's continuing subservience to 17th Street. Many displeased with the mayor were sure Denver again needed a breath of fresh air. Assorted politicians tried to provide it.

Miller Hudson, a former employee of Mountain Bell, had been a liberal state representative from North Denver from 1979 till 1982. His district was next to Peña's and the two had worked together closely in the House. Hudson was among those who had helped Peña rise in the legislature as House minority leader.

After pushing his fellow legislator's election in 1983 and serving a stormy term as chairman of the Denver Democratic Party, Hudson was disgusted by Peña's total subservience to special interests. By November 1985, he was ready to run for mayor. During the next year, the challenger sought to rebuild the élan and idealism Peña had successfully used in 1983.

The disillusioned Peña supporter ripped city hall's readiness to embrace "every hare-brained scheme that masquerades as economic development." Opposed to the callous ignorance of the Denver Planning Office, Hudson cited the work of Jane Jacobs as someone who understood how cities work and should function. Even so, the former representative made sure listeners knew he was fully committed to the development agenda. He explained his opposition to a pork-barrel subsidy for a new convention center: the handout actually delayed making the project a reality. Hudson embraced year-round daylight saving as a wonder-working solution to air pollution.

Given such equivocation, Hudson's campaign never took off. Many simply did not trust him. Insiders thought he was actually angling for a job in the Peña administration, not seriously seeking to change the city's direction. Before he had officially filed for a spot on the ballot, in February 1987, deeply in debt and unable to raise funds for what would become Denver's costliest mayoral election, Hudson dropped out.

The candidate subsequently endorsed Peña for reelection. Shortly after the mayor won his second term, Peña rewarded Hudson by appointing him manager of excise and license. Less than a year later, in May 1988, Peña ousted Hudson. The latter was not an ideal team player who was completely obedient to the mayor. In particular, Hudson was too critical of some of the administration's giveaways, notably its support of the anti-small business Transit Construction Authority in South Denver. The agency sought taxation power to build a private rail line between downtown and the Denver Tech Center. Its acting chairman, Chamber of Commerce chief and close Peña supporter Dick Fleming, reportedly demanded Hudson's head. The mayor readily delivered it.

A more durable challenger for mayor was Mike Licht. Born in Denver on May 23, 1931, he served as president of B'nai B'rith Lodge #171 in 1974. Once a powerhouse in the local Jewish community, the B'nai B'rith chapter had faded greatly since it sold its headquarters building at Colfax Avenue and Williams Street in 1964. Many dismissed it as nothing more than a vestige of the city's past. They did the same with Licht, a man proud of his origins in the West Colfax Jewish community.

A certified public accountant, Licht had worked for the city since 1958 in a variety of auditing and accounting jobs, including a stint with the Denver District Court. In the 1970s, he set his sights on Dr. Abraham Kauvar, manager of health and hospitals under McNichols. Licht complained about Kauvar's management of Denver General Hospital and the institution's cost overruns. Before long, Licht and Kauvar were virtually at war. The hospital was so disgusted with Licht's continued attacks that the accountant's photo was supposedly displayed in its emergency room with the caption "Do not revive this man."

Licht won a narrow, upset triumph as auditor in 1983. Initial results showed him losing to incumbent Charles Byrne, 58,360–58,572. A recount declared him the victor, 58,496–58,399. (The Denver Election Commission had no credibility in the race. In the fall of 1982, it had installed super-computerized voting machines. There was only one problem: they did not work. Other races besides auditor were disputed. After massive confusion in the 1982 primary and general elections, the election commission went back to having the populace use mechanical voting machines while it lost all public trust.)

As auditor, Licht was a loud watchdog, constantly barking and snapping at city hall. Reaching out to the public as no modern auditor had ever done, he staged his own public forums, taught classes on the auditor's role through Denver Free University, and issued annual reports including discussions of the city's heritage and traditions. He projected himself as a folksy politician who was in tune with the citizenry, opposed to the big boys of the mayor's office.

Author's Collection

*Mike Licht*

At first, Licht was the frontrunner in challenging Peña. He was ready with numerous barbs about how "Peña has done less with more" and badly run the city. As mayor, Licht would not "imagine a great city"; he would manage the great city Denver already was. The auditor claimed he had been forced continually to call the mayor to account when city contracts went to politically well-connected, out-of-town companies overbidding fully qualified local firms. Licht promised to bring the efficiency of an accountant to city hall.

The auditor's positions did not inspire confidence. This was illustrated by his wavering on Denver International Airport. Licht was initially against it, dismissing it as a scam pushed by "Feddy and the dreamers." His position changed after he was offered political support by developer Larry Mizel of MDC, a heavy promoter of the airport who had speculative holdings near it. When Licht reversed his position on the field, he alienated some of his previous supporters while exposing his unreliability—he could be turned as easily as any other venal politician. Other than the Mizel money, he had trouble raising campaign funds.

The candidate appeared a loose cannon. Much of city council and the political establishment hated the auditor. Licht had so shaken up the city government that members of council, loudly echoed by newspaper editors who did not want controversy, called for abolishing the elected nature of the auditor's post. The purpose was plain: individuals such as Licht must be prevented from ever again holding the job. Ruling Denver, it appeared, feared an auditor watchdog guarding the taxpayers against a corporate city hall.

Among Licht's most severe opponents were the mayor's youthful supporters. Joined by editors and reporters new to Denver, they had no use for the traditional city Licht sought to recall. Against the mayor's glowing vision of reshaping Denver on the basis of cities elsewhere, they were sure Licht personified Denver's cow-town heritage. As the auditor threatened to emerge as the premier alternative candidate for mayor, newspaper scrutiny of him soared. Reporters, fed by city hall, accused him of politicizing the auditor's office. Charges were widely publicized about him receiving improper donations from city employees. An auditing of the auditor's office showed Licht had used $7,000 in city funds for public relations. Though special investigations cleared him of any misdoings, the publicity severely affected his candidacy. By early 1987, Licht's star was rapidly fading.

## The Senator

Dennis J. Gallagher also pondered a run for mayor. Born in Denver on July 1, 1939, he was a third-generation resident. Holding a master's degree from Catholic University in Washington, D.C., he was an extremely devout Catholic who had been a classics professor at Regis College since 1967. He readily quoted Latin and Greek verses and drew upon his Irish heritage. In 1970, Gallagher was part of a group of insurgents who swept the Denver Democratic Party as he won election to the state House of Representatives from North Denver. After a couple of terms in the lower house, in 1974 Gallagher won a seat in the state Senate. He easily gained reelection during the next 12 years.

Supporters simply called Gallagher "the Senator." An affable, scholarly presence, he pushed historic preservation and freely imbibed on bar tours he led with his close companion, establishment historian Tom Noel. The politician was always ready with a quip and knew how properly to observe public ceremonies. Among those whom he encouraged to work closely with neighborhood activists was Federico Peña. When the future mayor first entered the legislature in 1979, Gallagher took him under his wing. The Senator sometimes hauled Peña with him to various neighborhood gatherings.

The politician's foremost accomplishment came in 1982 when he successfully pushed what became known as the Gallagher Amendment. An initiated change of the state constitution, it kept taxes on residential properties in check vis-à-vis commercial properties. In such a manner, business was supposed to bear the brunt of the costs of growth. The effort was a clear message: everyday citizens needed protection from a government primarily catering to 17th Street.

By 1987, Gallagher was extremely uneasy about the direction of city hall. Along with many of Peña's onetime supporters, he noted the administration had turned its back on its previous idealism. In private conversations Gallagher berated the mayor's anti-people, pro-development slant. Still, he hesitated to run for mayor. The Senator was a loyal Democrat who did not want to challenge one of his own.

Gallagher was among many liberal Democrats whom the Peña clique scorned. No sooner was Peña in office than relations soured between him and liberal members of city council. Nor did the mayor have good ties with others who had long challenged the McNichols–17th Street link. Instead of seeking to build coalitions with such former foes of city hall, the Peña administration demanded complete subservience. It excluded mavericks such as Gallagher and city councilwoman Cathy Donohue from its camp. They, in turn, freely shot barbs at the mayor.

While the Peña conservatives had little use for Gallagher, McNichols Democrats were more accommodating. They still hoped for a return of the pre-1983 state of affairs and desperately sought to field a candidate in 1987. Noting

Author's Collection

*Dennis Gallagher shaved off his beard as he ran for mayor in 1987.*

Gallagher's alienation from the mayor, they approached the Senator. Despite past bad blood between them and Gallagher, they noted their common commitment to yesterday's Denver and the glories of the old-fashioned Democratic machine. The McNichols operatives informed the Senator they were ready to back him if he ran against the incumbent. All the former mayor wanted was for Gallagher to shave off his beard. Such a physical move would symbolically show the contender's commitment to the status quo. Gallagher readily complied.

The Senator so entered the race, not as an opposition candidate who would finally redeem the promises for change Peña had short-circuited, but as a traditionalist recalling the days of Mayor Bill. Typical was his answer to a question at a candidate forum on whether, as mayor, he would continue to push an unpopular convention center despite a public vote rejecting it. Yes, was his determined answer. As a senator, he noted, he had worked to get legislative financing for the state capitalist effort. The candidate likewise firmly stated his commitment to a new airport. "There's a big job to be done! Let's get on with it" was his campaign slogan.

Despite Gallagher showing himself at one with the establishment in his eager desire to recreate the old-fashioned city machine, some McNichols' backers still found the Senator too radical. They did not forget his past clashes with city hall. This group, led by Neil Macey who had rallied the anti-Union Station convention center forces in conjunction with the Dikeou family, sought a candidate even further encrusted in the past. It found him in an undefeated politician who had plenty of experience as mayor, Tom Currigan.

Since leaving Denver to become vice president of Continental Airlines at the end of 1968, Currigan had been around. Fourteen years after bailing out as mayor, he returned to Denver in 1982, remaining as a consultant to the airline. The 66-year-old Currigan showed up at public forums recalling the glorious days of urban renewal during his tenure. He promised he would restore them if he were again elected mayor. The candidate vowed he would not complain about his salary or resign from office in midterm.

Currigan was an anachronism by 1987. Though people knowledgeable about Denver history recalled exactly who he was and what he had done, he did not strike a chord with new Denver. He also showed his age at candidate debates, coming across more as a vestige of yesterday than a dynamic figure who would set Denver back on the right course.

Clarke Watson was the contender who barbed the establishment in 1987. Another longtime Denverite, his brother, Lauren, headed the local Black Panther Party in the late 1960s. At that time Watson was caught between protest and crime. He was convicted of a felony as a youth when he participated in a 1971 robbery at the zoo. Since then, he stood out for his intense community work and political involvement.

Previously head of the Colorado Black Political Caucus, Watson was a dynamic orator who ripped the corporate subservience of city hall. Unlike the other candidates, he called for keeping the airport where it was while urging a public vote on where the convention center should be. Even as he livened up the campaign, some did not trust Watson. They thought him more interested in using the campaign to fish for influence and power than in making his pledges reality. They noted how, seeking political advantage, Watson readily denounced his brother.

## The Republican Candidate

The exact opposite of Watson—a boring, unimaginative presence—was the Republican challenger, Don Bain. A fifth-generation Denverite, he hailed from a family linked to banking, baking, and related developments. Over the years, the Bains had been everywhere, interrelated with virtually all of yesterday's Denver money. His parents had served in the General Assembly, on the school board, and taken numerous civic posts. Bain was part of the network of old Denver.

An East High graduate who had gone on to Yale University and Harvard Law School, Bain emerged as a senior member of the city's largest law firm, Holme, Roberts & Owen. During the 1960s and 1970s, the 55-year-old candidate had been the prototypical bluestocking Republican. Living adjacent to Cheesman Park at 833 Race Street, in the late 1960s he actively participated in efforts to establish a mountain-view ordinance limiting the heights of buildings constructed directly west of the park. Bain had also served on the board of neighborhood groups and supported various municipal improvement measures.

As a corporate lawyer, Bain represented big business. The candidate belonged to the Denver Country Club and other organizations of ruling class power and influence. Community service was his personal credo. Among his appointments had been the library commission and the board governing the Auraria Higher Education Center. He was an old-fashioned, service-oriented progressive who, without the Peña populist smoke screen, personified business-governmental cooperation.

There was nothing colorful about Bain. Not a flamboyant attorney or powerful speaker, he was a good, effective, sharp administrator who knew how to get things done. As part of big money, he was not awed by it. Supporters noted he would not be afraid occasionally to say no to 17th Street. On this basis, backers pushed him as a traditional Denverite who could effectively run the mayor's office.

The challenger had had close ties with the Republican Party for years. His campaign was something of a step back for the local Republicans. They had not put up a challenger for mayor since 1975. When the Republicans sought to run powerful candidates in 1971 and 1975, Joe Shoemaker and Charles Byrne respectively, many members of the party preferred to support McNichols over one of their own. Seeing Peña's vulnerability, Bain believed he could win. The Republicans eagerly lined up behind him.

Two others entered the mayor's race: Dave Daniels, a 32-year-old Alaska native, was the Libertarian Party's candidate; and Chuck Martinez, 55, who had worked for the Denver Department of Parks and Recreation for 24 years. Neither had much of an impact. As a Libertarian, Daniels readily spoke against the state capitalism underlying the Peña administration. Martinez noted how Peña did not treat veteran city workers well.

Author's Collection

*Don Bain*

Despite intense rhetoric, professional campaign consultants, and heavy advertising, the 1987 mayoral race was incredibly dull. None of the major candidates challenged the essential Peña agenda of the need for a new airport, convention center, growth, sprawl, and greatness. The *Rocky Mountain News*, in an unusually candid editorial, noted that all of the major candidates were reluctant "to offend any interest group."

Just as those dissatisfied with Mayor Bill had made "anyone but McNichols" their credo in 1983, four years later anti-Peña forces were desperately seeking someone against the incumbent. Developments since 1983, however, meant they did not have much from which to choose. A key Peña accomplishment had been gutting the forces of opposition that had repeatedly challenged McNichols in the late 1970s and early 1980s. Many were sure the officeholder was not the man for the job, but they had no organization or vision for a better candidate.

Given this abysmal climate, some anti-growth voters lined up behind Bain. They noted how he, a conservative Republican, would never be able to push the pro-business, pro-development programs of Peña without unleashing a storm of popular protest. Many in the business community agreed: Peña was more in tune with their aspirations than one of their own—Bain. A Hispanic Democrat and a supposed liberal as mayor, they were sure, could rally the public to their agenda far better than a 17th Street lawyer.

## Neighborhood Improvement Organizations

Side by side of the corporate community, Peña received powerful support from a sector which had intently battled the McNichols administration, neighborhood improvement organizations. Since the mid-1970s, they had burgeoned, projecting themselves as alternative voices to city hall. The incumbent cleverly made them part of his political machine.

Denver periodically had bursts of neighborhood activism. Assorted local citizen and homeowners groups date from at least the early 20th century. They formed a crucial constituency of the Ku Klux Klan in the 1920s.

When the Klan ran Denver in 1923–25, many neighborhood activists backed it. The Robert Speer League, an organization of various residential and business improvement associations, for example, endorsed the white supremacist group. The Klan's rhetoric appealed to the improvers. The hooded order promised to fight crime, preserve property values, and guard neighborhoods from "undesirable" elements. While the hate group specifically targeted Jews, blacks, Spanish-Americans, and Catholics, most improvement associations defined "undesirable" residents as those who failed to worship immaculate green lawns, stored beat-up cars in their backyards, or who failed to make an appreciation of home values their number-one concern.

Residential clubs did not amount to much after the collapse of the Klan. Once he had consolidated himself in power in 1925 upon the Klan's demise, Mayor Ben Stapleton had little use for such associations. He ran city hall through a machine. The administration only helped councilmen who supported it. (The Robert Speer League lingered on for many years, primarily functioning as a booster organization backing city hall.)

A new burst of citizen activism swept the city under Quigg Newton. In 1951, about 15 neighborhood improvement associations organized the Denver Civic Council as a coalition of residential groups. The mayor endorsed the conclave. To push it and its sponsoring groups, he proclaimed September 24–29, 1951, "Join Your Civic Club Week." The Denver Civic Council associated with a national organization of improvement groups, ACTION—the New York-based American Council To Improve Our Neighborhoods. Within a few years, the Mile High organization faded.

Most homeowner bureaus had extremely short lives. Residents usually formed them to demand a certain amenity such as paving alleys or flood-control efforts. Conversely, citizens organized to fight a specific threat, including city-sponsored urban renewal programs and school busing. Frequently, one or two activists were the heart and soul of a group. When they tired of fighting city hall, their organizations faded. In other cases, homeowners, seeing the negative impact city policies had on their neighborhoods, packed up and fled to suburbia rather than swallowing the urban renewal cure. Here and there, property covenants required all residents to belong to a homeowners' or condominium association. In yet other circumstances, especially in stable middle-class areas, the clubs were primarily social organizations, allowing locals a chance to meet their neighbors.

Many residents were not happy in the new areas of the city. No sooner had they moved to these promised utopian enclaves than problems appeared. Schools, streets, sewers, and parks were inadequate. They demanded governmental relief. When city hall suggested specific bond improvement districts as the way to finance these public works, homeowners sometimes opposed the increased assessments. They had paid enough already. But something had to be done. By organizing and screaming, they hoped to get a better treatment from the city. In response to such pres-

*The Sixth Avenue Parkway, looking east from Ash Street, in 1973. During the 1960s, city hall wished to devastate it and the surrounding neighborhood by transforming the road into an extension of the Sixth Avenue Freeway.*

sures, the bulk of Denver capital spending through the 1970s was on new sections. The message was plain: through organization citizens could successfully fight city hall.

Growth and city hall's disdain for old Denver also adversely impacted residents in some elite neighborhoods. Typical was the plan for the extension of the West Sixth Avenue Freeway. In conjunction with the state and federal government, the city built the road west from Kalamath Street during World War II to connect with an isolated armaments plant at Kipling Street (eventually the site of the Denver Federal Center). In the early 1960s, planners and traffic engineers proposed extending the freeway eastward from Kalamath Street. They saw it extending through the Seventh Avenue Parkway district before devastating property along Sixth Avenue Parkway east of Colorado Boulevard. In such a manner, the Sixth Avenue Freeway would tie Lowry Air Force Base and Aurora with the western suburbs.

Capitol Hill, Montclair, and Country Club homeowners, who saw their properties as negatively impacted by the superhighway, did not want the "improvement." Some were unhappy as it was. Rumors floated about banks red-lining them—drawing maps around the neighborhoods in red lines and refusing to finance mortgages in their areas. Those living near the Country Club fought back, forming

Preserve Our Way of Urban Residence (POWUR). The group told city hall to kill the freeway. Before long, the plans to extend the highway were permanently shelved.

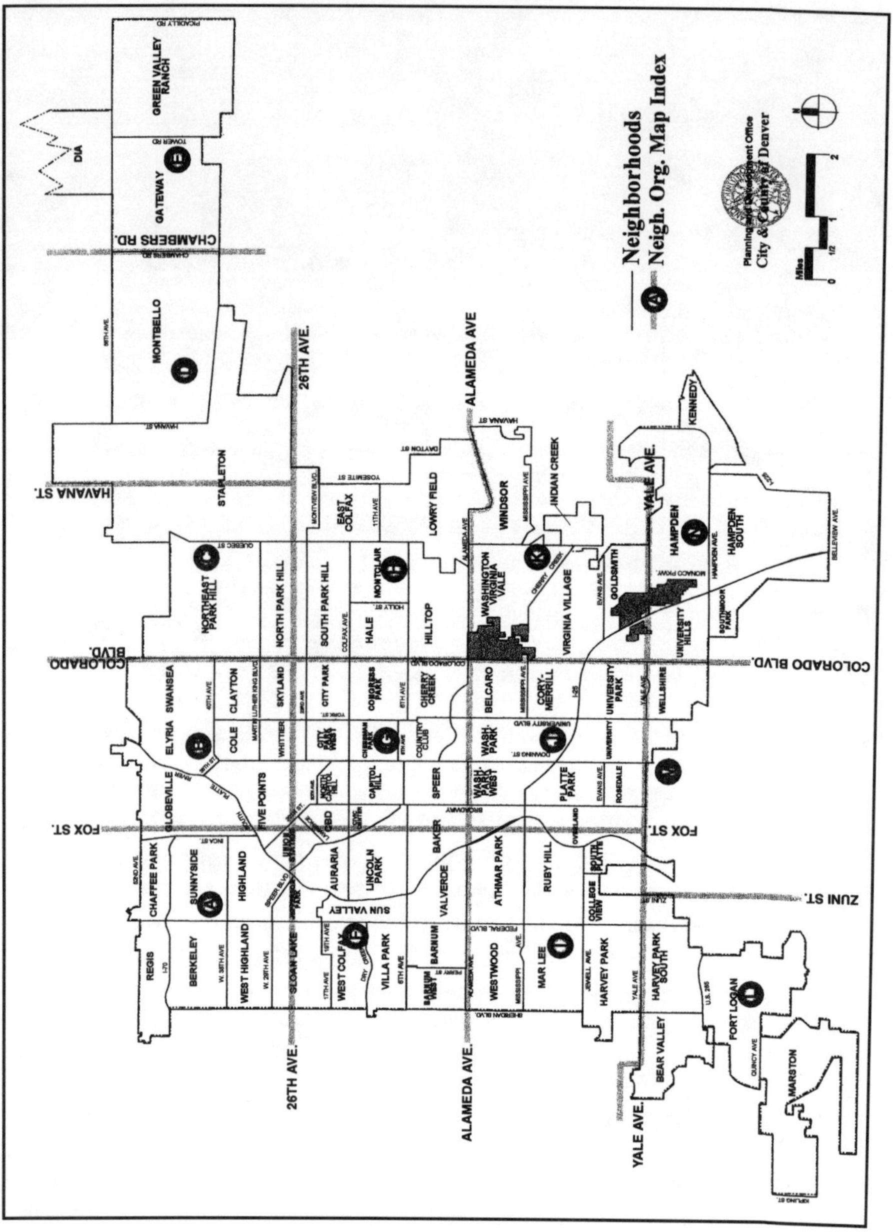

DPO

*The Denver Planning Office has issued elaborate maps of the city, specifying statistical planning units and recognized neighborhood associations.*

Other organizations came and went, protesting road and urban renewal programs. While the Denver Urban Renewal Authority (DURA) readily bulldozed over poor neighborhoods, now and then protesters won limited victories. McNichols was an astute enough politician to know when to withdraw from unwinnable fights.

One citizen triumph saw the defeat of a 1969–70 city hall effort to put a bridge over West 12th Avenue at Cherry Creek. The McNichols administration sought to place the bridge there in order to transform 11th and 12th avenues into paired one-way streets linking Cheesman Park at Humboldt Street with Lincoln Park at Mariposa Street. Not only did West Denver residents oppose it, so did those living on Capitol Hill. The latter organized as the Capitol Hill Congress. That club quickly decayed, torn apart by political and personal differences. Still, Capitol Hill activists saw they had to organize and speak out against city hall. Toward this end, they formed the Capitol Hill United Neighborhoods (CHUN) in 1971. Mostly dominated by liberal Democrats, the body continually clashed with the mayor over the fate of this section of town.

McNichols paid little heed to homeowner organizations. Power, he was clear, rested in the mayor's office. The foremost concern of city hall lay in the prosperity of business, especially the vitality of downtown. At one with 17th Street, the mayor had no doubt corporate domination was good for Denver. He was as deaf as the bankers and suburban real estate speculators to arguments about how cancerous growth was destroying the city's many fine and distinctive residential neighborhoods.

Even so, the McNichols administration oversaw a certain defining of neighborhoods. Many had rich traditions, dating back to the days when they were independent communities before Denver annexed them in the late 19th and early 20th centuries. Locals celebrated neighborhood customs and identities. Often a subdivision was more a state of mind, adopted by those living in it, than a specifically demarcated enclave. McNichols changed this.

## Neighborhood Definitions and Divisions

In the early 1970s, federal revenue-sharing and urban improvement moneys were available to cities to spruce up blighted areas. To get such funds, municipalities had to carve themselves into statistical planning units. The older the houses, the lower the car ownership, and the less a residential section looked like modern suburbia, the more blighted it was according to Department of Housing and Urban Development standards. An area so defined qualified to receive considerable sums so the city could rebuild it as part of what was deemed the Neighborhood Revitalization Program.

Desirous of the money, the McNichols administration painted Denver as a city filled with slums. During 1971–72 the Denver Planning Office (DPO) undertook a systematic survey of neighborhoods. It divided the town into 73 statistical planning units. (Others were subsequently added.) Often the names and borders chosen by the planners had little connection with the city's history or traditions.

One example was what the planning office labeled the Baker neighborhood. This consisted of land stretching between West Sixth and West Mississippi avenues from Broadway to the Platte River. The area encompassed a wide variety of people, structures, and usages. Not only had no one ever called the enclave Baker in the past, but many of its parts had no connections. Locals once knew the heart of the area, north of Alameda and along both sides of Broadway as Broadway Terrace. The land south of Alameda had been part of an independent Town of South Denver. The name Baker was taken from the presence of Baker Junior High School at West Sixth Avenue and Elati Street.

Another illustration of the nature of neighborhood definitions was how the DPO decreed the Highlands neighborhood, once the heart of the independent Town of Highlands to the west of Zuni Street in North Denver, "West Highland." According to the planners, it only covered the area west of Federal Boulevard. The West Highland designation confused Highlands with a historic section of North Denver east of Zuni Street, Highland.

The planning office labeled the land south of West Highland the "Sloan Lake Statistical Planning Unit." The name derived from the DPO's denotation of a body of water generations of Denverites had called Sloans Lake. DPO defined the Platte Park neighborhood as the enclave between Mississippi Avenue, Interstate 25, Evans Avenue, South Downing Street and South Broadway. It was named for Platt Park at South Logan Street and Florida Avenue, greenery recalling James Platt. The planning office, either not knowing this or how the park was spelled, dubbed it "Platte" Park as if it had some connection with the Platte River. Whenever possible, DPO declared neighborhoods "endangered" or "blighted."

Once federal funds started pouring in, thanks to such statistical planning unit designations, DPO drafted neighborhood plans. They were filled with unreliable history and information. In the name of democratic participation and to meet federal mandates, the planning office asked residents to come to meetings to help draft these documents, ones supposedly guiding the destinies of their areas. City council was supposed to consult the plans when pondering zoning and land use changes. It rarely paid attention to them. Officials only cited the plans as gospel when it was politically convenient to do so.

The plans were often sops, actions by city hall making it appear the mayor was doing something for people in residential enclaves. More relevant was how the McNichols administration transformed vacant and litter-filled lots into small corner parks. Despite such gestures, McNichols had poor ties with residents. Through the 1970s, ever more neighborhood groups appeared. Most dealt with nuts-and-bolts issues such as loose-running dogs and the lack of proper street sweeping and trash pickup. Traffic and noise were paramount concerns of these citizen leagues.

The groups were primarily reactive. Members rarely had a larger vision of the city or even basic knowledge of city politics or urban affairs. Those joining the organizations were drawn to them by an unease, noting forces and events beyond their control negatively impacted property values in their bailiwicks. The result was often an extreme parochialism. Larger issues and visions were absent from the statements and positions of the outfits. The organizations tended to attract political junkies who thrived on bureaucratic meetings and the belief they were exercising power.

In many cases, socially concerned residents joined the clubs. They enthusiastically turned out for lectures on the history of their areas. Generally, they were a world apart from those who ran the groups as political pressure organizations.

Homeowners predominated in improvement guilds. This shaped their contours. During the 1970s, newcomers started to discover pre-World War II Denver. Individuals who had grown up in the suburbs or were from faceless cities found the Mile High City filled with quaint, charming, and distinguished single-family houses. With a heavy application of elbow grease and commitment, they could be fixed up. Not only good places to live, these houses were excellent investments.

No sooner had the gentry started to move into old, poor neighborhoods such as Curtis Park, Broadway Terrace, and the heart of Capitol Hill than tensions arose between them and established residents. Many longtime denizens did not see their neighborhoods as blighted, but as tolerant, democratic sections with a flourishing live-and-let-live outlook. They did not care if their neighbors worshipped old cars and stashed them in their backyards. Others refused to kowtow to the god of green grass. They liked their crop of dandelions. Often the newcomers did not. They organized to do something about them.

Renters were common among the established residents of poorer neighborhoods. Virtually no laws protected them from rapacious landlords. Rundown properties were common. Slumlords were often slow to fix broken windows or put up new gutters. Nor was city council about to act to force landlord responsibility. When city councilman Sam Sandos pushed for a warrant of habitability in the mid-1980s, a majority of council either abstained from the measure or vehemently opposed it since they were landlords. The Sandos measure, consequently, went down to defeat. (Peña was silent on the issue.) Other than for a Capitol Hill Tenants Union functioning through the 1970s, those seeking to form renter groups had little success.

Photo by Phil Goodstein

*The mountains stand out west of Sloans Lake. The city called the body of water Sloan Lake.*

Photo by Phil Goodstein

*The trashed-out abandoned headquarters of the city's Community Development Agency on the 1400 block of Kalamath. Peña used the bureau to help build a neighborhood machine.*

The result was to make sections of Curtis Park and Highlands extremely eclectic. The old and new came together. One house or block might be immaculate, the next rundown. Despite a wave of renovation, much of the "blighted" character of the areas remained.

This rankled affluent settlers. As much as a missionary force invading another people's land, they sought to reshape these neighborhoods in their image. Echoing chambers of commerce and boards of Realtors, their credo was soaring real estate values—complete with higher rents. To make them a reality, they formed improvement associations as they lobbied city hall for better public services—frequently the city was lax in street sweeping and trash pickup in poor neighborhoods. Most of all, improvement groups demanded the administration enforce existing ordinances against fellow residents who liked the somewhat dilapidated status quo.

The newcomers and investors acclaimed themselves "stakeholders." Since they owned real property, they insisted they had a greater interest in the neighborhoods than did renters who might have been there for more than 50 years. Two classes of citizens apparently existed. Homeowners, these loud advocates of neighborhood groups implied, were better and had more rights than did the non-homeowners. Given this outlook, it was not surprising that few renters joined or supported the improvement organizations.

The stakeholders often exuded a condescending disdain for the poor. They saw thrift stores and pawn shops as awful neighborhood blights. Rather than treating these businesses as a natural part of the economy, members of uplift organizations hated them as open advertisements showing poor citizens still lived in the sections improvers had colonized. Leading neighborhood groups, such as CHUN, treated halls hiring day laborers as abominations. Those campaigning against them noted the businesses brought the wrong kind of people to their areas. They likewise saw tattoo parlors as blatant examples of degeneracy and decay. All such "undesirable" establishments, the stakeholders were sure, caused suburbanites to have the wrong impression of central Denver. Those voicing these views saw any businesses outside of their middle-class norms as evil incarnate. Fully in tune with suburbanites who sought to live in protected shells, the improvers demanded the city rezone commercial strips to eliminate and keep out any establishments they did not like.

There was sometimes a racial line in improvement associations. In marginal areas invaded by stakeholders, the groups were overwhelmingly white in what were otherwise black and brown neighborhoods. In the late 1990s, for example, the Whittier Neighborhood Association, encompassing the area east of Whittier School at 25th Avenue and Downing Street, primarily consisted of newly arrived white homeowners in a longtime African-American enclave primarily populated by renters.

## The Neighborhood Machine

Much of this parochialism and rhetoric lay well in the future—it was a product of a machine Peña cobbled together in 1987 to assure his reelection. Part of his coalition resulted from the deliberate transformation of the neighborhood groups. Before Peña became mayor, these organizations were constantly in opposition to city hall, frequently fighting the McNichols administration just to preserve the conditions as they were. The mayor categorically vetoed one of their foremost reforms: getting rid of some of the one-way streets cutting through residential neighborhoods. Since the elimination of the arterials would interfere with traffic flow and downtown commuters, McNichols would have nothing to do with it.

The one-way issue was indicative of the problematic approach of the neighborhood improvers. They did not want heavy traffic through their areas, but such individuals desired to quickly and freely drive through other sections of town. There was no alternate vision for traffic in the anti-one-way agitation, one questioning the sprawl making traffic such a problem. The neighborhood groups were not a unified opposition to the status quo or city hall; they were simply coalitions of concerned small property owners wanting a better shake from the city.

Some members of city council supported the improvement organizations. The 1975 elections saw three neighborhood-oriented individuals, Sam Sandos, Sal Carpio, and Cathy Donohue, gain membership on the body where they joined with Bill Roberts, a product of the Park Hill neighborhood movement. They pushed through a neighborhood notification ordinance in 1978. It required city agencies to inform registered neighborhood groups about applications for zoning changes, liquor licenses, and other municipal actions affecting the parts of town the improvers claimed to represent.

It was quite easy for a group to register with DPO as a neighborhood organization. Such associations constantly came and went. The notification measure immediately assisted groups with staying power. Thanks to it, neighborhood leaders knew what was going on. Given the media's generally vacuous reportage on neighborhoods, only through joining the groups and reviewing the city handouts could locals learn about many developments.

Members of the improvement associations noted they had shared problems with other clubs. Led by Bernie Jones, a professor at the University of Colorado at Denver who was a key figure in CHUN, activists sought to give coherence and direction to the neighborhood movement through forming Inter–Neighborhood Cooperation (INC) in 1975. Members of CHUN and Greater Park Hill Community Incorporated emerged as its leaders. Those wishing advice on how their neighborhoods could fight city hall often asked the established groups about how to proceed. INC participants noted diverse neighborhood councils had shared problems with rowdy bars, traffic, noise, dogs, and poor public services. By banding together, they could effectively pressure a city hall that did not care.

During the McNichols years, INC was something of a loyal opposition. Its leaders insisted city hall pay more attention to neighborhoods. Meetings of INC brought together community activists from across the city, giving them a chance to share information and compare tactics.

Like Denver municipal elections, most of the improvement groups were ostensibly nonpartisan. Just as the Democratic Party had a heavy hand in supporting certain favored "nonpartisan" candidates, it similarly influenced many neighborhood activists. Often there was a close overlap between leaders of some of the organizations and the Democratic Party. In no case was this more so than with CHUN. Its leadership virtually intertwined with the Capitol Hill Democratic Party.

In 1983, Federico Peña touched the neighborhood movement. He reached out to it, promising to consult and respect it. Leaders of the amelioration associations jumped on his bandwagon. In office, Peña named neighborhood activists to various ceremonial boards and commissions. The city also sought to address specific neighborhood concerns.

One-way streets were once more the exemplar. John Desmond had been a Peña supporter as well as a leader of the South Central Improvement Association (later the West Washington Park Neighborhood Association). He lived on South Grant Street, a busy, noisy one-way street. Peña named Desmond to the Denver Planning Board. As chairman of the commission, Desmond saw the board review one-way streets. Its study recommended eliminating some one-way streets in residential neighborhoods, especially in South Denver. Among those from which the city removed heavy traffic was South Grant Street.

Peña continued to reach out to neighborhood organizations. When possible, he attended their meetings. The city stepped up code enforcement against residents whose yards had too many dandelions or junked cars. Busybodies used their membership in the groups to get the city to pick on neighbors they did not like. Inspectors cited residents for such "violations" as having an old couch on a front porch or a washing machine by the side of their house.

Photo by L. C. McClure, DPL

*The Sullivan Gateway at Colfax and the Esplanade is shown shortly after its completion in 1919. It was among the many monuments the city neglected during the McNichols years when Denver turned its back on its City Beautiful heritage.*

A representative of the mayor's office usually was present at the monthly gatherings of INC. Time and again, city hall insisted it wanted to make neighborhoods part of the administration. No longer functioning as forces of opposition, as they had when they fought McNichols, the improvement clubs under Peña were increasingly supporters of city hall. This was vital as the 1987 campaign heated up. Neighborhood leaders overwhelmingly supported the mayor for reelection.

## The City Beautiful

As he sought to keep the mayor's office, Peña could not point to many accomplishments. Though firmly committed to a new convention center and airport, these projects remained on the drawing board. The place where the incumbent had primarily scored was that the city looked better than it had four years earlier. This stemmed from his embrace of the City Beautiful movement.

By the mid-19th century, most metropolises were disaster areas. Badly polluted, they had grown up during the industrial revolution with little planning or coordination. Robber barons frequently owned and plundered vital public amenities. City hall was usually in the hands of unscrupulous politicians who did the bidding of the business community. In response, both reform and revolutionary movements convulsed cities. Something had to be done.

Emperor Louis Napoleon of France took the initiative. During his reign from 1851 until 1870, he oversaw a total redesign of Paris. His goal was blunt: by eliminating twisting lanes and old buildings, the government could easily employ artillery against street rebels. So the middle class would not complain about the cost of urban renewal, Louis Napoleon sought to make Paris a work of art, a city filled with monumental buildings, parkways, trees, and fountains.

The French model awed 19th-century city planners. They wanted to transform cities from drab, poorly functioning industrial centers into veritable gardens. The public spaces at the center of the city, they announced, must not be ugly, polluting factories; on the contrary, they should become beautiful open spaces highlighting the citizenry's pride in the metropolis. They designed parkway systems whereby crucial roads converged in the heart of the city at the civic center. The latter was a park-like setting for gatherings and concerts. American advocates of the City Beautiful saw the civic center as a monument to democracy, a central park surrounded by inspiring, neoclassical libraries and city halls celebrating the government of, by, and for the people. While many of these ideas were formally postulated at the Chicago World's Fair of 1893, they went back at least to the time of Louis Napoleon if not to the original plans for Washington, D.C.

Denver embraced the City Beautiful at an early date. No sooner had the Mile High City established its permanence by the end of the Civil War than residents sought to improve the area. Real estate speculators were in the lead. They realized their lands were more valuable with trees and parks than as part of the desolate Great American Desert. Beginning with Curtis Park in 1868, developers gave the city land for open spaces as part of residential neighborhoods. Within a few years, irrigation canals lined numerous boulevards whereby Denver emerged as something of a garden city.

During the 1880s and 1890s, lovers of beauty and idealists joined real estate interests in procuring land for large, majestic public spaces, notably City, Cheesman, and Washington parks. The city laid out tree-lined parkways and boulevards. Even so, much of the City Beautiful agenda was still more pious hope than reality when Robert Speer became mayor in 1904. He showed the full, and very cynical, dimensions of this planning movement.

Above all else, Speer wanted to make Denver a city good for business. This, he believed, demanded improving the way it looked—an attractive, well-kept city would lure attractive, well-kept residents and industries. He consequently placed a heavy emphasis on developing parks and parkways. Many of the latter were located adjacent to property owned by Speer's friends, members of his administration, and key political and business backers. They greatly benefited by having the city improve the roads near their investments. Speer Boulevard, for example, linked city hall at 14th and Larimer streets with the Denver Country Club. Prior to taking office, Speer had been the key real estate broker in putting together the land deal leading to the establishment of the Denver Country Club at First Avenue and Gilpin Street in 1902.

Speer pulled out the City Beautiful whenever opponents accused him of corruption. The mayor, according to such reformers as Juvenile Judge Benjamin Barr

Lindsey, was the center of "The Beast," a vicious tiger composed of the leading utilities, banks, and corporations preying on the body politick. Whenever muckrakers exposed one of the Beast's dirty deals, the mayor quickly responded by announcing a new park or garden. Denver, Speer implied, could be a drab, honest city or a beautiful one.

Most of corporate Denver rallied to Speer. Flower and garden lovers also embraced him. When Speer died in office on May 14, 1918, ruling Denver commemorated him as a great builder who transformed a cow town into the Paris of the West. Subsidized histories of Denver have continued to spout this line. Despite a veritable beatification of the man, there was nothing specifically City Beautiful about the Speer administration. The reformers were at one with him about trees and parks. They differed on the means of getting them and whether their presence demanded city hall's total subservience to big-money interests and questionable real estate deals. The effusive praise of Speer has implied it did.

Even as Denver praised Speer as a great visionary, the City Beautiful image faded. As sprawl became the city's defining ideal after World War II, the City Beautiful was a faint vestige, symbolized by decaying statues and fountains. The administration no more cared about them than it did about its trees.

The City Beautiful movement noted how commanding, big trees added to the dignity and livability of the metropolis. Local landscape architects favored no species more than the American elm. The Speer administration encouraged homeowners to plant them along curbs. During the summer, the trees' branches formed veritable Gothic arches on residential streets. Beginning in the 1960s, Dutch elm disease destroyed upwards of 90 percent of Denver's American elms.

Photo by Phil Goodstein

*Artists have transformed diseased elm trees into elaborate street sculptures such as this one at 23rd Avenue and Ash Street.*

City hall was concerned. Dutch elm disease is highly contagious. The city forester's office ordered owners to destroy trees suffering from the blight. Residents often found this a traumatic, expensive experience costing upwards of $2,000 per tree. While requiring the removal of the diseased trees, the city did nothing to encourage a systematic replanting of trees in place of the dying ones. Blocks once having upwards of 20 majestic elms lining the curbs soon had none. These established sections often came to look like parts of new Denver where no efforts were ever made to plant street trees.

This was fine with the development crowd. To get people in and out of the suburbs, advocates of growth called for expanding roads. During the postwar era, highway engineers destroyed numerous street trees for more lanes of traffic. Federal and Colorado boulevards, for example, were once parkways. In the 1950s and 1960s they were converted into arterials virtually devoid of trees. The city took land, once reserved for East 46th Avenue and West 48th Avenue parkways, for Interstate 70. Where the freeway devastated parts of Rocky Mountain and Berkeley parks in North Denver, traffic engineers explained it was a "parkway."

As the trees disappeared, the city became bleaker. Nor did the city do much to maintain monuments and statues in the parks. From a center of summer activity attracting up to 10,000 visitors an evening, City Park under McNichols became a stark, sterile spot mostly patronized by rowdies who drove noisily around the central lake. The Civic Center, instead of serving as a meeting, gathering spot, was increasingly a hangout for drunks and drug dealers.

Peña announced plans to change all this. He and his backers again discovered trees. They encouraged residents to plant them as excellent investments. As in the days of Mayor Speer, the city sometimes gave trees away to locals promising to put them by the curbs in front of their houses. The administration, drawing on a 1982 bond issue, also found money to restore fountains and monuments. This was sometimes more rhetoric than reality. A case in point was the *Electric Fountain* in City Park.

The Speer administration installed the monument in the middle of the park's big lake in 1908 as the mayor sought reelection. In response to opposition complaints about Speer's nefarious dealings with brothel owners, real estate brokers, and utilities, his supporters cited the *Electric Fountain* as illustrative of the incumbent's continued improvement of the Mile High City. The device shot water high into the air, coloring it with a battery of lights. From Memorial Day to Labor Day, people rented paddle boats and sailed around the fountain and lake while the Denver Municipal Band serenaded them with concerts six nights a week.

The *Electric Fountain* was increasingly run-down by the 1970s. Few people came to the ever less frequent band concerts. The *Miss Denver*, a small cruise ship once sailing around City Park Lake, disappeared. Under McNichols, the city more or less neglected the fountain and adjacent bandstand and pavilion.

Peña oversaw a renovation of the fountain and bandstand in 1983–84. He declared Memorial Day 1984 "Fountain Day" when the city turned on all its working fountains as a sign of civic beauty. The mayor announced he would personally dedicate the redesigned *Electric Fountain* at six o'clock that evening.

Supporters of the fountain program urged the mayor to cut the ribbon later in the night. They explained it was only possible to properly appreciate the fountain's beauty after dark. The mayor was insistent about the six o'clock time. When the

Photo by Phil Goodstein

*Under Peña, the city turned its fountains back on in 1984, including the* Benedict Fountain *at 20th Avenue and Pennsylvania Street.*

fountain was turned on, Peña looked at it, chagrined. It appeared as nothing more than an aeration jet at a water sanitation plant. Nor was the fountain after dark nearly as impressive as it had been before it was improved. By the 1990s, it and the adjacent bandstand once more were in need of drastic restoration.

## "Civic Center Park"

The mayor also announced an effort to revive what his administration called "Civic Center Park." This was a vogue phrase of those having little understanding of Denver. The label "Civic Center Park" was redundant for the greenery between West Colfax and West 14th avenues from Broadway to Bannock Street. In the City Beautiful movement, a civic center is a park. "Civic Center Park" was a jarring term used by transplants who sought to impose their ignorance on the city. Efforts to educate them on this point were of no avail. Led by the planning office, these self-proclaimed guardians of Denver customs determinedly referred to the land as "Civic Center Park." Trendy individuals in other cities with historic civic centers likewise called them "Civic Center Park."

The Peña administration used the Civic Center for mega-celebrations. Once more it drew upon and distorted Denver traditions. This was seen in the Denver Partnership's reincarnation of the Festival of Mountain and Plain in 1983.

Beginning in 1896, the Mile High City attempted to stage an ornate fall Mardi Gras, the Festival of Mountain and Plain. It was a week-long spree during which residents partied heavily in early October. Masque balls, parades, and fireworks highlighted the affair. Cowboys and Indians came to town for the occasion, camping in City Park. To emphasize their presence, one year Festival of Mountain and Plain officials poured kerosene atop City Park Lake, setting the body of water afire to show the glamour of the whole shindig. The queen of the Slaves of the Silver Serpent, a young society woman, ruled over the festival. The celebration quickly faded. It was only held sporadically after the turn of the century until it gave up the ghost in 1912. Efforts to revive it over the years had little success.

The restored Festival of Mountain and Plain under Peña had nothing in common with the Denver custom. A preliminary effort, staged between October 14 and 16, 1983, was held on the 16th Street Mall. Mostly featuring street artists, it received little attention. The Denver Partnership converted the event for Labor Day weekend the next year when it emerged as "The Taste of Colorado." The downtown business association encouraged leading restaurants to get booths and sell samples of their food. There was no distinctive Denver or even western theme. On the contrary, the festival was modeled after a comparable food feast in Minneapolis. With the event held along Broadway next to "Civic Center Park," sponsors did nothing to educate the citizenry about precisely what the Civic Center was or

Photo by John Schoenwalter

*The Capitol Hill People's Fair was filled with numerous booths for unorthodox causes when it was held in front of East High School in the 1970s. Under Peña, it moved to a place the administration callously called "Civic Center Park," a location where the People's Fair became a sterile, generic beer bash.*

the meaning of the statues and monuments in it. In no time, the affair was essentially the utterly indistinct Festival of Greed and Gluttony.

Much the same was true with the Capitol Hill People's Fair. It dated from May 1972 when locals organized a gathering at Morey Junior High School as a neighborhood happening, complete with open stages. By the time the sponsoring Capitol Hill United Neighborhoods relocated the event from East High School to the Civic Center in 1987, the People's Fair had no specific Capitol Hill orientation. Nor was it much of a people's fair. The two-day event in June was nothing more than a big beer bash raising money for CHUN even as the improvement group continually moaned about alcohol abuse at local bars and liquor stores.

In 1991, CHUN revealed its executive director, Ron Hillstrom, had embezzled nearly $150,000 from People's Fair revenues. The group mostly used the moneys to perpetuate itself as the supposed voice of the neighborhood. The more CHUN made from the Civic Center event, the less connection it had with those living on Capitol Hill.

The Civic Center likewise became the home of a very non-ethnic Cinco de Mayo celebration in the mid-1990s. A summer theater in the park program then brought live drama to the park's Greek Theater. Landscaping improvements stemming from a 1989 bond issue restored antique street lamps and added flower gardens to the central gathering spot. Compared to the neglect of the McNichols administration, these actions were a strong affirmation of pride in Denver's past and present. All the while, the jarring "Civic Center Park" label remained. Some even used it to refer to buildings near the greenery.

Veteran *Denver Post* reporter Joanne Ditmer objected. The conscience of the City Beautiful crowd since the early 1960s, she frequently used her column to criticize some of the inane developments detracting from Denver's charms. Sick of the callous talk about "Civic Center Park," in the mid-1990s she loudly asserted it high time to junk the term as an insult to Denver traditions. Mayor Wellington Webb agreed. Assorted newspaper and broadcast accounts consequently again called the open space the Civic Center. Many city agencies, including the mayor's office, however, continued to refer to the greenery as "Civic Center Park."

By this time, the City Beautiful was as much part and parcel of Denver politics as it had been under Mayor Speer. Both Peña and Webb projected themselves as modern incarnations of the previous Denver boss. As much as Speer, they and their supporters implied the City Beautiful was synonymous with their administrations. The choice was between a more attractive Denver with growth, sprawl, and a total dominance by the business community or the desperate ugliness of oil-bust Denver. This was another theme dominating the 1987 mayoral campaign.

## The 1987 Campaign

Not only Peña, but most of the other candidates for mayor in 1987 praised the neighborhood movement. They proclaimed it the essence of citizen activism. City council publications called on residents to join improvement groups. Administration figures consulted politically well-connected members of these organizations as the voices of neighborhoods and of the people of Denver as a whole. CHUN leader Mike Henry closely supported Peña, leading opposition to any efforts to reduce the mayor's power. In this light, Inter–Neighborhood Cooperation appropriately hosted the first crucial mayoral debate in the 1987 election. The campaign's major themes were outlined at it. One was the demand for complete agreement on all controversial issues.

Sponsors of some candidate forums, including members of the League of Women Voters, continually bemoaned the bickering in local politics. Despite seemingly wide-scale public support for some of 17th Street's favored nostrums, including the convention center, airport, and light rail, these programs were invariably delayed. Their champions denied the delays stemmed from basic problems in the projects or lack of consensus on them; on the contrary, they blamed the postponements on personal disagreements between policy makers. They noted how members of city council continually clashed with each other and the mayor. Those demanding immediate action viewed the quarrels—not intrinsic problems or divisions in the community—as responsible for the stagnation marking Peña's first four years. What, the League and its cohorts wanted to know, would the candidates do to end this squabbling?

Advocates of a unified, nonpartisan city fully committed to growth were unhappy about some of the answers. Veteran city councilwoman Cathy Reynolds was blunt: she would do nothing. These so-called wrangles frequently represented strong differences of opinion about where the community was headed. The whole purpose of political debate was to bring out problems in various proposals. All too often, supposedly good ideas failed because they were poorly thought out and did not have any relationship to reality. Anybody who had seen the shoddiness of the planning office's programs readily granted this point.

Such an outlook did not bode well with the advocates of a no-dissent government. They wanted action. Conditions were so bad something had to be immediately done. There was no time or place for questions. Those ruthlessly demanding the convention center and airport dismissed doubters as irresponsible naysayers. Denver urgently needed a strong leader comparable to Speer who would ramrod all opposition to make the corporate agenda a reality. All the major candidates swore they would accomplish this: they would be bold leaders making sure popular distrust of the government did not interfere with development programs.

Even while the candidates equivocated on the tolerability of disagreement, those dissatisfied with city hall mulled the candidates, hoping one would emerge as an alternative to Peña. There was little from which to choose. After an initial flurry, few took the Currigan comeback seriously. Licht never overcame his flip-flop on the airport and the accusations of mismanagement of the auditor's office. Gallagher showed himself only a feeble effort to restore the image of the supposedly good McNichols years. By default, Bain came to the fore.

The candidate's campaign mirrored the man: it was there, it was a powerful force, but it was almost impossible to define. Unlike the other major contenders, Bain was a bit hesitant about the airport. It was such a major investment that maybe the city ought to review it thoroughly before plunging into it with the head-over-heels fast-track approach of Peña. The 17th Street attorney likewise ques-

Photo by Phil Goodstein

*"No loitering" signs popped up everywhere around the city in response to city hall's actions in making business associations and neighborhood groups the virtual private rulers of public streets.*

tioned some of the other business panaceas. On this basis, the Republican contender slowly separated himself from the pack as the challenger to the mayor.

Bain was unable to inspire audiences. Though a coherent speaker, he lacked Peña's extemporaneous appeal. He avoided some neighborhood debates, both because he came off poorly at them compared to the other candidates and due to the improvement organizations' semi-official support of the incumbent. Not only did he find the forums very hostile, but Bain believed they were more pep rallies than places to sway uncommitted voters. Powerful television ads were the heart of his campaign. In them, Bain effectively projected himself as the candidate of change. Those who did not like the mayor and were undecided about the race lined up behind the corporate lawyer. "Anybody but Peña" remained the cry of some of Bain's backers. As the anti-Peña challenger, the Denver native surged in the polls.

Bain's ascendancy was obvious on election day, May 19, when he led the pack, receiving 41.7 percent of the vote, 57,986, to Peña's 51,950 (37.1 percent). Gallagher trailed far behind with 17,974 (12.9 percent); Licht got 6,109 (4.4 percent); Currigan 3,051 (2.2 percent); and Watson 1,204 (.9 percent). Daniels and Martinez both received about .4 percent of the total. Since Bain failed to win a majority, he faced Peña in a June 16 runoff.

## The Runoff

Now that he was poised to become Denver's next mayor, Bain stalled. Instead of presenting an alternative to Peña or a program of action, he continued to focus on a glaring personal weakness of the incumbent—the mayor's insecurity. Not the airport, convention center, or corporate domination of the city, but Peña's paranoia, became Bain's dominating campaign theme.

Since Peña took office, the mayor's fears had been a city joke. A big police trailer was parked by his rather unkempt house in North Denver. The politician insisted he needed extra security. Everywhere Peña went, a corps of bodyguards surrounded him. At times, the mayor was easily nonplused, such as when he was jokingly introduced as the mayor of Aurora. In response, he went out of his way to insist he was really the mayor of Denver. Always perfectly dressed and groomed, appropriately prepared for ceremonies, Peña sometimes came across as Denver's Little Lord Fauntleroy.

Peña placed guards, operating metal detectors, at all entrances of city hall. People needing to visit the seat of their government had to submit to degrading searches at the hands of minimum-wage, private contract employees. The latter, often flaunted their power over those ordered to report to city hall for jury duty and other civic functions. Thanks to Peña, the security personnel had the power to decide who could enter city hall. (The mayor's security fixation and fear of the populace were not unique—virtually all of ruling America shared his anxieties. Guards were increasingly stationed at entrances to government buildings everywhere.)

Photo by John Schoenwalter

*During the 1970s, 1980s, and 1990s, "Father Fraud," as the Reverend Martin Philips was known, was an omnipresent character around town. In the same manner corporate developers asked for subsidies, he always had a basket ready for handouts.*

Later, as Secretary of Transportation, Peña put in new, extremely inconvenient rules about what kind of packages individuals could mail, citing the safety of airplanes. This was his response to the crash of a TWA flight over Long Island Sound in 1996. Though there was no evidence of a bomb bringing down the jet, the Peña program remained in effect. While the government embraced such burdensome measures targeting the everyday public, it was most questionable whether Peña, as Secretary of Transportation, protected travelers from literal fly-by-night airlines with outrageous safety records. The number of air crashes soared during his years running the Department of Transportation.

Bain played on the mayor's fears as he emerged as the prime challenger to Peña in April. His television advertisements showed hordes of bodyguards jogging through the city, guarding some unseen, but seemingly important character. In other words, Peña was such an insignificant force his bodyguards overshadowed the mayor. Instead of raising the larger issue about what the incumbent's fears said about the politician and the city, Bain made the security theme a personal one. In doing so, he revealed his lack of an alternative agenda.

In response to the Bain challenge, Peña forged a coalition. In the lead were minority voters. The mayor and activists in the Democratic Party insisted blacks and Hispanics should vote for one of their own. As was the case in 1983, Peña's supporters encouraged Latinos to register and vote. Gallagher agreed as he endorsed Peña.

Labor played a key role in the Peña campaign. Even more than the business community, it saw the convention center and airport as marvelous public works projects bringing jobs to construction workers. As it lined up behind the incumbent, the organized union movement made no mention of such past Peña policies as endorsing Coors Beer during the labor boycott or pushing a vindictive city prosecution against union organizers arrested at the Denver Tech Center for allegedly trespassing on the union-free enclave.

The election affirmed the construction trades domination of the area's labor movement. Members of the American Federation of State, County, and Municipal Employees—whose members had actually dealt with the Peña administration—preferred Licht and Gallagher over Peña. With the choice between Peña and Bain, the union movement put its full resources behind the mayor.

Neighborhood politicians firmly allied themselves with the incumbent. Opposed to McNichols, whom they had always had to fight, Peña had recognized them. Having received appointments on various boards, they were part of the team. Even though Bain had been an early participant in CHUN, he was not one of them. Peña, never an active member of an improvement association fighting city hall, was their man.

Feminists and gays also hopped on the Peña bandwagon. By this time, rumors freely and fiercely floated about Peña's sexual orientation. (He had hidden a past live-in relationship with a young, politically active mother at the time he was first elected to the legislature, fearing it would blemish his political opportunities.) Some joked that he might conveniently get married as part of the campaign to assure conservative voters he was heterosexual. Sure enough, as the mayor's race heated up, Peña was frequently accompanied by Ellen Hart, the woman to whom he soon announced his engagement. They married in 1988.

Most of all, the business community sided with Peña. As election day neared, 17th Street found itself more drawn to the mayor than the corporate lawyer. As a seeming outsider who did not have the experiences with local big money that Bain did, Peña readily made extra steps to show the business establishment that he was the mayor of the Denver Partnership.

With Dick Fleming, now the head of the Chamber of Commerce, in the forefront, leaders of corporate Denver made it clear they did not want laissez faire; on the contrary, their goal was an active partnership with city hall. Peña endlessly reminded them this was also his goal with his unending espousal of the "public/

private partnership." He was the man who would do the bidding of the Partnership and all who had worn the gigantic "BUILD IT" pins during the 1985 convention center campaign. It was more than coincidence that gigantic Peña buttons in 1987 were about the same size as the BUILD IT buttons—frequently the same people wore both.

Some sections of the business community backed Bain. They did not have nearly the dominance or publicity of the Partnership and real estate industry. The latter were sure, with his enthusiasm for a new airport, Peña was the best man to lead the city. Playing it safe, some corporate interests donated to both campaigns.

As traditional Republicans had qualms about Peña, the mayor recreated the old city machine. Similar to the political forces that dominated cities from the Civil War until World War II, it was a strange conglomeration. The heart of the old machine's voting strength lay in ethnic, immigrant voters. In exchange for supporting incumbents, politically well-connected voters got jobs from city hall or breaks in their troubles with authorities. The black and Hispanic communities now filled the niche of what were once called hyphenated-Americans. Just as immigrants had once seen electing a person of Irish or Italian or Polish descent as an emancipatory gesture, so now numerous blacks and Hispanics believed the same about putting a member of their group in office.

Photo by Phil Goodstein

*An empty liquor bottle replaces a missing street lamp at 34th Avenue and Gilpin Street, a sign of the less than successful city efforts to stress streetscaping as a solution to urban woes.*

Peña also benefited from a cynical program introduced by President Richard Nixon, set-asides. It called for a certain percentage of all federally funded construction work to go to registered minority (officially, "disadvantaged") contractors. The goal was to give them a strong stake in the system. Black capitalists, Nixon was sure, would be at one with white capitalists. In exchange for governmental contracts, they would readily turn their backs on African-American militants shouting for black power and a total reorganization of society.

The Nixon program was immediately popular with black business interests. Denver embraced it. Ordinances required the city to allocate a percentage of all municipal construction contracts to minority- and women-business enterprises. These moneys tended to flow to affluent members of the black, Hispanic, and feminist communities. African-Americans and Latino contractors, with the right connections, consequently, loudly endorsed Peña for reelection. They noted how the mayor's building efforts at the convention center and airport would create jobs for them. Echoed by the media and ruling Denver, they celebrated their success as victories of all blacks and Hispanics. An "Anglo" such as Bain, they implied, would leave them and their unskilled brothers and sisters out in the cold.

A similar politics of recognition was seen in the feminist and gay support of Peña. The mayor elevated individuals, openly noting their sexual preferences, to positions of power. They were now part of the establishment and saw no need to rock the boat. Added to them was a sprinkling of advocates of good government and the City Beautiful who were impressed by the mayor's numerous outreach measures.

## Funding the Machine

Most of all, government funds fueled the machine. A stated purpose of the revenue-sharing programs instituted by Nixon was to give local authorities greater control of federal moneys. Before long, city halls became spigots through which flowed community block development grants, national business revitalization efforts, and assorted handouts. The moneys went to people, businesses, and organizations with good political ties and those knowing how to play the bureaucratic procurement game.

Often the revenues were spent on fluff: uniform street awnings, quaint old-fashioned street lamps, and fake stone sidewalks. Already under Mayor McNichols, the city transformed neighborhood business blocks, such as parts of Broadway between Second and Bayaud avenues, the intersection of 23rd Avenue and Dexter Street, and sections of West 32nd Avenue near Lowell Street with these moneys. Whether the street improvements actually helped the neighborhoods and small merchants was questionable, but the areas often looked more enticing. Many benefiting from the handouts lined up behind city hall.

Property owners and business groups did not always maintain the improvements. This was compounded by the sometimes shoddy work on the projects. Before long, the phony stone sidewalks started to crumble while rampaging cars destroyed the lamps. The latter sometimes remained lying on the sidewalks for weeks on end. Eventually, the city machine came to the rescue. It awarded appropriations to revitalize the same areas all over again. In the process, city hall sought to show provincials it cared about their neck of the woods. The mayor's backers cited this as a prime reason to reelect the incumbent.

Peña took office when the Ronald Reagan administration claimed it was cutting pork out of the federal budget. Nonetheless, many of the urban development funds remained. In some cases, they actually increased—the Republican mantra was more money to localities and less federal control. Under Reagan, the social idealism of the Great Society disappeared, including revenue for low-income housing and residential participation in blight alleviation measures. The power of money remained.

The mayor knew how to use the sums. With the planning office taking the lead, the city sought to forge a partnership with neighborhood and business organizations. If property owners would band together and play by the city's rules, the city would appropriate funds for more street improvements, decorations, trees, lamps, banners, and other worthy projects for the areas the commercial associations claimed as their own. Peña's backers pointed to the streetscaping as evidence of the administration's commitment to the quality of life, residential neighborhoods, and civic beauty. Activists and contractors, including minorities with close political ties to city hall, gladly took the money. State capitalism was clearly the way to go, be it at the neighborhood level or with the corporate welfare of the convention center.

Some of the neighborhood money flowed through the Mayor's Office of Economic Development (MOED). That was another Peña incantation—economic development. Seemingly, city hall blessed any project promising to boost sales-tax revenues. The government sought to be something of a superbank: it lent money to promising businesses when no private lender would take the risk. MOED primarily targeted minority neighborhoods and contractors.

This wing of city hall did not always work directly with fledgling enterprises needing funds. It often operated through the Small Business Development Center of the Chamber of Commerce. This emphasized how those wanting city funds had to show themselves willing to follow in the steps of the organization of big business. The city even gave money to the Chamber's Small Business Development Center, using the latter to scout potential borrowers.

Peña confirmed the close link between neighborhoods, the planning office, and community development funds when he saw DPO elevated to permanent cabinet status as it emerged as the Office of Planning and Community Development. MOED, under Mayor Wellington Webb, increased its aspirations as the Mayor's Office of Economic Development–International Trade.

A sharing of power between the business community and city hall was another aspect of the machine. City hall encouraged commercial property owners to form business maintenance organizations. Beginning with the creation of an improvement district for the 16th Street Mall in 1982—a measure assuring the Denver Partnership would essentially rule the road—the city adopted a policy whereby landlords on business strips had governmental powers, including the ability to assess extra taxes to shape the boulevards in their own images.

Photo by Phil Goodstein

*Despite investing immense sums to place quaint street lamps along sidewalks as part of its commitment to city beautification and neighborhood improvement, city hall did little to improve walking conditions. Shown is a blocked-off, narrow, redesigned sidewalk on 13th Avenue east of Pennsylvania Street in the mid-1990s.*

With the assistance of the planning office, such districts were formed on the basis of one-dollar, one-vote, i.e., the quasi-governmental bodies were not forged by a democratic discussion and vote of all they impacted; on the contrary, they were based on property ownership. After leading business interests established such authorities, city hall gave the maintenance districts sizable sums for trees and uniform street awnings. Frequently there was a close linkage between the leaders of such organizations and the political establishment. By the late 1990s, 19 such districts existed. The federal government helped the city encourage their proliferation. The Department of Housing and Urban Development usually awarded the city about $11.5 million a year for community development block grants to pay for the district-administered street cosmetics. (Washington established the community block grant program in the mid-1970s to take over various Model Cities efforts dating from the Great Society of the mid-1960s.)

The emerging Peña machine got a substantial economic boost during the mayor's first term from the Denver Urban Renewal Authority. In 1984–85, the Skyline Urban Renewal Project was finally completed. Corporate Denver declared it a great success in ripping the heart and soul out of the central business district. DURA had about $26 million in the bank from the effort—the same amount Washington granted it in 1967 to destroy much of historic Larimer Street. Washington expected DURA to repay the loan.

The city did not want to let go of the capital. On the contrary, Congresswoman Pat Schroeder did her all to keep the money in Denver. With her assistance and that of city lobbyist Ron Brown, a powerful Washington insider who subsequently served in the Bill Clinton cabinet with Peña, Denver convinced the Reagan administration to turn the sum over to city hall. The Peña administration vowed to use the funds for loans to assure the continued renewal and improvement of the city, especially its stock of affordable housing. Once more, the mayor skillfully employed the revenue in gaining political support in the name of preservation and development. The old Temple Emanuel at 16th Avenue and Pearl Street, for example, was saved from demolition with money from the Skyline Project. Repayment of such loans quickly became problematic. Amidst a booming economy in the late 1990s/early 2000s, the stock of affordable housing was scarcer than ever.

Photo by Phil Goodstein

*The city readily lent funds to politically well-connected non-profits and developers to build housing and rearrange neighborhoods, including demolishing some of these structures on the 2400 block of Welton Street.*

Numerous other channels existed for getting city money. In some cases, for-profit ventures were tied to ostensibly non-profit community development corporations. (The term "development corporation" was usually a clue as to the business orientation of such ventures.) Often the non-profits were part and parcel of the for-profit enterprises—the latter supported the former to get tax breaks. Enterprise zones created a bewildering array of tax incentives and exemptions of which smart, politically well-connected operators took great advantage.

The non-profits often had marked agendas, seeking to modify behavior and enact social legislation as part of their "charitable" missions. Other times, they were fronts for private developers. The Winter Park Recreational Association, for example, often seemed primarily to function to assure the city-owned ski resort and nearby public lands were maintained in the interest of the private Arlberg Club. Even when they were simply "housing corporations," the non-profits had close linkages to banks, builders, and other parts of 17th Street. By avidly assisting and letting these non-profits do the public bidding, city hall assured the private sector would have a decisive say in Denver's destiny.

There were strong personal ties between the non-profits and city hall. In no case was this more apparent than with the Hunt Alternatives Fund. Bankrolled by oil heiress Swanee Hunt, there was a close overlap of its employees and members and former members of the Peña administration.

Similarly, the Piton Foundation, whose revenues stemmed from oil and real estate fortunes, aimed to influence the city's politics and quality of life. It openly sought a partnership with city hall and the business community. There was a frequent crossover between its functionaries and Peña political appointees. In other instances, the non-profits were something of patronage machines where supporters of city hall were rewarded with cushy, seemingly influential jobs.

The state government under governors Richard Lamm and Roy Romer encouraged this. Some Colorado agencies and commissions, such as the office of energy conservation, appeared to be little more than suppliers of posts for worthy Democrats. The Colorado Housing and Finance Authority existed as a strange quasi-public/private outfit. In addition to helping first-time homebuyers and operating rental properties, it channeled money to favored causes and concerns, including Six Flags Elitch Gardens and developments near Coors Field. It further helped provide money for certain neighborhood groups and "community development" outfits. The result was a strong patronage machine. Those who benefited from it had a marked incentive in seeing Peña's return to office.

While it courted the middle-class members of minority groups, city hall scorned the poor. Its glowing neighborhood and business plans had no place for the lower-class individuals. DPO, in association with neighborhood groups and maintenance districts, arrogantly dismissed people with limited incomes, substance abuse problems, the homeless, and street people as "undesirables." Part and parcel of city plans for increased business viability was ridding neighborhoods of people and places standing in the way of every section of town emerging as another Hilltop or Cherry Creek North. Backers endorsed ordinances prohibiting the poor from standing too long in specific areas as "quality of life" measures.

**Photo by Phil Goodstein**

*Under Peña, the city added medians to arterials as part of its commitment to the City Beautiful. In the process, it failed to provide bike lanes or better access for non-drivers. Eventually, under Mayor Wellington Webb, the administration responded by installing arcane bike route maps around town.*

Reflecting Peña's insistent corporate commitment, the machine was of business and for business. City hall insiders cynically used ethnicity and the mayor's supposed liberal incarnation to cloak this point and the essence of the Peña city hall. This was a national trend: the rise of a new political machine based on a combination of minority voters and businesses interests. During the 1987 race, Peña helped perfect it.

The surface of the machine was still extremely uneven as Peña fought for his political life against Bain in the runoff. None of the buy-off factors could be publicly mentioned—they hinted more than idealism and good government stood behind those who embraced the mayor. The exposure of the operations of the machine would help many residents realize why they were so uneasy about the incumbent. Countless citizens felt there was something utterly rotten about the Peña administration, but there was no voice to this conviction.

Bain benefited from this anxiety. Though the corporate attorney did not seek to uncloak the machine or offer a change from the status quo, he was not Peña. The

Republican was seemingly the last chance the city had before it was totally sold to project developers encouraging ever more sprawl.

A few of the feeble voices of the Denver opposition supported the challenger because they did not believe he could come close to Peña in carrying out the corporate agenda. If McNichols or a Republican had pulled some of the stunts at the heart of the Peña machine in handing out massive sums to cronies and business associates, they noted, the goody-goodies around the neighborhood movement and civil rights advocates would have screamed in rage. Against this, the incumbent cleverly used his cover as a Latino politician to cloak his capitulation to 17th Street.

The Peña forces successfully turned this point on its head. As the mayor sagged by more than 20 points in the polls, they readily resorted to demagogic rhetoric. Bain, they loudly declared, was the candidate of the old, racist, conservative establishment against the struggling, idealistic Hispanic Federico. The Peña campaign noted, unlike Bain, the rich lawyer who lived in a mansion with a commanding view of Cheesman Park and the mountains, the mayor was a newcomer from Texas who dwelt in a modest North Denver home. While Bain was a member of the Denver Country Club and had a 17th Street office, Peña had been a people's attorney, fighting against racism and for the equal opportunity of all.

Opposed to Bain, a past supporter of height-limitation ordinances, Peña had done nothing to push through such measures. Nonetheless, the mayor's backers asserted Bain would kowtow to developers erecting ugly towers blocking the mountains. The incumbent's adherents, in an extremely powerful, effective advertisement, likewise labeled Bain a polluters' attorney. The challenger's law firm had represented Shell Oil, a company which had befouled the Rocky Mountain Arsenal. Bain as mayor, they insisted, would give the corporate community a license to keep on polluting unlike the environmentalist in office. Even as the mayor's backers loudly voiced this assertion, Shell Oil donated $1,500 to the Peña campaign. More pertinently, the mayor was closely linked to the law firm of Brownstein Hyatt Farber & Strickland, an outfit representing numerous corporate polluters.

Facts did not matter. The Peña campaign was fueled by lies, moralism, and innuendo. Many of its loyalists believed their own rhetoric about serving as embattled defenders of progressive liberalism opposed to a reactionary ogre as personified by Bain. Any statement or means, apparently, justified the defense of such a civilization.

Typical was the outrage of the Peña camp when "Ño!" signs popped up around town. Designed to look like yard signs endorsing the mayor, they mocked the mayor's emphasis on the tilde in his name. Such expressions, Peña's backers loudly asserted, were racist. They were not dissuaded from this position when an anti-Peña Hispanic took credit for the signs.

The Democratic establishment fully lined up behind this approach. Roy Romer, Pat Schroeder, and Tim Wirth used their political influence to portray the reelection of Peña a life-and-death matter for the poor, struggling people of Denver against the corporate elite. The labor movement, which generally disdained class warfare rhetoric and bashing of the business community, heartily jumped on this bandwagon.

It paid off on election day, June 16, 1987, when Peña narrowly triumphed, 79,685 (51 percent) to 76,678 (49 percent). As had been the case in 1983, his margin of victory overwhelmingly came from the black, brown, and poorer sections of town. Once more there were rumblings about him importing thousands of non-Denver Hispanic voters. As was the case in 1983, the opposition failed to substantiate its claims.

Returned to office, the Texan was set to deliver his pro-corporate agenda. He marked this shortly after the election when he abandoned his North Denver residence for an elaborate mansion in old Park Hill. This was in the heart of the neighborhood demanding a new airport. Peña was posed to bring greatness for Denver. Rather than glory, the city reaped the savings and loan scandal.

## A Note on Sources:

I have closely observed the city's political scene over the past generation. Many of the comments stem from having attended various political forums and talking to the politicians mentioned in the text. Eventually, I hope to give my file on the 1987 election to the Auraria Archives.

The *Colorado Statesman* has been the gossip publication of local politicos in recent decades. It has frequently contained articles about the city's politics and the aspirations of the different wings of the Democratic Party. (During the late 1980s, it briefly changed its name to the *New Political Newspaper*.) Both daily and weekly newspapers have had many stories on the doings of various candidates and political insiders.

Miller Hudson's campaign views were expressed in his speech to the City Club delivered on February 10, 1987. He shared his thoughts with me in numerous informal conversations and reviewed a draft of this chapter. Hudson also discussed some of the stormy episodes in which he was involved in the local Democratic Party and his association with Peña while the two served together in the legislature. Biographies of various politicians who served in the General Assembly in the early 1980s are in Margaret Ackerman and Clela A. Rorex, *Colorado Legislative Almanac, 1981* (Boulder: Ackerman-Rorex Corporation, 1981).

Cindia Cleaver recalled Peña being introduced as "the mayor of Aurora" in the summer of 1986. I attended a Licht class on the auditor's role at Denver Free University and occasionally chatted with him about city politics. His 1983 auditor report gives his version of Denver history. The Abraham Kauvar papers in the DU Archives contain materials on the controversies over the administration of Denver General Hospital in the 1970s.

Dennis Gallagher casually discussed his involvement in the 1987 race. Don Bain granted me an interview about his participation in Denver politics. Dean Punké noted both his work for Bain and past involvement in many fights against the Currigan and McNichols administrations. He related the story about the Sixth Avenue Freeway and the emergence of POWUR. Reuben Espinosa, a key political operator who supported Currigan before joining Bain in the runoff, discussed his role in the campaign.

Mark Herwig, editor of the *Colorado Labor Advocate*, observed the labor movement's ardent support for Peña and the pressures on him to mute class warfare articles in the paper. Bob McRae and Jack B. Weil gave me the Republican Party's slant on the contest. Mike Davenport, Steve Schweitzberger, and Randi Lewis also reflected on the race. City council members Cathy Donohue, Cathy Reynolds, and Hiawatha Davis shared their views on city politics in interviews in early 1988. Dick Fleming loudly spoke out at public forums, noting how the business community opposed laissez faire. Jack McCroskey, proud of his role as a gadfly, took on those advocating a dissent-free democracy in personal conversations.

J. Joseph Huthmacher spells out the concept of the politics of recognition and the role of ethnic groups in elections in *Massachusetts People and Politics* (Cambridge: Harvard University Press, 1959). Also see David Burner, *The Politics of Provincialism* (New York: Knopf, 1970). Alexander B. Callow Jr., ed., *The City Boss in America* (New York: Oxford University Press, 1976), outlines the traditional view of the urban machine. Mike Royko, *Boss* (New York: Signet, 1971), examines the old-fashioned Richard J. Daley machine in Chicago.

*Community Renewal Program, Denver Neighborhood Analysis* (Denver: DPO, 1972), was the document in which the planning office defined the various statistical planning units. Billie Bramhall, the head of neighborhood planning under McNichols, shared her memories of the evolution of the program. She also noted the origins of the neighborhood notification ordinance and the character of city hall's relationship with neighborhoods during the McNichols administration. *Zoning and Land Use Guide for Neighborhood Organizations* ([Denver]: Inter–Neighborhood Cooperation, 1986), is a brief overview of the officious role of neighborhood organizations in city politics.

A book is desperately needed on the history and character of Denver neighborhood associations. Other than for a few INC publications and numerous DPO studies, nothing specifically focuses on the rise and power of the organizations. Goldberg, *Hooded Empire*, links improvement groups to the Klan. The James Atkins papers at CHS include materials on the Denver Civic Council. R. Laurie Simmons and Thomas H. Simmons, *Denver Neighborhood History Project* (Denver: DLPC and DPO, 1995), is a challenging, though extremely uneven and often superficial, look at some of the city's residential enclaves.

I review the character of improvement clubs in South Denver in my *South Denver Saga*, further examining the influence of CHUN and other neighborhood organizations on greater Capitol Hill in my *Ghosts of Denver*. Chuck Michaels, Bernie Jones, and Mike Henry shared memories about the forging of CHUN and INC. Chuck Nefzger recalled his early participation in CHUN and the emergence of various neighborhood development corporations in the late 1970s/early 1980s. John Desmond talked about his role in the Washington Park neighborhood. I focus on the one-way controversies in my *Denver's Capitol Hill* and *South Denver Saga*. Doug Linkhart discussed his role as head of INC in the mid-1980s. His successor, Bill Gross, also talked about the organization. I attended many of its meetings at the time, even briefly contributing a column to its monthly newsletter. INC issued sporadic annual reports in the late 1970s/early 1980s, listing its membership and activities of associated organizations.

Walt Young and Jim Hannifin gave me dissenting views about the neighborhood groups, noting how they have been run by petty, insecure manipulators. Hannifin further shared his observations about the workings of Congress Park Neighbors. Ron Yost joined him in recalling the Organization of Midtown Neighborhood Improvement and making cynical observations about city politics. Steve Savageau and Jim Raughton discussed the changing character of the Whittier neighborhood. Ed Natan chatted about the origins of a business improvement group, Uptown on the Hill. Stu MacPhail, Margot Crewe, and John Hand joined Young and Hannifin in giving me their impressions about the evolution of Colfax on the Hill and the Colfax Business Improvement District.

*Colorado and the American Renaissance, 1876–1917* (Denver: Denver Art Museum, 1980), notes the impact of the City Beautiful movement in the Centennial State and how it considerably predated Mayor Speer. Materials on the City Beautiful fill volumes by Tom Noel, notably his *Denver: The City Beautiful*, with Barbara Norgren; and *Mining Camp to Metropolis*, with Steve Leonard. Don Etter stressed the City Beautiful in his nomination of the city's park and parkway system to the National Register of Historic Places, *The Denver Park and Parkway System.* In personal conversations, he shared his knowledge of the city's legacy of civic beauty. So did longtime assistant manager of parks and recreation, Pat Gallavan. Jack Bruce, who was McNichols' city engineer, explained the workings of much of the road system and the Department of Public Works. Goodman, *After the Planners*, critically evaluates the City Beautiful tradition.

Ben Lindsey noted the character of ruling Denver under Speer, including its cynical use of the *Electric Fountain*, in *The Beast.* Bette Peters, *Denver's City Park*, covers the history of the fountain and City Park. I examine the park and the city's monuments in my "Monumental Denver"; and *Denver's Capitol Hill.* Tom Morris shared the story about Peña and the *Electric Fountain.* Veritable hagiographic treatments of Speer are Charles Johnson, *Denver's Mayor Speer*; and Edgar MacMechem, *Robert W. Speer.*

The papers of the Festival of Mountain and Plain are at CHS. The Denver Partnership heavily publicized the Taste of Colorado in its various newsletters and press handouts. Some are in the Government Documents section of DPL. I reflect on the evolution of the People's Fair in my *Ghosts of Denver.* Ed Thomas shared his recollections as president of CHUN at the time the Hillstrom swindle erupted. Bob Cameron talked about the Skyline Project and money. Billie Bramhall talked about the partnership aspirations of the Piton Foundation. Newspaper reportage about it and various community development foundations has been invariably upbeat.

# 8

# Banking on Savings and Loans

Denver found its identity in 1981 when "Dynasty" went on the air. A prime-time soap opera, the television show focused on the greed, lust, cynical manipulations, and buccaneering dominance of oil billionaire Blake Carrington. Insecure residents thrilled to see the Mile High City featured, even if most of the show was filmed out of state. If anything, Blake Carrington was a role model for the local nouveau riche: they eagerly aspired to emulate the worst of his characteristics. With the press touting them, they viewed themselves as visionaries as they devastated the city. They and Denver soon reaped their just deserts.

The loot-the-city-of-fools approach was exemplified by the savings and loan fiasco, an event closely linked to the oil bust and Denver's aspirations for greatness. As oil profits soared in the 1970s, investors poured money into office developments, structures immediately filled by petroleum companies paying high rents. The temporary demand for glasstowers ridiculously inflated land prices. Savings and loans, insurance companies, and real estate investment trusts freely lent sums to construct more office buildings. All corporate Denver believed the boom would never end. When the bubble burst, many of the investments were worthless.

The oil bust alone does not explain the real estate crash of the mid-1980s. Even more than the collapse of the petroleum balloon, the savings and loan fiasco was fueled by shortsightedness and shady business practices. Rather than following the traditional role of thrifts in generating steady profits by underwriting long-term home loans, the savings and loans increasingly focused on get-rich-quick development schemes in the late 1970s and early 1980s. Instead of prudently lending money on standing buildings, thrifts sought instant fortunes through speculative investments. Like the city planners and politicians, savings and loan executives were sure there was no limit to growth. To assure the permanent escalation of property values, thrift officers served as leaders of the Chamber of Commerce, loudly insisting untrammeled sprawl and a new airport were vital for the area.

No institution more championed development while engaging in questionable banking practices than Silverado Banking Savings & Loan. Its directors and large stockholders were pillars in the business community. The thrift was in the lead of bankrolling the drive for Denver International Airport. Silverado's subsequent notoriety illustrated the dubious core of 17th Street. The thrift's operations marked Denver as a wide-open city freely plundered by carpetbaggers.

Real estate magnate Franklin Burns helped found and finance the forerunner of Silverado on January 30, 1956, Mile High Savings and Loan. It had downtown and East Denver offices when it merged with Circle Savings of Littleton in June 1970. (That institution stemmed from Littleton Savings & Loan, chartered in May 1957. It changed its name to Circle Savings in 1963.) The combined Mile High Circle Savings had four locations. The thrift remained a small operation through the next decade. In 1980, when it was again known as simply Mile High Savings and Loan, the bank was the 26th largest thrift in the state with five branches.

As the oil boom swept the region, Mile High Savings was in transition. Burns sold it to investor W. James Metz in 1976–77 after the bank lost a sizable sum when a loan to a ski resort went bad. Before long, Metz was in trouble. Federal regulators sanctioned him for skimming money from the institution. Forcing Metz out as president, they suggested an upcoming Kansas banker as Mile High's chief, Michael R. Wise.

The nominee was a slick, nattily dressed, perfectly groomed upwardly mobile man in his thirties from Emporia, Kansas. After starting out as a suit salesman, Wise worked for the Federal Home Loan Bank of Topeka, the Washington agency overseeing Colorado savings and loans. The flashy executive married a banker's daughter and emerged as executive vice president/manager of Columbia Savings of Emporia. With his Boy Scout earnestness, Wise readily won favor in the eyes of those who judged individuals by outward appearances. Despite his success as the head of the Emporia Chamber of Commerce, Wise did not find the small-town atmosphere enough. The banker snapped at the opportunity to take over Mile High Savings in June 1979. Arguing that banking was more an information than a lending business, Wise transformed the thrift.

Noting the Queen City had numerous "mile high" monikers, from a dog track to a sports stadium, Wise pushed a glittering name for the institution. In 1980, he dubbed it Silverado Savings. About this time, he began a rapid growth campaign. Wise made it known Silverado was a place where people needing quick capital for speculative building projects could get financing. Its dollars fueled the growing real estate boom. Under Wise's management, the savings and loan quickly stood out as a key player in local development.

Greater Denver Chamber of Commerce
*Silverado chief Michael R. Wise*

The Kansas banker took over Silverado right when the savings and loan industry was in drastic transition. From a heavily regulated field, stemming from numerous banking frauds and failures in the past, beginning in 1977 Washington increasingly deregulated thrifts. The Federal Home Loan Bank slowly lifted the ceiling on the amount of interest a member institution could pay. While a savings and loan could offer more interest to bring in new sums, a governmental agency, the Federal Savings and Loan Insurance Corporation (FSLIC), guaranteed the safety of a depositor's money. This meant people putting funds in the high-yielding accounts at Silverado seemingly could not lose: their principal would be repaid despite how poorly the thrift managed their money.

While interest rates paid to depositors shot up to double-digit figures, many long-term housing loans were at low rates of interest, i.e., the bank received less for the money it lent out than what it paid to depositors. Silverado was not alone. Savings and loans every place were financially squeezed. The former Mile High Savings was virtually broke by 1980.

The thrift responded with an innovative marketing effort. Wise advertised Silverado was on the cutting edge of "go-go banking." After the further deregulation of savings and loans in 1982, Silverado changed its focus. Abandoning its traditional role of providing home mortgages, the thrift concentrated exclusively on commercial real estate and venture banking.

As oil fueled the soaring Denver economy, Silverado rode the wave. It financed shopping centers and idyllic subdivisions on the far fringes of the metropolis. It was involved in numerous land transactions near Denver International Airport. The bank's ability to lend money was enhanced when FSLIC hiked insurance on accounts from $40,000 to $100,000 in 1980. With the guarantee and the high interest rates, depositors flocked to Silverado.

From $83 million in assets when Wise took over, Silverado had about $250 million in 1982 when it became Silverado Bank Savings and Loan following its acquisition of Security Savings of Colorado Springs. Before long, the former Mile High Savings was the state's third largest thrift behind Bank Western (Western Federal Savings) and Columbia Savings. In addition to the Denver area, Silverado had branches in Breckenridge, Castle Rock, Colorado Springs, and Frisco. By 1983, it reported $370 million in assets.

The Federal Home Loan Bank sometimes questioned the bank's practices. As Silverado's assets quadrupled, the thrift's capital-to-loan ratio was less than 2.5

Photo by Phil Goodstein

*The Silverado headquarters at 3900 Mexico Avenue.*

percent—half of the 5-percent minimum required by federal regulations. Nonetheless, the federal agency overseeing Silverado failed to act. Wise was one of its own and Silverado appeared to be doing quite well. If anything, the regulators catered to the thrift's president. Wise served two terms on the board of the Federal Home Loan Bank of Topeka. When Wise flew out to visit the regulators in the Kansas city, Kermit Mowbray, the head of the Topeka branch of the federal agency, often sent a limousine to the airport to pick him up. With the Home Loan Bank's stamp of approval, Silverado again doubled its size in the early to mid-1980s. At the most, regulators suggested the savings and loan slow its frantic pace.

There was nothing unusual about Silverado lacking the minimum capital ratio. Most savings and loans were in the same boat as Silverado. Regulators responded by lowering the capital-to-loan ratio required at thrifts from 5 to 3 percent. They further allowed the banks to cite almost anything as assets, including speculative real estate holdings and nebulous goodwill. Under President Ronald Reagan, the government liberalized accounting rules to help savings and loans continue to thrive. Between the onset of deregulation in 1977 and 1982, Silverado's loan portfolio grew 800 percent. It was among the fast growing thrifts in the country.

Others in the savings and loan industry admired Silverado and its chief. In 1985, Wise joined the board of the United States League of Savings Institutions, a lobbying group for thrifts. In that post, he vehemently denounced efforts to rein in out-of-control savings and loans. He established close personal ties with M. Danny Wall, the chairman of the Federal Home Loan Bank in Washington. The League of Savings Institutions seriously pondered making Wise its president in 1988.

At the behest of Democratic Congressman Tim Wirth and the League of Saving Institutions, Wise was named president of the Federal Reserve's thrift advisory council. The Mile High banker also had close ties with Democratic Senator Donald Riegle of Michigan, a politician who once gave a private talk to the Silverado board. Craig Fuller, the chief of staff for Vice President George Bush, was another friend of Wise. Everybody in the industry knew the Silverado chief. Regulators treated him with great deference. Wise was something of the national personification of the savings and loan industry, an ace whom other thrift executives emulated.

## Bigger Fools

As the Colorado economy soared in the early 1980s, Silverado increasingly depended on the bigger fool theory of real estate investment: its loans might not be sound and a borrower could very well be a fool, but a bigger fool was always out there to whom a property owner could sell his holdings at a considerable gain. Minimal profits were realized from long-term loans; opposed to them, the thrift emphasized origination fees and profit-sharing in speculative transactions. Each time it made a loan, the bank tacked hefty up-front costs on to it. These fees immediately flowed back into Silverado's coffers. Many of the Silverado projects never materialized; they were paper developments designed for immediate sale at a great profit to another party, i.e., a bigger fool. The transaction allowed the lender to reap a tidy sum through closing one set of loans and opening another, complete with high fees to the new borrower.

The bank pushed ADC loans—money for the acquisition, development, and construction of a project. In these cases, the borrower never saw the costly up-front fees, money taken by the thrift in the process of generating the loan. Sometimes, Silverado bought back office buildings it had financed through these loans, structures it immediately sold at inflated prices. It often then carried the mortgage. In addition to the loans, Silverado accumulated further income from the real estate transactions.

These practices, added to the liberalized regulations and accounting rules, greatly benefited Silverado. Even as the oil bust loomed in 1982–84, the thrift was no longer on the verge of insolvency; on the contrary, the business press and politicians cited Silverado as a dynamic, highly profitable institution. The bank went out of its way to court wealthy depositors. Only people willing to sink a minimum of $10,000 into a certificate of deposit were welcomed there. Silverado scoured the country for them. It shunted locals with only nominal savings to lesser thrifts.

No longer making home loans by 1984, Silverado was, for all intents and purposes, a venture bank. To show its leadership in the corporate community, the savings and loan moved into an impressive headquarters near I-25 and South Colorado Boulevard. The thrift was frequently in the news as it financed assorted wildcat developers. From a capital of $250 million in 1982, Silverado claimed a worth of $2.7 billion by 1988. Its capital level then was .6 percent of assets.

Even after the peak of the oil boom had passed, Silverado kept growing rapidly. Often its initial loans were repaid by even larger loans to new owners of the same properties—there was an abundance of bigger fools. However, as the oil bust set in, many of its loans turned sour. By 1985, its problem loans and real estate foreclosures had increased tenfold from the 1983 level. While the thrift claimed a $12 million profit, regulators said it had actually lost $10 million. Wise fired Silverado's independent auditor, Ernst & Whinney, which called for the bank to report a loss of $15 million to $20 million. The Kansas whiz kid had had trouble with the company in the past as it sought to act as the watchdog it was supposed to be.

A rival accounting firm, Coopers & Lybrand, signed on as Silverado's auditor. It agreed with management: a $15 million loss was actually a $15 million profit. Lawyers justified the thrift's operations. Appraisers told it the properties on which

**Photo by Ann Bingham**

*The contrasting faces of the old Neusteter's at 16th and Stout streets. Silverado forced an artificially high loan on borrowers who sought to transform the former department store into apartments in the mid-1980s.*

it had lent money were worth all the bank claimed they were. Nonetheless, financial realities haunted Silverado.

As the bank's problems mounted, it required those seeking substantial loans to purchase stock in the firm. This provided a fresh source of capital. The practice also ensured the stockholders were at one with management in making even more risky loans—stockholders and borrowers alike were dependent on management remaining firmly in place. If only the idyllic days of the oil boom returned, management and stockholders agreed, Silverado's problems would be easily solved by a soaring real estate market.

Silverado did more than longingly hope for a return of the oil boom. It tried to make it a reality. Its officers and biggest borrowers played prominent roles in the Greater Denver Chamber of Commerce. That organization loudly called for building a new convention center and airport as a means of bailing out the suffering financial community. The goal was clear: state capitalism was needed to assure endless growth so Silverado could continue to profit.

By 1986, regulators had discovered 66 percent of Silverado's loans were at high risk; 22 percent were already bad. The Federal Home Loan Bank of Topeka charged the thrift was hiding problem loans by devious schemes to boost its capital. In spite of this, Silverado continued to report profits. Bonuses to officers increased. The board, for example, paid Wise $1.3 million compensation, including $724,000 in bonuses. Even as his income escalated, he had to raise more money to pay off huge loans he and majority owner Metz had taken to buy additional Silverado stock. Prosecutors later accused the two of using Silverado money to pay their personal debts.

As the office vacancy rate escalated in the mid-1980s, developments collapsed. Properties on which Silverado had made loans were not worth 50 cents on the dollar of what borrowers owed the thrift. Silverado kept the loans on book at full dollar value, adding to the outstanding balance the cost of taxes, maintenance, and marketing. In this manner, Silverado further inflated its assets. The more the economy shrank, the greater its net worth seemed to become. As the Denver market faltered, the thrift made equally unsound loans in Texas and California.

Typical of Silverado's bookkeeping legerdemain was a $26 million loan in 1986 to Colorado Investment Partners to convert the Neusteter Building, at the south corner of 16th and Stout streets, from a department store into 90 apartments and ground retail space. A limited partnership led by Silverado investors Jeff Selby and Allen Gersenberger, Colorado Investment Partners, acquired the 1924-vintage building after Neusteter's closed as a department store in December 1985. The developers figured it would cost about $13.2 million to transform the building.

Silverado insisted on the $26 million loan. Much of the capital was eaten away in up-front fees. These were put on the books as a Silverado profit. Before long, it became clear the Neusteter investment could not generate enough revenue to repay the $26 million outlay. Colorado Investment Partners defaulted on the loan in September 1988, leading to a $13.2 million loss for Silverado. The company redeveloping the Neusteter Building filed for bankruptcy under the pressure of the debt in June 1990.

## The Savings and Loan Blight

The former Mile High Savings was not alone. Other savings and loans, locally and nationally, engaged in equally problematic real estate ventures, loans, and investments. Among them was Columbia Savings. It was a storied firm, incorporated on August 31, 1929, as Columbia Savings Building and Loan, a partner of a stock brokerage, Columbia Securities Corporation. After the operation struggled during the Depression, Kenneth Kendal King gained control of it in 1937, building the bank into a local dynamo. In 1961, King sold Columbia to the Music Corporation of America, a firm emerging as a conglomerate, MCA Incorporated.

A 29-year-old prodigy, Daniel L. Ritchie, took charge of the thrift in 1960. He later moved up in the MCA world before holding a key post with Westinghouse. In 1989, Ritchie, a nonacademic, became head of the University of Denver. By this time, Columbia was a tattered part of the savings and loan scene.

The thrift's corporate owner spun off Columbia in 1982, an institution claiming more than a billion dollars in assets. The savings and loan had severely overexpanded and was hemorrhaging money. About the same time, MDC (Mizel Development Corporation), the parent company of Richmond Homes, a major home builder, targeted the historic Denver thrift.

Larry Mizel was the namesake of MDC and owner of the firm. He started its forerunner, Larry A. Mizel Investments, in 1965 while he was a law student at the University of Denver. After obtaining his degree in 1967, Mizel rapidly moved into local real estate, focusing on building apartment complexes in the southeast-

Photo by Phil Goodstein

*The Jewish Community Center named its performing arts complex the Mizel Family Cultural Arts Center after Larry Mizel, a key investor in Silverado Savings.*

ern area. He formed the Mizel Development Corporation in July 1972. In no time, it was a powerhouse of local residential construction.

A native of Tulsa, Oklahoma, Mizel collaborated with junk bond king Michael Milken as the home builder enlarged his development corporation. MDC came to control Imperial Savings of San Diego, a thrift with ties to Milken. Mizel also had links with Charles Keating's notorious Lincoln Savings and Loan of California. Deals between Lincoln Savings, MDC, and Silverado were common. As much as 80 percent of MDC's profits in the mid-1980s derived from deals associated with Silverado. MDC bought shares in California savings and loans that snapped up some of the junk bonds issued by Milken. When the junk bond market collapsed, many of these savings and loans went down with it.

Federal regulators responded slowly. They sensed something was drastically wrong, but the spirit of deregulation and Ronald Reagan's America meant they should mostly keep their hands off the thrifts. Silverado was, however, in violation of so many basic tenets of sound banking that the Federal Home Loan Bank of Topeka sought to learn more. A team of regulators started delving into the thrift's machinations in December 1986. They found a convoluted trail, front groups, traps, detours, smoke screens, paper profits, and a cloaking of losses. Nonetheless, the regulators still hesitated to use their powers. Since the Home Loan Bank had recommended Wise for the Silverado job, the staff did not want to embarrass those responsible for Wise's selection. Not only was Wise a member of the Home Loan Bank's board, but the regulatory agency had previously approved many of Silverado's bizarre schemes.

Economic reality forced the regulators to do something. In 1987, the Home Loan Bank finally moved to restrict Silverado's activities. The thrift, then claiming total assets of more than $2.2 billion, agreed it would not step out of bounds. Losses escalated. In August 1988, the bank reported 25 percent of its loans were bad and headed for foreclosure. It had to write off $198 million in problem loans. This came on top of another $75 million in bad loans it had already swallowed. Even with this, Silverado claimed it had earned $13.7 million in the first six months of the year. All it needed, Wise claimed in a newspaper advertisement, were new investors. The savings and loan's only mistake was placing too many eggs in the basket of commercial real estate loans. Silverado, the bank's head predicted confidently, would doubtlessly recover as soon as the economy corrected itself.

Silverado's frenzied support for convention centers and airports proved of no avail. The vastly over-built real estate market continued to slump. Even as the city began work on the Colorado Convention Center and committed itself to Denver International Airport, new sources of revenue dried up. The thrift failed in its efforts to sell mortgage-backed securities on Wall Street. Investors increasingly recognized Silverado's properties were nowhere near their book values.

The savings and loan required borrowers to take out ever bigger loans. Developers had to use the extra money to buy bad loans from Silverado. Only individuals desperate for cash agreed to Silverado's terms. It so continued to make loans on projects for far more than the property was worth or the revenue the venture could generate. Problem loans became worse than ever.

By 1988, 20 bank examiners were working full-time on Silverado, drawn to it from assignments throughout the entire midwestern regulatory region of the Topeka Home Loan Bank. Federal bank officials increasingly discovered losses and outright deceit by Silverado. The bank had $43 million in unreported losses, resulting in a negative net worth of $167 million.

Despite these findings, the regulatory agency still failed to move. Silverado had strong political ties with both the local and federal government. Though the evidence justified shutting down the rogue operation, the Home Loan Bank simply asked Silverado to no longer engage in risky operations. After months of squabbling, in October 1988 the thrift's board agreed to do as the regulators wished. By this time, the Silverado empire was rapidly cracking.

Bad loans and inflated real estate estimates were tearing the savings and loan apart. Backed by federal insurance, it raised its interest rates to depositors ever higher, sometimes paying them more than it was charging on its highly speculative loans. As the magnitude of Silverado's fraud was exposed, massive withdrawals of deposits racked the institution. The Home Loan Bank responded by trying to prop up Silverado, realizing its collapse might bring down much of the savings and loan industry as a whole. In August 1988, the Federal Home Loan Bank in Washington poured $450 million into the thrift to keep it temporarily afloat.

Silverado was hopeless. Efforts to bring it under control were of no avail. Still, it was not politically expedient to close the bank. Washington did not want the thrift's failure in the news during the 1988 presidential campaign. Neil Bush, the son of the Republican candidate, George Bush, had been on the Silverado board until his father received the nomination. By this time, some jokingly called the institution "Desperado Savings."

Political considerations continually overrode banking regulations. The Topeka Home Loan Bank knew it should immediately seize Silverado. It had no luck when it tried to force a sale of the institution. On September 12, the Topeka regulators called for FSLIC to take over the savings and loan. The Federal Home Loan Bank in Washington deferred action. Meanwhile, on October 23, the state of Colorado, noting Silverado was a state-chartered institution, belatedly moved against the runaway bank. State thrift commissioner David L. Paul informed Topeka he would shutter Silverado by the end of the month. In response, Washington ordered the Topeka authorities to delay closing the savings and loan for 45 days. Only on November 9, 1988, the day after George Bush's election as president, did federal regulators finally sign a letter ordering the Topeka branch to close the thrift a month later.

With Silverado executives receiving illicit advance notice of the federal action, regulators finally shut the savings and loan at 5:00 PM on December 9, 1988. Silverado had $200 million in problem loans. To help the public forget the debacle, the Home Loan Bank assigned the bank its old name, Mile High Savings, when it reopened the thrift on December 12.

The government sold Silverado's assets and its deposit customers to First Nationwide Bank, a subsidiary of Ford Motor Company. First Nationwide simultaneously bought another failed thrift, the MDC-influenced Columbia Savings. First

CHS

*Empire Savings, at 17th and California streets, tried to have an old West setting. Shown is its mock western village for the Rush to the Rockies Centennial in 1959. The Security Building is the tower on the left. That building was destroyed in 1992, four years after Empire Savings disappeared as a local thrift.*

Nationwide paid about $175 million for the two companies, forming them into a new Columbia Savings.

The Federal Savings and Loan Insurance Corporation promised to cover all of the $1.2 billion in liabilities to depositors of the two collapsed thrifts. In 1993, Norwest Banks of Colorado made Columbia part of its empire. By the time the dust of the savings and loan scandal had cleared, taxpayers were socked more than $1 billion to cover the operations of the pro-growth, pro-development, pro-airport, pro-great city Silverado.

The government and media targeted Wise as the scapegoat for Silverado's failure. Regulators banned him from the banking industry in January 1990. Generally, though, Wise and the others around Silverado weathered the storm. A grand jury indicted the bank chairman on September 10, 1992, for illegally diverting nearly a half million dollars of Silverado's money for his personal use. It also accused him of lying about his actions to regulators. Wise was acquitted of the charges in 1993.

After briefly returning to Kansas, Wise settled in Aspen as a mortgage lender. Within a few years, he was up to his old tricks. After passing a psychological review an investment partner demanded he take, Wise was back in business. The perfectly groomed banker again won the hearts and pocketbooks of affluent investors. He convinced them their moneys were safe in his hands. In 1998, while serving as president and chief executive officer of Cornerstone Private Capital, he admitted he had "misappropriated" $8.75 million from at least 38 investors in the real estate lending firm.

The federal courts slapped Wise's hands in 1999. As the evidence of the Silverado chief's new swindling came out, Wise reached a deal with prosecutors. He pleaded guilty to two counts of wire fraud. Though he failed to provide a payment schedule and claimed he lacked the resources, the banker vowed to pay complete restitution to his victims. Hearing this, the judge sentenced Wise to 42 months in a federal prison camp. Showing a fondness for Wise, who as ever projected himself as an earnest altar boy, the jurist stated his hope Wise could serve his term in Leavenworth near the banker's family in Emporia.

## Bill Walters and Kenneth Good

Silverado's biggest outside partner/investor, Bill Lester Walters, also came out of the scandal standing on his feet. A teammate of Gale Sayers on the University of Kansas football team in the early 1960s, Walters ran wild across the Denver real estate field in the 1970s and 1980s. The Kansan settled in town in 1972 as an architect. Before long, he began to invest in real estate. His principle was to use other people's money: he would design projects and let others pay for them. Walters shared the profits while others took the risks.

The architect prospered during the boom in the late 1970s. His enterprises soared in the early 1980s with the help of tax legislation promoting new real estate development. Seeing himself as the Donald Trump of the Rockies, Walters eventually possessed upwards of three million square feet of office space in the region.

Walters personified those eagerly seeking to build whatever and wherever they could regardless if there was a demand for the projects. Tax incentives, easy money from lenders such as Silverado, and the belief there was an endless supply of bigger fools, led to a massive expansion of the metropolitan area's borders. New malls and strip shopping centers appeared everywhere. Walters' house of cards began to collapse in 1986 when Washington rescinded some of the tax breaks encouraging his ventures.

By this time, Walters led the Greater Denver Chamber of Commerce. (Wise was treasurer of the group.) Under him and executive Dick Fleming, the booster organization promoted Denver as a veritable Oz, apparently a community where the art of humbug was the most valuable commodity of all. Newspapers estimated Walters' net worth at upwards of $200 million. They appraised his investments at $700 million. The booster's holdings included three banks, numerous office buildings, and tracts of real estate near what later became DIA. At the peak of his operations, he owned 24 million square feet of undeveloped land, real estate equal to the entire central business district.

The Galleria was a typical Walters/Silverado project in the mid-1980s, a super shopping center near the interchange of I-25 and I-225 on the Denver-Aurora line.

Silverado agreed to give Walters $18.5 million for the project. In return, the thrift received all sorts of overvalued property Walters promised to buy back in the future. The developer further agreed to invest $7 million in Silverado Financial Corporation, a holding company formed to hide some of Silverado's other schemes. Silverado joined Walters in advocating city subsidies for the Galleria. The Federico Peña administration ardently backed the plan. Though the Galleria never made it off the drawing board, Walters ordered workers to bulldoze environmentally sensitive wetlands for the project.

Greater Denver Chamber of Commerce

*Heavy Silverado investor Bill L. Walters led the Greater Denver Chamber of Commerce at the time the city committed itself to Denver International Airport while the thrift verged on collapse.*

As the oil bust deepened, Walters sank with it. By 1988, his equity was down to $47 million opposed to $170 million a year earlier. He eventually defaulted on $106 million in loans to Silverado. The Chamber chief filed for bankruptcy in November 1990. Nonetheless, Walters continued to lead the life of a millionaire. He drew on the $15.83 million he had given his second wife, his former secretary Jacqueline Brown, in a controversial pre-nuptial agreement they signed in 1986.

The courts discharged Walters from bankruptcy in 1993. The action effectively cleared him of between $220 million and $280 million in debts. He and his wife were allowed to keep a house worth more than $2 million in Englewood, a Rolls Royce, Ferrari, two Mercedes Benzes, a $1 million home in Vail, and other rich real estate and personal holdings. Rumors floated Walters might have stashed $20 million in the Isle of Jersey off the southern coast of England.

The story about Walters' hidden assets on the Channel Island stemmed from the divorce proceedings of an associate, John Dick. The holder of a law degree from the University of Toronto, Dick was part of the Canadian influx during the 1960s and 1970s. With William B. Pauls, Dick gained control of the Denver Tech Center. Living high with his wife, Elisabeth Flemmer, he dwelt in a 25-room mansion in Cherry Hills Village and showed up at affairs where new money flaunted its wealth.

The Dick marriage collapsed in 1987. Before long, the Canadian attorney, under court order to pay alimony and a settlement to his former wife, fled the region. He showed up living in a 16th-century manor house on the Isle of Jersey as the Seigneur of St. John. During the course of the long, controversial, and heavily publicized divorce proceedings, the charge was made Dick was hiding $20 million of Walters' assets there.

A close Walters associate, Kenneth Good, similarly managed to survive the Silverado collapse. From Wichita, Kansas, he graduated from Southern Methodist

University, setting up shop in Dallas as a real estate investor and developer in the late 1960s. After making and losing a fortune in Dallas by the time he was 26 and verging on bankruptcy in the mid-1970s, Good relocated to the Mile High City in 1977. Plunging into local real estate, the investor found his niche here, successfully developing condos on Capitol Hill.

By 1979, the Silverado borrower owned property worth more than $75 million. Good expanded his empire to Florida in 1985, running Gulfstream Land & Development Corporation. At the peak of his fortune, the entrepreneur invested in Argentine oil ventures. He projected himself as publicly concerned, serving on various public bodies and working with the Colorado Forum, a key 17th Street club trying to shape the area's growth contours.

Walters and Good frequently traded parcels with each other. Each time land was sold between them or other partners and investors, the property soared in value, allowing them to pocket considerable profits. Silverado financed some of these deals. Good and Walters were not only leading customers of the thrift, but something of collaborators with Wise. In 1984, to raise new capital for the bank, Wise arranged for Silverado to issue $15 million in stock to Walters and $14 million to Good in exchange for the bank acquiring some of their vastly over-valued real estate.

Good celebrated his opulence. He was a great man in a great city, strutting prominently at assorted parties and charity balls. The real estate wizard went out of his way to court important political officials. Among those praising him was Governor Richard Lamm. In November 1979, the governor named Good to a 21-member commission as part of the Front Range Project, an effort to check sprawl in the area. This was at the same time Good heavily profited from such cancerous growth.

The heavy Silverado borrower had other close ties to the Lamm administration. This came out in 1980–81 when Good focused on oil shale in western Colorado. He bought massive acreage near where oil corporations Exxon and Tosco planned the huge Colony Project, an effort backed by more than a billion dollars in loan guarantees from the state and federal government. Simultaneously, Good courted Paula Herzmark, the executive director of the Colorado Department of Local Affairs, the state agency overseeing the oil shale boom. The investor showered her with thousands of dollars worth of gifts. The 33-year-old Herzmark, a former head of Colorado Common Cause, admitted the 38-year-old Good was her lover. She sometimes signed her name Mrs. Kenneth Good.

The would-be shale oil entrepreneur was also a close friend of a key Lamm aide, Jim Monaghan. The latter, between stints working for the governor, served as a special consultant to the United States Synthetic Fuels Corporation during 1980–81, the federal agency pushing shale development. This was right before Good sought to take over Tosco. Much of this came out in lawsuits Tosco filed against Good in 1981. Before anything happened, the oil shale bubble burst in 1982.

Besides speeding around in a Maserati and flying in a private jet to Las Vegas and Monte Carlo with Walters for gambling sprees, Good was known for his 33,000-

Private Collection

*Kenneth Good*

square foot, $10 million house. He built it on five acres at 16 Lynn Road near Quincy Avenue and South University Boulevard in Cherry Hills Village. His palace included 15 bathrooms, six kitchens, world-class exercise facilities, and an indoor tennis court. Marble and slate floors graced the mansion, as did mirrored walls and a honeycombed wine cellar. The developer decorated it with works of art, declaring it a museum in its own right. Good was a customer of Cherry Creek National Bank, a financial institution owned by Walters.

The two investors fell out when Good took the side of Walters' first wife, Mary Lou Paulsen Walters, in Walters' divorce. Not only did Good start dating her, but he advised the society woman, who lived in the exclusive Polo Club neighborhood, about how her husband would try to hide his assets from her. As was the case in the Dick divorce, many of high society's financial practices were publicly aired in the dispute. "Dynasty" was not make-believe; it was a documentary on the oil, real estate, and banking buccaneers.

In addition to drawing funds from Silverado, Good also received financing for his speculative ventures from Columbia Savings, Capitol Federal Savings, and the First Interstate Bank. His losses at Silverado alone were about $32 million. When he filed for bankruptcy, he claimed to have only $99,000 in assets opposed to $99 million in liabilities.

By the time his empire collapsed in the late 1980s, Good had stashed money away in 174 private trust accounts. His huge mansion was abandoned and littered with broken glass. When it was opened to the public as the Junior Symphony Guild's Designer Showhouse in 1989, it was something of a white elephant symbolizing the grandiose savings and loan aspirations. The house sold for $2.5 million at an October 1989 auction. Columbia Savings, which had lent Good funds for the house, reported taking a major loss on it.

## The Vice President's Son

Good was close to a Texan who served on the Silverado board of directors, Neil Bush, son of George Bush. Other than for his father's influence, Bush brought nothing to the board. After receiving an MBA from Tulane, he arrived in oil-boom Denver in 1979 with his new bride, Sharon Smith, working as a landsman for Amoco. Parlaying his father's political and economic connections, he quickly emerged as part of young Denver high society, serving on the board of the Children's Museum while joining the Denver Club. His wife teamed up with Nancy Davis Zarif, the daughter of Marvin Davis, in a cookie company, Cookie Express. On this basis, Sharon Bush became chairwoman of a gala ball for Children's Hospital.

Neil and Sharon Bush were seemingly everywhere by the time George Bush was vice president. Scott Hinkley, the brother of unsuccessful Ronald Reagan assassin John Hinkley Jr., was among Neil's buddies. Ominously, the vice president's son was slated to have dinner with Scott Hinkley the same day John Hinkley shot Reagan in March 1981.

In January 1983, Neil Bush started his own oil exploration firm, JNB Exploration. Among those funding it were people who hoped support for Neil Bush would give them access to and influence with George Bush and other key Washington figures. Walters contributed $150,000 for JNB. An independent oil company invested another $150,000. Good acquired 25 percent of JNB, putting up $10,000 and arranging for a $1.8 million line of credit for the company from the Walters-owned Cherry Creek National Bank. He later lent Bush $100,000 to speculate in commodity markets based on a hot tip. (Good forgave the loan when the tip proved unfounded.) Bush's personal contribution to JNB was only $100.

The oil exploration company never found any marketable oil and quickly used up its line of credit at Cherry Creek National Bank. JNB collapsed in 1989. Meanwhile, in 1985, Michael Wise met Bush at a dinner party. Wanting to improve his connections with Washington where he had ties with the extremely powerful vice president, the Silverado chief asked Neil Bush to join the thrift's 11-member board. Despite no knowledge of banking, the vice president's son readily signed on as a well-paid director on August 22, 1985.

Rather than bothering to read regulatory reports critical of Silverado's management, Bush blessed the Wise regime. A member of the thrift's auditing committee, Bush sanctioned the bank's switching its auditor. Through his work on the compensation committee, he awarded massive pay raises and bonuses to Wise and other officers. In 1986, the director urged Silverado to grant a $900,000 letter of credit to Good, not disclosing some of his other deals with the speculator. He likewise readily authorized loans to Bill Walters, a partner/key investor in JNB. Far from rocking the boat, the outside director approved virtually every problematic action in which Silverado engaged. The Texan severed his connections with the thrift in August 1988 as his father ran for president while Silverado teetered on collapse. The local Republican Party thereupon honored Neil Bush by making him an elector for his father's campaign.

After George Bush won the presidency and the massive savings and loan swindle was exposed, Neil Bush became something of the poster boy for the unethical operations of the thrift industry—a scam leading to a taxpayer loss of more than $500 billion. Under George Bush, Washington readily agreed to pay the tab. Republicans charged a 1990 congressional investigation of Silverado, conducted by Texas Congressman Henry B. Gonzales, was actually more a Democratic ploy to embarrass the Bush family than a legitimate effort to expose the quagmire of corruption at the heart of Silverado and the entire savings and loan industry.

The Office of Thrift Supervision, the government agency dealing with the savings and loan morass, sought to punish Neil Bush for "one of the worst kinds of conflict of interest." The former director refused to admit he had done anything wrong. He refused to sign a consent decree banning him from the banking industry for life. Rather, seeking the spotlight, in 1990 the 35-year-old Bush held press conferences where he presented himself as the unfortunate persecuted victim of

Private Collection

*Neil Bush*

the thrift collapse simply because his father was president. Defiantly, he announced he might even run for Congress as a measure of vindication.

In December 1990, an administrative law judge ruled Bush had engaged in conflicts of interest as a Silverado board member. On April 18, 1991, the Office of Thrift Supervision affirmed the verdict. It ordered the president's son to cease and desist from ever engaging in comparable conflicts of interest as a bank director.

On May 29, 1991, Bush agreed to pay $50,000 as his share in ending a $200 million lawsuit the Federal Deposit Insurance Corporation, taking over from FSLIC, filed against 13 Silverado board members and officers in 1990. After long negotiations, a $49.5 million settlement was reached. Much of the money came from a $23 million defense fund the bank's directors had established for themselves in 1986 to cover any misdoings for which they might be found liable. Sherman & Howard, the bank's law firm, forked over $16.5 million stemming from its blessing of Silverado's actions. A day later, the government reached a further settlement with Silverado's independent auditor, Coopers & Lybrand. The company paid a $20 million fine after regulators showed how severely flawed its 1986 audit of the thrift had been.

In January 1988, Good named Bush to the board of the former's Gulfstream Land & Development Corporation, paying him $100,000 a year. Good's outfit failed in 1990. Meanwhile, with the help of cable television executive Bill Daniels, Bush set up another oil firm, Apex Energy. He simultaneously moved to a bigger, more impressive $500,000 home in a gated suburban community. Bush's new outfit, from which he received $160,000 annual salary, was no more successful than JNB Exploration had been. It collapsed in 1992, most of its $2.3 million capital guaranteed by federal Small Business Administration loans.

In face of continued failures, the president's son abandoned Denver for Houston in July 1991. He signed on there as a business adviser with a Daniels' company, TransMedia Communications. Before long, drawing on his father's political and economic associates, and money provided by Daniels, Bush was able to set up a new company, Interlink Management, where he worked as a consultant for international investments.

By the time Bush had exited from the Mile High scene, it was obvious Denver deserved the savings and loan crisis. While most of the bank failures were sparked by the oil collapse and the bursting of the speculative real estate bubble of the early 1980s, the roots of the bankruptcies were swindling, dishonesty, and greed.

Neil Bush was the personification of everything marking the operations of those who eagerly plundered the city. He was a politically connected operative whom people around Silverado thought could produce special favors for them.

Bush was only the most visible link between the thrift manipulators and the political establishment. Heavy Silverado borrower/investor Larry Mizel was also extremely active in this regard. He chaired a 1986 luncheon, attended by President Reagan, an affair generating more money for the Republican congressional campaign than did any other single function that year. In 1990, right when the savings and loan scandal and Neil Bush's links to Silverado were exposed, President George Bush attended a fund-raising luncheon in Colorado cochaired by Mizel and Walters.

Mizel's MDC was in the doldrums for some years after the savings and loan crash. Upon Silverado's collapse, it had to write off more than a $20 million investment in the thrift. At one point in 1990, MDC stock was selling for nine cents a share. Eventually, MDC recovered. Mizel had an estimated net worth of at least $100 million in the mid-1990s. He projected himself as a philanthropist, complete with the Mizel Museum of Judaica, a small institution celebrating the city's Jewish elite. The Jewish Community Center honored him, naming its performance complex the Mizel Family Cultural Arts Center.

There was nothing specifically Republican about the savings and loan scandal. While Alamosa attorney Carlos Lucero, an unsuccessful Democratic candidate for the party's nomination to the United States Senate in 1990 and 1992 sought to make the savings and loan scandal a crucial campaign issue, the corporate leadership of his party effectively ignored him. On the contrary, Governor Roy Romer and Mayor Federico Peña both received substantial financial campaign backing from Mizel. For a while, Romer attended frequent gatherings at Mizel's home. The governor and the mayor were also close to the law firm of Brownstein Hyatt Farber & Strickland. A principal of the firm, Norm Brownstein, a friend of Good, was the attorney who had drawn up some of the trusts through which Good allegedly hid his money.

## The Baron of Bad Deals

How the savings and loan scandal touched everyday people was illustrated in the fate of Highland Hill. This refers to the block on 15th Street in North Denver between Boulder and Central streets, just northwest of the Valley Highway (I-25). For years, it was an out-of-the way area. The city destroyed many nearby houses in the 1940s and 1950s to make way for the freeway. Francis Van Derbur, the head of Olinger Mortuary, owned most of the land.

Highland Hill took off in the mid-1970s as a funky, bohemian section filled with art galleries, used book and record stores, a kite shop, and the city's only true coffeehouse, Muddy Waters of the Platte. Usually called Muddy's, the last dated from 1975. Joe DeRose, a third generation Denverite, led the enterprise. He had been part of a small literary group that then found itself evicted from its meeting room at the Oxford Hotel when the rent was hiked from $35 to $175 a month. The club looked for a gathering spot in North Denver.

Photo by John Schoenwalter

*Muddy Waters of the Platte Coffeehouse, at 2557 15th Street, was among the institutions destroyed by the manipulations of real estate speculator Richard Rossmiller.*

Finances were a problem. Hoping to transform their group into a debating society, supporters believed they could meet the rent by running a bookstore. In the process, they would stimulate the minds of locals and encourage artists. Reviewing the economics, they realized the bookstore would not pay for itself. If they could get customers to buy a cup of coffee and a few food items, their store could make it. On this basis, they launched the coffeehouse, named for a famous blues musician. In no time, Muddy's was not only a restaurant and bookstore, but also had an experimental theater. Its coffee bar brought together countless unorthodox types after midnight. Chess players and political radicals frequented the spot, a place functioning as a center of alternative Denver.

As Muddy's flourished and other Highland Hill businesses emerged in the low-rent area, developers eyed the neighborhood. They believed the architecturally appealing section, placed on the National Register of Historic Places as a landmark district in July 1979, was too good for the likes of Muddy's. Against the current tenants, corporate Denver hoped to transform the block into a second Larimer Square. To achieve this, big-money players sought to depopulate the area. Locals repeatedly fought off such efforts to evict them from the business district they had made. State Representative Federico Peña, whose district included Highland Hill, supported Muddy's against 17th Street.

Richard Harmes "Dick" Rossmiller bought the land on the northeast side of Highland Hill in 1981 for $2.5 million. He immediately claimed the real estate was worth $5 million. On this basis, he secured a loan on the property for $3.3 million from Brighton Federal Savings. Locals vehemently fought his redevelopment plans.

The *Denver Post* came to refer to Rossmiller as "the Baron of Bad Deals." The owner of the Highland Hill property was another of the savings and loan highflyers who had collaborated with Silverado and Charles Keating in questionable real estate ventures. Much of what Rossmiller touched turned to dross. This included the North Denver venture. By the time Peña had become mayor and office and commercial vacancy rates were soaring, Rossmiller announced work would finally get underway on gentrifying Highland Hill. Shortly thereafter, a historic apartment building next to Muddy's mysteriously burnt down. About the same time, Brighton Federal Savings foreclosed on the land.

After a long fight, the thrift evicted Muddy's in late 1985. (A new Muddy's opened at 22nd and Champa streets in 1987, lasting until 1997.) New owners finally redeveloped the Highland Hill property in the image of corporate Denver. The project never came close to paying for itself. Buildings there stood mostly vacant for years.

Brighton Federal Savings swallowed massive losses on the Highland Hill venture. It also suffered major defaults from other Rossmiller ventures. By the time the thrift forced Muddy's from North Denver, FSLIC arranged for a branch of Household Finance to purchase the nearly insolvent Brighton Federal Savings on June 30, 1985. The government agency gave Household Bank of Westminster, California, $22 million to swallow the Denver-area thrift. The latter was swamped with $16 million in bad loans to Rossmiller.

The Baron of Bad Deals had haunted Denver real estate since the early 1970s. Between 1974 and 1978, he teamed up with Bill Walters in various transactions. Rossmiller was a heavy borrower from Mile High Savings before the thrift evolved into Silverado. Amidst the savings and loan debacle, claims were loudly made that Rossmiller had ties to both the Mafia and the CIA in some of his smoke-and-mirror investments.

The developer left a long streak of unpaid bills everywhere, especially borrowing from Walters' Cherry Creek National Bank and South Denver National Bank of Glendale. Rossmiller was also involved in the destruction of the South Broadway Montgomery Ward, an exchange leading to the collapse of Hill Financial Savings of Red Hill, Pennsylvania. That thrift had previously lent Rossmiller about $30 million to build the Mount Carbon Metropolitan District, an elaborate, 1,000-acre office-residential-retail complex, complete with an aquatic museum, in Jefferson County. The project was always a paper venture, one primarily designed to line Rossmiller's pockets.

Rossmiller introduced developer Allan Reiver to Hill Financial, getting a finder's fee and interest in the Broadway Plaza/Denver Design Center near Montgomery Ward, a much hyped venture on which Hill Financial lost about $80 million. All told, Rossmiller's total losses were estimated at $200 million to $300 million. He had interests in everything from hotels in Phoenix to an auto dealership in Oxnard, California. None were completely sound.

DURA

*The Denver Federal Reserve Bank, at the north corner of 17th and Arapahoe streets, was once the area's banking headquarters. The structure was torn down as part of the Skyline Urban Renewal Project in the late 1960s—the same fate experienced by many historic buildings targeted by savings and loan manipulators.*

The man behind the end of Muddy's also drained Brazosbanc of Texas. The Baron of Bad Deals had established connections with both it and Hill Financial through W. James Metz, the major stockholder in Silverado. First National Bank of Denver and Manufacturers Hanover Trust of New York were other institutions swallowing what the latter bank called "astronomical" Rossmiller losses. A Rossmiller project in Beaver Creek cost it $48 million.

During the peak of the oil boom, Rossmiller lived in opulence in the Casa da Vinci, his name for his $1.5 million mansion in Cherry Hills Village. It was filled with another million dollars worth of antiques, artwork, quaint furniture, and a 385-bottle collection of vintage wines. Besides real estate, Rossmiller dabbled in alchemy, claiming it was possible to distill valuable metals from mountain streams by using enzyme-activated wood chips. As his Colorado empire collapsed in 1989, Rossmiller relocated to San Diego where he declared bankruptcy on October 30 of that year, reporting personal debts of more than $55 million. In 1991, a federal bankruptcy judge stripped Rossmiller of immunity from paying his bills because he had withheld important financial information from the court. United States District Court Judge John Kane called Rossmiller's conduct "a study in arrogance."

As did the Chamber of Commerce, Denver Planning Office, leading politicians, and other boosters, Rossmiller blamed the "economy" for his financial failures. The oil crash, one and all claimed, was beyond their control. Rossmiller described himself and his collaborators as "just bright-eyed, bushy-tailed guys" who got eaten by the financial downturn.

In June 1993, Rossmiller pleaded guilty to five counts of fraud in Philadelphia. He admitted government charges of undertaking "a wide-ranging scheme" to defraud Hill Financial Savings of $70-plus million. The Denver high-flyer likewise conceded he had looted funds from Main Line Federal Savings & Loan of Villanova, Pennsylvania, for money slated for the Mount Carbon Metropolitan District. Prosecutors showed the Baron of Bad Deals had received a $23 million loan from the Villanova thrift to purchase a parcel costing about $6 million.

A week later, Rossmiller further pleaded guilty to five more counts of fraud for swindling Colorado financial institutions. Having a sudden attack of conscience, he announced he did not dispute the charges since a guilty plea was "the right thing to do." Denver Federal District Court Judge Zita Weinshienk sentenced him to three-and-a-half years in prison, ordering him to pay $1 million in restitution to the Federal Deposit Insurance Corporation. A Philadelphia federal judge, noting Rossmiller's crimes there were more serious than those in Denver, sentenced him to four-and-a-half years in prison, to be served concurrently with the Colorado term. The court also ordered him to pay $10 million in restitution. There is little record of him paying the sum.

Though many of the leaders of the savings and loan industry personally survived the fiasco, few of the thrifts did. Such longtime stalwarts as Silver State Savings, Western Federal Savings, Colorado Federal Savings, Majestic Savings, and Midland Federal Savings were bought up, merged, or became part of national bank chains. Other local outfits, such as Gibraltar Savings, American Federal Savings, Sierra Federal Savings, and Jefferson County Savings were long forgotten vestiges of the days when thrifts were a central part of the local banking scene.

## Penny Stocks

Besides attracting numerous savings and loan manipulators, Denver was also the home of penny stock operators. During the 1970s and 1980s, initial stock offerings came out right and left. Start-up companies often sold their stocks for a penny a share. Weak financial disclosure laws and a lack of oversight by the Denver district attorney and Colorado attorney general's offices greatly encouraged this. The Mile High City was a wide-open market where it was seemingly possible for manipulators to pull any and all strings.

The basic premise behind the penny stock market was *not* that the stocks were for promising concerns in need of capital; on the contrary, it was that plenty of money could be made by speculating in such stocks. Investment companies, sometimes fly-by-night operators, brought out initial public offerings for small companies. Brokers urged favored clients to buy ten or twenty thousand shares of stock at a penny a share. The marketing firm would thereupon report the stock offering had sold out and done extremely well. This boosted the price of the stock. Shortly thereafter, seeing the stock at five or ten cents a share, initial buyers sold out, making considerable profits. There was frequently more than a 100-percent spread between the bid and ask price of penny stocks, money pocketed by the firms selling them.

Governor Dick Lamm was among those profiting from penny stock investments. He did so with the help of the self-proclaimed "king of the penny stock market," Meyer Blinder. The son of a poor candy store owner, Blinder was born in

Brooklyn on September 16, 1921. He dropped out of school as a boy, hustling on the streets of New York. Eventually earning a night-school diploma, he had the business ethics of a street fighter. Blinder honed them by operating vending machines around New York after World War II.

In 1969, in collaboration with Mac Robinson, Blinder established Blinder Robinson & Company in Jersey City. It focused on over-the-counter stocks and underwriting small firms. Blinder Robinson opened its first branch on Long Island in 1970. During the next few years, it was a tiny operation, bringing out initial stock offerings at the minimum of ten cents a share. After buying the Denver-based Douglass & Company in 1977, Blinder Robinson relocated to the Mile High City. By this time, Mac Robinson had left the brokerage.

As Denver real estate soared, Blinder increased the firm's promotions. The company dropped the price of its initial offerings to a penny a share. More than anything, it recruited an eager corps of salesmen to hawk its products. Cold calling of prospects and the continual hounding of current customers to buy more were their preferred techniques. The boiler room outfit (slang for an unscrupulous stock brokerage) even had its own small radio station whereby Blinder personally delivered pep talks to the sales crew.

In 1983, Blinder Robinson moved into an ornate 10-story tower at 6455 South Yosemite Street. The penthouse included Blinder's office, a swimming pool, gymnasium, and a deluxe conference area. By this time, the firm was the leading penny stock brokerage in the country.

Photo by Phil Goodstein

*Market Center, on the south side of the 1600 block of Market Street, was a project by architect/developer Allan Reiver in the 1970s. In the 1980s he collaborated with the "Baron of Bad Deals," Richard Rossmiller, in the highly unsuccessful, fraud-haunted Broadway Plaza/Denver Design Center on South Broadway.*

Denver District Attorney Norm Early joined with Governor Lamm in praising Blinder as a model citizen, a man who visibly participated in charity campaigns. In 1986, both politicians, who opposed gambling in Colorado, wrote letters to Nevada authorities in support of Blinder's application for a casino license there. About this time, newspapers revealed Lamm had made a $49,000 profit on a $5,000 investment with Blinder Robinson. The governor responded to the disclosure by rescinding his support for the casino and offering to give his profit to charity. An investigation cleared Lamm of any misdoing. (Lamm's successor, Roy Romer, appointed Blinder Robinson's former general counsel in the early 1980s, Gregory Kellam Scott, to the Colorado Supreme Court in 1992. Before signing on with Blinder Robinson, Scott had been an attorney with the Securities and Exchange Commission.)

Stinging from the Lamm exposé, Blinder withdrew his application for the casino. He had pushed it through Cattle Baron, a subsidiary of Source Venture Capital Incorporated, which was part of the Denver-based Blinder International Enterprises. The last was Blinder's holding company. He had countless other front groups, divisions, and dodges.

By 1987, Blinder had an estimated net worth of upwards of $200 million. Already in 1985, with a $4.4 million salary, he was the highest paid executive in Colorado. He hiked his compensation to $9.4 million in 1986. The value of Blinder Robinson kept soaring. The parent company made $30 million in four hours when it went public in 1986. Then at the peak of its operations, Blinder Robinson had more than $100 million in revenue, 82 offices in 37 states, and 1,500-plus brokers. International holdings included a full-scale subsidiary in West Germany, operations in Hong Kong, and speculative interests in Indonesia, Switzerland, and China.

As was the case with the real estate speculators, Blinder's success was premised on the belief there was an endless supply of dupes who would buy the penny stocks for more than previous investors had. Lest there be any doubt about this, he was able successfully to bring out an issue for a company promising to extract gold by burning coal. Denver led the nation in penny stock manipulations.

About the same time the real estate, oil, and savings and loan bubbles were bursting, so did Blinder's empire. His company reported a $14.8 million loss in 1988. As the brokerage failed to find ever more suckers, charges of fraud dogged Blinder. Already in 1979–80, the Securities and Exchange Commission targeted him for a questionable $25 million stock transaction in association with American Leisure Corporation concerning an Atlantic City casino. Investigations, fines, court hearings, and appeals followed through the 1980s. Though juries kept ruling against Blinder and regulators slapped his hands, he managed to stay in business. By 1990, Blinder, Robinson was involved in nearly 400 lawsuits. As his troubles escalated in 1988, he increasingly focused on Hong Kong.

Beginning on November 19, 1988, 12 Internal Revenue Service agents, joined by two Securities and Exchange Commission investigators, swept through Blinder Robinson headquarters for a period of four days. They seized about a million documents, looking for information about specific individuals and companies. They also believed Blinder was engaged in securities fraud and money laundering. By this time, Blinder Robinson was rapidly collapsing. Investors who had purchased Blinder Robinson penny stocks discovered there were no new buyers for their holdings—their stock was not even worth a penny a share. *Forbes* exposed the firm as "Blind 'Em and Rob 'Em."

To cloak its devious reputation, on July 27, 1989, Blinder Robinson & Company changed its name to Intercontinental Enterprises. This was just after the Colorado Supreme Court upheld a 1988, $4.5 million civil judgment against Blinder Robinson. To avoid paying it, the company filed for Chapter 11 bankruptcy reorganization on July 30, 1989. Acting on a complaint from the Federal Securities Investor Protection Corporation, the judge ruled against the brokerage. The bankruptcy court, rather, appointed a trustee to oversee the firm's liquidation. Total assets were around $35 million compared to nearly $250 million in debts. Investors were lucky to get ten to 15 cents on the dollar.

In February 1990, a federal grand jury in Las Vegas indicted Blinder and four of his associates for racketeering, wire and securities fraud, and money laundering. On July 10, 1992, after a two-and-half-week trial, a jury found the 70-year-old Blinder guilty on all six counts. The prosecutor estimated Blinder's scams between 1984 and 1988 had bilked investors out of as much as $1 billion. The penny-stock king responded by cursing Assistant United States Attorney Howard Zlotnick, threatening to kill him. Sentenced to 46 months in prison and a $100,000 fine, Blinder was released in November 1995 after serving 40 months. Litigation surrounding the collapse of the firm continued into 2000. By then, the penny-stock frauds, savings and loan swindles and the oil bust had reshaped downtown.

## A Note on Sources:

Steve Wilmsen, *Silverado: Neil Bush and the Savings & Loan Scandal* (Washington: National Press Books, 1991), focuses on Denver savings and loans, especially Silverado. Unfortunately, the book is poorly written, filled with slang, and often is very short on details and specifics. Wilmsen gave his papers and sources for the book to CHS. The collection, #1532, is filled with newspaper clippings on Silverado, the thrift's newsletters, auditor's reports, the analysis of the Colorado Attorney General's office on Silverado, and the transcript of the Congressional hearing on Silverado, document 101–124.

The best overview of the thrift scandal is Martin Mayer, *The Greatest Ever Bank Robbery: The Collapse of the Savings & Loan Industry* (New York: Charles Scribner's Sons, 1990). It includes information about Silverado. Mayer lectured on the topic at the Jewish Community Center during a book festival when his volume came out. A good brief look at Silverado is "Rush for Gold: How Silverado Operated," *Time*, August 13, 1990, p. 52. Kathleen Day, *S&L Hell: The People and the Politics behind the $1 Trillion Savings and Loan Scandal* (New York: W. W. Norton, 1993), is a somewhat shallow examination of the scam. She includes a portrait of Neil Bush and the congressional investigation of him and Silverado. Also see James Ring Adams, *The Big Fix: Inside the Savings and Loan Scandal* (New York: Wiley, 1989); and Martin Lowy, *High Rollers: Inside the*

*Savings & Loan Debacle* (New York: Praeger, 1991). A rather cutesy look at Wise in Aspen is Tony Perez-Giese, "Wise Gal," *WW*, March 18, 1999, pp. 14–18.

Newspaper accounts sporadically mentioned Silverado's problems. There are clipping files on Silverado and the George Bush family at DPL, filled with materials about the thrift's fate. The library also has uneven clippings on other thrifts and such characters as Ken Good, Bill Walters, and Meyer Blinder. Colorado Forum portrayed itself on the cutting edge of Colorado in the mid-1980s, including a portrait of Ken Good in its *Business Leadership for Colorado's Future* (Denver: Colorado Forum, 1985).

The division of Savings & Loans of the Colorado Department of Regulatory Agencies, issued annual reports about the state's thrifts from 1979 until 1995, except for the crucial years of 1984–90. The documents mostly contain only the thrifts' officers, number of branches, assets, and liabilities. A statistical listing of the state's savings and loans in the late 1980s is found in the annual *Sheshunoff Savings & Loans Associations, Colorado* (Austin: Sheshunoff Information Services, 1986–90).

*Columbia Savings & Loan Association* ([Denver]: Columbia Savings, [1968]), is extremely superficial and filled with every hackneyed, booster cliché imaginable while telling little about the origins and evolution of the thrift. There are bits on Columbia in the file on Daniel Ritchie at the DU Archives. A much better booklet, looking at the actual evolution of a thrift, is First Federal Savings and Loan, *Seventy-fifth Diamond Anniversary* (Denver: First Federal Savings and Loan, 1960); and its subsequent *A Brief History of First Federal Savings* (Denver: First Federal Savings, 1965). Albin Wagner, *Brighton Reflections from Brighton Federal Savings* (Brighton: Brighton Federal Savings, 1976), has little on the financial institution.

The *Denver Post* sporadically covered Rossmiller's operations. It christened him "the Baron of Dead Deals," in a May 12, 1991, feature, p. 1A. A November 21, 1999, story, p. 1B, looks at the bond scams in the Mount Carbon Metropolitan District. Bryan Abas examined Rossmiller's numerous deals, claiming they and much of the savings and loan scam were connected to the Mafia and the CIA in "Ripoff Savings and Loan of Colorado," *WW*, April 18, 1990, pp. 10–24. Also see Steve Weinberg, "The Mob, the CIA, and the Savings and Loan Scandal," *Columbia Journalism Review*, November-December 1990, pp. 28–35. John Ashton noted the Highland Hill development in "Block-busters," *WW*, September 18, 1985, pp. 8–13. Joe DeRose recalled the origins and evolution of Muddy's, complete with its wars with Rossmiller and Brighton Savings. I tell the Broadway Plaza/Denver Design Center story in my *South Denver Saga*.

Matthew Schifrin, "Blinder Robinson—Blind 'em and Rob 'em," *Forbes*, April 20, 1987, pp. 33–38, is an exposé of brokerage. Also see *Forbes*, April 2, 1990, p. 10, and June 25, 1990, pp. 262–63; and *Business Week*, August 13, 1990, p. 100, and April 8, 1991, pp. 74–75. Court records document many of Meyer Blinder's manipulations. Greg O'Hara and Scott Briggs talked about the working of the penny stock market.

# 9

# Reshaping Downtown

The savings and loan fiasco, oil bust, real estate collapse, and penny stock fraud left Denver badly tattered. Under the impact of speculative money, most of downtown was completely destroyed and rebuilt in the 1960s, 1970s, and into the 1980s. The trendy investors dismissed as no account the low-scale buildings in which Denver had once taken pride. In their place, the corporate and political elite celebrated the generic glasstowers and faceless monoliths shaping the new skyline. Only when the full extent of the transformation had become clear by 1984, with the end of the oil boom and the many vacant lots dotting downtown, did members of the business community start to think there might be a better way.

The fate of the Masonic Building, at the east corner of 16th and Welton streets, illustrated the consensus Denver needed to preserve downtown's architectural heritage. Architect Frank Edbrooke designed it in 1890 as the region's central Masonic meeting hall. Numerous lodges gathered there over the years.

While the Masons continued to have the hall, packed with memorabilia, the fraternal group leased much of the building for offices and ground-floor retail. A tasteless remodeling in 1950 saw most of the windows filled in. Cambridge Development targeted the Masonic Building for redevelopment in 1984. The firm had gutted and redesigned Odd Fellows Hall at 1543–45 Champa Street in 1983. That structure, erected in 1887, was the headquarters of an order rivaling the Masons in influence.

A number of colorful restaurants and bars, notably the Dutch Mill, came and went from Odd Fellows Hall. Cambridge evicted all of the edifice's tenants, including Walter Garcia of Jerry Breen Florists. The shop had rented space at Odd Fellows Hall since the 1960s. Garcia relocated to the Masonic Building.

No sooner was Garcia settled in the 16th and Welton location than Cambridge again evicted him. Not believing he had received a fair deal from the developer at either Odd Fellows Hall or the Masonic Building, the florist set three fires in his shop at the latter in March 1984. A vicious blaze destroyed virtually the entire structure. Only its exterior walls remained standing.

By this time, the southwest side of the block between Glenarm Place and Welton Street on 16th Street was empty. With the Masonic Building also gone and no prospect of immediate construction, the block would be totally sterile. A community effort saved the Masonic Building, a structure rebuilt in its shell in 1985.

Though the renovation achieved great acclaim, Cambridge Development could not pay its $14.5 million cost. The firm lost the Masonic Building in March 1988 when First Interstate Bank foreclosed on a $7.3 million loan. The bank later sold the renovated edifice for about $1.45 million. (Figures in Cambridge Development were heavy investors in and borrowers from Silverado Savings.)

The fate of the Masonic Building illustrated the massive collapse of real estate values. An extremely high vacancy rate swept central Denver in the wake of the oil bust and savings and loan debacle. A solution: removing much of the existing office space from the market. Even as activists saved the Masonic Building, numerous other landmarks were demolished to reduce the oversupply of office space.

Such was the fate of the Security Building at the south corner of 17th and California streets. The 12-story structure, designed by the architectural firm of Fisher & Fisher, dated from 1927. For decades, it housed the offices of such financial powerhouses as Bosworth Sullivan and the Van Schaack real estate empire. Empire Savings bought it in 1974. Three years later, the thrift renamed the structure the Empire Savings Building. Incorporated on April 6, 1931, the savings and loan remodeled the lobby, giving it an Old West theme.

Empire Savings, taken over the Baldwin conglomerate in 1968, was brought down by the bankruptcy of its parent in the early 1980s. The thrift was subsequently sold repeatedly while it was engulfed in the problems of the savings and loan industry. Omaha-based Commercial Federal acquired Empire Savings in 1986, changing the bank's name to that of the Nebraska company in 1988. (Commercial Federal subsequently swallowed the state's oldest thrift, First Federal Bank, an institution dating from 1885.) The out-of-state owner sold the landmark 17th and California building to the Canadian Trizec Corporation in 1989.

The purchaser announced plans to demolish the Security Building. By this time, the structure was vacant. Seeing it unrentable and not wanting to pay taxes on it, Trizec aimed to tear it down for a parking lot. This was problematic. Not only was the property not zoned for parking, but preservationists expressed concern about the demolition of the Empire Savings Building. They feared its demise was only the beginning. A number of other distinguished former bank buildings were vacant along 17th Street. If owners had their way, they would tear down these remnants of historic Denver. Seventeenth Street, consequently, would become nothing more than a mix of glasstowers and parking lots.

Those pondering downtown's architectural future had good reason for their worries. Shortly before Trizec targeted the Security Building, the First Bank of Minneapolis (subsequently US Bank) destroyed the vacant Central Bank Building at 15th and Arapahoe streets in 1990. Though advocates of historic preservation lost the fight to save that structure, they gained momentum. They struck a chord in the community with their observation there had been enough downtown demolition. Instead of foolishly razing the 17th and California landmark for a sterile lot, they urged the city to retain the architectural fabric of the Wall Street of the Rockies. Under such pressure, the administration announced Trizec had to give Denver something in return for removing the Security Building. Only then would it permit a parking lot in its place.

The solution, when the Empire Savings Building came down in a controlled explosion on July 26, 1992, was a DUDE. This was a planning term for a downtown urban design element, an abstract sculpture dominating the corner of 17th and California streets. According to the city planners, the DUDE brought "sophisticated whimsy" to downtown, serving as a "combination of humor and practicality." Skeptics could see none of this; rather, they viewed the DUDE as something of a tombstone for a historic building.

Thanks to the efforts of preservationists, many 17th Street landmarks survived the oil boom and real estate bust. Few of the structures remained as offices. After the continual destruction of old hotels and downtown residential facilities in the 1970s and 1980s, developers transformed many of the surviving commercial structures into apartments/condos in the mid- to late 1990s. Typical was the Guaranty Bank Building at the north corner of 17th and Stout streets.

**Author's Collection**

*The Masonic Building, at the east corner of 16th Street and Glenarm Place, was rebuilt after fire almost consumed it in 1984.*

Brothers William E. and Arthur A. Fisher designed the ten-story structure for United States National Bank of Denver in 1921. The financial institution abandoned it in the mid-1950s shortly before it merged with Denver National Bank to form Denver-U.S. National Bank, a business eventually becoming United Bank and part of Norwest Banks and the Wells Fargo empire. The recently organized Guaranty Bank took over the Stout Street building.

The new tenant appreciated the edifice with its lush decorations, elaborate brickwork and stonework, plastered, decorated ceilings, and chandeliers. A generation later, amidst the oil boom, Guaranty Bank followed United States National Bank, leaving the structure for a highrise in lower downtown. Real estate speculator Bill Walters obtained the property in 1982 in association with Canadian investors and the Boettcher empire. He announced plans to raze the bank for a 35-story tower slated as the world headquarters of Silverado Savings. The skyscraper, he noted, was 65 percent preleased. Prior to calling in the wrecking crew, Walters gutted the building's interior.

Before anything more was done, the office market collapsed. The complex sat abandoned and decaying. As Walters' empire collapsed, FSLIC foreclosed on the property. Private investors bought the neglected highrise from the government. After receiving a considerable urban renewal subsidy, new owners, the Chotin Group, transformed the structure into apartments in 1996.

The 12-story First National Bank Building, across the street at the west corner of 17th and Stout streets, experienced a similar fate. Harry J. Edbrooke designed it for the city's commanding financial institution in 1911. When First National Bank abandoned the early skyscraper for the Murchison Tower at 17th and Welton streets in 1958, acclaimed landmark preservation architect Jim Sudler oversaw a sterile remodeling of the highrise. A much smaller financial institution, American National Bank, moved in.

Firstamerica Corporation of California took over American National Bank in the late 1950s. Later known as Western Bankcorp, it kept the Denver institution as American National Bank until 1981 when it was establishing a chain as First Interstate Bankcorp. It renamed the local concern First Interstate Bank of Denver. Then, in December 1982, First Interstate Bankcorp bought First National Bank. It abandoned the 17th and Stout structure for the Murchison Tower. By this time, the Stout Street landmark was owned by Urban Management Ltd., an Edmonton-based company. It bought it in 1979 from the University of Denver—the school had received the building as a gift in 1965. The old First National Bank structure became a typical Canadian holding: one slated for replacement with a monstrous glasstower. The office market collapsed before the new owners could wreck this part of 17th Street.

The Canadians lost the building to Rosewood Properties via foreclosure in the late 1980s. Caroline Hunt Schoellkopf, a half-sister of oil heiress Swanee Hunt, was a key figure in the new ownership company. In 1989, Rosewood announced plans to demolish the once prestigious office structure. This was staved off while asbestos was removed from the building. The former First National Bank headquarters changed hands a couple more times in the 1990s. Holtze Brothers Devel-

Photo by Phil Goodstein

*The old and new are seen looking north along 17th Street from California Street. The Equitable Building on the left remains offices; the old First National Bank Building in the center has become a hotel. Developers turned the Boston Building, behind it, into condos.*

opment owned it by the middle of the decade. With a $1.97 million subsidy from the Denver Urban Renewal Authority (DURA), the owners converted it into a luxury hotel. The renovation included undoing Jim Sudler's previous remodeling of the skyscraper.

Residences were also the fate of the Boston Building at the east corner of 17th and Champa streets. Its name derived from Boston capitalists who financed it in 1890 as offices to oversee their investments in the area. The Boettcher family acquired the Boston Building in 1924, making it the headquarters of Boettcher & Company. Bill Walters bought the Boston Building in the mid-1980s. In a frenzied real estate market, he sold the stone structure for $30 million in 1987 to William Pauls, the owner of the Denver Tech Center who was part of the Canadian crowd.

The transplant quickly discovered he had been taken. The edifice was nowhere near worth $30 million. Rather than trying to pay off the mortgage, Pauls walked away from it. Travelers Insurance foreclosed on the Boston Building. It sold the structure for $5 million in 1994. New owners cleared offices out of the landmark, converting it into condos in 1997–98. Parts of the Denver Dry, Railway Express, and Joslins buildings were among many other commercial and office structures transformed into hotels, lofts, and apartments.

Some structures, notably those housing low-income renters, were not as lucky. The fate of the Kenmark Hotel at the south corner of 17th and Welton streets was illustrative. Dating from the early 1890s, it was built as the Albert Hotel, a fine facility on upper 17th Street complementing the Brown Palace. The inn was drastically remodeled in 1910 when Frank Kirchhof signed a long lease to run it. He renamed it the Kaiserhof after a famous hotel in Berlin. Decorations included symbols of the Hohenzollern dynasty. The owner changed the name to the Kenmark during World War I to escape the Kaiserhof's pro-German implications.

In subsequent decades, the five-story structure remained part of the upper 17th Street hotel row. After the Dikeou family purchased it in 1965, the Kenmark emerged as a working-class residential hotel. By the 1980s, it was a vestige of yesterday's Denver. Retired coal miners, union organizers, and men who had built the country during the Depression lived there. A visit to it was a trip back in time.

The landmark was among many downtown working-class hotels in the 1970s. At the beginning of the oil boom, around 1974, there were an estimated 57 low-income lodges with 3,093 rooms in central Denver. By 1992, there were only nine such inns with 531 rooms. The Kenmark was among those intentionally destroyed.

Commercial Federal Savings obtained it in foreclosure from the Dikeou family. The thrift subsequently sold it to German investors. The new landlord kicked out the residents on June 1, 1991. Instead of seeing possibilities of renovating the structure, they tore it down in November 1995. Because it had housed the poor, apparently, preservationists and the subsidy crowd were not eager to save it. The owners failed to put up a DUDE, meaning the land, which was not zoned for parking, was simply left an unoccupied gravel-filled lot for some years.

Photo by L. C. McClure

*The Kenmark Hotel, at 17th and Welton streets, when it was the Albert Hotel in the late 19th century. Foreign investors destroyed the building in 1995.*

## Historic Denver

Voices of protest greeted the continued demolition of historic properties. They were a discordant chorus, ranging from lovers of old architecture to people who had worked or lived in the buildings to historians to members of high society to downtown interests who feared for their investments if all of the city's charms disappeared. The group doing the most to preserve and redevelop landmarks was Historic Denver Incorporated.

Under the pressure of those who called for saving some of Denver's old buildings, the city established the Denver Landmark Preservation Commission (DLPC) on March 6, 1967, to serve as a public guardian of distinguished structures. After the agency nominated a building as a landmark, city council had to ratify the act. The latter body invariably acted only with the consent of the property's owner. Once an edifice was officially decreed a landmark, DLPC had the power to protect its architectural integrity through a review of any proposed changes to the structure's exterior. This included preserving buildings in historic districts—blocks of houses or commercial structures whose groupings made them a central part of the city's architecture, history, and geography.

DLPC quickly proved a mostly ceremonial, ineffectual body. It began operations at the same time DURA was planning to demolish the heart of downtown through the Skyline Urban Renewal Project. When DLPC sought to save such landmarks as the Tabor Block, Cheesman Building, and old Federal Reserve Bank, DURA and city council quickly put landmark commission in its place as nothing more than an ornamental bureau that was not to interfere with the corporate reshaping of the Queen City.

Essentially, the bureau could only save landmarks whose owners wanted them preserved and declared landmarks. The law establishing DLPC was written to assure special interests, including the local chapter of the American Institute of Architects, controlled the agency. Society linkages and an old-boy network were crucial in determining who served on the board.

Private initiative, not the doings of DLPC, was at the heart of preservation efforts when rumors floated that the Molly Brown House at 1340 Pennsylvania Street was slated for destruction in the late 1960s. After numerous Capitol Hill mansions had been torn down, with many laments from DLPC but little opposition from city hall, it seemed the home of Denver's unsinkable lady might be next. This struck a raw chord.

Denver provincialism shone in the 1950s when the Broadway hit T*he Unsinkable Molly Brown* told the story of a poor girl who had married an affluent mining engineer in Leadville. Residents were even prouder when Hollywood made the musical into a feature film, proving Denver was a magical place. Even this did not appear enough to halt postwar Denver's hatred of its past. Molly Brown's local shrine, the fabled House of Lions, appeared doomed. The citizenry demanded action.

Ann Love, the wife of Governor John Love, was among those who urged saving the Molly Brown House in 1969–70. As first lady, Ann Love received various pleas from the populace as the conscience of her husband's administration. Though she had no power to act, she consulted with others in the state government. Led by state publicist Hal Haney, those sick of the devastation sweeping downtown and Capitol Hill rallied to save the House of Lions. In a whirlwind of energy, they managed to purchase the Molly Brown House and transform it into a museum celebrating Brown's role at about the time she sailed on the *Titanic*. Even before this became a reality, they decided to form a permanent organization to assist and encourage historic preservation, creating Historic Denver in 1970.

Far more than DLPC, Historic Denver developed lobbying influence. Politicians and citizens alike often referred to it as "the historical society," implying it had some sort of governmental power. Historic Denver often overshadowed the Colorado Historical Society and DLPC as the body acting to save vintage structures. The group grew into what it claimed was the nation's largest private historic preservation society with nearly 5,000 members.

The organization responded unevenly to the upheavals of the 1970s. In some cases, it failed despite desperately trying to save such storied edifices as the David Moffat Mansion at the northeast corner of Eighth Avenue and Grant Street. In other cases, it took the lead in helping get landmark designations for such structures as the Paramount Theater while it arranged funding to help renovate them. Historic Denver was primarily responsible for saving the houses on the Auraria campus composing Ninth Street Park.

Though supported by many well-to-do individuals, Historic Denver did not have the economic resources to stand up to the developers who were leveling countless landmarks at the peak of the oil boom. With city hall sitting on its hands and DLPC ineffective, Historic Denver could only lament the destruction of such gems as the Majestic Building at the northwest corner of 16th Street and Broadway and the adjacent Metropolitan Building at the east corner of 16th Street and Court Place. At the most, it worked to salvage some of their fixtures. Architects added those parts to new and refurbished buildings. The preservation group sometimes sought to collaborate with lenders and developers who were changing the face of the city. Leading bankers and real estate attorneys served on its board. As was the case with the Colorado Historical Society, a public body essentially controlled by private interests, Historic Denver placed corporate Denver on a pedestal. Its newspaper, *Historic Denver News*, frequently praised members of the business elite. On occasion, Historic Denver was mute when its financially well-connected backers leveled landmark-quality structures.

The preservationist group worked in tandem with the landmark commission. The latter got a new burst of energy in the 1980s as the memories of its defeats by DURA faded. By this time, in the wake of continued demolition of crucial landmarks, those calling for saving the best of Denver architecture got city council to strengthen DLPC's powers. The landmark commission managed to keep the Mayan Theater standing at the northeast corner of First Avenue and Broadway in 1984 when, for the first time, it convinced city council to declare a structure a landmark over the objections of the owner who wished to wreck the movie palace. Citizens sought to use DLPC's governmental power by pushing for large landmark districts. Their goal was to protect their neighborhoods from speculators, the anti-

Photo by Phil Goodstein

*The Molly Brown House at 1340 Pennsylvania Street.*

urban zoning code Denver had proudly adopted in the mid-1950s, and the ostentatious, intrusive, out-of-scale palaces increasingly besmirching such sections as Hilltop, Cherry Creek, and Washington Park.

Given the seemingly endless efforts to destroy everything associated with the Mile High City's past, Historic Denver was an unwitting voice of opposition. A celebration of old buildings became an outlet for those who felt something was wrong, that Denver was on an erratic path, but were not sure where it should be headed. Meanwhile, the city found itself faced with replacing a little of what the oil boom had destroyed. This was illustrated by the demolition of the Denver Theatre and the stillborn Centerstone project.

## Centerstone

Before the days of the 16th Street Mall, the Denver Theatre, at the west corner of 16th Street and Glenarm Place, was a prime downtown magnet. Occupying nearly a quarter of a block, the showplace opened on November 19, 1927, as the Mile High City's grandest movie palace. In addition to facilities for films, it included a full stage for live performances, a pipe organ, seven stories of balconies, and ornate decorations.

The Denver Theatre was hurting by the 1970s. Like most downtown cinemas, time had passed it by. National chains, owning and managing virtually all the city's movie houses, increasingly only showed films in sterile suburban multiplexes. These companies did not want to take the extra care and effort to make a place such as the Denver Theatre work. As downtown became ever more of a business district and less of a people place, patrons found it easier to go to a suburban multiplex than see a film at the Denver.

To bring in moviegoers, the Denver Theatre tried to emulate suburban facilities when the owner transformed it into twin screens. In 1976, it won a beer license. Neither effort helped. Revenues stagnated while property values soared. As the oil-boom metropolis bustled, memories of the Denver Theatre faded. In 1979, a year after work began on the 16th Street Mall, under pressure of escalating real estate prices, the cinema closed. The building was torn down in July 1980.

Cheesman Realty owned the land. It represented the real estate fortune of the Evans family. In the early 20th century, the son of pioneer governor John Evans, William Gray Evans, was the head of the powerful Denver Tramway Company. In 1908, his son, John Evans II, married Gladys Cheesman, the daughter of recently deceased Walter S. Cheesman who had owned the monopolistic Denver Union Water Company. Cheesman Realty was the result of the union of the two families.

Over the years, the Evans family projected itself as preservationists. John Evans II long served as president of the Colorado Historical Society. Even so, he and Cheesman Realty oversaw the knocking down of his landmark mansion at Cedar Avenue and South Race Street in 1964. Cheesman Realty likewise sanctioned the destruction of the Republic Building at the east corner of 16th Street and Tremont Place at the peak of the oil boom.

The fate of the latter embodied what old Denver and the frenzied real estate market of the late 1970s/early 1980s were all about. The U-shaped Republic Building arose between 1925 and 1928 with financing from Republic Drugs. Besides a drug store in the lobby, the edifice housed medical offices of the city's leading physicians. To advertise how the 12-story tower was the home of doctors, terracotta heads of smirking 1920esque physicians stared at passersby from above the first floor. Inside, brass-caged elevators, complete with attendants, took patients up to see the doctor.

In August 1977, Cheesman Realty agreed the Republic Building should become part of Denver's rapidly emerging Little Canada when it sold the edifice to Oxford-Ansco, the consortium owned by Canadian investors and Denver oil man Philip Anschutz. The firm planned to raze the landmark for a commanding skyscraper occupying the entire block between 16th and 17th streets and Tremont and Court places.

Mass protests ensued. The Republic Building was not any ordinary downtown structure, but part of the city's collective memory. It was the place where countless people had gone to see the doctor. Nor were physicians eager to exit the landmark. Some banded together, offering to buy the building. It was of no use. Cheesman Realty oversaw the demolition of the medical center in 1981 to make way for the faceless, sterile Republic Plaza.

The 56-story skyscraper, designed by the internationally acclaimed firm of Skidmore, Owings & Merrill, was a veritable clone of a tower in New Orleans. It did not work well. Red ink plagued the owners amidst the real estate collapse. The bust kept Reliance Plaza, a twin of Republic Plaza, from rising a block away where the Denver Theatre had stood.

At the time the theater was wrecked, Cheesman Realty, working with the Reliance Development of New York, hoped to put the 57-story, 1.4 million-square-

DPL

*The Denver Theatre at the west corner of 16th Street and Glenarm Place in 1931.*

foot Reliance Plaza on the block bordered by 15th and 16th streets from Tremont Place to Welton Street. In 1980, the Empire State firm opened the 36-story Amoco Building at the southeast corner of 17th Avenue and Broadway. Dick Fleming of the Denver Partnership helped recruit Reliance Development for the Cheesman project. Historic Denver eagerly endorsed the effort.

Reliance Development was much more skeptical of Denver than were locals. In April 1982, seeing the Mile High office market had potential problems, it walked away from the project. By this time, the adjacent block between Glenarm and Tremont places from 15th Street to 16th Street was also mostly vacant. Within a few years, all the structures on it were torn down for a massive parking lot.

Even as the city determinedly destroyed nearby residential structures to make way for the Colorado Convention Center, it hoped a developer would place an elaborate shopping complex on the vacant 16th Street property. The 1986 comprehensive downtown plan was based on the premise that such a center was an imminent reality. With a glutted office market, commercial construction was then at a standstill.

From the time it was obvious no more skyscrapers were going up after 1983, talk was heard about a public underwriting of Reliance Plaza. In 1984, a $40 million city subsidy was projected for a square-block project on the Cheesman land. Oxford-Ansco signed on. City hall's plans soared. So did those of the Denver Partnership. In connection with the adjacent empty block where Oxford-

Ansco also owned much of the real estate, boosters and developers proposed a veritable suburban shopping center. Planners and downtown interests wished for outside retail, ideally a Macy's, Neiman Marcus, or Saks Fifth Avenue, to anchor the project, a development now known as Centerstone.

Proponents urged tax-increment financing to pay for the effort. They pushed a favored urban renewal/state capitalist scheme. Instead of having revenues from the city-financed effort go directly into the general fund, under tax-increment financing, the new sales and property taxes generated by an urban renewal effort are placed in a special sinking fund to pay off the bondholders. The result: taxpayers receive no immediate benefit from their investment.

As they advocated this corporate welfare scheme, those around the Denver Partnership vehemently opposed efforts to redevelop the Cherry Creek Shopping Center. They feared if Cherry Creek came to the fore, their hopes for exclusive downtown retail and Centerstone would collapse. Part of the reason politicians and powerbrokers were so uninterested in saving the Denver Dry when it was taken over by the May Company in 1986–87 stemmed from their fear the store's continuing presence might detract from the city's ability to lure an outside, high-class chain into the city.

The Partnership, working with DURA, hired consultants to develop a "market rationale" for Centerstone. The highly paid experts produced optimistic projections for the effort. Even so, economic calculations about Centerstone did not make sense. In no time, the required subsidy doubled from $40 million to $80 million. By 1986, critical reviews estimated Centerstone would cost taxpayers about $171 million in the course of 25 years. The sum included the price of bonded indebtedness in addition to the revenues lost to the general fund through tax-increment financing. No private developer was willing take the plunge without getting public moneys.

Nor was land ownership completely clear. Besides Canadian concerns and Cheesman Realty, others had parcels on the proposed Centerstone land. They wanted top dollar for their properties. To try to break the log jam, city hall talked about DURA taking over the whole area. The urban renewal agency would use its condemnation powers to acquire all the real estate. Supporters argued the area between 14th and 16th streets from Cheyenne Place to Champa Street was blighted and as much in need of urban renewal as had been the Skyline District along the Larimer Street skid row. Were this believed, the logical conclusion was the entire redevelopment of downtown since World War II, complete with the 16th Street Mall and all the new building of the oil boom, had transformed the heart of 16th Street into a slum. At least city council thought as much when it created a 15-block downtown retail urban renewal district in May 1986.

Cheesman Realty loudly opposed the efforts to involve DURA in Centerstone. It feared it would not get the best price for its land. Other property owners agreed. They did not want DURA in their part of town. Skeptical members of city council likewise expressed their doubts. If the heart of downtown were blighted, the term was meaningless. It was nothing more than a cloak used by politically well-connected businesses to profit at the expense of others.

By this time, downtown fears of Cherry Creek had proven well founded. As plans for the mall were finalized in 1986, the hope of Denver haters—that outside retail would replace historic local stores—came to fruition when Saks Fifth Avenue and Neiman Marcus committed themselves to the center at First Avenue and Fillmore Street. The chains, realizing Denver was not rich enough for two of their exclusive stores, showed no interest in Centerstone. Nor was Macy's, Dillard's, or Nordstrom ready to sign on. The May D&F vigorously opposed suggestions it join the downtown project by expanding Centerstone to encompass its property between Court and Tremont places.

Though the planning office, DURA, and Denver Partnership continued to try to breathe life into Centerstone through the late 1980s and early 1990s, nothing happened. Missing were clear ownership of the land, a developer, anchors, and investors. In August 1989, the courts ordered DURA to return the land to the private owners. Seven months later, in March 1990, the judge further instructed DURA to pay the property owners $450,000 in legal fees.

The land remained a gigantic parking lot. Cheesman Realty optimistically talked about putting up its own project. Again, nothing happened. Only in 1995, after the Denver market had absorbed the massive losses generated by the oil bust and savings and loan scandal, were plans finalized for what was called the Entertainment and Fashion Pavilions on the two square-block area. To show the project, slated for occupancy by numerous generic national chains, was indeed in the Mile High City, the developers relabeled it Denver Pavilions. The 350,000-square foot edifice came in at about $107.5 million by the time it opened in November 1998. Included in the price was a $27 million DURA subsidy.

Author's Collection

*The Paramount Theater, at 1621 Glenarm Place, was the only downtown movie palace to escape destruction amidst the oil boom. Historic Denver transformed it into a general performance hall in the 1980s.*

Photo by Phil Goodstein

*To show the generic Denver Pavilions is indeed part of the Mile High City, it features a "great wall," spelling out the city's name.*

Bill Denton of Entertainment Development Group collaborated with Arthur Hill & Company in building the Denver Pavilions. He made no secret he wanted a trendy place. Instead of filling in the major voids in downtown shopping, notably the lack of a supermarket, hardware store, and Woolworth-like emporium, such fashionable mall stores as Virgin Records, Nike Town, Barnes & Noble, and the Hard Rock Cafe dominated Denver Pavilions. The urban renewal project also included a movie theater. Backers cited this as a great breakthrough. After the wave of oil-boom demolition, including the wrecking of the Denver Theatre, city hall and downtown boosters took credit for bringing back what they had previously scorned along 16th Street.

Denver bashers seized on the Pavilions project. Cheesman Realty hoped to top it off on the west side with an overbearing, 86-story highrise. The tower's advocates tore into the existing oil-boom skyline as bleak, ugly, and undistinguished. To get their latest tower approved, they vehemently denounced all the buildings of the postwar years, including those they had supported during the oil boom, notably Republic Plaza.

As its contribution to civic beauty and to show it was indeed a Colorado phenomenon, Denver Pavilions included a huge protruding sign, with letters around 35-feet-high, spelling out "DENVER." The promoters noted it was on "The Great Wall," proclaiming the project's and downtown's identity. Half of the $800,000, 356-foot-long sign was paid for by DURA. Such a banner was absolutely necessary, a spokesman for the Denver-hating Downtown Denver Partnership explained, so the 16th Street Mall would not look so much "like Wichita." Such an emphasis on cosmetics over substance also haunted the Denver Public Library.

## A Note on Sources:

Much of this chapter is based on personal observations, including working as a journalist in the mid-1980s during the Masonic Building fire and rebuilding campaign. I have consulted newspaper accounts on each of the buildings mentioned and, where they exist, files of DLPC and the listings of the National Register of Historic Places at CHS. Tom Noel, *Denver Landmarks*, gives brief, puffy looks at many of the downtown buildings. He also reviews them with Barbara Norgren in his *City Beautiful*.

The local branch of the American Institute of Architects put out a brochure, *The Denver Walking Tour*, c. 1985, celebrating the new and historic downtown structures. Also see Michael Paglia, Diane Wray, and Rodd Wheaton, *Denver: The Modern City* (Denver: Historic Denver, 1999). I examine the evolution of downtown shopping and banks in volume one, especially in the chapters on "Big Money" and "Malling 16th Street." My *Ghosts of Denver* contains a discussion of the evolution of the Cherry Creek Shopping Center.

Hal Haney recalled the campaign to save the Molly Brown House. Brown's life, career, and home are mentioned in the two modern biographies of her: Christine Whitacre, *Denver's Unsinkable Lady* (Denver: Historic Denver, 1984); and Kristen Iversen, *Molly Brown: Unraveling the Myth* (Boulder: Johnson Books, 1999.) *Historic Denver News* has reported downtown zoning and preservation controversies. Chuck Hillestead offered a scathing critique of Historic Denver in a two-part article, "What is Wrong with Historic Denver?" *Life on Capitol Hill*, July 1992 and August 1992.

Barbara Norgren talked about the operations of DLPC. Steve Leonard also shared his views about serving on the body. Langdon Morris, *Denver Landmarks*, is superior to a subsequent history of the city's landmarks, Noel, *Denver Landmarks*. I detail the fate of the Central Bank building in volume one. Adams, *Pioneer Western Bank*, treats the history of buildings housing First National Bank.

Bryan Abas, "A Big Stretch of the Imagination," *WW*, July 9, 1986, pp. 8–16, focuses on Centerstone and the role of Canadian developers. Breck, *John Evans*, is an insubstantial accolade to the Evans family, noting the origins of Cheesman Realty and the destruction of the Evans House. Scott Moore of Cheesman Realty talked about the company's operations during a brief phone interview in 1984. Zeckendorf, *Autobiography*, has a good discussion of the economics of downtown development, including the contrasting roles of landowners, builders, and managers.

Ann Morgan Woodward recalled the fight to save the Republic Building. Dianne Clark reminisced about the Denver Theatre. So did members of the Friends of the Mayan. Besides discussing the history of that cinema, they noted the evolution of movie palaces, both locally and nationally. I tell the Mayan story in my *South Denver Saga*.

# 10

# A Library in Crisis

No institution more typifies Denver's split personality than the city's foremost educational facility, the Denver Public Library (DPL). The city has mocked, ignored, attacked, and celebrated this vital resource. Supporters have often emphasized the library's trifles while city officials have undercut the institution's essence. DPL has both put together impressive collections and dispersed them. It has welcomed researchers and served as a fortress against them.

The library had a slow, tortured beginning. No sooner was Denver established than leaders agreed on the need for a reading room. Many supported this institution more because they believed a prosperous community had a library than because they actually wanted shared books and a source of community wisdom. Despite continued commitments, the Queen City struggled to create a true public library during its first 30 years.

Money was a prime consideration. While governmental funds were available for speculative railroad ventures, the library was a secondary consideration. Typical of the city's straits was an 1873 lottery designed to raise $50,000 seed money for the reading room. No sooner were the tickets sold than the operator skipped town with the proceeds. He was never caught.

During the 19th century, many fraternal societies, social clubs, and labor unions had libraries for their members and the community at large. Instead of working with everyday residents who appreciated books, newspapers, and magazines, a class bias was obvious when the city asked the Chamber of Commerce to take the lead in establishing a public library. On November 1, 1886, this body embodying corporate Denver started a subscription library of 3,000 volumes in its headquar-

Photo by L. C. McClure, DPL

*The Denver Public Library at West Colfax and Bannock Street.*

ters at the north corner of 14th and Lawrence streets. Three years later, Denver Public Schools opened a public library in East High School, on the block bordered by 19th, 20th, California, and Stout streets. That year, 1889, is the date noted as the true beginning of DPL. Beginning in 1891, the city regularly appropriated money for the venture.

Within a few years, the Chamber's library merged with the one at East High. The combined effort was officially decreed the Public Library of the City of Denver on August 13, 1898. By then, having outgrown its homes at East High and the Chamber of Commerce, the library leased space at 15th Street and Court Place. John Cotton Dana, who headed the institution from 1889 to 1897, introduced a popular open-shelf system, allowing readers to browse as opposed to the standard policy of having patrons request books on call slips. Even so, the library was not sure all books should be available to the public. In 1902, it banned *Huckleberry Finn* as "immoral and sacrilegious."

The city needed a true library building. DPL moved its collection of books to La Veta Place at the southeast corner of West Colfax Avenue and Bannock Street in 1903. Its new home was in an instant slum. Banker David Moffat financed the construction of La Veta Place in the early 1880s as Denver's first, elite, suburban luxury townhouse complex. Eventually, Augusta Tabor owned it, renting apartments to members of Denver high society. Following the silver crash of 1893 and her death in 1895, the property quickly went downhill. As the library moved in, bats flew from the once fashionable abode and bedbugs crawled out of layers of wallpaper. The solution was to tear down La Veta Place for a library building.

This was the era of the robber barons. One, Andrew Carnegie, sought to atone for the dirty deeds of the masters of capital by giving back to communities. A strong exponent of self-help and education, Carnegie financed public libraries. While DPL methodically drew up plans for a $400,000 building, a Denver booster, William L. Palm, independently approached Carnegie in 1902, asking him to help pay for the library. Carnegie responded to Palm's wish, granting the city $200,000. DPL had to hustle to get the rest of the money for the structure it put up where La Veta Place had stood. The library opened on February 15, 1910, in a $430,000 facility, with 300,000 volumes. Besides books, the library also had art works. It further included the Colorado Collection, a diverse array of newspaper clippings and other documents about Denver and the region.

An eight-member mayorally appointed commission oversaw the library. To assure a feminine touch, the 1904 city charter specified at least two of the commissioners be women. The charter further mandated a minimum annual city appropriation of $30,000 for the library.

Generally, members of high society served on the library board. In the forefront was Anne Evans (1871–1941). The daughter of territorial governor John Evans, she was on the commission from 1907 until 1940. Real estate developer Frederick R. Ross joined her. He was a board fixture from 1906 until his death in 1938, bequeathing the institution a trust fund for library construction. People with ties to city hall likewise were on the commission.

Politicians and boosters tended to support the library on a pragmatic basis: the institution was abstractly a good thing whereby Denver was a better community

Photo by Phil Goodstein

*Neighborhood activists forced the city to keep the Byers Library, at the southwest corner of West Seventh Avenue and Santa Fe Drive, open when the library administration sought to shut libraries in poorer sections of town in the early 1950s.*

for business since it had an impressive central library. These individuals often valued the library more for show than as a facility embodying the area's commitment to education and self-learning. On occasion, the prime qualification for the chief librarian was his ability to mix with members of the city's self-proclaimed smart set.

Patrons flocked to the library. In response to popular demand and new grants from Carnegie, DPL opened its first branches in 1912. These neighborhood libraries allowed the central institution to emerge as a reference facility, a source of knowledge, a collection of vital, rare, and expensive books never leaving the building. It was a place where anyone seeking to learn could go. The librarians were there to assist patrons, not to question the hows, whys, or wherefores of a researcher's investigations.

Generally, the library reflected the city. During the heyday of the Ku Klux Klan in the 1920s, efforts were made to reshape the library and its holdings in the image of that organization. A decade later, a church-sponsored censorship campaign targeted certain allegedly scurrilous and sex-filled books for elimination. Over the years, DPL banned such volumes as Ernest Hemingway's *A Farewell to Arms*, Tom Paine's *Age of Reason*, *Battle Cry* by Leon Uris, Sinclair Lewis' *Kingsblood Royal*, and *The Man with a Golden Army* by Nelson Algren.

Many opposed such limitations on books and the free flow of ideas. DPL, they insisted, must be a true library, housing books from all slants and perspectives in a tolerant, democratic, open-minded community. Though they lost some specific battles, advocates of a free press and free library generally emerged triumphant as DPL flourished as a distinguished regional center of books.

## Library Growth

The library continually grew. By 1935, the central building desperately needed an addition. The facility was badly overcrowded. DPL expanded operations, occupying nearby space at 15th Street and Cleveland Place for classes and forums. Not until 1947, did the city ask residents to approve a $2.5 million bond issue to make way for more books and storage space. Though the electorate said yes to the measure, it rejected a companion proposal to move the library through acquiring property for the facility as part of a concert hall/performing arts center. By their vote Denverites clearly preferred keeping the library where it was. City hall, scorning the existing building as old and as bad as everything else dating from the prewar epoch, insisted DPL move. Continual delays consequently occurred in city efforts to redress the library's lack of space.

DPL was in flux in the early 1950s. The library commission shut branch libraries in poor neighborhoods. The pro-development body implied lower-income individuals did not use or deserve these reading rooms. Consequently, it closed the Elyria branch at 47th Avenue and High Street on February 14, 1952. It also discontinued operations at the Dickinson Library at West Conejos Place and Hooker Street in 1954. Only a determined neighborhood fight saved the Byers Library at West Seventh Avenue and Santa Fe Drive. The library had already closed extension branches in Globeville and Valverde before World War II.

The Cosmopolitan branch, at 27th and Welton streets in the heart of Five Points, was an on-and-off operation during this epoch. It opened on October 5, 1939, as a library specifically geared to blacks, complete with "Race literature." DPL shuttered it on December 31, 1951, citing a lack of funds. One who pushed reestablishing it was the first African-American on the library commission, Oglesvie "Sonny" Lawson. In November 1974, with the assistance of federal funds, DPL recreated a branch at the Five Points Community Center at 2855 Tremont Place. The Bill McNichols administration aimed to shut it at the peak of the oil boom in 1979. City councilman Elvin Caldwell forced the mayor to retreat on this matter.

As DPL deprived old residential areas of library services, the commission pushed new buildings in emerging suburban sections. It also selected a site for the central library at the southwest corner of West 14th Avenue and Broadway. Car dealerships had previously been in the area. DPL kept part of the former O'Meara Ford showroom at West 14th Avenue and Acoma Street standing, converting the structure into the children's wing of the new facility. Modernistic architect Burnham Hoyt designed the $3.3 million edifice in conjunction with the firm of Fisher & Fisher. DPL opened its new home in 1956. Wits observed the central library looked like a car showroom.

From the start, the staff had severe problems with the building. Because of inflation, the structure was only two-thirds the size projected by the 1947 bond issue. Floors were uneven and the library was immediately overcrowded. Most of the books were in the basement, only retrievable by a call system. The library immediately expressed hope about expanding the building. Supporters noted the architect had designed the edifice for additions. From the outset, DPL made it known the new home would only meet its needs for about ten years.

The central institution continued to expand. Within the main branch were numerous subsections. Foremost was the Western History Department. Evolving out of the Colorado Collection and a Western Americana emphasis authorized in 1929, this part of the library was formed in 1935 to focus on all of the country west of the Mississippi River. Located on the fourth floor of the Burnham Hoyt edifice, the Western History Department concentrated on Denver. It was packed with rich collections of clippings, artwork, manuscripts, and memorabilia about the metropolitan area.

An outstanding genealogy department elsewhere in the library complemented Western History. A poetry collection was a treasure trove of 19th-century works. Songs from around the world highlighted a folklore/folk music collection. Books and materials on airplanes were stashed away in the Ross-Barrett Historical Aeronautics Collection. Even before the ecology movement took off in the 1970s, DPL had an excellent conservation library. The Metropolitan Adult Education Council held numerous classes at the library. The library further ran the Bibliographic Center for Research, an effort dating from 1935 in regional library cooperation.

The central branch was never all-embracing. It did not seek to mirror or compete with academic libraries. Staffers sometimes told researchers they were out of luck at DPL: if they needed more scholarly resources, they had better go to a university library.

CHS

*The 1956 Denver Public Library.*

The library hosted a wide variety of public functions. During the late 1970s, chess and checker players gathered in one room of the central branch. The 372-seat Wyer Auditorium in the basement served as the site for public hearings, concerts, movies, lectures, and library-sponsored programs.

The auditorium memorialized Malcolm Glenn Wyer (1877–1966). He headed the library between 1924 and 1951. Besides pushing Western History and the Bibliographic Center, Wyer helped establish the school of librarianship at the University of Denver (DU) in 1931. For years, there was a close working relationship between the college and DPL. Many graduates of the DU program took jobs at the library. They were often people who had grown up in Denver and the library and were proud to join the institution. Those who worked for the library had an élan as part of a vital team.

## Barbarians at the Gate

As Denver boomed in the 1970s, the central library suffered. Under Bill McNichols, the city had little use for DPL. In the early 1970s, some members of city council expressed outrage when they learned the library had revolutionary literature on public display, including the writings of Marx, Mao, and the new left. Generally, though, they left the library alone.

While Denver grew by leaps and bounds during the oil boom, city hall more or less ignored the library as a trivial appendage, something draining money from public coffers. Opposed to providing adequate library financing, the McNichols administration poured municipal funds into annexations, sports palaces, and highways. The administration let funding for the library stagnate while inflation soared. In 1972 and 1980, McNichols rejected proposals to include money to expand the central library in sweeping bond issues. (The 1972 ballot included a successful $1.5 million bond to build three branch libraries.)

Growth, in other words, was no friend of the library. Ruling Denver did not treat the central institution as a vital public service equal to police and fire protection; on the contrary, it dismissed DPL as a luxury. Right when promoters were insistently claiming growth was good since it promised new tax revenues for public services, the city shut the library on Sundays in 1977—the McNichols administration explained Denver could no longer afford to keep DPL open despite all the wealth the oil boom was allegedly creating. Though the library's budget increased at this time, it far trailed the cost of living. City hall's utter scorn for DPL was shown in January 1981 when the administration closed the main library on Thursdays.

This was only the beginning. Sometimes, the library dimmed lights during regular hours. Supposedly, this was to save energy. The reality was to make it a less friendly place for users—individuals with poor eyesight could not read there because the lighting was so bad. The administration cut 20 percent of the staff. Patrons found it harder to get books. Departments were consolidated. Only powerful public protests and opposition from city council prevented the McNichols administration from closing some of the branch libraries.

The 1956 building was showing its age. It had not been well constructed. The flat roof leaked and the structure often seemed a maze, continually redesigned as the library moved its holdings about. Many employees and friends of the library were sure the city had made a monumental blunder 25 years earlier when it committed itself to the 14th and Broadway building. The library administration stated it was "undesirable" to expand the main branch, an edifice it dismissed as a hopelessly obsolete relic of bad 1950s architecture.

The library was caught in the crossfire of disputes between Denver and the suburbs. Representatives from the latter dominated the General Assembly. Scorning and hating the Mile High City, legislators loudly made it known they would not appropriate any state funds for DPL. Denver claimed such revenues were vital. More than just Denverites patronized the central library. Its holdings and resources overshadowed those of all the suburban libraries combined. As the city

Photo by Phil Goodstein

*Bookstores complement the library in serving a literate community. Shown is Capitol Hill Books, at the southeast corner of Colfax Avenue and Grant Street.*

suffered from the financial crunch of the oil boom, DPL demanded the suburbs help pay for the main library as a statewide institution. When the legislature refused to provide funds in 1981, virtually declaring war on DPL and all city cultural institutions, the library struck back. In October 1981, it closed the main branch to non-Denverites.

For the next year, all people wishing to use the central library were required to display a library card upon entering the building. Nonresidents, including out-of-state researchers, had to pay high daily fees for access to its collections. A side consequence: the percentage of city residents holding library cards soared from 23.67 percent in 1980 to 48.5 percent by 1985.

Chief librarian Henry G. Shearouse, in office since 1969, projected DPL as the "university of the people." He clashed with the library commission over closing the building. He crusaded for more funds for the institution. The new Federico Peña administration treated him as a part and parcel of the McNichols regime. The library commission dismissed Shearouse in March 1984.

Educated, articulate, well-read suburbanites were angry about DPL shutting its doors to them. They called their representatives, demanding action. Under such pressure, a number of suburban systems agreed to help pay for DPL. Some library advocates called for an area-wide library district whereby DPL would no longer be a city institution, but a metropolitan one. While this did not make it off the drawing board, by 1985 state funding of the library was back at its previous level. Colorado then established a statewide library system. The central branch once more functioned as a free public library open to all who wished to use it.

## The Library's Mission

The library struggled to define its niche within the community when it held a major conference on June 15–16, 1984, entitled "Is There a Library in Your Future?" While city hall and the library commission had a well-set agenda for the institution, the forum did not work out according to plans. On the contrary, the meeting was actually a serious discussion of the crises faced by public libraries.

Leading librarians from across the country addressed the conclave. They discussed the educational role of a public library and why it must function as a center of knowledge, civilization, and community continuity. Libraries everywhere were beset by barbarians—politicians and administrators who could only define greatness in mass complexes lacking heart, soul, or substance. Unscrupulous forces, who wished to turn libraries into adjuncts of big business, threatened the basic principles of these educational institutions.

Many at the conference were highly skeptical of making libraries part of Mayor Peña's beloved public/private partnership. By giving the private sector a crucial role in determining the operations and fate of the library, the institution would betray its essential public service and mission. Not only would private money imply private control, but it would not assure any more funds for the library. Speakers from other cities noted how, when private financing had increased, public revenues for the library were often cut back by the politicians/philistines extolling the public/private partnership.

Dr. Vatran Gregorian, the head of the New York Public Library, delivered the keynote speech at a high-priced banquet at the Brown Palace. The audience was an affluent crowd, proud of the library and city hall's commitment to a corporate modernization of the institution. It hoped DPL was at a positive turning point, having overcome the worst of the McNichols regime.

DPL was not the only public library suffering at this period. New York City administrators had forged a model for Denver, closing the New York Public Library for two days a week in the late 1970s/early 1980s. Gregorian fought back. He was not only an administrator, but an effective missionary of the public library ideal. The barbarians, he noted, were not only at the gates, but had breached the walls of Denver by attacking its most vital educational/cultural institution. They had already closed DPL two days a week and were threatening even worse.

Gregorian cited the continual laments about wide-scale functional illiteracy, cultural ignorance, and historical amnesia in a country beset by an information explosion. The library was a guardian against this. Not simply a collection of books and documents, the library was a place organizing resources to help transform collections of raw information into knowledge. Otherwise, new technologies would only barrage the populace with endless trivia.

The library, the speaker emphasized, must take pride in its obscure and arcane holdings. While these collections might seem to have no value to the simple-minded today, their worth would be obvious tomorrow amidst a political upheaval, war, or discovery. The worst thing any central library could do was to dump such assets for momentary public acclaim via focusing on bestsellers and trendy topics. "The ABCs come before the PCs," he announced, rebutting the belief computers were the solution to all learning and research problems. Books would always be at the heart of a good library's holdings. It was the library's responsibility to protect the treasured volumes of yesterday despite all of the political and business pressures of today. Only cultural illiterates would tolerate a library junking its holdings based on temporary patron demands or circulation records.

The conference got good publicity. The library launched a campaign for public suggestions. Funding was restored to reopen the library on Thursdays and Sundays. The city and library commission agreed on the need to replace the 1956 building. Officially, the main branch had been at 100-percent capacity since 1967. A new head librarian, Dr. Rick J. Ashton, took charge in July 1985. Under him, many of the suggestions and lessons of the conference were turned on their heads.

There was, for example, the issue of the public/private partnership. Far from questioning whether the very concept was a total sellout of the public resources to the private sector, the library sought to market itself to corporate Denver. Time and again, promoters noted the central library had a very rich business collection. This allowed companies to save thousands of dollars while enhancing the corporate climate. The financial community should recognize this by embracing the library.

As it advertised its business holdings, the library ignored labor. Not only were there no major collections about unions, but there were few labor newspapers or journals in the periodicals section. Loud proponents of the library's collaboration

Photo by Phil Goodstein

*As part of the public/private partnership, the library sometimes closed during regular hours to host high-society affairs at the central building.*

with business pretended the subject had not been raised when critics suggested the library should hold labor history programs comparable to those it sponsored about business. (The Stephen Hart Library of the Colorado Historical Society mirrored DPL in this respect—it went out of its way to emphasize its business history collections. The Colorado Historical Society's monthly newspaper paid special attention to companies giving the organization considerable sums. Insofar as possible, the organization's corporate leadership treated labor as a nonexistent part of the Centennial State's past.)

While the library's business holdings soared, other sections were endangered. DPL dismantled its conservation library in the 1980s. Opposed to specialized collections geared for researchers, Ashton saw the central library as primarily a massive branch library, one focusing on bestsellers. The institution evaluated itself on the number of books checked out. It labeled patrons "customers."

Typical was the pronouncement of Carol King, head of DPL's collection development:

> We make a concerted effort to provide our customers with what they say they want. We've cut back on expensive, scholarly books and magazines that aren't

used much. Let the academics do the academic part. We're becoming a public library.

On this basis, the library abrogated all responsibility to serve as a center of knowledge and valuable, rare, controversial, and irreplaceable holdings. Instead, it sought to pander to a popular demand. Since "expensive, scholarly books and magazines" were not used much, they were treated as dead space that had to go. In their place, the central branch focused on trendy volumes, talking books, CDs, and other items readily available in bookstores. It discontinued branch library subscriptions to liberal magazines such as *The Nation* and *Z*. Librarians explained "customers" failed to check them out—those reading the periodicals in the library were of no account to the cost-accounting system favored by King and Ashton. In such a manner, the educational focus of the library was abandoned. This was how DPL was "becoming a public library."

Such actions outraged many veterans of the library, proud of its past educational accomplishments. The more DPL supposedly became a public library, the more staff morale plummeted. Some friends of the library were sure conditions were worse than during the bad times of McNichols. That mayor had only closed the library. Under Peña and Ashton, the heart of the facility was gutted. Frightened librarians, afraid to give their names to reporters, desperately sought to leak information about the mismanagement of the institution. They feared they might be punished or lose their jobs by going public. Chief librarian Ashton, they gossiped, had been called "Little Hitler" in his previous post as director of the Allen County Public Library in Fort Wayne, Indiana. He was, they lamented, living up to his reputation.

Newspapers were not interested in what was going on at DPL. On the contrary, they jumped on the library administration's bandwagon as it projected a destruction of resources and the public/private partnership as the city's future. They also rallied behind DPL's effort to construct a castle-like edifice as its new home.

## A Disney World Building

Debates whirled about such a structure. While all supporters of the library agreed the existing facility was inadequate, there was no consensus about where a new building should be, the nature of its design, or the fate of the 1956 edifice. Chief librarian Ashton's plan was simply to put the books in storage for a year or so while the existing building was razed and the replacement structure went up. In the meanwhile, the library would make a few volumes available for "customers" at a nearby hall.

Library lovers found Ashton's proposal inconceivably arrogant. The shutting of the facility implied it was not a crucial, indispensable asset educating people daily, but simply a showpiece, a glorified bookstore reflecting Denver's affluence. Those who would countenance such a closing scorned the library as only a decoration in the City Beautiful, something like parks, sculptures, and fountains. The adoption of such a perspective showed Dr. Gregorian had understated the threat to the library: vandals were now guarding the central treasures.

Photo by Doug Gerash

*The library turned an old Ford service structure into the children's section of the 1956 library. The sign was uncovered during construction of the new library in the mid-1990s.*

Little organized opposition existed to Ashton's plan. The main objection came from lovers of modern architecture. Not only had international design with flat roofs and blank walls swept the city and country after World War II, but its exponents embraced it as vital, modern art. They went out of their way to project themselves as sophisticates of beauty. Only the uncouth, they lamented, mocked the ugliness of the 1956 library. Actually, they loudly asserted, it was a masterpiece of enticing design. Like the emperor's new clothes, the beauty was too new to be seen. Before long, they were sure, everybody would join them in recognizing the loveliness of the 1956 structure. One and all would see the car showroom as a stunning example of the modern American renaissance. So Denver could always appreciate the international-style Denver Public Library, they managed to get the city to declare the dysfunctional postwar building a landmark.

This set the debate. The new library was *not* envisaged as a structure for library users—they were nothing more than "customers." On the contrary, it was primarily a statement of public architecture. Exterior design, not interior function and holdings, was its hallmark. The door was left open for a disaster.

While architects and their supporters insistently proclaimed the beauty of modern structures, the area was haunted by three very badly designed academic libraries. Penrose Library at the University of Denver, dedicated in 1972, was right next to busy Evans Avenue. Traffic noise easily came through the walls. In a different part of the library, a problem with the heating and cooling system led to a periodic banging noise every 15 or 20 seconds. Lights frequently flickered in areas set aside for reading.

The Auraria Library opened in the mid-1970s. With long halls, it was something of a noise corridor. There were few quiet areas where students could read. Lacking shades on windows, blinding sunlight sometimes made sections of the library unusable for study during parts of the day.

Norlin Library at the University of Colorado in Boulder was totally remodeled and expanded in the late 1970s. Lights were placed up to 50 feet above tables, producing inferior reading conditions. A poor heating and cooling system plagued the building. The inferior circulation system resulted in the destruction of a number of books by mildew and mold.

Ashton stated he was fully aware of such problems. He dismissed other tales about badly built, malfunctioning libraries as "urban folklore." He told doubters he knew what he was doing. "Thank you for your comments," he perfunctorily told those questioning his decisions as he proceeded on his path to erect the new library.

City hall fully supported Ashton. The Peña administration saw the new library as a crowning achievement, the third part of its triad with DIA and the convention center. With supporters selling the library as the signature piece of the city, in August 1990 DPL asked voters to approve a $91.6 million bond issue. Besides paying for the new library, the funds were to provide for four new branch libraries in addition to sweeping improvements of and expansions to 15 existing branches.

The library question shared the ballot with the vote for a new baseball stadium. While many questioned the latter, nobody doubted the former. Even critics, who noted the plans for the new library were nebulous and in the hands of arrogant, anti-public, pro-business administrators, muted their criticism. They feared if the

Photo by Phil Goodstein

*The Michael Graves Denver Public Library.*

library bond went down to defeat, the city might well again turn its back on this vital facility. They had nothing to worry about. The bond issue overwhelming passed, winning about 75 percent of the vote.

With the money in hand, debates once more raged about the nature of the building—nothing was said about the scope of its collections. The landmark designation of the 1956 building meant the new edifice was to incorporate it. The library commission held a national competition to select the designer. Twenty architects submitted bids. DPL selected three finalists. It placed models of their proposed library on display in the existing facility. Enthusiasts noisily raved over them, readily disrupting "customers" in the process. The library was not about books, knowledge, culture, or literacy their actions said; above all else, it was an architectural statement.

After a four-month review, in March 1991, an 11-member committee tabbed Michael Graves of Princeton, New Jersey, as the architect for the new building. He was responsible for theme-park hotels at Disney World. His proposal for DPL looked like an extension of them. (In 1999, Target commissioned Graves to design "giftware" for its stores.) Local architect Brian Klipp collaborated with Graves on the project.

The Graves library was not a coherent structure, but a mishmash of many different compounds in one. The facility looked like everything from a pencil point sticking into the air to a helicopter landing pad to a big drum. It prominently featured flat roofs in spite of the severe leakage problems the library had with the flat roof at its landmark building.

None of the parts of the Graves library fit in with the existing neoclassical architecture of the adjacent Civic Center. The closest the architect came to recognizing the proximity of the Civic Center was his proposal to line the structure with Indiana limestone, comparable to the stone at the Greek Theater and the 1956 showroom. As it turned out, precast concrete was used for the exterior of the library. The edifice lacked a uniform color whereby the Graves tower did not match the Civic Center or existing building. Imported limestone from Germany was used above the main entrance. It quickly crumbled: the building material was unable to withstand the Colorado climate. DPL had to replace it with granite in 1998. Nor were steps at the main entrance well-marked. Patrons sometimes stumbled on them. The library completely redesigned and rebuilt its Broadway entrance in 1999.

Such was the result of a structure primarily viewed as a signature piece. The new library was an isolated monolith standing apart from the neighborhood. Little of the neighborhood was left. The city destroyed most of the nearby buildings for a library parking lot to the south of 13th Avenue where it had once planned to place the convention center.

Graves made it clear he had no use for the architecture or traditions of Denver. When he came to town, he insistently made a point of staying at the only hotel with a design he liked, the generic Westin Hotel in the Tabor Center. Its interior was an indistinguishable clone of other modern hotels. The meaning was obvious: the Brown Palace, Oxford Hotel, and other 19th-century landmarks were thor-

Photo by Phil Goodstein

*Part of the new DPL looks like a pencil point sticking in the air.*

oughly obsolete—just like traditional conceptions of libraries designed for users and researchers.

With kazoos playing and "bookclappers" cheering—part of the library's elaborate public relations team—the city broke ground for the new library in 1992. Mayor Wellington Webb, who had worked in the library as a shelver as a teenager and headed the library commission at the time it hired Ashton, proudly declared "You can't have a great city without having a great library." The building was seven stories high with 404,450 square feet opposed to the 133,400 square feet of the 1956 edifice. The combined structure was the eighth largest public library in the country. The cost was $71.9 million. The other $19.7 million from the bond issue went to the branch libraries.

During the next few years, many of the branches were redesigned or rebuilt. In some cases, notably at the Park Hill Library, the remodeling was a vast improvements over a 1960s expansion which had threatened the building's historic character. In other cases, especially at Cherry Creek, the redesign looked as if it was deliberately left unfinished, filling the entrance to the library with an obstacle course. Nonetheless, the Cherry Creek branch was a well-conceived, ideally functioning building compared to the central library where abstract modernistic concepts were everything; the actual purpose of the library as a center of knowledge was nothing.

As work began on the signature piece of the modern Mile High City, there was the question of the what would happen to the existing central library during construction. Once more, the anti-research administration simply wanted to close it down. The "customers," noted Ashton, had been "severely inconvenienced for 25 years already." Another year or two would not make much difference since an architectural masterpiece would result. City council objected. Its members had a far greater appreciation of the value of the library than did the facility's leadership. Since hospitals, airports, and other vital public services do not close during reconstruction, council members decided, neither should the library.

Under such pressure, Ashton agreed to keep much of the central library open during construction of the Disney World annex. The library moved assorted collections from the building whereby patrons were denied access to them. The administration told some volunteers their services were no longer wanted—they might get in the way of construction and empire building. As the new edifice neared completion in late 1994, Ashton got his way when the whole central library was shut down for three months. No alternative hall was provided.

Users howled, but they were dismissed as cranks. They simply wanted their library and did not appreciate the demands of progress. DPL leadership forgot or scorned the words of Dr. Gregorian to the 1984 conference: the library is a center of culture, continuity, and civilization. No place proud of its central library would tolerate such a decision. Denver easily did.

## A Sick Building

The new building opened on March 25, 1995. Newspapers and 17th Street gloried in it as a dream come true. Led by mutual fund firms and Cadillac dealers, the private sector sponsored an elite, grand celebration. Crowds flocked in, curious to see the building.

The first thing they noticed was the noise. The entrance led to a three-story-high atrium, an empty sound chamber. Much of the library was still incomplete and numerous volumes were stacked on carts since many book shelves were not yet installed. Some collections, including biographies, were still inaccessible. Tables and chairs were rare in the stacks. Beepers sounded near the Western History Department, effectively breaking the concentration of "customers."

In a thoroughly venal move, the library plastered names of corporate sponsors and affluent individuals on the walls of the interior. No identification was given of exactly who these people were or how they had come to make their fortunes or assisted literacy. The implication: these companies and benefactors, not the people of Denver through a bond issue, were responsible for the building. The new edifice had no Wyer Auditorium. (DPL added a tiny Wyer foyer on the fifth floor in 1999.) Little at the facility honored librarians or authors; mostly, rather, it extolled big-money interests.

To note that architecture was the library's keynote, DPL designated the 1956 wing the Hoyt Library after its designer, Burnham Hoyt. That section held most of the central branch's circulating books. It functioned far better than the new structure or than it ever had as the main building.

The general reaction of everyday people to the Disney World piece was absolute amazement. They could not believe sophisticates hailed such a hodgepodge as the home of Denver's most vital learning resource. Patrons dismissed the Graves work as gaudy and garish. They mocked the tower as everything from a medieval village to the meanderings of a child with a play construction set to a southern California beach house. *Denver Post* columnist Tom Gavin, when asked how to find the library, gave the following directions: go south on the west side of Broadway from Colfax; when you start madly laughing at an absolutely ridiculous building, you will know you are in front of the library.

To show one and all that the Disney World clone was a joke, in October 1998, the library received a defining work of public art along West 14th Avenue outside the 1956 building, *The Yearling*. It was a tiny horse standing on a 20-foot-high steel chair designed by New York artist Donald Lipski. The library did not select the $150,000 work; Denver Art Museum did. In particular, a rich art lover who had been a Denver Art Museum curator, Nancy Tieken, foisted it on the library and people of Denver. An example of the public/private partnership in action, she used her wealth and influence to make sure that her tastes were those of the city.

The new library was not user friendly. It was designed whereby it was exceedingly hard to get from one floor to another or even across sections of the same floor. The administration considerably beefed up the security staff. Most of the guards were quite helpful and accommodating. They had a better sense of locations and collections than did some of the staff. Members of the security force sometimes even pulled files for users.

Nothing fazed the administration. As much as the proponents of the airport and convention center, it had a skilled public relations team. Promotion rather than actual resources, convenience of patrons, and access, was everything. Problems were ignored. Complaints about the building were left unanswered despite Ashton's request that "customers" send him "Dear Rick" letters with their questions about the facility.

Typical of how little the library cared for its holdings was the structure's roof. As had been foretold when the first plans for the building were unveiled, a flat roof meant water problems. Nor was Ashton's promise to take care of this carried out. On the contrary, water leakage was part and parcel of construction. This was confirmed during an extremely wet spring in 1995. Thousands of books and documents were damaged by a leaking roof in a section of the old building. Humidity caused further problems. Tarpaulins were used to protect other volumes.

Water problems continued when the new building opened. The tarpaulins came in handy to guard against its leaking roofs. Ceiling tiles became mottled. Mildew spots appeared. By Memorial Day weekend, water had leaked into the basement where nearly half-a million volumes were stored. The library dismissed this as a minor inconvenience. Actually, it was a sign of how poorly the building was designed and administered. Problems with leaking roofs continued into the late 1990s. The architectural masterpiece so proved as dysfunctional a building as the 1956 landmark. Far more books were damaged or destroyed by the building's bad design than by "customers."

Photo by Phil Goodstein

The Yearling *is the name of the horse atop the chair next to the 1956 wing of the central library.*

Some of the staff complained about the poor quality of air circulation in the library. They also lamented about having to walk forever to get various files for "customers." Those coming into or going out of the temple of books often had to pass through clouds of tobacco smoke. The administration did not even have the courtesy to isolate smoking spots to avoid such a nuisance.

Individuals seeking to use DPL quickly discovered far more prosaic problems with it. Foremost was terrible lighting. The main reading room of the Western History Department—the vastly overrated pride and joy of the facility—had constant shadows and glaring reflections. The administration paid no more heed to this shortcoming than any of the other problems with the showpiece. Instead of redressing the bad lighting, promoters of the library claimed the reading room was designed to look something like the base of an oil derrick. It had excellent acoustics whereby whispering in one part of the room could be heard in other parts of it.

Nor was the reading room conducive to research. The administration hated notebooks. It prevented "customers" from bringing them into the reading room. Instead of allowing patrons to use traditional writing materials, DPL encouraged them to use noisy, energy-consuming laptop computers. In other words, some library users, such as affluent computer addicts, were treated far more favorably than people who liked notebooks. Without notebooks, some users inadvertently pressed their cards and pieces of paper against old maps, newspapers, and manuscripts, thereby endangering the collections.

A pompous insecurity pervaded the Western History Department. All sorts of show security measures, which had never been found necessary in the old building, were imposed in the name of protecting manuscripts. Researchers using them were restricted to a special room that sometimes got quite crowded. Those looking at photos were assigned to a table where the lighting was even worse than in the rest of the library. A prissy, self-righteousness predominated some of the staff. Often these were the same librarians who were not concerned when damaged books were called to their attention or the unwitting damage caused by the prohibition of notebooks.

Nor was it easy to see some manuscripts at the library. Despite the cramping of the old library, requested materials would usually be brought to a patron within five minutes. Now, with the super secured new library with its luxurious spaces, those requesting to see special collections were often told the next day was the soonest they could examine them. Nor did the library have an efficient call system compared to the old building. Individuals needing to get materials not on the shelves sometimes had to wait for a librarian to call a clerk to run half a block away to get some clippings, photos, or books. (The library preferred having "customers" ask for help. Each time they did so, the administration registered another patron contact which it added to its "sales" record.)

None of this was surprising. As the library made it plain the private half of the public/private partnership dominated the facility, much of the administration projected itself as an exercise in power. A poor morale radiated in bad attitudes. Librarians sometimes did not know the full extent of the collections they served. On occasion, they would outright lie to patrons rather than making the extra effort to help users find a piece of information or a missing volume. Nor did the library aggressively seek public documents whereby its Government Documents section served as a depository of city records and actions.

This condescension toward researchers in the name of protecting rare holdings contrasted with the library's failure to guard its collections when they were threatened by the noise of a Grand Prix race right outside the windows of the old building in the early 1990s. Not only had the library administration failed emphatically to protest that the sporting affair could cause a crash endangering the library, but it readily closed the educational center for a few days on its account. It also sometimes closed the library early so it could host high society banquets in the main building. The heads of DPL so showed that, far more than protecting the institution's treasure trove of knowledge, they wanted to rule an empire.

## A Computer Fixation

Insofar as the library had a way of dealing with some of its heavily used, but fragile volumes, it was to seal them from "customers." It microfilmed assorted city directories and building permits. The job was often badly done. The microfilm was frequently hard to read and sometimes virtually illegible. The administration placed some microfilm readers in spots where the screens reflected the glare of outside windows. There were no curtains on the latter. Where reference volumes remained, there were frequently no nearby chairs or tables. The volumes were quite heavy and patrons had to haul them quite a distance before they could use them. "Customers" could not always keep from abusing the tomes in the process. Once more, the open impression was books were for show, not the convenience of the people of Denver.

The library had a computer fixation. Card catalogs disappeared for computer terminals. At first, the books listed on the computer catalog did not come close to having all the library's holdings on them. Old volumes, consequently, were virtually inaccessible. Sometimes, patrons only discovered these resources thanks to the extra effort of librarians and shelving clerks who went out of their way to find them. The computers were often exceedingly slow. Information on them was not always accurate. No sooner had DPL joined hands with local academic libraries in the Colorado Alliance of Research Libraries (CARL), where the collections of all the libraries were accessible via computer terminal, than the University of Colorado and Auraria libraries adopted alternative computer systems.

The terminals at DPL were continually modified. On-line computer systems, which increasingly replaced the simple CARL system, were not always as specific about the nature of holdings and ability to search the collection as were the machines they displaced. With the computer reliance, complete access to the holdings was often worse than it had been in the card catalog epoch.

When the computer system went down, a not infrequent event, the library was at a standstill. It was as if a vandal had nailed all the card catalogs shut. This did not embarrass DPL; on the contrary, it tried to explain away its keeping an irreplaceable reference card catalog in Western History—it feared other computer addicts would mock it for retaining the old efficient technology.

Photo by Phil Goodstein

*The former Warren Library, at the southeast corner of 34th Avenue and High Street, is today a church.*

Photo by Phil Goodstein

*The Pauline Robinson Library, at the northwest corner of 33rd Avenue and Holly Street, honors the city's first black librarian.*

Forgetting Dr. Gregorian's observation that "the ABCs come before the PCs," DPL increasingly relied on computers. Staffers at the facility, including non-trained assistants, simply told people to look at the Internet for answers to their questions. Not only did this ignore the highly selective and problematic nature of materials on the Internet, but it was a denial of the very purpose of a library. Any such institution worthy of its name is a collection of books, clippings, brochures, and other sources of information allowing a person to study and evaluate documents, judging their accuracy for himself. Opposed to this, seeing the library as a superfluous luxury, the administration projected the Internet as a replacement for basic library holdings. The educational institution was no longer a place where a seeker could discover how much myth and folklore was foisted on the public as fact via the advertising-filled Internet; it was simply a place encouraging them to rely on that dubious, trendy source.

With its computer fixation, the library even failed to provide basic sources of information for its "customers." Readily usable printed materials, notably bus schedules, disappeared from the library. People needing them—these sheets of paper had been part of the library for years—were once more told to check the Internet. For a while, the library did not even have the courtesy to stock tax forms.

Materials printed out from computer bases were frequently not nearly as concise as the actual documents the library once preserved. Computerized newspaper articles, for instance, did not include photos with them. Nor could a researcher get an idea of the placement and layout of the story—a clue to how the news was reported. Indexing to newspapers was incredibly superficial. Opposed to an excellent clipping index of local newspapers and magazines the library had kept for decades, it increasingly relied on a shallow, highly selective, gap-filled index prepared by Bell & Howell for the *Denver Post.* (Rather than hiring librarians to index documents, the library subscribed to outside indexing services.) Despite the heavy computer emphasis and voluminous amounts of information, the actual accessible indexing and materials on the 1990s were often far more scanty than those on the 1890s.

Among those eagerly applauding this was Governor Roy Romer. As a politician who frequently shifted his stances and denied past positions in his years in office from 1987 until 1999, he had no use for archives and community continuity. This, at least, was his clear message when he called for abolishing the Colorado State Archives in the early 1990s, citing state budget shortfalls. When massive protests ensued, he oversaw the imposition of stiff fees on people wishing to dig out records there. Even when the state had a budget surplus requiring it to refund some taxes in the late 1990s, the archive fees remained in place.

The library administration had little more appreciation of its own past than did the governor. DPL lacked well-indexed, readily accessible collections about its own buildings and projects. This was not surprising since the library considerably scaled back its clipping operations. A few librarians went so far as to ponder eliminating those crucial holdings.

Amidst the library's worship of the computer, it briefly appeared to take a stand of principle against eager censors. Demagogic politicians, who never cared for the integrity of the library, screamed that the prime purpose of the Internet was pornography. They feared Internet connections in the library would provide outlets through which youngsters could explore human sexuality. Various libraries sought to place filters and limits on computers. Governor Bill Owens, shortly after taking office in 1999, threatened to cut $2 million in state funding from public and school libraries if they did not engage in such censorship. DPL at least proclaimed the free use of its computer networks.

This created problems. The administration no longer allowed individuals to sit down and play each other in chess at the library as it once had. Locals, though, could play chess on the Internet in the library. Some hogged the machines all day for such games. Others employed the computers for personal e-mail. Librarians started to circulate near the monitors, chiding boys who might be laughing in front of a machines. DPL installed screens in the children's section. The library placed time limits on certain computers, requiring patrons to check-in on them via a library card.

Even as the computer became the dictator of the library, the machines were often exceedingly slow. Sometimes it took upwards of five minutes just to find if the library had a specific holding. Now and then, it had the book though the computer did not show the volume under its title or author. At other times, the machines locked up, rendering the library a prisoner of this technology. DPL's most valued accomplishment was making it easy for "customers" to renew books over the phone and place them on hold without the intervention of a live person.

## A Whorehouse for Rent

The ultimate insult the city gave friends and users of the library came in 1997 when it threatened the very safety of the building. This stemmed from Denver's hosting the Summit of the Eight. It was a make-believe event, a gathering of the heads of the seven most powerful capitalist countries who had banded together in an organization known as the Group of Seven (G-7). They were joined by the president of Russia. The G-7 annually convened. Its sessions were primarily for show. Little of substance ever came from such meetings. Denver took the bogus affair extremely seriously.

From the time the Mile High City snagged the conclave, area leaders made it known residents must sacrifice their everyday comforts so Denver could use the G-7 to market the city to the greedy and crass. Led by the media, insecure provincials rigorously tried to convince themselves they were really important since the world manipulators were coming to town. To assure the maximum inconvenience of the public, the politicians and police closed down crucial arterials. Newspapers barraged the citizenry with endless tripe about the summit. The result was to interfere with the daily routines of all except those who were super high society. Only at the last minute, though, did the wise planners of the media event decide precisely where the governmental leaders were to gather.

As the Summit of the Eight loomed, diplomatic experts, working with locals, decided to hold it at Denver Museum of Natural History in City Park. Nobody told the facility's owners—the people of Denver and the taxpayers who supported it through extra sales and property taxes—about this. Nor were individuals who took out memberships in the museum asked how they felt about transforming the

Photo by Phil Goodstein

*Highrises overwhelm the mountains as one looks west at the lake in City Park. The city initially sought to feature this view by holding the Summit of the Eight at the Museum of Natural History east of the lake. Shown is a 1999 summer concert of the Colorado Symphony.*

very nature and function of the cultural facility. On the contrary, officials simply planned to shut the museum so international politicians could assemble there.

The leaders of the world powers were to meet in a badly neglected and rarely appreciated museum lounge. Located on the western edge of the second floor of the museum, the room had a magnificent overview of the Rockies. This part of the museum was once a cherished amenity. Like the long closed-off main entrance on the west side of the museum, it was designed to give patrons a panorama of the mountains. Over the years, ignoring the view, the city let developers build high-rises west of the museum interfering with much of the mountain majesty. Rather than outrage, corporate Denver celebrated this. The boosters' most beloved photo of the city was the skyline blotting out the mountains as seen from City Park. To advertise this blemish on the city's natural amenities, ruling interests selected the museum as the ideal place to stuff the G-7.

There were intense police concerns about the summit. Both the Denver Police Department and Secret Service feared so-called terrorists might disrupt the event. In addition to the museum, the city planned to seal off most of City Park. Even at that, it was possible a missile or plane could bomb the premises. Security forces announced they would do their all to prevent this.

They never asked the larger question: If there were the slightest danger of massive destruction, how could a civilized city caring for its museum even consider having such an event in it. The leaders could be replaced in the case of a tragedy. It was impossible to duplicate many of the museum's rare holdings. The Denver haters gave no consideration to this. The most criticism directed at the museum came when the compromised cultural facility announced it was ousting a previously booked, fancy society wedding to make way for the diplomats.

Only after the arrogant forces celebrating the summit had readily disrupted the museum routine did they discover the museum would not work for the meeting. Having haughtily despised the institution's supporters, making it clear the facility was not for the people of Denver, but for international manipulators, the city and G-7 organizers were startled to discover the cultural institution had not been designed as a conference center. Immense costs loomed in redesigning it for the non-epochal event lasting less than a week. New electrical systems and communication outlets were necessary for the conference. The imperialist powers dispossessing Denverites from their museum were not about to pay for them. Therefore, the G-7 decided to go elsewhere. If this outfit had put up the money, city leaders and the museum administration would have readily destroyed the public institution for the summit. (As if it had something to hide or it seeing it had disgraced the old title, in May 2000 the facility changed its name to the Denver Museum of Nature & Science.)

When the museum backed out of the summit, the city decided to threaten an even more vital educational facility—the central Denver Public Library. When this was first suggested, the library administration showed its true colors. Far from loudly objecting, stating the main branch is the crucial gem of the city, an institution of, by, and for the people which must always be open and available to all who wish to learn, it readily announced it was for sale. Scorning and hating its "customers," DPL proclaimed its eagerness to kick out the people of Denver so the plotters of the New World Order could temporarily take possession of the main branch.

The only person in power to raise even a slight objection was a foremost advocate of selling out the library, Mayor Webb. He protested, not on the basis that the very principle of closing the library was a total insult to a literate community, but because the G-7 did not guarantee the right price for the use of his stable—apparently, the library was nothing more than a whorehouse he was ready to rent. With such a treatment of DPL, it was no wonder public relations lies about its beauty successfully drowned out the obvious fact the institution had abandoned its civic responsibility.

As was the case at the museum, security considerations for the summit paralyzed the city. Police fenced off the blocks surrounding the library. City hall decreed Denver Art Museum the personal preserve of international leaders. So was the Civic Center. Much of this was comparable to developments during the extremely unsuccessful, money-losing Grand Prix races in 1990 and 1991 when the city likewise turned the areas around the Civic Center into something of a prison camp.

Washington assisted Denver in increasing security efforts. The number-one goal was to prevent citizens from patronizing municipal cultural institutions. Authorities further welded down manhole covers and sealed sewer outlets with metal grates—apparently they needed to keep the politicians from sinking that low. The grates quickly clogged with leaves and litter, causing flash flooding after rain storms. This was another message why people should never dare walk in Denver. Inside the library, the security forces ripped out sections of lockers, leaving the scars for more than a year. The main reference section of the library was moved for the conclave, thereby threatening the key collection's integrity.

Even as they exercised this scornful hatred of Denver residents, the sponsors of the G-7 never asked whether the summit should be at the library. In case of a disaster, other politicians would emerge; nothing could ever replace many library resources. If there were the slightest danger—one requiring one-tenth of the police measures—no community with a dribbling of pride in its library would have allowed such a threat to its key educational center.

From the outset, there was a far better location for the summit than the museum or library. If such heavy security were needed, Denver already had a heavily guarded place, one isolated from the general public with conference areas—the Denver County Jail. The city could just as well have kicked out the prison's regulars in the same way the museum and library dealt with their patrons.

Those protesting the invasion of the library were dismissed as crackpots. Against them, the city pointed to the diplomatic affair as a sign of its greatness. Simultaneously, it adopted the policies of Prince Grigori Potemkin. He was prime minister under Tsar Catherine the Great in the late 18th century when massive poverty tore Russia apart, leading to powerful peasant revolts. Potemkin, the role model of pompous, deceitful, insecure manipulators, continually insisted the country was flourishing. Whenever the tsar traveled, he arranged for local authorities to place

Photo by John Schoenwalter

*Pope John Paul II stayed at the Basilica of the Immaculate Conception, at Colfax and Logan Street, during World Youth Day in 1993. The church subsequently welcomed the international dignitaries during the 1997 Summit of the Eight. The day after the conference ended, lightning struck and badly damaged the cathedral. More than one local saw the lightning strike as a sign from above about the church's failure to exorcise the evil wrought by those who readily shut the Denver Public Library for the conclave.*

beautiful facades in the villages through which she passed. These towns were so temporarily spruced up, displaying a phony beauty for her highness. As soon as Catherine had left, Potemkin's operatives removed the cosmetics and let the peasants return to their everyday misery. That was the essence of the G-7, an event at which nothing of substance happened.

Denver newspapers well realized the emptiness of the G-7 in 1998 when world leaders gathered in a villa outside of Birmingham, England. The Mile High media gave the summit minimal reportage. All their stories on it would have fit onto a page in one of their inflated sections on the Denver affair. They knew it was not worth wasting ink on an event primarily designed to make the foolish believe that something of importance was occurring.

The Summit of the Eight was Denver's second mega-event of the 1990s featuring a Potemkin Village. The first had come four years earlier, in August 1993, when Pope John Paul II came to the Mile High City for World Youth Day. This event drew around 186,000 visitors, mostly men and women in their late teens and early 20s. Compared to the G-7, it was an exuberant, democratic affair. People from diverse cultures mingled. Locals were able to view exclusive Vatican art work. Museums and libraries remained open. The Civic Center was a gathering place, one filled with impromptu debates, discussions, and friendships.

Despite the efforts of the police and policy makers, the pope even met a few everyday people. The city readily spread cosmetics on Colfax Avenue for his visit. Numerous street people disappeared from view during John Paul's stay at the Basilica of the Immaculate Conception at Logan Street and Colfax Avenue. The city gave some of the Colfax regulars lodging in jail.

The major fiasco of the pope's visit stemmed from the ineptitude of organizers of the event who were ready to manipulate the young people making the Denver pilgrimage. John Paul's service for the masses was at Cherry Creek State Park. Adolescents who had come to Denver were expected to make a trek there. To show their dedication and belief, they were encouraged to walk the 13-plus miles from the Civic Center to the reservoir.

The event occurred during a period of alternating rainy and very hot days. Visitors, out of shape or unused to Colorado's altitude, attempted to make the hike

**Photo by Phil Goodstein**

*Denver welcomed visitors during World Youth Day in 1993, an occasion marked by a visit from the pope when the library, art museum, and Civic Center were open to youths from around the world.*

on a 90-degree, humid day. Organizers failed to provide plenty of shaded and frequent rest stops for the pilgrims. On the contrary, profiteers lined the route, hoping to sell the youths drinks.

When the pilgrims finally made their way to the park, they found a crowded, muddy, and unsanitary meeting place. A paucity of portable toilets was compounded by a lack of space to move around as upwards of 200,000 turned out for the pope's public celebration. The result was massive heat stroke and suffering by individuals whom sponsors had encouraged to show their devotion by undertaking the challenging walk.

Events like the pope's visit and the Summit of the Eight were ruling Denver's glory. They were occasions through which a grasping business community sought to overcome its insecurities and hatred for its own city. Understanding this helps explain the very mixed views Denver's rulers have had of the library: On the one hand, they have basked in the new building, one usually open seven days a week opposed to the horrors of the McNichols years; on the other, their devotion to the library is show, not substance. In many ways, the same factors added up in a push for a new convention center and airport. They were also closely tied to real estate speculation and pork-barrel politics. Even while the build-it crowd succeeded on the library, it stumbled in efforts to create a massive new dam for the area, Two Forks. This leads to the vital role of water in the region.

## A Note on Sources:

Frederick J. Yonce, *The Denver Public Library: 100th Anniversary Celebration*, is a brief, official overview of the library's history. Lisa Backman of the library's Western History Department checked materials in the generally disorganized library archives for me. DPL has issued numerous brochures, newsletters, and reports. *The Outlook*, *The Inkling*, and *Dewey's Path* were among DPL internal publications, noting the people, policies, collections, and buildings of the institution. There are also annual reports by the library commission. In recent years, they have often read more like corporate/charity reports, extolling the members of the Friends of the Denver Public Library, than serious analyses of the institution. The reports and numerous other library publications are in the Government Documents section of DPL. Louisa Ward Arps, *Speaking of Books* (Denver: Denver Public Schools, 1941), includes floor plans of the old central library and maps of the city's branch libraries.

Nat Hentoff, *Free Speech for me—but not for Thee* (New York: HarperCollins, 1992), 21, notes DPL's purge of *Huckleberry Finn* in 1902. The William S. Friedman scrapbook at DPL includes materials on the 1930s censorship push. F. L. Merriam, "Open Shelves, Open Minds—and Open to Criticism?" *Denver: Monthly Magazine of the Good Life in Colorado*, July 1965, pp. 36–37, is a look at censorship issues at the library. *Westword*, October 8, 1988, p. 10, talked about some of the problems with DPL's Internet fixation. Michael Graves' career, including the library building, is in Karen Nichols, Lisa Burke, and Patrick Burke, eds., *Michael Graves: Buildings and Projects, 1990–94* (New York: Rizzoli, 1995).

Much of the comments on the modern library are based on personal experiences. I have been a heavy user of the library, especially of the Western History Department, for years. For a while, I was a volunteer there until I was told I was not wanted amidst the library's commitment to expansion. I attended the 1984 library conference and wrote it up, "The Trials and Tribulations of the Denver Public Library," *City Edition*, June 27, 1984. Many past and present staffers of the library have discussed the facility with me. Most requested anonymity, fearing retribution if their criticisms became known.

I especially wish to thank the staff of the Western History Department for its help and quality service in my various projects. Brit Kaur and Kathey Swan, former library employees, shared their insights as did retired librarian Helen Watts. The late Agie Maestroguisipie was not only a skilled librarian with an encyclopedic knowledge of Western History's photo collection, but also an astute observer of DPL. He shared his views on library developments with me. Jane Gould recalled libraries in the area, especially those at the University of Denver. Steve Fisher discussed Penrose Library, notably its special collections. George Barany, my advisor for my master's degree at DU, taught me the vital partnership between researchers and librarians.

The late Eleanor Gehres, longtime head of the Western History Department, reviewed a draft of this chapter. Carlos Martinez gave me a guard's perspective on operations at the downtown branch. Further thanks go to the librarians staffing the general reference desk and the Government Documents section. While now and then I have found librarians ignorant of the institution's holdings and not at all helpful, most are superbly committed to their jobs.

Dick Akeroyd Jr. talked about the library when he was acting director in 1984–85. Steve Savageau discussed serving on the library commission in the 1990s and the generally ineffective role of the body. Don Bain recalled his service on the commission in the mid-1980s. Pat Hodapp, a library publicist, firmly defended the institution. Bonnie McCune, Laura Christensen, Dennis Gallagher, and Tom Noel also gave me their views of the place. I have had assorted conversations with Rick Ashton about the library. His answers have been curt and officious, including "thank you for your concern," when I have expressed my belief that the library has been poorly managed and that the new building was hideously designed.

Newspaper reports and personal observations are the bases of the comments on the Summit of the Eight and World Youth Day. Valerie Abney and John Schoenwalter shared stories about the lightning strike at the Basilica of the Immaculate Conception.

# 11

# Water in the Great American Desert

Even as debates over transportation, air pollution, downtown, urban renewal, and corporate subsidies engulfed the Mile High City, the Denver Water Department (DWD) has operated with amazingly little publicity. It supplies the area with its most vital fluid: water. The agency illustrates how the city actually works.

From the time the first local pressurized water system began operations in 1872 until World War I, various private companies provided water to subscribers. Service was never very good while rates were often exorbitant. Walter Scott Cheesman consolidated assorted water firms into the Denver Union Water Company (DUWC) in October 1894. The company quickly emerged as a grasping monopoly. By the time of his death in 1907, locals widely hated Cheesman as a robber baron. His family atoned for his poor reputation by giving Denver $100,000 for a marble pavilion in exchange for the city naming a major park in Cheesman's memory.

DUWC interests often clashed with those of the city as a whole. Businessmen, who were not part of the utility clique, feared and hated the monopoly. They found themselves forced to pay extra water fees. Sections of corporate Denver loudly believed DUWC, through its high rates and poor service, was hindering the further real estate development of the area. Were the company to retain its unchecked power, it might limit the Mile High City's growth since Denver lacked a massive flow of cheap water. Simply put, the liquid was too valuable to leave its control in the hands of Cheesman's heirs and associates.

Reformers' efforts to establish a municipal water works were well underway by 1910 when voters authorized the creation of the Denver Public Utility Commission. The new body's mandate was to create and operate a city-owned water system. Though Mayor Robert Speer and his cohorts sought to block such a municipal utility, a drought during the middle teens settled the question. Water shortages loomed and DUWC was not able to provide adequate service. In the hope of assuring plenty of inexpensive water and opening up the potentials for massive growth, the electorate approved a $14 million bond issue in 1918 to buy the monopoly. On November 1 of that year, the Denver Water Department supplanted the Public Utility Commission, taking charge of the water works. By the late 1990s, the agency simply referred to itself as Denver Water.

A five-person board oversees the Water Department. Members serve staggered six-year terms, receiving a salary of $600 a year—their rate of compensation from 1918 into the 21st century. The mayor is responsible for appointing them. Once they are in office, neither the mayor nor any one else in the city has any direct control of the commissioners. Invariably board members have been individuals with strong ties to city hall and 17th Street. They have shared ruling Denver's views on water: the need for a plentiful and cheap supply.

Water is essential. Denver is on the fringe of the Great American Desert, a parched, arid zone where natural rainfall does not come close to providing the precipitation necessary to raise dependable crops. At an early day, farmers devised elaborate irrigation systems. Virtually from the time of the Pikes Peak gold rush, a detailed body of water law evolved based on the principle of prior appropriation: the first to use the water always has first right to it. The water must be employed productively. "Use it or lose it" has been the abbreviated description of the western attitude to this limited resource.

Even as water supplies have always been problematic, Denver has painted itself as a garden city, an oasis filled with lush green lawns and majestic trees. The landscaping requires immense amounts of water. Before a pressurized water system served all parts of Denver, the Mile High City was something of a little Venice, cut by numerous irrigation canals. Vestiges of them remain in the City Ditch in Washington Park, the Rocky Mountain Ditch in the Berkeley/Grand View neighborhood, the High Line Canal in sections of southeast Denver, and in assorted waterways meandering through agricultural remnants of suburbia.

Under the impetus of the City Beautiful movement, Denver became fixated with immaculate, well-trimmed, lawns. Many residents treated their yards as shrines. They spared no expense in opulently irrigating and fertilizing them. In the summer, some locals heavily watered sidewalks as waste water freely flowed down the gutters. Newspapers sponsored contests for who had the finest lawn. Promoters acclaimed the garden hose as a symbol of the Queen City's hopes, values, and aspirations. City inspectors readily cited those having too many dandelions, untrimmed grass, or the wrong kind of plants for maintaining a nuisance.

DWD

*The Denver Water Department's headquarters are near Lake Archer at West Tenth Avenue and the Platte River, the site of the city's earliest reservoir.*

The Water Board encouraged wasteful water usage. Few houses were metered. It billed customers on a flat rate based on an elaborate formula drawing on the number of rooms and taps in a house along with the square footage of its lot. The goal was to charge primarily for domestic usage while discounting water employed for the irrigation of lawns. The more water used, consequently, the less the cost. Besides, if Denver did not consume the water, California might very well claim all of Colorado's water resources as its own. These policies caused severe problems.

## Droughts

In the late 19th century, the forerunners of DWD began to develop mountain reserves. Such sources of water were crucial because of the region's sparse and irregular rainfalls. Denver has been plagued by a 20- to 30-year drought cycle. After years of sizable snow accumulations, dry winters resulted in minimal spring runoffs. By midsummer, there was not enough water for farmers and residents. Not only did such a drought spark the formation of the Denver Board of Water Commissioners in 1918, but a similar dearth of water caused severe problems in the 1930s. The eastern plains were part of the Dust Bowl and the Mile High City was parched. Only when workers converted the bore of the Moffat Tunnel into a water tunnel, bringing the life-giving liquid from the Fraser River on the Western Slope to Denver in 1936, was the city partially able to quench the drought. (A water project was part and parcel of the design of the Moffat Tunnel.)

The Mile High City was again running out of water in the 1950s. Another drought dried up the state. With well more than half of all the water used in the summer going to lawns and gardens, the Water Board imposed restrictions on landscape irrigation. Conditions were so bad Denver drew a blue line beyond which it would not annex—it did not have enough water to fuel unconstrained growth.

Using political influence with the Dwight Eisenhower administration, Mayor Will F. Nicholson (1955–59) received federal authorization for the city to build the

Dillon Reservoir and Roberts Tunnel to bring water from the Blue River on the Western Slope to the Mile High City. The immense project not only immediately relieved water shortages, but it provided for abundant growth. Supporters viewed it as a far-sighted effort to assure plentiful water into the 21st century. The remarks of Hudson Moore Jr., DWD president and an heir of Walter Cheesman, were apropos. When the first water from the Blue River flowed into town in 1964, he claimed not only were Denver's immediate water problems solved, but the city had enough supplies for "our lifetime."

Denver had more than enough water. The blue line disappeared as the city resumed its massive drive to grow ever more. The Water Board also provided plenty of water to the suburbs. It emerged as something of a utility in supplying the commodity to the growing communities outside of the City and County of Denver. These one-time isolated hamlets frequently lacked dependable water reserves of their own. They became foremost Denver Water Department customers. Thanks to the city agency, they were able to expand without having to invest in

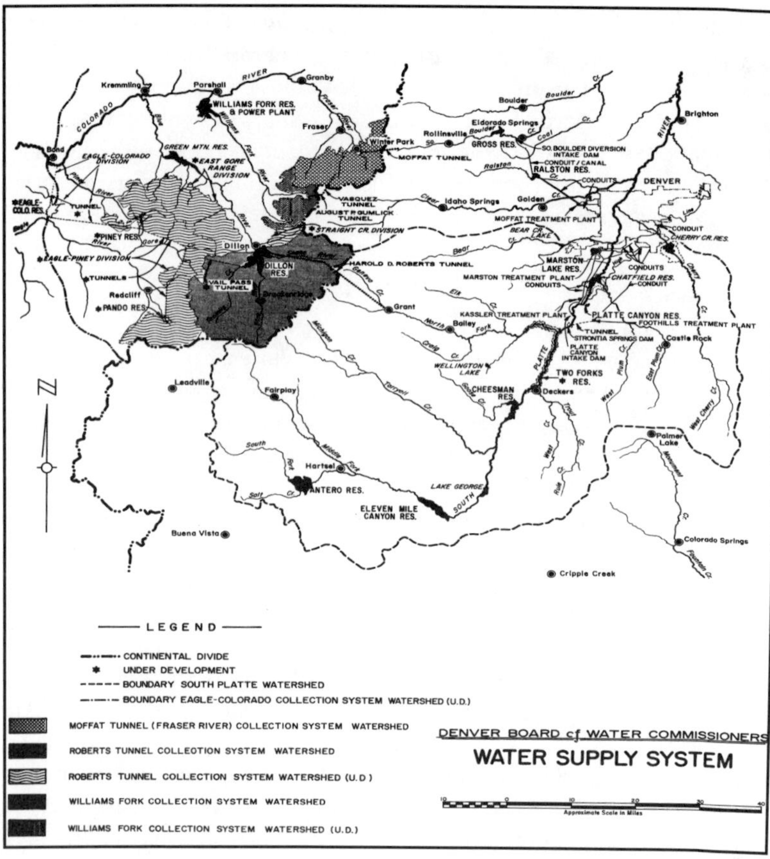


DWD

*Denver draws its water from both the South Platte basin and the Western Slope.*

their own water systems. Eventually, the Water Board came to have a 324-square mile service area in a city encompassing about 153 square miles. By the 1970s, it had more customers outside of Denver than it did in the city it was supposed to serve.

Water was literally a political football during the late 1960s. As suburban growth soared while Denver stalled, the city used its control of water to push annexations. The administration told residents in unincorporated areas that they had to join the city to get water. Some reluctantly did so. Others were outraged.

Many outside of Denver pointedly made it known they had moved from the City and County of Denver precisely because they hated and feared the evil town. Yes, they wanted the amenities of parks, museums, libraries, and water, but they did not want Denver and its grasping politicians and minorities. Now, however, it appeared the choice was between Denver water and Denver control or no water at all. This was a powerful spur to a suburban revolt in the early 1970s. While school busing was the primary goad in the passage of the Poundstone Amendment in 1974, resentment over water policies helped rally the suburbs against the Mile High City.

New water shortages loomed by this time. The excess water from the Blue River/Dillon Reservoir project quickly disappeared. Residents continued to water sidewalks in over-irrigating their lawns. DWD seemingly encouraged such profligacy: the greater the water use, the more urgent it was to undertake new projects, developments, and procurements. A Parkinson's Law of water existed: no matter how much was supplied, there was never enough. Besides, through new water projects, Denver could poise itself for further growth. Enthusiasts noted Colorado had enough water resources for a population of 14 million residents.

As the suburbs came to overshadow Denver, overwhelmingly surpassing it in population in the 1970s, some started to question DWD's role in developing additional water resources. Hudson Moore had been right in 1964: with the Blue River project, Denver did have enough water for its future needs. The suburbs did not. Despite the Poundstone Amendment and the suburbs' scorn for Denver, they fully expected the Water Board to provide their water.

According to city charter, Denver Water must supply plentiful water to residents at rates "as low as good service will permit." Beyond this, it is authorized to sell excess water to non-Denverites. Such outside customers must bear the full cost of the service. The utility must not sell suburbanites any water coming at the price of depriving city dwellers of an adequate supply.

As the drought cycle reappeared in the mid-1970s, Denver Water Department was in a fix. The number of suburban subscribers had come to equal those in the city. DWD had provided so much water to the suburbs, basing its revenues on those sales, it could not cut back on these services.

To guard against this, and prevent the Denver agency from gouging them, suburban politicians and developers sought to transform DWD into an outright public utility, regulated by the state Public Utilities Commission. Only in that manner could they assure their future water. On no account, did they want to let Denver Water have the ability to bite back at the suburbs as the latter freely scorned the city. Nor did members of the Water Board, sharing the 17th Street growth ethic, care to engage in war with the suburbs.

Some Denverites joined with suburbanites during the 1970s and 1980s in unsuccessful efforts to transform DWD into a metropolitan service entity. DWD had pondered this for years. A 1959 city charter amendment had authorized the agency to take such a step.

Failure was more due to the suburbs than Denver. Under Mayor Bill McNichols, the Mile High City pushed for metropolitan cooperation through establishing an elected board overseeing the entire region. While the Queen City repeatedly voted yes for the effort, the suburbs always rejected it. Suburban efforts to have the General Assembly remove the Water Department from the city similarly failed.

The key force in supporting the Mile High City in the latter fight, ironically, was a longtime opponent of DWD—Western Slope interests. Virtually from the beginnings of the city utility, those living on the other side of the Continental Divide have bitterly opposed the Water Board. Every drop of water Denver takes from the Western Slope, they have moaned, is another nail in their area's economic coffin. But Denver has demanded water. While 90 percent of Coloradans live on the Front Range, 70 percent of the area's water flows on the other side of the state. Developers in this part of Colorado have believed their section has stagnated precisely because Denver has drained its water.

A new division in Colorado politics confronted Western Slope politicians and builders. Over the years, they had been able to hold their own against Denver by allying with the suburbs against the wicked capital. If the suburbs won their battles against the Water Board, the Western Slope feared a gigantic, unchecked water procurement vacuum would unite Denver and the suburbs against it.

## Environmentalists

A fourth force entered the equation: environmentalists. By the early 1970s, as their movement surged, they realized how ecologically devastating dams were. They saw DWD as an unchecked bulldozer, destroying pristine mountain areas for massive water projects. Far from benefiting residents, the new efforts only promised cancerous growth, sprawl, and pollution. By reining in the Water Board, conservationists hoped to forge a sound future for the Centennial State.

Denver Water vehemently fought the environmentalists. It projected itself as a friend of the earth. Growth, the Water Board and its backers insisted, was bound to come. Either the Board of Water Commissioners took the lead for the metropolitan region by arranging new water projects as part of an integrated system with a slight ecological awareness or various jurisdictions would engage in haphazard water procurement efforts far more devastating than the worst dam environmentalists could imagine.

The result was a tangled and temporary set of alliances, intrigue, back-stabbing, and double-dealing among those supporting and opposing various water procurement efforts. The extremely conservative, pro-development property owners on the Western Slope, for example, temporarily allied themselves with Front Range environmentalists in opposing more Denver water projects. DWD awarded Western Slope communities extra shares of its immense water development rights in exchange for their collaboration in its efforts. These exceedingly convoluted deals rarely got much media play since they were far beyond the grasp of news agencies. Newspapers and television only focused on water when it was too polluted or lacking in supply.

Water was too fundamental to be ignored. With suburban water shortages looming, on July 11, 1972, the Water Board asked Denverites to authorize a $200 million bond issue as part of a 12-year, $355 million effort to increase the system's capacity. Many city residents were hesitant. Republican State Senator John Bermingham of Denver, a long-time critic of DWD, claimed bond advocates staged a "really phony, misleading, and dishonest" campaign—the new capacity was not needed. Denver had plenty of water thanks to the Blue River project. The new supplies were not for the Mile High City; they were designed to fuel growth, annexation, and sprawl. As it was, Bermingham noted, the Water Board was a "political monster" with unguided, unlimited power. Passage of the bond would only make it worse. He estimated Denver customers were already paying 25 percent too much to help the system expand for the suburbs.

DWD admitted it had enough water for Denver. The money, it conceded, was to help provide more of the liquid for the suburbs. Seen in this light, suburban interests heavily lobbied for the bond. So did real estate developers. As usual, the Denver Chamber of Commerce was a foremost supporter.

Some groups that usually endorsed such bond issues and municipal improvements, including the League of Women Voters, had second thoughts. They noted DWD's request for more money was a poorly presented mishmash of various pro-

DWD

*The early 20th-century Cheesman Dam on the South Platte River created the city's first major mountain reservoir.*

DWD

*The Strontia Springs Dam is part of the extremely controversial Foothills Project.*

posals. The bond issue was more designed to strengthen the Water Department's power than serve the citizenry. The environmentalist Colorado Open Space Council loudly urged its defeat. The electorate rejected the issue 23,595–27,349. This was the first water bond to fail since 1925.

Responding to the defeat, the Water Board announced it would restrict further sales to the suburbs. It followed this by imposing tap fees on new homes in 1973. Unlike the rest of city hall and corporate Denver, the department argued growth had to pay its own way. The bond election showed city residents were not eager to have DWD subsidize further development by giving water away to the suburbs.

By this time, Denver Water charged suburban subscribers about 40 percent more than it did for comparable city service. Just as the suburbs charged in their lawsuit, DWD treated them as a profit-making utility. In November 1973, vowing to make money from its continued suburban operations, the Water Department convinced Denverites to approve a scaled-down $160 million bond for the 12-year capital construction agenda. It stated it would not raise rates on city residents to pay for system expansions. Despite this pledge, the Water Board considerably hiked Denver fees in 1975 and again in 1976. The city increasingly used water as its key bargaining chip in relations with the suburbs.

Some of the towns ringing the city responded by seeking to break free of dependency on Denver water. Aurora was in the lead. In partnership with Colorado

Springs, it began the Homestake Creek project near Vail in 1963. (Aurora had pondered the effort since the 1950s.) This investment eventually provided the growing town with an independent supply of water. The result was breathtaking: when other suburbs found their growth limited by water shortages in the 1970s, Aurora soared ahead, emerging as a virtual second city to Denver.

After a series of dry years in the mid-1970s, the Water Board reluctantly imposed restrictions on summer lawn watering in 1977. DWD fined those who flagrantly wasted water by carelessly running it down sidewalks and streets. Even so, water usage soared. Though the Queen City's population stagnated between 1960 and 1990, Denver used more water in the latter year than it did in the former.

Much of the sprawl and increased water usage occurred under an ostensibly liberal, ecologically aware governor, Richard Lamm (1975–87). He established numerous commissions to study the impact of growth. His administration talked about wise land usage and shared resources. Foremost of Lamm's efforts was the Metropolitan Water Roundtable. It called for cooperation of Denver area water suppliers, pushing for a uniform state water policy. A primary hope was developers and environmentalists could compromise on water issues.

## Foothills

The Foothills Treatment Plant illustrated the water wars. With the money from the 1973 bond issue in hand, DWD announced plans for an elaborate project on the South Platte River near Roxborough Park, 30 miles southwest of town. The agency had seriously pondered it since 1955 as a combined reservoir, treatment plant, and tunnel system. Nothing was done then since the Water Board gave its full attention to constructing the Dillon Reservoir. As sprawl drained the waters from the Blue River diversion, the Board of Water Commissioners was finally ready to make Foothills a reality.

The Water Board pushed Foothills when the environmental forces were at high tide, having recently defeated the 1976 Winter Olympics. After years of debate, the city water agency moved ahead. A series of political confrontations, threats, and deals followed. At one point, the Denver Water Department sued environmentalist groups for standing in its way. In response, on August 15, 1978, through such groups as American Rivers, Colorado Open Space Council, and Concerned Citizens for the Upper South Platte River, ecologists counter-sued to block the construction of Foothills. They specifically feared the Strontia Springs Dam there was too large. The entire effort would devastate the South Platte River. Not only that, but the Foothills project was badly designed and guaranteed the city would again soon run short of water.

Foothills rapidly escalated in price. DWD estimated its cost at $70.2 million in 1973. By 1975, the agency conceded it would come in at least at $134.8 million. The project also kept growing in size. At one point, the Water Board projected it as so huge it could handle virtually every drop of South Platte water.

Various federal bureaus intervened. Often the departments of the Interior and Agriculture were at odds on the effort. On March 2, 1979, water interests and

Photo by Phil Goodstein

*Residents frequently water sidewalks. The more water they use in the process, the more eagerly the Denver Water Department has sought to develop new water supplies.*

developers, having reached a compromise with environmentalists over the lawsuits, signed a consent decree. Known as the Foothills Agreement, it permitted the Water Board to build a smaller dam than initially proposed at Strontia Springs and go ahead with the Foothills Treatment Plant. In return, the Water Board agreed to establish a citizens' advisory committee, one for which ecologists readily volunteered. Simultaneously, DWD committed itself to developing a conservation plan.

The Water Board completed the first phase of the Foothills project in 1983. Its opening allowed DWD to lift lawn watering restrictions. When completed, the Foothills plant increased the department's ability to treat raw water by 500 million gallons a day. Combined with the passing of the drought of the late 1970s, this effectively ended the water shortages haunting Denver since the early 1970s. More than that, Foothills provided an immense reservoir of new water for suburban growth.

(Foothills came in right about the time Denver Water conceded its Kassler Treatment Plant in Waterton Canyon was severely contaminated with trichloroethylene. The chemicals came from the nearby Martin Marietta/Air Force rocket plant. Residents in the southwestern suburbs, especially around Friendly Hills, claimed a strong trail of disease and death stemmed from illegal dumping of chemicals and polluted water contaminated at the missile factory. Though legal discovery procedures documented the massive pollution originating at Martin Marietta, the courts killed citizen suits against the company, Water Board, and state health authorities. Even so, seeing the severe problems at Kassler, in 1985, after Foothills opened, DWD placed the Waterton Canyon facility on standby status. The Environmental Protection Agency subsequently declared the Martin location the "Air Force Superfund Site at Lockheed Martin.")

As part of the Foothills Agreement, the Water Board admitted customers wasted too much water. One solution was xeriscaping. Derived from the Greek word for dry, *xeros*, it is a landscaping technique encouraging lawns and gardens which require little irrigation.

Xeriscaping features native plants and ground cover. With the assistance of the Botanic Gardens, DWD planted attractive demonstration xeriscape lawns. They were extremely expensive, requiring consultations with and commissions to landscape architects. Such gardens sometimes took years to mature. Here and there, homeowner associations protested residents having xeriscapes, claiming they infringed on the uniform lawns and beauty of neighborhoods.

The city of Denver did not provide leadership on xeriscaping. It installed few such gardens in its parks. On the contrary, computerized sprinkler systems watered city greenery in the middle of rain storms while water freely sprayed onto the streets along parkways and boulevard medians. With the end of fines for water waste after the opening of Foothills, the level of runoff water again soared. Sidewalks were as well irrigated as ever.

Another conservation project also stalled, a water recycling plant. For years, the city had pondered reusing its waste water. The hope was engineers could devise some method to purify water from downstream runoff, putting it immediately back into the system. Denver Water built a Potable Reuse Demonstration Plant north of the city along the Platte near the central water treatment facility. Despite great publicity and promise, little came of it. By the end of the millennium, new talk was heard of the effort even after the experimental facility had been closed for some years. (The city lacked rights to take waste water from the stream. It worked to gain them, hoping to use the water to irrigate new golf courses.)

As the reuse effort stalled, DWD decided to meter all Denver customers in the mid-1980s. It had long pondered this measure. Homeowners who wanted meters were welcomed to install them at their own cost—possibly one to two thousand dollars. Faced with this disincentive, most residents preferred to do without meters. As renewed water shortages loomed, the Water Board agreed with environmentalists: meters would save more than enough water to pay for their installation. Denver Water so announced it would pay for the installation of meters in the 87,500 homes on flat rates.

Some homeowners were eager to get meters. They found the flat rates bewildering. Often the ones who wanted meters the most had the hardest time getting DWD to install them. Once they surmounted the bureaucratic obstacle, customers found having a water meter was well worth the effort: their bills were cut in half. Opposed to Water Board projections, they did not use much water for irrigation for their small lawns. Especially in central Denver, a good deal of the yards had long been paved over for parking.

The Water Board had not expected metering would result in a reduction of revenues. As income plunged, it announced it had to hike water rates—residents were saving too much water. Charges from the wastewater management division of the city soared. Those using minimal water found themselves subjected to departmental audits. The utility claimed they might be cheating it since they were using so little water compared to the estimates under the flat-rate system.

## Two Forks

Despite the water saved by meters, DWD had its eyes on greater projects. Foremost was Two Forks. This was its name for a super dam about 50 miles south of Denver near the junction of the north and south forks of the South Platte River. The 615-foot-high dam was to create a 300-foot-deep lake, flooding nearly 20 miles of the river, including deluging the town of Deckers. The 1.1 million acre-foot reservoir promised to provide enough water for more than four million residents.

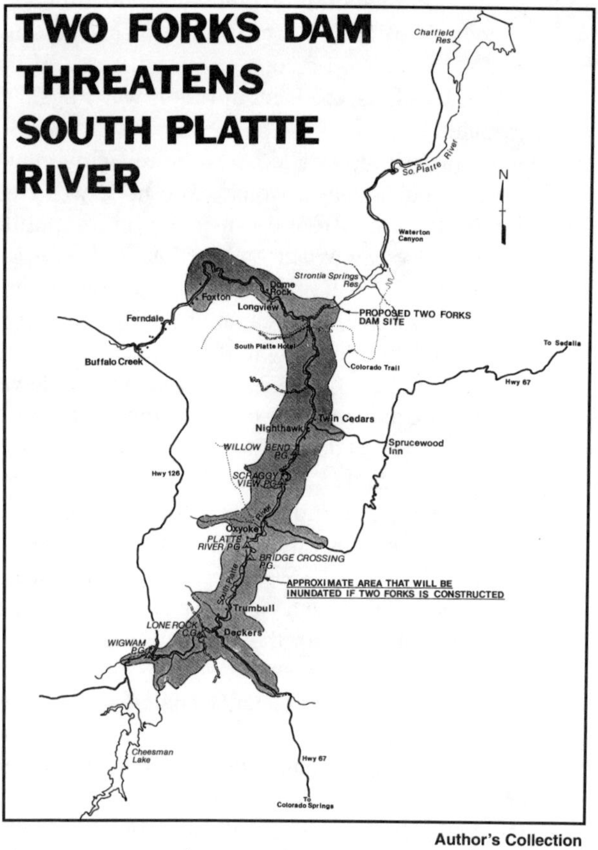


Author's Collection

*An environmentalist map shows the impact of Two Forks on the Platte River.*

Water procurers had pondered the project since the 1890s. The Denver Union Water Company rejected it at that time in favor of building Cheesman Dam a few miles up stream. The push for a reservoir at the confluence percolated for years. In 1929, for example, the Water Board pulled a permit to build a hydroelectric dam there. Nothing happened then or during the water shortages of the 1950s when growth advocates called Two Forks an urgent necessity. As was the case with Foothills, the Blue River project sidetracked Two Forks.

From the beginning, there was a close linkage between Foothills and Two Forks. DWD made no secret that a prime purpose of Foothills was to provide for the water treatment capacity required by the flow of Two Forks. Indeed, no sooner was Foothills finally under construction in the late 1970s, with more treatment capacity than there was water storage supply, did the Water Board turn its attention to Two Forks. If nothing else, Two Forks would create a surplus of water, mandating another treatment plant.

Mayor McNichols projected Two Forks as an example of Denver-suburban cooperation. In 1982, DWD reached an agreement with 43 suburban water districts and suppliers to build the dam. The purpose was plain: to spur growth and assure suburban water supplies. The suburbs admitted this, agreeing to pay for 80 to 90 percent of the project. The Water Board estimated its share of the effort was upwards of $397 million. Water for Metropolitan Denver, a group headquartered in the Denver Tech Center, was in the forefront of pushing the effort.

Ever since the Water Board had encountered turbulence over Foothills and saw its 1972 bond proposal suffer defeat, the business-oriented body had readily courted the suburbs. Serving them, not Denver residents, was increasingly its goal as DWD continued to broaden its empire while the city's population stagnated. Seventeenth Street sanctioned this approach and commitment to Two Forks. Only with a secure water system in place could the metropolitan area double and triple in size. It saw the dam as a matter of faith assuring Denver's future greatness.

Two Forks troubled outdoors enthusiasts. They realized it would destroy some of the finest fishing spots in North America. Middle-class environmentalists were similarly hesitant about the dam. Their opposition to it, they hastened to explain, was not because they were against growth—they no longer embraced such a heresy. On the contrary, they argued Two Forks was extremely wasteful. More economic and ecologically sound water procurement measures were possible in its stead. When the conservationists found the establishment unwilling to budge on Two Forks, they turned to the federal government.

The Environmental Protection Act requires a developer to file an environmental-impact statement (EIS) on any project receiving governmental funds or threatening the ecology of public lands. Such analyses are par for the course on all water efforts. DWD had immense experience with them. It expected the Two Forks study, conducted by the Army Corps of Engineers, to cost $6.7 million when it authorized the mandatory effort in the early 1980s.

The EIS presented a myriad of problems. Instead of coming in on budget for the 1984 projected completion date, the tab for the undertaking soared to more than $22 million by 1985. By 1987, a draft was 600 pages long plus another thousand pages of appendices. The cost was nearly $35 million. DWD manager Bill Miller called it "a monster" and the "state's biggest growth industry." About 75 separate contractors got commissions in compiling the EIS.

The complexity of the EIS reflected the sharp divisions within the area. Many residents did not share the corporate commitment to growth. They treasured Colorado for its open, unpolluted spaces. Such individuals feared Two Forks would destroy the area's amenities for suburban ticky-tacky. Even those settling in the far suburbs hesitated about Two Forks. Now that they had established themselves in idyllic abodes, they did not want new growth and neighbors. Two Forks, they realized, might blemish their dream homes.

As controversy raged about Two Forks, the dam had a foremost champion—a politician endorsed for election and reelection by the organized environmentalist movement—Federico Peña. From the onset of his administration, he had shown himself at one with the old power structure on water issues. After months of delay in filling two empty seats on the water commission, he named two veteran water attorneys to the body, Charles G. Jordan and 1983 mayoral challenger Monte Pascoe. In June 1985, Jordan resigned from the board to became a special assistant to the manager of the department.

In 1987, as Peña faced the fight of his political life for reelection, many environmentalists sat on their hands. They were not pleased by the mayor's enthusiasm for Two Forks. Only when it appeared Republican challenger Don Bain might win did the Sierra Club, the leadership of which had close links to the Democrats, endorse the pro-water development incumbent. In exchange, the mayor promised environmentalists that they could suggest one of their own for the Water Board as long as their candidate was not a vehement foe of the department. In particular, Peña did not want the environmentalists to nominate longtime DWD critic John Bermingham.

The leaders of the ecology groups readily complied. In August 1987, along with commercial real estate broker Donald L. Kortz of Fuller & Company, Peña named attorney Malcolm M. Murray to the water board. The latter, part of the Lamm crowd, had created the Denver Environmental Coalition in 1987, an ad hoc group of environmental activists who pushed Peña's reelection. Though Murray opposed Two Forks, his presence on the Water Board made no difference since Peña remained a Two Forks enthusiast.

As concerns about Two Forks multiplied and environmentalists fought it, Peña insisted the effort was vital for Denver greatness. Denver International Airport would require far more water than Stapleton. Development of the Platte floodplain and other parts of the city likewise demanded new water resources. Besides, Two Forks was a far better solution than pumping up ground water or stealing water from agricultural areas.

State and suburban politics also impacted the Two Forks debate. On April 7, 1986, the Colorado Supreme Court threw out the 1973 suit filed by Jefferson, Adams, and Arapahoe counties against the Water Board demanding state regulation of the Denver Water Department as a utility. On November 8, 1982, District Court Judge William Ela of Mesa County had ruled for the suburbs. He took the

Colorado Environmental Coalition

*A kayaker makes his way along the Platte River in an area threatened by Two Forks.*

case after all Denver District Court judges had recused themselves. In reversing the trial judge's verdict, the high court ruled Denver's home rule status, combined with nebulous state regulations over municipally owned water services, meant the Water Department was beyond the reach of the state Public Utilities Commission. The suburbs, consequently, had to work ever more closely with Denver in pushing Two Forks.

By this time, Denver Water was optimistic about Two Forks. The agency was sure it would complete the project within ten years. Supporters did not expect any real difficulties from the Army Corps of Engineers' analysis of the proposal. They knew the federal agency had seemingly never found a dam it did not like. Amidst environmentalist charges of sloppy review, irregularities, and an obvious pro-development slant, the Corps authorized Two Forks in June 1988. Peña, the suburbs, and the growth crowd praised the military's decision.

The Army agency conceded Two Forks had numerous environmental problems. The dam "would be extremely damaging to recreation, threatened and endangered species, vegetation, wildlife, aquatic life, water quality, and to visual and cultural resources." But, with appropriate mitigation, it was possible to overcome these difficulties. Besides, Two Forks was vital for Denver's water future. On this basis, the Corps approved the environmental-impact statement. Thanks to this move, the Water Board could finally move ahead with the dam.

Governor Roy Romer gave the Corps a green light on Two Forks. Elected to office in 1986 with environmentalist support and seeing mass opposition to the project, the new governor initially proceeded cautiously on the dam. While he did not give the effort a ringing endorsement, he did not oppose it. Nor did he offer any alternative to it.

The Corps realized Two Forks was more a political than an environmental issue. It loudly hinted it would follow the governor's wishes on the dam. Romer, in turn, knowing the Army agency was likely to okay the effort, announced he would let the federal body take the lead. The governor admitted his hesitancy. More than anything else, he feared a public vote on Two Forks. Such a referendum, he observed, could recreate the idealism and élan of those who had shot down the 1976 Winter Olympics. By avoiding a vote and endorsing the Corps' decision, the governor acted to help Two Forks become a reality.

Environmentalists, outdoors groups, and those opposed to cancerous growth were not ready to accept the Corps' verdict. Federal conservationist groups, including the Environmental Defense Fund, Audubon Society, and American Rivers, joined the fray. Mobilizing their Washington clout, they saw Two Forks as an ecological disaster. In addition to destroying the heart of the Platte River, the dam would adversely affect at least 50 other mountain streams.

Coloradans opposing Two Forks found allies in Nebraska. Politicians and growth interests there feared the dam would deprive the Cornhusker State of an adequate flow of Platte River water. They were inspired by Kansas, a state eventually winning a long-standing suit against Colorado over the flow of Arkansas River water. Senator James Exon of Nebraska led the charge against Two Forks. Some in Colorado saw him doing far more to protect their interests than any members of the Centennial State's congressional delegation. The latter either publicly supported Two Forks or, like Pat Schroeder, were largely silent about it.

With the 1988 presidential election looming, the opposition sought to make Two Forks a campaign issue. The Ronald Reagan administration agreed to let the Environmental Protection Agency (EPA) review Two Forks. The Republicans needed to make some gesture to show their environmental concern. Two Forks was an ideal subject. A review of it would not have any meaningful impact on the election or national developments—or so cynics argued.

The more it looked at Two Forks, the more problems EPA found. It agreed with the environmentalists: the construction of Two Forks would violate existing environmental laws and might well prove extremely ecologically devastating. Noting Two Forks specifically violated the Clean Water Act, on March 24, 1989, EPA began what was called a 404c, a veto of the effort based on section 404c of the Clean Water Act.

Supporters of Two Forks screamed in protest. Here they had agreed to a long, expensive EIS whereby the Army Corps of Engineers had approved Two Forks. Now, thanks to the federal busybodies, the effort was dead. Angrily arguing that EPA had stepped out of bounds, they got Washington to order EPA to reconsider its

Colorado Environmental Coalition

*Environmentalists called on Washington to designate the South Platte River near Deckers a "wild and scenic" river.*

decision. The agency sustained its veto on August 29 when it noted further research upheld its anti-Two Forks verdict.

While critics pointed out Two Forks threatened the ecology of the Platte River, developers continued to insist growth was bound to come. Two Forks was the only sound way of procuring water for it. At least 17 Denver area communities, they noted, already had "serious water supply issues." National figures in the Republican Party, including its chairman Lee Atwater, argued the EPA veto was preposterous. They cited it as they talked about reducing the agency's power.

Peña was among those loudly joining the Republicans in calling for the overturn of the veto to permit the construction of Two Forks. His remarks were poignant at a public hearing before the EPA review panel. In a speech worthy of a reactionary southern, demagogic state's rights Democrat, Peña tore into EPA: it did not understand Denver or Colorado water issues. It was nothing more than an intrusive, arrogant, Washington body, one lacking any justification in coming to town and telling the Mile High City what it could and should do with its water resources. Two Forks was vital to Denver. If EPA knew the region, it would realize as much. As it was, it should authorize the release of federal funds so the project should go ahead.

"Give us the money and leave us alone!" has been the historic cry of western water developers. The liberal, environmentalist-backed mayor fully echoed them.

Governor Romer likewise pushed for a revival of Two Forks. The federal agency failed to heed the governor or mayor. Two Forks was dead.

## Ecological Devastation

While conservationists celebrated Two Forks' demise, developers undertook all sorts of ecologically devastating water procurement efforts in its wake. Farmers on the eastern plains sold their water rights to Denver suburbs. Environmentalist ex-governor Lamm joined American Water Development Incorporated, an effort to pump water out of the San Luis Valley for Denver sprawl. Builders increasingly tapped ground water for their instant communities.

The environmentalists had obviously failed: They had focused on the smaller issue of the horrors of Two Forks while not addressing the larger issue of growth. Their success in killing Two Forks possibly created far worse problems than what would have occurred with the authorization of the dam. By the beginning of the 21st century, debate on growth was again intense. Environmentalists, though, were minor role-players. Suburbanites, who feared how badly sprawl was affecting their bailiwicks, rather, took the lead in arguing for action to better shape the region's future.

The fight over Two Forks produced no winners. Bad water projects remained. DWD critics never addressed the reasons corporate Denver so wanted the dam. In light of this, it is not surprising debates on water procurement remained dismal. As much as with Two Forks, opponents tended to concentrate on arcane ecological and legal matters, studiously avoiding the larger question of water for what.

Compared to the bulldozers ramming through sports stadiums, the convention center, and airport, at least voices of opposition were loudly heard in the Two Forks debate. In this instance, environmentalists realized officials in Washington, far removed from the petty intrigues of Denver politics, had a far greater appreciation of the amenities of the Platte River than did the local power elite. This perspective led some politically active members of the ecology movement to support a proposal to hand control of the Platte to a federal agency.

In June 1988, seeing Denver water interests could not be trusted to protect the South Platte River, with the support of environmentalists, the United States Forest Service recommended designating a 48-mile stretch of the stream in the mountains, including its North Fork, a "wild and scenic" river. This would prevent any future dams or developments along or near the Platte. The area in question included land targeted by Two Forks.

The "wild and scenic" designation had been pondered since 1968 when Congress passed the Wild and Scenic River Act. Though nothing immediately happened with this suggestion, ecologists revived it every few years. After Two Forks was dead, DWD called for metropolitan cooperation on the Platte canyon. As an alternative to the Forest Service's "wild and scenic" river, it sought to team up with the Colorado Department of Parks, the Jefferson County Open Space Council, and other public entities to keep control of the Platte. Under their direction, Denver Water promised, it would transform the river into a jointly managed riparian park.

Meanwhile, the city encouraged developers to build in the Platte floodplain. This included environmentally sensitive land in the suburbs next to Chatfield Arboretum. Many around Mayor Wellington Webb eagerly endorsed the latter project.

During the 1980s, the environmentalists had been so committed to blocking Two Forks that they did little to question other ecologically devastating projects tearing through the Denver area. In particular, they paid little heed to Denver International Airport. On the contrary, despite the way politicians whom they had endorsed supported Two Forks, they continued to play the politics-as-usual game. Many of their leaders retained their links with the Democrats. More often than not, they lined up behind the latter's political fortunes as opposed to formulating a green agenda. This lack of choices was illustrated by the 1991 mayoral election.

## A Note on Sources:

DWD has a rich archives, containing its many newsletters, studies, brochures, and photos. They are complemented by thick clipping collections and holdings on water controversies at DPL and CHS. The Government Documents section of DPL also has many Denver Water documents. In addition to these sources, literature on water in Colorado is immense. The Colorado Water Conservation Board has issued numerous studies. There are also many papers by the Metropolitan Water Roundtable and the Colorado Water Quality Control Commission. Then there are the reports of the Army Corps of Engineers. Many are also on file at the Government Documents section. The University of Colorado sponsored an annual Western Resources Conference in the 1960s, publishing numerous papers related to water.

*Colorado Water* (Denver: League of Women Voters, 1975), is an introduction to the subject. The standard work on the origins of DWD is Earl Mosley, "History of the Denver Water System, 1859–1919." Clyde Lyndon King, *History of the Government of Denver*, specifically documents the deals of the water monopoly. Breck, *John Evans*, includes an uncritical accolade to Cheesman. Carol Edmonds, *Wayne Aspinall: Mr. Chairman*, is a developer-financed biography of a western Colorado congressman who was a foremost dam, water-procurement exponent. Steven F. Mehls, Carol J. Drake, and James E. Fell Jr., *Aurora: Gateway to the Rockies*, notes the Homestake Creek project.

Ed Ruetz of DWD freely talked about the utility's operations and history. Trina McGuire of the agency also answered my questions. John Bermingham and Mick Spano shared their past clashes with and thoughts about the Water Board. John Morris discussed water issues in a 1985 interview. Don Thompson of the Sierra Club and I have had sporadic conversations over the years about the stances of the environmentalist movement. Rocky Smith noted his views on water in the early 1980s. Mike Davenport read a draft of the chapter and recalled his work in opposition to Two Forks.

I looked at the operations of DWD in a three-part article, "Water in the Desert," *City Edition*, March 6, 13, 20, 1985. Board members Monte Pascoe, Charles Jordan, Meg Pugsley, Dale Shaffer, and John A. Yelenick all discussed its operations. So did Manger Bill Miller. Besides attending Water Board and environmentalist meetings as part of my research, I also went to many public hearings in the 1980s about Two Forks. I was present when Peña addressed EPA about the veto.

Colorado Environmental Coalition papers at DPL, focusing on 1965–1993, are a gold mine on water issues, especially boxes 8, 24, 47, 69. In addition to numerous governmental studies on Two Forks and Foothills, the collection contains rich newspaper clippings and press releases on the issues. The archive embodies something of the statements of the vague "environmentalist" label on water issues. Included are many papers issued by John Bermingham lambasting DWD. Particularly valuable are his *Foothills: $135 million in the Wrong Place* (Denver: Water Users Alliance, 1978); and idem, *A Dozen and More Myths about Foothills* (Denver: Water Users Alliance, 1977).

The collection further contains immense materials on wild and scenic rivers. It has assorted publications of the Audubon Society and Sierra Club. *The Ark*, the newsletter of Denver Zero Population Growth in the 1970s, focused on the link between water projects and real estate development. Also present are materials from the Colorado Rivers Coalition. The boxes include Colorado Open Space Council records and papers from the Rocky Mountain Center on the Environment (ROMCOE). The latter was an extremely influential environmentalist group in the 1970s. There is also information on the Colorado Environmental Caucus of the 1980s. The records contain correspondence between various conservationist leaders with Governor Lamm and Mayor Peña. Materials document the environmentalist support of Peña.

Mark Kindley, "Behind the Lines in the Water War: The Foothills–Two Forks Connection," *Denver Magazine*, August 1978, pp. 32–35, 68, is a good treatment of the subject. John J. Vierthaler discussed the lawsuits relating to the Kassler Treatment Plant. Also see the letter to the editor from Adrienne Anderson, who teaches in the Environmental Studies Program at the University of Colorado-Boulder and worked with the Friendly Hills community against the Water Board, in *DP*, December 16, 1999, p. 10B. Some of the best reportage on Two Forks was in the *Omaha World-Herald*. Opposing the dam, that paper provided a far more critical look at the dam than Denver newspapers usually did. The late Harriet Collick kindly provided me with clippings from the Omaha daily. *Colorado Gardener* has included articles about how neighborhood improvers and city inspectors have cited those with naturalistic landscaping for having weeds.

Robert C. Hoffman and Keith Fletcher, *America's Rivers: An Assessment of State River Conservation Programs* (Washington: River Conservation Fund, 1984), connects the debate over the Platte with the national push to save river resources. Cecil Kuhne, "Down a Paper River," *River Runner*, August 1988, pp. 22–25, reflects on the Wild and Scenic River Act. The newsletter of the American Rivers Conservation Council, *American Rivers*, also discussed the character of the Platte and the threat of water developments. Cheryl Jacobs noted developments near Chatfield Arboretum.

# 12

# Webb Wins

Federico Peña had an acute sense of timing, knowing when to plunge into a controversy and when to steer clear of it. He perceived his dynamism as mayor was dissipating as the city entered the final decade of the 20th century. Despite his extravagant claims, numerous problems loomed at DIA, a project not close to its promised 1992 opening. Many still hated Peña, recalling his betrayal of his 1983 hope and the dirty tone of his 1987 campaign. He knew he would face another stiff challenge if he sought reelection in 1991.

In April 1988, less than a year after his 1987 triumph, the mayor narrowly escaped a recall effort. City employees launched it in January 1988, disgusted by what they perceived as the mayor's inept management. Though their specific accusations against Peña were vague, they were clear on one point: he had treated them shamefully. Their effort collapsed when they came in 2,000 signatures short of the 39,091 they needed for their drive. Some who circulated the petitions against Peña reported receiving threats for daring oppose the mayor.

Even while avoiding the recall, Peña realized the failed promises of the airport and convention center could easily haunt him during a third term. All this led him to announce on November 28, 1990, that he would not seek reelection in May 1991. He explained he wanted to spend more time with his growing family.

After leaving office, Peña set himself up as a financial guru. In November 1991 he started to form the money management firm of Peña Investment Advisors. It was, he proclaimed, a Hispanic-owned operation, one encouraging Latinos to serve Wall Street. Cable television magnate Bill Daniels was a key investor in the firm. (About the same time, Daniels also advanced funds to Neil Bush to work as a consultant for international investments.) Charles Ansbacher, the husband of oil heiress Swanee Hunt, joined Daniels in underwriting Peña's company. Both, non-Hispanics, had ardently supported the mayor's pro-business actions.

No sooner did Peña Investment Advisors begin operations in April 1992 than it got its first client, US West. The phone company, which had worked closely with the former mayor in pushing sprawl and DIA, turned over $10 million to the firm from its pension fund. This came a day after the *Rocky Mountain News* reported Peña's outfit hoped to manage $15 million in funds by the end of its first year.

As his organization prospered, Peña wanted more. In July 1992, despite previously rejecting offers to join leading law firms in order to form Peña Investment Advisors, the former mayor signed on with the politically charged law firm of Brownstein Hyatt Farber & Strickland. Named "of counsel" with the outfit, he oversaw a new unit dealing with trade between the United States, Canada, and Mexico. Peña simultaneously operated his investment company.

This continued for about six months. Bill Clinton's election as president affected Peña's fortunes. The former Arkansas governor had close ties with such conservative, pro-business Democrats as Governor Roy Romer and Senator Tim Wirth. They, along with Peña, were clones of Clinton—Democrats who sought to prove the party's conservatism and commitment to corporate domination while projecting a liberal veneer. As much as Peña, Clinton forever extolled the "public/private partnership."

Brownstein Hyatt Farber & Strickland had linkages to the new president. At first, it appeared a politician whom the law firm had firmly supported in Congress, Tim Wirth, would join the Clinton cabinet. Wirth won a seat in the House of Representatives in the 1974 Watergate election to represent Boulder and the northern Denver suburbs. At first, Wirth portrayed himself as a committed liberal and idealistic environmentalist. Usually, the farther a project was from Colorado, the more ardently Wirth favored it. He won his race for the Senate in 1986. The politician had ties with the conservative Democratic Leadership Council, a group surging to the control of the Democratic Party. In Congress, Wirth was a foremost champion of cable television interests. Detractors sometimes called him the Senator from Tele-Communications Incorporated. (To help pave the way for cable television companies, Wirth pushed the breakup of the old AT&T monopoly. That corporation favored the measure, wishing to concentrate on profitable new communication technologies over old-fashioned local phone service.)

Wirth did not seek reelection to the Senate in 1992. Rather, he roundly denounced the body in the *New York Times*. This, and some of his other actions, alienated many of his cohorts in Congress. If Clinton recommended Wirth for the cabinet, the former senator would have likely faced a tough confirmation battle.

As a post for Wirth loomed, Peña insisted he was not interested in joining the Clinton team. When Wirth's fortunes faded, Clinton nominated Peña to head the Department of Transportation. By this time the president-elect had named Henry Cisneros, the former mayor of San Antonio, Secretary of Housing and Urban Development. The Texas Latino, who had previously assisted Peña in forming Peña Investment Advisors, recommended Clinton bring the former mayor of Denver to

Photo by Phil Goodstein

*Since Federico Peña successfully used yard signs in his 1983 campaign, countless such signs have spouted up prior to elections.*

Washington. Not only did the president need another Hispanic for his cabinet, but Peña was apparently a great expert in transportation thanks to pushing through DIA. (Peña sold his interest in his investment company at a good profit on going to Washington.)

After four years of undistinguished service as Secretary of Transportation, Peña talked about leaving Washington. Once more, he noted he wanted to spend more time with his family. Nonetheless, he remained the right man of the right ethnicity at the right time. After he quit as Secretary of Transportation, Clinton named Peña Secretary of Energy. Some in Denver were grateful for the nomination: it kept Peña out of town. In mid-1998, again citing a concern for his family, Peña left Washington. The "populist" ex-mayor returned to the city as a senior adviser for Vestar Capital Partners, a $3.5 billion, New York-based firm specializing in management buyouts, recapitalizations, and growth capital investments. Shortly after he left the Department of Energy, the agency was plunged into massive controversy over its questionable protection of nuclear secrets. Once more, the politician had shown an outstanding sense of timing.

## Peña's Successor

No clear successor stood out to Peña in 1991. Nobody in his cabinet was a head-over-shoulders heir to the mayor. Nor had any member of city council established himself as the mayor's loyalest, truest champion. Rather, the lawyer who had followed Dale Tooley as district attorney—Norman S. "Norm" Early Jr.—was the establishment's candidate to keep the Peña machine in place.

Like Peña, Early was a migrant to Denver. Born on November 14, 1945, he had grown up in Washington, D.C., attending an all-black school until he was in fourth grade. The son of a mail carrier, he lived with his mother and stepfather, both middle-class employees of the federal government. Early was a good student who received an academic and athletic scholarship to American University in his home city. By this time, the six-foot two-inch-tall, 200-pound young man was known as "Stormin' Norman," the most popular student in his class.

Early broke away from Washington after graduating from American University in 1967 to attend law school at the University of Illinois. There he gained a social conscience, caught up in the political upheavals of the day. Upon receiving his degree in 1970, he headed to the Mile High City, drawn to the area by friends. He arrived as a "Reggie."

Author's Collection

*Norm Early was the frontrunner in the race to succeed Federico Peña as mayor in 1991.*

Reginald Heber Smith was a wealthy New York lawyer who left his money to a trust to provide free legal services for the poor. In the late 1960s/early 1970s, idealistic young attorneys avidly competed to become "Reggies," as recent graduates of law schools receiving grants from the Reginald Heber Smith Foundation were known. Denver legal aid was eager to have Early, its first black attorney, step on board.

The young lawyer quickly became involved in the local Democratic Party, loudly advocating more blacks in office. At first, he was extremely distrustful of the district attorney's office. By 1973, however, after Early's Reggie had expired, District Attorney Dale Tooley offered the Washington native a job as a community affairs/outreach deputy district attorney. Realizing it was time to move on, Early hesitatingly accepted the post. In no time, he emerged as a slashing prosecutor. An eager politician on the make, Early handled a number of high-profile cases, including police shootings. In the latter circumstances, he usually cleared the police officers of any misdoing.

When Tooley resigned in January 1983 to run for mayor, Governor Richard Lamm named Early his successor. The announcement thrilled black Denver. The African-American community had been recognized. One of its own was finally a top city official. Among those firmly endorsing Early's appointment as district attorney was a member of the Lamm cabinet, Wellington Webb.

When Early sought election to the district attorney's post in his own right in 1984, Bert Gallegos challenged him. The latter initially won election to the General Assembly as a Democrat in 1956. In the House, he successfully pushed civil rights and fair housing legislation. After Gallegos failed to gain renomination to the legislature in 1962, he scorned the Democrats for the Republicans. After unsuccessfully seeking a number of posts under the banner of the GOP, in 1971 Gallegos joined those vehemently opposing school busing when he was elected to the board of education. A year later he quit the school position for a job with the Nixon administration in Washington where he helped destroy the remnants of the Office of Economic Opportunity. Running as a longtime community activist, Gallegos mocked Early as an unknown who had suddenly descended on Denver and had taken over the district attorney's office.

The challenger's attack failed dismally. More voters were aware of and knew about Early than remembered Gallegos. The district attorney had no trouble remaining in office. Early similarly coasted to reelection in 1988. In 1990, he made headlines when he refused to become the first African-American member of the Cherry Hills Country Club. The prosecutor loudly announced he had rejected the invitation since the longtime anti-black, anti-Semitic bastion did not have any full women members; otherwise, he was comfortable with the country club scene.

Unlike Tooley, Early did not use the district attorney's office as a bully pulpit to keep the city honest. He was the district attorney right when the penny stock and savings and loan frauds soared. His office did little to try to check them. Instead of rocking the boat or mounting crusades against white-collar criminals, Early showed up at charity functions and supported worthy causes. A telegenic man, he quickly became part of establishment Denver.

Pundits immediately tabbed the district attorney the favorite to succeed Peña. Early had not questioned any of the incumbent's programs and was a firm advocate of continuing to push the airport and the rest of the development agenda. His team included many individuals who had worked closely with Peña. Such tycoons as Bill Coors, real estate broker John Fuller, contractor Linda Alvarado, dairy king Dick Robinson, bond dealer Lee White, and airport land speculator Gary Antonoff prominently served on the Early campaign committee.

The candidate was at a loss when the *Rocky Mountain News* asked him to list three issues on which he disagreed with the mayor. This led the paper to observe, "if you like Mayor Federico Peña, you probably are going to love Norm Early." In response, the district attorney sought to establish himself as an independent challenger, vigorously denying he was a Peña clone. Cole Finegan, an operative of the law firm of Brownstein Hyatt Farber & Strickland—Peña's future employer—was the district attorney's campaign manager. Chris Romer, the bond dealer son of the governor, also played a key role in the Early challenge. It was headquartered at the site of the failed Broadway Plaza at 601 South Broadway.

## Rival Candidates

As the district attorney emerged as the candidate of the status quo, some hoped an alternative would emerge. None did. Don Bain was once more the Republican challenger to the conservative, pro-business Democratic city hall. His main attraction since his defeat four years earlier was that he had done nothing. At a time when Early had firmly endorsed the 1989 airport election, Bain grudgingly supported the measure. (He was the next-door neighbor and longtime political associate of William B. Chenoweth who helped lead the anti-airport opposition.) As the full dimensions, costs, and bad management of DIA loomed in 1991, Bain announced there was no reason to rush the project. Nothing, he observed, would be hurt by a couple of years delay on it. Prior to the campaign, he had sarcastically dismissed Peña's exultation of the effort as a form of "religious veneration."

Bain once more emphasized he was not Peña. In contrast to the incumbent, who readily did the bidding of 17th Street, Bain promised he would be a strong, independent mayor who would stand up "against the special interests at city hall, not cozy up to them." Faced with the racially/ethnically charged machine Peña had successfully built with the business establishment, Bain's lack of charisma hurt him. No longer the unknown of 1987, political analysts dismissed him as a very politically incorrect, white male Republican who lacked what it took to continue the corporate domination of Denver. The newspapers also found Bain an easy target, lambasting him as a vestige of the city's past. He was not a slick, young candidate like Peña or Early.

A challenger who rivaled Early as the establishment's candidate was Wellington Edward Webb. Since his defeat in the 1983 mayoral election, the six-foot four-inch-tall former basketball star had smoothed many of his edges. He shaved off his beard. Harvard's Kennedy School of Government saw Webb as a potential urban leader, selecting him for its Senior Executive Program. He polished his image there. Back in Denver, Webb remained director of regulatory agencies under Governor Lamm until the latter left office in January 1987. Webb thereupon ran for auditor.

Under Mike Licht, the auditor's office was highly visible from 1983 until 1987. Webb promised, if elected, he would take it out of the limelight. Stability, not controversy, was the proper goal of the auditor. The candidate announced he was a team player. The implication: he would abrogate the main function of the elected auditor's post as a fiercely independent watchdog of the commonweal against a free-spending administration. While four others sought the auditor's job, Webb easily swept the race, winning 63.4 percent of the vote in the June runoff.

Big-money interests rallied to Webb's campaign for auditor. He proudly noted the support of United Bank chairman Berne Hart, Bank of Denver president Walt Emery, power broker attorney Norm Brownstein, developer Gary Antonoff, bond dealer Lee White, and real estate magnate Robert F. Hackstaff. In office, Webb delivered on his promise of not rocking the boat—the auditor was extremely silent while costs soared at DIA. Now he sought his reward by becoming mayor.

Other candidates entered the fray. Errol Stevens was a long-time city functionary who had been Bill McNichols' right-hand man in coping most ineptly with the Christmas blizzard. He readily supported state capitalist subsidies. His main complaint was not about the direction of Denver, but its specific operation. As a veteran insider, he vowed, he would be the ideal city manager. A Park Hill resident, he hoped to win the neighborhood activist vote. Toward this end, he called for making neighborhood groups a formal part of the city administration. The leaders

Photo by Phil Goodstein

*Wellington Webb*

of improvement associations, though, paid him little heed. They mostly committed themselves to Webb and Early.

Steve Schweitzberger, who soon moved to the suburbs and later emerged as a leading Christian Columbine parent in the wake of the massacre at the school, again sought to make his views known. Political novices Larry G. Walsh and George D. Knapp also ran, but nobody knew who they were or paid much attention to them. The Socialist Workers Party no longer had a Denver presence. Nor did any other radical party field a candidate. No challenger stood out as a skeptical opponent of the total business domination of the city.

A Hispanic candidate was also missing. Some Latinos initially hoped to keep one of their own in city hall. Politically prominent Mexican-American politicians talked about recruiting a well-known officeholder such as former state Senator Paul Sandoval, state Representative Don Mares, or Councilwoman Debbie Ortega for the race. None wished to run for mayor. They teamed up, rather, to elect Tim Sandos, the son of Sam Sandos, as councilman at large. The advocates of the politics of ethnic recognition agreed 1991 was an African-American year. This quickly proved problematic.

## The Ascendancy of Wellington Webb

With two high-profile black politicians seeking the mayor's post, the election became racially charged. The middle-class black establishment was primarily in Early's camp. Some of its political activists were unhappy about Webb taking on their candidate. Denver's time for a black mayor had come and Early, they insisted, was the man for the job. These ideologues feared Webb's entry into the race would divide the black/Hispanic vote, leading to a runoff in which Bain would triumph as the white candidate. In the same manner they made race a primary consideration, they were sure white Denver would automatically support one of its own against a pro-development African-American.

Using this as a pretext, Early's black supporters loudly called for Webb to drop his candidacy in April. Not only did Webb refuse to heed this call, but it was obvious that Early was not *the* black candidate. There were political fissures within African-American Denver. The Webb-Early division reflected them.

Whereas Early was the candidate of the professional, upscale blacks—some of whom, like the district attorney, lived in southeast Denver—Webb appealed to traditional black, working-class East Denver. As one who had grown up in the Mile High City, he projected himself as the contender who was in tune with the traditions and people of black Denver and the city as a whole.

The more success black politicians had, the greater became the rivalries within the African-American Democratic Party. The division between Webb and Early was far more than one of class or geography. By the early 1980s, there were two very distinct political factions among Five Points and Park Hill blacks. Usually, they turned on personalities, not on political differences. The Webb-Early rivalry reflected this split. Generally, Park Hill blacks who supported the Peña status quo, such as Bill Roberts, Happy Haynes, Regis Groff, and Gloria Tanner, lined up behind Early. Against them, former Park Hill state Representative Arie Taylor, who had long clashed with Tanner and Groff, strongly endorsed Webb.

Photo by Phil Goodstein

*There is no question Wellington Webb has been sold in this picture of his 1999 campaign headquarters at 1525 Josephine, the former home of the Metro Denver Fair Housing Center.*

The auditor loudly rejected calls by African-Americans to withdraw from the contest. He openly attacked what he claimed was their shameful race-baiting. Webb announced he was in the mayor's race for the distance. Besides, his campaign was looking up. After starting out as a poor third in the polls with 12–15 percent against Early's 39–42 percent and Bain's 21–22 percent, by April Webb was steadily gaining support. Establishment politicos who could not stomach Bain and did not like Early rallied to Webb. Even so, his campaign was broke. Political professionals viewed it as hopeless.

In an act of desperation, Webb, who was still an avid basketball player, stated that he would walk the city in the three weeks before the May 21 election. His campaign signs showed a pair of big tennis shoes as the former state legislator strolled daily with his supporters through various parts of town. He stopped and chatted with passersby about what they thought of the city, where it should be headed, and what the next mayor must do. Rather than returning home each evening, he stayed with supporters in all parts of the city.

Projecting himself as a veritable David against Early the Goliath, Webb came across as a very friendly, congenial contender who understood the Mile High City. His advisers did their all to romanticize the walk. They used the theme song from *Rocky* as Webb marched 240 miles through the city.

Webb went out of his way to attend election forums. Early, like Bain, was often absent from them. The heavily favored district attorney appeared to pattern himself on Tooley's failed 1983 mayoral campaign. Instead of directly seeking contact with members of the electorate as Webb did, the frontrunner projected himself as the heir apparent, depending mostly on the electronic media to make himself known to the populace. Early was omnipresent at charity fund-raisers and prominent social events, but nowhere in sight where real voters sought to meet him.

This backfired on the frontrunner. Those going to the debates in the hope of directly seeing the men who wanted to guide the city's destiny came away with the conclusion that if Early was too busy to attend their forums, he would be too busy to attend to their needs as mayor. As often as not, people turning out for the forums left with the resolve to vote for someone else.

As Early stagnated, Webb rose in the polls. By the time he started walking the city in early May, he had pulled even with Bain. The latter's campaign went nowhere. Instead of dealing with the actual issues facing the city and how he would free himself from the big-money interests of which he was part, Bain bitterly attacked Early's use of plea bargains as district attorney. This gave the impression he was running for district attorney, not mayor. Such a campaign did nothing to inspire voters, especially those sick of the Peña great city projects.

Among those fiercely counterattacking Bain was Webb. The latter focused more on the Republican's faults than Early's politics. Webb castigated Bain for having doubts about DIA. He also noted Bain, unlike himself, had not been a fervid supporter of a 1990 effort to hike the sales tax to build a baseball stadium and give away the public purse to the major league franchise. By turning his guns on Bain, Webb simultaneously sought election as both the opposition and establishment candidate. Among those contributing heavily to his campaign were underwriters of bond issues at Denver International Airport. He had dealt with some of them as auditor.

Webb's strategy worked. By the time of the election, he was the alternative to Early. The district attorney received a commanding plurality on May 21, 50,360 (40.8 percent). Webb came in second with 36,874 (29.8 percent), trailed by Bain with 33,233 (26.9 percent). Schweitzberger was a distant fourth with 1,600 (1.2 percent). The other candidates failed to register on the charts. Early had spent nearly $13.71 a vote compared to Webb's $4.83.

The contenders echoed the themes established in the election during the runoff. Webb portrayed himself as the people's candidate, the outsider who literally ran on a shoestring against the smug, conservative, establishment Early. Bain then helped Webb paint himself as the opposition challenger. The unsuccessful Republican candidate loudly urged his backers to support Webb in the runoff.

(Later, Bain stated Early's defeat was his foremost goal. During the primary campaign, despite the urging of the Early camp, Bain determinedly refused to attack Webb. He saw the latter could win over Early while he would invariably lose a runoff with the district attorney.)

Early failed to respond to the Webb insurgency. As much as he had in the primary, he simply presented himself as Peña's successor, doing little to mobilize voters who had neither supported him nor Webb in the May election. The district attorney failed to point out the glaring contradiction of Webb's campaign. Despite the auditor's self-portrait as the outsider and the candidate of change, Webb repeatedly vowed he was fully committed the Peña agenda. Instead of exposing Webb's facade, Early accepted it. The frontrunner's effort to become mayor was even more lackluster in the runoff than it had been in the initial vote. Early paid the price of his inept campaign on June 18 when Webb overwhelmed him. The auditor swept all sections of the city, 66,511 (57.7 percent) to 48,702 (42.3 percent).

(After his defeat for mayor, Early stated he had no interest in again running for district attorney. Despite this, he easily won reelection to the job in 1992. Six months later, he announced he was quitting as of June 4, 1993, to become an employee of the military-industrial complex, taking a job with Lockheed Information Management Services. He noted he had rejected a post with the Department of Justice in Washington because he wanted to stay in Denver. The former district attorney remained active in the community, serving on assorted appointed boards. In 1998, he was a key supporter in getting corporate welfare for the Denver Broncos by having the citizenry agree to a raise in the sales tax to build the team a new stadium.)

## Webb in Office

In office, Webb quickly showed he was part of the machine. The 1991 election had illustrated its power: the runoff was a choice between two of its own. Though there were startling personal contrasts between Webb and Peña, it was business as usual at city hall. Webb's main problems as mayor stemmed from accusations of cronyism, especially when politically well-connected black entrepreneurs got

Photo by John Schoenwalter

*Wilma Webb loudly came across as the city's cultural queen during her husband's first term. She is shown flanked by Wellington Webb and Governor Roy Romer.*

whopping city contracts. Story after story detailed how Webb's friends and political supporters received interest-free loans and special deals from the city. Problems his sons encountered with the law and city revenue authorities also plagued the mayor.

DIA haunted Webb. From the beginning, he had firmly supported Peña on the project. Now he reaped its fruits. When he readily vowed to keep previous mayor's pledges about it, the airport's bad design, cost overruns, extravagant promises, and totally inefficient luggage system engulfed him.

Wilma J. Webb, the mayor's wife, embarrassed her husband. After Webb left the state House of Representatives for a federal post in 1977, the local Democratic Party appointed King Trimble, a close Webb political colleague, to fill the seat. The latter resigned in 1980 after he successfully ran for city council to replace Elvin Caldwell. The Democrats thereupon tabbed Wilma Webb for the legislature. She was unopposed for the post in both the 1980 primary and general election.

Born in Denver on May 17, 1943, Wilma Webb was the daughter of Frank and Faye Jerdine. She had attended Manual High School with her future husband. The two had little relation then. After both went through other spouses and divorces, they married in 1971. By this time, she was an activist in her own right in the Democratic Party.

The mayor's wife was among those swept into politics by the school busing upheavals. She emerged as an articulate speaker. Her major achievement in the legislature came in 1984 when she pushed through a Martin Luther King holiday. Standing by her husband's side, she helped him in his 1983 mayoral bid and 1987 run for the auditor's seat. Together, the Webbs were very much a political couple. Wilma Webb remained in the House until deciding not to seek reelection in 1992.

Once her husband was ensconced in city hall, Wilma Webb asserted herself. More than the first lady, she seemed co-mayor with her spouse. It was no secret she was angling for a federal job. She failed, though, to become director of the Denver Mint. Wits claimed "Wilmington" Webb ran the city.

Styling herself as a cultural maven, Wilma Webb emerged as head of the Mayor's Commission on Art, Culture, and Film. Established in October 1991, the body gave the mayor's wife an important municipal position. As its chairwoman, she muscled in on the public art program at DIA, selecting sites for works despite their doubtful engineering merits. She also sought to change the selection process for public art whereby race was a primary consideration. Wilma Webb, pictured by critics as a cultural queen, let one and all know "I am a musician, I am an artist, I have written."

"My mother told me many years ago that politics is an art," she told the press. Despite this, Wilma Webb managed to alienate many, both within and without the arts community. Rather than studying the subjects on which she commented, she

Photo by John Schoenwalter

*Turmoil marked the police department under Webb. Shown are members of the SWAT team/gang unit ready for action in 1992.*

sometimes revealed her ignorance. Such was the case with her speech at the fifteenth anniversary concert of Boettcher Concert Hall on March 4, 1993. In a snide move, showing an utter contempt for its audience, the Colorado Symphony forced people who bought tickets to a music program to listen to Wilma Webb talk about famous pianist "Van Cleeburn." Denver, she erroneously continued, was one of "only four cities in the world" blessed with a concert hall in the round. The others were "Berlin, Mexico City, and Asia." Musicians rustled their sheet music while members of the chorus had to restrain their laughter. Concert-goers found themselves insulted by having Webb as part of the program.

As she increasingly revealed her arrogance and caused her husband political problems, Wilma Webb resigned as chairwoman of the art commission in the summer of 1993. Finally, in October 1997, she achieved her goal of a federal job. The Clinton administration named her the regional director of the Department of Labor—a position Washington had left vacant for nearly five years, a sign of how little the Democrats thought about the post and the local labor movement. Congresswoman Diana DeGette was among the key figures in helping the mayor's wife get this office. Before DeGette won election in 1996 to replace Pat Schroeder, rumors had been hot and heavy about Wilma Webb seeking the open House seat.

## Police Turmoil

Even as Wellington Webb oversaw the opening of DIA and the city hosted the pope and the Summit of the Eight, central Denver was increasingly perceived as a violence-filled, mean, dangerous place. Controversy swirled around the police department beginning with the mayor's first police chief, Jim Collier.

A lieutenant at the time of Webb's election, Collier was apparently appointed chief thanks to favors the mayor owed him. No sooner had Collier taken office in September 1991 than numerous officers made it known they were extremely unhappy with the chief's administration. As turmoil wracked the department, Collier asked for exemption from the residency rule.

In 1978, four years after the passage of the Poundstone Amendment, Denver struck back at suburbanites who sought to live off the city when it required municipal employees—including members of the police department—to live within the City and County of Denver. The measure was partly in response to the large number of Denver's finest who deliberately turned their backs on the Mile High City. Apparently, they feared police protection was so bad they could not tolerate dwelling in the city they patrolled. This was at a time when Denver was increasingly torn by complaints about extreme police brutality. Advocates of the residency requirement argued the law was necessary to keep officers from being nothing but members of an occupying, mercenary army who had no pride in or identification with the city they sought to serve and protect. Voters repeatedly affirmed the residency rule during the next 15 years.

Collier was among the police officers who did not like living in Denver. Despite serving as chief, he told the mayor he preferred to make Arapahoe County his home. Webb was unwilling to give the head of the department special dispensa-

Photo by Phil Goodstein

*Concerned citizens protested police brutality under Webb. The mayor responded by unsuccessfully trying to limit such demonstrations.*

tion from the residency rule. He used Collier's request as a convenient pretext to dismiss the chief in September 1992.

Dave Michaud succeeded Collier as police chief. Under him, complaints about police brutality soared. Simultaneously, black violence, crime, and social problems haunted Denver. Between May and October 1993, the city was torn by "the summer of violence." It was a terrible time when the sons and daughters of the civil rights generation in Park Hill readily resorted to guns and shot one another and innocent bystanders. In the same manner as oil buccaneers, savings and loan scoundrels, and other outside investors saw the Mile High City ripe for the plucking, national gangs moved in, recruiting black youths for their criminal enterprises. The more the police, receiving sizable federal grants to combat gangs, warned about the imminent arrival of the drug-dealing syndicates, the more young men joined these organizations, notably the Crips and the Bloods. Before long, the gangs expanded to other ethnic and racial groups.

The mayor replied with coercive police actions. Foremost were curfew enforcement and sweeps targeting adolescents—especially Chicanos and African-Americans—precisely because they were minority teenagers. Far from seeking to make them part of the community, city hall targeted these young men and women because of their age. Instead of basking in the magnanimity of secure power, city hall showed itself vindictive and petty. The youths responded in kind. Violence rather than celebration became part of festivals such as Cinco de Mayo.

The administration branded adolescents who hung out on the 16th Street Mall, including homeless kids and runaways, "mall rats." The implication: they were subhuman vermin whom the city must exterminate. Not only did the police step up harassment of them, but city hall pondered completely destroying the landscaping of Skyline Park near 16th and Arapahoe streets to keep the youths away.

Insofar as the police roughly dealt with minors, blacks, and Chicanos, some thought Bill McNichols was still mayor. Police violence had receded from the headlines during the Peña years. Even as city hall embraced a crude administrative mentality, seeking to show how tough it was on trifling code enforcement, the Peña administration purged some of the old practices and brutal officers who had had free rein under Art Dill, McNichols' police chief from 1972 until 1983. Recalling his past opposition to untrammeled police violence, an early Webb act was establishing an extremely weak civilian review board of the police. Virtually powerless, it received little support from city hall. The police department openly scorned it, refusing to cooperate in its investigations.

As police brutality again became a frequent front-page item under Webb, most black community leaders sided with the mayor. With a black in office, the African-American political-business class supported the incumbent's policies. These middle- and upper-class individuals hated the young African-American punks as much as did any conservative white suburbanite. Typical was the silence of the middle-class black civil rights advocates about Webb's efforts to stifle street dissent, especially on police violence.

End the Politics of Cruelty was a group protesting police brutality. It staged some small demonstrations demanding reforms in the police department. In response, in 1998 Webb demanded those holding public rallies pay for special police escorts while having insurance policies to cover any damage stemming from their protests. The purpose was to make it virtually impossible for tiny organizations to hold visible rallies. While he targeted such political demonstrations, Webb did nothing to impose comparable costs on those supporting football rallies despite the violence stemming from football fans' celebrations. Not only were the Broncos' Super Bowl triumphs marked by massive vandalism, but a September 1999 University of Colorado-Colorado State University football game at Mile High Stadium saw extreme police gassing of spectators. The police restrained themselves, however, when Bronco fans freely threw ice-packed snowballs at members of the Oakland Raiders during a Monday night game in November 1999.

On New Year's eve 1999/2000, lower downtown was a virtual occupied territory. With police everywhere, the department was ready for a riot, threatening mass violence should revelers try anything. The only permissible activities, city hall implied, were extremely high-priced affairs. Its efforts were successful: Denver's year 2000 celebration was a somnolent nonevent. By this time, the police readily cited street people for spitting and other trivial infractions. The number one purpose, apparently, was to show they were in charge. Webb encouraged harsher ordinances to provide for even more severe crackdowns.

There was a precedent for the Webb administration's measures: the action of Jim Crow politicians in dealing with civil rights protests in the 1960s. Southern mayors and sheriffs then claimed they had to limit the demonstrations in the name of public safety and the expenses possibly resulting from rowdy crowds. Instead of seeing this parallel and expressing outrage over Webb's efforts to stifle dissent, the black middle class backed the mayor. They were now in power and were not about to rock the boat.

Besides, their man in city hall delivered for the machine. Developers continued to receive subsidies. Labor likewise endorsed the mayor for at least not totally undercutting unions. Prominent black, Latino, and women politicians were recognized, named to commissions and high posts in the Webb administration. Tax breaks for corporations parading under the banner of non-profit community development increasingly became a way of life. The message was clear: great dividends accrued to those who worked within the system. The machine rewarded those who backed it. Webb pointed to the new library, Elitch's, Coors Field, and light rail as his accomplishments.

Instead of redressing the causes of urban breakdown whereby the police did not want to live in the city while many citizens distrusted the law enforcement personnel, even more than Peña, Webb touted himself as a champion of the City Beautiful. He readily drew his inspiration from the dirty deals of Robert Speer. Just like the mayor of early 20th-century Denver, Webb stressed parks and gardens whenever opponents or the press exposed outrageous municipal deeds. As with Peña and others idealizing the City Beautiful, Webb had a fixation on graffiti. He and his kind saw such scribblings as a foremost blight on civic pulchritude.

As the Peña administration spouted about why Denver had to become a great city, a senseless mutilation of property by taggers soared. More than anything, it was advertisement of a vandal's alienation. Peña readily declared war on those resorting to graffiti. His administration primarily focused on murals and political comments sprayed on the sterile concrete walls embanking Cherry Creek near the Platte River. The mayor bemoaned this commentary as a defacement of public property. The more Peña decried graffiti, the worse it became. It was increasingly less political while crude scribblings supplanted artistic statements.

Graffiti was a natural target. The city could do something about it. Police patrols and spy cameras could and did catch taggers. Citizens got a sense of accomplishment when they joined together on clean-up days. Dealing with graffiti was a manageable effort, unlike programs to redress school failure, social breakdown, anomie, slum housing, and the increasingly nasty interpersonal relations in the city.

The last came out in road rage. As sprawl continued, traffic soared. Having to drive for miles to get anyplace, motorists frequently became jealous of any insults or perceived attempts to infringe on their space. Not only were pedestrians and bicyclists treated as hunted animals, but other motorists were sometimes physically attacked for some transgression on the road. More than one shooting resulted from such a breakdown of community. Under Webb, the rights of pedestrians disappeared as right turns on red were permitted downtown. His administration took down some mid-block traffic control signals designed to control speeding on one-way streets in residential areas.

Photo by Phil Goodstein

*The statues atop the Sullivan Gateway in front of East High School at Colfax and the City Park Esplanade were renovated during the Webb administration, part of the mayor's commitment to city beautification.*

In response to complaints about speeding, Webb introduced the use of spy cameras run by a for-profit private contractor. Those nabbed by the devices—only drivers of in-state cars with legible license plates—were fined. Not only was there little due process in the system, but it was virtually a permit for wealthy drivers to speed since no points were deducted from their licenses. Far more than controlling speeding, the effort was primarily a revenue-producing device.

Even so, the mayor claimed to support traffic calming measures. More often than not, they were primarily efforts to get traffic off one street and onto another, especially in sections of South Denver. The more Webb undertook extra efforts to provide for more on-street parking along one-ways, the worse and more dangerous traffic became. Still, a major Webb constituency, neighborhood associations, heavily endorsed the effort.

## The Neighborhood Movement

By the time Webb sought reelection in 1995, nothing remained of the neighborhood movement of the 1970s. Instead of an aroused group of citizens who distrusted and readily fought city hall, leaders of improvement associations were essentially extensions of the administration. Webb encouraged this, helping channel city money and control to these activists. Members of city council made it sound as if membership in such a band was a prerequisite for good citizenship—only the unconcerned would not belong.

Neighborhood bureaus were ever more bastions of conservative, middle-class, homeowners. Generally, they did not come close to encompassing the people in the areas they sought to represent. Their memberships were often quite small, sometimes not more than ten or 20 people in neighborhoods with upwards of ten thousand residents. Often the leadership was self-encrusted where the groups operated more like exclusive social clubs than democratic political organizations open to all who wished to belong.

In some areas rival associations existed—personal considerations more than political differences frequently were at the heart of the divisions. In others, individuals known to dissent from the existing leadership were not informed about meetings. The bands were not mini-governments, reflecting the debates, differences, and diversity of a pluralistic society; more often than not, they were expressions of a few insecure citizens who wanted to impose their values and lifestyles on others.

This came out at their meetings where an extreme anger and intolerance sometimes pervaded. Far from seeking to educate themselves through studying urban issues, activists let themselves be guided by their opinions—they might even resent factual corrections of their stances. Some members were quite vindictive, acting as if they were negotiating a bitter divorce. Others simply sought power. A few activists pretended as if, through enacting their personal preferences, they were wise solons assuring the prosperity of the region.

Many of the improvement organizations were short-lived. The two with the most sway and staying power—the Greater Park Hill Community Incorporated and the Capitol Hill United Neighborhoods—both survived by having independent funding mechanisms. In the Park Hill case, churches helped underwrite the group, an association providing many social-welfare functions. The Capitol Hill

Photo by Phil Goodstein

*What some call art, others dismiss as graffiti. Shown is such a panel on the alley of the 1300 block between Ogden and Corona streets.*

United Neighborhoods was only able to continue operations thanks to the revenue it raised from the Capitol Hill People's Fair. Neither organization had a smooth link or dynamic interaction with residents who lived in the massive areas they claimed to embody.

Money was at the crux of the neighborhood machine. Webb revealed this in 1998. As had other mayors, he urged a bond issue to spruce up the city, including road work, better recreational facilities, renovated police stations, and libraries. Rather than presenting the request for such general obligation bonds as a sensible housekeeping measure, he claimed a $98.6 million package was for "neighborhoods." He appointed improvement association activists to a bonds-need committee to confirm this. It seemed as if a side goal were to maintain an administration slush fund.

No sooner was the money from the bond issue approved than city hall revealed it had a different agenda. Despite promising specific road and park improvements in campaign materials, it immediately reversed course on some of them. Typical was the effort to divert funds from an extension of 51st Avenue east of Emerson Street in Globeville. Right after the election, city officials, led by Councilwoman Debbie Ortega, discovered the promised project was laid out all wrong.

Instead of seeking delay whereby officials could set the effort right and again consult with the voters, Ortega called, with virtually no advanced notice, a special neighborhood meeting at 3:00 PM on a workday. There, in a place only accessible by automobile in a poor neighborhood where many individuals did not own cars, a motorcade of the latest pickup trucks, sports utility vehicles, and the neighborhood association leader's unscratched, late-model BMW, headed to the isolated spot. About ten citizens were present in addition to as many city officials. The majority of the residents agreed with the councilwoman. She cited this as evidence that the neighborhood agreed with her views, so validating the rejection of the bond election promises.

Despite the urgent "neighborhood" authorization of the Globeville revision, the matter did not come before city council for nearly a year. Then, showing the hasty incompetence of the change's backers, the city had to delay the measure because supporters had written the measure to authorize work on 51st Street, not 51st Avenue.

An opponent of the city's bait-and-switch bond issue, Bill Good, complained the city had towed away his many junk cars from his nearby property at 51st Avenue and Clarkson Street in a mostly weed-filled, industrial area. The courts repeatedly slapped Good's hands for stashing unauthorized vehicles on his land. He claimed the sanctions were city revenge against him for protesting Councilwoman Ortega's actions.

This was a minor example of the neighborhood machine. In some ways, when Webb talked about empowering neighborhoods, he specifically meant giving authority to snoops who wanted to use the city to enforce their aesthetic values over property owners and residents they did not like. In particular, the alliance of improvement associations and city hall set their sights on the institutions and customs of lower-class individuals. The improvers specifically hoped to eliminate tattoo parlors and day labor halls. They saw beat-up cars in backyards as a complete abomination.

The Webb administration increasingly showed itself to have a politically driven agenda of code enforcement. A prime target was Colorado Springs activist Douglas Bruce who owned slum properties in the Mile High City. The political establishment painted him as the epitome of evil, especially after he had pushed through his Taxpayer Bill of Rights in 1992. The city struck back by citing Bruce for numerous property violations.

The Denver County Court rubber-stamped city hall, finding Bruce guilty of maintaining nuisances. It subjected him to considerable fines and possible imprisonment. When the case came to appeal, the higher court found severe problems with the case. The appellate body ruled the Denver County Court had thoroughly inadequate records whereupon it threw out Bruce's conviction. Critics of city hall found the slumlord's assertion most plausible that the prosecution was more a politically inspired ploy than an actual effort to improve Denver. Meanwhile, to rid the city of slum properties, city hall sometimes ordered the demolition of old houses and apartment buildings. The net effect was to reduce the total housing stock for low-income individuals.

Most of those targeted by city hall, often small homeowners, were not as rich or visible as Bruce. Nor were they able to fight back. They consequently found themselves subjected to stiff penalties for failing to please the dandelion police. City hall strengthened this approach. Rather than having skilled medical professionals work as health inspectors, under Webb and Peña, the city turned the jobs over to a neighborhood support service. Seeing how some residents increasingly feared the city inspectors as a force of governmental harassment and repression, Webb—a strong advocate of gun control—authorized the arming of zoning inspectors. In other cases, code enforcement officials regularly toured neighborhoods with specially appointed community police officers.

Council passed laws giving the police wide discretionary powers. Foremost was the right to confiscate property that might have been involved in a crime. The authorities did not have to prove the property, including houses and automobiles, was actually used in the offense or a direct link existed between the property and the disruption of the peace. Critics loudly feared the authorities might use the ordinance to enrich the city's coffers; the law gave government officials an incentive to find anything they did not like a nuisance.

To strengthen this system, city hall closely worked with a coalition of improvement associations, Inter–Neighborhood Cooperation (INC), to establish a system of "neighborhood ambassadors" or "neighborhood preservationists." They were the block captains of the Webb-neighborhood machine. The mayor accepted volunteers, closely allied with the neighborhood movement, as opposed to trained city officials, to review controversial land uses and landscaping. In 1999, the neighborhood ambassadors began conducting block-by-block searches seeking code violations. They targeted cars parked on unpaved surfaces, improper outdoor storage, and weeds. The preservationists sometimes interpreted the last to include natural landscaping and efforts to cut down on water-wasteful bluegrass lawns.

Photo by Phil Goodstein

*City councilwoman Debbie Ortega speaks at an "emergency" neighborhood meeting in Globeville in 1998. Like the mayor, she projected herself as a foremost champion of improvement associations.*

The Neighborhood Resource Center, a nonprofit with close ties to city hall, openly advocated giving improvement associations this neo-governmental role. Doug Linkhart, a former head of INC, who was appointed to seats in the state House and Senate, served as the Resource Center's executive director. In partnership with Webb, his group handed out 27 checks for $1,000 each to well-connected neighborhood groups in July 1999. The stated purpose was to improve connections between the associations and city hall. The fixation on trifling code enforcement strengthened the link. More money followed in 2000.

The neighborhood preservationists were part of another Webb effort to strengthen a neighborhood machine—community policing. A buzzword of the 1990s, community policing was often little more than the old-fashioned, common-sense notion that police should be friends and neighbors of the people they served, not members of an occupying army. It was nowhere close to proposals during the 1960s and 1970s calling for police to live in the neighborhoods they patrolled while working with democratically elected community boards. On the contrary, most officers who had joined the force before the imposition of the residency rule deliberately lived outside the city. The police union repeatedly launched efforts to overturn the requirement. It succeeded in 1998 with virtually no effective opposition from the mayor or neighborhood advocates of community policing.

At times, community policing had ominous implications. In the guise of giving public power to neighborhood groups, the department assigned certain policemen and women to work specifically with neighborhood activists as community relations officers. Politically favored neighborhood groups had recommendation and veto power as to whom the department selected as the community's officer. By giving improvement organizations such authority, the police acted as if the clubs were the neighborhoods/people of Denver.

Seen in this light, it was not surprising how those in the know were given pager numbers for their neighborhood police officer. He was expected to answer their calls in preference to those of ordinary citizens who would simply call the central dispatch number. This was an open sign of the power and influence of neighborhood groups—the police were their personal tool. A 1998 survey of the Capitol Hill neighborhood, sponsored by the district attorney's office and slanted in favor of community policing, showed 88 percent of the respondents did not know their neighborhood police officers. Individuals living in unfavored parts of town, notably poorer and minority sections, who did not have strong neighborhood organizations or who chose not to belong to them, sometimes complained the police failed to respond to their calls.

In places, neighborhood officers were appointed after a citizen group had asked for one. Sometimes, the improvers provided supplies for the officer, such as buying a bicycle for Patrolman Troy Ortega who was assigned to the Congress Park area in 1998. In other words, more affluent neighborhoods with politically well-connected associations got better police service than poorer areas where people treasured their privacy and independence. It was another reason why the busybodies active in the improvement groups rallied to city hall.

The federal government supported Webb in developing the neighborhood machine. Weed and Seed was a special program under President Bill Clinton. The Department of Justice awarded cities sizable grants to establish partnerships between the police and concerned residents in marginal areas. The idea was to weed out undesirable elements, residents, and practices. In their place, the groups were to plant the seeds of middle-class domination and control. In no time, local programs were mired in controversies between different factions. Critics accused Councilman Hiawatha Davis of using a Weed and Seed effort near Cole Junior High School to advance his political fortunes. Residents in North Denver, who were on the outs with those who ran the Highland Weed and Seed program, noted how its director, Paul Roybal, had a long criminal record. But Roybal had good connections. His brother-in-law was Butch Montoya, the manager of safety, i.e., the city official overseeing the police department.

In 1999, Montoya reversed Police Chief Tom Sanchez, ordering the department to hire a cadet, Ellis Johnson, who was an admitted thief with a past record of drug abuse. Johnson, reportedly, boasted of his insider ties with the Civil Service Commission, the agency overseeing police personnel. Shortly thereafter, as the department suffered intense scrutiny, complete with charges of brutality, mismanagement, and outright police perjury and killings, Webb ousted Sanchez as police chief in February 2000. Montoya remained in place. More Civil Service Commissions scandals followed.

District Attorney Bill Ritter, whom Governor Roy Romer appointed to succeed Norm Early in 1993, supported the status quo. If anything, Ritter sought to jump

Photo by Phil Goodstein

*A mural at the Cole Weed and Seed storefront, at 1842 33rd Avenue, could easily be dismissed as graffiti, a foremost abomination according to many middle-class neighborhood activists.*

on the neighborhood bandwagon. Under him, the district attorney's office formed justice councils in 1998 in collaboration with the police and improvement organizations. This led to community accountability boards. They consisted of neighborhood goody-goodies who, collaborating closely with the police and district attorney's office, had the power to decide the appropriate community service for juvenile offenders who had been caught engaging in petty vandalism. The district attorney claimed the sentences imposed by the councils were not punishment for the guilty, but "solutions and agreements" as part of a "restorative justice" system.

Even as the administration used such rhetoric to cloak the modern machine, it could not hide the strong affinities between the Webb-neighborhood coalition and the old urban machine. In particular, the administration had close ties to public utilities. Traditionally, the power, transit, and phone companies had virtually incestuous relations with city hall. The modern machine reflected this in connection with the new utility player, cable television. In many cities, cable firms won monopolistic franchises through virtual bribery and ties with the political elite.

Subscribers widely hated Denver's cable provider, Mile Hi Cablevision/Tele-Communications Incorporated (TCI) for its lousy service, exorbitant rates, and broken promises. The company won the franchise in 1984, virtually renting key political activists and community leaders. The utility had offered them special stock deals for community access channels in exchange for help in procuring the franchise, a business deal painted as a civil rights triumph.

AT&T took over TCI in February-March 1999. Shortly thereafter, it had to renew the franchise. The Webb administration eagerly catered to the firm. Members of city council, who authorized the deal—including recipients of AT&T campaign donations—campaigned for voters to approve the agreement. The AT&T and city seals were placed side by side, noting the close unity of the two. Council aides called voters, soliciting for the issue in the November 1999 election.

Most of all, the utility provided evidence of the direct payoffs of the machine. AT&T hired key Webb backers as it sought to win the election. Among them were Greg Kolomitz, Webb's campaign manager in the May 1999 mayoral election. He was a key player in CRL Associates, a powerful Denver lobbying firm representing AT&T. Ken Smith, a former Webb campaigner, took a leave of absence as aide to Councilwoman Joyce Foster to push the deal as assistant campaign manager. Michael Devereaux, Webb's stepbrother, was in charge of getting out the pro-AT&T vote.

The Denver Neighborhood Cable Partnership was the bogus title of the pro-franchise group. Walter Keller, whose family had long had close ties with the North Denver Democratic Party, served as the group's treasurer. Simultaneously, he received city loans to operate a North Denver bed and breakfast. The Denver Neighborhood Cable Partnership's phone solicitors were extremely obnoxious and uninformed about the issues.

The AT&T steamroller specifically provided money and jobs for activists in the neighborhood machine. Dick Bjurstrom, the head of INC, was in the lead. He received at least $8,038 for putting the "neighborhood" seal on the issue. Isabella Allen, a Montbello neighborhood activist heavily involved in the Democratic Party, received $25,000 in 1998 from the Webb administration to push the "neighborhood" bond issue. AT&T paid her more than $5,000 in 1999. For the most part, however, the neighborhood activists gave away their skills and influence, wanting to show their team spirit and membership in the machine. With their help, the AT&T franchise breezed to victory.

## The 1995 Election

By serving as the mayor of neighborhood busybodies, attacking graffiti, advocating the City Beautiful, catering to 17th Street, arranging for business deals and subsidies, and hailing the glories of DIA, Webb had proven himself as the same cut of Bill McNichols and Federico Peña as the May 1995 municipal elections loomed. He sought reelection. Governor Romer was in the forefront of those endorsing him. So did many improvement associations and environmentalists. Leading black and Hispano politicians and business people lined up behind him, a man showing the system worked for them.

Many supported Webb on a very basic, personal level. The politician was approachable. He had an open house once a month when people with city problems could inform him of their woes. Webb also staged televised community meetings. Though they were primarily designed to sell his development agenda and code enforcement fixation, everyday citizens used the chance to talk back to him and denounce some of his pro-corporate policies. Opposed to the untouchable McNichols or the robot-like Peña, Webb retained a basic humanity as mayor.

Even so, unease haunted the city. Not only violence, but a feeling of restlessness pulsated. The elections were once more a time for the citizenry to blow off

Author's Collection
*Mary DeGroot*

steam. As was the case in past contests, rival candidates concentrated on secondary issues. No organized opposition existed to the Webb machine. In this void, Mary DeGroot unwittingly became the challenger.

A native of Sioux Falls, South Dakota, DeGroot came to Denver in 1974. After graduating with a degree in medical technology from South Dakota State University, she had worked at local hospitals. Going back to school, she earned a bachelor's degree in economics from Metropolitan State College of Denver in 1981, becoming a cost analyst for Mountain Bell. By the time she sought election to city council in 1987, she was a manager of budget and regulatory affairs for AT&T.

DeGroot lived in the Bonnie Brae neighborhood. Her husband, Bill, was a longtime activist in the Democratic Party. In late 1982, as the 1983 municipal elections loomed, he emerged as vice-chairman of the local Democratic Party when the incumbent resigned. Bill DeGroot hoped to use his post to win election as party chairman in early 1983.

By the time Bill DeGroot launched his campaign, both the Peña and Webb forces—who targeted city hall—had lined up behind the candidacy of former state representative Miller Hudson. He urged Bill DeGroot not to challenge him for the post. The latter, though, was sure his time had come. Hudson easily triumphed in the contest. Bill DeGroot long sulked over his defeat. He subsequently emerged as a high official in the Urban Drainage and Flood Control District. His wife, meanwhile, carried the family's political torch.

Aged 35 in 1987, Mary DeGroot campaigned door-to-door in South Denver with her two-year-old daughter for council against conservative incumbent John Silchia. He was an outspoken libertarian who questioned many of the basic premises of Denver state capitalism. Opposed to him, DeGroot had close ties with the Democratic Party and had been a member of Governor Romer's inaugural committee. She proclaimed city council should avoid confrontation with the mayor. Anything else would slow "the business of moving Denver forward."

DeGroot easily defeated Silchia, 7,994–5,250. On council, she firmly supported the convention center. In January 1989, when public doubts were expressed about DIA, DeGroot scorned suggestions for a council public hearing on the matter. The issue, she stated, had already been decided. Not only did she never question the project, but she failed to stand out as a councilwoman. Nobody looked to her for leadership as a principled critic of the mayor or Denver's direction. The legislator had no trouble gaining reelection in 1991.

The challenger did *not* campaign for mayor as an alternative in 1995. The heart of DeGroot's campaign was the promise she would be a better city manager than Webb. Denver, the councilwoman asserted, had to emerge as a vibrant place attracting new employers catering to middle-income workers. To assure this, she put together a trite "100 Steps Toward Denver's Future," filled with commonplace utterances and suggestions. Pointing to some of the troubling personal business deals of Webb, she claimed the issue was "cronyism and mismanagement versus ethics and common sense." On practical issues, including the power of the neighborhood machine, she was virtually indistinguishable from Webb.

Bob Crider also challenged Webb for the mayor's post. A Denver native who had graduated from Manual High School, he had worked as a truck driver. The school busing controversies of the late 1960s politically mobilized him. A close friend, Ted Hackworth, encouraged Crider. An anti-busing activist in southwest Denver, Hackworth later served on the school board and city council. Crider followed in Hackworth's footsteps, gaining election with Hackworth as an anti-busing candidate to the school board in 1971. In 1979, Crider won a spot as councilman at large.

A very friendly man, the 56-year-old Crider sometimes appeared to lose control of city council meetings when he served as its president. Still, he projected a seat-of-the-pants wisdom against many of the schemes of the Peña administration. While he had lined up behind the airport, he was not part and parcel of the slick young men and women who had run the city since 1983. Though Crider was a registered Democrat, the Republicans sometimes claimed him as one of their own.

In 1991, Crider had swept to victory as auditor, promising he would carefully monitor the contracts for the "$1.4 billion" airport. While he sometimes squawked about Webb's handling of the city and raised questions concerning municipal finances as the city's watchdog, Crider did nothing to assert himself in the airport

Photo by Phil Goodstein

*This yard sign shows how Wellington Webb successfully portrayed his 1998 request for a bond issue as a matter of supporting "our neighborhoods."*

controversies. On the contrary, as he ran for mayor in 1995, Crider was something of an echo of Webb's 1991 campaign: a challenger who sought to prove he could do an even better job of maintaining the status quo than the incumbent.

John Frew was the ultra-loyalist candidate. In previous years, the 39-year-old Iowa-born contender had emerged as an inside fixer, a staffer for Senator Tim Wirth who had led the push for public subsidies for a baseball stadium. Frew was a key player in winning the 1988 Adams County and 1989 Denver votes for DIA. Far from apologizing about the need for ever more handouts to developers, Frew celebrated them. A Park Hill resident, he was essentially Peña and Webb combined—but without the ethnic or racial coloring. In contrast, Crider was the candidate of community continuity. No radicals or even fringe candidates entered the 1995 fray.

To limit the change any new administration might immediately bring, in the early 1990s reformers increased the time between the election and the inauguration of the mayor. The city, consequently, moved elections from mid-May to the first week of the month. It further delayed the inauguration of those elected from the first of July to the middle of the month. The 1995 election was the first year of the new date for elections, leading to a vote on May 2. The swearing-in was changed for 1999.

Given the candidates and background, the campaign was incredibly dull. There was once more the feeling something was wrong, but none of Webb's challengers stood out as bold alternatives to the status quo. They failed to pinpoint why the city suffered from such unease and violence. Still, voters again showed a longing for change from corporate domination when DeGroot won a narrow plurality over Webb 43,338 (42.9 percent) to 42,860 (42.5 percent). Crider was an also-ran with 9,714 (9.6 percent). Frew came in last with 5,058 (5 percent).

Political commentators noted Webb had taken blacks and Hispanics for granted. The machine had slipped, not turning out the vote of those who primarily voted on the basis of race and ethnicity. Against marginal turnouts in the machine-dominated sections, DeGroot had done quite well in the traditional white enclaves of southeast Denver.

The results startled Webb. He was in danger of losing his post. His supporters and those benefiting from the machine mobilized in mass for the runoff. As had been the case in the 1987 runoff election between Peña and Bain, the mayor's backers sought to polarize the city. They portrayed the contest as a choice between a liberal black and a suburban white. Some of the incumbent's advocates personally degraded DeGroot, claiming she was too stupid to serve as mayor. The Webb camp further noted some of DeGroot's dubious deals, especially what appeared to be promises of high posts to influential police officers in exchange for their support.

Even less than in the primary campaign, the candidates failed to address any substantive issues during the runoff. DeGroot was at one with Webb in pretending there was no machine. Nor did she say anything to challenge the 17th Street domination of the city. Essentially, the mayoral election was a popularity contest. Only race and gender issues enlivened it.

The politically active wing of the women's movement was generally closely tied to the Democratic Party and the Peña-Webb machine. Though they did not mobilize in mass for DeGroot, some women were attracted to her because she was a woman. Others had no identification with her—DeGroot had never been on the cutting edge of feminist fights. Cynics argued conservatives would decide the election based on whom they hated more: continued rule by a black or the ascendancy of a woman.

Voters answered the question on June 6, 1995. Webb was the victorious candidate of the status quo, burying DeGroot by 66,884 (54.1 percent) to 56,725 (45.9 percent). The machine showed its ability to get a heavy, pro-Webb vote in minority neighborhoods. President Clinton, celebrating the triumph of a fellow corporate Democrat, was quick to phone the mayor with his congratulations. The message was clear: the machine was in control. Reelection was Webb's reward for his past granting token recognition of various minority- and women-business enterprises, strengthening neighborhood associations, and assuring the unchecked domination of big money.

## Webb's Consolidation

Heads rolled in the wake of Webb's reelection. Members of the police department who had supported DeGroot felt the sting of the machine. Division chief Miriam Reed, in particular, was demoted to captain due to her outspoken support of the challenger. She achieved little in her suit against the city complaining about her treatment.

Webb emerged as the head of the United States Conference of Mayors, fully supporting the Clinton administration. The president named Webb to various commissions, including serving as a representative to the coercive, violence-filled World Trade Organization conclave in Seattle in late 1999, an event Denver had sought to host. The city continued to hand out corporate subsidies. No active movements of opposition emerged. A few black ideologues who supported the mayor were quick to denounce any opposition to Webb as racially inspired.

During his 1991 campaign, Webb had vowed he would not seek a third term. By 1998, his pledge had no more substance than his unfulfilled promise not to accept a $10,000 salary hike as mayor or to allow council to confirm his cabinet appointments. On the contrary, the increasingly pompous Webb lubricated his ties with 17th Street as he sought to remain in city hall in 1999. Riding on a wave of economic prosperity, he was the right leader for Denver—a politician making all the appropriate gestures while endlessly lecturing on manners—as he served as a partner with banks and real estate interests.

The 1999 mayoral election was irredeemably turgid. As they had during other periods of corporate Democratic control, Republicans failed to mount a challenger. On the contrary, such conservative Republicans as Bill Coors and Bill Daniels readily contributed to the Webb campaign. Both moguls had had close ties with city hall from the time Webb took office. Other stalwarts of 17th Street, including former US West head Richard McCormick and Republican Party leader Bruce Benson, visibly backed the self-proclaimed liberal Democratic incumbent.

Photo by Phil Goodstein

*Don Mares, elected auditor in 1995, was among Denver's upcoming politicians as the city entered the 21st century.*

No Latino challenged for the mayor's post in 1999. The consensus was Webb could not be defeated. Therefore, political aspirants decided 1999 was an era of good feelings as they eyed the 2003 race. At the most, two African-Americans, who were dissatisfied with Webb's total capitulation to the white establishment, joined the race. One was a concerned black preacher, Gill Ford, who had clashed with the mayor over police brutality. The other, Stephannie Huey, claimed she was married to Jesus. They attacked the mayor for not doing enough for black Denver. Richard Grimes, a barber and sperm bank owner who had spent time in jail for illegally practicing law, also threw his hat in the ring. His only complaint was Webb's reneging on his no-third term vow.

Essentially, there was no race. Candidate forums were few and far between. Nor did anyone challenge incumbent auditor Don Mares. As he retained the post, his campaign virtually announced the politician's mayoral ambitions in 2003. (Generally, Mares was extremely silent as auditor in overseeing questionable city expenses and the problematic doings of the Civil Service Commission.)

The only color in city council contests was where the police union pushed "Mr. Leather," a past homosexual beauty champion, Kevin Shancady, against sitting councilman Ed Thomas. The latter, a retired police officer, had been critical of many of the operations of the department. Despite the police union backing Shancady, the incumbent easily cruised to reelection. So did all his veteran cohorts—there was only one open council seat. For all sitting members of council, this was their last hurrah. Seeing Denver politics were designed to perpetuate the status quo, voters had endorsed term limits prior to the 1995 elections, restricting all subsequent candidates to two terms in office.

Few pretended a lively election was underway. Veteran political consultant Eric Sondermann openly mocked the contest. "What race? They had more competitive elections in Soviet Russia," he stated. The only question was whether Webb could easily get more than 75 percent of the vote. He received just over 80 percent of the minimal ballots cast.

Ruling Denver greeted the returns as a pat on the back. Council responded to the low turnout by attempting to make it harder for citizens to place voter initiatives on the ballot. The righteous members of the citizen legislature feared it was too easy for the public to be heard. The triumph also produced an amazingly incompetent arrogance. Notable was the Webb administration's selection of retired county, district, and federal judge Sherman Finesilver to swear in the office-holders. About six weeks after the inauguration, a legal review showed Finesilver did not have the capacity to give the oaths. The mayor, council, election commissioners, and auditor consequently had to be again sworn into office.

Webb took his triumph as a confirmation of the status quo. If anything, his elitist policies became more pronounced. His treatment of Sonny Lawson Park, at 23rd and Welton streets, exemplified this. Generations of Denverites had played competitive softball on its lighted field. They shared the park with the many different faces of Five Points, including drunks who lounged about the greenery.

Few used the athletic facilities by the 1980s. The city demolished the old press box behind the softball field. It locked the public restrooms along 23rd Street. (City hall renamed the road Park Avenue West in 1990 to give the boulevard a more distinguished designation.) Especially with the massive slum displacement stemming from the renovation of lower downtown and the area near Coors Field, the park was increasingly a gathering point for those unable to fit in with the middle-class ethic. Winos and drug abusers hung out on the eastern edge of the park.

By the late 1990s, this was too much for the Webb administration. Encouraged by urban homesteaders, self-portrayed as fearless pioneers who were rescuing the fine Victorian houses of the neighborhood from the poor, a prime goal was the transformation of Five Points from a black, working-class neighborhood into a real estate speculation zone. City hall helped finance projects to allow first-time homebuyers to get places in the neighborhood. The Denver Housing Authority (DHA) destroyed some of its projects in the area. In place of poor residents, it worked to bring in middle-class and aspiring upper-class residents. The goal was to integrate them with the low-income denizens. With the full encouragement of Washington and assistance from federal programs, the city agency projected the new homeowners as role models for the long-time Five Pointers.

As with any uplift operation, DHA had a strong, condescending, middle-class bias. Its operations implied the low-income residents, who had long been in the neighborhood, were some sort of inferior breed who needed inspiration from their betters. (At the same time city hall pushed programs to have affluent, middle-class whites colonize historic lower-income neighborhoods populated by people of color, the Lowry Redevelopment Authority—the body charged with rebuilding the former Air Force base into a planned community—vehemently opposed efforts to have mixed housing there where the poor would live among the rich.)

Webb's planning director, Jennifer Moulton, was blunt about the city's strategy of economic cleansing of the poor from Five Points and Curtis Park. Gentrification, she announced in a Brookings Institution study, was a "benchmark of success." Parking lots separating Five Points and other lower-income sections ringing downtown, the high city official explained, composed "an intimidating moat" making a trip into downtown "unappealing" to suburban commuters. By driving out the poor and misfits, the city hoped to make such communities "attractive to private sector investment in market housing."

Given this background, the Webb administration's treatment of Sonny Lawson Park was not surprising. In 1998, it placed spy cameras in the greenery. Their

Photo by Phil Goodstein

*The fenced-off Sonny Lawson Park at 23rd and Welton streets.*

purpose was to keep locals from engaging in supposedly anti-social actions in the one-square block open space. The police assigned special patrols to the park. City hall claimed "the neighborhood" had requested these measures. The administration more or less defined "the neighborhood" as members of middle-class, homeowner associations who wanted to transform the face of the area. Locals who opposed the police-state actions complained the city had not informed them of the meetings and plans.

These efforts failed to produce the desired results. Consequently, in June 1999, shortly after Webb's reelection, with the eager support of a nearby restaurant owner whose eatery blared loud music onto the street, the city fenced off the entire park. Only those with permits were allowed to use the greenery. (The restaurant owner had a special key to the park.) Public pressure forced the city frequently to keep the gates to the park open.

Having attempted to deprive locals of their park, the city worked with an ostensible nonprofit housing developer, Northeast Denver Housing, to buy nearby houses on the 2400 block of Welton Street, giving the group a $468,000 interest-free loan. This was done in the name of making home ownership possible for individuals approaching middle-income levels. The actual result was the displacement of existing low-income residents and the Catholic Workers' well-respected, long-established soup-kitchen. (No sooner had the group relocated its facility in the abandoned Cathedral School at 1836 Logan Street than the city, pushed by neighborhood improvement groups, ordered the kitchen evicted in September 1999. The Webb administration explained the food line was in violation of the zoning of the increasingly less tolerant, ever more gentrified North Capitol Hill.)

Politically conscious locals saw these moves as direct attacks on them. The fencing of the park was a symbolic gating of the neighborhood as a whole. At the insistence of city hall and "the neighborhood," operators of nearby shelters were also forced to fence off their facilities. Both on- and off-duty police patrolled the area, targeting the homeless. Exponents of these measures endlessly cited the need to fight drug-dealers as a prime reason for these measures.

Not everybody was pleased. Some residents noted they had long lived near Five Points and Lawson Park precisely because they preferred the diversity and openness of old Denver compared to the gated, exclusive sections of suburbia. The mayor's action was an announcement that the latter were Denver's destiny.

Protesters were only marginal voices. Had Bill McNichols sought to implement such measures as mayor in the 1970s, there would have been a storm of protest from the black, Chicano, and liberal communities. Those backing city hall, including the members of the machine, did nothing to protest Webb's action. On the contrary, the neighborhood movement praised the mayor more than ever for precisely such deeds. Webb further called for severe crackdowns on the poor in downtown; he did nothing, however, to protest the mass, rowdy alcoholism of affluent drunks in lower downtown.

As the city eagerly pushed upper-class developments in the historic abodes of the city's down-and-out denizens along old Larimer Street, near Coors Field, and the Platte floodplain, tensions grew among the homeless. In the fall of 1999, a wave of murders saw the deaths of seven street people. The police blamed "mall rats"—teenagers hanging out on the 16th Street Mall—for the killings.

This was a minor aberration to 17th Street's triumph under Webb. The metropolitan area continued to sprawl. Besides, under Webb, Denver had reached its destiny: It was the home of the world's greatest airport, an appropriate conclusion in pondering Denver in our time.

## A Note on Sources:

Peña's career after leaving city hall is treated in newspaper accounts. Mike Davenport and Peter Boyles noted the US West financing of Peña Investment Advisers. Deborah L. Tucker, *To Make a Mayor* (Lanham, MD: University Press of America, 1995), is a pro-Webb, almost reverential portrait of his triumph in the 1991 election. *For the Record* was a monthly voting report of city council actions in the mid-1990s. It also reported on the 1995 election.

Walter Gerash recalled Norm Early's service as district attorney. Tom Bastien remembered Early's initial involvement in the local Democratic Party. Mary DeGroot talked about her role on council while she still held the office. Miller Hudson discussed his clash with Bill DeGroot in the race for Democratic Party chairman. He reviewed a draft of this chapter. Don Bain recalled the 1991 campaign. I observed the mayoral races, keeping files on them. There are also clipping files on the elections and candidates at DPL.

INC has issued newsletters. So have many of the neighborhood groups. Various city and neighborhood cooperation bulletins have appeared, including *Resource News*. Doug Linkhart briefly observed his role in neighborhood efforts.

*Life on Capitol Hill* was often filled with the platitudes of the advocates of a coercive neighborhood government. Articles in it heralded community policing and neighborhood preservationists. It has had endless pieces extolling the neighborhood organizations. Though more restrained, *Washington Park Profile* has done the same. Other looks at Denver neighborhoods and their groups are sometimes found in the *Southwest Denver Herald-Dispatch* and *North Denver Tribune*. I examine the workings of Capitol Hill neighborhood groups in detail in my *Ghosts of Denver*.

Bill Good informed me of his wars with Debbie Ortega and the city. I was present at the "emergency" neighborhood meeting on 51st Avenue. Also see Harrison Fletcher, "One Man's Junk," *WW*, February 24, 2000, pp. 9, 11.

The October 24, 1999, *DP*, p. 1A, noted the Webb-AT&T machine. Stephen Keating, *Cutthroat*, reports on the dirty deeds behind cable franchises. He describes Wirth as the Senator from TCI. T. R. Witcher, "The Revolution will not be Televised," *WW*, March 30, 2000, pp. 17–23, notes the cynical ethnic/racial politics behind how Mile Hi Cablevision originally won the Denver franchise. Clyde Lyndon King, *History of the Government of Denver*, examines the power of utilities in the old city machine.

The Minoru Yasui papers at Auraria and the CCR papers at DPL include materials on police brutality, efforts at better police-community relations, and studies of youth gangs. Ed Thomas and Dave Michaud talked about neighborhood policing. Jim Hannifin discussed the Congress Park Neighbors crime committee and how it procured a neighborhood police office and provided him with a bicycle. *Life on Capitol Hill* has heavily stressed the wonders of community police officers. Maxine Lankford informed me of the doings of End the Politics of Cruelty. I observed some of its rallies.

The September 13, 1999, *DP*, p. 1B, had a portrait of Paul Roybal and the controversies surrounding the Highland Weed and Seed office. In 1995, *Westword* looked at the Cole Weed and Seed problems. Cheryl Jacobs, Jay Katz, and Jeremy Ferguson talked about the Capitol Hill Weed and Seed. The *Curtis Park Times*, the newsletter of the Curtis Park Neighbors Incorporated, generally supported the city's actions at Lawson Park and in increased code enforcement. Walt Young shared his observations about these matters, including his discussions with city officials about the neighborhood preservationist efforts. He called my attention to Jennifer Moulton's remarks about gentrification, providing me with a copy of her statement and his response to it. Her study is "Ten Steps to a Living Downtown," a discussion paper prepared for the Brookings Institution Center on Urban and Metropolitan Policy, October 1999. Tony Robinson critiqued it in the February 7, 2000, *RMN*.

*Denver Voice*, a monthly newspaper, sought to express the views of the "homeless, formerly homeless, and disenfranchised" in the late 1990s into 2000. It carried many exposés about the city's war on the poor, including the many petty harassments directed at street people by the police and city officials under Wellington Webb. The paper noted the fencing of Lawson Park, the displacement of the Catholic Worker soup kitchen, and the deaths of the homeless.

# 13

# DIA: Disaster In Action

With Denver immersed in the fallout from the oil bust, looted by savings and loan scoundrels, and unable to produce convention center magic, in the mid-1980s Mayor Federico Peña sought to conjure up another means of restoring a runaway economy and corporate domination via a new airport. By 1986, the push for such a facility was the heart and soul of his administration. With virtually no consultation with the citizenry—a prime 1983 Peña election promise—he embraced creating the world's greatest airport. As was typical of Peña's years as mayor, Denver International Airport (DIA) was a cynical real estate ploy disguised by demagogic rhetoric.

The mayor explained DIA was vitally necessary because the city's airport, Stapleton International Airport, was no good. As much as the post-World War II generation, the great city rhetoric of Peña reeked with a contempt for the Mile High City. Denver haters dismissed all facilities as obsolete, poorly built, or hopelessly out of date. No place was this more obvious than in the mayor's treatment of the airfield.

A lot of myths exist about the origins of Stapleton, tales readily cited by DIA's backers. In particular, contrary to their claims, Stapleton was not a bold, imaginative effort against an anti-airport city. The field, rather, was fully in tune with the special deals and handouts associated with the public/private partnership.

In the 1920s, corporate Denver, insecure as ever, dreaded the city might get left behind by the growing field of civil aviation. The Chamber of Commerce com-

CHS

*Denver Municipal Airport shortly after it opened in 1929.*

plained mightily when Washington chose Cheyenne over Denver as a transcontinental depot for the developing air mail system. While the Wyoming city connected with Chicago and San Francisco, all Denver air mail routes had to go through Cheyenne. Fearful locals, readily believing business domination via state capitalist subsidies was everything, readily forecast the Mile High City's doom. If the Queen City, they gloomily predicted, did not engage in spectacular municipal efforts to procure direct, transcontinental airmail routes and passenger carriers, the Wyoming city would supplant it.

In many ways, the demand for governmental action in securing aviation links was a repeat of the railroad hysteria of the late 1860s. Ignoring the region's natural amenities over Cheyenne, promoters paid $6.5 million for a $2 million Denver Pacific Railroad to link the Mile High City with Cheyenne after the Union Pacific routed its transcontinental trains through Wyoming. Even as Denver invested in the line, the railroad industry well knew there was a lot more economic potential in Colorado, with its mineral resources and water, than in Wyoming. The Union Pacific had originally planned a feeder route south from the Cowboy State. However, since Denver was willing to pay for the railroad, the Wall Street firm naturally expected a subsidy from the Mile High City.

Even as Cheyenne emerged as a transfer point for the nascent civil aviation industry, airlines realized Denver, with its population and industries, was a far better crossroads than Cheyenne could ever be. The Wyoming stop was only a makeshift—it was easier for early planes to fly over the continental divide in Wyoming than over the high Colorado Rockies. As technology advanced, Denver developed as an aviation center.

Numerous small commercial airports popped up around the city in the 1920s. They were joined by the city's first Lowry Field. Occupying 120 acres, it stretched from approximately 38th Avenue to the Union Pacific Railroad tracks between Dahlia and Holly streets. Promoters designed the base to house the 120th Observation Squadron of the Colorado Air National Guard. It honored Lieutenant Francis Brown Lowry, an aerial photographer and son of a prominent Denver politician, who was killed in action on September 26, 1918. Among the businessmen sponsoring the field was mortician George W. Olinger. This seemed apropos. In response to a crash at Lowry shortly after it opened in 1924, the *Denver Post* observed the new airport would "keep the cemeteries hopeful."

While some civil aviation flights operated out of Lowry, other airfields came and went. This was the trend everywhere. In response, Secretary of Commerce Herbert Hoover called on metropolises to establish municipally owned and operated airports. The Post Office Department encouraged civil aviation by heavily subsidizing air mail routes on selected commercial carriers. All this added up to a general consensus by 1926: Denver needed a municipal airport.

The key dispute was where to locate the facility. The most logical suggestion was expanding Lowry. Proponents urged redesigning the facility so commercial carriers could share it with the military. *Denver Post* publisher Frederick Bonfils, who owned land near the Air National Guard base, wanted his property selected. Others called for using the adjacent real estate west of Lowry, farmland of Clayton Boys College which later became the Park Hill Golf Course. Humphreys Field at 26th Avenue and Oneida Street (also known as Vest Field, Western Airport, and Higley Field) was likewise touted. So was Denver Union Airport (sometimes called Park Hill Field, Hayden Air Field, and Curtiss or Curtiss-Wright Field) north of Lowry between 48th and 52nd avenues from Dahlia Street to Holly Street. Though rivals appeared in other parts of town, including near Overland Park, the southern suburbs, and in Dupont near 76th Avenue and Brighton Road, the consensus was to locate the airport in the far northeastern section of Denver.

Despite the existing air facilities near Lowry, in 1928 Mayor Ben Stapleton selected land owned by a close political associate, H. Brown Cannon. The head of the Windsor Dairy Farm, Cannon had served on numerous appointed bodies while pushing the Denver Convention & Visitors Bureau. His site centered at 32nd Avenue and Wabash Street. That real estate, mostly a dairy farm and undeveloped property, was called the Sand Creek site. Some mocked it as "Rattlesnake Hollow." Stories abounded about how Cannon got the land. According to one version, he acquired it through a close confederate, Mike Penrose of the London Dairy, who had his home there. Another account claimed Cannon bought the property for back taxes. A popular third report insisted Cannon simply stole it.

Bonfils, unhappy to lose the airport to Cannon, tore into the project as "Stapleton's Folly" or "Simpleton's Sand Dunes." Neither he nor anybody else questioned the need for a municipal airport—the whole debate was where to locate it and the questionable means city hall used to procure the land.

Denver Municipal Airport opened on a square-mile plot bordered by Ulster and Dayton streets from 26th Avenue to 38th Avenue on October 17, 1929. It literally took off in the 1930s with the coming of the DC-3. Trunk-line carriers United and Continental airlines arrived in 1937.

By World War II, the field was an air crossroads. In a measure of fulsome praise to Stapleton, who served as mayor from 1923 until 1931 and 1935 until 1947, the city renamed the facility Stapleton Airfield on August 25, 1944. (After a second Lowry Air Force Base, near Sixth Avenue and Quebec Street, began operations in 1937–38, Mountain States Aviation took possession of the 38th and Dahlia location. It ran Combs Airpark there, named for the company's president, Harry B. Combs, until January 1949.)

Growth was a constant at Stapleton. By 1945, it had more than doubled in size. Already in May 1943, the city eyed a 2,000-acre site for a second municipal airport to handle general aviation. Council appropriated money for the project, announcing Denver aimed to acquire the land between South Broadway and South University Boulevard south of the High Line Canal. Arapahoe County bitterly opposed the effort. In January 1945, over the latter's protests, the Colorado Supreme Court authorized Denver to begin land condemnation proceedings to acquire the real estate. Before long, the push for the field soon sputtered to a end. After sitting on 728 acres there, Denver sold the land in August 1958. There was already too much nearby residential and commercial building, it explained, to make the airport feasible.

The city, Chamber of Commerce, and aeronautics interests pondered other airport plans by the end of World War II. Some hoped to expand commercial operations to the new Lowry. Others believed Buckley Field would become part of the Denver civil aviation matrix.

In 1947, a group of administrators and professors at Colorado Woman's College, at Montview Boulevard and Quebec Street, urged relocating the airport some

Photo by Phil Goodstein

*A hangar from Combs Airpark, the site of the first Lowry Field, remained in place on the 3800 block of Dahlia Street into the 21st century.*

miles away to a deliberately isolated country spot. The next year, city councilman Ernest P. Marranzino echoed them. Not only did he work to force the closure of Combs Airpark, the last private air strip in the city, but he also suggested moving Stapleton. Denver's natural residential growth, he proclaimed, was to the northeast. The airport should fly elsewhere. Despite his lament, it was full growth ahead at Stapleton during the postwar epoch.

## Stapleton's Growth

The airfield soared as commercial aviation burgeoned in the 1950s. Not only did Continental Airlines have its headquarters at Stapleton, so did such regional carriers as Frontier and Western airlines. Cross-country flights frequently stopped at it for refueling. The *Rocky Mountain News* ceaselessly campaigned to "make Denver the nation's air center."

The city continually increased Stapleton's capacity. From 504,657 passengers in 1947, the field served more than a million passengers by 1955. The airport expanded in size, going east toward Peoria Street, south to Montview Boulevard, north to beyond 56th Avenue, and west nearly to Quebec Street.

Many individuals sought to live right next door to the airport. Developers filled the land in new Park Hill directly west of the airfield with houses. Realtors readily sold them to young families and airport workers. The city was concerned about residential development encroaching too closely on the airport. The Quigg Newton administration drew a line at Quebec Street in the early 1950s east of which it permitted no further houses.

In 1953, the city lengthened the main east-west runway, assuring more flights over new Park Hill. The airport racket increased in 1959 with the advent of jet operations. Those living west of Stapleton sometimes found conversations impossible for upwards of five minutes at a time since they were barraged by the jets.

Airport promoters did not care. Those who did not like the noise, they noted, could move. Besides, mostly blacks were starting to settle in areas directly under Stapleton flight paths. Though engineers undertook efforts to rearrange runways and flight patterns to move the noise from residential sections, the din remained. Ever more flights swept over sections where people lived.

City hall and 17th Street were unending in noting the Denver field was among the busiest airports in the country. In the pious hope Stapleton would emerge as a center of worldwide aviation, in early 1964 the Denver Chamber of Commerce asked the city to rename the facility Denver International Airport. In response, city council agreed to designate the old Denver Municipal Airport "Stapleton International Airport" to mark the field's 35th anniversary on October 17–18, 1964. Not until December 1, 1968, did the international part of the name become a reality when flights from Calgary, Canada, came directly to the Mile High City.

By this time, residential development had started to encompass the eastern borders of the airfield. Sections of Aurora grew up north of Fitzsimons. On September 11, 1965, Denver annexed Montbello, the development bordered approximately by Havana Street, Chambers Road, Smith Road, and 56th Avenue. This was land directly to the north and northeast of the airport. The real estate, once the Joe

Miller Ranch, was planned by Miller's grandson, Micky Miller, in association with Aetna Insurance, Perlmack, and Chicago investors, as an idyllic planned community. City hall heartily embraced it as the model of Denver's future. Neither the Currigan administration pushing Montbello nor Aurora politicians supporting annexations and developments east of Stapleton gave much thought to how these neighborhoods would impact the growth of Stapleton or the noise problems associated with the airport.

Operations at Stapleton also affected Lowry Air Force Base. Locals were concerned about periodic accidents at the latter. They were outraged by a crash on Hilltop on December 3, 1951, when a B-29 smashed into a house at 70 South Dahlia Street, killing eight crew members. In response, the Lowry commander announced the only way to assure no more incidents was to remove flight operations. But an Air Force base without flight operations, he observed, was an oxymoron. Denverites vowed they did not want to lose Lowry and resolved they would bear the burden of crashes to keep the military installation open.

DU Archives

*Micky Miller was a key player in the development of Montbello.*

By the early 1960s, flights at Lowry increasingly interfered with those at Stapleton. The Pentagon responded by phasing out Lowry air operations. When the last planes flew from the base in 1966, the Air Force announced it hoped to close Lowry as an obsolete facility. Advocates of commercial aviation thereupon loudly called for keeping the Air Force base's runways intact—they could be used for future Stapleton expansion. Little was done to implement this suggestion since Lowry remained operating as an Air Force technical training facility until September 1994.

Even with the abandonment of flights from Lowry, Stapleton was still limited in its flight patterns—air operations south of the airport also heavily impacted residential neighborhoods. With blockages to the east, west, and south, the logical direction for Stapleton takeoffs, landings, and further growth was to the north. The Rocky Mountain Arsenal stood in the way.

## The Rocky Mountain Arsenal

As the United States geared up for World War II, the War Department feared the military might have to deploy chemical and biological agents despite their prohibition by the Geneva Convention on the rules of war. The Pentagon needed a place to manufacture and store mustard gas and related weaponry. To accomplish as much, in 1940 Washington selected a 27-square-mile tract northeast of Denver, approximately bordered by Quebec Street and Buckley Road from 56th

Avenue to Highway 2 to 96th Avenue as the home of the Rocky Mountain Arsenal. The Army Chemical Corps began producing chemical and incendiary weapons there in 1942. The Army used napalm and phosphorus bombs manufactured at the Arsenal in both World War II and Korea. The Pentagon stored other chemical and biological weapons at the plant.

Washington placed the Arsenal on standby status after World War II. In 1947, Shell Oil and other private companies leased parts of the facility as a place to manufacture pesticides and related toxic substances. Shell dumped its wastes from the operations into the ground. With the advent of the Korean War, the Pentagon reactivated the Arsenal. The military declared it a permanent base in 1954.

The Army manufactured ever more deadly weapons there. Foremost were 21,108 M-34 bombs. They consisted of packages of GB nerve gas the Army began to produce in 1953. A highly volatile, colorless, odorless, liquid weapon, GB nerve gas paralyzes the body's muscles. Within minutes to hours of exposure to GB, either by skin contact or inhalation, a victim falls into convulsions, dying of asphyxiation resulting from the paralysis of the respiratory muscles. The Arsenal was also home of hundreds of M-55 rockets containing packets of GB nerve gas.

The Army continued to produce chemical and biological agents at the Rocky Mountain Arsenal until 1957. It often stored the deadly weapons in steel canisters. The military frequently placed the containers in the open fields, meaning the biological and chemical agents were exposed to the elements. Before long these dangerous substances were leaking into the air and the ground. The Arsenal was a disaster waiting to explode. A fire, earthquake, tornado, or other natural disaster could have set off a holocaust there.

Combined with the pesticides, the result was to turn the Arsenal into an exceedingly polluted site. Ground water was contaminated. Thousands of birds died after nesting in the area or drinking the water. Mysterious illnesses struck cattle, sheep, and humans in the vicinity. Crops withered and died when irrigated with water contaminated at the Arsenal. After initially denying any responsibility, the Army agreed something should be done. Its solutions exacerbated the problem.

The managers of the Arsenal tried placing some of the hazardous waste into so-called sealed lakes. Water fowl landed on these ponds, soon dying. The chemicals also leaked into the earth and further contaminated groundwater. Even worse was an effort to pump the wastes 12,000 feet into the ground right where the Derby Fault runs along the front range of the Rocky Mountains.

No sooner did the pumping begin in 1962 than Denver was rattled by a continuous series of earthquakes. They were the first notable tremors in the area since 1882. During the next few years, the Colorado School of Mines recorded 1,589 earthquakes in the region. Led by consulting geologist David Evans, some scientists immediately saw a link between the tremors and the pumping at the Arsenal. The military vehemently denied any connection until it suspended the pumping in mid-1963 when the tremors more or less abated. No sooner did the Arsenal again shoot the wastes deep into the ground in 1964 than the earthquakes resumed. Finally, in February 1966, the Arsenal halted further pumping. Before long, the earth was no longer shaking.

CHS

*Citizens protested the poisons at the Rocky Mountain Arsenal in the 1970s.*

Unable to dispose of the wastes deep into the ground, the Army planned to transport some of the Arsenal poisons to New Jersey whence it was to dump them into the Atlantic Ocean. When environmentalists blocked the effort, the military stashed 27,000 tons of the chemical and biological weapons in 170 railroad cars on the Arsenal. They were located right beneath the flight paths of Stapleton. This led the Federal Aviation Administration to caution pilots about the dangerous proximity of the Arsenal when flying into and out of Denver. A study by the National Academy of Sciences recommended removing all the chemical and biological agents from the Arsenal to a sparsely populated region.

Though countless members of the public were loudly alarmed by the Arsenal, ruling Denver did not care. Time and again, politicians and business leaders spoke favorably about the base, noting it was a patriotic employer undertaking all possible safety precautions. These were often the same individuals who had denied pumping at the Arsenal was responsible for the earthquakes.

As Stapleton grew in the 1950s, it increasingly headed toward the Arsenal. Bit by bit, Denver arranged to procure sections of the terrain for airport expansion. New runways on this land north of I-70, the city explained, would doubtlessly redress Stapleton's noise problems. In 1959, Mayor Will F. Nicholson told the Army Denver would eventually need all of the Arsenal's real estate for the airport. Even as Stapleton came to encompass parts of the Arsenal to past 64th Avenue in the 1960s, there were fears much of the old chemical/biological bomb plant was hopelessly polluted. Flights or airport expansion in that direction could easily produce a disaster.

## Noise and Deregulation

With no place to expand, air noise escalated with the growth of Stapleton in the 1960s. Not only were the neighborhoods right beneath the flight paths heavily impacted by the jet racket, but so were exclusive residential enclaves miles away. Downtown workers also frequently heard the annoying drone of planes coming and going from the airfield.

Even as jet clamor was an increasing plague of urban life, city hall celebrated the continual expansion of the airport. At the most, when massive residential and environmentalist opposition arose to the incredibly noisy supersonic jets, the city reluctantly ruled such planes were not to use Stapleton. Another Pentagon present to Denver in the mid-1960s aggravated the fear of supersonic flights: sonic booms were frequent for a few years as military aircraft flew at supersonic speeds over the city.

There seemed no limit to the demand for commercial aviation. Union Station became a veritable mausoleum by the 1970s as passenger trains virtually disappeared. The number of passengers flying into and out of Stapleton leaped from one year to the next. New facilities sprouted up about the airport. A hotel/convention/meeting district emerged along Quebec Street directly west of the airport to the north of 32nd Avenue.

The airport generally operated smoothly. A series of concourses linked the main terminal with the loading gates. The result was a walkable, manageable facility. Unlike other cities, Denver travelers were not at the mercy of high-tech conveyances subject to mechanical breakdowns. Stapleton was also relatively close to the central business district. The Chamber of Commerce highlighted this in its sell Denver efforts. The city, it noted, was blessed by an airport allowing visitors easily and inexpensively to get into and out of town.

Numbers illustrate the growth of Stapleton. In 1955, it handled 1.2 million passengers. By 1960, it reached the two million mark. Five years later, this was up to 3.3 million. In 1970, the facility handled 7.4 million passengers. Twelve

*The Stapleton terminal around the end of World War II.* CHS

million travelers used it in 1975. They increased to 15.3 million in 1977. In an epochal year, 1978, 18.9 wayfarers came and went from the facility. About half those coming and going from Stapleton were connecting passengers.

Developments in 1978 stressed Stapleton's vital role in providing for travelers switching planes. Washington deregulated the airlines that year. From the start of commercial aviation in the 1920s, the federal government had overseen all aspects of the industry, nurturing and subsidizing airlines, mandating their fares, and checking the levels of service. Now, carriers were virtually free to do as they pleased.

An immediate impact of deregulation was decreasing fares at centrally located airports. More people flew, attracted by discounts airlines offered to fill empty seats. At times, air connections were the only way of getting to certain locations. Here and there, it was cheaper to fly than take the bus to other metropolises.

The airlines used deregulation to change the nature of their air routes. They dumped the existing system of origin and destination flights as too costly. Areas off the beaten path suffered as national carriers eliminated service. A system of hubs and spokes connected cities. Airlines designated certain airports as aviation centers where they linked most of their flights. This meant a passenger often had to change planes midway through a trip. Each time the traveler landed or took off registered as a passenger flight at an airport. In other words, though the total number of people traveling was the same, under the hub-and-spoke system the passenger count increased because of more flight transfers. This increased total air operations everywhere.

Stapleton was the exemplar of the new system. Even before deregulation, it served as a hub. Flights from many small towns in adjacent states via regional carriers connected with transcontinental routes at Denver. Unlike most other big city airports, only served by one hub operation, Stapleton was the center for three national carriers: United, Continental, and Frontier.

Upon deregulation, enplanements at Stapleton surged by nearly 50 percent. From 20.8 million passengers in 1980, the Denver airport was handling 29.9 million people in 1985. More than ever, Stapleton was a natural crossroads, a place connecting flights from the east and west. The threefold competition at Stapleton made other carriers think Denver's airport was a special place they should serve. Delta, American, and Eastern airlines all mulled possible expansion into it. TWA had major operations there with 40 flights a day. The result was spirited competition at the field. Fares, consequently, were quite reasonable for locals.

Growth had severe costs. Stapleton became increasingly cramped. Travelers sometimes encountered delays stemming from the massive popularity of the facility. Intrusive noise from the field continued to vex people living miles away. Shortcuts during the 1960s and 1970s led to poorly designed runways. Their alignment was such that, during bad weather, Stapleton was unable to handle simultaneous takeoffs and landings.

After President Ronald Reagan busted the strike of air controllers in 1981, the commercial aviation system was in chaos. Flights were frequently delayed at all airports. As a hub, Stapleton suffered the impact. It was compounded by bad weather across the country. When other hubs were shut down, connecting flights at Stapleton were postponed or canceled. The result was all-too-frequent backups in flights coming into and going out of Denver.

Bad traffic direction by the city in the wake of the 1982 Christmas blizzard left many stranded at the airport. The paralysis of Stapleton during the blizzard showed the urgency of redesigning the field. The demands of the deregulated aviation industry had outgrown the 1929 airport. Nobody, though, was ready to junk Stapleton in the early 1980s for an exceedingly expensive new airport.

## Pondering a New Airport

All politicians agreed about the need for action on Stapleton during the 1983 mayoral election. Challenger Federico Peña echoed incumbent Bill McNichols: Stapleton was a fundamentally sound facility in need of enlargement. By carefully working with the Pentagon, clean, unpolluted land on the southern edge of the Rocky Mountain Arsenal could be used to realign the facility's runways to take Stapleton into the 21st century.

The city had reflected on replacing Stapleton for years. In 1967, the airport announced it hoped to have a totally new facility in place by the early 1980s, at which time Stapleton would be used exclusively for general aviation. Nothing came of this. Still, the idea lingered. In 1978, McNichols again pondered a new airport, one costing upwards of $2 billion and taking 25 to 30 years to build. He soon reneged on the idea, noting its incredibly high costs. Rather, by 1982, he had firmed up his plans for Stapleton's thriving future. At a cost of $1.4 billion, he hoped to see the airport grow onto the Arsenal. In March 1983, shortly before McNichols left office, the city hired a Washington law firm to negotiate with the Army over acquiring the Arsenal land.

(Environmentalists filed lawsuits against the Arsenal in the 1970s. The inept management of the facility came out in 1977 when the FBI revealed it had arrested the Arsenal's adjutant, Captain Gregory Alberico. He was convicted of selling the base's explosives and equipment to FBI operatives in a sting operation.

(The Army quit dumping toxic materials at the Arsenal in 1981. The military subsequently destroyed or moved its chemical and biological weapons from the area. Shell Oil closed its pesticide plant at the facility in 1982. The Environmental Protection Agency oversaw a massive cleanup. Eventually, a suit forced Shell and other corporate polluters to join with the Army in paying the costs of repairing the environmental damage. In the 1990s, to show the Arsenal was no longer "the most poisoned place on earth," the government renamed the base the "Rocky Mountain Wildlife Refuge." Denver officials celebrated the land as an environmental park/nature reserve. By 2000, Commerce City hoped to annex some of the western section of the Arsenal for residential development.)

As the city pushed an airport expansion onto the Arsenal, Denver took pride in Stapleton. Not only was it well located for the demands of local air travelers, but it was a money-maker. Despite the continual expansions, the airport was easily in the black, producing more revenue than it needed to pay off existing debts and operational costs. Some of those moneys poured into the city's general fund, reducing the strain of municipal taxation.

Nor were the delays that bad at Stapleton. Other crucial airports, such as Hartsfield in Atlanta, JFK in New York, O'Hare in Chicago, and Newark International, had more and worse delays—often with fewer flights than at Stapleton. As late as 1987, the city's annual report on Stapleton claimed the Denver airport had a great record of facilitating on-time performance. Insofar as delays were a problem, they could be solved by airport expansion, the realignment of the runways, and the installation of new equipment. In other words, a new airport was not needed to redress them.

Still, suggestions for a totally new airport continued to percolate. One idea was to isolate the field from the city. Passengers and employees would get to it by limited-access freeways and high-speed trains. Careful land use would assure nothing was built near the facility resulting in conflicts between residents and the demands of aviation.

Such proposals never got anywhere. Their crucial failure was economic: Stapleton was a major employer. Investors eyed the land around it for airport-related businesses. A new field, they insisted, would destroy this economic potential. The aviation center, in other words, must not be separate from the city; on the contrary, it was a crucial part of the integrated business community.

DU Archives

*An aerial overview of Stapleton in the early 1950s. Colfax is the road in the foreground.*

Government agencies undertook countless studies about Stapleton's potential and future. The Denver Regional Council of Governments (DRCOG) was in the lead. Local politicians created it in 1955 as the Inter-County Regional Planning Association. (Forerunners dated back to the Denver Regional Planning Association of 1938.) As the suburbs surged and the body took on an independent identity, it changed its name to DRCOG in 1968. It was a rather powerless body bringing together representatives from the various units of government throughout the area. Though DRCOG was unable to implement decisions, its clout came from federal legislation requiring metropolitan areas have specifically designated transportation planning agencies. Without them, Washington would not grant communities funds for highways, transit systems, and airports.

As the area's transportation planning agency, DRCOG's primary role was to help metropolitan Denver procure federal moneys. Reflecting the business domination of local governments, DRCOG was at one with the Chamber of Commerce in the belief an increased demand for transportation was a constant. Its projections always showed the area's numbers soaring: growth demanded ever more federal revenues and handouts to politically well-connected contractors. In 1980, DRCOG had concocted fanciful figures about commuting demand via public transportation to push an unsuccessful tax increase to build a light rail system.

Adams County, which wanted a new airport east of the Arsenal, asked DRCOG to conduct a study on Stapleton's future in 1973. The agency concluded a new field might be necessary were Stapleton unable to grow onto the Arsenal. DRCOG again looked at the field's future in 1980 in response to a 1978 Denver request. The premise of the survey was the number of passengers at Stapleton would exponentially escalate. The planners accepted the immense increase of travelers since deregulation as the permanent model of the future. By the turn of the millennium, according to the DRCOG calculations, Denver would need a facility capable of handling upwards of 100 million passengers a year. Even so, after reviewing six possible sites for a new airport, the study reported the expansion of Stapleton was the best choice. The survey's authors observed the exact future of the airfield was more a political decision than a technical one. There was nothing, they concluded, intrinsically wrong with the existing airport.

Not only had Peña agreed with this stance in his 1983 mayoral campaign, but he had issued a joint statement with contender Dale Tooley backing an expansion onto the Arsenal. During the campaign, the future mayor bitterly tore into rival Monte Pascoe when the latter suggested moving the airport east of the Arsenal. Peña confirmed his opposition to relocating the field on taking office in July 1983. At the city's behest, DRCOG endorsed Stapleton's growth to the north as the airport sought to swallow more sections of the Arsenal.

Politicians in Adams County vehemently opposed this decision. Peña soon joined them in arguing expansion of Stapleton was a foolhardy enterprise. As he consolidated himself as mayor in 1983–84, Peña's views on the airport flip-flopped. After initial great promise in city hall, his administration stagnated. Not only were officials often arrogant and ignorant about the way the city worked, but they did not seem to accomplish anything. Meanwhile, the economy was in a tailspin.

CHS

*Stapleton Airport in the mid-1960s, shortly after a semicircular traffic connection was completed to the main terminal.*

Hopes for a gigantic convention center encountered repeated roadblocks. Nor did water procurement projects materialize. The more Peña drifted as the impact of the oil crash grew ever worse, the more the mayor and his advisors saw the urgent necessity of a bold stroke to reverse the city's misfortunes.

In this climate, Peña eagerly embraced building a new airport. Not only would it end the standstill in construction stemming from the real estate collapse, but it would be a lasting monument, commemorating his administration to future generations. A new airport was a bold initiative to counter the devastation left by the frenzied growth of the late 1970s/early 1980s. Most of all, a new airport would spur growth comparable to that of the McNichols years while it allowed Denver to breach the limitations of the Poundstone Amendment with the city annexing suburban land for the project.

No one event led Peña to reverse his airport stance. At first, his position wavered. In February 1984, he began secret negotiations with Adams County over a new field. By mid-1984, the mayor had totally changed his 1983 posture. Expansion of Stapleton onto the Arsenal land, Peña concluded, was a disaster waiting to happen. The only logical decision to assure Denver's future was a brand new airport. The field was the Mile High destiny. Henceforth, the Peña administration willingly undertook any expense necessary to make it a reality.

From the start, the mayor was convinced the new airport would be directly east of the Rocky Mountain Arsenal on land Denver would get from Adams County. The site was closely linked to the real estate fortunes in this part of the metropolitan area. In the late 1960s, corporate Denver viewed Montbello as a daring success. The instant, overnight community was extremely profitable for Micky Miller and Aetna Insurance. This convinced other investors that Denver was on the verge of a massive expansion to the northeast of Montbello. They speculated in land in this part of the region. Despite their hopes, little happened. During the 1970s, the metropolitan area sprawled to the northwest, southwest, and southeast while minimal development occurred to the northeast. By then, Montbello was a deeply troubled community, rent asunder by social and racial tensions. Residents charged it was a cheap, shoddy division lacking its fair share of municipal services.

This was an afterthought. As land values stagnated northeast of Montbello, speculators noted the Rocky Mountain Arsenal stood in the way of the development of the corridor. As long as the bomb factory was constantly in the news with its severe environmental problems, real estate interests knew they would have a hard time selling houses right by it. Stapleton similarly was a barrier to northeastern sprawl. Even so, the city encouraged residential growth in the area, including at Green Valley Ranch near 48th Avenue and Tower Road. This neighborhood, developed by brothers Lee, Ted, and Harvey Alpert of the Alpert Corporation, was simultaneously an exurban community and part of the City and County of Denver.

As the idea of the new airport grew, developers saw places like Green Valley Ranch as potential gateways to the aviation facility. The Alpert Corporation encouraged this vision. On November 28, 1984, it sold Denver 644 acres of Adams County land for $19.5 million for a new airport. The Alpert family had bought the real estate three months earlier for $4.4 million. Despite the inflated price, the city subsequently decided this property was not the right place for the new airport.

CHS

*Stapleton was a walkable, manageable facility with a set of concourse arms stretching out from the terminal.*

Other real estate in the far northeastern quadrant frequently changed hands in the mid-1980s as different buyers purchased it in the hope it might become the center of the airport. Some politically well-connected old Denver families, notably the Fulenwiders and Van Schaacks, held onto land in the area, sure Denver would yet expand to the northeast. All this added up to a change of direction in city policy on the airport in 1984–85 when DIA became Denver's destiny.

## Adams County Politics

Far more than simply a place for airplanes to take off and land, city hall embraced the airport as an economic generator. With new buildings always going up while sections of Stapleton were continually remodeled, the field was a prime source of contracts, jobs, and political influence. On occasion, when the city needed to provide somebody a job, the individual landed up at the airport. The Denver Police Department tended to dump its problem officers at the Stapleton command. In virtually all aspects, properly handled, the airport was a gold mine and a rich center of power and influence for the mayor. A new airport would magnify all these tendencies.

Denver was not the only community to see the airport as a source of funds and profits. Onetime rural towns, notably Watkins and Bennett near the southeastern edge of Adams County, sought airport greatness. Front Range Airport, a small regional facility, began operations near those communities in August 1984. It quickly emerged as the area's third busiest aviation facility behind Stapleton and Centennial airports. Optimists believed there was no reason Front Range could not grow into the area's prime airport. Close to I-70 and railroad tracks, it was otherwise isolated enough from the Queen City whereby no one would complain about noise from jet operations. Besides, by massively expanding Front Range, a set of hotels, restaurants, and businesses would pop up around the airport. Land speculators there eagerly pushed a massive expansion of the field.

The Peña administration insisted the new airport be part and parcel of the City and County of Denver. Since there was not enough land within the city's existing borders, the administration eyed property to the north and east of the Rocky Mountain Arsenal, Green Valley Ranch, and Montbello for the field. This was land Adams County fiercely called its own.

From the onset of the airport debate, Adams County interests primarily wanted a cut of the action. For decades, this county to the north and east of Denver had the most colorful politics of any jurisdiction within the metropolitan area. In addition to agricultural areas, Adams County encompassed such traditional blue-collar enclaves as Commerce City and suburban white-collar communities as Westminster. Most residents were newcomers who had little involvement with or knowledge of the county government. Against them, the commanding politicians had connections going back for decades. They frequently accused one another of pandering to special interests, making inside deals, and receiving payoffs. Wirepullers frolicked in Brighton, the seat of Adams County.

Typical of the county's politics was the fate of a member of its three-person board of commissioners. Ronald D. Nichol was badly injured in a helicopter crash on October 10, 1985. When some of his opponents heard this, they lamented he had not been killed in the wreck. By this time, Nichol had repeatedly clashed with fellow commissioners Steve Cramer and Leo Younger. After Nichol won election to the body in 1982, commission votes were invariably two to one against him. His fellow board members, Nichol charged, often failed to inform him of decisions they had reached in private. Among the subjects on which they differed was Denver's new airport. Newspaper stories accused all three of accepting suspicious campaign donations in return for authorizing zoning changes on land slated near what became DIA.

Stapleton was long a bone of contention between Denver and Adams County. Already in 1968, Adams County called for the end of all expansion at the airport. Ideally, it wanted Stapleton removed elsewhere. The county readily lobbied federal officials and threatened court action against Denver, especially as the city continued to acquire Arsenal land for the growth of the airfield. The county's protests were of little avail.

Aurora joined Adams County in 1975 in opposing the spread of the airport onto the Arsenal. Both jurisdictions feared a greater Stapleton would increase the power of Denver and keep airport profits from the suburbs. Mayor McNichols was ready to fight them on this subject when he was defeated for reelection in 1983. Peña, initially, sought to follow in his predecessor's footsteps. But as the economy soured and the land speculation potential of a new airport became irresistible, Adams County commissioners Younger and Cramer offered Denver a deal: they would allow Denver to annex parts of Adams County for a new field if their county received a percentage of the contracts and concessions at the landing strip.

Simultaneously, the corporate community started to rally in favor of a new facility. (Only in 1991 was the new field generally called Denver International Airport. Prior to then, the city often designated it New Stapleton, the relocated Stapleton, the new airport, or sometimes the New World Airport.) In June 1984, the Denver Chamber of Commerce joined with the MetroNorth Chamber, a body largely composed of Adams County business interests, in pushing for the air facility east of the Rocky Mountain Arsenal.

As the proponent of a great city, Peña did not think small about the airport. He projected his field of dreams as encompassing 30 to 40 square miles—Denver then had a total land mass of 111 square miles. (DIA eventually covered 53 square miles in a City and County of Denver of 153 square miles—some existing city land was used for the field.) The real estate, annexed from Adams County, would provide space for Denver to grow with the airport. DIA would serve as the city's identity well into the next century.

New airport champions insisted the project was urgent. They observed the continued increase of passengers and flights at Stapleton. With three separate hubs, the airport was often congested. Some outsiders hated flying through Denver, fearing delays. Not enplaning or disembarking passengers who generated revenue to the city, they were simply individuals changing flights at Stapleton because they had no other choice but passing through Denver on account of the hub-and-spoke operations. Though such travelers brought little to the metropolis,

CHS

*Quebec Street, in the middle of the photo, marked the demarcation line between the Park Hill neighborhood and Stapleton Airport.*

Denver wanted these passengers. Were a new airport not built to accommodate them, city hall and the Chamber of Commerce feared, Salt Lake City or Kansas City would build facilities stealing such wayfarers from the Queen City. Rival airlines to United, Continental, and Frontier noted how congested Stapleton was compared to their operations, ones successfully avoiding the Mile High morass.

Citing the endless growth at Stapleton, the inefficiency of its operations, and the potential growth provided by a new airport, on January 28, 1985, Peña formally committed the Mile High City to Denver International Airport. That day he signed an agreement with Adams County. In exchange for allowing Denver to annex land directly east of the Arsenal for the airport, Adams County would get a share of the airport proceeds. In particular, its residents would not need to meet Denver's residency rule at the new field.

Peña envisaged a super airport, one putting Stapleton to shame. Opposed to Stapleton's five runways on 4,679 acres, the Adams County field would have eight runways on 34,000 acres. Engineers would design flight paths to assure jet operations had virtually no noise impact on Denver or Adams County residents. High-tech conveyances would whiz passengers from their cars into the planes through ultramodern terminals and concourses. The Adams County agreement specified the airport of the future would be in full operation no later than 2000. Once it opened, no aircraft could use Stapleton.

Not everybody was happy about the commitment to a new airport. Businesses near Stapleton saw themselves endangered. People who had selected home sites east of the Arsenal likewise objected—they wanted to remain far from the city. An anti-airport group emerged protesting the proposed new field. There was nothing wrong with Stapleton, it insisted, that could not be solved by expansion of the facility onto the Arsenal.

The Federal Aviation Administration (FAA) had previously agreed the question of an airport was a political choice, not an aeronautics decision. Now it endorsed the new airport. After the Denver staff of FAA pointed to the city's problematic planning for DIA, Peña exploded in anger. In March 1987, the mayor announced "I want these local monkeys off my back." Congresswoman Pat Schroeder responded by using her clout to get FAA to endorse the airport. She explained the Denver district office of the regulatory agency had "exceeded its jurisdiction" by pointing out the new airport's problems. The local head of FAA who had opposed Denver International Airport found himself shipped to Seattle. George Brewer replaced him. He set up shop next to the city's aviation director, George Doughty, developing a cozy relationship with him as the Federal Aviation Authority became a foremost advocate of the new field.

A new Denver airport, FAA noted, was vital to the country's civil aviation system. Unlike the consensus of 1983, when candidates and FAA agreed an expansion onto the Arsenal could solve the technical problems of the layout of Stapleton's runways, FAA concluded only a new airport could make Denver the center of the country's flight system. On this basis, supplemented by the growth potential of a new airport, Peña canceled efforts to modify and expand runways at Stapleton. It was cheaper, he concluded, to pay billions for a new facility than move a few obstacles making it impossible to modify Stapleton runways. (The city nonetheless added a sixth runway to Stapleton in the mid-1980s.)

Even as Denver committed itself to a new airport, commercial aviation was again drastically changing. By the mid-1980s, as the deregulation boom faded, many airlines reduced or ceased operations. After peaking at nearly 35 million passengers with 525,000 aircraft operations in 1986, the total number of flights and passengers at Stapleton started to decline. The Denver field served an ever smaller percentage of the nation's air passengers.

Delays likewise declined as the civil aviation system overcame the chaos induced by the breaking of the 1981 air controllers' strike. Even during the worst of its congestion, Stapleton ranked well below most key American airports in the number of delays per thousand flights. When the national average of flight delays went up in 1986, Denver's went down. Nor did the new airport resolve the delays caused by bad weather at Stapleton. The land selected was more apt to experience prairie blizzards than Stapleton. While new technology was supposed to address the problem of flight operations in bad weather, there was no reason those systems could not be installed at Stapleton.

In other words, there was nothing intrinsically wrong with Stapleton requiring its replacement with a new airport. As with the mayor's commitment to DIA, FAA's decision was political. It appeared to want the experience of having a major new airport. The last one in the country had opened at Dallas–Fort Worth in 1974. Since then, numerous cities had shied away from the massive investment needed to open new airfields. Ignoring this, FAA produced fantastic flight projection numbers for DIA, numbers with no more relationship to reality than those manufactured by DRCOG. It also saw DIA as a wonderful chance to experiment with a facility where planes might taxi at high speeds to get to isolated runways. (Supposedly, FAA so backed DIA it vowed that, if planes did not come to the new field, the agency would force airlines to use the facility.)

Despite Peña's January 1985 proclamation, little happened immediately. The commitment to a new airport got minimal front-page attention. Throughout the first two-thirds of 1985, attention on the mayor focused on his push for a convention center in the Platte floodplain. When voters overwhelmingly rejected the issue and mayor in October, Peña announced his response the next day: the new airport was the city's salvation. Nothing would stand in the way of its completion as soon as possible.

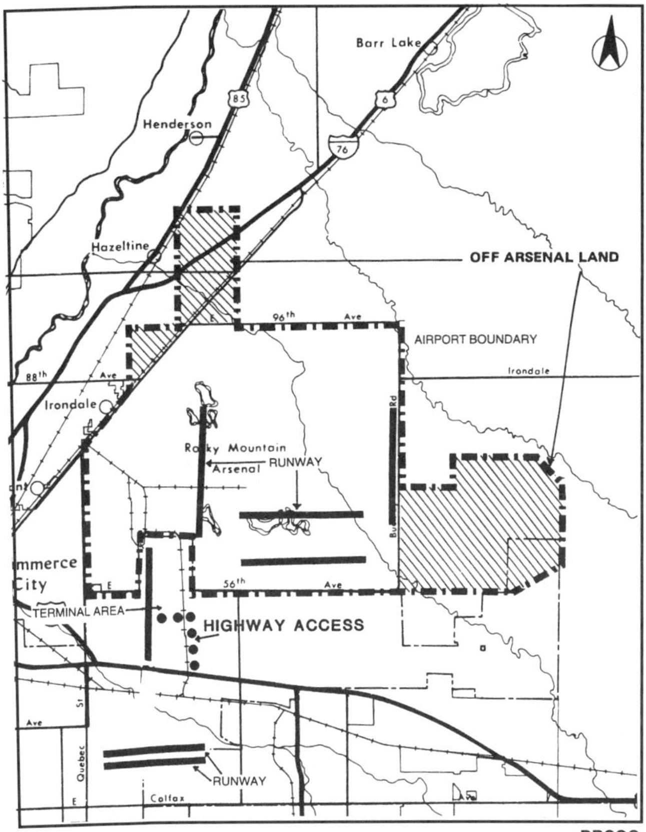


DRCOG

*This 1983 map shows the city's plans to expand onto the Rocky Mountain Arsenal. Peña opposed such growth, fearing the former military base's extreme pollution. It also interfered with DIA's real estate speculation potential.*

CHS

*A Frontier flight attendant checks her uniform in the early 1950s. The airline did not survive the push for DIA.*

## Reaganomics

As he did with many of his corporate handouts and pro-development projects, Peña justified the airport by his general endorsement of Reaganomics. Ostensibly a liberal Democrat who was supposedly at odds with the conservative revolution sweeping Washington in the 1980s, Peña had amazing ideological affinities with the president. Reagan argued tax breaks for the rich and concessions to corporate America would trickle down to the poor. Peña echoed him: by showering city funds on developers, builders, and speculators, the wealthy would create new jobs for the poor at the airport. City-commissioned consultants echoed the mayor. The administration asked these outside wizards to review the site of a new airport and the future of Stapleton.

Not surprisingly, the experts reported exactly what the city wanted to hear. In the course of 1984–85, the engineering/consulting/architectural firm of Howard Needles Tammen & Bergendoff (HNTB) examined half a dozen sites, all to the north or east of Stapleton, for the new airport. Echoing city hall, it concluded a location just east of the Rocky Mountain Arsenal was the ideal spot for DIA. HNTB dismissed all negative factors while emphasizing the positive ones justifying this decision.

About the same time the mayor cited the report to justify his airport decision, HNTB suffered a disaster in early October 1985. It had designed the Walnut Street Viaduct, linking the new Colfax Viaduct with Auraria. During the course of the construction, the workers, following nebulous plans, failed to place a ten-inch concrete support atop a pillar, leading to the collapse of the bridge. One worker was killed and another suffered severe, permanent injuries. Once the viaduct was rebuilt and finally opened, the city often had to close it during cold weather because it was right next to an oxygen/nitrogen plant. Steam from the cooling tower produced an impenetrable fog on the HNTB-designed road on winter mornings.

Even as the mayor committed Denver to DIA, work began on additions to Stapleton. Regardless of how soon the ultramodern facility opened, the city explained, the expansions were necessary to meet the immediate crush of passengers. A prime goal was the completion of a new Concourse E. In September 1984, however, the city scrapped plans for a 30-gate concourse American Airlines hoped to use for a Stapleton hub.

Continental and United airlines were not enthusiastic about junking Stapleton. They liked the existing field and feared a new airport would only hike their costs. Meanwhile, the operator of the third hub at Stapleton—Frontier Airlines—was hurting badly.

As hub operations at Denver soared, literal fly-by-night operations briefly popped up at Stapleton. Among them was People Express. Northwest, Eastern, Southwest, and Piedmont airlines also expanded their operations into Stapleton. Before long, supply overwhelmed demand. The novelty of deregulation and flying was spent. More and more seats were empty on flights into and out of Stapleton. Airline financial losses escalated. None suffered more than Frontier.

Formed in 1950 from a merger of Monarch, Challenger, and Arizona airlines, Frontier was a locally based carrier. It grew rapidly with deregulation. By May 1982, with 120 flights a day out of Stapleton compared to Continental's 110 and United's 96, it was the hub's largest carrier, accounting for 24.3 percent of the Denver market. As Peña committed Denver to DIA, Frontier was in a tailspin, badly hemorrhaging red ink. It sold many of its assets to United. This did not help. People Express bought Frontier in October 1985. The operation shut down on August 24, 1986. The community loudly lamented the fate of Frontier's 4,700 employees. Even as city hall was gung-ho about the need for a gigantic new airport, Stapleton was down to two hubs.

The mayor minimized Frontier's failure. He was sure the airport would soon be back up to three hub operations, if not four. Optimistic stories appeared suggesting Eastern Airlines could not resist Denver and would open a hub at the new airfield. The city also courted American Airlines as a hub. Though such cheerful blather greeted Frontier's demise, the fate of the Continental hub was also extremely nebulous.

Continental turned its back on the Mile High City in July 1963 when it moved its corporate headquarters to Los Angeles. Nonetheless, many locals remained strongly loyal to the former Denver corporation. They had grown up with the airline and recalled the glory days of its maverick president Robert Six.

Little other than memories of Six remained at Continental by the 1980s when Continental was the plaything of Frank Lorenzo. The ultimate airline pirate, Lorenzo ran Continental into the ground with poor service and questionable financial operations. Continental Airlines filed for bankruptcy in 1983. Lorenzo, with the full backing of corporate America and the courts, used the occasion to crush the airline's unions.

Striking Continental workers received none of the sympathy corporate Denver extended to Frontier workers who lost their positions. Many Continental employees never held another airline post. The strike was as devastating to Denver air transportation as was the failure of Frontier. It was an open statement about the changing nature of airline employment. Whereas previously airline workers had been on the cutting edge of the labor force, often receiving top dollar for their professions, the breaking of the Continental strike meant, henceforth, many airline jobs would be low-paying, subservient ones. Workers with pride in themselves and their union were not wanted.

Strikebreaking was nothing to the administration of the labor-backed Peña administration. Rather than shunning Lorenzo as a pariah for his vicious actions in destroying the integrity of Continental and mistreating its employees, the local establishment feted the airline. Continental was the "official" airline of Denver. In exchange for providing a few free flights for celebrities, Continental had its name splashed on all sorts of civic ventures, celebrations, and film festivals. Even so, the Lorenzo airline balked about DIA—Continental argued the rewards of the new airport did not justify its costs.

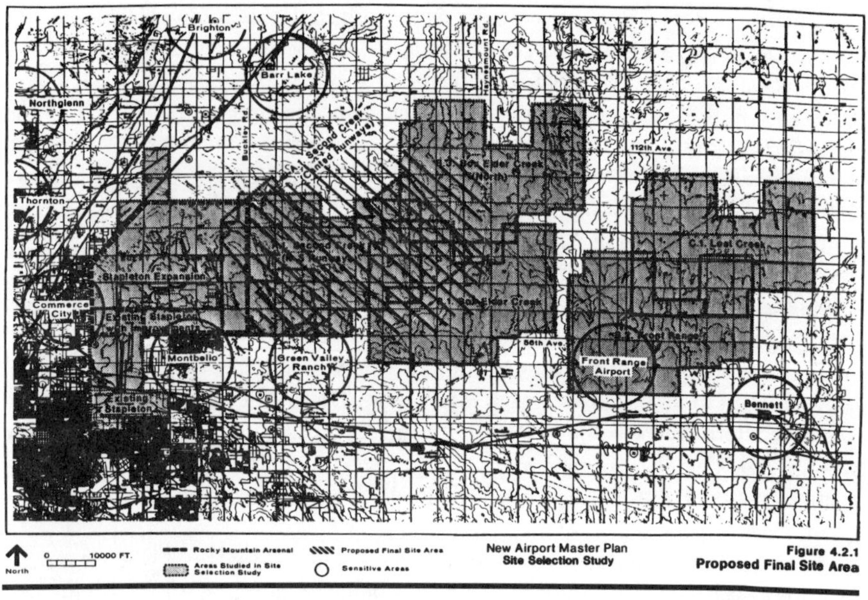


Author's Collection

*Initially, DIA was supposed to be directly east of the Rocky Mountain Arsenal, as shown on this 1986 map.*

City hall did not believe this for a minute. It commissioned further studies, noting the wonderful benefits of the airfield of the future. The Colorado Forum, a key 17th Street group pushing DIA, coordinated an analysis of the new airport's economic impact. Its report, released on September 9, 1986, asserted DIA would not only create 41,000 jobs by 1995, but it would revive the slumped office market, generate new retail, and create a great city. By 2010, the mayor hopefully proclaimed on reading the study, the thriving aviation center alone would produce 54,000 new jobs. DIA would be responsible for more than 10 percent of the total Colorado economy. The promised results were "so astounding," Peña announced, "we have got to figure out a way to build this airport faster than 1993." He listed 1992 as the target date to open the field.

No claim was too extravagant for the administration as it fully pushed DIA. Even as they asserted Denver had to build the airport to prevent Salt Lake City or Kansas City from preempting Denver's aviation business, the field's backers cited geographic determinism as key to the airport's destiny. According to boosters, Denver was ideally situated halfway between Tokyo and Frankfurt as the aviation center of the world. All the Mile High City needed to do was to build the airport and international flights and travelers would flock to Denver from all points on the globe. In an open advertisement Denver was overcoming its provincial isolation, the Peña administration planned DIA with customs facilities equal or superior to those at Los Angeles and New York airports.

Opposed to Stapleton's 108 working gates, DIA would have a minimum of 120 gates when it opened, soon growing to 206 gates. Besides aviation, the field would develop into a business center, complete with 40 million to 50 million square feet of commercial, office, and industrial space compared to the 23 million square feet of downtown office space. According to city hall, the project was a virtual godsend. As big business touted the new airport, it was obvious a prime purpose of the field was to overcome all of the insecurity and doubts about Denver held by carpetbaggers and the corporate community.

From the outset, the exact costs of DIA were nebulous. Stapleton was generating a surplus. In addition to paying for its operations and bonded indebtedness, it poured about $30 million a year into the city's general fund. Besides, it was easy for employees to reach Stapleton. They did not have to spend countless hours getting to work there.

None of this was included in the cost projections for DIA. It was to encompass a 30- to 53-square-mile parcel, create anywhere from 20,000 to 90,000 new jobs, and generate $5.1 billion in new business annually. By 2010, this would be up to $8.2 billion. Best of all, the airport would only cost $1.35 billion, i.e., a price less than McNichols' planned $1.4 billion expansion onto the Arsenal. Washington, the mayor was sure, would likely pay $1 billion of that. Existing airport funds would easily finance the rest. (Another scenario listed an airport price of $1.5 billion. Washington would allocate Denver $500 million of this. The city would then sell Stapleton for $500 million, meaning it would have no problem in raising the additional $500 million from airport revenues.) In this manner, Peña presented DIA as a no-lose proposition.

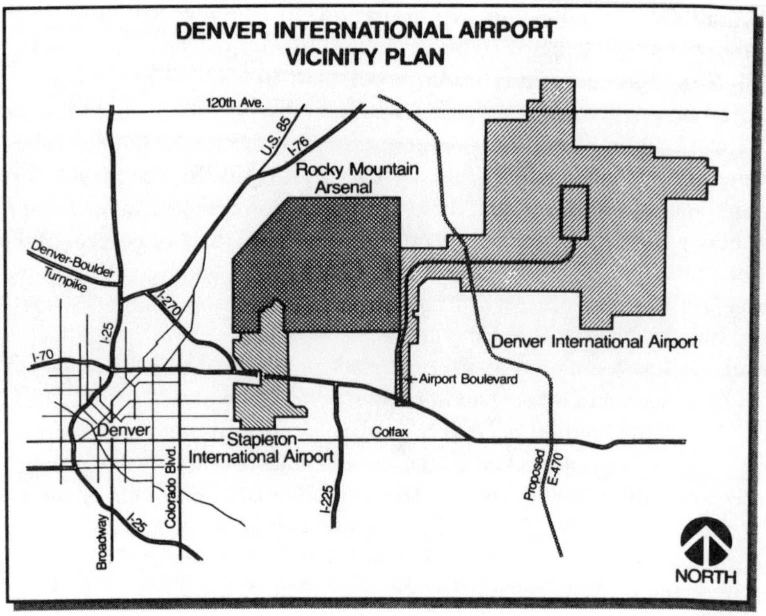


DRCOG

*DIA overwhelms residential Denver in size.*

There would be nothing small, puny, or second-rate about DIA. The great city's airport would occupy twice as much ground as Manhattan. FAA retained its projections that the Denver airport would handle 100 million passengers a year by 2000. The field would have two times the capacity and load of the world's busiest airport, Chicago's O'Hare.

Nor would DIA inconvenience residents. Advocates continually vowed the city would not impose any extra passenger access fees. Even if the field suffered from a financial crunch, such tolls would not exist because the federal government prohibited them. At the most, passenger charges for the airlines would be about $7–8, a dollar or two more than at Stapleton—the efficiencies of DIA would more than compensate for the additional cost. George Doughty, whom Peña named aviation director in 1984, stated it was "absolutely crazy" to think such expenses could go much higher.

By 1986, consequently, the effort to make DIA a reality was in full swing. Supporters had no doubt the facility would cure all the problems Denver had reaped from its eager embrace of cancerous growth since World War II. The field of dreams would assure sprawl was a permanent part of the local scene, another mark of greatness. Labor unions eagerly signed onto the project, hoping the construction trades would get all of the promised 10,000 building jobs there. Many minority contractors, most of whom were nonunion, were eager to get a cut of the action through government-mandated set-asides. They readily added their voices to the clamor for the airport. On this basis, Peña made the airport into a populist project:

it would help the poor, blacks, Latinos, and labor; only the most selfish, witless old fogeys questioned it. Even so, United and Continental balked.

The opposition of the airlines to DIA did not dissuade the city from relentlessly pursuing the field. Far from making the airport part of his beloved public/private partnership, the mayor was ready to dictate to the airlines on precisely how they would support the new field. Apparently, the only private interests worthy of joining the Peña partnership were real estate firms, investors, and contractors who stood ready to profit from the airport deal.

The mayor's ideological slant was crucial in shaping DIA. Not seeing the airlines as worthy partners, the city never sat down and worked with them on the project. On the contrary, it resolved to build the airport first and then force the airlines to come to terms with it. The project, the mayor repeatedly insisted, was so wonderful not a minute's delay was tolerable. So even while the exact users of the airport were unknown, design work got underway on DIA.

From the outset, the city planned to pay for the field with revenue bonds. Income generated by the airport, including additional tolls on airlines, would pay off the loans. Such a revenue stream, Peña continually noted, meant Denver taxpayers would not have to pay anything for the field. He was sure the airport would be up and running by 1992. To make sure this was a reality, Denver promised bondholders quick payoffs on the financial obligations.

As city hall loudly announced DIA was Denver's salvation, the long-awaited Concourse E opened at Stapleton in June 1987. Far from a lively, packed center of air traffic and burgeoning passenger numbers, it was a morgue. After nearly ten years of airline deregulation, the price of the policy was in full bloom: massive bankruptcies by air carriers and a spewing of red ink by others.

Traffic declined at Stapleton. From a peak of 34.7 million passengers in 1986, it was down to 34.1 million in 1987; 31.8 million in 1988; 27.6 million in 1989; and 27.4 million in 1990. The decreasing demand showed there was no need for the increased supply of gates at the existing facility. At most, city hall saw the decline of passengers as a minor aberration. The new airport would naturally attract more travelers and airlines—everybody would want to fly through DIA.

## Land Speculation

Corporate Colorado loudly backed Peña on the airport. The more obvious it was that the frenzied growth in the 1970s and early 1980s had led to the bankruptcies, foreclosures, and business failures of the mid-1980s, the more investors were eager to have the city build DIA. Right at the time the drive for the great airport got in full gear in early 1987, the Denver Chamber of Commerce changed its name to the Greater Denver Chamber of Commerce. It loudly announced the new field was vital for the business of greater Denver as a whole.

Many Chamber members had direct interests in building and real estate projects at or around DIA. No sooner did the first rumors percolate in 1984 about the airport arising east of the Rocky Mountain Arsenal than land speculators seized on the opportunity. In the forefront was MDC, the nation's fifth-largest home builder.

Owner Larry Mizel had close connections with both the Republican Reagan administration and the Democratic Peña city hall.

Though the oil/real estate collapse paralyzed most of the city's building by 1986, MDC was still going strong. Mizel and his chief operative, David Mandarich, heavily used the company's political clout, actively intervening in that year's gubernatorial election in which Roy Romer replaced Richard Lamm as the state's chief executive. From his first day in office, Romer was at one with Peña in pushing Denver International Airport.

MDC sometimes asked its subcontractors to assist it in channeling money to pro-development candidates. The home builder poured funds into crucial campaigns right when debates over the airport raged at fever pitch. Politicians it favored agreed a new airport was vital to Denver's future. (The powerhouse law firm of Brownstein Hyatt Farber & Strickland, which had extremely cozy ties with the Peña and Romer administrations, represented MDC, the Chamber of Commerce, Silverado Savings, and Bill Walters. Simultaneously Brownstein Hyatt was in the vanguard of lobbying Congress to provide federal funds for DIA.)

From the very first ponderings of the new airport under Peña, Mizel was a key player. In addition to running MDC, he also headed Omnibancorp. An associate there was Phil Winn, a powerful Republican politician who held key posts in the Reagan administration. In 1984, Omnibank Southeast, on whose board Winn sat, lent $500,000 to Tower 64 Limited Partnership, an outfit led by Gregory Kent and Michael Blumenthal. They used the money to acquire 317 acres along Tower Road between 64th and 72nd avenues—prime airport real estate. Kent and Blumenthal, in turn, liberally contributed to Adams County commissioners who authorized rezoning the land for residential use just before the Denver–Adams County agreement.

On December 26, 1984, immediately after Peña first announced plans for the airport east of the Arsenal, MDC began to acquire land and options on 877 acres from Union Pacific Land Resources on what was known as the Upland Tract. This referred to property between roughly 40th and 48th avenues from Chambers Road to Tower Road. It was situated right along the central access corridor to the proposed new facility. In the course of the next year, various MDC front groups, many with key connections to Silverado Savings, traded these parcels among themselves. At the same time, MDC bought $6 million in convertible Silverado preferred stock. At its peak, MDC had a $43 million investment in Silverado.

The development company paid about 69 to 94 cents a square foot for Upland Tract properties. An appraisal stated the land was worth about 10 to 12 cents a square foot for simple farming. Should, however, the airport corridor pass through the property, the evaluator continued, the real estate would have a value of $8 to $12 a square foot. Translated, this meant land MDC bought for $4,000 an acre would be worth upwards of $522,000 an acre once DIA boomed.

Mizel continued to play an active role in DIA land deals and political developments during the last half of the 1980s. Right after Mizel met with the mayor in September 1986, for instance, Peña announced the accelerated DIA construction schedule. When an election on the airport loomed in Adams County in the spring

Photo by Phil Goodstein

*After closing as an Air Force base in 1994, Lowry rapidly emerged as a community filled with luxurious homes. Promoters of DIA were sure it would spark comparable developments at Stapleton. Shown are new houses on South Quebec Street just north of Alameda Avenue on the former Lowry land in 1998.*

of 1988, Mizel swore he only had minimal holdings near the airport. He explained he supported DIA as an important public works project good for the region.

The city bought some land from MDC near the proposed airport for about $40,000 an acre in 1986. Shortly after this transaction, MDC acquired another 1,300 acres in the vicinity. In 1987, MDC contributed at least $34,000 to the Peña mayoral campaign. Upon the mayor's reelection, Mizel emerged as the voice of the business community loudly backing Peña on the airport. The developer had easy access to city hall.

In connection with MDC, manipulators around Silverado Savings also eagerly bought property near the new airport. They set up Silverado Elektra, a landholding company, to fuel the thrift's speculative purchases. Among the Silverado investments was the Little Buckaroo Ranch, a 39-acre dry wheat farm, near 38th Avenue and Tower Road, adjacent to MDC's Upland Tract. The smoke-and-mirrors savings and loan bought it for $1.5 million in 1984, right when the airport was pondered. As DIA started to approach reality, Silverado sold the Little Buckaroo in the summer of 1985 for $3.7 million to Wayne Gardenswartz, a former executive with MDC. Silverado helped provide the financing for this bleak acreage, land little more than a dirt farm and a few buildings. Gardenswartz was essentially a straw buyer for MDC. The development firm lent him $1.1 million for a down payment on the deal.

The next year, 1986, as it was obvious Denver was going ahead with DIA, Gardenswartz/MDC found a new buyer for the Little Buckaroo, Craig Balnicke, another former MDC executive. He paid nearly $4.3 million for the land with the help of a $3.8 million loan from Silverado. Though MDC was entitled to profits from the deal, the loan was written whereby the developer was not responsible for paying any part of the principal. In September 1993, the Federal Deposit Insurance Corporation, which had taken possession of the Little Buckaroo in the wake of the savings and loan debacle, sold the land at auction for $325,000.

Silverado investor Bill Walters was chairman of the Greater Denver Chamber of Commerce when it heavily pushed DIA. (The thrift's president Michael Wise was the group's treasurer.) The Chamber chief bought 4,000 acres in the airport area in December 1985, with the help of a $26 million loan from the savings and loan. Walters subsequently got another $11 million from Silverado for a couple of other purchases amounting to nearly 2,500 acres. All in all, Silverado put up $70 million-plus for speculative land investments near the airport. With Walters and MDC, it amassed more than 10,000 acres in the area. If nothing else, DIA was the last hope for Silverado Savings.

As Chamber leaders lined up to profit from DIA, the organization gave no consideration to possible negative repercussions from the new airport. Instead of seeing DIA as an extremely expensive investment, one cautiously considered, the foremost advocates of the new airport—many, such as Chamber chief Dick Flem-

**Author's Collection**

*Insecurity and a complete vehicular dominance are the keynotes of this brochure for DIA.*

ing, who had only recently arrived in the city and would be gone within a few years—showed their scorn for the people of Denver. If nothing else, DIA was designed as a newcomers' place. Treating other cities as their true homes, these backers were individuals who frequently flew. They supported DIA as a sign of their ostentatious triumph in the cow town they had colonized.

Airport backers scornfully ignored Stapleton's advantages to the downtown business community. Peña and the Chamber had no use for the existing field's relative proximity to the central city. They gave no account to how, with the easy access of Stapleton, travelers passing through the area might venture off their itineraries to visit the heart of Denver. Against this, in a new facility isolated from downtown, these potential tourists would likely skip an excursion to the central business district. The jet set might ignore Denver altogether, flying directly to Aspen or Vail.

There was also the possibility the airport might be a flop. The frenzied construction pace, the promised minimal costs, the perceived miracle benefits, and the lack of airline cooperation could easily backfire. The price of the project might get out of hand. Nor was there any guarantee that the heralded, but unproven, technologies slated for DIA would work. In such circumstances, far from an amenity, the airport would be a black eye for Denver, one showing the foolish greed of the business community and a gullible citizenry. Such a fiasco would prove a sure reason for any sensible person or investor to stay away from the Mile High City.

Neither the business community nor politicians pondered these possibilities. As the Chamber of Commerce and Silverado crowd poured money into the DIA campaign, establishment Denver dismissed any questioning of the airport as damnable heresy. Nothing, the Peña administration repeatedly informed the citizenry, could possibly could go wrong with the venture.

The media heartily embraced the project. Their leaders were often closely tied with the Chamber. Roger Ogden, who headed Channel Nine and then Channel Four, served as chairman of the Chamber. Bill Hornby, a retired *Denver Post* senior editor, wrote a book praising the Chamber's front group on the airport, the Greater Denver Corporation. Other broadcast and newspaper executives likewise had ties with those standing to benefit from DIA. Television and published news accounts projected the impression of a wide consensus in favor of the effort.

One doubter was Bill McNichols. In an outspoken moment, he opposed the venture, calling it a "mirage. . . . It is an unfortunate thing when people embrace a fleeting picture painted in the sky." Other than for this, he mostly kept his peace. He gave no more leadership to those doubting the effort than he did to promoting harmony in the Queen City while he was mayor. Even so, McNichols' observance illustrated why he had to go in 1983: he was old Denver, an obsolete encumbrance to Mile High greatness who no longer served the interests of the business community. His successor did.

Far from echoing McNichols' criticism of DIA, none of the main contenders to Peña made the airport an issue in the 1987 election. Rather than challenging the project and the hasty, unquestioning, miracle-producing tone of the mayor, they asserted they could do an even better job than the incumbent in getting it done.

Even so, Peña's reelection was a vote for the airport. The mayor's return to office was a sign the city would move at full speed ahead on DIA.

## Roy Romer and DIA

The new governor, Roy Romer, fully echoed the mayor on the field. Romer took office in January 1987, a drastic change in pace and tone from his predecessor, Richard Lamm. The latter had ridden his opposition to the Winter Olympics to win election as the state's chief executive in 1974. During Lamm's 12 years in office, Colorado experienced massive growth. The governor never formulated an effective program of action to deal with cancerous sprawl. Nor did he do much to prevent the oil boom from draining the state and collapsing in a massive depression. On the contrary, Lamm generally had a laissez-faire approach. At the most, he was Governor Gloom for his dreary predictions about where the state and country were headed. He failed to sketch a way the Centennial State could recover from the oil bust.

Romer, on the other hand, celebrated development and business domination. No sooner was he elected, with generous contributions from the development/building industry—including about $100,000 from Silverado-MDC-Walters—than the new governor swore he would "make sure the airport happens." He named Mizel to the Colorado Economic Development Council. There the home builder called for using the state organization's $1.4 million budget to push DIA.

The state's chief executive quickly projected himself as supergovernor, one who was everywhere and did everything. Critics mocked him as "Governor Roamer" as the politician traveled far and wide trying to market Colorado and bring business to it. His message was plain: the state was for sale to wealthy corporations ready to invest in it. DIA was a sign of how serious the Centennial State was to provide facilities to assure international air access.

The business community gave DIA far more than paper support. In November 1986, the Chamber of Commerce formed the Greater Denver Corporation, a political action committee advocating projects good for big business. The voice of corporate Denver raised $5 million from 587 sponsors. Half of the Greater Denver Corporation's budget went to lobbying for DIA.

From the outset, the Greater Denver Corporation had something to hide. At least it acted to cloak its revenue stream. The Chamber of Commerce successfully pushed legislation through the General Assembly to keep the Greater Denver Corporation's list of donors secret. This was at a time when reformers loudly demanded the public disclosure of big-money contributors who influenced politicians and public issues. Despite the governor's support, the voice of big business eventually lost a court case brought by former state Representative John Davoren. The court ordered it to reveal the names of those giving funds to the Greater Denver Corporation. Even as its nefarious role in buying support for DIA came out, the Chamber remained a close collaborator with the governor and mayor—it was the "private" side of the public/private partnership. This was obvious in 1991 when the city awarded it, without competitive bidding, a $325,000 contract to promote DIA.

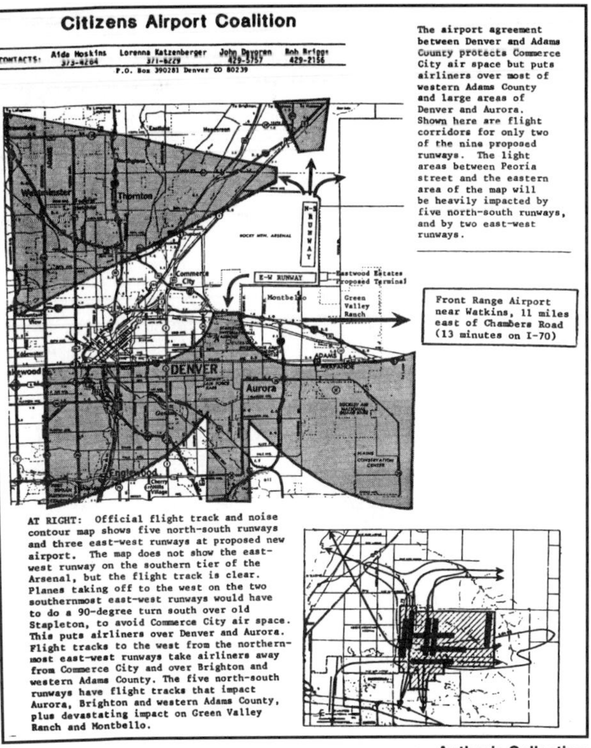


**Author's Collection**

*Citizens Airport Coalition was an Adams County group opposed to DIA.*

## The Adams County Election

With Peña reelected and the rest of the political and economic establishment behind him, Denver was ready to breach the Poundstone Amendment for the new airport. Denver, according to the legislation, could annex suburban land if the commissioners and the people in the county so affected authorized the measure. The city struck a deal with Adams County leaders in January 1988, permitting Denver to annex about 45 square miles east of the Arsenal for the airport. Not only were Adams County residents exempted from Denver's residency requirement at the speculative facility, but Adams County would share the fruits of airport development. Denver promised to finance Adams County roads leading to the new airport and give Adams County $8 million for improvements of the small Front Range Airport near Watkins.

Before the annexation could become a reality, Adams County voters had to approve it. This was cause for great concern. Unlike residents in Arapahoe County, who readily supported build-it projects, Adams County residents had a reputation for conservative caution. They frequently voted no on various improvements and economic elixirs, including Coors Field, light rail, and E-470. County commissioners continued to squabble. Unlike the Chamber/Peña/Romer cabal, its political establishment was not of one mind about DIA.

Some Adams County residents feared the new field. They noted Denver claimed it had to move the airport because of Stapleton's noise impact. If planes from the existing airport caused noise pollution over Denver, they feared, the jets would do the same over their enclaves. The projected flight patterns of DIA took aircraft over numerous residential sections of Adams County.

Peña continually cited noise problems to show DIA was vital. For years, residents of Park Hill had complained about the endless drone of planes. City promises to solve the problem were never kept. In 1981, Greater Park Hill Community sued to force the city to cease and desist the nuisance.

Right after Peña decided DIA was Denver's salvation, the city settled the lawsuit in 1985 on terms highly favorable to the neighborhood group. Denver vowed to build a new airport to replace Stapleton. Once DIA was operating, the agreement stated, there would be no more flights out of the old field. This would allow Park Hill to resume its rightful place as the idyllic, elite enclave it was supposed to be. The mayor repeatedly cited the Park Hill settlement as evidence of why the city was legally obliged to build DIA. Peña moved to an elite section of Park Hill shortly after his 1987 reelection.

Events like this were more than coincidence. Or so Adams County skeptics believed as a special election approached on May 17, 1988, on the annexation and airport. The electorate appeared about evenly divided on the issue. Consultants and political aficionados alike agreed on one thing: Peña was not popular in Adams County. He would best help the airport effort by staying away.

Romer, rather, took the lead. Like a plague on Adams County residents, the governor was omnipresent. The politician reaped immense publicity by getting up extremely early each morning and eating oatmeal at the greasy spoons and breakfast spots of blue-collar workers. Everywhere citizens turned, Romer was present, ready to buttonhole them and preach the glories of DIA. Unions likewise heavily endorsed the effort, recruiting thousands of volunteers. They noted the high unemployment rate in the county. The solution was obvious: Build DIA!

The business elite tabbed John Frew to lead Adams County Partners in Progress for a New Airport, a front group of the Greater Denver Chamber pushing a yes vote in Adams County. The campaign chief was an operative for Democratic United States Senator Tim Wirth. He had previously managed the aborted Gary Hart for president campaign in 1987. Between stints in the political world, Frew worked for Printon, Kane & Company, a New Jersey-based investment firm. Printon, Kane "lent" Frew, paying his salary, to the airport advocates.

Partners in Progress noted it did not want to appear too fancy or too well heeled, knowing such an image would easily lose it support. It desperately sought to present itself as a grassroots Adams County emanation, not a product of 17th Street. Even so, the pro-DIA group had virtually unlimited funds. Among those campaigning for the airport were employees of Silverado Savings. That bank shipped its workers (ostensibly "volunteers") into Adams County to canvass neighborhoods.

An organized but extremely fractured opposition emerged. One anti-DIA association was Ordinary People for a Better Adams County. It represented the Van Aire community, about 100 families who owned private planes and a landing strip between 157th and 160th avenues from Gun Club Road to Harvest Mile Road, about seven miles north of the planned facility. The extremely affluent residents often had hangars for their small planes next to their houses. They saw their enclave and lifestyle endangered by the coming of DIA.

A veteran community activist, Reuben Espinosa, led a second organization, the Committee for a Better Airport. A Denver native and skilled political operative, Espinosa had been a key figure in pushing Peña's election in 1983. Before long, he soured on the administration. In 1985, he coordinated the opposition that successfully shot down the floodplain convention center. More than anything, Espinosa managed to feed many stories about DIA's problems to *Denver Post* reporter Bob Kowalski. The latter quickly emerged as the *Post*'s star investigator with front-page exposés about the airport's problems. (Before long, the *Post* transferred Kowalski to Washington, D.C.)

The Committee for a Better Airport evolved into the Citizens Airport Coalition. It focused on the massive noise potential of DIA. Receiving money from Watkins' interests, it urged moving aviation operations to Front Range Airport. (Stop Denver's Rip-Off of Adams County was another anti-DIA group, essentially a one-man operation of Hal Shroyer, a key player in the county's Republican Party.)

Business interests around Stapleton formed the Committee for a New Stapleton Airport. The organization also called on Adams County voters to reject the annexation. Neither it nor the other leagues were well funded. Opposed to the $1 million-plus war budget of the airport supporters, they had less than $100,000 at their disposal. Much to the surprise of DIA advocates, none of the opponents questioned Partners in Progress' money stream.

There was no rational debate of the airport issues in the 1988 Adams County campaign. Opponents tried to bring out the extreme costs of DIA. They noted it was flirting with disaster to build the field before the airlines had signed on. The location of DIA, critics observed, was such that noise would not go away. Many were sure a redesign of Stapleton, not a new airport, was the best way to deal with the existing airport's inefficiencies.

Photo by Phil Goodstein

*The United Airlines flight training center at the northeast corner of 32nd Avenue and Quebec Street was among Stapleton's many auxiliary operations.*

DIA backers never convincingly refuted the opposition's charges. Instead of dealing with the practical issues of how the new airport would impact everyday residents, proponents presented DIA as salvation. If nothing else, the new airport was a sign of greatness. Prosperity, enlightenment, jobs, growth, and culture were all easily to be had by simply voting yes.

Polls showed a toss-up in the week before the election. Corporate Denver responded with an unending barrage of propaganda, combined with the hands-on appeal of labor unions in the weekend before the vote. There was approximately one pro-airport lobbyist/canvasser/volunteer in the county then for every ten voters. This provided the difference. A last-minute infusion of money from Chamber of Commerce front groups, along with labor's get-out-the-vote effort, led to DIA's triumph by 56 percent, 34,070, to 44 percent, 26,928.

Supporters had contingency plans about how to respond in case they lost the election. Some pondered going ahead with the annexation despite an anti-airport vote. Though they did not have to worry about this, negative feelings about the field remained. In August 1988, Leo Younger, the Democratic incumbent commissioner supporting DIA, lost his bid for renomination to Elaine Valente. In November, campaigning against the airport, Brighton councilman Jim Nelms defeated pro-DIA Republican commissioner Steve Cramer. In no time, Nelms stood out as the only elected official in the region who loudly blasted the new airfield.

## The Denver Opposition

Only after Adams County had supported the annexation did Denverites finally realize the reality of DIA. Not all were happy about it. Until then, many simply figured the new airport was one of Peña's harmless fantasies, something satisfying his construction fixation. Now they saw the need for action to prevent the mayor's bad dream from becoming the city's future.

Veteran activist Richard Young was among those questioning the project. A graduate of the University of Michigan law school, he joined the bar in 1960 and established himself in the Mile High City. In no time, he was involved in Park Hill issues, serving as the chairman of the Park Hill Action Committee in 1962–63. He left the post at the behest of Mayor Tom Currigan to lead the city's Commission on Community Relations. In 1966, Young emerged as chairman of the Metro Denver Fair Housing Center. He quickly built it into a housing development empire as the group received considerable federal and foundation funding. In 1983, he won promotion to rear admiral in the Naval Reserves.

Remaining in Park Hill, Young was a bosom buddy of Dale Tooley. He managed the candidate's 1971 mayoral campaign. Two month's after the challenger's defeat, Young, in a move reeking of machine politics, was elected chairman of the Denver Democratic Party at Tooley's behest when the incumbent resigned. Young held the post until 1976, serving as something of a "reform" boss.

Typical of how Young behaved as Democratic chairman was his treatment of Pat Schroeder in 1972 when she called to inform him she was running for Congress: he hung up on her. (Schroeder's husband, Jim, knew Young, having worked

Photo of picture at Park Hill Library

*Veteran political activist Dick Young pushed a vote on DIA in early 1989.*

as an attorney for the Metropolitan Housing Development Corporation, a subsidiary of the Metro Denver Fair Housing Center.)

By the time Peña was mayor, Young was increasingly forgotten as a remnant of yesterday's very ungreat city. Nonetheless, as a veteran insider, Young's loud public stance against DIA was ominous. It showed not everybody, including those in Park Hill, supported the airport. Many in the neighborhood and city were openly skeptical about the project. They did not believe the mayor's vows it would magically solve noise problems. Nor did they think it a wise investment.

William B. Chenoweth joined Young in strongly opposing DIA. He was the son of J. Edgar Chenoweth, who represented southern Colorado in Congress from 1941 to 1949 and 1951 to 1965. The Denver resident developed a political career of his own. After serving as a Republican in the Colorado House of Representatives in 1955–56 and winning election to the state Senate in 1960, William Chenoweth unsuccessfully ran for Congress in 1962 against incumbent Byron Rogers. The politician eventually became an encrusted incumbent on the generally do-nothing Moffat Tunnel Commission. (The body awakened to life in the 1990s after Chenoweth left it, challenging some of the giveaways to and land grabs of the elite Arlberg Club near Winter Park on property under its jurisdiction. The General Assembly responded by abolishing the Moffat Tunnel Commission.)

An advertising executive, Chenoweth was a key Republican campaign adviser. In 1970, he helped Mike McKevitt gain election to Congress over pro-school busing attorney Craig Barnes. The next year, Chenoweth led Republicans for McNichols. He was in the forefront in helping McNichols defeat Tooley. More than anyone else, Chenoweth was the loud public figure who virulently branded the future district attorney the head of the "Tooley-Barnes bunch." The openly implied message was Tooley was a radical extremist who should be rejected as much as Barnes. Any means, fair or foul, were justified to achieve such an end.

A mutual acquaintance suggested Young and Chenoweth forget about their differences stemming from the 1971 mayoral election. The threat of DIA united them in action. McNichols encouraged them to lead a drive against it. According to Young, despite the former mayor's public silence, McNichols was even more vehement than they were in questioning the field of schemes.

John D. MacFarlane was another prominent voice urging the mayor to slow down and think twice about the project. After serving as a Democrat in the legislature from Pueblo and as state attorney general from 1975 until 1983, the veteran politician was manager of safety under Peña between 1985 and 1987. Initially, he firmly supported DIA and Two Forks. Leaving Denver, MacFarlane ventured to Southern California where he worked for the Net Air International Corporation. There he saw a great city and the future DIA promised Denver. He hated it. MacFarlane consequently turned his back on the Peña vision, openly speaking out against the airport. Other members of the old-line establishment noted DIA was such a massive investment that the city must proceed cautiously on it.

Not only was the field extremely expensive, opponents of the airport pointed out, but it could adversely affect Denver's destiny. The city had enough problems as it was with sprawl and air pollution. Building a new airport miles away from downtown would only aggravate them. The airport would emphasize the metropolis' total dependence on motor vehicles since there was nothing in the basic plans and design of the facility to link it with the central city via a high-speed rapid transit system. Aurora, they observed, would benefit far more from the project than the Mile High City.

Real estate and business interests were blunt about Denver International Airport's potential profits. They spoke of a 50-year build-up area. Far from having the new airport deliberately isolated from residential and business communities, exponents of the airfield wanted to create a virtual second city next to the facility. This, doubters noted, could drain life, vitality, and services from vibrant Denver neighborhoods and downtown.

To try to get a hearing about these matters, on January 5, 1989, Young and Chenoweth wrote Peña a public letter, asking him to reconsider his hasty commitment to the airport. They pointed to the declining traffic at Stapleton. A review of the numbers, they insisted, raised more questions about the field than the mayor's office had answered. The evidence was "certainly no basis on which to justify the largest public construction project in the history of Colorado."

The letter touched a raw nerve. Young and Chenoweth received numerous calls from locals who were sick of Peña and the airport. Many everyday citizens asked the two to mount a crusade against it. Anti-airport feelings rapidly grew. Newspapers increasingly published stories pointing out some of the mayor's suspicious promises about the field.

At first, Peña's aides simply brushed aside the objections: There was nothing new in any of the points raised by Young and Chenoweth. The city had already thoroughly dealt with all these problems. Nor was there anything to worry about. When this response failed to calm concerns about DIA, the mayor publicly responded to the letter. Instead of dealing with the doubts, he attacked Young, Chenoweth, and others who dared knock the wisdom of DIA. He particularly blasted Young. The sudden opponent of the field had not been involved in previous airport public hearings or spoken out when it mattered. Besides, the time for debate had passed. Peña was blunt: Denver International Airport was a given; there was no place for second-thoughts about or further discussion of the matter.

City council joined the mayor in fervently embracing the airport. Having heard what it wanted from the administration, it did not desire any public input on the field. Since council had already endorsed DIA, members expected the citizenry to go along with the decision of their elected representatives. As incertitude failed to go away, questions remained unanswered, and the Young-Chenoweth appeal expanded, council slowly realized it had to do something to redress the growing airport unease. Reversing its decision on January 17, council asked residents to come to city hall on Thursday, February 2, to speak out concerning this project designed to change thc face of the Mile High City.

Even as it announced the hearing, council made it plain the public could tell it nothing to change the city's commitment to DIA. The mayor echoed council. After vehemently opposing the public hearing, stating the whole matter had been debated to death, Peña endorsed the airing of the citizenry's views on DIA. The forum, he was sure, would prove the massive public sentiment behind the effort. It would illustrate how the forces of opposition were nothing more than a few isolated malcontents. He arranged to tilt the hearing to prove his case.

Council gave residents the wide impression the forum would be conducted on a democratic basis. In particular, members of the public would speak in the order

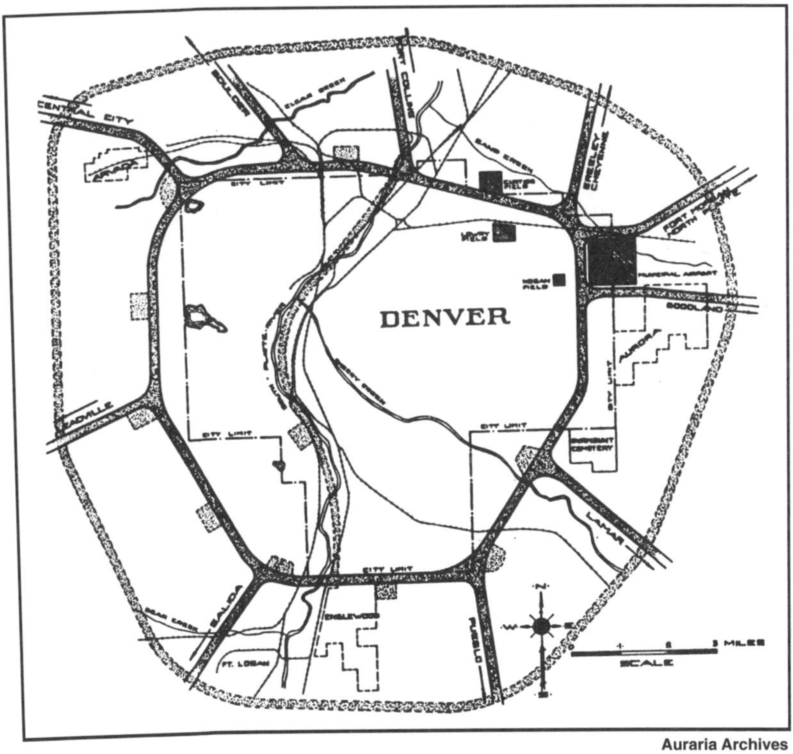


Auraria Archives

*In the 1930s, the city believed federal authorities would soon outlaw flights over cities. The solution was an air loop, paralleled by a beltway, around the city for flights to other regional communities. Not only was this suggestion never implemented, but by the 1980s noise problems were why the city claimed DIA was an urgent necessity.*

Photo by Phil Goodstein

*Federico Peña occupied this house at 700 Franklin Street when he returned to Denver from Washington in 1998. It was previously the home of Susan Barnes-Gelt, who helped stack the February 1989 city council hearing on DIA.*

in which they signed up. Many citizens, wanting to be heard, descended on city hall hours before the hearing to get their place in line. More than 300 concerned residents packed council chambers for the event on a five-below-zero night.

Rather than hosting an honest debate on the airport, the director of city council, John Bennett, stacked the hearing. At the behest of a key Peña aide, Susan Barnes-Gelt, whose then husband led the Democratic Party, he arranged to have politically connected, articulate airport advocates go first. Council permitted them plenty of time to state their case. This move assured DIA backers got prime television coverage on the evening news.

Not until after 10:00 PM did council call the first anti-DIA speaker. Many who had sat around and waited for hours on end found themselves ordered to cut their remarks short once they had the floor. Eventually, council told numerous individuals on the speakers' list they had to come back the next day if they still desired to have their say.

When the slanted nature of the hearing was exposed, members of council claimed to have no knowledge of it. They did nothing to atone for it. Bennett retained his post. Susan Barnes-Gelt went on from performing such deeds for the mayor's office and local Democratic Party to win election as city councilwoman-at-large in 1995. When Peña returned to Denver from Washington in 1998, Barnes-Gelt arranged for him to move into her mansion at 700 Franklin Street.

Other public hearings had comparable formats. The organizers heard what they wished: the citizenry fully supported the airport. To make sure this was the message, selected speakers who endorsed the airport went first. After they had their say, others were limited to brief statements. In some cases, pro-airport sponsors told citizens at "public hearings" that they were not permitted to make comments. On the contrary, organizers limited everyday people hoping to denounce DIA to asking one question each when they were given the floor. Airport ideologues thereupon dismissed those protesting such proceedings as angry, uncouth ignoramuses who did not deserve the chance to air their views.

Any doubts about DIA, the mayor, city council, and the Greater Denver Chamber made clear, were impermissible delusions. Typical was the fate of Mike Bell, a senior financial analyst for Boettcher & Company, an underwriter of DIA bonds. In reviewing the securities and the project, Bell wrote a somewhat critical report about the airport. It would be no great loss, he concluded, for the city to continue to operate Stapleton while mothballing the new field. Learning of the study, representatives of the Peña administration met with top Boettcher executives. The latter agreed to suppress the survey and destroy the computer files supporting its conclusions. (By this time, Boettcher & Company was badly hurting, stemming from poor investments and management decisions. Kemper Securities of Chicago had taken it over in 1985 in the wake of the oil crash. As DIA approached takeoff in 1992, Boettcher & Company ceased to exist.)

Opposed to the fate of the critical Boettcher report, the business community praised Will F. Nicholson Jr., the chairman of Colorado National Bank (CNB). That pillar of the establishment published a review noting the great economic development wrought by airports in Kansas City, Dallas, and Atlanta. DIA backers seized upon it, showing DIA would do the same for Denver.

At the same time Nicholson and CNB committed themselves to DIA, the financial institution was engulfed in a sea of red ink stemming from bad loans and questionable investments. Within a few years, far from growing with DIA, CNB sold out to a Minnesota concern, First Bank. The latter relabeled it part of the generic US Bank in 1998. At the time of the airport debate, CNB owned 1,280 acres near DIA.

Among those heartily supporting DIA was CNB board member Gary Antonoff. He was another investor in Adams County real estate, having led the charge for the airport. Right about the time plans for DIA were finalized in 1986, he borrowed $3.5 million from CNB to pay for a project on the fringe areas of DIA. Antonoff later defaulted on the loan, settling with the bank for $500,000.

## The Denver Airport Election

As the DIA enthusiasts increasingly showed their greed and intolerance, Young, Chenoweth, and other opponents suggested a public vote on the issue. Calling for a citizen initiative, they hoped to place the matter on the ballot. Echoing the most fervent supporters of the 1976 Winter Olympics, Peña and the Greater Denver Chamber dismissed this as a ridiculous fantasy. The issue had been decided. Elected leaders had endorsed the project. The city had already spent $236 million for airport land. It was high time to award construction contracts and have work get underway. There was no time or place for a vote.

Opponents would not go away. When city hall made it clear nothing would change its commitment to the airport, opposition surged. Critics played on the mayor's fear of a vote, calling for an election. Young and Chenoweth formed a group called "Let's Vote." They launched a petition drive on January 21.

When it appeared something might result from this, the airport's boosters became increasingly nervous. They knew there was a groundswell of doubt about the project. By allowing opposition forces to petition for an election, those questioning DIA would have an opportunity to grow roots and touch the nerve of the community. Moreover, an initiated election would spell delay on DIA. With doubts looming about the outcome of such a vote, Wall Street would be hesitant about buying airport bonds. This might postpone or even kill what the Peña administration believed was a vitally urgent project. The mayor continued to insist DIA had to be built as soon as possible.

Among those dismissing an airport election as a foolish fantasy was the League of Women Voters (LWV). The issue, it explained, was too complex for a referendum. This was in tune with the organization, one increasingly lining up as a highly partisan backer of the Democrats and build-it projects. Republican state Senator Ted Strickland of Westminster claimed as much. After losing the 1978 and 1986 gubernatorial races, he noted LWV's slanted role, branding it the "League of Women Vipers." He quickly apologized for his remark.

The LWV position was at one with the rest of the DIA crowd. The airport's supporters continually implied voters were too stupid to see the wisdom of the expensive, hasty effort. If at all possible, the Chamber/Peña DIA backers hoped to silence the airport opposition.

Questioners remained. The louder city hall rejected a public vote on DIA, the more opponents flourished. The mayor was increasingly running scared, desperately appearing to want to hide something the electorate might discover in an airport vote. It seemed possible DIA might become a replay of the entire fiasco of the 1976 Winter Olympics.

Some key Peña advisers had actively fought the Olympics and knew the lesson of that referendum. City hall, finding itself unable to muzzle exponents of an election, realized it had to head off airport opponents with a direct blow. To prevent DIA doubters from gathering strength and momentum via an initiative from below, in March 1989 the mayor and city council agreed to hold a DIA vote on May 16, 1989, the same day as a previously scheduled school board election.

It was no contest. The entire political and economic establishment mobilized for the vote. Arms were freely twisted, coercion was used, special concessions were offered, and promises were made to get people to vote for the airport. Chenoweth found himself barraged with hate mail. Most of it came from old political and social cronies with whom he had worked for years. Young's law business dried up. Rumors freely floated those consulting him were coerced to see other attorneys.

DIA backers heavily lobbied the newspapers on their coverage of the airport and election. They wanted the publications only to print good, positive, pro-airport news. Aviation director Doughty called *Denver Post* editors to account when

Photo by John Schoenwalter

*Governor Roy Romer stated he would "roll over and crush" anybody who stood in the way of DIA.*

the paper printed an article suggesting some DIA promises would not easily become reality. The build-it set also reviled popular *Rocky Mountain News* anti-airport columnist Gene Amole.

Signs popped up around town, announcing residents' support for the airport. Few anti signs were present. When homeowners put them up, they found their signs destroyed virtually overnight. In the lead of encouraging such behavior was Governor Romer who loudly announced he was going to "roll over and crush" all opponents of the airport. "They're like gnats," he continued, nuisances it was necessary to forcefully swat away.

The governor's comments came during a press conference at the ultra-ruling class Denver Athletic Club on January 19. Leaders of the Chamber of Commerce and key businessmen surrounded him. None voiced any qualms about Romer's threats. The only crucial figure supporting the airport who was immediately unhappy with the governor's violent ultimatum was Romer. The next day, he apologized for his remarks, fearing they too bluntly showed the iron fist of 17th Street.

Actually, Romer's remarks were a rare moment of candor. They came right at the time when gang violence and social breakdown soared in the Mile High City. He showed the government was the foremost exponent of using crude physical force in bulldozing anyone who stood in a person's or cause's way. Seen in this light, it was no wonder the level of road rage and public rudeness soared during Romer's 12 years as governor. During his tenure the number of inmates in the state's correction system more than tripled from 4,327 to 14,288 prisoners. The politician's statement revealed the vicious core of the establishment's etiquette.

Young mocked the governor's threat. "Do we have a governor of the people or do we have a spokesman for the special interest groups, the ones that are going to make millions of dollars of profits off this project?" he asked. Romer's answer was the election would not harm ruling Denver. On the contrary, reverting to his persona as a liberal, populist Democrat, he lamented, by delaying the project, the election would hurt the poor who would fail to get desperately needed airport jobs.

City hall offered inducements to those lining up behind the airport. Peña approached neighborhood and local business groups. In places, he appeared to promise them city favors in exchange for signing on to the airport. The Denver Board of Realtors pressured members to go along. Opposition was not a simple questioning of DIA; it was viewed as a rejection of everything the local power elite held dear. The airport was beyond rational consideration; rather, it was worshipped as a municipal religion.

The forces of opposition were not united. Young and Chenoweth organized themselves into Vote No. Their organization had little popular outreach or financial resources. Many veteran community activists and neighborhood improvers were either silent about DIA or firmly approved it. As with Romer and Peña, they were loyal members of the Democratic Party, an organization freely scorning its former chairman. The Democratic machine was at one with the Greater Denver Chamber on the airport. The Republicans likewise were generally behind the effort. Virtually none of the anti-McNichols constituency, which had helped elect Peña in 1983, even existed by this time, much less spoke out on DIA.

Nor were environmentalists a force in the DIA debate. They showed some concern about it increasing sprawl and dependency on the automobile. Generally, though, their attention during the late 1980s was on Two Forks—the push for it occurred at the same time DIA was imminent. More than dealing with the politics and economics of the airport, friends of the earth expressed concern DIA flights might impact eagles nesting near Barr Lake. (Some who claimed to speak on

Photo by Phil Goodstein

*The Doubletree Hotel at the northwest corner of 32nd Avenue and Quebec Street anchored a hotel row adjacent to Stapleton. Property owners there opposed DIA.*

behalf of the environment were eager DIA advocates. In particular, *Denver Post* columnist Mark Obmascik smeared airport opponents as dolts who did not know what Denver greatness was about.)

Save Our Stapleton was another voice speaking out against the new airport. It consisted of landowners, hotels, and other businesses near Stapleton. The group's members saw their main source of revenue about to disappear, supplanted by land speculations far to the east. When Save Our Stapleton hired conservative Republican strategist Roger Ailes to prepare ads against DIA, airport advocates exploded. They cited the outsider's intervention into the airport debate as carpetbaggery run amuck. Opposed to this non-Denverite who dared oppose the Queen City's salvation, they projected themselves as good-old Denver boys and girls who were behind the Mile High City's destiny.

John Frew, who had pulled the strings on the Adams County vote, was the establishment's man in pushing the referendum. He headed Let's Vote YES, an organization dominated by representatives of the Greater Denver Chamber, Denver Partnership, and the mayor's office. Except in name and direct financing, it was a virtual city agency. Builders and speculators, who hoped to reap a fortune from the project, were in the lead of underwriting it.

Organized labor, fully committed to class collaboration and tailing behind businesses usually bitterly opposed to and hating unions, added its voice to the pro-airport campaign. So did minority and feminist politicians and business groups. The mayor readily promised them a share of all DIA contracts. The Peña machine of 1987 was operating at full flower. This was his alliance of blacks, Hispanics, feminists, neighborhood do-gooders, and labor. They rallied under a populist banner while they embraced and advanced the agenda of the corporate elite.

As in the 1988 Adams County election there was no free, fair, and open debate of the airport in the election. It was an affirmation of creed. The wording of the ballot issue said as much:

> In order to create jobs, stimulate the local economy and meet future air transportation needs of Denver and Colorado, shall the City and County of Denver construct an airport on land annexed from Adams County in 1988, using airport-related revenues and, except for that portion of the tax on aviation fuel required by federal law to be used for aviation purposes, using no city taxes?

The biased language of the ballot proposal did not matter. The referendum was nonbinding. In other words, there was no legal outlet for voters if the new airport failed to create jobs, stimulate the local economy, or meet future air transportation needs, while it drained public taxes. The phrasing was simply window-dressing, an expression of the DIA wonder.

Nor did the referendum provide any limit on the projected price of the airport. The city vowed it would only cost \$1.7 billion, up from the earlier estimates of \$1.35 billion and \$1.5 billion. Opposed to the previously announced 120 gates, it would only have 94 gates. Without question, it would serve 38 million passengers by 1993 compared to the 27.6 million people who used Stapleton in 1989. Amidst the hoopla, critics noted, the more expensive new airport was smaller than the one city hall had promised in 1985. With 94 gates, DIA did not have as much capacity as Stapleton did with 111 gates.

Supporters failed to deal with these points. An insulting barrage questioning an individual's heritage and commitment to Denver was the uniform response to doubts about DIA. Nor did the airport's supporters want any of its questionable cost projections mentioned. They angrily screamed when a *Rocky Mountain News* reporter revealed city hall's $1.7 billion figure did not include $281 million in hidden construction costs. The role of the newspapers, DIA's advocates repeatedly and openly implied, was not to keep the government honest and expose politicians' lies; on the contrary, they viewed the media as the city's ipso facto mouthpieces. The newspapers' duty, according to corporate airport backers, was to arouse the populace and line them up behind this urgently necessary endeavor without which the Mile High City would shrink out of view.

**Author's Collection**

*Bill Chenoweth was among the vestiges of Denver's past opposing DIA.*

Airport ideologues vehemently rejected all assertions the new facility would be very expensive. When Continental and United estimated the airport might cost as much as $2.7 billion in 1988, aviation director Doughty angrily rebutted them. He could build a four-runway, 100-gate airport for $1.2 billion. The only way DIA could cost $2.7 billion was "if you gold-plate the terminal building."

In light of the glib promises, arm-twisting, the financial sway of the business community and city hall, the seeming bribes, and the ad hominem attacks and intimidation marking the airport campaign, the vote did not come down to a decision about whether DIA was a well-designed project crucially needed to meet the demands of the city and its air travelers; rather, it was a measure of faith. The choice was between growing into a prosperous great city or decaying into a hick, depressed, insignificant cow town. On this basis, the pressure against airport doubters easily paid off. Forty-one percent of the city's 271,409 registered voters trooped to the polls on election day, May 16. Sixty-three percent supported the airport, 70,122, against 37 percent naysayers, 41,754.

Airport advocates outspent foes by at least three to one. Most of the anti money came from Save Our Stapleton, which raised $283,999. The Young-Chenoweth forces spent $42,748. Opposed to this, the city hall–Greater Denver Chamber partnership reported revenues of $1,060,750. Among its most generous supporters were the same ones who had contributed to the 1988 Adams County election: Public Service, Colorado Ski Country USA (of which John Frew was later the director), US West, Brownstein Hyatt Farber & Strickland, Silverado Savings, Bill Walters, MDC, and real estate, construction, and development firms. Translated, the money meant the pro-airport forces had spent about $15 for each vote. A "no" vote had cost about $8.

In the wake of the airport triumph, Young's law business collapsed. Specializing in estates and trusts, he had considerable assets receivable in fiduciary accounts. Suffering financial problems in the face of the election, without authorization, he unethically borrowed funds from a client in 1989. Though he paid the money back with full interest, the anti-DIA attorney repeated this impropriety three more times.

The Colorado Bar Association discovered the violation, leading it to suspend Young's license to practice law on November 16, 1992. On December 6, 1993, the Colorado Supreme Court disbarred Young. It noted unauthorized borrowing from clients meant almost automatic disbarment. Young's previous contributions to the community, no prior record of discipline, cooperation in the investigation, and restitution of all missing funds with interest were not sufficient mitigation to stay this penalty.

At the same time Young was engaged in the conduct bringing about his disbarment, a leading pro-airport attorney, Linwood Tyronne Holt, also violated legal ethics. Holt was a close friend and supporter of Wellington Webb. In 1987, he prominently served on the committee pushing Webb's election as auditor. The lawyer played a key role in the 1991 Webb mayoral campaign.

The pro-airport Holt subsequently became bond counsel for Pryor, McClendon, Counts & Company of Philadelphia, an underwriting firm heavily contributing to the Webb campaign. The city awarded it 27.7 percent of a $600 million DIA bond. The company earned $1.4 million from the job.

Holt failed to file any federal or state income taxes between 1980 and 1987. Nor did he pay any state withholding taxes while he had smoked marijuana for years. The mayor's buddy had used cocaine from 1981 until November 1988. When this came out—and Holt admitted the charges—the disciplinary committee of the Colorado Bar Association recommended the Supreme Court suspend the attorney for six months. Reviewing the report, the court noted it had suspended lawyers for three years in comparable cases. Observing Holt's contributions to the community, good faith in rectifying the problems, remorse, and enrollment in a drug rehabilitation program, in August 1992 the court decided the politically well-connected attorney deserved a suspension of one year and one day. Anti-airport activists saw the mild discipline of Holt compared to Young's disbarment as typical of the political fate of those who dared speak out against DIA.

## Moving DIA

With the voter authorization for DIA, it was full steam ahead on the new facility. By this time the exact location of the airport had changed; it had drifted northeast from the initially selected site just east of the Rocky Mountain Arsenal. From the time Denver and Adams County had signed the memorandum of understanding committing the city to the new airport in January 1985, DIA had been creeping away from the military post.

According to city hall, the land directly east of the Arsenal would not do for technical reasons. As the world's greatest and busiest airport, the original site was not large enough. DIA would have up to five separate concourses linked by a mile-long subway. Twelve runways, rather than the planned eight, were required. Operations along them might interfere with military flights out of Buckley Field near Sixth Avenue and Buckley Road if DIA were next to the Arsenal.

The old military nerve gas center, the city repeatedly insisted, was too polluted for even contemplating airport expansion on or next to it. Despite this, local officials did not object when the property was decreed a nature preserve schoolchildren were welcome to visit. That youths could now play on the Arsenal showed something else was afoot with the airport location. The real reason the area directly east of the Arsenal would not do was because it interfered with DIA's primary goal of real estate promotion.

Were the airport right next to the Arsenal, growth could not occur between the city and DIA—the Arsenal stood in the way. The field, its sponsors repeatedly stressed, was a magnificent economic generator leading to immense construction and a thriving adjacent business center. Only by moving the airport north and east of the Arsenal was such development possible. Having the airport further to the north would also better connect the field with speculative projects in Adams County.

This meant bait-and-switch tactics. The land sold to Denverites as the initial headquarters of the airport in 1985–86 was not where DIA was built. Between the time Peña embraced the facility as Denver's salvation in 1984–85 and January 1988, city hall announced four different sites as the exact place of the field. Only as the Adams County election loomed did Peña select the final real estate: 34,000 acres roughly bordered by the seven-mile stretch between 56th and 112th avenues from what was then Buckley Road on the west (later known as Airport Boulevard

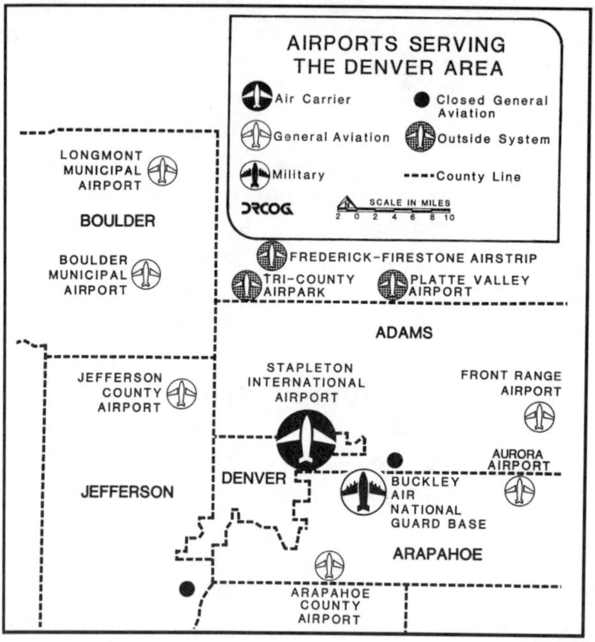

DRCOG

*In addition to Stapleton, there were other area airfields in the 1980s.*

and Peña Boulevard) the 16900 east block, to Hayesmont Road, the 29700 east block, eight miles to the east. The plot covered 53 square miles.

The city broke ground for DIA on September 28, 1989. Sponsors announced it was not simply going to be an airport, but a work of art. The terminal would be a statement of civic beauty. Inside, travelers would be beguiled by more than $8 million worth of paintings, mosaics, and sculptures. A fabric roof would stretch across the main terminal, recalling the Queen City was once the home of teepees and was situated next to the mountains. DIA would be a visitor's introduction to the Denver wonderland, the beginning of a marvelous Mile High adventure. By this time, DIA's cost had climbed to well over $2 billion. The field of dreams was seemingly about to become reality.

With the land acquired, the project approved, and ground broken, DIA essentially disappeared from the charts for the next couple of years. While the city awarded contracts and work began, the media paid little attention to the project. Nobody was more muted about the effort than city auditor Wellington Webb. Rather than closely watching DIA, continually calling the public's attention to questionable contracts and cost overruns occurring there, he said little. This was not surprising. Webb vigorously supported the airport. Besides, many of those winning contracts had strong political ties, including Webb supporters who received disadvantaged-business enterprise quotas at DIA.

A foremost Hispanic contractor was Alvarado Construction. No sooner was Peña mayor than the firm burgeoned as an important player in receiving city jobs, particularly along Santa Fe Drive south of West Colfax Avenue. The company's DIA role came out after it had received $13.4 million to erect the ten-story airport administration building. In the middle of the job, a crucial column toppled on February 25, 1992, as members of the construction crew tried to place a steel beam on the seventh floor. Two workers were killed in the accident. The Occupational Safety and Health Administration concluded the structure was in "imminent danger" of collapse.

Investigations revealed the problematic nature of the contract. Alvarado had originally been the low bidder in 1991, coming in at $12.5 million. A standard review showed the Alvarado offer was deeply flawed. In addition to technical problems with the proposal, the company failed to provide adequate quotas of women- and minority-business enterprises as stipulated by airport rules. Regular procedures dictated awarding the contract to the number-two bidder, PCL Construction, which had offered to do the job for $12.6 million. Instead of following them, with the authorization of Peña, the manager of public works, Bill Roberts, ordered a rebid of the contract to assure Alvarado got the job.

After the accident, the former mayor met with aviation director Doughty about what should be done. Initially Peña's story about how Alvarado won the contract was nebulous. As with any politician having something to hide, Peña suddenly claimed he had no memory of how Alvarado procured the job. By the time the building was in the headlines, Alvarado's owners, Linda and Robert Alvarado, were investors in Peña Investment Advisers, the company Peña formed after leaving city hall. (Bill Roberts' construction firm subsequently collaborated with Al-

Photo by Phil Goodstein

*The sterile headquarters of the politically well-connected Alvarado Construction at 1266 Santa Fe Drive.*

varado Construction as a lead contractor in building a new publicly financed stadium for the Denver Broncos.)

Rather than deeply digging into what was really going on at DIA, the press was generally filled with hoopla concerning the project. A slick public relations effort poured out voluminous materials about the emerging wonder of the world. Promoters readily moved the mountains. Graphics portraying the beauty of the main terminal showed the Rockies as virtually within reach. This was only appropriate: much of the terrain selected for DIA was quite hilly and a prime construction effort was leveling the land. Some of the runways were virtual earth-filled dams, with cuts as great as 40 feet and fills in excess of a hundred feet.

While the administration proclaimed the glories of the coming DIA, it ignored practical matters. In particular, there was no effort to build a rail link to the airport. If Denver were serious about reducing air pollution or providing alternatives to the automobile, a rail connection would have been the first priority of the project. The line would have originally hauled workers and materials to the airport. On the facility's opening, it would emerge as the main connection to bring passengers to the field. The expense would have been less than building a superhighway to the airport, especially when all the extra travel costs of individual motorists were taken into account. One estimate placed such charges at upwards of a $1 billion a year plus the tragedies of automobile accidents caused by all the additional driving.

The rail link was not built because of the very nature of DIA. For one thing, a rail line implied an integrated overview of the project. That was not part of the hasty, miracle-mongering tone of the airport. For another, having a rail line as the primary means of access to DIA would have interfered with the predominant land speculation purposes of the field. A fixed rail system would not easily serve properties adjacent to the airport—they were all designed for automotive access. Hence, there was no good transportation connection with Peña's field. Workers and construction equipment had to use unpaved and two-lane roads to reach the airport.

## Costs Soar

As auditor and media oversight vanished from DIA, costs soared. Since the administration claimed the airport was so inexpensive, it designed the main terminal as a jewel, complete with a floor of polished granite. Initially, the city planned to use terrazzo for the floor. In 1992, it switched to specially imported epoxy-impregnated glass fiber nine-millimeter-thick tiles made of stones from around the world. Not only were the new tiles, half the thickness of standard flooring, apt to crack, but they were also extremely slippery. The flooring material came in well above twice budget. By the time the city discovered obvious difficulties with the tiles, their manufacturer, Teconomaiera of Italy, was bankrupt while the contractor only had enough tiles for 80 percent of the floor. In places, consequently, DIA used terrazzo and carpeting rather than the tiles.

In addition to extra funds spent fixing this problem, covers were needed for placement atop the floors whenever it rained or snowed. Inside, the tiles suffered from immense leakage from planter boxes placed on the floor. Within three years of DIA's opening, airport officials concluded the planters were hopelessly cracked and needed replacement at a cost of $120,000.

Ceilings towered nearly one hundred feet above the ground of the terminal. Architects designed a translucent woven-fiberglass roof for it with an insulation value of R-2 (a well-constructed house has an insulation of R-30). In other words, the airport was not ecologically sound. It was built in such a manner to assure high energy consumption. Far from seeing any problems with this, airport backers praised architect Curt Fentress of Fentress Bradburn and Associates for the effort. They celebrated him for finally giving Denver its signature piece.

(The city initially tabbed the Perez Group of New Orleans to design the terminal. The Louisiana firm proposed three glass-and-steel towers resembling Aztec pyramids as the keynote of the airport. The Peña administration was not happy with the suggestion. In 1990, it called for the powerful, politically well-connected local firm of Fentress Bradburn to review the Perez scheme. Before long, Fentress Bradburn convinced city hall to substitute the tent-like structure for the pyramids. Architect James Bradburn of the partnership insisted the city use the Teconomaiera tiles over terrazzo.)

The airport was designed to assure high maintenance costs. For example, there was no easy means for crews to reach light bulbs in the center of extremely high concourse ceilings. DIA, consequently, had to budget more than a quarter million dollars a year to change light bulbs.

Poor insulation and high energy use were fine with gas and electric supplier Public Service, a key backer of the airport. It had donated $300,000 to the Greater

Photo by Bob Weinberg

*Acres of parking lots front the main DIA terminal, an energy-inefficient building pushed by an environmentalist-backed mayor.*

Denver Corporation as part of 17th Street's efforts to win elections for DIA. The new airport was a chance for the utility to expand its market, capital investments, profits, and empire. It bitterly opposed suggestions the city build an efficient municipally owned and operated power plant as part of the project. Despite recommendations by city engineers that DIA have a municipal power plant, the mayor backed Public Service.

While the utility estimated it would spend about $16 million to $20 million to bring power to the airport, it hoped to earn as much as $8.5 million a year by having the energy monopoly there. Increased demands at DIA led the way as power usage surged in the Denver area as a whole in the late 1990s. By the time the airport was in full operation in 1998, Denver suffered blackouts and energy shortages during extremely hot weather—the demand for electricity was more than Public Service could provide after it had sponsored the energy-hungry DIA.

US West joined Public Service in advocating DIA. It invested $400,000 into the vote yes campaign. The phone company pushed "shared tenant service." This was Peña's beloved public/private partnership in action: essentially the public entity of the airport turned over the phone/communications system to the private US West. The latter had the right to operate the airport as a miniature city, negotiating rates with users, long-distance companies, and all others needing a wide array of telecommunication services. Though Denver could have generated $3 million to $8.7 million a year by maintaining phone service as a city/airport function, the private sector in US West walked off with the profits.

By the time these giveaways were firmly in place, it was obvious DIA was not going to be anywhere near the size or scope of the promised facility. Not only was it scaled back from 120 to 94 gates, but only six runways, not the promised eight or 12, would be in place. The city placed the proposed 40-million to 50-million square feet of commercial, office, and industrial space on the back burner. By 1990, costs were well above $2 billion.

As it was increasingly clear DIA would not deliver on the original pledges, voices of opposition were once more heard. Some claimed it was still not too late to turn back, mothballing the entire project. *Rocky Mountain News*' columnist Gene Amole exposed the mendacity of the effort in many pieces. He labeled it "The Incredible Shrinking Airport." Over at the *Post*, Tom Gavin insisted DIA stood for Dumbbell International Airport. Others claimed DIA meant deceitful, incompetent administration, or Denver Idiotic Airport.

Planners were not fazed by the critics or cutbacks. They touted an "airport gateway development." This was their term for a seven-square-mile new city fronting DIA. It was part of the 50-year buildout—the projected period it would take for the real estate venture to mature around the field. Virtually from the time Peña announced the city's commitment to DIA, the business press had story after story optimistically informing readers about hotels, commercial buildings, and residential developments slated near the airport.

The last were emphasized. A 1988 study called for eight to ten thousand units of single-family housing in the 4,500-acre gateway area. Prominently featured was the 225-acre Gateway Village, ultimately to grow to 1,100 homes. None of the airport exponents saw the slightest irony in pushing residential units despite the city citing airplane noise as a primary reason for closing Stapleton.

Boosters were positively lyrical in describing the wonders of the gateway. As one drove out of DIA, he would find himself

> immediately greeted with a breathtaking view of the Rocky Mountains. As you travel along Airport Boulevard, your senses are filled with colors and landscaping in tune with the rolling plains, blue sky and majestic mountain peaks. . . . Wildlife habitats such as wetlands and streambeds have been carefully protected and a nature area and golf course have been established.

All of it, complete with "distinctively . . . broad parkways and a series of lively town squares" was to be in place, including the hotels and offices, by the time the airport opened in 1992. The media echoed this. Rather than investigating exactly what was happening at DIA, they acted as cheerleaders, repeating city inanities.

The more the Peña administration emphasized the gateway, the greater was the decline in passenger traffic at Stapleton. Within five years after the city had concluded DIA was absolutely necessary because Stapleton could never keep up with the projected demand, usage of the existing airport was down more than 20 percent from a peak of 34,706,474 passengers in 1986 to 27,432,989 in 1990. Suddenly there was a mocking new explanation of why DIA was urgently needed: Stapleton was too big. Only a smaller new airport could properly serve the city.

## The Continental Agreement

As commercial aviation slumped, Continental Airlines struggled. Its head, Frank Lorenzo, riding high on his union-busting, established an aviation empire through

UPDATE SUMMER 1990

# Denver International Airport

# NEW DENVER AIRPORT TAKES OFF!

## Bond Sales Skyrocket!

*Investors from throughout the nation gave Denver's new airport a strong vote of confidence last month when they snapped up $704 million in bonds, far exceeding the city's goal.*

The bond money will help fuel the airport's design and construction. Essentially, the bonds are a loan from investors. They are to be repaid with money generated by the new airport through such sources as airline fees and parking. Denver tax money cannot be used to repay the bonds, and Denver taxpayers are not at risk.

Lead national underwriter Goldman, Sachs & Co. had set a goal of $600 million in sales. But demand was strong from the start and $704 million in bonds were easily sold. Denver plans to sell up to $2 billion in bonds by the time the new airport opens in 1993.

Colorado investors bought between $25 million and $50 million of the bonds. The average interest rate turned out more favorable than analysts expected at 8.63 percent.

Denver Officials and bond experts were jubilant at the outcome. "This bodes tremendously well for the rest of the program," said Goldman, Sach's bond expert Ellen Jewett. ■

## Denver and Continental Sign New Airport Agreement

On March 19, the City and County of Denver and Continental Airlines reached an agreement on construction and leasing arrangements at Denver International Airport. "We look forward to this partnership and cooperative endeavor to build tomorrow's airport today," Mayor Peña commented.

"This is an historic day for Denver, the State of Colorado, the national air transportation system and Continental's nearly 7,000 employees," said Continental Chairman Frank Lorenzo.

**"This is an historic day for Denver..."**

Both the City and County of Denver and Continental Airlines agreed on the importance of reaching an agreement at a time when a major carrier's commitment could positively affect interest costs of the project.

Among the key elements of the agreement are:

- Stapleton International Airport will be closed to flight operations and sold or leased for other uses when Denver International Airport opens. At least 75% of the proceeds will be used to offset the airport revenue bonds. The remaining 25% will be used for other airport projects.
- Agreement reached with the FAA to phase construction of the new airfield consistent with traffic needs.
- Cost of construction will be limited to $1.922 billion, excluding land acquisition costs.
- Profits derived from airport concessions will be shared between Denver and the airline lessees.

*Continued on page 2*

*Conceptual model of Denver International Airport Concourse*

**Author's Collection**

*The city endlessly promoted DIA to the citizenry in a wide variety of newsletters.*

Texas Air. He eventually came to control Frontier, People Express, and Eastern Airlines. He ran each into the ground. Continental, a far cry from "the proud bird with a golden tail" (its advertising slogan in the 1960s), was known for poor service, overbookings, lost luggage, and frequent flight cancelations. It simultaneously sought to surpass United as Denver's busiest airline. The result was even more losses, leading to Lorenzo's ouster in 1990.

By then Continental was deeply in debt to the City and County of Denver. Many of its bills at Stapleton were unpaid. Lorenzo addressed the costs owed before he left Continental when he reached an agreement with the city on March 19, 1990, whereby Continental agreed to move to DIA. It was a "historic day for Denver," noted Lorenzo in an official DIA publication. The airline would take 30 gates in Concourse A, the section nearest the main terminal. Included was space for 15 commuter aircraft. The carrier would put up an air freight facility, maintenance hangar, and flight kitchen. Financing would stem from $73 million in DIA revenue bonds—the city would pay for them since it could sell the bonds cheaper than the private business.

In exchange for the airline signing on at DIA, the city forgave many of Continental's debts. At the time of the agreement, Continental operated 160 flights a day out of Stapleton where it leased 24 gates. City hall estimated the total economic impact of the deal was about $100 million—a sign of DIA's promise and prosperity.

The Continental deal heavily impacted the cost of the airport. The city readily agreed to make sweeping modifications at the facility for the airline, necessitating expensive change orders and the redesign of already completed work. The pact, for example, called for moving four international gates from the main terminal—they were DIA's pride—to Concourse A, quite a distance from the slated headquarters of the Customs Service.

Even more poignant was the bridge. To allow passengers to walk to their flights, the agreement mandated a bridge between Concourse A and the terminal. The linkage meant jumbo jets could not use the area between Concourse A and the main terminal since the walkway and other obstacles were placed in the way of the gigantic planes. Even with the modifications, city hall insisted DIA would still only cost $1.92 billion. That, the mayor's office was forced to add, did not include land acquisition costs.

Shortly after Continental's agreement with DIA and Lorenzo's departure from the airline, the carrier again plunged into bankruptcy on December 3, 1990. This allowed Continental to free itself from its DIA obligations. Nonetheless, the changes at the airport were implemented based on the March 1990 contract. Using its bankruptcy leverage, Continental negotiated a new pact in August 1992.

The firm now only took 20 gates on Concourse A. Sixteen were only for five years, i.e., Continental did not have a long-term commitment to DIA. The airline simultaneously pushed a Cleveland hub over its Denver operations. Still, the city granted the carrier $55 million to customize its space. Denver also reimbursed the airline for more than $3 million Continental still owed the city for Stapleton fees. The accord seemed a total city giveaway, an act of desperation to assure DIA would indeed have two hub carriers when it opened.

By this time—the summer of 1992 when DIA was originally to have begun operations under Peña's most optimistic scenario—observers estimated the airport's price at anywhere from $2.5 billion to $4.2 billion. Nobody knew the exact costs. A labyrinth of hidden charges, fees, enterprise funds, land deals, interest expenses, and lost revenues at Stapleton led different accountants to come up with various amounts. The administration, airport, and auditor each appeared to have different sets of books on the project. All agreed the undertaking was not cheap. DIA would likely come in at more than twice as much as Peña had promised.

As costs soared, the city reneged on another vow: Denver passengers would not be socked with extra fees. In October 1990, Congress passed the Aviation Safety and Capacity Expansion Act. It permitted the Secretary of Transportation to impose passenger facility charges of up to $3 a ticket to pay for the expansion or improvement of an airport. Denver heartily embraced this measure. Passengers flying into and out of Stapleton had the maximum $3 charge added to their tickets.

Meanwhile, Continental's losses at Denver escalated. Many only flew it because United was booked. As the carrier tried to head off terminal bankruptcy, Continental figured Denver was not worth the effort. With ever more fees looming at DIA, it feared it might lose nearly $10 million a month if it maintained its full Denver operations. To avoid this, Continental drastically reduced operations at Stapleton. These accelerated after it emerged from bankruptcy in April 1993.

In 1987, Continental surpassed United at Stapleton with 236 daily flights compared to the latter's 218. United soon regained its lead over Continental. Nonetheless, Continental increased its considerable Stapleton operation to 285 daily departures in February 1992. This was just before it gave up on Denver. As DIA's opening approached, Continental began to eliminate its Mile High presence. The carrier was down to 165 daily flights in August 1993. These decreased to 148 in January 1994, then to 59 in September of that year. Four gates, not 20, were all it needed at DIA. Continental only had 19 flights a day out of Denver when the new airport opened in 1995. United, in contrast, had 280 departures.

The only sizable Denver facility Continental wished to retain was its maintenance plant at Stapleton. To use it, a few flights a week would have to come into and go out of the old airport. This was heresy to DIA's backers: Stapleton must close. All the land speculation, noise promises, and presumptions of DIA were based on that. There was a fear if any flights were allowed out of Stapleton once DIA opened, passengers would continue to embrace the working old airport over the costly new one. Consequently, despite readily showering outside firms with inducements to come to Colorado and create jobs, Denver loudly said NO! to Continental's request to keep the Stapleton operation going. The latter, consequently, took 1,500 relatively well-paying jobs out of the Mile High City.

## The New World Airport Commission

The loss of jobs was of no account to the booster establishment. As DIA approached its promised opening date, the city cranked up the publicity machine. With the backing of corporate Denver, the Webb administration created a pretentious New World Airport Commission in April 1992. Berne Hart of United Bank and W. W. "Peter" Grant IV of Colorado National Bank cochaired the private corporation with the mayor's wife, Wilma Webb.

The husband of Texas oil billionaire heiress Swanee Hunt, Charles Ansbacher, was the New World Airport Commission's president and chief executive officer. By this time, Hunt had close ties with DIA backers. After Peña left office in 1991, she hired many of his staffers to promote her various Mile High ventures. Ansbacher was a leading financial backer of Peña Investment Advisers.

Society-page aspirants signed on to the New World Airport Commission. Corporations helped underwrite its efforts to celebrate DIA. Before long, nearly $1 million in city funds had been poured into the body's coffers. Most of this money came from the enterprise fund at Stapleton. Wilma Webb tried to dictate art placement at DIA, including a terminal fountain atop a crucial electrical transformer. The art work, known as *Mountain Mirage*, was only completed in November 1999, coming in at a cost far above initial estimates.

The New World Airport Commission touted the artistic wonders of DIA, complete with plans for an art show in the empty, unopened terminal in March 1994. (In 1988, prior to the coming of the New World Airport Commission, the city

Photo by Phil Goodstein

*Leo Tanguma's* In Peace & Harmony with Nature *is among DIA's many art works.*

named Ansbacher the head of an effort to assure DIA was designed with the arts in mind. The more turbulence DIA encountered, the more supporters projected the facility as much an art museum as an airport.) The Ansbacher propaganda outfit commissioned poets to praise the wondrous new field. It asked musicians to use their skills to celebrate this monument to Mile High greatness.

Denver did not think small about DIA. Ideally, Ansbacher announced, the first two planes to touch down would be those carrying Pope John Paul II and President Bill Clinton. The landings would show one and all that Denver was the pivot of the universe. The New World Airport would so serve as the center of the New World Order. (A key backer of Clinton's foreign policy was Swanee Hunt whom the president named American ambassador to Austria in the summer of 1993 after she gave his 1992 campaign more than $250,000.)

The corporate-dominated New World Airport Commission muscled its way into the educational system. It printed free curriculum guides for elementary schools, ones it circulated as part of a "Young Person's Airport Program." The goal was to incorporate the marvels of the airport into daily lessons. This was part of the commission's goal to "celebrate the construction" of DIA. Mayor Webb echoed the propaganda effort, calling it "an effort to move the real world into the classroom." Included in the pro-airport package were 45 lessons and a video tour of the facility, complete with a description of the control building as the "Terror Tower." There was nothing in the packets about the public debates and doubts about the airport.

Such praise was necessary because DIA was in crisis—it was a terror. As the price soared, the city reduced DIA from 94 to 84 gates in January 1991. From six runways, it was down to five. Opposed to an earlier FAA estimate of 55 million passengers in 1995, it was expected only to handle 34 million that year. (It actually had 31 million passengers.) As the airport shrank further, the city claimed it was saving $150 million extra by cutting out useless gates and other facilities. Bloated DIA had gone on a rigorous diet.

By this time the city had sold hundreds of millions of dollars of airport bonds. Washington approved federal funds to help Denver. As construction costs escalated while the actual size and capacity of DIA decreased, some Wall Street analysts started to question whether the airport would come in anywhere near the original budget or the 1992 completion date. In face of this, on March 12, 1991, the bond-rating firm of Standard & Poor dropped its rating to BBB- on DIA bonds, one step above the junk level. Interest on the notes ranged from 8 to 14 percent. Comparable, A-rated bonds then yielded about 5 percent.

Throughout the vital construction period, a crucial player remained missing: United Airlines. It continued to question the need for the facility, especially with the massive extra costs associated with flying into and out of the new field. United's doubts escalated when it saw the numerous concessions Continental received for signing on at the facility. The rival airline naturally wanted the same. Besides, as

Photo by Phil Goodstein

*Concourse B is wider than other airport facilities, a sign of United Airlines' dominance at DIA.*

Continental declined, United realized it had greater power than ever and readily sought to take advantage of it.

About the same time work began on DIA, United upgraded its Stapleton facilities. Naturally, it did not want to lose its investment by simply moving to the high-priced new field. Even as the city made the super airport a matter of faith in 1987, United was squabbling with Denver over payments it owed the city at Stapleton.

As the Peña administration went ahead with DIA despite United's opposition, the airline responded by reducing its presence in the Mile High City. Between 1987 and 1989, it moved aircraft out of Stapleton for a new hub at Dulles International Airport in Washington. United head Stephen Wolf raged "I never fought anything so hard in my life" as the new airport. The message was clear: unless the city negotiated with the airline as an equal, United might follow Continental and likewise leave town—or such was the bluster.

Actually, United needed a Mile High link. Stapleton was key to its national operations. The airline was reaching capacity at its Chicago headquarters. Denver was a future center for growth. When it was obvious DIA was going ahead, United knew it had to negotiate. Peña wanted to have it in the fold before he left office.

In June 1991, the lame-duck mayor signed a 30-year lease with United for DIA. The dominant airline agreed to take all of Concourse B, a facility the city agreed to lengthen and widen. Opposed to the rest of the airport, Concourse B had double sets of escalators and moving walkways. United's deal provided space for 31 narrow-body jets, 11 wide-body jets, and numerous commuter planes. The airline further promised to bring about 1,500 reservation jobs to Denver. For signing on to DIA, the city forgave $44 million in United debts at Stapleton.

A further part of the deal called for Denver to build a $160 million United hangar at DIA. Opposed to the traditional airport practice of having the airlines design and pay for their own buildings, the city was to pay these costs, including the massive sums required for United to customize Concourse B. This was necessary to assure DIA was an integrated facility. Besides, as was the case with Continental, city bonds cost less than the corporate airline bonds.

This closing act of Peña at DIA gave United a major say in airport design. For example, its maintenance hangar was placed on land slated for a future Concourse E. That proposed passenger facility was dropped. Many of United's requests impacted vital, already constructed areas of the airport. They required massive, expensive changes. Foremost was the nature of the baggage system.

## A Space-Age Baggage System

United noted the existing plans for the airport were a sprawling blob. The city had placed so much emphasis on greatness and aesthetics that it had failed to properly address the practical means of moving luggage from the terminal to the planes. It urged some sort of automated way of hauling bags at DIA. The administration agreed that using tugs and carts would be too slow for the sleek, modernistic, gigantic facility. The city concluded a destination-coded vehicle luggage system was needed to link Concourse B, serving United, with the terminal.

A destination-coded vehicle baggage system was technical jargon for fancy, independent luggage carriers speeding through the airport on conveyor belts. The operation would quickly transport suitcases from the check-in counters directly to the appropriate airplane loading zone. Sponsors promised this high-tech gadgetry would allow luggage to always beat a passenger to the terminal. It would prove DIA was *the* international aviation leader.

No airport had installed a destination-coded vehicle baggage system. The one promised for DIA was more a theoretical concept than a working reality. At the most, BAE Automated Systems, the contractor selected for the job, had a problematic model of the operation functioning in a Dallas warehouse. The company had never tested it at an actual airport. The proposed mechanism included 4,000 computer-guided fiberglass carts along 22 miles of steel tracks. Ideally, it would deliver 225 bags a minute.

Such a mechanism was to shine at DIA. Not only would the space-age system serve Concourse B, but, since other airlines demanded parity with United, the city promised to place the destination-coded vehicle baggage technique in all the airport. BAE was not sure it could immediately install such a working luggage operation, one lacking any provision for skis or golf bags. Still, the administration was convinced nothing could go wrong with this program worthy of George Jetson. (There were no serious rival bidders to BAE for the project.)

The commitment to the high-tech means of transporting bags required the construction of a new level inside the main terminal to handle the suitcases—the original design and construction lacked such a means of moving luggage. DIA also needed a totally modified electrical system and changes in structural steel support and the plumbing system to make the baggage technology a reality. This meant sweeping modifications of completed work.

The city's hasty, impatient demand to build DIA before the airlines had signed on was starting to tell. The immediate result of the commitment to the destination-coded baggage technique was another round of cost escalations. Delays in the rush job likewise resulted. United pointed to them, noting a provision in its contract. Because of continued city postponements and failures to carry out its promises, United was able to back out of its end of the agreement to add 1,500 jobs to its reservations department. Rather than creating new jobs, it merely moved Denver reservation workers from locations elsewhere to unoccupied space the airline had near Stapleton.

By now, the summer of 1991, United was sure Denver was a gullible city. Seeing how local authorities freely gave away public money to private entities, it wanted more. To get it, the airline announced it was pondering building a huge maintenance facility in the Mile High City. The plant might employ 4,500 workers. The cost was simple: the government had to grant United a package of more than $600 million in tax credits, concessions, and even cash payments.

Governor Romer eagerly snapped at the bait. He called a special session of the General Assembly to give United the appropriate bribe. The legislature went along. Although opponents, citing provisions in the Colorado constitution prohibiting giveaways to railroads and other transportation entities, argued this was a blatantly

Photo by Phil Goodstein

*The DIA space-age luggage system never worked as promised.*

unconstitutional move, the Colorado Supreme Court upheld the governor's position. Despite the offered subsidies, United opted to take its facility to Indianapolis. Once it was operating there, many in the Indiana city wondered what had happened to all of the promised benefits—most failed to materialize.

Even with the cutbacks occasioned by the shrinking number of gates and runways, DIA's cost had escalated to $2.7 billion by the time Peña left office at the end of June 1991. The United agreement specified this was the airport's maximum price. The pact further specified the airline's cost per revenue passenger would never exceed $20 in 1990 dollars. If United found the expense of bringing passengers to and from Denver greater than this, it had the right to cancel the lease.

The baggage system, stemming from Peña's lame-duck deal, haunted DIA. The new way of handling luggage was supposed to cost $193 million. Another $100 million was required to modify much of the airport stemming from previous work. Yet more money was spent on redesigning a nearby garage impacted by tunnels for the new luggage technique.

In the fast-track approach endorsed by the mayor, the foremost goal was to get the airport up and running as soon as possible. This tactic provided for no margin of error or overview of larger problems. On the contrary, the city actually believed its own promises about how inexpensive this wondrous, economic generator would prove. By the time Peña left office, change order after change order was needed. Much of DIA had to be completely rebuilt in 1992 and 1993—the original design was inappropriate for a working facility. As a result, construction contracts for the concourses, terminal, runways, and other aspects of the airport, which had originally come in at $1.427 billion, soared. Before long, their price was $1.871 billion. This was only the beginning.

## Freight Operations

The Peña administration treated DIA as a monopoly. Not only were passenger carriers expected to accept city's terms, so were commercial shippers. City hall observed there were no rival world-class airports in the region. Therefore, cargo operators would have to take what they got at DIA. Planners isolated these major airport users at the far northern edge of the facility, away from highways and easy communication and transportation.

The new airport, however, was not the only choice for freight carriers. Virtually from the time Peña had committed himself to DIA, the 3,100-acre Front Range Airport near Watkins, only about three miles away from the eastern border of DIA, sought to emerge as the region's airport. Supporters noted Front Range was not much further from downtown than DIA. Unlike the new facility, Front Range, near I-70 and the Union Pacific tracks, had well-established transportation facilities in place. As the city backtracked on many DIA promises while the airport's costs soared, Front Range advocates promoted CenterPort, an exclusive international freight-shipping operation at their field.

City hall initially ignored CenterPort. In a burst of its usual populist demagogy, the Peña/Webb administration insisted it would not give in to the cargo carrier demands. It was firmly convinced the freight airlines had no alternative but signing on at DIA at the city's terms.

But they did have a choice. As Denver proved inflexible at the badly designed DIA, Federal Express, United Parcel Service, Emery Worldwide, and Airborne

Photo by Dick Davis, DPL

*The Jefferson County Airport at its dedication on June 4, 1967. Its sponsors feared the impact of CenterPort at Front Range Airport on local aviation.*

Express signed letters of intent with CenterPort in early 1992. The proposal called for a three-mile land bridge connecting Front Range with DIA. As much as the Denver field, Front Range aimed to emerge as the cargo center of world aviation, linking up directly with Japan.

An optimistic newspaper account claimed CenterPort might create up to 59,000 jobs, adding $190 million to the economy. This inflated rhetoric struck home with Denver officials who issued the same kind of propaganda and bought it. City hall increasingly viewed Front Range as a serious threat. In reaction, the administration loudly objected to the upstart project. DIA backers complained the Adams County facility lacked the adequate capacity and safety designs for jumbo jet operations. FAA sustained Front Range.

United Airlines also protested the CenterPort plans. If freight operations were taken from DIA, it believed, passenger costs would increase while the airline would have a hard time connecting its freight service with the other firms. Jefferson County, fearful of the impact of Front Range on its airport near Broomfield, joined United in claiming the Front Range operation might endanger the environment. The Sierra Club likewise signed on to the anti–Front Range campaign. The goal was to force an environmental-impact statement and reviews. The effect would delay CenterPort for years past the opening of DIA. Amidst this, on November 23, 1992, FAA announced Front Range was inadequate for international freight operations, effectively killing the effort.

By this time, the cargo carriers had made their point: they were not absolutely dependent on DIA. The Webb administration offered them sweeping concessions to abandon Front Range for the new airport. Rather than isolating them from the rest of the field on the north side, the city moved freight operations to the south side. On this basis, the freight companies signed on at DIA in 1993. Denver paid $63 million to relocate their facilities, spending another $100 million in related construction costs stemming from the last-minute changes.

(After DIA opened, the relative proximity of Front Range impacted the new field's safety. Pilots of small, private craft sometimes confused DIA runways with those of Front Range. As many as 20 pilots of small craft mistakenly tried to land at DIA in the course of 1995–99. This came out in October 1999 when a private plane landed on a DIA runway where a passenger jet was about to take off.)

The fate of private aviation was also in flux at DIA. Opposed to the original mandate of an airport only for commercial carriers, private planes gained access to the new facility. Comparable changes, shifts, and reverses were par for the course on subject after subject in 1989–93. As the reality of the airport set in, it was obvious the Peña/Webb team had paid no attention to details or long-term considerations in the frenzied push to make this land speculation project a reality.

More problems loomed. Some of the original construction work was extremely shoddy. Permeable bentonite soil underlay parts of the airport. As yet unused runways started to crack, as did parts of buildings. This necessitated adding deep pylons to the basement of some buildings to keep them from moving and heaving. Concourse A suffered fractures on its north end where concrete buckled and windows broke. The poor construction and bentonite base resulted in structural damage to the bridge linking the terminal with Concourse A. Carpeting in Concourse C, among the first buildings completed at DIA, required replacement before one passenger flew out of it.

A main utility tunnel totally flooded in a rainstorm during the early 1990s. Contractors did not have enough pumps to bail it out. In May 1993, many of those working in and near the tunnel were sick. They blamed their illness on fungi in the tunnel. The location of massive electrical transformers was a second thought. They were not designed as part and parcel of the project. Charges were loudly heard that concrete paving lacked enough cement. Lawsuits documented how badly the runways were built. There might not have been sufficient reinforcing steel dowels in them. Even as the price of haste was soaring, the tone of an urgent rush job continued. Payments on bonds were coming due.

Security dealers eagerly marketed DIA obligations. Newspaper accounts proudly reported how quickly investors snapped them up—the airport must obviously be a good prospect to get so many ready buyers. The bonds often sold for a discount, i.e., Denver received less than a hundred cents on the dollar for them. Wall Street continued to list DIA notes at near junk levels. This hiked the interest rates and the cost of the project. Thanks to a booming economy with decreasing interest rates, the city was able to refinance some of the bonds.

As delays and shoddy construction plagued DIA, the field's exact cost was more nebulous than ever. By August 1992, newspaper accounts put it at $3.2 billion. Before long, the price was more than $4 billion. None of these cost factors took intangibles into account: What exactly was the price of servicing the debts? How much money would Stapleton have made if the city had committed itself to the Arsenal expansion? Would the airport pay for the extra expenses of increased police and fire protection or would the city finance them through greater general city expenses and the overall budget of public safety services? When all the hidden costs were added, by 1993 critics were readily stating DIA cost upwards of $10 billion.

## Airport Turnover

DIA lacked steady administration. Officials came and went from the project. Not only did Peña leave office as problems loomed at DIA, but a year later, in June 1992, aviation director Doughty exited the scene to become the head of the tiny Lehigh-Northampton regional airfield in Allentown, Pennsylvania. About the same time, Wellington Webb's manager of public works, Bill Smith, the number two man on the airport under Peña who had played a crucial role in the design of DIA, died of brain cancer. Robert Boulware, the field's prime publicist, was reassigned in March 1993. Ginger Evans, the head of construction who temporarily replaced Doughty, quit in December 1993.

Before long, a completely different team was in charge. The newcomers often turned their backs on previous airport promises and commitments. Jim DeLong, formerly the director of the Philadelphia airport, emerged as the city's aviation chief in early 1993. He quickly took pride in DIA as his special project, repeating every extravagant vow about it. Under him, questionable personnel moves bounced city employees to and from positions of airport responsibility. The city's Career Service Authority ruled against the administrator on some of these transfers.

Photo by Phil Goodstein

*A bust recalls Bill Smith, a key operative in the Peña and Webb administrations in pushing DIA.*

The only permanent fixture at DIA was Roy Romer. He remained in office, easily reelected in 1990 and 1994. In both elections, the Republicans put up extremely weak candidates. It often seemed Romer, with his urgent endorsement of state capitalism, was more the Republicans' man than the GOP's standard-bearer. Though the governor was a fervid DIA supporter from the beginning, he distanced himself from the project as the airport encountered turbulence. Meanwhile, Mayor Wellington Webb stood out as its prime apologist.

From its inception, Webb backed DIA as fully as Peña. After remaining mostly silent about questionable airport expenses during his tenure as auditor between 1987 and 1991, Webb made support of the airport a prime plank in his 1991 mayoral campaign. He lambasted rival Don Bain for daring to suggest a two-year moratorium on the field during which the project could catch its breath. In office, Webb resolutely endorsed the work of the airport planners.

As DIA problems escalated under Webb, Doughty berated the mayor for running the airport into the ground. The former aviation chief asserted he had been pushed out, citing the wrath of the mayor's chief of staff, Venita Vinson, a former functionary of Congresswoman Pat Schroeder. The latter was a firm DIA supporter, setting up various federal deals on the airport with Peña and Webb. (Shortly after Vinson ousted Doughty, she abandoned city hall when it was revealed she had not filed an income tax return in years). DIA opponents claimed Vinson was not responsible for Doughty's departure. He was forced out, they explained, because no one any longer believed his numerous vows about DIA.)

Vinson's fate was typical of the cronyism and special favors surrounding Webb on the airport. As he sought reelection in May 1995, his opponent, Mary DeGroot, targeted such misdoings, pledging she would be a far better administrator of the project than Webb had been. In response, the mayor announced he would expect the resignation of all his political appointees for a second term. When it appeared this might mean DeLong's head as aviation director, Moody's, a powerful Wall Street rating firm, demanded continuity of management at DIA to keep it from lowering the bonds to an even worse level. Webb thereupon affirmed he was behind DeLong and the rest of the airport team. (More than one-fifth of the mayor's total contributions in his reelection campaign came from people with direct interests in advancing DIA.)

DeLong stayed on as DIA chief until May 15, 1998, when he left to take a job at a regional airport in Louisville, Kentucky, a field with about one-tenth the traffic volume of DIA. A city administrator, who had no experience in running a first-class airport, Bruce Baumgartner, replaced him. The latter's primary qualification appeared to be his political loyalty to the mayor.

## Delayed Openings

During his first term, Webb continually suffered because it was not clear when DIA would open. The original Peña goal of 1992 was increasingly problematic. Not only was the airport drastically over budget, but it was also considerably behind schedule. By the spring of 1993, most of the physical construction, including the change orders, was finished. Architectural and newspaper critics raved about DIA as a Disneyland on the high prairie plains, a virtual eighth wonder of the world. In October 1992, Webb announced DIA would commence operations on October 29, 1993, right in time for Halloween.

Nobody knowledgeable about DIA believed city hall's prediction. By early 1993, the super automated baggage system was finally in place. There was only one problem: it did not work. The electrical system was thoroughly inadequate and bags were frequently lost or destroyed in test runs. No alternative or backup means of transporting luggage was in place. Once the city signed on to the space-age technology, it made little provision for what might happen in case of a computer or electrical outage. There were no rights-of-way between the terminal and concourses for a traditional tug-and-cart system. By this time the city had eliminated pedestrian walkways between the concourses to save money.

Other problems also loomed at DIA. As the city reviewed the plant, it realized the airport was no place near completion. Consequently, on March 2, 1993, Webb postponed DIA's opening until December 19, at the height of the Christmas rush season. That, apparently, was just what airport users deserved: those flying out of the airport at major holidays were often newcomers who were going to visit their real homes and families elsewhere. The opening of any mega-project is invariably associated with glitches the best of planners cannot fully address. By starting DIA operations at a busy period, the city assured travelers the maximum inconvenience. Seemingly, this is what the new airport was all about.

The breathing time was insufficient to make the luggage system function properly. Modification after modification followed on the high-tech conveyances through the summer of 1993. Consultants and engineers examined the effort, seeking a magical wand to make the George Jetson-operation work as promised. More delays followed. Believing only a little more fine tuning was needed, on October 25, the mayor postponed the opening of the airport until March 9, 1994.

By now, controversy raged over the baggage system. As problems loomed, the city refused to award builder BAE the operational contract. Claiming the Dallas-based company did not have enough minority and women employees, the Webb administration awarded the job of running the highly complex mechanism to Aircraft Service International of Miami. That company suddenly found itself trying

DPL

*Perez and Associates of New Orleans initially envisaged the DIA terminal resembling a glass-and-brick Aztec temple.*

to master an operation of which it had virtually zero knowledge. The system continued to fail to perform adequately.

Nothing fazed Webb about the airport. Though problem after problem popped up, he remained sure DIA was Denver's destiny. The third effort to open it would surely prove a charm. The *Denver Post* was among those believing March 9, 1994, would finally inaugurate the great city's airport. To mark the epochal occasion, it got advertisers to invest in an elaborate DIA opening celebration issue. The special section was already on the presses when, on February 28, 1994, Webb announced a further postponement to May 2. Despite this, the *Post* printed the grandiose opening edition. By doing so, the paper showed it did not have the slightest idea of what was going on at DIA—if its reporters or editors had been on the ball, they would have told the advertising department to hold back on the special section. Of course, it was quite possible the pro-business, pro-airport management of the *Post* did not want to hear such news; it might have ordered the supplement to proceed since it believed city hall over its own news staff. (To show it was equal with the *Post*, the *News* subsequently published a comparable celebration issue on May 8 for another non-opening of the airport.)

Nor did the rest of the establishment appear to have any doubts about city hall's extravagant airport promises. Like the management of the newspapers, it seemed to live in a world of make-believe about the airport. The propaganda efforts to celebrate the project were stepped up, with a full barrage of media ploys. Already in November 1993, the New World Airport Commission staged a grand "dedication" ball at DIA, complete with the Colorado Symphony Orchestra serenading the impending opening of the pork-barrel, badly delayed project. The Symphony scorned actual concert audiences by interrupting regular performances with accolades to DIA.

By the spring of 1994, Webb reluctantly realized the field of dreams had severe problems. The breakdowns in the automated baggage system were not caused by one or two easily resolvable problems, but were endemic to its very design. Only by a complete reworking of luggage-handling patterns could DIA open within a year. Not wanting to be caught short again, in May the mayor announced an indefinite delay in the day scheduled for Denver's grandest event.

By this time, interest on bonds was coming due. The city had to pay more than a $1 million a day in interest charges for the money-eating, non-revenue producing, non-opened DIA. It used, in part, money from the principal received in bond sales to meet its obligations. This was essentially a Ponzi scheme: an effort to pay interest on existing loans by borrowing ever greater sums. Wall Street expressed its doubts about how viable the bonds were when it downgraded them to junk quality in response to the latest postponement. Webb, in turn, named a blue-ribbon panel of leading business people to five task forces to do something about the disaster in action. The public/private partnership meant corporate Denver was to dictate public policy stemming from the problems the airport had produced.

The business interests taking charge at the airport represented 17th Street. They were a world apart from small merchants who had signed contracts at DIA for space in the terminal and concourses. The latter found themselves getting no return on their heavy investments there.

One politically well-connected concessionaire, Paradies Shops, was in the limelight. Local black investors and airport backers encouraged the out-of-town op-

Photo by Phil Goodstein

*The 327-foot high main control tower at DIA.*

erator to win shopping spaces as a disadvantaged-business enterprise. The city removed Paradies from the action shortly after the contractor was convicted of 84 counts of bribery in a federal court in January 1994 for actions it had undertaken at the Atlanta airport. Once more questions were asked if DIA had anything to do with air transportation and the convenience of the people of Denver or whether it was an elaborate real estate scam, lubricated with minority contracts crucial to the Peña/Webb machine. Illustrating the latter was news of how Mayor Webb's brother, former police officer Joe Webb, gained employment as a representative of some DIA concession bidders.

Stores were key to DIA's operations. The airport was designed to look like an extended shopping mall. Numerous fast-food joints and gift shops were to service travelers who would likely have to spend hours on end waiting for flights at the totally isolated facility. The ironic message: despite all the hype about its efficiency, DIA was designed for delays. As bored passengers, faced with endless waits, swarmed in the terminal and concourses, they would spend ever more at the shopping arcade. When customer advocates expressed fears concessionaires might gouge travelers, the city required national chains to agree their DIA prices would be competitive with their non-airport operations.

One and all were aware of DIA by now. The airport was an international laughing stock. Commentators everywhere dismissed the Queen City as a town of fools for agreeing to the project. Merchants sold T-shirts with question marks about DIA's true opening date. "Done in awhile" was the popular response to the question of what DIA meant. It was discovered a road slated for the far eastern edge of the airport, the 29300 east block, Flat Brook Street, had inadvertently been printed as Flat Broke Street on the city engineer's map of the project. Some did not believe this was a mistake.

The establishment continued to make the airport a matter of faith. Story after story appeared about how wonderful it would be. Similarly, the vilification of all airport opponents continued. When this author presented a lecture in April 1994 on the history of local civil aviation, including the problems of DIA, the *Denver Post* reported it as "comedian rips mayor" on airport.

Finally, with continued escalating costs, leaking roofs, and inadequate venting systems, on January 31, 1995, Webb declared DIA's time had finally come. Depending on a totally modified, traditional tug-and-cart means of handling luggage, the airport opened on February 28, 1995. With Peña and Webb in the lead, the city cranked up the publicity machine for the occasion. Few of the accounts hailing DIA's opening mentioned how the administration had to divert the first plane landing at the field because the jetway did not work at the gate where the celebrity-filled flight was supposed to discharge its passengers.

(Upon the opening of the airport, the city more or less abandoned the destination-coded vehicle baggage system to United Airlines. The operation only functioned in one direction. Clashes between the carrier and luggage contractor BAE led each to sue the other on March 8, 1996. With closed lips and providing few details, United and BAE reached an out-of-court agreement on their dispute in September 1997. Included in the settlement was a payment of $3 million the city had withheld from BAE stemming from problems with the system. Though the automated luggage system did not serve Concourse A, airlines there had to pay millions of dollars to help finance this means of hauling suitcases.)

DIA's ostensible price was $4.9 billion. With all the hidden costs, including capitalized interest, tenant construction bills, the expense of closing Stapleton and the write-off of the existing value of the old airport's facilities, $361 million in extra interest associated with the delay in opening, and questionable land acquisition charges, some who had been active in the anti-airport campaign calculated DIA actually had come in at more than $12 billion.

Actually, nobody really knew the true price of DIA. Figures ranged from about $4.9 billion to $5.3 billion to $6 billion to $11.3 billion to the $12 billion figure and beyond. Many of the costs were intangibles: extra charges the city would have to pay for years because of DIA's isolation from the city. Added to them were the price of growth, sprawl, pollution, increased travel, and higher energy consumption. There were also the expenses of the extra time and money passengers and airport employees had to spend to get to the remote facility.

On a more prosaic level, DIA's reality could be measured against the promises on which it had been sold. Instead of the planned 120 gates, it had 84 gates, some of which did not have jetways. Five runways, down from the original estimate of eight or 12, were operating. Passenger fees, exclusive of the $3 passenger surcharge, were estimated at nearly $18.80 a trip contrasted to around $6.50 at Stapleton. Opposed to the 41,000 jobs it was supposed to produce, about 22,000 people worked at DIA—nearly 3,000 fewer than had been employed at Stapleton when the new airport was first launched. (The city aviation department employed 814 full-time personnel in 1997 in contrast to the 316 who worked for the agency in 1985.)

After all the smoke had cleared and $232 million extra had been spent on the automated baggage system, only bits and pieces of it worked. Passengers went out of their way to take additional carry-on luggage rather than depend on the baggage system. As late as 1998—three years after the airport opened—major breakdowns in equipment were occurring. Denver had been sold a super-luxury sedan by Peña and had received an Edsel in its place.

## Peña Boulevard

This was only the beginning of DIA's convoluted history. No sooner was the airport open than crucial problems appeared. Poor connections existed between the field and the metropolis. Having scorned a rail system to get workers and construction materials to DIA, the city naturally failed to have a rail line in place for travelers and employees to reach the airport. Despite his verbal support of mass transit, Peña's actions increased Denver's dependency on the automobile by making highway access the only feasible way to get to DIA. In September 1992, the city fawningly dubbed the road connecting I-70 with the facility "Peña Boulevard." Originally proposed as Airport Boulevard, the street's designation meant everyone would remember the mayor's commitment to poor transportation de-

Photo by Phil Goodstein

*Passengers line up to pass through security gates at DIA.*

sign. Instead of a multi-lane superhighway, Peña Boulevard, like the rest of the airport, turned out a lot less than promised with only a couple of lanes in each direction.

The true goal of DIA was exposed when Denver did the seemingly unthinkable—reject federal funds for Peña Boulevard. The Federal Highway Administration offered the city $75 million for the road. The money came with strings attached: the highway was to have limited access, connecting only with I-70, the future E-470, and the airport. Since the entire purpose of DIA was to facilitate land development near the field, the administration declined the grant. Airport bond money paid for Peña Boulevard. The freeway was laid out as the spine of the gateway area. Peña Boulevard was not just to get people to DIA; it was the base for a speculative, sprawl city around the field of dreams.

The highway's route confirmed this. Though DIA is approximately 18 miles from downtown, vehicles taking the shortest route from the City & County Building to the terminal rack up about 27.3 miles. The mayor's avenue intentionally weaves on its route from I-70 to DIA to best serve the landowners and speculators in the area. At the same time the airport was going up, the city hired a real estate professional to market DIA to out-of-state businesses in the hope they might locate in and around it, especially along the circuitous Peña Boulevard.

While ostensibly a freeway, Peña Boulevard included a toll. Drivers entering the airport had to pass through a plaza four miles from the terminal where they received a timed parking ticket. There was no charge if the vehicle left the airport within half an hour. It was, however, virtually impossible to meet this time frame. From day one, the plaza was backed up, mostly for those wanting to get out of the airport. In response to massive complaints it took more than a half hour to exit from the airport, the city modified the free time to 70 minutes.

This slightly alleviated problems. Nonetheless, delays at the exit remained so bad the airport sometimes had to "vent" or "flush" the waiting vehicles, letting them through without paying their parking fees. The administration readily admitted it lost thousands of dollars every time it did this, but it had no choice: the toll area was so badly designed there was no other alternative.

By 1998, the solution was to spend millions of dollars on moving and totally redesigning the plaza. This central feature, the administration realized, was at the wrong spot. DIA also needed more parking garages since the existing facilities did not meet the demand. The covered parking garages leaked water. Drivers leaving passengers off at the airport had to drive an extra three-mile loop to get from the terminal to the garages. To save money, the city had eliminated access ramps from the check-in level to the parking areas.

Photo by Phil Goodstein

*The main building at DIA is officially the Elroy B. Jeppesen Terminal, recalling a local who was an international pioneer in aviation mapping.*

Rental car facilities were poorly located. As a captive market, people seeking to rent a vehicle appeared targeted for the greatest possible inconvenience. The city placed extra fees on all cars rented at the airport. Those moneys went to help pay for both the rental car structures—far isolated from the terminal—and the costs of the airport itself. That was Denver's ethos: visitors were victims, individuals on whom the city imposed all sorts of extra charges in the name of economic development.

Nor was there decent transportation for airport employees. They were provided with parking lots of their own from which they took shuttle buses to their jobs. Such vehicles had to negotiate through the airport where planes were taxiing. Since no cars were supposed to share this space with the aircraft, DIA was not designed for shuttle buses near the runways. Crashes and near collisions between the buses, service trucks, and planes were all too frequent.

## Whiteout

As DIA's shortcomings and failed promises plagued travelers and employees, the city often grasped at straws. The air train was an example. After the city had determinedly resolved *not* to put in a rail link as the first necessity of DIA, access along Peña Boulevard proved hideously bad, expensive, and problematic. Champions of public transportation and DIA responded by advocating a commuter train between DIA and downtown. They called for it to use the Union Pacific tracks from Union Station to a connection at Stapleton from which new tracks would extend to DIA.

The airlines protested. The air train was another added cost. The price of rights-of-way alone was estimated at $20 million. The air train, sponsors hoped, would be part of the Regional Transportation District's elaborate efforts to install an integrated passenger rail system throughout the city. It went down when voters rejected RTD's poorly conceived Guide the Ride in November 1997.

The vote came shortly after the reality of Peña Boulevard was exposed. As airport costs escalated, the city cut back on the road. Workers planted only a few trees while they failed to install snow fences all along it. The City Beautiful crowd, noting Peña Boulevard was actually a "parkway," dismissed the latter as far too ugly for the wonderful aesthetics of DIA. This foible quickly told.

No sooner had the airport opened than blizzards sometimes forced the city to close the mayor's road. One person who realized Peña Boulevard was not the best way to get to Denver from the airport was Roy Romer. In October 1997, more than 20 inches of snow stranded travelers at DIA. The airport ostensibly remained open even though television news shots showed the runways were not cleared of snow. The blizzard made the highway almost impassable. The governor flew back into the area from Washington, D.C., via Salt Lake City, returning to Denver by car, rather than risking a trip to the airport he had so ruthlessly promoted.

Though no ordinary travelers could make it into or out of DIA amidst the October 1997 snowstorm, members of the Denver Broncos did. Needing to fly to a Monday night game in Buffalo, the city arranged a special convoy to get the players to the field bad weather was never supposed to affect. Supposedly, an Army

Humvee led the Bronco caravan—Peña Boulevard was so poorly designed rugged military vehicles were needed to negotiate it.

Assistance of the National Guard was further necessary because people were stranded on the highway and DIA lacked snowplows to rescue them. Nobody could find the key to the shack where the administration kept the field's few insufficient snowplows. The Department of Public Works and airport disputed over which agency was responsible for clearing the snow off Peña Boulevard. Aurora and Denver likewise clashed over their jurisdiction over the road leading to DIA.

Though this was simply the most publicized instance, other blizzards had previously paralyzed Peña Boulevard and the airport. Despite pompous official pronouncements that DIA remained open, it ceased all operations during periods of extremely heavy snow and winds. Microbursts also closed it down. Strong winds were far worse at DIA than they had been at Stapleton. On occasion, when the wind blew from the wrong direction, DIA was able to use only two of its five runways.

Already on April 9–11, 1995, a few inches of snow incapacitated DIA. Peña Boulevard was a driver's nightmare; even city plows slipped off the road. While the administration announced DIA was operating with virtually no problems, airlines reported delays on an average of 52 minutes per flight.

When a blizzard swept the field in October 1995, a landing 727 almost crashed into an airport service Chevy Suburban parked on the wrong runway. Visibility was zero and the driver could not see he was on runway 35 left rather than on 35 right. In the middle of the storm, the airport's ultramodern control tower almost flooded, swamped by leaking windows. There were blind spots around the airport where ground radar could not pick up certain objects such as the Chevy Suburban. The airport had to halt all flights for 45 minutes. Peña Boulevard was backed up 6 miles. Shortly thereafter, the administration admitted the high-tech, advanced weather radar system at DIA suffered from frequent breakdowns.

Even when Peña Boulevard was not ostensibly closed by a blizzard, DIA still experienced severe weather delays. A March 1998 snowfall, for example, forced the cancelation of 75 to 80 percent of commuter flights in addition to many national routes. Veteran travelers could not recall such sweeping elimination of flights at Stapleton.

Nor was DIA equipped with decent ground transportation systems during bad weather. Often shuttle buses going to outlying parking lots and car rental facilities were severely overloaded. People found themselves having to wait in blowing snow for the vehicles. Even when the city claimed to fix these problems, more weather-induced problems followed. During a spring storm on Thursday, April 22, 1999, for example, United canceled nearly a third of its DIA flights because of massive delays stemming from deicing aircraft in the heavy, wet snow. The all-weather promises proved as empty as the rest of the vows concerning the project.

The city vehemently denied DIA suffered from any delays. Even as airlines reported 5,136 delays to FAA in arrivals and departures from the airport during its first year, the Webb administration claimed there had been zero delays at the field. It got away with this by defining delays as only flights postponed because of FAA

CHS

*The original Frontier Airlines evolved out of Monarch Air Lines. A new Frontier Airlines emerged as a competitor to United at DIA.*

interventions. (FAA flight interventions are responsible for about 3 percent of total flight delays.) Almost 20 percent of all DIA flights continued to suffer delays during the field's first five years. Stapleton, in contrast, had 17.65 percent flight delays during its last year of operation.

(When Peña was Secretary of Transportation, the government changed its definition of flight delays. Previously, FAA had reported them by minutes of postponements. Stapleton had averaged a little more than 14 minutes per delay. By the time DIA was operating, FAA only defined a delay as a flight 15 minutes late in coming or going. Denver, as a result, suddenly had no delays.)

Odors permeated parts of the concourses. Mice and poor hygiene haunted Concourse C. One time, the city had to close the toll booths when a nearby sewer line broke. Structural damage from shifting soils continued. The subway, linking the terminal with the concourses, was not always dependable. The train system could not easily handle maximum passenger volumes, leading to long waits.

The people mover illustrated the utter scorn DIA officials had for travelers. The poor construction and administration of the airport came out when a guide wheel on a subway car went haywire on Sunday, April 26, 1998. The train halted between concourses B and C, stranding the passengers there. There was no communication between airport authorities and the passengers in the cramped cars. Some riders eventually forced their way out of the train, only to find all the emergency exits along the subway tunnel locked. With a total security fixation and minimal concern about safety, a disaster could have easily resulted had there been a fire with the sealed-off exits.

DIA had no satisfactory alternative to the train system. The result was massive congestion. It was nearly nine hours before the airport resumed normal operations. Instead of admitting another part of DIA had proven inadequately conceived and ineptly managed with 1,400 stoppages in the airport's first three years, DIA officials claimed the shuttle system worked 99.7 percent of the time, i.e., three out of every thousand passengers did not matter and should expect inconvenience. This arrogant nothing-can-go-wrong attitude taught travelers a lesson:

steer clear of DIA if at all possible. The city did its all to assure locals had no choice but continued subjection to this condescending treatment. All workers and passengers thus paid for the bungling at the heart of the project. By 1999, seeing severe problems with the train system would not go away, the city talked about totally redesigning the subway.

Realizing DIA was the product of an overbearing, haughty incompetence, people flying out of it had to budget an extra hour to get to the airport and arrive in plenty of time before their flights. Airlines required passengers to board the plane at least 15 minutes before takeoff. They also strictly limited the size and amount of carry-on luggage. All this was at a facility sold to the public as a field urgently necessary to save passengers ten or fifteen minutes on the flight delays into and out of Stapleton. Travelers spent yet more time on planes since the jets had to taxi considerable distances at slow speeds to get to the sprawled-out runways.

Simultaneously, millions of extra miles were driven by commuters on Peña Boulevard. From a fare of 50 cents to $1.00 to take Regional Transportation District service to Stapleton, minimum bus fares to DIA were $4.00. From an average $12 cab fare to Stapleton, travelers had to pay about $38 to $40 for a ride to the new facility. The result was obvious: rather than benefiting from DIA, locals had to pay more, spend more time coming and going, and receive worse treatment than had been the case at the old airport. DIA employees found themselves locked into longer work days because of the extra commuting time. They received no extra compensation.

The airport employed more minimum-wage janitors and security personnel than it had at Stapleton. These, apparently, were the mayor and governor's promised jobs for blacks and Hispanics. Few new high-paying airline positions existed at DIA or went to Peña's alleged constituency. If anything, DIA was a smaller operation than Stapleton. It also drained people's pocketbooks. This came out in the escalating price of airline tickets.

## Higher Fares

With Continental severely curtailing its Mile High operations in the last months of 1994, United was the only national hub carrier with full operations at DIA. As a virtual monopoly, it raised fares to what the market would bear. Compared to the mid-1980s when Stapleton was "the fare wars capital of the world" with the lowest prices of any major hub airport, tickets for flights out of DIA were among the most expensive anyplace. The cost of trips out of DIA by June 1995 was 46 percent above those sold at Stapleton a year earlier.

United hiked its prices. On January 27, 1995, the carrier announced the imposition of a $20 extra charge on each way of round-trip tickets originating at DIA as of March 6, 1995, to pay for the more than $210 million increased rents and fees it faced at the new field. (Some of United's extra expenses stemmed from its agreement to have the airport, rather than the airline, provide crucial services.)

Rivals sought to break the United monopoly. Western Pacific Airlines was in the lead. Local entrepreneurs founded it in 1995 as a discount carrier flying into and out of Colorado Springs. Offering fares less than a half of those charged at

DIA—including for flights touching down in Denver on their way to and from Colorado Springs, Western Pacific, known as WestPac, hoped to attract passengers from the southern suburbs. (It often took less time for such flyers to get to the Colorado Springs airport than DIA.)

The idea of a southern suburban airport had been on the drawing board for years. When Peña first proposed DIA, investors around the Denver Tech Center suggested a new airport south of the city. As Stapleton phased out small aviation in the 1960s, Arapahoe County opened its own field south of Arapahoe Road along South Peoria Street in May 1968. Originally designed for private planes and air shows as the Arapahoe County Airport, the 1,360-acre plot grew into the nation's 11th busiest airport in small craft operations by 1984 when it was designated Centennial Airport. John Andrews of Centennial Express Airlines insistently pushed for the right to begin commercial passenger operations out of it. Though residents and county commissioners bitterly opposed his efforts, fearing the noise and congestion, local authorities gave developers a green light to build homes beneath Centennial flight paths. (Severe topographical and altitude problems limited the potential of creating a major airport farther south of the metropolis.)

**Photo by Phil Goodstein**

Mountain Mirage *is the name of the fountain in the center of the Great Hall at the main DIA terminal.*

Western Pacific struck a raw nerve. By the time it began flying, many locals hated DIA. Forgetting the panacea-business campaign behind it, passengers wondered how voters had been so foolish as to approve the field. (Already in the summer of 1989, only a few months after the Denver airport election, polls showed a majority of locals doubting the wisdom of DIA.) Those who did not like the new field, or who sought lower fares, flocked to WestPac flights in Colorado Springs. That city's airport traffic surged 75 percent in 1995, leading Colorado Springs to undertake massive additions to its field.

Airlines found their price of doing business in Denver had gone from $80 million annually at Stapleton to $300 million a year at DIA. While the city claimed DIA's efficiencies saved airlines $1.70 a passenger, this did not come close to meeting the extra $220 million in costs. Connecting passengers, who made up about 55 to 60 percent of the total people using the Denver facility, sometimes tried to avoid having to fly through the corruption-haunted project.

Nonetheless, DIA pulled in some start-up airlines. Besides WestPac, other carriers sought to compete with United. Continental subleased some of its gates to them. Many only lasted a short time, such as MarkAir and Reno Air. Three regional carriers, GP Express, Maverick, and Mountain Air Express, quickly failed at the new facility. Established firms, notably Southwest Airlines, refused to use DIA because of its high costs. Opposed to 54 airlines at Stapleton in 1994, there were 14 carriers at DIA in 1998.

Side by side of WestPac, a new Frontier Airlines completed its first flight on July 5, 1994. It included several airline professionals who had been around the old operation and were still proud of Frontier's independence and tenacity. They believed there was a niche for such an operation at DIA. As Frontier literally took off with discounted fares from DIA, United lowered its prices. It also matched WestPac fares in Colorado Springs. The latter airline increasingly focused more on Denver than on Colorado Springs.

Despite receiving very favorable press, WestPac continually lost money. As the upstart carrier sunk into financial distress, it moved the bulk of its operations to Denver from Colorado Springs in June 1997. WestPac drew up plans for a merger with Frontier. It also worked out promotional deals with supermarket chain King Soopers and talked about receiving city rebates on aviation fuel taxes in the name of economic development.

Nothing helped. The start-up carrier plunged ever deeper into debt. Its merger with Frontier collapsed when Western Pacific filed for bankruptcy on October 5, 1997. Creditors tightened the screws, leading WestPac to shut down on February 4, 1998. Far from encouraging airlines, DIA beckoned as their graveyard.

Among those turning their back on DIA were members of the jet set. Rather than fly through Denver on their way to posh ski resorts, they wanted direct service to them. As DIA ironed out its kinks, nonstop service began to Sardy Field in Aspen from Los Angeles, Dallas, Atlanta, and Chicago. Comparable nonstop routes flew into Vail and other mountain areas. Walker Field in Grand Junction also surged. Utah offered itself as a skiing alternative to Colorado since visitors there would not have to worry about the horrors of DIA.

The demise of WestPac further helped United consolidate a virtual stranglehold at DIA. Fares for local flyers once more soared. Out-of-town passengers, simply making connections at the airport, however, benefited. As a hub operation, United used DIA to connect many cross-country flights. The high costs of the airport required United to maximize the number of travelers passing through Denver and switching planes at the field. The effect was to hold down the corporation's average per passenger expenses. For example, while a round-trip Denver-Wichita package in 1999 cost $1,164, a passenger going from Chicago to San Francisco via DIA only paid $710 for a round-trip fare. The expense of the same flight on United directly between Chicago and San Francisco was about $2,000. A November 1999 American Express travel-service report listed DIA as having the highest business fares of any of the 40 fields it surveyed. The price of an average Denver flight, it observed, increased 32 percent between September 1998 and September 1999.

## Lawsuits and Investigations

As problem after problem with DIA came out, bondholders grew increasingly uneasy about their securities. After snapping up the notes, some investors complained DIA was besmirched by controversy and potential scandal. They claimed they had been duped, arguing the severe shortcomings of the baggage system had not been properly disclosed by security dealers and in prospectuses. Those holding DIA financial obligations filed four separate suits against the bond dealers and the city. Denver denied liability, noting the problems of the airport had been publicly reported. More than that, the airport bonds were being paid off. Upon the

Photo by Tom Noel, DPL

*Centennial Airport emerged as the area's second busiest field after it opened in 1968. This photo dates from the late 1980s.*

Photo by Phil Goodstein

*United's hangar occupies land originally slated for Concourse E at DIA.*

opening of DIA, Wall Street again rated the bonds above junk level.

With absolutely no hoopla and only carrying minimal wire-service reports, local newspapers informed readers the suits had been settled for $4.5 million in December 1997. Five investment firms marketing the bonds—Dain Rauscher, Goldman Sachs, Lazard Frères, Lehman Brothers, and Piper Jaffray—paid the cost. Denver, noted city attorney Dan Muse, did not pay anything.

Reportage on the bond suit was typical. While the newspapers chronicled some of the continuing problems at DIA, their emphasis was continually upbeat. The great city's airport had taken off. Even as lawsuits raged over the baggage system, the *Rocky Mountain News* blazoned "DIA Bags Rolling at Last." As much as anything, the newspapers seemed to want to convince themselves and the business establishment that DIA was not a fiasco.

The media generally ignored the airport's continuing financial problems. Stapleton reported a net income of $25,911,000 in its last full year, 1994. DIA, in contrast, lost a whopping $141,272,000 during 1995. Losses continued through the end of the decade with an $89,920,000 deficit in 1996; $68,483,000 loss in 1997; and $48,515,000 in red ink in 1998. Bonded indebtedness increased from $3,957,515,000 in 1995 to $4,106,095,000 in 1998 while equity plunged from $835,184,000 during DIA's first year to $728,298,000 by 1998. All the while, the city continued to sell new DIA bonds to meet continuing expenses and interest on the old bonds.

New construction and repairs were a constant at the airport. Within its first five years, a good deal of DIA had to be redone. It almost seemed as if the city had wanted shoddy work on the project: the maintenance contracts were a fresh source of city influence and rewards.

Airport boosters were proud numerous investigations did not turn up any flagrant corruption or misdoing. Probes by both the Colorado attorney general's office and the Denver district attorney could not find any specific crimes behind the massive DIA cost escalation, bungling, and delays. In other words, it was the lies, gullibility, and ineptitude of the Peña and Webb administrations, compounded by the mindless boosterism of the Greater Denver Chamber, which were primarily responsible for the disaster.

This point was affirmed by national probes, including ones conducted by the Securities and Exchange Commission, General Accounting Office, and Federal Aviation Administration. While some questionable activities were exposed, no egregious swindles or felonies were revealed. On the contrary, DIA was typical of what was once cynically termed "honest corruption": through playing by the Byzantine rules of affirmative action, land speculation, public contracts, campaign donations, consultant commissions, and creating a new airport, people around the Peña/Webb machine did quite well.

Typical was the role of disadvantaged-business enterprises. The contracts specifically set aside for companies owned by blacks, Hispanos, and women naturally went to upper-middle- and upper-class concerns, usually ones already well established. Often these were nonunion firms having few minority workers. Arthur Fletcher, the chairman of the United States Civil Rights Commission, emphasized this in August 1992. Reviewing DIA, he issued a study stating it was questionable if minorities and women had been "provided with equal employment" at the field.

Already in 1987, reports revealed how millions of dollars in city work reserved for minorities went into the pockets of companies owned or controlled by white men. The supposed "disadvantaged" firms were simply front groups for those who already dominated the building industry. Other minority contractors had excellent political connections. Among them were associates of Bill Roberts, a former city councilman from Park Hill.

During the 1970s, Roberts continually battled the McNichols administration. Projecting himself as a liberal champion of everyday people opposed to the 17th Street-dominated city hall, the politician openly sought greater council power over the mayor. This changed with the election of Federico Peña. Before long, Roberts was a firm supporter of city building projects. He was in the lead of busting the principle of council courtesy in the late 1980s whereby members of council deferred to the opinion of the representative whose district was the center of a zoning controversy. Against it, Roberts wanted more building and development. In 1990, Roberts resigned from council to become manager of public works under Peña, a key job in promoting the new airport.

As a contractor, Roberts had little use for unions. Still, labor had to be rewarded for its heavy support of the airport. It did not get much. The city awarded the first multimillion-dollar contract at DIA to a nonunion firm from Minneapolis. Rather than hiring locals, the corporation imported out-of-state workers. Eventually, some union members got DIA jobs. Labor as a whole gained no respect in the city. Denver remained an anti-union climate where 17th Street treated organized labor as an aberration. Unions subsequently got minimal backing from city hall and the corporate airport community when they unsuccessfully called on voters to raise the Denver minimum wage and give city workers the right to engage in collective bargaining.

This was not surprising. From the outset, promises to help labor and minorities at DIA were mere window-dressing. Only by engaging in such populist rhetoric could the Peña/Webb machine cloak its role in serving land speculators. As much as the old city machine of a hundred years ago, the political machine of the 1980s, 1990s, and into the 2000s was fully in tune with the most grasping wing of the business community, the one seeing the public/private partnership as an ideal means of draining the public purse.

DIA was built in the era of the second great American barbecue. Just as in the epoch following the Civil War, when the prime role of the federal government was to assist major investors and the dominant robber barons, the same was true in the late 20th century. The airport came to fruition at a time of virtually unrestrained corporate growth, mergers, political influence, questionable campaign donations, and an open celebration of business as the country's finest achievement. Under such stalwart Democrats as Webb, Romer, and Peña, Denver, as illustrated by DIA, was a national model. Not surprisingly, both Peña and Romer went on to hold high national posts under corporate Democratic President Bill Clinton.

## Box Elder Farms

The Republicans were equally involved with DIA. This stood out in the savings and loan link to the airport. Under President George Bush, few were called into account for the massive robbery. The airport once more illustrated how the public/private partnership assisted financial manipulators.

Virtually from the time Peña committed Denver to the airport, adjacent land prices soared. The city bought waterless real estate, worth little except for dry farming, for an average of $6,700 an acre for DIA. Silverado Savings' speculative investments fueled soaring costs. In one instance, property went for $107,000 an acre. In its hasty drive to get the airport completed as soon as possible—especially before the savings and loan bubble burst—city hall readily paid ridiculous prices for the parcels where DIA arose.

Members of the Fulenwider and Van Schaack families, both representing old Denver fortunes, were among those benefiting from airport land deals. DIA is centered on Box Elder Farms, a series of small ranches on the high, dry, prairie plains. Box Elder Creek, known as Terrapin Creek or Running Creek in the 19th century, is among the streams draining the area. The Smoky Hill North Trail had a stage coach station along the brook in the 1860s. Cattle ranches and farms were nearby into the 1930s. At that time, real estate investor Lloyd C. "Cal" Fulenwider, in connection with Van Schaack & Company, started buying land near Box Elder Creek for back taxes. By 1939, Fulenwider won title to the property after a court battle when he owned more than 40,000 acres. Until the real estate was contemplated for DIA, Box Elder Farms were mostly leased by tenant farmers.

DIA made all the difference in land use and values. In 1988, the Fulenwider and Van Schaack families disposed of much of the land when they sold 14,300 acres to the city for $52.3 million. The Peña administration claimed this was a bargain: the Van Schaacks and Fulenwiders had asked $143 million for the real estate. The Box Elder section consisted of 42 percent of DIA's total 34,000 acres.

When the city first considered the airport, the Fulenwiders and Van Schaacks hired academic consultants who praised the effort. They simultaneously retained

Photo by Phil Goodstein

*An 893 Eaglerock hangs in Concourse B at DIA. It recalls how the Alexander Airplane Company was a local aircraft manufacturer in the late 1920s-early 1930s.*

key tracts along Peña Boulevard for future development. Peña's chief airport consultant, James "Skip" Spensley, was personally close to the Fulenwiders. Spensley had negotiated Denver's deal with Adams County on DIA.

While the mayor claimed he was shocked by the appearance of impropriety of Spensley's connections, other linkages existed between the Fulenwiders and the Peña family. In the mid-1970s, as development to the northeast of Denver stalled, the Fulenwiders hired the Houston consulting firm of CRS Sirrine for suggestions about ways of improving the value of Box Elder Farms. A senior vice president of the Texas outfit was William Peña, an uncle of Mayor Peña.

Lest any doubts remained about the connections between the airport location and land speculation, Fulenwider Investments squelched them in December 1994 when it donated two miles of right-of-way for E-470 near DIA. E-470 was another developer effort. Promoters pushed it in the 1980s as a far eastern beltway, a 46-mile toll road linking I-25 at C-470 in Douglas County with I-25 near 160th Avenue in Adams County via the eastern edge of Aurora and the western edge of DIA. Bill Walters and developer Burt Heimlich, both of whom were associated with Silverado Savings, were among its foremost advocates.

Power broker attorney Tom Strickland called E-470 an urgent necessity as the head of Governor Lamm's State Transportation Commission. Strickland, as a partner in the law firm of Brownstein Hyatt Farber & Strickland, also served as an attorney for MDC and Silverado in some of their land dealings near DIA. He was secretary of the New World Airport Commission. A partner in Brownstein Hyatt Farber & Strickland (previously Brownstein, Hyatt Farber & Madden and subsequently Brownstein Farber & Hyatt), Norm Brownstein, was on the MDC board, a firm involved in numerous DIA deals.

The goal of E-470 was simple. Just as the completion of the previous eastern beltway, I-270, had spurred massive growth and development in Aurora, the new superhighway would do the same. Initially, developers were so sure of the profitability of the highway that they confidently announced they would build E-470 with private funds. Before long, they hedged. "Private funds" came to include tax-free municipal bonds sold in 1986. Further "private funds," used to back the bonds, were $10 additional registration fees tacked on all vehicles in Adams, Douglas, and Arapahoe counties. Even with this, E-470 stagnated. A small section between I-25 and Parker Road opened as a toll road, but did not generate enough revenue to keep expanding the project despite vigorous support from Arapahoe County politicians. By linking the expressway to DIA, E-470 investors hoped to assure development around the airport. Aurora politicians expected as many as 70,000 new residents, living in high-class homes, would populate a two-mile-wide corridor along the 12-mile strip of E-470 through the suburb.

In the wake of the Fulenwider donation to E-470, Van Schaack Holdings stated it might donate three more miles of right-of-way near the airport for the expressway. The Fulenwider and Van Schaack interests each owned about 7,000 acres in the area. Their land more or less followed the proposed route of E-470 between 56th and 120th avenues. E-470 intersected with Peña Boulevard at 76th Avenue.

The toll road also illustrated how local history is written. In 1997, when E-470 ended at Parker Road, a slick, glossy volume by Tom Noel, cosponsored by Historic Denver Incorporated, appeared, *Mile High City: An Illustrated History of Denver*. Three-fifths of the volume was portraits of "partners in Denver," firms and businesses paying more than $2,500 each for inclusion in the history. In the advertisement for Brownstein Hyatt Farber & Strickland, the book heralded E-470 as "a badly-needed new expressway that now connects Aurora and Denver International Airport with the southern and northern suburbs." In other words, facts were conveniently invented to give a better spin to DIA and its highway scams. (Noel claimed he did not write this, but simply accepted the law firm's puff piece.)

E-470 sponsors did not conduct an environmental-impact statement for the roadway. Since it was supposedly a privately funded effort, the highway's politically well-connected backers were able to get the federal authorities to waive the requisite. Foes of the throughway could not expect any help on this matter from the United States Attorney for Colorado in 1999—Tom Strickland. Meanwhile, northwestern suburban land developers avidly pitched a "Northwest Parkway." Voters had previously overwhelmingly rejected the project by a nearly eight-to-one vote on February 8, 1989, when it was marketed to them in the guise of W-470. Supporters of the Northwest Parkway did not bother asking the electorate its opinion of their new highway effort.

While the value of Van Schaack holdings near the airport soared with the coming of DIA, a feud ripped the family. During the early 1980s, the Van Schaacks and Fulenwiders had a falling out over Box Elder Farms, leading to lengthy litigation resolved in 1986 when they equally divided the land. They healed the rift when they were both able to profitably sell much of Box Elder Farms to the city for the airport.

As DIA reached fruition, the Van Schaack family no longer owned the commercial real estate brokerage of Van Schaack & Company. That outfit came under

Photo by Phil Goodstein

*The formal entry to Gateway Park, near 48th Avenue and Peña Boulevard, a commercial-residential development on land sold by the Fulenwider family in 1995, real estate illustrating DIA's land speculation potential.*

the control of MDC. Van Schaack & Company went bankrupt in the wake of the oil crash and savings and loan debacle. A Wall Street outfit, NRT Incorporated, eventually took it over. By that time, Beth Van Schaack, the widow of Henry C. Van Schaack Jr., had sued her in-laws in Denver district court, claiming they had conspired to deprive her of an appropriate share of the airport land. A jury awarded her $750,000 in April 1991.

Upon the opening of DIA, Fulenwider actions further illustrated the airport's land speculation potential. Among the family's investments were Buffalo Hills Ranch at 112th Avenue and Chambers Road and the South Cargo Area of DIA at 56th Avenue and Harvest Mile Road. A February 1994 newspaper story told how the Fulenwiders were expected to sell the land for a hotel near 72nd Avenue and Tower Road so DIA would not be totally isolated when it opened. WorldPort, on the south side of Peña Boulevard near DIA, was a central Fulenwider project, one for which it asked $65 million in city bonds in 2000 to make airport freight operations part of the DIA center of the universe. The Sunrise Ranch at 88th Avenue and Tower Road was the heart of the Van Schaack DIA holdings. The *Denver Post* estimated the worth of both the Fulenwider and Van Schaack families at between $50 million to $100 million by the time the airport was a reality.

Some of the suspect DIA-inspired land deals came out in a 1991 Colorado attorney general's probe into the field. The report observed the city likely paid ten times too much for some of the real estate, especially a 644-acre parcel known as Section 11. The property was worth about $3,000 to $4,000 an acre; Denver paid about $30,000 an acre for it.

The investigation focused on the role of MDC. The firm had pumped $120,000 into the pro-airport campaign while it had speculated in airport land. The attorney general's report concluded "probable cause exists to believe that MDC committed numerous criminal violations relating to election laws." However, since the statute of limitations had expired, it did not file any charges. In a related case, six executives and corporate subsidiaries of MDC pleaded guilty to illegal political money-laundering in the 1980s. They received slight slaps on the wrist.

Nor was the City and County of Denver successful in seeking legal redress for cost overruns at DIA. In October 1996, it went to trial in a suit against Fentress Bradburn and Associates, the firm designing the $432 million main terminal. The structure was originally only supposed to have cost $165 million. Even as the administration gloried in the aesthetics of the interior, known as "the Great Hall," it accused the architects of breaching "their duty of reasonable care and skill," leading to design errors and omissions resulting in $30 million in overcharges and damages. The city only asked for $15 million—the amount covered by insurance. The jury ruled in favor of the defendants: bad city management, not misdoings by the architects, was responsible for the extra costs.

New expenses continually popped up. In 1999, for example, $5.8 million was budgeted to deal with the unforeseen development that the year 2000 followed 1999—DIA computers had not taken this basic into account. By this time, the facility's runway lights were already obsolete and in need of replacement. Work was unending on repairing runways where slabs jutted up from the permeable soils. Planes blew tires on hitting the obstructions. Now and then, aircraft veered off the 150-foot-wide runways, landing strips 50 feet narrower than those at Stapleton.

## Noise Problems

Other schemes came out at the airport. One was to store radioactive dirt there. Since the 1970s, Denver had been haunted by the time before World War I when it was proud of its role as the "radium capital of the world." Some city streets were marginally radioactive, having been built up with dirt taken from radium mills. The solution in the late 1990s was to ship such contaminated soils to DIA awaiting their removal to a safer, more permanent site. The Webb administration seriously pondered this plan after the city had vehemently opposed expanding Stapleton onto the Rocky Mountain Arsenal because of the possible contamination of fringe areas of the latter. Now Denver seemed ready to have planes take off and land in an area to which it brought radioactive waste.

Change had to occur since the "international" in DIA was more pretense than reality. By geographic location, the Denver field was essentially a connection point for flights to other cities in North America. With the high altitude, existing commercial jet planes were not suited for direct flights to Japan. Despite this, in the pious wish Denver would yet become a port city, airport boosters continually talked about bringing nonstop flights from Europe and Asia to DIA.

As massive international connections remained glaringly absent from DIA, the field's champions were sure the completion of a 16,000-foot-long sixth runway, opposed to the five operating 12,000-foot-long runways, would make direct intercontinental travel the facility's keynote. If the promised sixth runway only became a reality, the city and media continually informed residents, all the operational problems of the world's greatest airport would be solved. This led *Westword* sarcastically to remark the proposed runway would be "long enough for nonstop space flights to Jupiter or 747s to Tokyo, whichever comes first." Even though the sixth runway was not completed as part of the original DIA, a city fire station was installed to serve it. (Denver's high altitude limits the range and capacity of jets. A longer runway would do little to redress this physical problem.)

A prime reason the sixth runway only remained on the drawing board was the lack of funds. As DIA became a laughingstock in the early 1990s, Congress saw it would not do to have additional federal aviation money poured into the boondoggle. Expressing anger at some of the Colorado politicians, Congress voted to prohibit any federal revenues from going to the sixth runway. In this manner, some observed how congressmen outside of Colorado did more to protect Denverites from the grasping DIA crowd than did any local politicians. Similarly, Colorado found itself in a fight with North Carolina over possible direct air access with London—the whole issue was used to obscure the fact there was little need or demand for nonstop flights between Denver and Europe. Jubilation greeted the introduction of nonstop service to London in the fall of 1998. Not mentioned was how direct European service had come and gone from Stapleton.

All the while, city hall pleaded for the sixth runway. It would not only provide an easy outlet for international travelers, but would also solve delay problems at the airport where they were not supposed to exist. Flight backups occurred at DIA just as they did at Stapleton.

Even as Hartsfield Airport in Atlanta, with four runways, handled twice as many flight operations as DIA, the city pushed for a sixth and even a seventh runway. Apparently, despite all the claims about the field's efficiency, these ex-

Photo by Phil Goodstein

*Even as DIA caused noise problems, the city heralded new residences near the field such as Legacy Gateway Park on 48th Avenue east of Chambers Road.*

pansions were vitally necessary to solve the new airport's shortcomings. (One study reported the sixth runway would save less than a minute per flight.)

The runway was also projected as a solution to another DIA plague: noise pollution. Far from alleviating the nuisance, the field of schemes dispersed and spread it over great parts of the metropolitan area. No sooner was the airport open than complaints poured in about its racket.

Many were from suburbanites who had deliberately located themselves far from the wicked city. Now evil Denver was coming to them via the airport, bringing its noise. They were not happy about the din caused by the airport designed to assure quiet for residential enclaves.

A good deal of the noise complaints came from Denver residents. They lived in neighborhoods supposedly outside the noise corridors of Stapleton. Nonetheless, they had constantly been disturbed by the roar of jet planes. The same remained true once DIA opened. Airplane noise was as bad as ever. Many of the flight routes from DIA continued to take jets over Denver residential enclaves. In other cases, with the Stapleton routes gone, private planes and military craft buzzed obnoxiously over the city.

City hall denied there was a problem. Nobody was more insistent than Mayor Webb. In the middle of an outdoor press conference, a loud jet interrupted him in an area supposedly never impacted by airport noise. Waiting for the sound to cease, he observed the plane causing the racket was not from DIA. In other words, since DIA was not responsible, there was no noise problem.

Opposed to the mayor, some suburban politicians, including congressional representatives, sought to redress constituent complaints about noise. Until the city ceased and desisted in generating noise from Denver International Airport, they fought any more federal money for the project. Adams County authorities were torn by this controversy. They sold the airport to residents with the promise of imposing fines of up to $500,000 per violation on Denver if planes exceeded noise maximums. But the airport was so designed it was impossible for the planes not to constantly insult the eardrums of people living within 20 miles of it. During an Adams County lawsuit against Denver over the noise in 1999, witnesses revealed how houses had been built near the airport as part of the field's logical economic development—they were naturally badly affected by jet noise. Adams County produced a Denver consultant's report showing the promised sixth runway not only would do nothing to redress DIA's racket, but might well increase the clamor.

Denver witnesses explained away the Adams County uproar. Skip Spensley, who had headed the city's New Airport Office, asserted the Denver–Adams County compact was only intended to protect existing residents from the DIA hubbub. Apparently, the airport was planned in such a manner that new growth—part and parcel of the reason for its creation—would always be impacted by aircraft noise.

In October 1999, the trial judge awarded Adams County $4 million for noise violations at DIA for the period between February 1995 and February 1996—the airport's first year when the Peña promises were immediately revealed as hollow. Talk was heard of more suits and fines for the field's many subsequent violations of the phony vows about no airport din.

Photo by John Schoenwalter

*Far from a bustling center of life, parts of DIA are where weary travelers can find quiet and rest.*

The DIA racket should have been expected. FAA noise maps at Stapleton had little relationship to reality. They were more idealistic conceptions of where airplane noise might be heard than actual studies of where it permeated. As with all the other factors behind the location of DIA, noise considerations were manipulated to justify city decisions.

## The Fate of Stapleton

At least residents did not have to worry about noise from Stapleton. Virtually from the time of the first commitment to DIA, airport advocates feared efforts would be made to maintain or reopen Stapleton once DIA was operating. Knowing such an action would severely impact the new field, they consequently made sure Stapleton would never again be used for flights.

DIA backers argued Stapleton was extremely valuable real estate. Once the new airport supplanted it, they insisted, new buyers would eagerly snap up the old field's land. A worthy developer would quickly transform Stapleton into a vibrant part of the expanding City and County of Denver. Prospectuses for airport bonds confidently predicted the sale of the old field would bring the city $100 million. Even at this, the sum was $400 million less than what Peña had estimated as Stapleton's price when he first pushed DIA.

Little immediately happened with the old airport property. The city took no account of the heavy pollution and clean-up costs stemming from Stapleton's long use as an airfield. While Denver gave subsidies to some businesses to move operations to vacant Stapleton facilities, the land sat mostly empty. A pie-in-the-sky effort to move the Smithsonian's National Air and Space Museum there not only flopped, but earned Denver the enmity of some Washington-area congressmen who wanted to keep the tourist attraction close to the capital.

As DIA became the area's flight center, the old airport rapidly decayed into an eyesore. Former mayoral candidate, McNichols aide, and DIA booster Errol Stevens headed Stapleton 2000. With an annual budget of $850,000, his group was charged with trying to do something with the former field.

In addition to paying people to push the redevelopment of Stapleton, the city spent nearly $5 million a year for policing and maintaining the ex-airport. Airlines objected. They claimed the administration was using DIA funds to take care of a non-airport operation. Every penny the city spent on non-DIA costs, the airlines figured, was another penny they would have to pay for the high-priced facility.

The city scaled down the revenue it expected to get from Stapleton to about $75 million. Before long, the Stapleton Redevelopment Foundation overshadowed Stapleton 2000. This agency dated from the late 1980s when it was obvious something would have to be done with the old airport upon the opening of DIA.

The Stapleton Redevelopment Foundation was essentially a front group for the Chamber of Commerce. This point was confirmed in July 1999 when its chief, investment banker Harry T. Lewis Jr., became Chamber's chair-elect. At the same time he led the Stapleton effort, Lewis also directed the Metro Denver Network, the arm of the Chamber which had supplanted the Greater Denver Corporation as the business group's political wing. The Metro Denver Network was at one with its predecessor in emphasizing the economic potentials of DIA. Lewis, a former partner of Boettcher & Company, was further a trustee of the extremely influential Boettcher Foundation. He was part of the Colorado Forum, the 17th Street group which had touted the economic wonders of DIA in the mid-1980s.

A Stapleton Redevelopment Foundation study urged the city to create a private, nonprofit to oversee the metamorphosis of the old airport. This led the Webb administration, working closely with the corporate community and the Denver Urban Renewal Authority, to establish the Stapleton Development Corporation in

Photo by Phil Goodstein

*An RTD park-and-ride occupied a former parking lot at Stapleton after DIA opened.*

1995. That group quickly pushed Stapleton 2000 aside. In no time, the new organization, despite its ostensible public role, operated extremely secretively. During the 1990s, the Stapleton Redevelopment Foundation/Stapleton Development Corporation received more than $4 million from the city, leading corporations, and philanthropies. United Airlines, Norwest Banks, US West, and Public Service were foremost contributors to the supposed "charitable" effort.

By the late 1990s, the most heavily used part of the abandoned Stapleton was a park-and-ride from which employees and passengers could catch buses to DIA. Developers announced they wanted to destroy the covered parking areas—a central part of this amenity. The Stapleton Development Corporation, overseeing the property, clashed with RTD in 1998 over who should pay for police protection of the lots.

Planners remained unfazed by past failures. They drew up ever more scenarios for Stapleton. The city projected the former field's 4,700 acres as a marvelous planned community, complete with luscious parks, bikeways along Sand Creek, a golf course, and other recreational facilities. Sand dunes were to reappear on the prairie north of I-70. Eight mixed-use villages would literally blossom in the middle of the open space.

In promises reminiscent of the way the city sold DIA, promoters vowed a $2.5 billion investment in the former Stapleton land would bring research and development parks, environmental technology centers, trendy shops, and swarming, high-class residential neighborhoods. Money from developers, private grants, tax-increment financing, and the city parks budget was to pay for all of it.

Nothing happened immediately. For some time, the Stapleton Development Corporation appeared more a paper organization spewing out idealistic sketches than an agency making promises reality. Real estate attorney Harvey E. Deutsch stepped into the breach in 1997. In the heyday of Silverado Savings, Deutsch stood by the side of the head of the Greater Denver Chamber, Bill Walters. The lawyer had also pushed for housing developments near DIA. He announced he was ready to buy up all of the Stapleton land for around $30 million. In face of the fiasco haunting the property since air operations had moved out, some took him seriously.

Though the Deutsch bid faded, the city resolved it had to expend millions of additional funds in demolishing the existing buildings at Stapleton. Many were modern structures in excellent shape. Far from seeking to find creative uses for the latter, the Stapleton Development Corporation gloried in the destruction of the remnants of a working airport during the final years of the 20th century. Nothing was to remain of Stapleton reminding residents of the massive inconvenience of DIA.

The Stapleton Development Corporation even clashed with its sponsor, the city of Denver. According to a 1994 airport deal, the city spent nearly $300,000 to renovate a hangar at the about-to-be-closed airfield as the training academy for the police department. No rent was charged on the building for five years in exchange for a steady police presence at the abandoned airport. By 1998, the Stapleton Development Corporation was reneging on this promise. Despite being ostensibly a city agency, it behaved like a typical developer trying to squeeze every penny it could out of tenants. Newspaper lawsuits forced it to open some of its records to the public.

On October 19, 1998, Denver selected Forest City Development of Cleveland as Stapleton's savior. With rhetoric comparable to anything ever coming out of the Peña administration, Forest City vowed to turn the former airport into a bustling commercial district with 17 million square free of commercial space. The center was to employ 35,000 workers. Twenty to thirty thousand people would live on the former airport grounds. To assure the perpetuation of the city machine, 10 percent of the land was promised at below-market prices to minorities, complete with set-aside contracts.

The total purchase and funding package was listed at $127.85 million for 3,000 acres to a company that was a generous contributor to the 1999 Webb reelection campaign. Forest City was poised to get $294 million, more than twice the purchase sum, back from the city through subsidies via tax-increment financing. The developer further stood to reap at least another $31.5 million from tax credits for bringing jobs to an enterprise zone. The airport's backers once more informed residents how salvation had arrived. Despite all the publicity, the final deal was delayed well into 2000.

## The DIA Success

The continued hoopla over Stapleton showed the airport backers' success. After five years of operation, at great cost and massive inconveniences, the city ironed out some of DIA's wrinkles. Passengers became used to the fact they had no alternative to the new field, resignedly driving extra distances and paying increased fees so they could live in the town with the world's most pompous airport.

Even as airlines required passengers to arrive ever earlier before flights, travelers experienced worse flight delays than at Stapleton. From a 81.7 percent on-time performance in May 1999, only 65.1 percent of DIA flights were on time in May 2000—the fourth worst of any major airport in the country. Far from solving national air congestion, the latter became worse after DIA opened. The field's cost per passenger slowly went down, though they were still more than twice what they had been at Stapleton. By 1999, United talked about expanding Concourse B while moving some of its gates to Concourse A. This allowed DIA champions to note the airport was virtually full—in a facility with fewer gates than at Stapleton. Repeating the same mindless numbers Peña had used to promote DIA, airport champions were sure DIA would surge to 206 gates serving 110 million passengers a year by 2020.

By the time Webb was easily reelected as mayor in 1999, DIA was a non-issue. Locals swallowed the airport's extra costs of time and money as facts of life. Besides, the Denver economy was again booming. Most of the new economic prosperity was more the product of national developments and the end of a cyclical slump than it was of any DIA-induced magic.

Among those aiding the boom were Californians. During the 1990s, Colorado experienced a mass influx of people who had soured on the Golden State. Compared to the Pacific Coast's inflated real estate market, they found the price of Denver homes most reasonable. The newcomers quickly drove up local land prices while patronizing DIA—it was as sprawled out as the world they had left. By 2000, many locals were loudly decrying the consequent cancerous growth. In other words, the prime goal of Peña and Romer in relentlessly pushing DIA was backfiring on the community's quality of life.

With a majority of connecting travelers, traffic at DIA surged to about 35 million passengers in 1997, about the same number who had used Stapleton at its peak year in 1986. Approximately 38 million flew in and out of the airport in 1999. Even so, total flight operations at DIA remained considerably below projections. Averaging 494,884 per year during DIA's first five years, they were fewer than the 520,667 in 1986 at Stapleton's peak. With a bustling economy, low interest rates, and yet more bond sales, the city was able to make payments on the airport debts.

Newspapers continued to report new developments near DIA, including hotels, office headquarters, and, most of all, residential facilities. A building boom was projected for Bennett and Watkins east of DIA as the entire I-70 corridor far east of the city was seen as a rich speculative zone for the next 25 to 50 years. The long-term prospects of the speculators were starting to pay off. The business domination of Denver was assured as the city moved into the 21st century.

## A Note on Sources:

Stapleton Airport is treated by Jeff Miller, *Stapleton International Airport: The First Fifty Years* (Boulder: Pruett, 1983). After the book appeared, drawing on it, he wrote "An Airport in Place," *Colorado Heritage*, 1984:3, pp. 2–16, in which he argued Stapleton was here to stay and talk about moving the airport was idle speculation. Articles in *Municipal Facts*, a city publication in the late 1920s, note city hall's decision to open Denver Municipal Airport, especially "Denver—Seaport of the Sky," September-October 1929, pp. 2–3. Also see *Souvenir Program* on the dedication of Denver Municipal Airport, October 17–20, 1929 (Denver: n.p., 1929). CHS manuscript collection 1640 includes various city public relations statements and brief historical portraits of Stapleton during the 1950s, 1960s, and 1970s. Patricia A. and Jack E. Fletcher, *The Historic Windsor Farm* (Yuma, AZ: Sun Graphics, 1982), mentions Brown Cannon and his Stapleton real estate dealings.

The standard mythology about Stapleton and how it forged the way for DIA is in Thomas J. Noel, "Unexplored Western Skies: Denver International Airport," *Journal of the West*, 30:1 (January 1991), 90–100. Frank Harper, "Colorado's Forgotten Airbase: The Original Lowry Field," *Colorado Heritage*, Autumn 1994, pp. 2–11, deals with that facility. Also see Nolie Mumey, *Epitome of the Semi-Centennial History of Colorado's Airmail* (Denver: Range Press, 1977).

The Hilltop crash is noted by Alice Millett Bakemeier, *Hilltop Heritage*; and "Transcript of Proceedings of Hilltop Protest Meeting," held at Graland School, December 5, 1951. At copy is at DPL. In it, Dave Davis, representing the city Department of Aeronautics, notes the Newton administration's efforts to restrict residential development near Stapleton to the west of Quebec Street.

Byron Johnson recalled his fights as a congressman against the Rocky Mountain Arsenal. Clippings and brochures on it are in the Denver Women's International League for Peace and Freedom papers at the Auraria Archives. Rachel Carson noted its pollution in her classic *Silent Spring* (Boston: Houghton Mifflin, 1962). Walter Gerash allowed me to examine the records of a lawsuit he filed against the Arsenal in 1970. The Federal District Court immediately dismissed it at the request of the Army. See *McQueary* v. *Laird*, 449 F.2d 608. Gerash also let me see his file on Gregory Alberico. Newspapers extensively reported the earthquakes in the 1960s and the analyses of David Evans.

David N. Wetzel gives a brief, positive overview of Denver International Airport in "The Road to DIA," *Colorado Heritage*, Winter 2000, pp. 30–34. He thoughtfully critiqued a draft of this chapter and provided layout suggestions for the volume. The airport's architecture, especially the terminal, is featured in Roger A. Chandler, *Fentress Bradburn Architects*.

The key book on DIA is Paul Stephen Dempsey, Andrew R. Goetz, and Joseph S. Szyliowicz, *Denver International Airport: Lessons Learned*. This 1997-volume notes the numerous deceits, failures, cost overruns, and problems of the airport. See the review in the *Naysayer*, January 1998. Dempsey, a professor of law specializing in transportation issues at the University of Denver and a vice-chairman and director of the new Frontier Airlines, was initially a supporter of DIA. He takes on United Airlines in his *Unfriendly Skies over Colorado: United Airlines Fortress Hub Monopoly at Denver* ([Denver]: Frontier Airlines, 1997). This work is subsequent to the DIA book, written as part of a Frontier legal campaign against United. In *Unfriendly Skies*, Dempsey makes United responsible for the failure of the baggage system and the delay of opening Denver International Airport.

Michael Boyd, of the Golden-based Aviation Systems Research Corporation, was a persistent critic of DIA. Newspapers frequently quoted him. An interview with him is in *DP Empire*, March 17, 1996, p. 8. Also see the March 6, 1994, *DP*, p. 1H. He issued *Airports: USA*, frequently commenting about DIA in its *Quarterly* and *Traffic Bulletin*. A special section of the April 1995 issue of the former, pp. 20–25, notes DIA's failures during its first months of operation.

Jim Buck, known as Robin during the DIA campaign, was also outspoken in opposing the new airport, highly publicizing its problems. He shared his thoughts with me on DIA, including his articles in *The Villager*. Buck reviewed a draft of this chapter and helped me strengthen it, providing me with data about DIA operations and delays. He noted DIA's cost could be up to $16 billion.

Paul Earle, "Batman"—Buck's cohort in fighting DIA—also reviewed a draft of the chapter. Buck and Earle provided me access to their files, including the analysis of the airport's geology by William A. Thompson. Included was their briefing book, presented to the House of Representative's transportation committee on May 2, 1991, containing anti-airport statements and documents from Dick Young, Bill Chenoweth, Tom Currigan, Bill McNichols, and others. The two further gave me copies of many critical clippings on the DIA from *Forbes*, *Wall Street Journal*, *US News & World Report*, *Time, Newsweek*, and other prominent publications. Peter Boyles also provided me with anti-DIA information. He looked at an early version of the text.

*Innerline* was a newsletter focusing on Stapleton. United Airlines reports on local developments in its employee magazine, *The Hub and Spoke*. Steven F. Mehls, *Denver International Airport Historic Resources: Multiple Property Listing* (Denver: Colorado Historical Society, 1992), reviews the history of land use and ownership on the land selected for DIA.

The January 23, 1995, *High Country News*, pp. 10–20, points out many of DIA's foibles. A bitter, conservative attack on DIA is Michael Fumento, "Federico's Folly," *American Spectator*, December 1993, pp. 42–49. James A. Barnes, "Cleared for Takeoff," *National Journal*, September 18, 1993, pp. 2237–41, notes the politics of CenterPort. An interesting statement is the September 2, 1993, circular letter on DIA by Robert G. Lesher of Lesher Partners Incorporated. Councilman Ed Thomas allowed me to look at his voluminous file on DIA. His collection also has materials on the fate of Stapleton.

Manuscript 1666 at CHS focuses on DIA, including architectural sketches, contractor puff pieces, and city news releases and brochures promoting the facility. The archive includes numerous DIA press handouts, justifying every move of the airport administration. It further includes critical newspaper clippings, both from the local and national press. There are also transcripts from television and radio broadcasts about the airport. The collection has materials on the Stapleton Noise Advisory Committee and the environmental-impact statements for both the expansion of Stapleton and DIA. Copies of *DIA Art*, the newsletter of those pushing the paintings at the airport, are in the holding. Airport advocates issued an unending stream of propaganda for the facility, including the bulletin, *Partners in Progress for a New Airport*.

There are countless airport studies and reports, including by the Denver Planning Office, DRCOG, and independent consultants, in both the Western History and Government Document departments of DPL. Unfortunately, the latter are very sporadic: the library has not sought to serve as a depository of city reports and proclamations. FAA documents are also uneven on Denver International Airport. As Secretary of Transportation, Peña completely reshaped the agency's records and reports.

A letter from Peña to the people of Denver, dated March 15, 1985, spells out the Adams County agreement and memo of understanding. *Regional Economic Impact of Stapleton International Airport and Future Airport Development: Summary Report* (Denver: Colorado Forum, September 1986), lists DIA's ability to create jobs. The New World Airport Commission issued an *Official Souvenir Program* (Westminster: Publishing Housing, 1994), for the non-opening of DIA in the spring of 1994. There are annual reports for both Stapleton and DIA.

Among the DRCOG studies are: *Financing Airport Capital Improvements in the Denver Region* (1984); *Final Report Metropolitan Airport Study* (1983), which is closely related to the Peat Marwick Mitchell's consultant report, *Metropolitan Airport Study* (1983); Peat Marwick Mitchell, *Site Evaluation* (1982); and Coopers & Lybrand, *Rocky Mountain Arsenal and Stapleton International Airport Expansion* (1983).

Peat Marwick Mitchell, *Airport Master Plan: Stapleton International Airport* (Denver: City and County of Denver, 1981), noted the city's commitment to expanding Stapleton through relocating its runways. HNTB's reports include *Denver Stapleton International Airport: Alternative Configurations for a New Airport* (February 1985); and *Site Selection Study* (September 1986).

I discuss the controversy over the 1976 Winter Olympics in volume one. Mike Davenport and Reuben Espinosa shared their memories of fighting DIA. Gary Oakley also recalled his activity against the field of dreams. He led a group, Concerned Coloradans Association, which called for scrapping the airport in 1992. It issued *Denver International Airport: A Second Look.* A letter to the editor by Richard Becker notes the public hearing process on DIA during the debates in 1988–89, *WW*, July 30, 1998, p. 4. Ed McGuire also gave me his perspective on the 1989 election. Figures on DIA losses are taken from annual auditor reports and the mayor's budget.

Jack McCroskey critically dissected the financial problems with the entire Peña economic scenario on the project in personal discussions. Bill Rourke talked about the civil aviation matrix. Jim Betts gave me a personal tour of DIA before it opened, noting the architecture and the field's design. He also provided me with information about the baggage system. Allen L. Jones recalled the police command at Stapleton. Pat Angell discussed working for United Airlines and how the new airport affected everyday airport employees.

Robert J. Sterling's biography of Robert Six, *Maverick*, focuses on the history of Continental. Kelly Lyons and other former Continental employees shared many stories about working for the airline and the 1983 strike. Noel, *Rocky Mountain Gold*, describes the origins of Frontier Airlines. Kate Engel recalled working for the original Frontier. The defunct carrier's papers are at CHS.

*People* v. *Young*, *Colorado Lawyer*, 23:2 (February 1994), 480, notes the disbarment of Richard Young. There is a biographical sketch of Young at the Park Hill Library. *Cervi's Journal* noted some of his boss-like actions in the Democratic Party in the early 1970s. Jerry Kopel recalled Young's close ties to Dale Tooley. The disciplining of Holt is *People* v. *Holt*, *Colorado Lawyer*, 21:9 (September 1992), 2048–49.

The Chamber of Commerce boasts of the nefarious deeds of the Greater Denver Corporation in William H. Hornby, *Eye on the Horizon.* Wilmsen, *Silverado*, notes the thrift's involvement in airport land deals. He also discusses the MDC and its involvement in the 1986 and 1987 elections. His Silverado collection at CHS includes the Colorado Attorney General's report by Robert R. Gallagher, issued in March 1991, noting the MDC-Silverado link and the development corporation's massive campaign contributions.

The ties between Gary Antonoff, the Colorado National Bank, Silverado Savings, the Peña administration, and land speculation in Adams County are discussed in Eric Dexheimer, "Turning Water into Whine," *WW*, August 20, 1998, pp. 19–28. US West celebrated its success at DIA with a pamphlet, *For a Better Colorado* (Denver: US West, n.d.), in collaboration with the city. A copy is in the DIA papers at CHS.

Articles by Bob Kowalski in the *Denver Post* were the best investigative journalism in the local media during the heart of the DIA debates in 1987–89. He especially exposed some of the MDC deals. Jodi Enda had some good articles about the airport in the *Rocky Mountain News*. Gene Amole columns in the *News* consistently berated the project.

An overview of the airport is "DIA: Dream to Disappointment," *DP*, February 12, 1995. Also see David Chandler, "Cash Landing," *WW*, February 17, 1993, pp. 14–21; idem, "Collision Course," *WW*, March 3, 1993, pp. 17–19; idem, "Small Craft Warnings," *WW*, January 12, 1994, pp. 15–20. *Westword* also had some other good barbs on the airport. Compared to the coverage in the *Post* and *News*, *Westword* was far and away the region's best newspaper in having a slight grasp of what was going on at DIA.

The Robert Lesher letter of September 2, 1993, notes the links between the Fulenwiders and William Peña. DPL has clipping files on the Fulenwider and Van Schaack families. Newspapers reported the demise of Van Schaack & Company. Mehls, *DIA Historic Resources*, traces the evolution of Box Elder Farms.

There was immense newspaper reportage on E-470. An advertising supplement to the October 24, 1999, *DP* stressed the real estate developments near the highway and DIA. A story in the December 6, 1999, *DP* noted the push for 70,000 people along the E-470 corridor. Noel, *Mile High City*, includes a discussion of the toll road and the work of Brownstein Hyatt Farber & Strickland in sponsoring it. He personally informed me that the law firm was the author of the text.

Vernon Parrington developed the theme of the "Great American Barbecue" after the Civil War in *The Beginnings of Critical Realism in America: 1860–1920* (New York: Harcourt, Brace & World, 1930). The dirty deeds of corporate America during that epoch are detailed by Matthew Josephson in *The Robber Barons* (New York: Harcourt, Brace & World, 1934). George Washington Plunkitt revealed the nature of "honest corruption" and the city machine in William L. Riordon, recorder, *Plunkitt of Tammany Hall* (New York: Dutton, 1963).

*Congress Park News*, the newsletter of the Congress Park Neighbors noted the increased noise problems over neighborhoods upon the opening of DIA. Kathi Anderson, aide to city councilman Ed Thomas, reported she received many complaints over the aviation racket. Newspapers reported the Adams County lawsuit on DIA.

The Stapleton Redevelopment Foundation spelled out its vision for the former airport in *Stapleton Development Plan: Integrating Jobs, Environment and Community* (Denver: Stapleton Redevelopment Foundation, 1995). Newspapers have reported the doings of the Stapleton Development Corporation. The *Denver Post* noted its suits forcing the agency to open up its records. Tom Gleason talked about its operations in a phone interview. Andy Van de Voorde, "The Jet Set," *WW*, September 25, 1997, pp. 15–21, discusses the fate of Stapleton. A propaganda tract extolling the redevelopment of the former airport is William A. Barnes, "Stapleton Gets Ready for Liftoff," *Urban Land* 57:4 (April 1998), 67–70, 116.

# Bibliography

Virtually from Denver's founding amidst the Pikes Peak gold rush in 1858–1859, local leaders have sought to justify themselves. Through the 19th century, businessmen readily financed histories of the community. These tomes included glowing biographical sketches of the books' backers and praise for the corporate establishment.

Starting with the first volume on the city's past, Junius Wharton's 1866 *History of the City of Denver from Its Earliest Times*, the tomes, written by journalists, extolled local financial leaders. Frequently, they were more booster tracts, reassuring an insecure community about its future, than studies of the people, politics, economics, and forces shaping the area.

Assorted volumes appeared as Denver emerged as a metropolis in the last 30 years of the 19th century. They often provide good material on early bankers and investors and include irreplaceable pictorial sketches of the area. Completely lacking, however, is any meaningful discussion of the lives of everyday workers. William B. Vickers' 1880 *History of the City of Denver*, and Jerome Smiley's monumental *History of Denver*, stand out as the best volumes from this epoch.

The latter, published in 1901 by a daily newspaper, the *Denver Times*, was a virtual encyclopedic listing of reputable early Denver businesses. The book is filled with long lists of names of monied individuals. Sidebars include portraits of city leaders and underwriters of the volume. Smiley, who later worked as a curator for the Colorado Historical Society, dismisses Indians, blacks, and Hispanics as of virtually no account in the forging of the city. Nor does he have much truck with gamblers, prostitutes, and other marginal elements. He is blunt in his condemnation of those failing to embrace the Chamber of Commerce ethic while he extravagantly praises the powers that be.

Opposed to Smiley, another early 20th-century work critically examined Denver's past and power relations, Clyde Lyndon King's *History of the Government of Denver in Specific Reference to its Relation to Public Service Companies.*

The book appeared in 1911, right at the flood tide of Progressivism. King, a forthright reformer, noted the extremely corrupt core of the city's politics, tying the malfeasance to the special deals and interests of utility corporations. The author called for solving these problems through having fewer elected officials, nonpartisan government, and a greater reliance on professional experts. His views helped shape a complete restructuring of the municipal government in 1912–13 when reformers took hold of city hall.

Nobody sought to document this last development. King's book was soon forgotten. The closest effort at a history of the Mile High City in ensuing decades was Gene Fowler's *Timber Line* (1933). Written by a former local newspaper reporter who was a leading Hearst columnist in New York, the book is ostensibly the story of the *Denver Post*. Fowler romanticizes the area, filling the book with tall tales and colorful personalities. Unfortunately, the volume is not factually trustworthy. Nor does *Timber Line* contain any probing into the heart of the community or examination of the forces that made possible the outrageous conduct of the *Denver Post*. (A subsequent 1976 official history of the *Post*, *Thunder in the Rockies* by Bill Hosokawa, is not nearly as good. Not only is the book primarily an accolade to the post-World War II paper under Helen Bonfils and Palmer Hoyt, but it lacks an overview of the city.)

Equally unreliable were numerous brochures on Denver, including some of its colorful characters, by Caroline Bancroft (1900–1985). From the time she started writing about "old timers" for the *Denver Post* in 1928 until her death, she projected herself as the guardian sentinel of the city's past. She readily filled her writing with fabricated dialogue. No more than Smiley or Fowler did she show any larger vision or understanding of the competing interests at the heart of the metropolis.

Much the same is true with most tracts by members of the Denver Posse of Westerners. From the 1930s into the 1970s, some of its members, notably Forbes Parkhill, Nolie Mumey, and Fred Mazzulla, produced a wide array of books and pamphlets. Often most entertaining reading, they are sometimes more tall tales than meaningful examinations of Denver's past.

Not until the centennial of the Rush to the Rockies in 1959 did a serious examination of Denver appear, *The First Hundred Years*, by Robert L. Perkin. Ostensibly a history of the *Rocky Mountain News*, it is the best overall volume ever published on Denver. Besides looking at the foibles of the *News* and its founding editor, William Newton Byers, Perkin notes the city's underside. He deals with the cynical manipulations of railroad promoters, politicians, and hate-mongers. As a veteran *News* writer, Perkin glossed over many of the paper's problems in the mid-century; nonetheless, he brought life and drama to the reality of the Mile High City as no one had ever done.

The same year, 1959, saw the publication of Louisa Ward Arps' *Denver in Slices*. Based on an early Channel Six show on the Mile High City's past, Arps, a longtime librarian for Denver Public Schools, sketched some of the city's colorful figures. Here one gets an introductory look at Buffalo Bill, takes a trip to Elitch's, explores the problems of drinking water, discovers the history of the Mint, and learns about the trauma of floods. Though *Denver in Slices* lacks a penetrating overview, the volume is an excellent introduction to the Queen City.

Another inviting look at the city is *Denver: A Pictorial History*, by William C. Jones and Kenton Forrest. Published in 1973, it not only provides numerous quality photos highlighting the evolution of the community, but includes a solid text where the authors tie the schools, the government, high society, floods, fires, and scoundrels into the fabric of the community. Forrest, a retired school teacher, has written numerous other volumes on the area, mostly dealing with railroads, transit, and public facilities. Jones, in collaboration with his wife Bettyann, has put together some other Colorado pictorial histories, concentrating on such photographers as William Henry Jackson, Harry Buckwalter, and L. C. McClure.

Not until 1977 did an academic historian attempt to tackle the totality of Denver. Lyle W. Dorsett was then a promising urban historian at the University of Denver (DU) who lived in Boulder and had taught at the University of Colorado in 1971–72. A native of Kansas City, Missouri, he received his degree from the University of Missouri. Primarily a student of Kansas City history, Dorsett had previously published on the Thomas J. Pendergast machine. In seminars, the professor insisted graduate students become probing professionals who question all facts and assumptions.

Simultaneously, Dorsett worked with the chairman of the DU history department, Allen duPont Breck. The latter has written numerous accolades to ruling Denver, including a subsidized history of the Jewish community, a vacuous portrait of the University of Denver, and effusive hagiographies of William Gray Evans and John Evans II. Breck's books are anything but the critical histories Dorsett pushed on his students.

George Cranmer and Ben Stapleton Jr., veterans of the past corporate domination of the Mile High City, approached Breck and the University of Denver in the early 1970s, requesting a modern history of the city. Dorsett received a leave of absence, with generous donations from the corporate community, to produce the work, *The Queen City*. Pruett Publishing of Boulder issued it as volume one of a multi-volume series on western cities. The DU professor joined with noted Kansas City historian Andrew Theodore Brown to write, *KC: A History of Kansas City, Missouri*, (1978) as part of this project.

*The Queen City* starts out with Dorsett placing Denver in the rubric of urban history, interpreting it through a booster perspective prevalent in studies of Kansas City. He showed himself fully aware of the elites, tensions, competing groups, nationalities, and races which make up a community. Side by side of this, he sought to praise Denver's business masters. The result, at first, was virtually two different volumes in one: Dorsett paired a chapter on the social setting and everyday people with one hailing the corporate leadership. Before long, the latter overwhelmed the former. Following in the footpaths of Breck, Dorsett was quick to condemn critics of the oligarchy, but was vague on specifics of why challengers had so lambasted the ruling elite. Especially with the chapters on Mayor Ben Stapleton and postwar Denver, the *Queen City* was at one with Smiley in being little more than a paean to the present.

Within a few years of the *Queen City*'s publication, Dorsett emerged as a fundamentalist Christian, moving to a church academy, Wheaton College, in Illinois. Michael McCarthy updated *Queen City* for a second edition in 1986. He failed to fill in many of the gaps Dorsett left, including little on such basic developments as the 1965 flood and the wars over school busing. The overall result is unsatisfying. The volume observes there is something beyond the previous puffy accounts in Denver's past, but fails to deliver on its promise.

Much the same is true with Stephen J. Leonard and Thomas J. Noel's 1990 volume, *Denver: Mining Camp to Metropolis*. The book is both a collaboration and sections separately written by the two. They did not have the courtesy in their introduction to specify this or who wrote what parts of the book. This is typical: the volume systematically beats about the bush and fails to analyze most of the crucial issues that have divided Denver. Captions on pictures are extremely vague and unsatisfying.

A product of a Jesuit education at Regis College, Leonard is the longtime chairman of the Metropolitan State College of Denver history department. Reflecting some of the problems with the school, the department under him has often had nebulous academic standards. Disgruntled part-time faculty members have charged he has pressured them to change grades. Leonard has sometimes urged associates not to tilt against windmills or rock the boat. The book reflects such views.

Noel, the city's best-known historian, is a skilled writer and an even better publicist. The author of more than 20 books on the region, his doctoral dissertation formed the basis of one of his best volumes, *The City and the Saloon* (1982). Far more than a look at Denver's drinking establishments before World War I, it examines the social, political, and economic roles of bars and how they related to the development of the metropolis.

Unfortunately, Noel did not keep up this pace in subsequent volumes. He has been at his best when focusing on architecture. His 1987 *Denver: The City Beautiful*, with Barbara Norgren, is an impressive look at the forces shaping the physical appearance of the city. No place in the volume, however, does Noel note why some forceful critics have condemned the City Beautiful movement as a sham. On the contrary, he has been something of an ideologue for Federico Peña, Wellington Webb, and others who have used the City Beautiful to cloak other issues. In the process, Noel has emerged as the historian sanctifying the status quo.

Avoidance of the debates shaping Denver's character fatally flaws *Mining Camp to Metropolis*. Compared to an early journal article by Noel, "All Hail the Denver Pacific: Denver's First Railroad," *Colorado Magazine*, 50:2 (Spring 1973), 91–116, in which he critically examined the problematic nature of the procurement of the city's inaugural railroad in 1870, the Leonard-Noel volume does not mention the divisions and questionable financing at the heart of the measure. This is only one example of the study's omission of community differences and a failure to question, much less expose, the business leadership.

Opposed to Dorsett, who goes out of his way to justify the actions of 17th Street, at places Leonard and Noel do not even admit the corporate community has central directing agencies. Far from seeking to educate readers about how disputes have shaped the city, the authors are eager not to offend anyone. Their joint personality comes across as that of Dr. Pangloss, Candide's tutor in asserting this is the best possible of all existing worlds. They confirmed this in a subsequent volume, with Kevin E. Rucker, *Colorado Givers: A History of Philanthropic Heroes*. Among those they unquestioningly celebrate is Reverend Jim Goodheart, a preacher who swindled $25,000-plus from a homeless shelter in the 1920s.

The deletion of uncomfortable facts severely blemishes much of Noel's publications. He has often taken money from the business elite about which he writes. His *Rocky Mountain Gold* (1979) and *Mile High City: An Illustrated History of Denver* (1997), are both filled with paid tributes to ruling Denver. Some of his other books are nothing more than superficial sets of lists that are of little value. In places, they are error-filled.

On occasion, Noel has not been above fabricating photos, especially a sham shot of early settler William McGaa in *Rocky Mountain Gold*. (The picture he offers of McGaa is actually a touched-up shot of his close companion, veteran politician Dennis Gallagher.) Noel's cynical use of the photo showed a contempt for both readers and future scholars who might believe the graphic is legitimate.

Various other works exist on Denver, including corporate histories, papers by graduate students, and Ph.D. dissertations. DPL, CHS, and the Auraria Archives all have rich holdings on the area. During the 1960s and 1970s, *Colorado Magazine* published numerous path-breaking articles on the state's past. David Halaas gives a brief, positive overview of the area's historiography in "The History of Denver Histories," *Colorado Heritage*, Summer 1991, pp. 35–39. Halaas reviewed a draft of this essay.

Historians are affected by the same pressures, values, and influences as anyone else. In this volume, my bias has been obvious: the belief the triumph of big money is not synonymous with the aspirations and hopes of everyday citizens. I discuss the specific works on the different subjects in the essays "a note on sources" at the end of each chapter. In addition to the books cited there, I have sought to draw on the rich literature on the area, including the following:


Abbott, Carl, Stephen J. Leonard, and David McComb. *Colorado: A History of the Centennial State*. Boulder: Colorado Associated University Press, 1982.

Abrams, Jeanne. *Blazing the Tuberculosis Trail*. Denver: Colorado Historical Society, 1990.

Ackland, Len. *Making a Real Killing: Rocky Flats and the Nuclear West*. Albuquerque: University of New Mexico Press, 1999.

Adams, Eugene H., Lyle W. Dorsett, and Robert S. Pulcipher. *The Pioneer Western Bank*. Denver: First Interstate Bank of Denver, 1984.

Allen, Frederick S., et al. *The University of Colorado, 1876–1976*. New York: Harcourt Brace Jovanovich, 1976.

Arps, Louisa Ward. *Denver in Slices*. Denver: Sage Books, 1959.

________. *From Cemetery to Conservatory*. Denver: Botanic Gardens, 1980.

Athearn, Robert G. *The Coloradans*. Albuquerque: University of New Mexico Press, 1976.

________. *The Denver & Rio Grande Western Railroad*. Lincoln: University of Nebraska Press, 1977.

Baker, James H., and Leroy Hafen, editors. *History of Colorado*. Five volumes. Denver: Linderman Company, 1927.

Bakke, Diane, and Jackie Davis. *Places around the Bases*. Englewood: Westcliffe Publishers, 1995.

Bancroft, Caroline. *Mile High Denver*. Denver: By the Author, 1952.

Bakemeier, Alice Millett. *Hilltop Heritage: A History and Guide to a Denver Neighborhood*. Denver: Cranmer Park/Hilltop Civic Association, 1997.

Ballast, David Kent. *The Denver Chronicle*. Houston: Gulf Publishing, 1995.

Barker, Bill, and Jackie Lewin. *Denver!* Garden City: Doubleday, 1972.

Barnes, Henry A. *The Man with Red and Green Eyes*. New York: Dutton, 1965.

Batschelet, Ralph J. *The Flick and I*. Smithtown, NY: Exposition Press, 1981.

Baum, Dan. *Citizen Coors*. New York: William Morrow, 2000.

Bean, Geraldine B. *Charles Boettcher: A Study in Pioneer Western Enterprise*. Boulder: Westview Press, 1976.

Beshoar, Barron B. *Hippocrates in a Red Vest: The Biography of a Frontier Doctor*. Palo Alto, CA: American West Publishing Company, 1973.

________. *Out of the Depths*. Denver: Golden Bell, 1942.

Betz, Larry. *Globeville: Part of Colorado's Past*. Denver: Larry Betz, 1972.

Bluemel, Elinor. *Florence Sabin: Colorado Woman of the Century*. Boulder: University of Colorado Press, n.d.

Breck, Allen duPont. *A Centennial History of the Jews of Colorado, 1859–1959*. Denver: University of Denver/Hirschfeld Press, 1961.

________. *The Episcopal Church in Colorado, 1860–1963*. Denver: Big Mountain Press, 1963.

________. *From Denver to the World: A Companion to the History of the University of Denver, 1864–1989*. Denver: University of Denver, 1989.

________. *John Evans of Denver*. Boulder: Pruett, 1972.

________. *William Gray Evans, 1855–1924*. Denver: University of Denver Department of History, 1964.

Brenneman, Bill. *Miracle on Cherry Creek*. Denver: World Press, 1973.

Brettell, Richard. *Historic Denver*. Denver: Historic Denver, 1973.

Byers, William N. *Encyclopedia of Biography of Colorado*. Chicago: Century Publishing Company, 1901.

Chandler, Roger A. *Fentress Bradburn Architects*. Washington: Studio Press, 1995.

*Colorado and the American Renaissance, 1876–1917*. Denver: Denver Art Museum, 1980.

*Colorado Year Book*. Denver: Colorado State Planning Division, 1918–64.

Colorado Legislative Council. *Presidents and Speakers of the Colorado General Assembly*. Denver: Eastwood Printing, 1980.

*Colorado: The Superstar State*. Baton Rouge: Moran Publishing Company, 1979.

Cooper, Arthur B. *The Story of Our Presbytery of Denver, 1870–1950*. Denver: n.p., 1950.

Creel, George. *Rebel at Large*. New York: G. P. Putnam's Sons, 1947.
Dallas, Sandra. *Cherry Creek Gothic*. Norman: University of Oklahoma Press, 1971.
Davis, Lawrence J. *The Billionaire Shell Game*. New York: Doubleday, 1998.
Davis, Sally, and Betty Baldwin. *Denver Dwellings and Descendants*. Denver: Sage Books, 1963.
Davis, William E. *Glory Colorado! A History of the University of Colorado, 1858–1963*. Boulder: Pruett, 1965.
De Baca, Vincent C., editor. *La Gente: Hispano History and Life in Colorado*. Denver: Colorado Historical Society, 1998.
DeBoer, S. R. *Around the Seasons in Denver*. Denver: Smith-Brooks 1948.
________. "Plans, Parks, and People," *The Greenthumb*, 29:5 (December 1972), 142–212.
Dempsey, Paul Stephen, Andrew R. Goetz, and Joseph S. Szyliowicz. *Denver International Airport: Lessons Learned*. New York: McGraw-Hill, 1997.
Denton, James A. *Rocky Mountain Radical: Myron W. Reed, Christian Socialist*. Albuquerque: University of New Mexico Press, 1997.
Dorsett, Lyle, and Michael McCarthy. *The Queen City*. Second edition. Boulder: Pruett, 1986.
Downing, Sybil, and Robert E. Smith. *Tom Patterson: Colorado Crusader for Change*. Niwot: University Press of Colorado, 1995.
Eason, Catherine McGuire, and J. Terry Heming. *United States Court of Appeals: Tenth Circuit 60th Anniversary*. [Denver]: [Tenth Circuit Court of Appeals], 1989.
Eatwell, John M., editor. *Denver's Golden Days and Apothecary Palaces*. Denver: Antique Bottle Collectors of Colorado, 1971.
Edmonds, Carol. *Wayne Aspinall: Mr. Chairman*. Lakewood: Crown Point, 1980.
Ekstrand, Margaret E., and Thomas J. Noel. *The University Club of Denver: The First Hundred Years*. Denver: University Club of Denver, 1991.
Eitemiller, David. *Historic Tours: Denver*. [Denver]: n.p., 1977.
Engle, Morey. *Denver Comes of Age: The Postwar Photography of Morey Engle*. Boulder: Johnson Books, 1994.
Engle, Morey, and Bernard Kelly. *Denver's Man with a Camera: The Photographs of Harry Rhoads*. Evergreen: Cordillera Press, 1989.
Etter, Don. *Auraria: Where Denver Began*. [Boulder]: Colorado Associated University Press, 1972.
________. *The Denver Park and Parkway System*. Denver: National Register Theme Nomination prepared for the Colorado Historical Society, 1986.
________. *Denver University Park: Four Walking Tours*. [Denver]: Graphic Impressions, 1974.
Fallis, Edwina. *When Denver and I Were Young*. Denver: Big Mountain Press, 1956.
Fell, James E., Jr. *Ores to Metals: The Rocky Mountain Smelting Industry*. Lincoln: University of Nebraska Press, 1979.

Ferril, Thomas Hornsby. *I Hate Thursday*. New York: Harper & Brothers, 1946.

Ferril, Thomas Hornsby, and Helen Ferril. *The Rocky Mountain Herald Reader*. New York: Morrow, 1966.

Ferril, Will. *Profiles of Colorado*. Denver: Western Press Bureau, 1911.

Fishell, Dave. *Towers of Healing: The First 125 Years of Denver's Saint Joseph Hospital*. Denver: Saint Joseph Hospital, 2000.

Fletcher, Jack E., and Patricia A. *Colorado's Cowtown*. Yuma, AZ: Jack E. and Patricia A. Fletcher, 1981.

Follawsbee, Robert, and Leonard R. Sawyer. *Floods in Colorado*. Washington: United States Geological Survey, 1948.

Forrest, Kenton. *The Railroads of Coors Field: A Brief History of Railroading in the Vicinity of Coors Field*. Golden: Colorado Railroad Museum, 1995.

Forrest, Kenton, and Charles Albi. *Denver's Railroads*. Revised edition. Golden: Colorado Railroad Museum, 1986.

Forrest, Kenton, Gene McKeever, and Raymond McAllister. *History of the Public Schools of Denver*. Denver: Tramway Press, 1989.

Fowler, Gene. *A Solo in Tom-Toms*. New York: Viking Press, 1946.

________. *Timber Line*. New York: Covici Friede, 1933.

Gibson, Barbara. *The City Club of Denver, 1922–1997*. Denver: City Club, 1999.

*The Glory that was Gold*. Third edition. Denver: Central City Opera House Association, 1940.

Goff, Kenneth. *The History of Sheridan, Colorado*. Englewood: Sheridan Historical Association, 1957.

Goldberg, Robert. *Hooded Empire: The Ku Klux Klan in Colorado*. Urbana: University of Illinois Press, 1981.

Goodstein, Phil. *Denver Streets: Names, Numbers, Locations, Logic*. Second edition. Denver: New Social Publications, 1995.

________. *Denver's Capitol Hill*. Denver: Life Publications, 1988.

________. *Exploring Jewish Colorado*. Denver: Center for Judaic Studies, University of Denver, 1992.

________. *The Ghosts of Denver: Capitol Hill*. Denver: New Social Publications, 1996.

________. "Monumental Denver," *Colorado Heritage*, No. 3 (1987), 34–43.

________. *The Seamy Side of Denver*. Denver: New Social Publications, 1993.

________. *South Denver Saga*. Denver: New Social Publications, 1991.

Goodstein, Phil, and Walter Gerash. *Murders in the Bank Vault*. Denver: New Social Publications, 1998.

Gressley, Gene M. *Bankers and Cattlemen*. Lincoln: University of Nebraska Press, 1966.

Griswold, Don, and Jean Griswold. *Colorado's Century of "Cities."* [Denver]: Smith-Brooks Printing Company, 1958.

Grand Lodge AF&AM of Colorado. *Centennial Celebration*. n.p.: n.p., [1961].

Gunther, John. *Inside USA*. Harper & Brothers, 1946, 1947.

Gurtler, Jack, and Corinne Hunt. *The Elitch Garden Story: Memories of Jack Gurtler*. Boulder: Rocky Mountain Writers Guild, 1982.

Hackenburg, Herbert J. *Muttering Machines to Laser Beams: A History of Mountain Bell*. Denver: Mountain Bell, 1986.

Hafen, Leroy, editor. *Colorado and Its People*. Four volumes. New York: Lewis Historical Publishing Company, 1948.

Halaas, David. *Boom Town Newspapers*. Albuquerque: University of New Mexico Press, 1981.

________. *Fairmount and Historic Colorado*. Denver: Fairmount Cemetery Association, 1976.

Hall, Frank. *History of the State of Colorado*. Chicago: Blakely, 1889.

Hansen, James E. *Democracy's College in the Centennial State: A History of Colorado State University*. Ft. Collins: Colorado State University, 1977.

Haro, Juan. *The Ultimate Betrayal*. Pittsburgh: Dorrance Publishing, 1998.

Haywood, William D. *Bill Haywood's Book*. New York: International Publishers, 1929.

Heber, Francine, Kenneth Fuller, and David Wetzel. *Robert S. Roeschlaub: Architect of the Emerging West*. Denver: Colorado Historical Society, 1988.

Hicks, Dave. *Denver History*. [Denver]: A-T-P, 1980.

________. *Aurora from the Beginning*. Denver: Egan Printing, 1977.

________. *Englewood from the Beginning*. Denver: A-T-P, 1971.

________. *Littleton from the Beginning*. Denver: Egan Printing, 1975.

Hill, Alice Polk. *Colorado Pioneers in Picture and Story*. Denver: Brock Haffen Press, 1915.

*Historic Building Inventory*. Revised edition. Denver: City and County of Denver, 1981.

*Histories of the Denver Public Schools*. Denver: Denver Public Schools, n.d.

*The History of the Albany, Denver*. [Denver]: Albany Hotel, [n.d.].

Hornby, William H. *Eye on the Horizon: The Greater Denver Corporation, 1987–95*. Denver: Greater Denver Corporation and Denver Metro Chamber of Commerce, 1995.

________. *The Law Out West: Holland & Hart, 1947–1989*. Denver: Holland & Hart, 1989.

________. *Voice of Empire*. Denver: Colorado Historical Society, 1992.

Hosokawa, Bill. *Thunder in the Rockies*. New York: Morrow, 1976.

Hunt, Corinne. *The Brown Palace Story*. [Boulder]: A Rocky Mountain Writers Guild Publication, 1982.

Hunt, Inez, and Wanetta W. Draper. *To Colorado's Restless Ghosts*. Denver: Sage Books, 1960.

Jackson, Kenneth. *The Ku Klux Klan and the City*. New York: Oxford University Press, 1967.

Jefferson County Historical Commission. *From Scratch: A History of Jefferson County, Colorado*. [Golden]: Jefferson County Historical Commission, 1985.

Johnson, Charles. *Denver's Mayor Speer*. Denver: Green Mountain Press, 1969.

________. *The D&F Tower*. Denver: Tower Press, 1977.

Johnson, Frank Thomas. *Autobiography of a Centenarian*. Denver: Big Mountain Press, 1961.

Jones, William C., and Kenton Forrest. *Denver: A Pictorial History.* Boulder: Pruett, 1974.

Jones, William C., and Elizabeth B. Jones, compilers. *Photo by McClure.* Boulder: Pruett, 1983.

Jones, William C., F. Hol Wagner Jr., Gene McKeever, and Kenton Forrest. *Mile High Trolleys.* Second edition. Boulder: Pruett, 1975.

Kal, Doris. *Fragile Advocate: Remembrance of a Legendary Lawyer.* Aurora: Verbal Imagery, 1975.

Kania, Alan J., and Diane Hartman. *The Bench and the Bar: A Centennial View of Denver's Legal History.* Denver: Denver Bar Association, 1993.

Keating, Stephen. *Cutthroat: High Stakes and Killer Moves on the Electronic Frontier.* Boulder: Johnson Books, 1999.

Kelly, George V. *The Old Gray Mayors of Denver.* Boulder: Pruett, 1974.

King, Clyde Lyndon. *History of the Government of Denver in Specific Reference to its Relation to Public Service Companies.* Denver: Fisher Books, 1911.

Kirby, Linda K. *Heritage of Heroes: Trinity Methodist Church, 1859–1988.* Denver: Trinity Methodist Church, 1988.

Kirkpatrick, Terry. *The South Platte River Greenway Trail.* Englewood: Trails 'n Tales Publishing, 1998.

Knight, Harold. *Working in Colorado.* Boulder: Colorado Labor Education and Research, 1971.

Kohl, Edith Eudora. *Denver's Historic Mansions.* Denver: Sage Books, 1957.

Kostka, William. *The Pre-Prohibition History of Adolph Coors Company, 1873–1933.* n.p.: Coors, n.d.

Lamm, Richard, and Duane Smith. *Pioneers & Politicians.* Boulder: Pruett, 1984.

Larsen, Charles. *The Good Fight: The Life and Times of Ben B. Lindsey.* Chicago: Quadrangle, 1972.

Larson, Robert W. *Populism in the Mountain West.* [Albuquerque]: University of New Mexico Press, 1986.

Leonard, Stephen. *Trials and Triumphs.* Niwot: University Press of Colorado, 1993.

Leonard, Stephen, and Tom Noel. *Denver: Mining Camp to Metropolis.* Niwot: University Press of Colorado, 1990.

Lindsey, Benjamin Barr, and Harvey O'Higgins. *The Beast.* New York: Doubleday, Page & Company, 1910.

Lindsey, Benjamin Barr, with Rube Borough. *The Dangerous Life.* New York: Liverright, 1931.

Loevy, Robert D. *The Flawed Path to the Governorship 1994.* Lanham, MD: University Press of America, 1996.

Logan, James K., editor. *The Federal Courts of the Tenth Circuit: A History.* Denver: Tenth Circuit Court of Appeals, 1992.

Lukas, J. Anthony. *Big Trouble.* New York: Simon & Schuster, 1997.

Lusky, Sam, and Bill Peery. *The Denver Excitement: The Story behind the City.* Denver: Challenger Publications, n.d.

MacMechem, Edgar C. *Robert W. Speer.* Denver: Smith-Brooks, 1919.

Marshall, Helen Lowrie, with photographs by Olga Seybert. *Have You Ever seen Denver?* Denver: Victoria Publishing, 1971.

McEncore, Donna. *Denver Renewed: A History of the Denver Urban Renewal Authority*. Denver: Denver Foundation, 1992.

McFadden, Carl V., and Leona M. McFadden. *Early Aurora*. Aurora: Aurora Technical Company, 1978.

McGiffert, Michael. *The Higher Learning in Colorado*. Denver: Sage Books, 1964.

McQuarie, Robert J., and C. W. Buchholtz. *Littleton, Colorado: Settlement to Centennial*. Littleton: Littleton Historical Museum, 1990.

McWilliams, Carey. *Ill Fares the Land*. Boston: Little, Brown, 1942.

Mehls, Steven F., Carol J. Drake, and James E. Fell Jr. *Aurora: Gateway to the Rockies*. [Evergreen]: Cordillera Press, 1985.

Melrose, Frances. *Rocky Mountain Memories*. Denver: Denver Publishing Company, 1986.

Miller, Jeff. *Stapleton International Airport: The First Fifty Years*. Boulder: Pruett, 1983.

Monnett, John H., and Michael McCarthy. *Colorado Profiles*. Evergreen: Cordillera Press, 1987.

Morris, Langdon E. *Denver Landmarks*. Denver: C. W. Cleworth, 1979.

Mosley, Earl. "History of the Denver Water System, 1859–1919." Denver: Unpublished Manuscript, 1966.

Mumey, Nolie. *History of the Early Settlements of Denver*. Glendale, CA: Arthur H. Clark Company, 1942.

Muntz, Geoffrey L., and Alan S. Wuth. *A Path Through Time: A Guide to the Platte River Greenway*. Frederick, CO: Jende-Hagan, 1983.

Natan, Ed. *Discover the Heart of Denver*. Denver: Natan & Associates, 1986.

Noel, Tom. *The City and the Saloon*. Lincoln: University of Nebraska Press, 1982.

________. *Colorado Catholicism*. Boulder: University Press of Colorado, 1989.

________. *The Denver Athletic Club*. Denver: Denver Athletic Club, 1984.

________. *Denver Landmarks & Historic Districts*. Niwot: University Press of Colorado, 1996.

________. *Denver's Larimer Street*. Denver: Historic Denver, 1981.

________. "Gay Bars and the Emergence of Denver's Homosexual Community," *Social Science Journal*, 15:2 (April 1978), 59–74.

________. *Growing Through History with Colorado: The Colorado National Banks*. Denver: Colorado National Bank, 1987.

________. *Mile High City: An Illustrated History of Denver*. Denver: Heritage Media Corporation, 1997.

________. *Richthofen's Montclair*. Boulder: Pruett, 1978.

________. *Rocky Mountain Gold*. Tulsa: Continental Heritage Press, 1980.

Noel, Tom, and Barbara Norgren. *Denver: The City Beautiful*. Denver: Historic Denver, 1987.

Noel, Tom, with Stephen J. Leonard and Kevin E. Rucker. *Colorado Givers: A History of Philanthropic Heroes.* Niwot: University Press of Colorado, 1998.

Norland, Jim. *Fifty Years of Mostly Fun.* Cherry Hills, CO: Cherry Hills Country Club, 1972.

Paglia, Michael, Diane Wray, and Rodd Wheaton, *Denver: The Modern City.* Denver: Historic Denver, 1999.

Parkhill, Forbes. *The Law Goes West. Denver*: Sage Books, 1956.

________. *The Wildest of the West.* New York: Holt, 1951.

Patterson, George James, Jr. *The Unassimilated Greeks of Denver.* New York: AMS Press, 1989.

Perkin, Robert L. *The First Hundred Years.* Garden City: Doubleday, 1959.

Peters, Bette, Louise Farrah, and Lee Peters. *Denver's City Park.* Boulder: Johnson Publishing Company, 1986.

Peterson, Nancy, and Cle Cervi. *The Women Who Made Headlines.* Denver: Denver Woman's Press Club, 1998.

Quillen, Ed. *Deep in the Heart of the Rockies.* Westcliffe, CO: Music Mountain Press, 1998.

*Report of the Cherry Creek Flood Commission.* Denver: Smith-Brooks, 1913.

Robert, Chaer. *An Interview with Helen Peterson.* Denver: Agency for Human Rights, 1997.

Rountree, Russ. *Western Oil Reporter's Rocky Mountain Oil History.* Denver: Hart Publications, 1984.

Schlosser, Elizabeth. *Modern Art in Denver (1919–1960): Eleven Denver Artists.* Denver: Ocean View Books, 1993.

Schroeder, Pat. *24 Years of House Work . . . and the Place is Still a Mess.* Kansas City: Andrews McMell, 1998.

*Los Seis de Boulder.* Alamosa: n.p., 1994.

Seligson, Harry, and George E. Bardwell. *Labor-Management Relations in Colorado.* Denver: Sage Books, 1961.

Serling, Robert J. *Maverick: The Story of Robert Six and Continental Airlines.* Garden City: Doubleday, 1974.

Shikes, Robert H. *Rocky Mountain Medicine.* Boulder: Johnson, 1986.

Shikes, Robert H., and Henry N. Claman. *The University of Colorado School of Medicine: A Centennial History, 1883–1983.* Denver: University of Colorado Board of Regents, 1983.

Shoemaker, Joe, with Leonard A. Stevens. *Returning the Platte to the People.* Westminster: Greenway Foundation, 1981.

Simmons, R. Laurie, and Thomas H. Simmons. *Denver Neighborhood History Project.* Denver: Denver Landmark Preservation Commission and Denver Planning Office, 1995.

Singular, Stephen. *Talked to Death: The Life and Murder of Alan Berg.* New York: Beech Tree Books, 1987.

Sinclair, Upton. *Mountain City.* New York: Boni, 1930.

Smiley, Jerome. *History of Denver.* Denver: *Denver Times*, 1901/Old American Publishing Company, 1978.

________. *A Semi-Centennial History of the State of Colorado*. Two volumes. Chicago: Lewis Publishing Company, 1913.

Smith, Jean W., and Elaine C. Walsh. *Queen of the Hill*. Denver: Colorado Historical Society, 1979.

Smith, Marion. *Westminster Then & Now*. Westminster: City, 1976.

Sprague, Marshall. *Colorado: A Bicentennial History*. New York: Norton, 1976.

Sprague, Marshall, et al. *Enchanted Central City*. Denver: Central City Opera House Association, n.d.

Spring, Agnes Wright. *Denver's Historic Markers, Memorials, Statues and Parks*. Denver: Colorado State Historical Society, 1959.

Stansell, Harold L. *Regis: On the Crest of the West*. Denver: Regis, 1977.

Stone, Wilber Fiske, editor. *History of Colorado*. Five volumes. Chicago: S. J. Clarke Publishing Company, 1918.

Student, Annette L. *Discover Colorado: Historic Denver Tours*. Two volumes. Aurora: By the Author, 1990.

Swearingen, Tom, editor. *The Cooperative Century: The Colorado Cattlemen's Association, 1867–1967*. [Denver]: Colorado Cattlemen's Association, 1967.

Templin, J. Alton, Allen D. Breck, and Martin Rist, editors. *The Methodist, Evangelical, and United Brethren Churches in the Rockies, 1859–1976*. [Denver]: Rocky Mountain Conference of the United Methodist Church, 1977.

Tooley, Dale. *I'd Rather Be in Denver*. Denver: Colorado Legal Publishing Company, 1985.

Turk, Gayle, editor. *A Denver Collage*. [Denver]: n.p., n.d.

Ubbelhode, Carl, Maxine Benson, and Duane A. Smith. *A Colorado History*. Seventh edition. Boulder: Pruett, 1995.

________., editors. *A Colorado Reader*. Second edition. Boulder: Pruett, 1982.

Uchill, Ida. *Pioneers, Peddlers, and Tsadikim*. Denver: Sage Books, 1957.

Van Cise, Philip. *Fighting the Underworld*. Boston: Houghton Mifflin, 1936.

Van Wyck, Millie. *The Town of South Denver*. Boulder: Pruett, 1991.

Varnell, Jeanne. *Women of Consequence*. Boulder: Johnson Books, 1999.

Vervalin, Gene. *West Denver: The Story of an American High School*. Boulder: EHV Publications, 1985.

Vickers, William B. *History of the City of Denver*. Chicago: O. L. Baskin & Company, 1880.

Vigil, Ernesto. *The Crusade for Justice: The Chicano Movement in Denver*. Madison: University of Wisconsin Press, 1999.

Wagner, Albin. *Brighton Reflections from Brighton Federal Savings on the Bicentennial Years, 1776–1976*. Brighton: [Brighton Federal Savings], [1976].

Wahlberg, Edgar M. *Voices in the Darkness*. Boulder: Roberts Rinehart, 1983.

Walsh, Elaine C., and Jean W. Smith. *Victoria of Civic Center*. Denver: Colorado Historical Society, 1984.

Wells, Bud. *The Colorado Car Book: The Climb to the Automobile's Centennial*. Boulder: Johnson Printing, 1996.

West, William Allen. *Curtis Park: A Denver Neighborhood*. Boulder: Colorado Associated University Press, 1980.

Westminster Citizens Advisory Committee. *History of Westminster, Colorado, 1911–1961*. Westminster: Westminster Citizens Advisory Committee, 1961.

Wharton, Junius W. *History of the City of Denver from Its Earliest Times*. Denver: Byers and Dailey, 1866.

Wheat Ridge Historical Committee. *History of Pioneer Wheat Ridge*. Wheat Ridge: City of Wheat Ridge, 1971.

Whitacre, Christine. *The Denver Club: 1880–1995*. Denver: Historic Denver, 1998.

White, Ed. *Cactus Club: Its Prickly Past*. Denver: Cactus Club, 1995.

Whiteside, James. *Colorado: A Sports History*. Niwot: University Press of Colorado 1999.

Wiberg, Ruth Eloise. *Rediscovering Northwest Denver*. Denver: Northwest Denver Books, 1976.

Widmann, Nancy L. *The East Seventh Avenue Historic District*. Denver: East Seventh Avenue Historic District, 1992.

________. *Sherman-Grant Historic District*. Denver: Preservation and Public History Research, 1997.

Wilcox, Pat, editor. *Lakewood, Colorado—An Illustrated Biography*. Lakewood: Twenty-fifth Birthday Commission, 1994.

________. *Seventy-Six Centennial Stories of Lakewood*. Lakewood: Lakewood Centennial-Bicentennial Commission 1976.

Wiley, Peter, and Robert Gottlieb. *Empires in the Sun: The Rise of the New American West*. Tucson: University of Arizona Press, 1982.

Wilk, Diane. *The Potter-Highlands Historic District*. Denver: Historic Denver, 1997.

Wilmsen, Steven. *Silverado*. Washington, DC: National Press Books, 1991.

*The WPA Guide to 1930s Colorado*. Introduction by Tom Noel. Lawrence, Kansas: University of Kansas Press, 1987.

[Yonce, Fred.] *The Denver Public Library: 100th Anniversary Celebration*. [Denver]: [Denver Public Library], [1989].

Zamonski, Stanley W., and Teddy Keller. *The Fifty-Niners*. Denver: Sage Books, 1961.

Zeckendorf, William, with Edward McCreary. *The Autobiography of William Zeckendorf*. New York: Holt, Rinehart and Winston, 1970.

Zellinger, Michael Jay, editor. *West Side Story Relived*. Denver: West Side Reunion Committee, 1987.

# Index